POLITICAL THOUGHT IN AMERICA

AN ANTHOLOGY

POLITICAL THOUGHT

IN
SECOND EDITION

AMERICA

AN ANTHOLOGY

Edited by

Michael B. Levy

WAVELAND
PRESS, INC.
Long Grove, Illinois

For information about this book, contact:
    Waveland Press, Inc.
    4180 IL Route 83, Suite 101
    Long Grove, IL 60047-9580
    (847) 634-0081
    info@waveland.com
    www.waveland.com

10-digit ISBN 0-88133-688-2
13-digit ISBN 978-0-88133-688-7

Printed in the United States of America

17   16   15   14   13   12

To the memory of my grandparents,
Europeans who made a New World

Foreword to the Second Edition

Students of Western political theory have long begun their studies with explorations of the grand tradition—canons of great works from Plato and Aristotle through Karl Marx, typically stopping along the way at St. Augustine, Thomas Aquinas, Machiavelli, Hobbes, Locke, and Rousseau. While the canons may expand to include Cicero, Calvin, Hegel, or Burke, a relatively small group of classics has long been taken to represent the essence of the political thinking produced by Western civilization.

Teachers of these classic works often differ over how they should be taught. Should they be studied primarily as historical documents? Must we extensively study the political, social, and economic contexts in which they were written? Or, instead, are these works timeless statements of political wisdom that speak to one another across the ages? Given the heat of these debates about critical method, it is striking how much consensus exists concerning which great works comprise the grand tradition. Yet a glance at the course syllabi of introductory political thought courses throughout the Western world establishes this agreement rather clearly.

The prominent place of these works in the study of political theory immediately raises two important points for the American student. First, no American political theorist's works are considered of this rank. American political theory has been virtually excluded from the grand tradition. Second, and critically important to the teacher of American political thought, there is no analogous canon in the history of American theory. While most courses in American political theory probably include *Federalist No. 10* and the Declaration of Independence—hardly full-blown philosophical treatises even if they are brilliant political tracts—there is little agreement about what or whom else such a study *must* include. Differences abound over both what has been influential and what has been conceptually significant.

Perhaps, some suggest, the paucity of universally recognized great works is simply a consequence of the United States' short, if remarkably successful, national history. Few should expect a nation of a little over 200 years' experience to have produced a grand tradition that would be recognized as such by themselves and the rest of the world alike. Others, taking their cue from the Frenchman Alexis de Tocqueville, have interpreted the absence of such a tradition as a consequence of national character. Americans, he felt, were a people moved by direct experience and not by self-conscious reflection or words. "The spirit of America is averse to general ideas," Tocqueville wrote in *Democracy in America* (1835), "and does not seek theoretical discoveries."

At the same time that Ralph Waldo Emerson bemoaned the absence of an authentic American literature, Tocqueville dismissed American political· thought. Those who required American lessons in the art of republican government needed to learn from "their example rather than from their teachings." Abstraction required leisure and a devotion to the joys of contemplation which were foreign to the spirit of an energetic, democratic, and commercial society such as the United States. However, Tocqueville also noted an American appreciation for the "utility of knowledge" and an eagerness for its practical application. Theoretical discoveries might be largely the work of the Old World, but Americans eagerly sought to apply these findings to their pursuit of worldly affairs.

True to this spirit, much of the best American political thought has come from political activists, the practitioners of the political arts. The writings and speeches of statesmen, jurists, clergymen, reformers, and politically active academics have provided Americans with a real, if different, tradition of political theory. While it is true that most great European and classical political theory has been written with concrete political ends in mind, the nature of the audience has often demanded a philosophical style foreign to most Americans. Writing to mass democratic audiences, the practical creators of American political thought have rarely seen the need to lay bare every premise or perfect each floor of their intellectual edifices. Moreover as inheritors of European, and especially English, intellectual traditions, they often have borrowed heavily from foreign ideas and creatively applied them to American circumstances. American activists qua theorists always have attempted to persuade in order to support a new course of public action. Choices publicly made have required that they be publicly defended or attacked. From this process has come serious political thought.

The absence of a large body of systematic political philosophy written in the nineteenth and early twentieth centuries should not lead one to assume otherwise. *The Federalist Papers* exemplify this much broader American phenomenon. Borrowing from European philosophers such as Hume and Montesquieu, its authors defended the new constitution and at the same time offered "a new science of politics" which was quite fresh and original. If one takes the tenth *Federalist Paper,* for example, and carefully explicates its assumptions about human nature and society, one finds a rather complete and sophisticated political theory that invites critical study and appreciation. Written for its practical effect, however, the authors of *The Federalist Papers* made little effort to detail every element in their entire system of thought. Their mass audience did not require it and probably would not have responded very well to it. What is true of *The Federalist Papers* has been equally true throughout much of American history.

If not classic political theory, these writings nonetheless have functioned as all great political theory has in the past. Political thought has always attempted to make men and women see their world with new eyes, believing that with new vision come new acts. Scholars such as Sheldon Wolin have emphasized that political theory is a creative activity that always has attempted to give order and meaning to a political world that appears to be in chaos. Thus people who live in a period of change find themselves unable to accept many of the ideas and beliefs that they have inherited. Once the "facts" of their lives differ from the "facts" that have made sense in the past, many seek out a clearer picture of what the world is and what it ought to be.

By way of illustration, we can look at the way Americans began to alter their views about Great Britain in the years just prior to the Revolution. In 1774, most Americans saw themselves as loyal—if disgruntled—subjects of the British Crown. Perhaps they believed that some of the details of their colony's relationship with England ought to be different, but they fully accepted the right of the mother country and Crown to govern and their obligation as colonial subjects to obey. Like the child who accepts and respects without question parental authority, Englishmen in America prior to the Revolutionary era accepted these beliefs and values as part of their political world.

By 1776, their view had changed. British colonials began to think of themselves loosely as Americans. They viewed the British differently and began to think that a new and different political order might be proper for men and women in their circumstances. Using the language of political philosophy, they began to see new "facts" and thus new "values." For example, in the view of many colonials, the British had begun to treat them as their wards instead of their children. The relationship seemed less that of a parent to a child and more that of a master to a servant, less one of nurturance and more one of exploitation. Once this shift in perception occurred, other shifts in beliefs and values could follow, as well.

Hadn't Americans cleared the wilderness and created colonial governing bodies and outposts of Western civilization without a great deal of involvement from the Crown? Perhaps then the English and colonial Americans were equal? Perhaps the authority to govern could only come from common consent, not natural subservience or inherited prerogative. If so, the Americans had the right to decide for themselves whether the British were protecting their rights as free and independent human beings. Perhaps these rights could only be protected in a self-governing new republic? And so on.

Notice that each of these beliefs required a shift in the way we conceptualized our political world. This is the activity of political theory, creating new lenses, or dusting off old lenses, so that we can see the "facts" of our political world more clearly. Then we can proceed to make sense of their implications.

Seen in this way, political theory, like any other scientific theory, tries to create an explanation or "covering principle" for events that could not be explained otherwise. Thus the theory of the "social contract" explains how a person can be free and at the same time subject to the authority of government in much the same way that the theory of gravity explains why objects fall to the ground. To the extent that either of these theories gives order to the world for those that live in it, people continue to accept them as true. If the logic falters or too many facts accumulate that don't fit the theory—and alternative theories seem to explain more—then older theories are replaced by newer and more powerful ones.

In another sense, however, the philosophical assumptions of most political theorists differ from those of most natural and physical scientists. First, political theorists (and social scientists in general) study human beings—individuals with free and variable wills subject to untold numbers of influences. Therefore, the degree of certainty that can be attained is necessarily less than in the natural and physical sciences.

Second, most political theorists do not accept—or are uncomfortable with—the rigid distinction between "facts" and "values" that characterizes most scientific thinking. Most of the political theory that has been written in the United States and elsewhere assumes that knowing the "facts" about how human beings live their lives inevitably leads us in the direction of "values," that is, a sense of how human beings ought to live their lives. Moreover, the reverse is also true. The values or culture of an investigator greatly influence the questions asked, the facts seen, and the interpretations placed on them.

This refusal to always accept the hard and fast distinction between facts and values (or empirical and normative statements) bothers many social scientists who have been reared in the positivist tradition. But it is impossible to understand what most political theorists are doing unless we see that their empirical and normative missions closely intertwine. An activity (writing political theory) that aims at getting people to do something because they *ought to do it*, must first convince them that the world really *is* as the theorist believes it to be.

For example, in the tenth *Federalist Paper*, James Madison tries to explain how the new constitution helps control narrow, selfish interest groups (factions). Madison assumes as fact that factions create "mischief" and threaten republican government, that republican government is suitable as the proper government of men, and that the government he is describing is truly "republican." These are judgments about the nature of mankind and government that leave facts and values hopelessly intertwined, yet they are intelligible both to those who make the judgments and those who receive them. Thus the debate between Federalist and Antifederalist in 1787, old liberal and new liberal in 1932, or liberal and new leftists in 1968 are all debates over the "facts" of legitimate government and the common good. From the perspective of those who speak it, such language simply can not be split into discrete categories labeled "fact" and "value." This is true of political thought in America and elsewhere.

If a political theory addresses a specific audience concerned with specific problems in a specific time and place, it is also true that political theories in general address a set of perennial questions. What is human nature? When is power and authority legitimate? Who should rule? What rights, if any, do individuals hold independent of the political order? What is the relationship between politics and other realms of activity such as religion or commerce? While it is true that every theorist does not always answer every one of these questions explicitly, we can usually answer them implicitly when he or she remains silent.

Because American theory is practical, American theorists often have not addressed or answered each of the so-called perennial questions in a rigorous fashion. As a result, American theory is best studied in context—intellectual, political, economic, and so on—as a conceptual activity aimed at influencing specific and tangible ends. By locating a work in its context, the student of American political thought can better understand what a given theorist intended by his words, how he altered earlier beliefs or meanings, and what he retained from earlier theoretical traditions. In this way as well, students can fill in what a theory implies, as well as what it explicitly states.

The structure of this book follows this perception. American political thought is a public, practically directed activity. The text builds on Robert Dahl's view that America has, after much debate and conflict, made a series of "historical commitments" or public decisions that have fundamentally altered the course of the American polity. Each of these changes brought with it a different or revised political vision and established a political language that continued to outline the contours of the political world for following generations.

Accordingly, the book is organized around the public debates that have surrounded those six "historical commitments" which I believe have defined contemporary America: (1) independence, (2) the extended federal republic and constitution, (3) an egalitarian market democracy (including Jacksonian democracy and emancipation), (4) industrial capitalism, (5) social democracy and the welfare state capitalism, and (6) American internationalism. Each of these was a major departure from past political and social practice, and each required public political argument to help justify the change. The fact that the language used to justify each of these decisions may not be wholly compatible helps further explain some of the conflict in American politics and alerts the reader to some of the linguistic and philosophical resources available within the American tradition to those who debate political alternatives.

The book contains seven parts, beginning with a contextual introduction "Europeans in the Wilderness" and followed by a part for each of the six decisions mentioned above. In Parts II through VII, each section begins with the Old Orthodoxy, or the political language and set of arguments that must be defeated. This is followed by the New Orthodoxy, the political theory that best legitimates the new historical commitment and that forms the basis of a political language that remains part of American political culture. (In Part V, there is no Old Orthodoxy since the New Orthodoxy of the preceding section represents that position.) Each part concludes with a Voices of Dissent section, which reminds us of alternatives not taken and potential political languages available for future political discourse.

It is clear from this approach that this text emphasizes structures of thought rather than famous thinkers. While many of the individuals who appear in these pages are famous for their writings or for other deeds, many are not. Each selection appears because it offers an example of a significant political perspective that adds to our understanding of American political thinking, American activities, and politics in general. As we have seen, many of these selections, taken in isolation, do not present complete political theories. However, if underlying assumptions are brought to light and words placed in their proper intellectual and historical context, a much fuller philosophical position should emerge. Students will then be able to evaluate these views in light of their own, investigate them for internal consistency, compare them to alternative perspectives, and discuss the significance of each for contemporary political problems.

The second edition of this anthology retains the basic structure of the first edition, while it attempts to build up areas that were either thin or in need of further clarification. In many instances, the suggestion for a specific change or addition came from students or faculty who used the text. The most significant additions can be found in Part I, in which I have given more orthodox Puritan writers a larger voice. Although a good case can be made for doing this on historical grounds, my reasons are largely conceptual and contemporary. In many respects, the relationships between state and society, and state and church, remain vexing. Students can better understand these relationships, and our unending attempts to put them in their proper perspectives, if they study the early writings of both orthodox and more individualistic, liberal Puritan thinkers. Important writers now expand especially the discourses of Part IV on the nineteenth century republic, Part V on industrial capitalism, and Part VI on the emergence of social democracy.

In addition, the introductions to each Part and to each writer have also been expanded so that students can better understand political theory as an intellectual and practical activity, and the place of American political thought within the larger tradition of political theory. The introductions further explore the tension between political theory as a body of thought that clarifies contemporary versus perennial questions.

The twenty pieces new to this edition include works by John Winthrop, Nathaniel Ward, Thomas Jefferson, certain Antifederalists, Walt Whitman, Frances Wright, Henry David Thoreau, Abraham Lincoln, Henry George, Charlotte Perkins Gilman, W. E. B. DuBois, Martin Luther King, Jr., Betty Friedan, Students for a Democratic Society, Randolph Bourne, Jeanne Kirkpatrick, and Christopher Layne. As in the first edition, each new entry is included in the volume for the purpose of helping students develop a fuller appreciation of a specific political or philosophical problem, whether the work itself is well or little known.

As far as possible I have attempted to edit each text in a way that faithfully exposes the kernel of an author's thought. I have attempted to avoid imposing my own interpretation on each text while striving to present a conceptually coherent anthology. In the end, I hope that the editing and the brief introductions only enhance what must be the most important experience that each student brings away from this study—the individual and personal encounter with an original, primary source.

Michael B. Levy

Contents

PART IV

Extending the Democratic Republic: Liberty, Equality, and the Open Marketplace

PART V

The Republic as Industrial Capitalism: Social Darwinism and the New Inequality

PART VI

The Republic as Social Democracy: Reining in the Market

PART VII

The Republic as World Power: Internationalism, Intervention, and a World Safe for Democracy

PART I

The Context: Europeans in the Wilderness

The men and women who use ideas and words to change their world are themselves products of that world. Simply, political theory, no matter how universal its intent, is written by people with particular histories who are confronting particular problems. Even the most radical political theories, those that attempt to make the world anew, are in part products of an inherited past that is economic, social, cultural, and intellectual in character.

The commanding influence of America's physical and economic environment has long impressed many observers who have tried to explain the "American mind." Hector St. John de Crevecoeur, a Frenchman living in America in the years just before our Revolution, believed the experience of confronting and taming the wilderness had transformed Europeans living in the New World into a "new race" of people—Americans. Since Americans were a new people, reasoned Crevecoeur, they needed a new "science of politics" appropriate to the conditions—the "facts"—of American life.

A half-century later, his fellow countryman Alexis de Tocqueville refined Crevecoeur's insight by suggesting that the easy availability of land was the key to the American character, and thus, politics. Unlike their European brethren, most Americans could own land, and thus were "born equal" without having to fight a social revolution to become so. For Tocqueville, as for Crevecoeur, Americans were creatures of experience. Their political thought simply reflected their physical and economic environment. Readily available land made it far more likely that men would own property, and thus be able to vote. Widely dispersed settlements made local self-government appropriate. Subsequently a political philosophy concluding that equal citizenship rights and republican self-government were proper for people seemed to grow naturally in America's political soil.

However, we would do well to remember that the men and women who first settled the Atlantic seaboard brought with them a rich and varied intellectual heritage, and this also influenced how they viewed their political world. Since the American colonists maintained constant contact with their mother country, Great Britain, the colonies continued to absorb those British ideas best-suited to specific American conditions.

Many of the most enduring ideas in American political thought have their roots in two dramatic events in the history of seventeenth century England and, for that matter, Western civilization—the English Civil War or Puritan Revolution (1648) and the Glorious Revolution (1688). While these events differed vastly, the first ending in the beheading of the king, the second in a peaceful transition to a new king and enlarged parliamentary power, both spawned political philosophers who spoke *for* the rights of Englishmen and *against* the divine rights of kings. In place of unlimited royal power, defenders of Parliament spoke of representative and republican government, individual rights, and rule of law.

It would be a mistake, nonetheless, to equate these theorists with modern democrats. For most Englishmen, government was the prerogative of landed gentlemen who in turn would represent other landed gentlemen, that is, the heads of the great families who owned the nation's soil. A few more egalitarian souls such as the Levellers in 1648 conceived of a more equal and democratic republic, but their assessments did not find immediate favor in Britain or on the other side of the Atlantic. Nevertheless, most who resisted the arbitrary power of the Crown believed that legitimate governments were created by free men. To remain free, they needed to create representative institutions of government; if kings were to remain as a part of that governing order, they had to function in a role prescribed by the nation's constitution. These theorists agreed that the nation was not the king's private preserve, and its people were not the king's private servants. Thus, if the royal family were to govern at all, they were to do so as the public's servants bound by a social contract with the people. All of these ideas were commonplace in England during the seventeenth century, and they reappeared in force a century later in North America.

Many opponents of the Crown in seventeenth century England were Puritans of various stripes. Puritans and their descendents settled Massachusetts Bay and other New England colonies, and their influence on American political culture and thought has been enormous. Puritans believed that the Church of England had grown corrupt. In their view, the church was filled with pomp and ritual devoid of religious meaning. Therefore, they believed that the church stood in the way of true Protestant reformation in England. The Puritan goal was to "purify" the church and return it to the simplicity and honest fellowship of the congregations they had read about in the New Testament.

Puritans believed that each individual could read Scripture and arrive at a personal understanding of truth and duty. At the same time, they maintained that all believers could agree on what truth and duty entailed. Obviously, such religious individualism threatened Puritan communities with anarchy. However, orthodox Puritans believed that those who received God's gift of "grace" were also capable of arriving at a common understanding of His will. Properly instructed by their elders—men of tremendous authority in Puritan communities—each community could join with others to form a renewed national church. As you can imagine, Puritans did not fully agree among themselves on the exact structure that a renewed national church would take, and these differences led to many debates and sectarian splits.

Nevertheless, Puritans shared a common belief that church members were the "elect" chosen by God to come together and freely build a renewed religious community. At the heart of the Puritan idea was the belief in a "covenant"—a freely chosen commitment that bound all individuals to one another and them and their church to God. The idea of the covenant gave expression to a core Puritan belief that has had tremendous influence beyond the bounds of theology: institutions, whether religious, political, or social, are legitimate only if they are grounded in freely given individual consent.

Yet many who began as Puritans believed that orthodox Puritan communities had become too rigid or too centralized for both the individual and cooperative search for the truth. Radical separatists believed that they had to remove themselves from any relationship with the existing Church of England and create a purified alternative. Independents refused altogether to accept any centralized church authority. In America, these tendencies later cohered into a natural preference for decentralization and local government in both church and state.

The more extreme views of many Independents helped give root to a tradition of religious toleration and the desire for separation of church and state. Afraid that they could be forced to conform to the theocratic politics of their Puritan brethren as well as the Church of England, many Dissenters, Seekers, Independents, and Antinomians sought to limit the power of government over private life. By giving special emphasis to the values of individual conscience and individual consent already present in Puritanism, these early religious dissenters articulated values that later became commonplace in American political thought.

As significant as religious thinking was, other intellectual traditions also greatly influenced American views on politics. In the eighteenth century, American colonists began to read and assimilate a variety of more secular British political writing. They read with great favor seventeenth-century agrarian republicans such as James Harrington and the early eighteenth-century *Letters of Cato* by Trenchard and Gordon. The agrarian republicans believed that the power of both the Crown and the great feudal lords could only be broken by a representative form of government that included the smaller landed gentry as full members.

Harrington believed that broadly representative government could only exist and remain stable if society was comprised of a large, roughly equal, self-sufficient landowning class. He placed great emphasis on the special "virtue" of the independent farmer and, conversely, noted the corrupt, fawning nature of those gentlemen who made up the king's court. While Harrington's special audience was the small gentry of England, his analysis found ready favor at the time of the American Revolution among colonial farmers living on the periphery of the English empire. In its American context, as we will see later, Harrington's landed class took on a far more egalitarian and democratic cast.

In addition, Americans read Whig jurists such as Coke and his eighteenth-century heir Blackstone, and absorbed their arguments about the rights of Englishmen under the law. The general Whig contention that "mixed government," that is, the shared rule of king, lords, and commons, was the key to English liberty also found a wide American audience, as did the Whig view that the domination of any one estate or branch spelled constitutional corruption and decay.

From republican and Whig theorists of the later seventeenth century—Algernon Sydney, James Tyrell, and John Locke—Americans received a set of political arguments that stressed the importance of natural rights belonging to individuals regardless of government or law. The protection of these rights was the reason for creating government, and their violation was grounds for resistance. This belief in natural rights, so central to what later political theorists have labeled "liberal individualism," was easily grafted onto older religious beliefs about natural and divine law. The older natural-law tradition maintained that just positive law needed to reflect the divine or transcendent order. From this perspective, law was not so much made as discovered. When adapted by Americans opposing new laws dictated by the English Crown, both the natural-law and natural-rights traditions bolstered the American contention that English laws such as the Stamp Act were unjust and thus not legally binding.

In the following part, we will examine writings that give the flavor of political thinking in America before the Stamp Act of 1765 and the Revolutionary era that followed. Before the Stamp Act, most political writing in America was couched in religious language and addressed, at least in part, religious issues. As a result, it is striking to compare writings from the seventeenth and early eighteenth centuries with later texts such as the Declaration of Independence and *The Federalist Papers*. However, it is also clear that many of the political writings from the Revolution and the Founding borrowed heavily from ideas developed during earlier theological disputes.

For a variety of reasons, contemporary Americans often look back at these writings to discover whether early Americans were either "conservative" or "liberal." Ironically, both Ronald Reagan and Walter Mondale cited John Winthrop's *Model of Christian Charity* during the 1984 presidential campaign. In truth, these writings are neither liberal nor conservative in our contemporary American understanding of these words. However American liberalism and conservatism—both deeply rooted in American soil—echo various themes found in all of these early writings.

The student may be alternately inspired and repelled by many of the arguments found here. But rather than claim any given theorist or body of thoughts as "proof" of the correctness of one's own position, the student must first try to understand these authors in their own terms and in their own contexts. Then, and only then, will students understand how their own views developed and how they may or may not remain appropriate for America in the late twentieth century.

The first four selections in this part—*A Model of Christian Charity, A Little Speech on Liberty, A Platform of Church Discipline,* and *The Simple Cobbler of Aggawam*—all represent orthodox Puritan writings on proper Christian community. They emphasize the strong mutual ties that bind each person to others, the need for discipline and authority in a community, and the role of the civil government as an instrument of church policy.

In contrast, Roger Williams represents the dissenting tradition in Protestant thinking, which holds many of the same values and beliefs found in orthodox Puritanism but reaches different conclusions. If individuals are to read scripture and come to a personal understanding of God's will, argues Williams, then they must be free to do so without the discipline of the civil authorities. This debate is an early and important example of an ongoing American search for the appropriate separation of church and state and over the appropriate limit of state interference in personal life.

John Wise's *A Vindication* discusses the role of centralized church bodies in the governance of local churches. He combines secular arguments about natural rights and natural law with scriptural arguments about ecclesiastical governance. It is a classic example of how theological writing influences secular political theory and vice versa.

In these ostensibly religious texts, we can see important tensions in American political thought: how to balance individualism, community, and legitimate authority in a free political and/or theological order. Each of these writers begins with *individuals,* moved by conscience and direct religious experience, and then tries to imagine a community that combines their innate freedom with a harmonious life shared in common. These tensions between individual and community, equality and authority, remain constant themes in the American quest for political understanding.

In the final selection, we read Hector St. John de Crevecoeur's *Letters from an American Farmer.* As we have seen, Crevecoeur emphasizes the material, rather than intellectual, roots of emerging American political beliefs. Crevecoeur's discussion of the equality and individualism, which he finds coupled with a spirit of local cooperation, echoes many republican themes that are critical components of American political thought from the Revolution to the present.

In short, as Americans in the decade preceding the Revolution began to articulate their grievances with England and offer alternative visions of political order, they were far from simple men of the wilderness. They were a special type of Englishmen, transformed by their experiences, and selectively drawing upon inherited traditions of thought. Ironically, the Americans who made the revolution against England justified their actions with ideas chosen from their English past, applying them to the American present and future.

John Winthrop, 1588–1649

John Winthrop was born near Suffolk, England. His grandfather, Adam Winthrop, had been a rich clothier and bought the manor of Groton in 1544. John's father, also Adam, was a successful lawyer, and John later followed his father's footsteps after studying at Trinity College, Cambridge, and at Gray's Inn. Although raised in the Church of England, Winthrop exhibited a religious intensity at an early age that soon led him to Puritanism.

After the second of his four wives died, and suffering a great deal of disillusionment with political and religious life in England, Winthrop felt himself drawn to the "intended Plantation in New England." In 1629 he was elected governor of the Massachusetts Bay Colony, and in 1630 he arrived in Salem, Massachusetts, with a group of settlers who had sailed on the *Arbella*. Winthrop lived in Massachusetts until his death nineteen years later and served as governor twelve of those years.

Fortunately for posterity, Winthrop kept a journal of his activities and thoughts. One of his most famous lay sermons *"A Modell of Christian Charity"* was delivered aboard the *Arbella* and preserved in his journal. In it Winthrop challenged his fellow Puritans to create a "City upon a Hill" (Matthew 5:14) that will stand as an example of Godliness for all mankind. This providential role for Massachusetts has inspired many generations of Americans who have accepted this ideal for the entire nation.

In the "Modell," Winthrop expressed an ideal of Christian community and common sharing. At the same time, he espoused an acceptance of inequality that may seem fixed and static to contemporary Americans. In fact, throughout his career as governor, Winthrop was criticized by many for distrust of the assembled freemen and his preference for authority exercised by the colony's magistrates.

In 1637, Winthrop attacked the Antinomian teachings of Anne Hutchinson and banned her from Massachusetts. His debate with Henry Vane over her fate remains an important early example of the tension between individual liberty and communal authority in Puritan thought.

Winthrop addressed this tension in a famous speech before the General Court in 1645, after he successfully withstood an impeachment proceeding. "A Little Speech on Liberty" distinguished between "natural liberty" and "civil liberty." Winthrop argued that freedom could only be experienced in a Christian community in which civil and ecclesiastical authority combined to provide discipline and rightful authority.

John Winthrop

A Modell of Christian Charity (1630)

V = u   u = v

Written
On Boarde the Arrabella,
On the Attlantick Ocean.
By the Honorable JOHN WINTHROP, Esq.

In His passage, (with the great Company of Religious people, of which Christian Tribes he was the Brave Leader and famous Governor;) from the Island of Great Brittaine, to New-England in the North America.

Anno 1630.

CHRISTIAN CHARITIES.

A Modell Hereof

God Almightie in his most holy and wise providence hath soe disposed of the Condicion of mankinde, as in all times some must be rich some poore, some highe and eminent in power and dignitie; others meane and in subieccion.

The Reason Hereof

1. REAS: First, to hold conformity with the rest of his workes, being delighted to shewe forthe the glory of his wisdome in the variety and differance of the Creatures and the glory of his power, in ordering all these differences for the preservacion and good of the whole, and the glory of his greatnes that as it is the glory of princes to haue many officers, soe this great King will haue many Stewards

counting himselfe more honoured in dispenceing his guifts to man by man, then if hee did it by his owne immediate hand.

2. REAS: Secondly, That he might haue the more occasion to manifest the worke of his Spirit: first, vpon the wicked in moderateing and restraineing them: soe that the riche and mighty should not eate vpp the poore, nor the poore, and dispised rise vpp against theire superiours, and shake off theire yoake; 2ly in the regenerate in exerciseing his graces in them, as in the greate ones, theire loue mercy, gentlenes, temperance etc., in the poore and inferiour sorte, theire faithe patience, obedience etc:

3. REAS: Thirdly, That every man might haue need of other, and from hence they might be all knitt more nearly together in the Bond of brotherly affeccion; from hence it appeares plainely that noe man is made more honourable than another or more wealthy etc., out of any perticuler and singuler respect to himselfe but for the glory of his Creator and the Common good of the Creature, Man; Therefore God still reserues the propperty of these guifts to himselfe as Ezek. 16:17. he there calls wealthe his gold and his silver etc. Prov. 3:9. he claimes theire seruice as his due[.] honour the Lord with thy riches etc. . . . There is likewise a double Lawe by which wee are regulated in our conversacion one towardes another: in both the former respects, the lawe of nature and the lawe of grace, or the morrall lawe or the lawe of the gospell, to omitt the rule of Justice as not propperly belonging to this purpose otherwise

SOURCE: Stewart Mitchell, ed., *Winthrop Papers* (Boston: Massachusetts Historical Society, 1929).

then it may fall into consideracion in some perticuler Cases; By the first of these lawes man as he was enabled soe withall [is] commaunded to loue his neighbour as himselfe[.] vpon this ground stands all the precepts of the morrall lawe, which concernes our dealings with men. To apply this to the works of mercy this lawe requires two things[,] first that every man afford his help to another in every want or distresse Secondly, That hee performe this out of the same affeccion, which makes him carefull of his owne good according to that of our Saviour Math. [7:12] Whatsoever ye would that men should doe to you. This was practised by Abraham and Lott in entertaineing the Angells and the old man of Gibea.

The Lawe of Grace or the Gospell hath some differance from the former as in these respectes first the lawe of nature was giuen to man in the estate of innocency; this of the gospell in the estate of regeneracy: 2ly, the former propounds one man to another, as the same fleshe and Image of god, this as a brother in Christ allsoe, and in the Communion of the same spirit and soe teacheth vs to put a difference betweene Christians and others. Doe good to all especially to the household of faith [Gal. 6:10]; vpon this ground the Israelites were to putt a difference betweene the brethren of such as were strangers though not of the Canaanites. 3ly. The Lawe of nature could giue noe rules for dealeing with enemies for all to be considered as freinds in the estate of innocency, but the Gospell commaunds loue to an enemy. proofe. If thine Enemie hunger feede him; Loue your Enemies doe good to them that hate you Math. 5:44.

This Lawe of the Gospell propoundes likewise a difference of seasons and occasions: there is a time when a christian must sell all and giue to the poore as they did in the Apostles times. There is a tyme allsoe when a christian (though they giue not all yet) must giue beyond theire abillity as they of Macedonia

Cor. 2:6. likewise community of perills calls for extraordinary liberallity and soe doth Community in some speciall seruice for the Churche. Lastly, when there is noe other meanes whereby our Christian brother may be releiued in this distresse wee must help him beyond our ability, rather than tempt God, in putting him vpon help by miraculous or extraordinary meanes.

This duty of mercy is exercised in the kindes, Giueing, lending, and forgiueing. . . .

QUESTION: What rule must wee obserue in lending?

ANSWER: Thou must obserue whether thy brother hath present or probable, or possible meanes of repayeing thee, if ther be none of these, thou must giue him according to his necessity, rather than lend him as hee requires: if he hath present meanes of repayeing thee, thou art to looke at him, not as an Act of mercy, but by way of Commerce; wherein thou arte to walke by the rule of Justice, but, if his meanes of repayeing thee be onely probable or possible then is hee an obiect of thy mercy thou must lend him, though there be danger of looseing it Deut. 15:7. If any of thy brethren be poore etc. thou shalt lend him sufficient that men might not shift off this duty by the apparent hazzard, he tells them that though the Yeare of Jubile were at hand (when he must remitt it, if hee were not able to repay it before) yet he must lend him and that chearefully; it may not greiue thee to giue him (saith hee) and because some might obiect, why soe I should soone impoverishe my selfe and my family, he adds with all thy Worke etc. for our Saviour Math. 5:42. From him that would borrow of thee turne not away.

QUESTION: What rule must wee obserue in forgiueing?

ANSWER: Whether thou didst lend by way of Commerce or in mercy, if he haue noething to pay thee [thou] must forgiue him (except in cause where thou hast a surety or a lawfull pleadge) Deut. 15:2. Every seauenth yeare the Creditor was to quitt that which hee lent to his brother if hee were poore as appeares ver: 8[4]: saue when there shall be noe poore with thee. In all these and like

Cases Christ was a generall rule Math. 7:22. Whatsoever ye would that men should doe to you doe yee the same to them allsoe.

QUESTION: What rule must wee obserue and walke by in cause of Community of perill?

ANSWER: The same as before, but with more enlargement towards others and lesse respect towards our selues, and our owne right hence it was that in the primitiue Churche they sold all [,] had all things in Common, neither did any man say that that which he possessed was his owne [Acts 2:44–45; 4:32–35] likewise in theire returne out of the Captiuity, because the worke was greate for the restoreing of the church and the danger of enemies was Common to all Nehemiah exhortes the Jewes to liberallity and readiness in remitting theire debtes to theire brethren, and disposeth liberally of his owne to such as wanted and stands not vpon his owne due, which hee might haue demaunded of them, thus did some of our forefathers in times of persecucion here in England, and soe did many of the faithfull in other Churches whereof wee keepe an honourable remembrance of them. . . .

The diffinition which the Scripture giues vs of loue is this Loue is the bond of perfection [Col. 3:14]. First, it is a bond, or ligament. 2ly, it makes the worke perfect. There is noe body but consistes of partes and that which knitts these partes together giues the body its perfeccion, because it makes each parte soe contiguous to other as thereby they doe mutually participate with eache other, both in strengthe and infirmity in pleasure and paine, to instance in the most perfect of all bodies, Christ and his church make one body: the severall partes of this body considered aparte before they were vnited were as disproportionate and as much disordering as soe many contrary quallities or elements but when christ comes and by his spirit and loue knitts all these partes to himselfe and each to other, it become the most perfect and best proportioned body in the world Eph. 4:16. Christ by whome all the body being knitt together by every ioynt for the furniture thereof according to the effectuall power which is in

the measure of every perfeccion of partes a glorious body without spott or wrinckle the ligaments hereof being Christ or his loue for Christ is loue 1 John 4:8. Soe this definition is right Loue is the bond of perfeccion.

From hence wee may frame these Conclusions.

1. first all true Christians are of one body in Christ 1. Cor. 12:12–13. 17. [27.] Ye are the body of Christ and members of [your?] parte.

2ly. The ligamentes of this body which knitt together are loue.

3ly. Noe body can be perfect which wants its propper ligamentes.

4ly. All the partes of this body being thus vnited are made soe contiguous in a speciall relacion as they must needes partake of each others strength and infirmity, ioy, and sorrowe, weale and woe. 1. Cor. 12:26. If one member suffers all suffer with it, if one be in honour, all reioyce with it.

5ly. This sensiblenes and Sympathy of each others Condicions will necessarily infuse into each parte a natiue desire and endeavour, to strengthen defend preserue and comfort the other.

To insist a little on this Conclusion being the product of all the former the truthe hereof will appeare both by precept and patterne i. John 3:10. yee ought to lay downe your liues for the brethren Gal. 6:2. beare ye one anothers burthens and soe fulfill the lawe of Christ . . .

The next consideracion is how this loue comes to be wrought; Adam in his first estate was a perfect modell of mankinde in all theire generacions, and in him this loue was perfected in regard of the habit, but Adam Rent in himselfe from his Creator, rent all his posterity allsoe one from another, whence it comes that every man is borne with this principle in him, to loue and seeke himselfe onely and thus a man continueth till Christ comes and takes possession of the soule, and infuseth another principle of loue to God and our brother, and this latter haueing continuall supply from Christ, as the head and roote by which hee is vnited get the predominency in the soule, soe by little and little expells the former 1 John 4:7. loue cometh of god and every one that loueth is borne of god, soe that this loue is the fruite of the new birthe, and none can haue it but the new Creature, now when this quallity is thus formed in the soules of men it workes like the Spirit vpon the drie bones Ezek. 37:[7] bone came to bone, it gathers together the scattered bones or perfect old man Adam and knitts them into one body againe in Christ whereby a man is become againe a liueing soule.

The third Consideracion is concerning the exercise of this loue, which is twofold, inward or outward, the outward hath beene handled in the former preface of this discourse, for vnfolding the other wee must take in our way that maxime of philosophy, Simile simili gaudet or like will to like; for as it is things which are carried with disafeccion to eache other, the ground of it is from a dissimilitude or [blank] ariseing from the contrary or different nature of the things themselues, soe the ground of loue is an apprehension of some resemblance in the things loued to that which affectes it, this is the cause why the Lord loues the Creature, soe farre as it hath any of his Image in it, he loues his elect because they are like himselfe, he beholds them in his beloued sonne; soe a mother loues her childe, because shee throughly conceiues a resemblance of herselfe in it. Thus it is betweene the members of Christ, each discernes by the worke of the spirit his owne Image and resemblance in another, and therefore cannot but loue him as he loues himselfe; Now when the soule which is of a sociable nature findes anything like to it selfe, it is like Adam when Eue was brought to him, shee must haue it one with herselfe this is fleshe of my fleshe (saith shee) and bone of my bone shee conceiues a greate delighte in it, therefore shee desires nearenes and familiarity with it: . . .

From the former Consideracions ariseth these Conclusions.

1. First. This loue among Christians is a reall thing not Imaginarie.

2ly. This loue is as absolutely necessary to the being of the body of Christ, as the sinewes and other ligaments of a naturall body are to the being of that body.

3ly. This loue is a divine Spirituall nature free, actiue strong Couragious permanent vnder valueing all things beneathe its propper obiect, and of all the graces this makes vs nearer to resemble the virtues of our heavenly father.

4ly. It restes in the loue and wellfare of its beloued, for the full and certaine knowledge of these truthes concerning the nature vse, [and] excellency of this grace, that which the holy ghost hath left recorded 1. Cor. 13. may giue full satisfaccion which is needfull for every true member of this louely body of the Lord Jesus, to worke vpon theire heartes, by prayer meditacion continuall exercise at least of the speciall [blank] of this grace till Christ be formed in them and they in him all in eache other knitt together by this bond of loue.

It rests now to make some applicacion of this discourse by the present designe which gaue the occasion of writeing of it. Herein are 4 things to be propounded: first the persons, 2ly, the worke, 3ly, the end, 4ly the meanes.

1. For the persons, wee are a Company professing our selues fellow members of Christ, In which respect only though wee were absent from eache other many miles, and had our imploymentes as farre distant, yet wee ought to account our selues knitt together by this bond of loue, and liue in the exercise of it, if wee would haue comforte of our being in Christ, this was notorious in the practise of the Christians in former times. . . .

2ly. for the Worke wee haue in hand, it is by a mutuall consent through a speciall overruleing providence, and a more then an ordinary approbation of the Churches of Christ to seeke out a place of Cohabitation and Consorteshipp vnder a due forme of Government both ciuill and ecclesiasticall. In such cases as this the care of the publique must oversway all private respects, by which not only conscience, but meare Ciuill pollicy doth binde vs; for it is a true rule that perticuler Estates cannott subsist in the ruine of the publique.

3ly. The end is to improue our liues to doe more seruice to the Lord the comforte and encrease of the body of christe whereof wee are members that our selues and posterity may be the better preserued from the Common corrupcions of this euill world to serue the Lord and worke out our Salvacion vnder the power and purity of his holy Ordinances.

4ly. for the meanes whereby this must bee effected, they are 2fold, a Conformity with the worke and end wee aime at, these wee see are extraordinary, therefore wee must not content our selues with vsuall ordinary meanes whatsoever wee did or ought to haue done when wee liued in England, the same must wee doe and more allsoe where wee goe; That which the most in theire Churches maineteine as a truthe in profession onely, wee must bring into familiar and constant practise, as in this duty of loue we must loue brotherly without dissimulation, wee must loue one another with a pure hearte feruently wee must beare one anothers burtheens, wee must not looke onely on our owne things, but allsoe on the things of our brethren, neither must wee think that the lord will beare with such faileings at our hands as hee dothe from those among whome wee haue liued, and that for 3 Reasons.

1. In regard of the more neare bond of mariage, betweene him and vs, wherein he hath taken vs to be his after a most strickt and peculiar manner which will make him the more Jealous of our loue and obedience soe he tells the people of Israell, you onely haue I knowne of all the families of the Earthe

therefore will I punishe you for your Transgressions.

2ly. because the lord will be sanctified in them that come neare him. Wee know that there were many that corrupted the seruice of the Lord some setting vpp Alters before his owne, others offering both strange fire and strange Sacrifices allsoe; yet there came noe fire from heaven, or other sudden Judgment vpon them as did vpon Nadab and Abihu [Lev. 10:1–2] whoe yet wee may thinke did not sinne presumptuously.

3ly. When God giues a speciall Commission he lookes to haue it stricktly obserued in every Article, when hee gaue Saule a Commission to destroy Amaleck hee indented with him vpon certaine Articles and because hee failed in one of the least, and that vpon a faire pretence, it lost him the kingdome, which should haue beene his reward, if hee had obserued his Commission [I Sam. 15; 28:16–18]; Thus stands the cause betweene God and vs, wee are entered into Covenant with him for this worke, wee haue taken out a Commission, the Lord hath giuen vs leaue to drawe our owne Articles wee haue professed to enterprise these Accions vpon these and these ends, wee haue herevpon besought him of favour and blessing; Now if the Lord shall please to heare vs, and bring vs in peace to the place wee desire, then hath hee ratified this Covenant and sealed our Commission, [and] will expect a strickt performance of the Articles contained in it, but if wee shall neglect the observacion of these Articles which are the ends wee haue propounded, and dissembling with our God, shall fall to embrace this present world and prosecute our carnall intencions, seekeing great things for our selues and our posterity, the Lord will surely breake out in wrathe against vs be revenged of such a periured people and make vs knowe the price of the breache of such a Covenant.

Now the onely way to avoyde this shipwracke and to provide for our posterity is to followe the Counsell of Micah, to doe Justly, to loue mercy, to walke humbly with our God, for this end wee must be knitt together in this worke as one man, wee must entertainee each other in brotherly Affeccion, wee must be willing to abridge our selues of our super-fluities, for the supply of others necessities, wee must vphold a familiar Commerce together in all meekenes, gentlenes, patience and liberallity, wee must delight in eache other, make others Condicions our owne reioyce together, mourne together, labour, and suffer together, allwayes haueing before our eyes our Commission and Community in the worke, our Community as members of the same body, soe shall wee keepe the vnitie of the spirit in the bond of peace, the Lord will be our God and delight to dwell among vs, as his owne people and will commaund a blessing vpon vs in all our wayes, soe that wee shall see much more of his wisdome power goodnes and truthe then formerly wee haue beene acquainted with, wee shall finde that the God of Israell is among vs, when tenn of vs shall be able to resist a thousand of our enemies, when hee shall make vs a prayse and glory, that men shall say of succeeding plantacions: the lord make it like that of New England; for wee must Consider that wee shall be as a Citty vpon a Hill, the Eies of all people are vppon vs; soe that if wee shall deale falsely with our god in this worke wee haue vndertaken and soe cause him to withdrawe his present help from vs, wee shall be made a story and a by-word through the world, wee shall open the mouthes of enemies to speake euill of the wayes of god and all professours for Gods sake; wee shall shame the faces of many of gods worthy seruants, and cause theire prayers to be turned into Cursses vpon vs till wee be consumed out of the good land whether wee are goeing; And to shutt vpp this Discourse with that exhortacion of Moses that faithfull seruant of the Lord in his last farewell to Israell Deut. 30: [15–19]. Beloued there is now sett before vs life, and good, deathe and euill in that wee are Commaunded this day to loue the Lord our God, and to loue one another to walke in his wayes and to keepe his Commaundements and his Ordinance, and his lawes, and the Articles of our Covenant with him that wee may liue and be multiplyed, and that the Lord our God may blesse vs in the land whether wee goe to possesse it: But if our heartes shall turne away soe that wee will not obey, but shall be seduced and worshipp other Gods our pleasures, and proffitts, and serue them; it is propounded vnto vs this day, wee shall surely perishe out of the good Land whether wee passe over this vast Sea to possesse it;

Therefore lett vs choose life,
that wee, and our Seede,
may liue; by obeying his
voyce, and cleaueing to him,
for hee is our life, and
our prosperity.

John Winthrop

A Little Speech on Liberty (1645)

I suppose something may be expected from me, upon this charge that is befallen me, which moves me to speak now to you. Yet I intend not to intermeddle in the proceedings of the Court, or with any of the persons concerned therein. Only I bless God that I see an issue of this troublesome business. I also acknowledge the justice of the Court, and, for mine own part, I am well satisfied, I was publicly charged, and I am publicly and legally acquitted, which is all I did expect or desire. . . .

The great questions that have troubled the country are about the authority of the magistrates and the liberty of the people. It is yourselves who have called us to this office; and being called by you, we have our authority from God, in way of an ordinance, such as hath the image of God eminently stamped upon it, the contempt and violation whereof hath been vindicated with examples of divine vengeance. I entreat you to consider that when you choose magistrates, you take them from among yourselves, men subject to like passions as you are. Therefore, when you see infirmities in us, you should reflect upon your own; and that would make you bear the more with us, and not be severe censurers of the failings of your magistrates, when you have continual experience of the like infirmities in yourselves

SOURCE: John Winthrop, *The History of New England from 1630 to 1649,* ed. James Savage (Boston: Thomas B. Wait and Son, 1826).

and others. We account him a good servant who breaks not his covenant. The covenant between you and us is the oath you have taken of us, which is to this purpose, that we shall govern you and judge your causes by the rules of God's law and our own, according to our best skill. When you agree with a workman to build you a ship or house, etc., he undertakes as well for his skill as for his faithfulness, for it is his profession, and you pay him for both. But when you call one to be a magistrate, he doth not profess nor undertake to have sufficient skill for that office, nor can you furnish him with gifts, etc.; therefore you must run the hazard of his skill and ability. But if he fail in faithfulness, which by his oath he is bound unto, that he must answer for. If it fall out that the case be clear to common apprehension and the rule clear also, if he transgress here, the error is not in the skill but in the evil of the will: it must be required of him. But if the case be doubtful or the rule doubtful to men of such understanding and parts as your magistrates are, if your magistrates should err here, yourselves must bear it.

For the other point concerning liberty, I observe a great mistake in the country about that. There is a twofold liberty—natural (I mean as our nature is now corrupt), and civil or federal. The first is common to man, with beasts and other creatures. By this, man, as he stands in relation to man simply, hath liberty to do what he lists; it is a liberty to evil as well as to good. This liberty is incompatible and inconsistent with authority, and cannot endure the least restraint of the most just authority. The exercise and maintaining of this liberty makes men grow more evil and in time to be worse than brute beasts: *omnes sumus licentia deteriores.* This is that great enemy of truth and peace, that wild beast, which all the ordinances of God are bent against to restrain and subdue it.

The other kind of liberty I call civil or federal; it may also be termed moral, in reference to the covenant between God and man in the moral law, and the politic covenants and constitutions amongst men themselves. This liberty is the proper end and object of authority and cannot subsist without it; and it is a liberty to that only which is good, just, and honest. This liberty you are to stand for, with the hazard not only of your goods, but of your lives, if need be. Whatsoever crosseth this is not authority, but distemper thereof. This liberty is maintained and exercised in a way of subjection to authority; it is of the same kind of liberty wherewith Christ hath made us free. The woman's own choice makes such a man her husband; yet being so chosen, he is her lord, and she is to be subject to him, yet in a way of liberty, not of bondage; and a true wife accounts her subjection her honor and freedom, and would not think her condition safe and free but in her subjection to her husband's authority. Such is the liberty of the church under the authority of Christ, her king and husband; his yoke is so easy and sweet to her as a bride's ornaments; and if through frowardness or wantonness, etc., she shake it off at any time, she is at no rest in her spirit until she take it up again; and whether her lord smiles upon her and embraceth her in his arms, or whether he frowns or rebukes, or smites her, she apprehends the sweetness of his love in all, and is refreshed, supported, and instructed by every such dispensation of his authority over her. On the other side, ye know who they are that complain of this yoke and say, let us break their bands, etc., we will not have this man to rule over us.

Even so, brethren, it will be between you and your magistrates. If you stand for your natural, corrupt liberties and will do what is good in your own eyes, you will not endure the least weight of authority, but will murmur, and oppose, and be always striving to shake off that yoke. But if you will be satisfied to enjoy such civil and lawful liberties, such as Christ allows you, then will you quietly and cheerfully submit unto that authority which is set over you, in all the administrations of it, for yoor good. Wherein, if we fail at any time, we hope we shall be willing, by God's assistance, to hearken to good advice from any of you or in any other way of God. So shall your liberties be preserved, in upholding the honor and power of authority amongst you.

A Platform of Church Discipline, 1649

In 1648, a church synod in Massachusetts directed John Cotton, Richard Mather, and Ralph Partridge to draw up a scriptural "model of church government," which was adopted by the General Court one year later. The document outlined the orthodox Puritan approach to church government and the relationship between church and state. The fact that the document was drawn up by the highest church organization (the synod) and then adopted by the most significant secular institution speaks volumes about the close ties between church and state in Puritan thought and practice.

The *Platform* presents a good example of the Puritan concern for local church government and the desire to balance the authority of the elders with the participation of the members. It offers a clear discussion of the idea of the "Covenant," which provided the grounding for all legitimate institutions, and a good example of the Puritan view on church-state relations. Simply, the state was to aid the church in its mission without interfering in its activities or prerogatives.

The view on church-state relations in *A Platform* shows the guiding hand of John Cotton, the leading spokesman for theocracy among the Puritan clergy. Cotton was both extremely distrustful of democracy and intolerant of religious diversity. For Cotton, the church was to set the tone for civil government. Religious and scriptural ethics as expounded by the church were to guide the life of "the Plantation," even in the realm of commerce and trade. Thus, membership in the political order required membership in the church.

While Cotton expressed the Puritan orthodoxy, this was not the only view in Massachusetts. Cotton's intellectual battles with Roger Williams on the subject of religious toleration remain classics in American political thought, with Williams making the case for extreme toleration although still from a religious perspective.

A Platform of Church Discipline (1649)

Gathered out of the Word of God, and Agreed upon by the Elders and Messengers of the Churches Assembled in the Synod, at Cambridge, in New-England, to be Presented to the Churches and General Court for their Consideration and Acceptance in the Lord, the 8th Month, Anno 1649

CHAPTER I

Of the Form of Church-Government; And That It Is One, Immutable, and Prescribed in the Word

1. Ecclesiastical polity, or church-government or discipline, is nothing else but that form and order that is to be observed in the church of Christ upon earth, both for the constitution of it, and all the administrations that therein are to be performed.

2. Church-government is considered in a double respect, either in regard of the parts of government themselves, or necessary circumstances thereof. The parts of government are prescribed in the word, because the Lord Jesus Christ, (Heb. iii. 5, 6; Exo. xxv. 40; 2 Tim. iii. 16,) the King and Law-giver in his church, is no less faithful in the house of God, than was Moses, who from the Lord delivered a form and pattern of government to the children of Israel in the Old Testament; and the

holy Scriptures are now also so perfect as they are able to make the man of God perfect, and thoroughly furnished unto every good work; and therefore doubtless to the well-ordering of the house of God.

3. The parts of church-government are all of them exactly described in the word of God, (1 Tim. iii. 15; 1 Chr. xv. 13; Exod. ii. 4; 1 Tim. vi. 13. 16; Heb. xii. 27, 28; 1 Cor. xv. 24,) being parts or means of instituted worship according to the second commandment, and therefore to continue one and the same unto the appearing of our Lord Jesus Christ, as a kingdom that cannot be shaken, until he shall deliver it up unto God, even to the Father. (Deut. xii. 32; Ezek. xlv. 8; 1 Kin. xii. 31, 32, 33.) So that it is not left in the power of men, officers, churches, or any state in the world, to add, or diminish, or alter any thing in the least measure therein.

4. The necessary circumstances, as time and place, &c., belonging unto order and decency, are not so left unto men, as that, under pretence of them, they may thrust their own inventions upon the churches, (2 Kin. xii.; Exo. xx. 19; Isa. xxviii. 13; Col. i. 22, 23.) being circumscribed in the word with many

Source: Cotton Mather, *Magnalia Christi Americana*, ed. Rev. Thomas Robbins (Hartford, Conn.: Silas Andrus and Sons, 1853).

general limitations, where they are determined with respect to the matter to be neither worship it self, nor circumstances separable from worship. (Acts xv. 28; Mat. xv. 9; 1 Cor. xi. 23, and viii. 34.) In respect of their end, they must be done unto edification; in respect of the manner, decently and in order, according to the nature of the things themselves, and civil and church custom. Doth not even nature its self teach you? Yea, they are in some sort determined particularly—namely, that they be done in such a manner as, all circumstances considered, is most expedient for edification: (1 Cor. xiv. 26, and xiv. 40, and xi. 14. 16 and xiv. 12. 19; Acts xv. 28.) So as, if there be no error of man concerning their determination, the determining of them is to be accounted as if it were divine.

CHAPTER II

Of the Nature of the Catholick Church in General, and in Special of a Particular Visible Church

1. The catholick church is the whole company of those that are elected, redeemed, and in time effectually called from the state of sin and death unto a state of grace and salvation in Jesus Christ.

2. This church is either triumphant or militant. Triumphant, the number of them who are glorified in heaven; militant, the number of them who are conflicting with their enemies upon earth.

3. This militant church is to be consider'd as invisible and visible. (2 Tim. ii. 19; Rev. ii. 17; 1 Cor. vi. 17; Eph. iii. 17; Rom. i. 8; 1 Thes. i. 8; Isa. ii. 2; 1 Tim. vi. 12.) Invisible, in respect to their relation, wherein they stand to Christ as a body unto the head, being united unto him by the Spirit of God and faith in their hearts. Visible, in respect of the profession of their faith, in their persons, and in particular churches. And so there may be acknowledged an universal visible church.

4. The members of the militant visible church, considered either as not yet in church order, or walking according to the church order of the gospel. (Acts xix. 1; Col. ii. 5; Mat. xviii. 17; 1 Cor. v. 12.) In order, and so besides the spiritual union and communion common to all believers, they enjoy moreover an union and communion ecclesiastical, political. So we deny an universal visible church.

5. The state of the members of the militant visible church, walking in order, was either before the law, (Gen. xviii. 19; Exod. xix. 6,) economical, that is, in families; or under the law, national; or since the coming of Christ, only congregational (the term *independent*, we approve not): therefore neither national, provincial, nor classical.

6. A congregational church is by the institution of Christ a part of the militant visible church, consisting of a company of saints by calling, united into one body by an holy covenant, for the publique worship of God, and the mutual edification of one another in the fellowship of the Lord Jesus. (1 Cor. xiv. 23. 36, and i. 2, and xii. 27; Ex. xix. 5, 6; Deut. xxix. 1, and 9 to 15; Acts ii. 42; 1 Cor. xiv. 26.)

CHAPTER III

Of the Matter of the Visible Church, Soth in Respect of Quality and Quantity

1. The matter of the visible church are saints by calling.

2. By saints, we understand—1, Such as have not only attained the knowledge of the principles of religion, and are free from gross and open scandals, but also do, together with the profession of their faith and repentance, walk in blameless obedience to the word, so as that in charitable discretion they may be accounted saints by calling. (tho' perhaps some or more of them be unsound and hypocrites inwardly) because the members of such particular churches are commonly by the Holy Ghost called "saints and faithful brethren in

Christ;" and sundry churches have been reproved for receiving, and suffering such persons to continue in fellowship among them, as have been offensive and scandalous; the name of God also, by this means, is blasphemed, and the holy things of God defiled and profaned, the hearts of the godly grieved, and the wicked themselves hardened and holpen forward to damnation. (1 Cor. i. 2; Eph. i. 1; Heb. vi. 1; 1 Cor. i. 5; Ro. xv. 14; Psalm 1. 16, 17; Acts viii. 37; Mat. iii. 6; Ro. vi. 17; 1 Cor. i. 2; Phil. i. 2; Col. i. 2; Eph. i. 1; 1 Cor. v. 2. 13; Rev. ii. 14, 15. 20; Ezek. xliv. 7. 9, and xxiii. 38, 39; Numb. xix. 20; Hag. ii. 13, 14; 1 Cor. xi. 27. 29; Psa. xxxvii. 21; 1 Cor. v. 6; 2 Cor. vii. 14.) The example of such doth endanger the sanctity of others, a little leaven leaveneth the whole lump. 2, The children of such who are also holy.

3. The members of churches, tho' orderly constituted, may in time degenerate, and grow corrupt and scandalous, which, tho' they ought not to be tolerated in the church, yet their continuance therein, thro' the defect of the execution of discipline and just censures, doth not immediately dissolve the being of a church, as appears in the church of Israel. and the churches of Galatia and Corinth, Pergamos and Thyatira. (Rev. ii. 14, 15; and xxi. 21.)

4. The matter of the church, in respect of its *quantity*, ought not to be of greater number than may ordinarily meet together conveniently in one place; (1 Cor. xiv. 21; Mat. xviii. 17,) nor ordinarily fewer than may conveniently carry on church-work. Hence, when the holy Scripture makes mention of the saints combined into a church estate in a town or city, where was but one congregation, it usually calleth those saints ["the church"] in the singular number, as "the church of the Thessalonians." "the church of Smyrna, Philadelphia," &c.; (Rom. xvi. 1; 1 Thes. i. 1: Rev. ii. 28, and iii. 7,) but when it speaketh of the saints in a nation or province, wherein there were sundry congregations, it frequently and usually calleth them by the name of ["churches"] in the plural number, as the "churches of Asia, Galatia, Macedonia," and the like: (1 Cor. xvi. 1. 19; Gal. i. 2; 2 Cor. viii. 1; Thes. ii. 14,) which is further confirmed by what is written of sundry of those churches in particular, how they were assembled and met together the whole church in one place, as the church at Jerusalem, the church at Antioch, the church at Corinth and Cenchrea, tho' it were more near to Corinth, it being the port thereof, and answerable to a village: yet being a distinct congregation from Corinth, it had a church of its own, as well as Corinth had. (Acts ii. 46, and v. 12. and vi. 2, and xiv. 27. and xv. 38; 1 Cor. v. 4, and xiv. 23; Rom. xvi. 1).

CHAPTER IV

Of the Form of the Visible Church, and of Church Covenant

1. Saints by calling must have a visible political union among themselves, or else they are not yet a particular church, (1 Cor. xii. 27; 1 Tim. iii. 15; Eph. ii. 22; 1 Cor. xii. 15, 16, 17,) as those similitudes hold forth, which the Scripture makes use of to shew the nature of particular churches; as a *body,* a *building, house, hands, eyes, feet* and other members, must be united, or else (remaining separate) are not a body. Stones, timber, tho' squared, hewen and polished, are not an house, until they are compacted and united: (Rev. ii.) so saints or believers in judgment of charity, are not a church unless orderly knit together.

2. Particular churches cannot be distinguished one from another but by their forms. Ephesus is not Smyrna, nor Pergamos Thyatira; but each one a distinct society of itself, having officers of their own, which had not the charge of others; virtues of their own, for which others are not praised; corruptions of their own, for which others are not blamed.

3. This form is the *visible covenant*, agreement or consent, whereby they give up themselves unto the Lord, to the observing of the ordinances of Christ together in the same society, which is usually call'd the "church covenant." (Ex. xix. 5. 8; Deut. xxix. 12, 13: Zec. xi. 14. and ix. 11,) for we see not otherwise how members can have church-power over one another mutually. The comparing of each particular church to a *city*, and unto a *spouse*, (Eph. ii. 19; 2 Cor. xi. 2,) seemeth to conclude not only a form, but that that form is by way of covenant. The covenant, as it was that which made the family of Abraham and children of Israel to be a church and people unto God, (Gen. xvii. 7; Eph. ii. 12. 18,) so is it that which now makes the several societies of Gentile believers to be churches in these days.

4. This voluntary agreement, consent or covenant—for all these are here taken for the same—altho' the more express and plain it is, the more fully it puts us in mind of our mutual duty; and stirreth us up to it, and leaveth less room for the questioning of the truth of the church-estate of a company of professors, and the truth of membership of particular persons; yet we conceive the substance of it is kept where there is real agreement and consent of a company of faithful persons to meet constantly together in one congregation, for the publick worship of God, and their mutual edification: which real agreement and consent they do express by their constant practice in coming together for the publick worship of God and by their religious subjection unto the ordinances of God there: (Exod. xix. 5, and xx. 8, and xxiv. 3. 17; Josh. xxiv. 18 to 24; Psal. l. 5; Neh. ix. 38, and x. 1; Gen. xvii.; Deut. xxix.) the rather, if we do consider how Scripture-covenants have been entred into, not only expressly by word of mouth, but by sacrifice, by hand-writing and seal; and also sometimes by silent consent, without any writing or expression of words at all. . . .

CHAPTER X

Of the Power of the Church and Its Presbytery

1. Supreme and Lordly power over all the churches upon earth doth only belong to Jesus Christ, who is king of the church, and the head thereof (Ps. ii. 6; Eph. i. 21, 22; Isa. ix. 6; Mat. xxviii. 18.) He hath the government upon his shoulders, and hath all power given to him, both in heaven and earth.

2. A company of professed believers, ecclesiastically confederate, as they are a church before they have officers, and without them; so even in that estate, subordinate church-power (Acts i. 23, and xiv. 23. and vi. 3. 4; Mat. xviii. 17; 1 Cor. v. 4, 5,) under Christ delegated to them by him, doth belong to them in such a manner as is before expressed. CHAP. V. Sec. 2, and as flowing from the very nature and essence of a church; it being natural unto all bodies, and so unto a church-body, to be furnished with sufficient power for its own preservation and subsistence.

3. This government of the church (Rev. iii. 7; 1 Cor. v. 12.) is a mixt government (and so has been acknowledged, long before the term of *independency* was heard of); in respect of Christ, the head and king of the church, and the Sovereign Power residing in him, and exercised by him, it is a *monarchy:* in respect of the body or brotherhood of the church, and power from Christ granted unto them (1 Tim. v. 27.) it resembles a *democracy* in respect of the presbytery and power committed unto them, it is an *aristocracy.*

4. The Sovereign Power, which is peculiar unto Christ, is exercised—1. In calling the church out of the world into an holy fellowship with himself. (Gal. i. 4; Rev. v. 8, 9; Mat. xxviii. 20; Eph. iv. 8. 11; Jam. iv. 12; Is. xxxiii. 22; 1 Tim. iii. 15; 2 Cor. x. 4, 5; Is. xxxii. 2; Luke i. 71.) 2, In instituting the ordinances of his worship, and appointing his ministers and officers for the dispensing of them. 3, In giving laws for the ordering of all our ways, and the ways of his house. 4, In giving power and life to all his institutions, and to his people by them. 5, In protecting and delivering his church against and from all the enemies of their peace.

5. The power granted by Christ unto the body of the church and brotherhood, is a *prerogative* or *privilege* which the church doth exercise—1. In *choosing* their own officers, whether elders or deacons. (Acts vi. 3. 5. and xiv. 23, and ix. 26; Mat. xviii. 15, 16, 17.) 2, In *admission* of these members; and therefore there is great reason they should have power to remove any from their fellowship again. Hence, in case of offence, any brother hath power to convince and admonish an offending brother: and, in case of not hearing him, to take one or two more to set on the admonition: and in case of not hearing them, to proceed to tell the church: and as his offence may require, the whole church has power to proceed to the censure of him, whether by admonition or excommunication: (Tit. iii. 10; Col. iv. 17; Mat. xviii. 17; 2 Cor. ii. 7, 8.) and upon his repentance to restore him again unto his former communion.

6. In case an elder offend incorrigibly, the matter so requiring, as the church had power to call him to office, so they have power according to order (the counsel of other churches, where it may be had, directing thereto) to remove him from his office, and being now but a member, (Col. iv. 17; Ro. xvi. 17; Mat. xviii. 17,) in case he add contumacy to his sin, the church, that had power to receive him into their fellowship, hath also the same power to cast him out that they have concerning any other member.

7. Church-government or rule is placed by Christ in the officers of the church, (1 Tim. v. 17; Heb. xiii. 17; 1 Thes. v. 12,) who are therefore called *rulers,* while they rule with God: yet, in case of male-administration, they are subject to the power of the church, as hath been said before. (Rom. xii. 8; 1 Tim.

v. 17; 1 Cor. xii. 28, 29; Heb. xiii. 7. 17.) The Holy Ghost frequently—yea, always—where it mentioneth church-rule and church government, ascribeth it to elders: whereas the work and duty of the people is expressed in the phrase of "obeying their elders," and "submitting themselves unto them in the Lord." So as it is manifest that an organick or compleat church is a body politick, consisting of some that are governours and some that are governed in the Lord.

8. The power which Christ hath committed to the elders is to feed and rule the church of God, and accordingly to call the church together upon any weighty occasion: (Acts xx. 28, and vi. 2; Numb. xvi. 12; Ezek. xivi. 10; Acts xiii. 15; Hos. iv. 4.) when the members so called, without just cause, may not refuse to come, nor when they are come, depart before they are dismissed, nor speak in the church, before they have leave from the elders, nor continue so doing when they require silence; nor may they oppose or contradict the judgment or sentence of the elders, without sufficient and weighty cause, because such practices are manifestly contrary unto order and government, and inlets of disturbance, and tend to confusion.

9. It belongs also unto the elders before to examine any officers or members before they be received of the church, (Rev. ii. 2; 1 Tim. v. 19; Acts xxi. 18. 22, 23; 1 Cor. v. 4, 5,) to receive the accusations brought to the church, and to prepare them for the churches hearing. In handling of offences and other matters before the church, they have power to declare and publish the will of God touching the same, and to pronounce sentence with the consent of the church. (Numb. vi. 23 to 26.) Lastly, They have power, when they dismiss the people, to bless them in the name of the Lord.

10. This power of government in the elders doth not any wise prejudice the power of privilege in the brotherhood; as neither the power of privilege in the brethren, doth prejudice the power of government in the elders. (Acts xiv. 15. 23, and vi. 2; 1 Cor. v. 4; 2 Cor. ii. 6, 7,) but they may sweetly agree together; as we may see in the example of the apostles, furnished with the greatest church-power, who took in the *concurrence* and *consent* of the brethren in church-administrations. Also that Scripture (2 Cor. ii. 9, and x. 6) doth declare that what the churches were to *act* and to *do* in these matters, they were to do in a way of obedience, and that not only to the direction of the apostles, but also of their ordinary elders. (Heb. xiii. 17.)

11. From the promises, namely, that the ordinary power of government belonging only to the elders, power of privilege remaining with the brotherhood, (as the power of judgment in matters of censure and power of liberty in matters of liberty,) it followeth that in an organick church and right administration, all church-acts proceed after the manner of a mixt administration, so as no church-act can be consummated or perfected without the consent of both. . . .

CHAPTER XIII

Of Church-Members, Their Removal from One Church to Another, and of Recommendation and Dismission

1. Church-members may not remove or depart from the church, and so one from another as they please, nor without just and weighty cause, but ought to live and dwell together, (Heb. x. 25,) forasmuch as they are commanded not to forsake the assembling of themselves together. Such departure tends to the dissolution and ruine of the body, as the pulling of stones and pieces of timber from the building, and of members from the natural body, tend to the destruction of the whole.

2. It is, therefore, the duty of church-members, in such times and places, where counsel may be had, to consult with the church

whereof they are members (Pro. xi. 16,) about their removal, that, accordingly, they having their approbation, may be encouraged, or otherwise desist. They who are joined with consent, should not depart without consent, except forced thereunto.

3. If a member's departure be manifestly unsafe and sinful, the church may not consent thereunto; for in so doing, (Ro. xiv. 23,) they should not act in faith, and should partake with him in his sin. (1 Tim. v. 22.) If the case be doubtful and the person not to be persuaded, (Acts xxi. 14,) it seemeth best to leave the matter unto God, and not forcibly to detain him.

4. Just reasons for a member's removal of himself from the church, are—1, If a man cannot continue without partaking in sin. (Eph. v. 11.) 2, In case of personal persecution: (Acts ix. 25. 29, 30, and viii. 1,) so Paul departed from the disciples at Damascus; also, in case of general persecution, when all are scattered. In case of real, and not only pretended want of competent subsistence, a door being opened for better supply in another place, (Neh. xiii. 20,) together with the means of spiritual edification. In these or like cases, a member may lawfully remove, and the church cannot lawfully detain him.

5. To separate from a church, either out of contempt of their holy fellowship, (2 Tim. iv. 10,) or out of covetousness, or for greater enlargements, with just grief to the church, or out of schism, or want of love, and out of a spirit of contention in respect of some unkindness, of some evil only *conceived* or *indeed* in the church, which might and should be tolerated and healed with a spirit of meekness, and of which evil the church is not yet convinced (tho' perhaps himself be) nor admonished; for these or the like reasons, to withdraw from publique communion to word or seals, or censures, is unlawful and sinful.

6. Such members as have orderly moved their habitation, ought to join themselves unto the church in order (Isa. lvi. 8,) where they do inhabit, (Acts ix. 26,) if it may be; otherwise, they can neither perform the duties nor receive the priviledges of members. Such an example, tolerated in some, is apt to corrupt others, which, if many should follow, would threaten the dissolution and confusion of churches, contrary to the Scripture (1 Cor. xiv. 33.)

7. Order requires that a member thus removing, have letters testimonial and of dismission from the church (Act. xviii. 27,) whereof he yet is, unto the church whereunto he desireth to be joined, lest the church should be deluded; that the church may receive him in faith, and not be corrupted in receiving deceivers and false brethren. Until the person dismissed be received unto another church, he ceaseth not by his letters of dismission to be a member of the church whereof he was. The church cannot make a member *no* member but by excommunication.

8. If a member be called to remove only for a time where a church is (Rom. xvi. 1, 2,) letters of recommendation are requisite and sufficient for communion with that church (2 Cor. iii. 1) in the ordinances and in their watch; as Phoebe, a servant of the church at Cenchrea, had a letter written for her to the church at Rome, that she might be received as becometh saints.

9. Such letters of recommendation and dismission (Acts xviii. 27) were written for Apollos, for Marcus to the Colossians, (Col. iv. 10,) for Phoebe to the Romans, (Rom. xvi. 1,) for sundry other churches. (2 Cor. iii. 5.) And the apostle tells us that some persons, not sufficiently known otherwise, have special need of such letters, tho' he, for his part, had no need thereof. The use of them is to be a benefit and help to the party for whom they are written, and for the furthering of his receiving among the saints, in the place whereto he goeth, and the due satisfaction of them in their receiving of him.

CHAPTER XIV

Of Excommunication and Other Censures

1. The censures of the church are appointed by Christ for the preventing, removing and healing of offences in the church; (1 Tim. v. 20; Jude 19; Deu. xiii. 11: 1 Cor. v. 6; Rom. ii. 24; Rev. ii. 14, 15, 16. 20,) for the reclaiming and gaining of offending brethren; for the deterring others from the like offences; for purging out the leaven which may infect the whole lump; for vindicating the honour of Christ and of his church, and the holy profession of the gospel; and for preventing of the wrath of God, that may justly fall upon the church, if they should suffer his covenant and the seals thereof to be profaned by notorious and obstinate offenders.

2. If an offence be private, (Mat. v. 23, 24,) (one brother offending another) the offender is to go and acknowledge his repentance for it unto his offended brother, who is then to forgive him; but if the offender neglect or refuse to do it, the brother offended is to go, and convince and admonish him of it, between themselves privately: if therefore the offender be brought to repent of his offence, the admonisher has won his brother: but if the offender hear not his brother, the brother of the offended is to take with him one or two more, (verse 16,) that in the mouth of two or three witnesses every word may be established, (whether the word of admonition, if the offender receive it; or the word of complaint, if he refuse it,) for if he refuse it, (verse 17,) the offended brother is by the mouth of the elders to tell the church, and if he hear the church, and declare the same by penitent confession, he is recovered and gained: And if the church discern him to be willing to hear, yet not fully convinced of his offence, as in case of heresie, they are to dispence to him a publick admonition; which, declaring the offender to lye under the publick offence of the church, doth thereby with-hold or suspend him from the holy fellowship of the Lord's Supper, till his offence be removed by penitent confession. If he still continue obstinate, they are to cast him out by excommunication.

3. But if the offence be more publick at first, and of a more hainous and criminal nature, (1 Cor. v. 4. 8, 11,) to wit, such as are condemned by the light of nature; then the church, without such gradual proceeding, is to cast out the offender from their holy communion, for the further mortifying of his sin, and the healing of his soul in the day of the Lord Jesus.

4. In dealing with an offender, great care is to be taken that we be neither over-strict or rigorous, nor too indulgent or remiss: our proceeding herein ought to be with a spirit of meekness, considering ourselves, lest we also be tempted, (Gal. vi. 1,) and that the best of us have need of much forgiveness from the Lord. (Math. xviii. 34, 35.) Yet the winning and healing of the offender's soul being the end of these endeavours, (Ezek. xiii. 10,) we must not daub with untempered mortar, nor heal the wounds of our brethren slightly. On some, have compassion; others, save with fear.

5. While the offender remains excommunicate, (Mat. xviii. 17.) the church is to refrain from all member-like communion with him in spiritual things, (1 Cor. v. 11,) and also from all familiar communion with him in civil things, (2 Thes. iii. 6. 14,) farther than the necessity of natural or domestical or civil relations do require; and are therefore to forbear to eat and drink with him, that he may be ashamed.

6. Excommunication being a spiritual punishment, it doth not prejudice the excommunicate in, or deprive him of his civil rights, and therefore toucheth not princes or magistrates in respect of their civil dignity or authority; (1 Cor. xiv. 24, 25,) and the excommunicate being but as a publican and a heathen, (2 Thes. iii. 14,) heathens being lawfully permitted to hear the *word* in church-assemblies,

we acknowledge therefore the like liberty of hearing the word may be permitted to persons excommunicate that is permitted unto heathen. And because we are not without hope of his recovery, we are not to account him as an enemy, but to admonish him as a brother. . . .

CHAPTER XV

Of the Communion of Churches One with Another

1. Altho' *churches* be distinct, and therefore may not be confounded one with another, and equal, and therefore have not dominion one over another; (Rev. i. 4; Cant. viii. 8; Rom. xvi. 16; 1 Cor. xvi. 19; Acts xv. 23; Rev. ii. 1,) yet all the churches ought to preserve *church-communion* one with another, because they are all united unto Christ, not only as a mystical, but as a political head: whence is derived a communion suitable thereunto.

2. The communion of churches is exercised several ways. (Cant. viii. 8.) 1, By way of *mutual care* in taking thought for one another's welfare. 2, By way of *consultation* one with another, when we have occasion to require the judgment and counsel of other churches, touching any person or cause, wherewith they may be better acquainted than our selves; (Acts xv. 2,) as the church of Antioch consulted with the Apostles and elders of the church at Jerusalem, about the question of circumcision of the Gentiles, and about the false teachers that broached that doctrine. . . .

3. A way, then, of communion of churches, is by way of *admonition;* to wit, in case any public offence be found in a church, which they either discern not, or are slow in proceeding to use the means for the removing and healing of. Paul had no authority over Peter, yet when he saw Peter not walking with a right foot, he publickly rebuked him before the church. (Gal. ii. 11 to 14.) Tho' churches have no more authority one over another, than one apostle had over another, yet, as one apostle might admonish another, so may one church admonish another, and yet without usurpation. (Matth. xviii. 15, 16, 17, by proportion.) . . .

4. A fourth way of communion with churches, is by way of *participation:* the members of one church occasionally coming to another, we willingly admit them to partake with them at the Lord's table, (1 Cor. xii. 13,) it being the seal of our communion not only with Christ, not only with the members of our own church, but also of all the churches of the saints: In which regard we refuse not to baptize their children presented to us, if either their own minister be absent, or such a fruit of holy fellowship be desired with us. In like cases, such churches as are furnished with more ministers than one, do willingly afford one of their own ministers to supply the absence or place of a sick minister of another church for a needful season. . . .

CHAPTER XVI

Of Synods

1. Synods, orderly assembled, (Acts xv. 2 to 15,) and rightly proceeding according to the pattern, (Acts xv.) we acknowledge as the ordinance of Christ: and tho' not absolutely necessary to the being, yet many times, thro' the iniquity of men and perverseness of times, necessary to the well-being of churches, for the establishment of truth and peace therein. . . .

4. It belongeth unto synods and councils to debate and determine controversies of faith and cases of conscience; (Acts xv. 1, 2. 6, 7: 1 Chr. xv. 13; 2 Chr. xxix. 6, 7; Acts xv. 24. 28, 29,) to clear from the word holy directions for the holy worship of God and good government of the church; to bear witness against mal-administration and corruption in doctrine or manners, in any particular church;

and to give directions for the reformation thereof: not to exercise church-censures in way of discipline, nor any other act of church-authority or jurisdiction which that presidential synod did forbear.

5. The synod's directions and determinations, so far as consonant to the word of God, are to be received with reverence and submission; not only for their agreement therewith, (Acts xv.) (which is the principal ground thereof, and without which they bind not at all,) but also, secondarily, for the power whereby they are made, as being an ordinance of God appointed thereunto in his word.

6. Because it is difficult, if not impossible, for many churches to come together in one place, in their members universally; therefore they may assemble by their delegates or messengers, as the church at Antioch went not all to Jerusalem, but some select men for that purpose (Acts xv. 2.) Because none are or should be more fit to know the state of the churches, nor to advise of ways for the good thereof, than elders; therefore it is fit that, in the choice of the messengers for such assemblies, they have special respect unto such; yet, inasmuch as not only Paul and Barnabas, but certain others also, (Acts xv. 2. 22, 23,) were sent to Jerusalem from Antioch, (Acts xv.) and when they were come to Jerusalem, not only the apostles and elders, but other bretheren, also do assemble and meet about the matter; therefore synods are to consist both of elders and other church-members, endued with gifts, and sent by the churches, not excluding the presence of any bretheren in the churches.

CHAPTER XVII

Of the Civil Magistrate's Power in Matters Ecclesiastical

1. It is lawful, profitable and necessary for Christians to gather themselves together into church estate, and therein to exercise all the ordinances of Christ, according unto the word, (Acts ii. 41. 47, and iv. 1, 2, 3,) although the consent of the magistrate could not be had thereunto: because the apostles and Christians in their time did frequently thus practise, when the magistrates, being all of them Jewish and Pagan, and most persecuting enemies, would give no countenance or consent to such matters.

2. Church-government stands in no opposition to civil government of commonwealths, nor any way intrencheth upon the authority of civil magistrates in their jurisdictions; nor any whit weakeneth their hands in governing, but rather strengtheneth them, and furthereth the people in yielding more hearty and conscionable obedience to them, whatsoever some ill affected persons to the ways of Christ have suggested, to alienate the affections of kings and princes from the ordinances of Christ; as if the kingdom of Christ in his church could not rise and stand, without the falling and weakening of their government, which is also of Christ, (Isa. xlix. 23,) whereas the contrary is most true, that they may both stand together and flourish, the one being helpful unto the other, in their distinct and due administrations.

3. The power and authority of magistrates is not for the restraining of churches (Rom. xiii. 4; 1 Tim. ii. 2,) or any other good works, but for helping in and furthering thereof; and therefore the consent and countenance of magistrates, when it may be had, is not to be slighted, or lightly esteemed; but, on the contrary, it is part of that honor due to Christian magistrates to desire and crave their consent and approbation therein; which being obtained, the churches may then proceed in their way with much more encouragement and comfort.

4. It is not in the power of magistrates to compel their subjects to become church-members, and to partake of the Lord's Supper; (Ezek. xliv. 7. 9,) for the priests are reproved that brought unworthy ones into the sanctuary: (1 Cor. v. 11;) then it was unlawful for the priests, so it is as unlawful to be done by civil magistrates; those whom the church is to cast out, if they were in, the magistrate ought not to thrust them into the church, nor to hold them therein.

5. As it is unlawful for church-officers to meddle with the sword of the magistrate, (Mat. ii. 25, 26,) so it is unlawful for the magistrate to meddle with the work proper to church-officers. The acts of Moses and David, who were not only princes but prophets, were extraordinary, therefore not inimitable. Against such usurpation the Lord witnessed by smiting Uzziah with leprosie for presuming to offer incense. (2 Chr. xxvi. 16, 17.)

Nathaniel Ward, 1578–1652

Nathaniel Ward was born in Haverhill, England, the son of a Puritan minister. He studied law at Emmanuel College, Cambridge, and later practiced law in England. On a trip to Heidelberg, he met the theologian David Pareus who convinced him to enter the ministry. After serving as minister to British merchants at Elbing, Prussia, Ward returned to Britain and preached Puritan doctrine in a Church of England congregation. Bishop Laud, ally of the Stuart kings and leading opponent of the Puritans, presented charges of nonconformity against Ward, and in 1633 removed him from his position.

Ward then migrated to Massachusetts, joining the Reverend Thomas Parker at Ipswich (which the Indians called Aggawam).

In 1638, Ward resigned his pastorate due to failing health, but soon accepted an offer from the General Court to help prepare a legal code for Massachusetts. The "Body of Liberties" codified the laws of Massachusetts and is one of the earliest contributions to the American constitutional tradition.

It would be a mistake, however, to confuse Ward's concern for enumerating the civil liberties of Massachusetts' citizens with the concerns of contemporary civil libertarians. Ward's most famous work, *The Simple Cobbler of Aggawam* (published under the pseudonym of Theodore de la Guard), was a clear and strident attack on the idea of religious toleration. The Puritans had not come to Massachusetts simply to find religious liberty, but rather to create a religious community capable of regenerating the people and the Church of England. Ward held to this view even as many English Puritans joined with other sectaries and Independents in Oliver Cromwell's New Model Army to promote "toleration" in England in the 1640s. Simply, Ward and the Puritans of New England by and large held to more orthodox views.

In 1647, the year of the *Simple Cobbler*'s publication, Ward returned to England where he spent his remaining years.

Nathaniel Ward

The Simple Cobbler of Aggawam, 1647

. . . I dare take upon me, to be the Herald of *New-England* so far, as to proclaim to the World, in the name of our Colony, that all Familists, Antinomians, Anabaptists, and other Enthusiasts shall have free Liberty to keep away from us, and such as will come to be gone as fast as they can, the sooner the better.

Secondly, I dare aver, that God doth no where in his word tolerate Christian States, to give Tolerations to such adversaries of his Truth, if they have power in their hands to suppress them. . . .

SOURCE: *Tracts and Other Papers,* ed. Peter Force (Washington, D.C., 1844).

If the Devil might have his free option, I believe he would ask nothing else, but liberty to enfranchize all false Religions, and to embondage the true; nor should he need: It is much to be feared that lax Tolerations upon State-pretences and planting necessities, will be the next subtle Stratagem he will spread to distaste the Truth of God, and supplant the Peace of the Churches. Tolerations in things tolerable, exquisitely drawn out by the lines of the Scripture, and pencil of the Spirit, are the sacred favours of Truth, the due latitudes of Love, the fair Compartments of Christian fraternity: but irregular dispensations, dealt forth by the facilities of men, are the frontiers of error, the redoubts of Schism, the perilous irritaments of carnal and spiritual enmity.

My heart hath naturally detested four things: The standing of the Aprocrypha in the Bible; Foreigners dwelling in my Country, to crowd out Native Subjects into the corners of the Earth; Alchymized Coins; Tolerations of divers Religions, or of one Religion in segregant shapes: He that willingly assents to the last, if he examines his heart by daylight, his Conscience will tell him, he is either an Atheist, or an Heretic, or an Hypocrite, or at best a captive to some Lust: . . .

To tolerate more than indifferences, is not to deal indifferently with God: He that doth it, takes his Scepter out of his hand, and bids him stand by. Who hath to do to institute Religion but God. The power of all Religion and Ordinances, lies in their Purity: their Purity in their Simplicity: then are mixtures pernicious. I lived in a City, where a Papist Preached in one Church, a Lutheran in another, a Calvinist in a third; a Lutheran one part of the day, a Calvinist the other, in the same Pulpit: the Religion of that Place was but motly and meagre, their affections Leopard-like.

If the whole Creature should conspire to do the Creator a mischief, or offer him an insolency, it would be in nothing more, than in erecting untruths against his Truth, or by sophisticating his Truths with humane medleys: the removing of some one iota in Scripture, may draw out all the life, and traverse all the Truth of the whole Bible: but to authorize an untruth, by a Toleration of State, is to build a sconce against the walls of Heaven, to batter God out of his Chair: . . .

That State is wise, that will improve all pains and patience rather to compose, than tolerate differences in Religion. There is no divine Truth, but hath much Celestial fire in it from the Spirit of Truth: nor no irreligious untruth, without its proportion of Antifire from the spirit of Error to contradict it: the zeal of the one, the virulency of the other, must necessar-

ily kindle Combustions. Fiery diseases seated in the Spirit, imbroil the whole frame of the body: others more external and cool, are less dangerous. They which divide in Religion, divide in God; they who divide in him, divide beyond *Genus Generalissimum*, where there is no reconciliation, without atonement; that is, without uniting in him, who is One, and in his Truth, which is also one. . . .

And prudent are those Christians, that will rather give what may be given, than hazard all by yielding nothing. To sell all Peace of Country, to buy some Peace of Conscience unseasonably, is more avarice than thrift, imprudence than patience: they deal not equally, that set any Truth of God at such a rate; but they deal wisely that will stay till the Market is fallen. . . .

He that is willing to tolerate any Religion, or discrepant way of Religion, besides his own, unless it be in matters merely indifferent, either doubts of his own, or is not sincere in it.

He that is willing to tolerate any unsound Opinion, that his own may also be tolerated, though never so sound, will for a need hang God's Bible at the Devil's girdle.

Every toleration of false Religions, or Opinions hath as many Errors and Sins in it, as all the false Religions and Opinions it tolerates, and one sound one more.

That State that will give Liberty of Conscience in matters of Religion, must give Liberty of Conscience and Conversation in their Moral Laws, or else the Fiddle will be out of Tune, and some of the strings crack. . . .

It is said, That Men ought to have Liberty of their Conscience, and that it is Persecution to debar them of it: I can rather stand amazed than reply to this: it is an astonishment to think that the brains of men should be parboiled in such impious ignorance; Let all the wits under the Heavens lay their heads together and find an Assertion worse than this (one excepted) I will Petition to be chosen the universal Idiot of the World. . . .

How all Religions should enjoy their liberty, Justice its due regularity, Civil cohabitation moral honesty, in one and the same Jurisdiction, is beyond the Artique of my comprehension. If the whole conclave of Hell can so compromise, exadverse, and diametrical contradictions, as to compolitize such a multi-monstrous maufrey of heteroclytes and quicquidlibets quietly; I trust I may say with all humble reverence, they can do more than the Senate of Heaven. . . .

Roger Williams, 1603–1683

Born in London and educated at Cambridge with the help of the lawyer Sir Edward Coke, Williams took holy orders in the Church of England. However, he soon became a Puritan and emigrated to the Massachusetts Bay Colony in 1631. Restless in his quest for religious truth, Williams became a Baptist and finally a Seeker, that is, one who subscribed to basic Christian tenets without adopting a formal sectarian creed.

While in Massachusetts, Williams began to openly criticize Puritan attempts to create a theocratic state and further angered Puritan leaders when he questioned the right of colonists to occupy Indian lands without paying full compensation. As a consequence of his actions, Williams was banished from Massachusetts Bay in 1636. He fled south, bought land from the Indians, and helped establish the colony of Rhode Island. Influenced by Williams's views, Rhode Island eliminated religious requirements for suffrage, held frequent elections, and created popular forms of government including "initiative" and "recall."

In 1643, Williams returned to England to obtain a royal charter that would protect Rhode Island's independence against the claims of Massachusetts. While there, he wrote *The Bloody Tenent of Persecution for Cause of Conscience*, attacking John Cotton's writings which had advocated an active state role in enforcing church discipline. Written in the same year as *Areopagitica*, John Milton's famous defense of free conscience, *The Bloody Tenent* is one of the earliest and most passionate arguments in Anglo-American thought for religious toleration, freedom of conscience, and separation of church and state.

The following passages from *The Bloody Tenent* take the form of a dialogue between Peace and Truth (who represents the views of Roger Williams).

Roger Williams

The Bloudy Tenent of Persecution for Cause of Conscience (1644)

INTRODUCTION

First, that the blood of so many hundred thousand souls of *Protestants* and *Papists*, spilt in the *Wars* of *present* and *former Ages,* for their respective *Consciences,* is not *required* nor *accepted* by *Jesus Christ* the *Prince* of *Peace.*

Secondly, Pregnant *Scriptures* and *Arguments* are throughout the Worke proposed against the *Doctrine* of *Persecution* for *cause of Conscience.*

Thirdly, Satisfactorie Answers are given to *Scriptures,* and *objections* produced by Mr. *Calvin, Beza,* Mr. *Cotton,* and the Ministers of the New England Church and others former and later, tending to prove the *Doctrine* of *Persecution* for Cause of *Conscience.*

Fourthly, The *Doctrine* of *Persecution* for cause of *Conscience,* is proved guilty of all the *blood* of the *Soules* crying for *vengeance* under the *Alter.*

Fifthly, All *Civill States* with their *Officers* of *justice* in their respective *constitutions* and *administrations* are proved *essentially Civil,* and therefore not *judges, Governours* or *Defendours* of the *Spirituall* or *Christian State* and *Worship.*

Sixthly, It is the will and command of *God,* that since the comming of his Sonne the *Lord Jesus* a *permission* of the most *Paganish, Jewish, Turkish* or *Antichristian consciences* and *worships,*

SOURCE: Roger Williams, *The Bloody Tenent of Persecution for Cause of Conscience* (London: 1644).

be granted to *all* men in all *Nations* and *Countries:* and they are onely to bee *fought* against with that *Sword* which is only (in *Soule matters*) able to conquer to wit the *Sword of Gods spirit,* the *Word of God.*

Seventhly, the *state* of the Land of *Israel,* the *Kings* and *people* thereof in *Peace & War,* is proved *figurative* and *ceremoniall,* and no *patterne* nor *president* for any *Kingdoms* or *civill state* in the *world* to follow.

Eightly, *God* requireth not an *uniformity* of *Religion* to be *inacted* and *inforced* in any *civill state;* which inforced *uniformity* (sooner or later) is the greatest occasion of *civill Warre, ravishing* of *conscience, persecution* of *Christ Jesus* in his *servants,* and of the *hypocrisie* and *destruction* of *millions* of *souls.*

Ninthly, In holding an inforced *uniformity* of *Religion* in a *civill state,* we must necessarily *disclaime* our desires and hopes of the *Jews conversion* to *Christ.*

Tenthly, An inforced *uniformity* of *Religion* throughout a *Nation* or *Civill state,* confounds the *Civill* and *Religious,* denies the principles of Christianity and civility, and that *Jesus Christ* is come in the flesh.

Eleventhly, The permission of other *consciences* and *worships* that a state professeth, only can (according to God) procure a firme and lasting *peace,* (good *assurance* being taken according to the *wisdome* of the *civill state* for *uniformity* of *civil obedience* from all sorts).

Twelfthly, lastly, true *civility* and *Christianity* may both flourish in a *State* or *Kingdome,* notwithstanding the *permission* of diverse and contrary *conscience,* either of *Jew* or *Gentile.* . . .

TO EVERY COURTEOUS READER

While I plead the Cause of *Truth* and *Innociencie* against the bloody *Doctrine* of *Persecution* for cause of *conscience,* I judge it not unfit to give *alarme* to my selfe, and all men to prepare to be *persecuted* or hunted for cause of *conscience.*

Whether thou standest charged with 10 or but *3 Talents,* if thou huntest any for cause of *conscience,* how canst thou say thou followest the *Lambe* of *God* who so abhorr'd that practice?

If *Paul,* if *Jesus Christ* were present here at *London,* and the *questions* were proposed what *Religion* would they approve of: The *Papists, Prelatists, Presbyterians, Independents, &c.* would each say, Of mine, of mine.

But put the second *question,* if one of the severall sorts should by *major vote* attaine the *Sword* of steele: what weapons doth *Christ Jesus* authorize them to fight with in His cause? Doe not all men hate the *persecutor,* and every *conscience* true or false complaine of *cruelty, tyranny? &c.*

Two *mountaines* of *crying guilt* lye heavie upon the backes of All that name the name of *Christ* in the eyes of *Jewes, Turkes* and *Pagans.*

First, The blasphemies of their *Idolatrous inventions, superstitions,* and most *unchristian conversations.*

Secondly, the bloody irreligious and inhumane *oppressions* and *destructions* under the maske or vaile of the Name of *Christ, &c.*

O how like is the *jealous Jehova,* the consuming fire to end these *present slaughters* in a greater slaughter of the holy Witnesses? *Rev. 11.*

Six years preaching of so much Truth of *Christ* (as that time afforded in *K. Edwards* dayes) kindles the flames of *Q. Maries* blood persecutions.

Who can now but expect that after so many scores of yeares *preaching* and *professing* of more *Truth,* and amongst so many great *contentions* amongst the very best of *Protestants,* a fierie furnace should be heat, and who sets not now the *fires* kindling? . . .

In vaine have *English Parliaments* permitted *English Bibles* in the poorest *English* houses, and the simplist man or woman to search the Scriptures, if yet against their soules perswasion from the Scripture, they should be forced (as if they lived in *Spaine* or *Rome* it selfe without the sight of a *Bible*) to beleeve as the Church beleeves.

Fourthly, having tried, we must hold fast, *1 Thessal. 5.* upon the losse of a Crowne, *Revel. 13.* we must not let goe for all the fleabitings of the present afflictions, *&c.* having bought Truth deare, we must not sell it cheape, not the least graine of it for the whole World, no not for the saving of Soules, though our owne most precious; least of all for the bitter sweetning of a little vanishing pleasure.

For a little puffe of credit and reputation from the changeable breath of uncertaine sons of men.

For the broken bagges of Riches on Eagles wings: For a dreame of these, any or all of these which on our death-bed vanish and leave tormenting stings behinde them: Oh how much better is it from the love of Truth, from the love of the Father of lights, from whence it comes, from the love of the Sonne of God, who is the way and the Truth, to say as he, *John 18.37.* For this end was I borne, and for this end came I into the World that I might beare witnesse to the Truth.

A REPLY TO THE AFORESAID ANSWER OF MR. COTTON IN A CONFERENCE BETWEEN TRUTH AND PEACE . . .

Chap. III

Truth. In the Answer Mr. *Cotton* first layes downe severall *distinctions* and *conclusions* of his owne, tending to prove persecution.

Secondly, *Answers* to the *Scriptures*, and *Arguments* proposed against *persecution*.

Peace. The first distinction is this: By persecution for cause of *Conscience*, "I conceive you meane either for professing some point of *doctrine* which you beleeve in *conscience* to be the *truth*, or for *practising* some worke which you beleeve in *conscience* to be a *religious* dutie."

Truth, I acknowledge that to molest any person, *Jew* or *Gentile*, for either professing *doctrine*, or practising *worship* meerly *religions* or spirituall, it is to persecute him, and such a person (whatever his *doctrine* or *practice* be true or false) suffereth persecution for *conscience*.

But withall I desire it may bee well observed, that this *distinction* is not full and complete: For beside this that a man may be persecuted because he holdeth or practiseth what he beleeves in *conscience* to be a *Truth*, (as *Daniel* did, for which he was cast into the *Lyons* den, *Dan. 6*) and many thousands of *Christians*, because they durst not cease to *preach* and *practise* what they beleeved was by *God* commanded, as the *Apostles* answered (*Acts 4 & 5*). I say besides this a man may also be persecuted, because hee dares not be *constrained* to yeeld obedience to such *doctrines* and *worships* as are by men invented and appointed. So the three famous *Jewes* were cast into the fiery furnace for refusing to fall downe (in a *non-conformity* to the whole conforming world) before the golden *Image*, Dan. 3.21. So thousands of *Christs witnesses* (and of late in those bloudy *Marian* dayes) have rather chose to yeeld their *bodies* to all sorts of *torments*, then to subscribe to *doctrines*, or practise *worships* unto which the States and Times (as *Nabuchadnezzer* to his golden *Image*) have compelled and urged them.

A chaste *wife* will not onely abhorre to be restrained from her *husbands bed,* as adulterous and polluted, but also abhore (if not much more) to bee constrained to the *bed* of a *stranger*. And what is abominable in *corporall*, is much more loathsome in *spirituall whoredomes* and defilement.

The Spouse of *Christ Jesus* who could not finde her soules beloved in the *wayes* of his *worship* and *Ministery*, (*Cant. 1.3.* and *5*. Chapters) abhorred to turne aside to other *Flockes*, *Worships, &c.* and to imbrace the bosome of a false *Christe, Cant. 1. 8.*

Chap. VI

Peace. The next *distinction* concerning the manner of *persons* holding forth the aforesaid *practices* (not onely the *waightier duties* of the *Law*, but points of *doctrines* and *worship* lesse principall.)

"Some (saith he) hold them forth in a *meeke* and *peaceable* way: some "with such *arrogance* and *impetuousnesse*, as of it selfe tendeth to the "disturbance of *civill peace.*"

Truth. In the examination of this *distinction* we shall discusse,

First, what is *civill Peace*, (wherein we shall vindicate thy name the better.)

Secondly, what it is to hold forth a Doctrine or Practice in this *impetuousnesse* or *arrogancy*.

First, for *civill peace*, what is it but *pax civitatis* the peace of the citie, whether an *English* City, *Scotch*, or *Irish* Citie, or further abroad, *French*, *Spanish, Turkish City, &c.*

Thus it pleased the Father of *Lights* to define it, *Jerem. 29. 7*. Pray for the *peace* of the *City;* which *peace* of the *City*, or *Citizens*, so compacted in a *civill* way of *union*, may be intire, unbroken, safe, &c. notwithstanding so many thousands of *Gods people* the *Jewes*, were there in *bondage*, and would neither be *constrained* to the *worship* of the Citie *Babell*, nor restrained from so much of the *worship* of the true *God*, as they then could practice, as is plaine in the practice of the 3 Worthies, *Shadrach, Misack,* and *Abednego*, as also of *Daniel, Dan. 3 & Dan. 6*. (the peace of the *City* or *Kingdome*, being a far different Peace from the Peace of the *Religion* or Spirituall *Worship*, maintained & professed of the Citizens. This *Peace* of their *worship* which *worship* also in some Cities being various) being a false Peace, *Gods people* were and ought to be *Nonconformitants*, not daring either to be *restrained* from the *true*, or *constrained* to *false worship*, and yet without *breach* of the Civill or *Citie-peace*, properly so called.

Peace. Hence it is that so many glorious and flourishing *Cities* of the World maintaine their *Civill* peace, yea the very *Americans &* wildest *Pagans* keep the peace of their *Towns* or *Cities*; though neither in one nor the other can any man prove a true *Church* of God in those places, and consequently no spirituall and heavenly peace: The Peace *Spirituall* (whether true or false) being of a higher and farre different nature from the Peace of the place or people, being meerly and essentially *civill* and *humane*.

Truth. O how lost are the sonnes of men in this point? To illustrate this: The *Church* or *company* of *worshippers* (whether true or false) is like unto a Body or Colledge of *Physitians* in a *Citie*; like unto a *Corporation*, *Society*, or *Company* of *East-Indie* or *Turkish-Merchants*, or any other *Societie* or *Company* in *London*: Which Companies may hold their *Courts*, keep their *Records*, hold *disputations*; and in matters concerning their *Societies*, may dissent, divide, breake into *Schismes* and *Factions*, sue and implead each other at the *Law*, yea wholly breake up and dissolve into pieces and nothing, and yet the *peace* of the *Citie* not be in the least measure impaired or disturbed; because the *essence* or being of the *Citie*, and so the *well-being* and *peace* thereof is essentially distinct from those particular *Societies*; the *Citie-Courts*, *Citie-Lawes*, *Citie-punnishments* distinct from theirs. The *Citie* was before them, and stands absolute and intire, when such a *Corporation* or *Society* is taken down. For instance further, The *City* or *Civill State* of *Ephesus* was essentially distinct from the *worship* of *Diana* in the Citie, or of the *whole city*. Againe, the *Church* of *Christ* in *Ephesus* (which were Gods people, converted and call'd out from the *worship* of that *City* unto *Christiantie* or *worship* of *God* in *Christ*) was distinct from both.

Now suppose that *God* remove the *Candle-ship* of the *Citie of Ephesus* should be altered:

yet (if men be true and honestly ingenuous to *Citie-covenants*, *Combinations* and *Principles*) all this might be without the least impeachment or infringement of the Peace of the *City* of *Ephesus*.

Thus in the Citie of *Smirna* was the Citie it selfe or Civill estate one thing, The Spirituall or Religious state of *Smirna* another; The Church of *Christ* in *Smirna*, distinct from them both; and the *Synagogue* of the *Jews*, whether literally *Jewes* (as some thinke) or mystically, false *Christians*, (as others) called the *Synagogue* of *Sathan*, Revel. 2. distinct from all these. And notwithstanding these spirituall oppositions in point of *Worship* and *Religion*, yet heare we not the least noyse (nor need we, if Men keep but the Bond of *Civility*) of any *Civill breach*, or *breach* of *Civill peace* amongst them: and to persecute Gods people there for Religion, that only was a breach of Civilitie itself.

2. Ob. Peace. It will here be said, Whence then ariseth civill dissentions and uproares about matters of Religion?

Truth. I answer: When a Kingdome or State, Towne or Family, lyes and lives in the guilt of a false God, false Christ, false worship: no wonder if sore eyes be troubled at the appearance of the light, be it never so sweet: No wonder if a body full of corrupt humours be troubled at strong (though wholsome) Physick? If persons sleepy and loving to sleepe be troubled at the noise of shrill (though silver) alarams: No wonder if *Adonijah* and all his company be amazed and troubled at the sound of the right Heyre *King Solomon, 1 King. 1.* If the Husbandmen were troubled when the Lord of the Vineyard sent servant after servant, and at last his onely Sonne, and they beat, and wounded, and kill'd even the Sonne himself, because they meant themselves to seize upon the inheritance, unto which they had no right, *Matth. 21. 38.*

Chap. XVII

Peace. I shall not trouble you (deare Truth) but with one conclusion more, which is this: *viz.* That if a man hold forth errour with *a, boysterous* and *arrogant* spirit, to the disturbance of the civill Peace, he ought to be punished, &c.

Truth. To this I have spoken too, confessing that if any man commit ought of those things which *Paul* was accused of (*Act. 25.11*) he ought not to be spared, yea he ought not, as *Paul* saith, in such cases to refuse to dye.

But if the *matter* be of another *nature*, a spirituall and divine *nature, I have written before in many cases, and might in many more, that the Worship* which a State professeth may bee *contradicted* and *preached* against, and yet no breach of *Civill Peace.* And if a *breach* follow, it is not made by such *doctrines*, but by the boysterous and violent opposers of them.

Such persons onely breake the *Cities* or *Kingdomes* peace, who cry out for *prison* and *Swords* against such who croste their *judgement* or *practice* in *Religion.* For as *Josephs* misstris accused *Joseph* of *uncleannesse*, and calls out for civill violence against him, when *Joseph* was chaste, and her *selfe* guilty: So commonly the meeke and *peacable* of the earth are traduced as *Rebells, factions, peace-breakers*, although they deale not with the *State* or *State-matters*, but *matters* of *divine* and *spirituall* nature, when their *traducers* are the onely *unpeacable*, and guilty of *breach* of *Civill Peace.*

Chap. XXXVII

. . . First, if the *Civill Magistrate* be a *Christian*, a *Disciple* or follower of the meeke *Lamb* of God, he is bound to be far from destroying the *bodies of men*, for refusing to receive the *Lord Jesus Christ*, for otherwise hee should not know (according to this speech of the *Lord Jesus*) what *spirit* he was of, yea and to be ignorant of the sweet end of the coming of the *Son of Man*, which was not to destroy the *bodies of Men*, but to save both *bodies* and *soules, vers. 55. 56.*

Secondly, if the *Civill Magistrate*, being a *Christian*, gifted, *prophesise* in the *Church*, 1

Corinth. 1. 14. although the *Lord Jesus Christ*, whom they in their owne persons hold forth, shall be refused, yet they are here forbidden to call for fire from *heaven*, that is, to produce or inflict any corporall *judgements* upon such *offenders*, remembering the end of the *Lord Jesus* his comming, not to *destroy* mens lives, but to *save* them.

Lastly, this also concernes the *conscience* of the *Civill Magistrate*, as he is bound to preserve the *civill peace* and quiet of the *place* and people under him, he is bound to suffer no man to breake the *Civill Peace*, by laying hands of *violence* upon any, though as vile as the *Samaritanes* for not receiving of the *Lord Jesus Christ.*

It is indeed the *ignorance* and blinde *zeale* of the second *Beast*, the *false Prophet, Rev. 13. 13.* to perswade the *civill Powers* of the earth to persecute the Saints, that is, to bring fiery *judgements* upon them in a *judiciall way*, and to pronounce that such *judgements* of *imprisonments, banishment, death*, proceed from Gods righteous *vengeance* upon such *Hereticks.* So dealt divers *Bishops* in *France*, and *England* too in Queene *Maries* dayes with the Saints of God at their putting to death, declaiming against them in their Sermons to the people, and proclaiming that these persecutions even unto death were *Gods just judgements from heaven upon these Hereticks.*

Chap. XXXIX

. . . It becomes not the *Spirit* of the *Gospel* to convert *Aliens* to the Faith (such as the *Samaritanes*, and the unconverted *Christians* in *Crete*) with *Fire* and *Brimstone.*

Secondly, be they *oppositions within*, and *Church members* (as the Answerer speaks) become *scandelous* in *doctrine*, (I speake not of *scandals* against the *civill State*, which the *civill Magistrate* ought to punish) it is the *Lord* onely (as this Scripture of *Timothy* implyes) who is able to give them *repentance*, and recover them out of *Sathans* snare: to which end also he hath appointed those holy and dreadfull *cen-*

sures in his *Church* or *Kingdome*. True it is, the *Sword* may make (as once the *Lord* complained, *Isa. 10*.) a whole *Nation* of *Hypocrites:* But to recover a Soule from *Sathan* by *repentance,* and to bring them from *Antichristian doctrine* or *worship,* to the *doctrine* or *worship Christian,* in the least true *internall* or *externall* submission, that only works the *All-powerfull God,* by the *Sword* of his Spirit in the hand of his *Spirituall officers.*

What a most wofull proofe thereof have the *Nations* of the Earth given in all *Ages?* And to seeke no further then our *native* Soyle, within a few scores of yeeres, how many wonderfull *changes* in *Religion* hath the *whole Kingdome* made, according to the *change* of the *Governours* thereof, in the severall *Religions* which they themselves imbraced! *Henry* the 7 finds and leaves the *kingdome* absolutely *Popish. Henry* the *8* casts it into a *mould* half *Popish* halfe *Protestant. Edward* the *6.* brings forth an *Edition* all *Protestant.* Queene *Mary* within few yeares defaceth *Edwards* worke, and renders the *Kingdome* (after her Grandfather *Hen 7* his pattern) all *Papish. Maries* short *life* and *Religion* ends together: and *Elizabeth* reviveth her Brother *Edwards* Modell, all Protestant: And some eminent *Witnesses* of Gods Truth against *Antichrist,* have enclined to believe, that before the downfall of that *Beast,* England must once againe bow down her faire Neck to his proud usurping yoake and foot.

Peace. It hath been *Englands* sinfull shame, to fashion & change their *Garments* and *Religions* with wondrous *ease* and *lightness,* as a *higher Power,* a *stronger Sword* hath prevailed; after the ancient patterne of *Nebuchadnezzars* bowing the whole world in one most solemne *uniformitie* of *worship* to his *Golden Image,* Dan. 3.

Chap. XL

. . . Accordingly an *unbelieving* Soule being dead in sinne (although he be changed from one *worship* to another, like a dead man shifted into severall changes of *apparell*) cannot please *God,* Heb. 11. and consequently, whatever such an *unbelieving & unregenerate* person acts in *Worship* or *Religion,* it is but sinne, *Rom. 14.* *Preaching* sinne, *praying* (though without beads or booke) sinne; *breaking of bread,* or *Lords supper* finne, yea as odious as the oblation of Swines *blood,* a Dogs *neck,* or *killing of a Man.* Isa. 66.

But *Faith* it is that *gift* which proceeds alone from the *Father* of Lights, *Phil. 1. 29.* and till he please to make his *light* arise and open the eyes of blind sinners, their soules shall lie fast asleep (and the faster, in that a *Sword* of steele compells them to a *worship* in *hypocrise*) in the dungeons of *Spirituall darknesse* and *Sathans slavery.*

Peace. I adde, that a *civill Sword* (as wofull experience in all ages hath proved) is so far from bringing or helping forward an *opposite* in *Religion* to *repentance,* that *Magistrates* sinne grievously against the *works* of God and *blood* of Soules, by such proceedings. Because as (commonly) the suffrings of *false* and *Antichristian Teachers* harden their *followers,* who being blind, by this meanes are occasioned to tumble into the *ditch of Hell* after their *blind leaders,* with more inflamed zeale of lying confidence. So secondly, *violence* and a *Sword* of *steele* begets such an *impression* in the sufferers, all such *mysticall* wolves must spiritually and mystically so be slain. And the *Witnesses* of *Truth,* Revel. 11. speake fire, and kill all that hurt them, by that *fierie* Word of *God,* and that two-edged *Sword* in their hand, *Psal. 149.*

But oh what streames of the *blood* of Saints have been and must be shed (untill the *Lambe* have obtained the Victorie, *Revel. 17.*) by this unmercifull (and in the state of the New *Testament,* when the *Church* is spread all the World over) most *bloody doctrine,* viz. The *wolves* (Hereticks) are to be driven away, their braines *knocked* out and *killed,* the poore sheepe to be preserved for whom Christ died, &c.

Is not this to take *Christ Jesus,* and make him a temporall *King* by force? *John 6.15.* Is not this to make his *Kingdome* of this *world*, to set up a *civill* and temporall *Israel*, to bound out new *Earthly holy Lands* of *Canaan*, yea and to set up a *Spanish Inquisition* in all parts of the *World*, to the speedy destruction of thousands, yea of millions of Soules, and the frustrating of the sweet *end* of the comming of the *Lord Jesus*, to wit, to save *mens soules* (and to that end not to destroy their *bodies*) by his own blood?

Chap. LIV

. . . It is *evill* (faith he) to tolerate notorious evill doers, seducing Teachers, scandalous livers.

In which speech I observe 2 evills:

First that this *Proposition* is too large and generall, because the *Rule* admits of *exception*, and that according to the will of *God*.

1. It is true, that *Evill* cannot alter its nature, but it is alway *Evill*, as *darkness* is alway *darkness*, yet

2. It must be remembered, that it is one thing to *command*, to *conceale*, to *councell*, to *approve Evill*, and another thing to *permit* and *suffer Evill* with *protestation* against it, or *dislike* of it, at least without *approbation* of it.

Lastly, this *sufferance* or *permission* of *Evill* is not for its own sake, but for the sake of *Good*, which puts a respect of *Goodness* upon such *permission*.

Hence it is, that for *Gods* owne *Glorie* sake (which is the highest Good) he endures, that is, *permits* or *suffers* the *Vessels of Wrath, Rom. 9.* And therefore although he be of pure eyes, and can behold no iniquitie, yet his pure eyes patiently and quietly beholds and permits all the *idolatries* and *prophanations*, all the *thefts* and *rapines*, all the *whoredomes* and *abominations*, all the *murthers* and *poysonings;* and yet I say, for his *glory* sake he is patient, and long permits.

Hence for his peoples sake (which is the next Good in his Son) he is oftentimes pleased to permit and suffer the wicked to enjoy a longer *reprise.* Therefore he gave *Paul* all the *lives* that were in the ship, *Acts. 27.*

Therefore he would not so soone have destroyed *Sodome,* but granted a longer *permission,* had there been but 10 righteous, *Gen. 19.* Therefore, *Jerem. 5.* had he found some to have stood in the *gap,* he would have spared others. Therefore gave he *Jesabel* a time or space, *Revel. 2.*

Therefore for his Glory sake hath he permitted longer *great sinners,* who afterward have perished in their season, as we see in the case of *Ahab,* the *Ninevites* and *Amorites, &c.*

Hence, it pleased the *Lord* not onely to permit the many *evills* against his owne honourable ordinance of *Mariage* in the world, but was pleased after a wonderfull manner to suffer that sin of many wives in *Abraham, Jacob, David, Solomon,* yea with some expression which seeme to pay *approbation as 2 Sam. 12.*

Peace.   It may be said, this is no *patterne* for us, because *God* is above Law, and an absolute *Soveraigne.*

Truth.   I answer, although wee finde him sometime dispensing with his Law, yet we never finde him deny himselfe, or utter a *falsehood:* And therefore when it crosseth not an absolute *Rule* to *permit* and tolerate (as in the case of the permission of the *Soules* and *consciences* of all men in the world, I have shewne and shall shew further it doth not) it will not hinder our being *holy* as hee is holy in all manner of conversation.

Chap. LV

Truth.   I Proceed. Hence it is that some Generals of Armies, and Governours of Cities, Townes, &c. doe, and (as those former instances prove) lawfully permit some evill persons and practices: As for instance, in the *civill State,* usury, for the preventing of a *greater evill* in the *civill Body, as stealing robbing, murthering, perishing* of the poore, and the hindrance or stop of *commerce* and dealing in the *Commonwealth.* Just like *Physicians,* wisely permitting noysome *humours,* and sometimes *diseases,* when the *cure* or *purging* would prove more dangerous to the *destruction* of the *whole,* a *weake* or *crazy* body, and specially at such a *time.*

Thus in many other instances it *pleased* the *Father of lights* the *God of Israel,* to permit that people especially in the matter of their demand of a *King,* (wherein he pleaded that himselfe as well as *Samuel* was rejected.)

This *ground,* to wit, for a *common good* of the *whole,* is the same with that of the *Lord Jesus* commanding *The Tares* to be permitted in the *World,* because other wise the *good wheat* should be indangered to be rooted up out of the *Field* or *World also,* as well as the *Tares:* and therefore for the good sake the *Tares,* which are indeed *evill,* were to be permitted: Yea and for the generall good of the *whole world,* the field it selfe, which for want of this obedience to the command of *Christ,* hath beene and is laid waste and desolate, with the fury and rage of *civill War,* professedly raised and maintained (as all States professe for the maintenance of one *true Religion* (after the patterne of that typicall land of *Canaan)* and to suppress and pluck up these Tares of *false Prophets* and false Professors, *Antichristians, Hereticks, &c.* out of the world.

Hence *illa lachryma:* hence *Germanics, Irelands,* and now *Englands* teares and dreadfull *desolations,* which ought to have beene, and may bee for the future (by obedience to the command of the *Lord Jesus,* concerning the permission of Tares to live in the *world* though not in the *Church)* I say ought to have beene, and may be mercifully prevented.

Chap. LVI

Peace. Pray descend now to the second *evill* which you observe in the *Answerers position, viz.* that it would bee *evill* to tolerate notorious *evill doers, seducing teachers, &c.*

Truth. I say, the *evill* is, that he most improperly and confusedly joynes and couples *seducing teachers* with *scandalous livers.*

Peace. But is it not true that the world is full of *seducing teachers,* and is it not true that *seducing teachers* are *notorious evill doers?*

Truth. I answer: far be it from me to deny either: and yet in two things I shall discover the great *evill* of this joyning and coupling *seducing teachers, and scandalous livers* as one adequate or proper object of the Magistrates care and worke to suppress and punish.

First, it is not an *Homogeneall* (as we speake) but an *Heterogeneall* commixture of joyning together of things most different in kindes and natures, as if they were both of one consideration.

For who knowes not but that many *seducing teachers,* either of the *Paganish, Jewish, Turkish, Antichristian* Religion may be clear and free from *scandalous offences* in their life, as also from *disobedience* to the Civill Lawes of a State? Yea the *Answerer* himselfe hath elsewhere granted, that if the Lawes of a *Civill State* be not broken, the *Peace* is not broken.

Againe, who knowes not that a *seducing teacher* properly sinnes against a *Church* or Spirituall estate and Lawes of it, and therefore ought most properly and onely to bee dealt withall in such a way, and by such weapons as the *Lord Jesus* himselfe hath appointed *gainsayers, opposites* and *disobedients* (either within his Church or without) to be *convinced, repelled, resisted,* and *slaine* withall.

Whereas *scandalous offendours* against *Parents,* against *Magistrates* in the 5 Command. and so against the *life, chastity, goods* or *goodname* in the rest, is properly transgression against the Civill State and Commonweale, or the worldly state of Men: And therefore consequently if the World or Civill State ought to be preserved by *Civill Governments* or *Governours;* such scandalous offendours ought not to be tolerated, but supprest according to the wisdome and prudence of the said *Government.*

Secondly, as there is a fallacious conjoyning and confounding together persons of severall kindes and natures, differing as much as Spirit and Flesh, Heaven and Earth each from other. So is there a silent and implicite *justification* to all the unrighteous and *cruell proceedings* of *Jews* and *Gentiles* against all the Prophets of *God*, the *Lord Jesus* himselfe, and all His Messengers and Witnesses, whom their Accusers have ever so coupled and mixed with notorious *evill doers* and *scandalous livers*.

Elijah was a *troubler* of the *State; Jeremy* weakned the hand of the people: yea *Moses* made the people neglect their worke: the *Jewes* built the Rebellious and bad City: the three Worthies regarded not the command of the King: *Christ Jesus* deceived the People, was a *conjurer* and a *traytor* against *Cesar* in being King of the Jewes (indeed He was so spiritually over the true Jew the Christian) therefore He was numbred with *notorious evill doers,* and hailed to the Gallowes between two Malefactours.

Hence *Paul* and all true Messengers of *Jesus Christ* are esteemed seducing and seditious teachers and turners of the World upside downe: Yea and to my knowledge (I speake with honourable respect to the *Answerer,* so far as he hath laboured for many truths of *Christ,* the *Answerer* himselfe hath drunke of this cup to be esteemed a *seducing Teacher.*

John Wise, 1652–1725

A rather obscure Congregationalist minister in rural Massachusetts, Wise wrote two works defending the Congregationalist tradition of separate and independent local churches (*The Churches Quarrel Espoused* in 1713 and *A Vindication of the Government of New England Churches* in 1717). He directed these works at the *Proposals* (1705) of Increase and Cotton Mather who had suggested that New England churches be governed by an association of church ministers along Presbyterian lines. Although written too late to influence this debate, Wise's defense of democratic church government made popular reading when *A Vindication* was reprinted in 1772, selling 1,133 copies just prior to the Revolution.

Wise broke new ground in American political thought by defending local democratic *church government* by first defending democracy as the best form of *civil government.* Furthermore, he went beyond more common arguments drawn from Scripture and the structure of the early (allegedly pure) church, to present arguments based on the "light of nature" or reason.

Although influenced more by the Dutch philosopher Samuel Pufendorf than the Englishman John Locke, Wise was one of the first American writers to use the language of individual natural rights that had recently become common among English Whigs in their struggle with the Crown. By the revolutionary war, however, natural rights arguments became standard on this side of the Atlantic as well.

While making an essentially theological point, John Wise's place in American political thought is significant indeed. Historian Vernon Parrington's words still apply:

> The struggle for ecclesiastical democracy was a forerunner of the struggle
> for political democracy which was to be the business of the next century;

and in founding his ecclesiasticism upon the doctrine of natural rights, John Wise was an early witness to the new order of thought.

The passages below are taken from Part II of *A Vindication.*

John Wise

A Vindication of the Government of New England Churches (1717)

The Constitution of *New England* CHURCHES, as settled by their Platform, may be fairly Justified, from *Antiquity;* The *Light of Nature; Holy Scripture;* and from the *Noble* and *Excellent Nature* of the *Constitution* it self. And lastly from the *Providence of God* dignifying of it.

* * * * *

CHAP. II

I. I Shall disclose several Principles of Natural Knowledge; plainly discovering the Law of Nature; or the true sentiments of Natural Reason, with Respect to Mans Being and Government And in this Essay I shall peculiarly confine the discourse to two heads, *viz*

1. Of the Natural [in distinction to the Civil] and then,

2. Of the Civil Being of Man. And I shall Principally take Baron *Puffendorff* for my Chief Guide and Spokes-man.

I. I shall consider Man in a state of Natural Being, as a Free-Born Subject under the

Crown of Heaven, and owing Homage to none but God himself. It is certain Civil Government in General, is a very Admirable Result of Providence, and an Incomparable Benefit to Man-kind, yet must needs be acknowledged to be the Effect of Humane Free-Compacts and not of Divine Institution; it is the Produce of Mans Reason, of Humane and Rational Combinations, and not from any direct Orders of Infinite Wisdom, in any positive Law wherein is drawn up this or that Scheme of Civil Government. Government [says the Lord *Warrington*] is necessary—in that no Society of Men can Subsist without it; and that Particular Form of Government is necessary which best suits the Temper and Inclination of a People. Nothing can be Gods Ordinance, but what he has particularly Declared to be such; there is no particular Form of Civil Government described in Gods Word, neither does Nature prompt it. The Government of the *Jews* was changed five Times. Government is not formed by Nature, as other Births or Productions; If it were, it would be the same in all Countries; because Nature keeps the same Method, in the same thing, in all Climates.

* * * * *

SOURCE: John Wise, *A Vindication of The Government of New England Churches* (1717). Gainesville, Florida: Scholar's Facsimiles & Reprints, 1958.

1. The Prime Immunity in Mans State, is that he is most properly the Subject of the Law of Nature. He is the Favourite Animal on Earth; in that this Part of Gods Image, *viz.* Reason is Congenate with his Nature, wherein by a Law Immutable, Instampt upon his Frame, God has provided a Rule for Men in all their Actions, obliging each one to the performance of that which is Right, not only as to Justice, but likewise as to all other Moral Vertues, the which is nothing but the Dictate of Right Reason founded in the Soul of Man . . . That which is to be drawn from Mans Reason, flowing from the true Current of that Faculty, when unperverted, may be said to be the Law of Nature; on which account, the Holy Scriptures declare it written on Mens hearts. For being indowed with a Soul, you may know from your self, how, and what you ought to act, Rom. 2.14. *These having not a Law, are a Law to themselves.* So that the meaning is, when we acknowledge the Law of Nature to be the dictate of Right Reason, we must mean that the Understanding of Man is Endowed with such a power, as to be able, from the Contemplation of humane Condition to discover a necessity of Living agreeably with this Law: And likewise to find out some Principle, by which the Precepts of it, may be clearly and solidly Demonstrated. The way to discover the Law of Nature in our own state, is by a narrow Watch, and accurate Contemplation of our Natural Condition, and propensions. . . .

. . . But more Particularly in pursuing our Condition for the discovery of the Law of Nature, this is very obvious to view, *viz.*

1. A Principle of Self-Love, & Self-Preservation, is very predominant in every Mans Being.

2. A Sociable Disposition.

3. An Affection of Love to Man-kind in General. And to give such Sentiments the force of a Law, we must suppose a God who takes care of all Mankind, and has thus obliged each one, as a Subject of higher Principles of Being, then meer Instincts. For that all Law properly considered, supposes a capable Subject, and a Superior Power; And the Law of God which is Binding, is published by the Dictates of Right Reason as other ways: Therefore says *Plutarch, To follow God and obey reason is the same thing.* But moreover that God has Established the Law of Nature, as the General Rule of Government, is further Illustrable from the many Sanctions in Providence, and from the Peace and Guilt of Conscience in them that either obey, or violate the Law of Nature. But moreover, the foundation of the Law of Nature with relation to Government, may be thus Discovered. *scil.* Man is a Creature extreamly desirous of his own Preservation; of himself he is plainly Exposed to many Wants, unable to secure his own safety, and Maintenance without the Assistance of his fellows; and he is also able of returning Kindness by the furtherance of mutual Good; But yet Man is often found to be Malicious, Insolent, and easily Provoked, and as powerful in Effecting mischief, as he is ready in designing it. Now that such a Creature may be Preserved, it is necessary that he be Sociable; that is, that he be capable and disposed to unite himself to those of his own species, and to Regulate himself towards them, that they may have no fair Reason to do him harm; but rather incline to promote his Interests, and secure his Rights and Concerns. This then is a Fundamental Law of Nature, that every Man as far as in him lies, do maintain a Sociableness with others, agreeable with the main end and disposition of humane Nature in general. For this is very apparent, that Reason and Society render Man the most potent of all Creatures. And Finally, from the Principles of Sociableness it follows as a fundamental Law of Nature, that Man is not so Wedded to his own Interest, but that he can make the Common good the mark of his Aim: And hence he becomes Capacitated to enter into a Civil State by the Law of Nature; for without this property in Nature, *viz.* Sociableness, which is for

Cementing of parts, every Government would soon moulder and dissolve.

2. The Second Great Immunity of Man is an Original Liberty Instampt upon his Rational Nature. He that intrudes upon this Liberty, Violates the Law of Nature. In this Disclosure I shall wave the Consideration of Mans Moral Turpitude, but shall view him Physically as a Creature which God has made and furnished essentially with many Enobling Immunities, which render him the most August Animal in the World, and still, whatever has happened since his Creation, he remains at the upper-end of Nature, and as such is a Creature of a very Noble Character. For as to his Dominion, the whole frame of the Lower Part of the Universe is devoted to his use, and at his Command; and his Liberty under the Conduct of Right Reason, is equal with his trust. Which Liberty may be briefly Considered, Internally as to his Mind, and Externally as to his Person. . . .

3. The Third Capital Immunity belonging to Mans Nature, is an equality amongst Men; Which is not to be denied by the Law of Nature, till Man has Resigned himself with all his Rights for the sake of a Civil State; and then his Personal Liberty and Equality is to be cherished, and preserved to the highest degree, as will consist with all just destinctions amongst Men of Honour, and shall be agreeable with the publick Good. For Man has a high valuation of himself, and the passion seems to lay its first foundation [not in Pride, but] really in the high and admirable Frame and Constitution of Humane Nature.

. . . Since then Human Nature agrees equally with all persons; and since no one can live a Sociable Life with another that does not own or Respect him as a Man; It follows as a Command of the Law of Nature, that every Man Esteem and treat another as one who is naturally his Equal or who is a Man as well as Reasons that greatly Illustrate this Equality, *viz.* that we all Derive our Being from one stock, the same Common Father of humane Race. . . .

And also that our Bodies are Composed of matter, frail, brittle, and lyable to be destroyed by thousand Accidents; we all owe our Existence to the same Method of propagation. The Noblest Mortal in his Entrance on to the Stage of Life, is not distinguished by any pomp or of passage from the lowest of Mankind; and our Life hastens to the same General Mark: Death observes no Ceremony, but Knocks as loud at the Barriers of the Court, as at the Door of the Cottage. This Equality being admitted, bears a very great force in maintaining Peace and Friendship amongst Men. For that he who would use the Assistance of others, in promoting his own Advantage, ought as freely to be at their service, when they want his help on the like Occasions. *One Good turn Requires another*, is the Common Proverb; for otherwise he must need esteem others unequal to himself, who constantly demands their Aid, and as constantly denies his own.

. . . Yet we must note, that there is room for an Answer, *scil.* That it would be the greatest absurdity to believe, that Nature actually Invests the Wise with a Sovereignity over the weak; or with a Right of forcing them against their Wills; for that no Sovereignty can be Established, unless some Humane Deed, or Covenant Precede: Nor does Natural fitness for Government make a Man presently Governour over another; for that as *Ulpian* says, *by a Natural Right all Men are born free;* and Nature having set all Men upon a Level and made them Equals, no Servitude or Subjection can be conceived without Inequality; and this cannot be made without Usurpation or Force in others, or Voluntary Compliance in those who Resign their freedom, and give away their Degree of Natural Being. . . .

(The Forms of Government)

I. The Forms of a Regular State are three only, which Forms arise from the proper and particular Subject, in which the Supream Power Resides. As,

1. A Democracy, which is when the Sovereign Power is Lodged in a Council consisting of all the Members, and where every Member has the Priviledge of a Vote. This Form of Government, appears in the greatest part of the World to have been the most Ancient. For that Reason seems to shew it to be most probable, that when Men [being Originally in a condition of Natural Freedom and Equality] had thoughts of joyning in a Civil Body, would without question be inclined to Administer their common Affairs, by their common Judgment, and so must necessarily to gratifie that Inclination establish a Democracy; neither can it be rationally imagined, that Fathers of Families being yet Free and Independent, should in a moment, or little time take off their long delight in governing their own Affairs, & Devolve all upon some single Sovereign Commander; for that it seems to have been thought more Equitable, that what belonged to all, should be managed by all, when all had entered by Compact into one Community. . . .

2. The Second Species of Regular Government, is an Aristocracy; and this is said then to be Constituted when the People, or Assembly United by a first Covenant, and having thereby cast themselves into the first Rudiments of a State; do then by Common Decree, Devolve the Sovereign Power, on a Council consisting of some Select Members; and these having accepted of the Designation, are then properly invested with Sovereign Command; and then an Aristocracy is formed.

3. The Third Species of a Regular Government, is a Monarchy which is settled when the Sovereign Power is confered on some one worthy Person. It differs from the former, because a Monarch who is but one Person in Natural, as well as in Moral account, & so is furnished with an Immediate Power of Exercising Sovereign Command in all Instances of Government; but the fore named must needs have Particular Time and Place assigned; but the Power and Authority is Equal in each.

2. Mixt Governments, which are various and of divers kinds [not now to be Enumerated] yet possibly the fairest in the World is that which has a Regular Monarchy; [in Distinction to what is Dispotick] settled upon a Noble Democracy as its Basis. And each part of the Government is so adjusted by Pacts and Laws that renders the whole Constitution an *Elisium*. It is said of the *British* Empire, *That it is such a Monarchy, as that by the necessary subordinate Occurrence of the Lords and Commons, in the Making and Repealing all Statutes or Acts of Parliament; it hath the main Advantages of an Aristocracy, and of a Democracy, and yet free from the Disadvantages and Evils of either. It is such a Monarchy, as by most Admirable Temperament affords very much to the Industry, Liberty, and Happiness of the Subject, and reserves enough for the Majesty and Prerogative of any King, who will own his People as Subjects, not as Slaves. It is a Kingdom, that of all the Kingdoms of the World, is most like to the Kingdom of Jesus Christ, whose Yoke is easie, and Burden light.* . . .

2. In special I shall now proceed to Enquire, Whether any of the aforesaid Species of regular, unmixt Governments, can with any good shew of Reason be predicable of the Church of Christ on Earth. If the Churches of Christ, as Churches, are either the Object or Subject of a Sovereign Power intrusted in the hands of Man, then most certainly one of the fore-cited Schemes of a perfect Government will be applicable to it.

Before I pursue the Enquiry, it may not be improper to pause, & make some Caution here, by distinguishing between that which may have some Resemblance of Civil Power, and the thing it self; and to the Power of Churches is but a faint Resemblance of Civil Power; it comes in reality nothing near to the thing it self; for the one is truly Coercive, the other perswasive; the one is Sovereign Power, the other is Delegated and Ministerial: But not to delay, I shall proceed with my Enquiry, and therein shall endeavour to humour the several great Claimers of Government in the Church of Christ. And

1. I shall begin with a Monarchy. It's certain, his Holiness, either by reasonable Pleas, or powerful Cheats, has assumed an absolute and universal Sovereignty; this fills his Cathedral Chair, and is adorned with a Triple Crown and in Defence thereof does protest, *The Almighty has made him both Key-keeper of Heaven and Hell, with the adjacent Territories of Purgetory, and vested in him an absolute Sovereignty over the Christian World.* And his Right has so far prevailed, that Princes and Civil Monarchy hold their Crowns and Donations as his Dutiful Sons, and Loyal Subjects; he therefore decks himself with the Spoils of the Divine Attributes, stiling himself, *Our Lord God, Optimum, Maximum et supremum numen in Terris;* a God on Earth, a visible Deity, and that his Power is absolute, & his Wisdom infallible. . . .

But I have no occasion to pursue this Remark with tedious Demonstrations: It's very plain, it's written with Blood in Capital Letters, to be Read at Midnight by the Flames of *Smithfield,* and other such like consecrated Fires. That the Government of this Ecclesiastical Monarch has instead of Sanctifying, absolutely Debaucht the World, and subverted all good Christianity in it. So that without the least shew of any vain presumption we may Infer, That God and wise Nature were never Propitious to the Birth of this Monster.

An Aristocracy which places the Supream Power in a Select Company of choice Persons. Here I freely acknowledge were the Gospel Ministry Established the Subject of this Power, *viz.* To Will and Do, in all Church Affairs without controul, etc. This Government might do to support the Church in its most valuable Rights, etc. If we could be assured they would make the Scripture, and not their private Will, the Rule of their Personal and Ministerial Actions: And indeed upon these terms any Species of Government, might serve the great design of Redemption; but considering how great an Interest is imbarkt, and how frail a bottom we trust, though we should rely upon the best of Men, especially if we remember what is in the hearts of Good Men, [*viz.* Much ignorance, abundance of small ends, many times cloked with a high Pretence in Religion; Pride Skulking and often breeding revenge upon a small affront; and blown up by a pretended Zeal; Yet really and truly by nothing more Divine then Interest, or ill Nature] and also considering how very uncertain we are of the real goodness of those we esteem good Men; and also how impossible it is to secure the Intail of it to Successors: And also if we remind how Christianity by the foresaid Principle has been peel'd, rob'd and spoiled already; it cannot consist with the Light of Nature to venture again upon such Perils, especially if we can find a safer way home. More Distinctly.

It is very plain [allowing me to speak Emblematically] the Primitive Constitution of the Churches was a Democracy, as appears by the foregoing Parallel. But after the Christian Churches were received into the favour of the Imperial Court, under the Dominion of *Constantine* the Great; there being many Praeliminaries which had furnished the Ministers with a disposition thereunto, they quickly deprived the Fraternities of their Rights in the Government of the Churches, when they were once provided of a plentiful maintenance through the Liberality of *Constantine,* that when Christianity was so Luxuriantly treated, as by his great Bounty, and Noble settlement, it is said there was a Voice heard from Heaven, saying, *Now is Poyson poured into the Church.* But the subversion of the Constitution, is a story too long now to tell. . . .

The Right of the People did not remain unhurt through many Ages; neither could it well be otherways, but that it must be lost, or much diminished. *Zonaras* does confess that heretofore Byshops were chosen by the Suffrage of the People. But many Seditions happening among them; it was Decreed that every Bishop should hereafter be chosen by the Authority of the Bishops of every province. The cause seemed to be so very specious, that nothing could be more Decent, or more Conducive to the safety of the Common-Wealth.

Yet [says my Author] if you do well weigh the business, you must needs acknowledge nothing could have happened more Pernicious or Destructive to the Church of God. For soon after these things came to pass, it is very obvious, that Tyranny over the Consciences of the faithful; and an Intolerable Pride every where grew Rampant among the guides of the Church. Yet there was one thing still very needful to be done; and that was to Establish or Confirm the Power which the Metropolitans and Bishops had acquired to themselves. Therefore they fell to it Tooth and Nail to drive away the Fraternity from all Interest in Elections: And alas Poor hearts! They began to sleep with both Ears; that then was scarce any Enemy left to Interrupt, or Controul the Conquerors. This was the manner of the Clergy till they had made themselves the Subjects of all Power and then acted Arbitrarily, and did what they pleased in the Church of God.

But let the learned, knowing World, consider, what the Issue of all this was, *scil.* what a wretched capacity the drowsiness & cowardize of the People; and the Usurpation and Ambition of the Ministry brought the Professing World into. If those who were truely Godly on both sides had in a few Ages lookt down from Heaven, and had Eyed the following Centurys, they might have beheld a world of matter for sorrowful Impressions; to think that they themselves had Occasioned the Ruin of Millions, by their remiss and passive temper in one sort; and too much humouring, and nourishing Pride, and high conceits of themselves and others, in the other; when as if they had stood firm to the Government as left settled by the Apostles; they had certainly prevented an Apostacy that has damned, and confounded a great part of about Thirty Generations of Men, Women, and Children. . . .

So doleful a Contemplation is it to think

the World should be destroyed by those Men, who by God were Ordained to save it!

In a Word, an Aristocracy is a dangerous Constitution in the Church of Christ, as it possesses the Presbytery of all Church Power: What has been observed sufficiently Evinces it. And not only so but from the Nature of the Constitution, for it has no more Barrier to it, against the Ambition, Insults, and Arbitrary measures of Men, then an absolute Monarchy. But to abbreviate; it seems most agreeable with the light of Nature, that if there be any of the Regular Government settled in the Church of God it must needs be.

3. A Democracy. This is a form of Government, which the Light of Nature does highly value, & often directs to as most agreeable to the Just and Natural Prerogatives of Humane Beings. This was of great account, in the early times of the World. And not only so, but upon the Experience of several Thousand years, after the World had been tumbled, and tost from one Species of Government to another, at a great Expence of Blood and Treasure, many of the wise Nations of the World have sheltered themselves under it again; or at least have blendished, and balanced their Governments with it.

It is certainly a great Truth, *scil.* That Mans Original Liberty after it is Resigned, [yet under due Restrictions] ought to be Cherished in all wise Governments; or otherwise a man in making himself a Subject, he alters himself from a Freeman, into a Slave, which to do is Repugnant to the Law of Nature. Also the Natural Equality of Men amongst Men must be duly favoured; in that Government was never Established by God or Nature, to give one Man a Prerogative to insult over another; therefore in a Civil, as well as in a Natural State of Being, a just Equality is to be indulged so far as that every Man is bound to Honour every Man, which is agreeable both with Nature and Religion, I Pet. 2. 17. *Honour all men.*—The End of all good Government is to Cultivate Humanity, and Promote the happiness of all, and the good of every Man in all his Rights, his Life, Liberty, Estate, Honour, etc. without injury or abuse done to any. Then certainly it cannot easily be thought, that a company of Men, that shall enter into a voluntary Compact, to hold all Power in their own hands, thereby to use and improve their united force, wisdom, riches and strength for the Common and Particular good of every Member, as is the Nature of a Democracy; I say it cannot be that this sort of Constitution, will so readily furnish those in Government with an appetite, or disposition to prey upon each other, or imbezle the common Stock; as some Particular Persons may be apt to do when set off, and Intrusted with the same Power. And moreover this appears very Natural, that when the aforesaid Government or Power, settled in all, when they have Elected certain capable Persons to Minister in their affairs, and the said Ministers remain accountable to the Assembly; these Officers must needs be under the influence of many wise cautions from their own thoughts [as well as under confinement by their Commission] in their whole Administration: And from thence it must needs follow that they will be more apt, and inclined to steer Right for the main Point, *viz.* The peculiar good, and benefit of the whole, and every particular Member fairly and sincerely. And why may not these stand for every Rational Pleas in Church Order?

Hector St. John de Crevecoeur, 1735–1813

Born in Normandy, France, Crevecoeur came to the New World as a mapmaker with the French Army in Canada. After the French defeat at the hands of the British, Crevecoeur chose to remain in the New World, traveling and working throughout New England and the Middle Atlantic Colonies. By 1764, he had settled in upstate New York, farming and writing about life in America.

During the Revolution, Crevecoeur left America and spent time in France and Britain, where he published his *Letters from an American Farmer*. Like his fellow countryman Alexis de Tocqueville half a century later, Crevecoeur brought the keen eye of the outsider to America's shores. He saw in America—with its absence of inherited titles and its abundance of land—the perfect environment for a new politics and a new race of man.

While clearly influenced by the French romantics and physiocrats, Crevecoeur also echoes the agrarian ethos of the English republican tradition. His vision of America, praised by Washington and Franklin and so compatible with that of Thomas Jefferson, shows a very important strand in American thinking that both complemented and at times contradicted the individualistic natural rights tradition. Both traditions were important elements in the "colonial mind" on the eve of the American Revolution.

The following passages are taken from Letter III "What Is an American?"

Hector St. John de Crevecoeur

Letters from an American Farmer (1782)

"WHAT IS AN AMERICAN?"

I wish I could be acquainted with the feelings and thoughts which must agitate the heart and present themselves to the mind of an enlightened Englishman, when he first lands on this continent. He must greatly rejoice that he lived at a time to see this fair country discovered and settled; he must necessarily feel a share of national pride, when he views the chain of settlements which embellishes these extended shores. When he says to himself, this is the work of my countrymen, who, when convulsed by factions, afflicted by a variety of miseries and wants, restless and impatient, took refuge here. They brought along with them their national genius, to which they principally owe what liberty they enjoy, and what substance they possess. Here he sees the industry of his native country displayed in a new manner, and traces in their works the embryos of all the arts, sciences, and ingenuity which flourish in Europe. Here he beholds fair cities, substantial villages, extensive fields, an immense country filled with decent houses, good roads, orchards, meadows, and bridges, where an hundred years ago all was wild, woody, and uncultivated! What a train of pleasing ideas this fair spectacle must suggest; it is a prospect which must inspire a good citizen with the most heartfelt pleasure. The difficulty consists in the manner of viewing so extensive a scene. He is arrived

SOURCE: *Letters from An American Farmer* (New York: Everyman's Library, 1951), "Letter III."

on a new continent; a modern society offers itself to his contemplation, different from what he had hitherto seen. It is not composed, as in Europe, of great lords who possess everything, and of a herd of people who have nothing. Here are no aristocratical families, no courts, no kings, no bishops, no ecclesiastical dominion, no invisible power giving to a few a very visible one; no great manufacturers employing thousands, no great refinements of luxury. The rich and the poor are not so far removed from each other as they are in Europe. Some few towns excepted, we are all tillers of the earth, from Nova Scotia to West Florida. We are a people of cultivators, scattered over an immense territory, communicating with each other by means of good roads and navigable rivers, united by the silken bands of mild government, all respecting the laws, without dreading their power, because they are equitable. We are all animated with the spirit of an industry which is unfettered and unrestrained, because each person works for himself. If he travels through our rural districts he views not the hostile castle, and the haughty mansion, contrasted with the clay-built hut and miserable cabin, where cattle and men help to keep each other warm, and dwell in meanness, smoke, and indigence. A pleasing uniformity of decent competence appears throughout our habitations. The meanest of our log-houses is a dry and comfortable habitation. Lawyer or merchant are the fairest titles our towns afford; that of a farmer is the only appellation of the rural inhabitants of our country. It must take some time ere he can reconcile himself to our dictionary, which is but short in words of dignity, and names of honour. There, on a Sunday, he sees a congregation of respectable farmers and their wives, all clad in neat homespun, well mounted, or riding in their own humble waggons. There is not among them an esquire, saving the unlettered magistrate. There he sees a parson as simple as his flock, a farmer who does not riot on the labour of others. We have no princes, for whom we toil, starve, and bleed: we are the most perfect society now existing in the world. Here man is free as he ought to be; nor is this pleasing equality so transitory as many others are. Many ages will not see the shores of our great lakes replenished with inland nations, nor the unknown bounds of North America entirely peopled. Who can tell how far it extends? Who can tell the millions of men whom it will feed and contain? for no European foot has as yet travelled half the extent of this mighty continent! . . .

In this great American asylum, the poor of Europe have by some means met together, and in consequence of various causes; to what purpose should they ask one another what countrymen they are? Alas, two thirds of them had no country. Can a wretch who wanders about who works and starves, whose life is a continual scene of sore affliction or pinching penury; can that man call England or any other kingdom his country? A country that had no bread for him, whose fields procured him no harvest, who met with nothing but the frowns of the rich, the severity of the laws, with jails and punishments; who owned not a single foot of the extensive surface of this planet? No! urged by a variety of motives, here they came. Every thing has tended to regenerate them; new laws, a new mode of living, a new social system; here they are become men: in Europe they were as so many useless plants, wanting vegetative mould, and refreshing showers; they withered, and were mowed down by want, hunger, and war; but

now by the power of transplantation, like all other plants they have taken root and flourished! Formerly they were not numbered in any civil lists of their country, except in those of the poor; here they rank as citizens. By what invisible power has this surprising metamorphosis been performed? By that of the laws and that of their industry. The laws, the indulgent laws, protect them as they arrive, stamping on them the symbol of adoption; they receive ample rewards for their labours; these accumulated rewards procure them lands; those lands confer on them the title of freemen, and to that title every benefit is affixed which men can possibly require. This is the great operation daily performed by our laws. From whence proceed these laws? From our government. Whence the government? It is derived from the original genius and strong desire of the people ratified and confirmed by the crown. This is the great chain which links us all, this is the picture which every province exhibits, Nova Scotia excepted. There the crown has done all; either there were no people who had genius, or it was not much attended to: the consequence is, that the province is very thinly inhabited indeed; the power of the crown in conjunction with the musketos has prevented men from settling there. Yet some parts of it flourished once, and it contained a mild harmless set of people. But for the fault of a few leaders, the whole were banished. The greatest political error the crown ever committed in America, was to cut off men from a country which wanted nothing but men!

What attachment can a poor European emigrant have for a country where he had nothing? The knowledge of the language, the love of a few kindred as poor as himself, were the only cords that tied him: his country is now that which gives him land, bread, protection, and consequence: *Ubi panis ibi patria*, is the motto of all emigrants. What then is the American, this new man? He is either an European, or the descendant of an European, hence that strange mixture of blood, which you will find in no other country. I could point out to you a family whose grandfather was an Englishman, whose wife was Dutch, whose son married a French woman, and whose present four sons have now four wives of different nations. *He* is an American, who, leaving behind him all his ancient prejudices and manners, receives new ones from the new mode of life he has embraced, the new government he obeys, and the new rank he holds. He becomes an American by being received in the broad lap of our great *Alma Mater.* Here individuals of all nations are melted into a new race of men whose labours and posterity will one day cause great changes in the world. Americans are the western pilgrims, who are carrying along with them that great mass of arts, sciences, vigour, and industry which began long since in the east; they will finish the great circle. The Americans were once scattered all over Europe; here they are incorporated into one of the finest systems of population which has ever appeared, and which will hereafter become distinct by the power of the different climates they inhabit. The American ought therefore to love this country much better than that wherein either he or his forefathers were born. Here the rewards of his industry follow with equal steps the progress of his labour; his labour is founded on the basis of nature, *self-interest;* can it want a stronger allurement? Wives and children, who before in vain demanded of him a morsel of bread, now, fat and frolicsome, gladly help their father to clear those fields whence exuberant crops are to arise to feed and to clothe them all; without any part being claimed, either by a despotic prince, a rich abbot, or a mighty lord. Here religion demands but little of him; a small voluntary salary to the minister, and gratitude to God; can he refuse these? The American is a new man, who acts upon new principles; he must therefore entertain new ideas, and form new opinions. From involuntary idleness, servile dependence, penury, and useless labour, he has passed to toils of a very different nature, rewarded by ample subsistence—This is an American. . . .

PART II

Establishing an Independent Republic: The Languages of Revolution

Prior to the 1760s, the American colonies had felt themselves to be virtually self-governing. Although the Navigation Acts technically limited American production and trade, in practice they were ignored by all parties involved. Moreover, colonial legislatures were free to raise and spend their own revenues, exercising a great degree of sovereign authority.

Such benign neglect ended after the French and Indian War. Needing revenues to repay the war debt and hoping to strengthen the British economy at the expense of her European rivals, Britain began to tax the colonies and fashion an imperial economy. Colonial merchants were no longer free to trade with whomever they chose, but instead were increasingly forced to sell to Britain or to countries that Britain approved for trade. Moreover, American producers were hampered from making or selling anything that might compete with British manufacturers and traders. As a result, the American colonies saw rights that had previously been theirs now being rescinded.

This growing exercise of authority by the British government startled many Americans and violated their sense of justice. For the first time, British power seemed arbitrary. Having been nearly self-governing for a century and a half, the American colonists thought they had already established an appropriate relationship between themselves and the mother country. The Revenue Act of 1764, the Stamp Act of 1765, and the Townshend Acts of 1767 met immediate American resistance, and a torrent of political argument followed on all sides.

By the time the united colonies declared their independence from Britain in July of 1776, Americans had been participating in this public feud for twelve years. During this period, American leaders and public philosophers developed a series of political arguments to justify their resistance and finally their total break with British rule. The Declaration of Independence did not spring out of nowhere in 1776, nor did it vanish after the Revolution was won. The Declaration grew out of a long process, and it is no exaggeration to claim that it expressed a core set of American beliefs that have remained central to our view of politics.

Of course, many Americans disapproved of the resistance altogether and urged their fellow colonists to obey existing authority. Daniel Leonard, using a Whig analysis similar to that of the resistance, claimed that the British Constitution was a mixed regime of king, lords, and commons. To deny Parliament the right to tax the colonies meant to recognize only the rule of the king, and thus to destroy the essence of the British political order and British liberty. In a mixed constitution, Whigs of all types argued, power was dispersed among three elements of the political and social order. Thus no one estate could dominate, and all could exercise their legitimate rights and privileges. Although most Whig theorists were on the side of the resistance, some like Leonard used Whig ideas to urge obedience to both king and Parliament.

Other loyalists, or Tories, such as Anglican minister Samuel Seabury, feared that disobedience opened the door to anarchy. Another Anglican minister, Jonathon Boucher, argued that all people had a religious obligation to obey their rulers. Boucher went even further, suggesting that the divine right of kings was rooted in "patriarchal power" derived from the Biblical Adam. In Boucher's view, men had no natural rights, and thus no rights had been violated by the British. Such traditional appeals to authority, however, elicited little public response.

American Whigs held almost unanimously that governments were humanly created institutions, even if they fulfilled divinely approved purposes. The obligation to obey any individual or set of institutions was by no means absolute. Writers such as James Otis (1764), John Adams (1765), John Dickinson (1767), and James Wilson (1774) agreed that the British (Whig) Constitution was indeed fundamental to an Englishman's liberty on both sides of the Atlantic, but they also held that the power of Parliament over the colonies was limited because the colonies remained unrepresented, and taxation without representation violated their rights as Englishmen. Thus, they thought that the colonists should largely govern themselves through their colonial legislatures. The ultimate logic of these arguments pointed toward a dominion status, with each colony combining home rule through its own legislature with an obligation to obey the Crown. However, events soon undermined the moderate Whig analysis.

Later American Whigs felt compelled to consider total separation. They argued that the Crown had corrupted Parliament by, in effect, buying off Parliamentary seats. With the independence of that body compromised and the balance of the constitution destroyed, Americans believed that the Crown was now free through Parliament to burden the colonies with taxes to pay for a luxurious and wasteful royal court. Accordingly, American Whigs— Samuel Langdon is one good example—claimed that a return to a more virtuous, more pure constitutional order was impossible as long as Americans maintained ties to the decadent British. Either the British themselves must return to "first principles" or Americans needed to create separate, alternative institutions. As we shall see, Langdon's rhetoric rang with echoes of Whig, republican, and Puritan ideas.

The few who advocated a total break with the mother country adopted a radical political language that decried the mixed government of England altogether. Unlike the Whigs who had dominated political discourse until 1776, radical republicans such as Thomas Paine completely rejected the monarchical and aristocratic elements of the British Constitution. Although not typical, Paine found sympathetic ears among many Americans. He contributed an individualistic, egalitarian, and democratic political language to the dispute, which by 1776 made it easier to reject British institutions and seek revolutionary change.

The final dissolution of ties to Great Britain was proclaimed in the magnificent language of Thomas Jefferson's Declaration of Independence. In that document, Jefferson borrowed heavily from the individualistic natural-rights philosophy of John Locke and Algernon Sydney. Following in Paine's footsteps, he made no mention of the mixed constitution and instead spoke of the natural equality of all men and their possession of inalienable rights. If the social contract was broken and rights violated, the Declaration argued, the aggrieved had the right to revolution.

Although written as a justification for revolution, Jefferson's words hinted at a complete conception of politics that later scholars have called "liberal individualism." Jefferson himself held more varied and even conflicting views—for example, he was an ardent agrarian and feared the growth of cities and industry that unbridled individualism ironically helped create. Nevertheless, the commitment to equal rights so prominently displayed in the Declaration has continued to give legitimacy to all the future generations who have sought to make rights more equal. Quite simply, the document designed to justify a specific revolution has continued to revolutionize American life. All those who have fought for universal suffrage and civil rights for blacks and women have found a ready weapon in Jefferson's Declaration of Independence. Moreover, Jefferson's commitment to individualism and limited government has continued to animate many in political life. However, in the twentieth century, at least, this side of Jefferson often has appealed to individuals who differed strongly with those inspired by his egalitarianism.

In short, the struggle for revolution fixed many political theories in the American consciousness: constitutionalism, Whig republicanism, egalitarian republicanism, and the natural-rights philosophy of liberal individualism. In various guises and differing situations, these political languages have reappeared throughout the history of American politics.

The Old Orthodoxy

The Loyalist Plea for Obedience

Samuel Seabury, 1729–1796

Anglican minister and trained physician, Samuel Seabury was an articulate opponent of the American independence movement.

Ordained in 1753, Seabury served as a missionary and then minister in New Jersey and New York state. In 1774, he wrote a series of attacks on the Continental Congress under the pen name of "A Westchester Farmer," which were in turn answered by Alexander Hamilton, then a student at King's (Columbia) College.

During the Revolution, Seabury provided information for the British Army. After the war, he helped oversee the Loyalist exodus to Nova Scotia and then returned to England.

Unwilling to offend the new American republic, the Anglican Church refused to send Seabury back to the United States. However, he soon returned as a bishop in the Scottish Episcopal Church and later helped found the Protestant Episcopal Church of America.

Seabury was a conservative who emphasized the importance of authority and order in both church and state. Even as bishop in the new American Episcopal Church, he fought against proposals to include laity in the church general assembly. In his writings, he emphasized the indivisibility of sovereignty and the importance of obedience to sovereign authority. Like many seventeenth- and eighteenth-century Anglicans, Seabury believed independence in religion produced republicans in government, and he disapproved of both.

In the passages below, taken from *The Letters of a Westchester Farmer*, Seabury echoes Thomas Hobbes instead of the Whig, John Locke. He warns the colonists that disobedience will lead to a chaotic state of nature—"Anarchy, riots, and brutal force"—without a trace of the peaceful security that has traditionally belonged to Englishmen.

Samuel Seabury

A View of the Controversy between Great Britain and Her Colonies (1774)

SIR—you have done me the honour "to bestow some notice upon" a little pamphlet which I lately published, entitled, *Free Thoughts on the Proceedings of the Continental Congress,* in a Piece which you call, *A full Vindication of the Measures of the Congress, from the Calumnies of their Enemies.* My present business shall be to examine your Vindication, and see whether it *fully* exculpates *the measures of the Congress,* from the charges brought against them by the friends of order and good government. This task I shall endeavour to perform, with all that freedom of thought and expression, which, as an *Englishman* I have a right to; and which never shall be wrested from me, either by *yourself* or the *Congress.* . . .

You begin your vindication with such an air of importance, and such pomposity of expression, as I scarce ever met with before—"It was hardly to be expected that any man *could* be so *presumptous,* as *openly* to controvert the *equity, wisdom* and *authority* of the measures adopted by the Congress: an assembly truly respectable on *every* account!—whether we consider the characters of the men, who composed it; the number and dignity of their constituents, or the important ends for which they were appointed."—Mere explosions of the wind of vanity! Three grains of consideration

would have prevented such a sentence from ever seeing the light.

It has ever been esteemed the privilege of Englishmen to canvass freely, the proceedings of every branch of the legislature; to examine into all public measures; to point out the errors that are committed in the administration of the government, and to censure without fear the conduct of all persons in public stations, whose conduct shall appear to deserve it. The exercise of this right has always been considered as one of the grand pillars which support our present happy constitution. The liberty taken with the *King, Lords* and *Commons* in many late publications in England, must convince every man, that the English nation retains, unimpaired, this right of bringing the most respectable characters before the tribunal of the public: and is an incontestible proof that the nation is not enslaved. Nor is this privilege exercised with less freedom in America than England. Did not the Congress? Do not you yourself? Does not every pidler in politics, who calls himself a *son of liberty,* take the licence of censuring and condemning the conduct of the *King,* the *Lords,* and the *Commons,* the supreme sovereign authority of the whole British Empire? Blush then at your own effrontery, in endeavouring to intimidate your countrymen from exercising this Right with regard to the Congress. . . .

I have no inclination to scrutinize the char-

SOURCE: Samuel Seabury, *Letters of a Westchester Farmer* (White Plains, N.Y.: Westchester Historical Society, 1930).

acters of men, who composed the Congress. It is not the dignity of their private characters, but their public conduct as *Delegates* that comes under my examination. The manner in which they were chosen was subversive of all law, and of the very constitution of the province. After they had met they were only a popular assembly, without check or controul, and therefore unqualified to make laws, or to pass ordinances. Upon supposition that they had been chosen by all the people with one voice, they could be only the servants of the people; and every individual must have had a right to animadvert on their conduct, and to have censured it where he thought it wrong. *We* think, Sir, that we have a double right to do so, seeing they were chosen by a party only, and have endeavoured to tyrannize over the whole people. . . .

I wish you had explicitly declared to the public your ideas of the *natural rights of mankind*. Man in a *state of nature* may be considered as perfectly free from all restraints of law and government: And then the *weak* must submit to the *strong*. From such a state, I confess, I have a violent aversion. I think the form of government we lately enjoyed a much more eligible state to live in: And cannot help regretting our having *lost* it, by the *equity*, *wisdom*, and *authority* of the Congress, who have introduced in the room of it, confusion and violence; where all must submit to the power of a mob.

You have taken some pains to prove what would readily have been granted you—that *liberty* is a very *good* thing, and *slavery* a very *bad* thing. But then I must think that liberty under a *King, Lords* and *Commons* is as good as liberty under a republican Congress: And that slavery under a republican Congress is as bad, at least, as slavery under a *King, Lords* and *Commons*: And upon the whole, that *liberty* under the supreme authority and protection of Great-Britain, is infinitely preferable to *slavery* under an American Congress. I will also agree with you, "that Americans are intitled to freedom." I will go further: I will own and acknowledge that not only *Americans*, but *Africans, Europeans, Asiaticks*, all men, of all countries and degrees, of all sizes and complexions, have a right to as much freedom as is consistent with the security of civil society: And I hope you will not think me an "enemy to the *natural* "rights of mankind" because I cannot wish them more. We must however remember, that more liberty may, without inconvenience, be allowed to individuals in a small government, than can be admitted of in a large empire.

But when you assert that "since Americans have not by any act of theirs impowered the British parliament to make laws for them, it follows they can have no just authority to do it," you advance a position subversive of that dependence which all colonies must, from their very nature, have on the mother country.—By the British parliament, I suppose you mean the supreme legislative authority, the King, Lords and Commons, because no other authority in England has a right to make laws to bind the kingdom, and consequently no authority to make laws to bind the colonies. In this sense I shall understand, and use the phrase *British parliament*.

Now the dependence of the colonies on the mother-country has ever been acknowledged. It is an impropriety of speech to talk of an independent colony. The words *independency* and *colony*, convey contradictory ideas: much like *killing* and *sparing*. As soon as a colony becomes independent on its parent state, it ceases to be any longer a colony; just as when you *kill* a sheep, you cease to *spare* him. The British colonies make a part of the British Empire. As parts of the body they must be subject to the general laws of the body. To talk of a colony independent of the mother-country, is no better sense than to talk of a limb independent of the body to which it belongs.

In every government there must be a supreme, absolute authority lodged somewhere.

In arbitrary governments this power is in the monarch; in aristocratical governments, in the nobles; in democratical, in the people; or the deputies of their electing. Our own government being a mixture of all these kinds, the supreme authority is vested in the King, Nobles and People, i.e. the King, House of Lords, and House of Commons elected by the people. This supreme authority extends as far as the British dominions extend. To suppose a part of the British dominions which is not subject to the power of the British legislature, is no better sense than to suppose a country, at one and the same time, to be, and not to be a part of the British dominions. If therefore the colony of New-York be a part of the British dominions, the colony of New-York is subject, and dependent on the supreme legislative authority of Great-Britain.

Legislation is not an inherent right in the colonies. Many colonies have been established, and subsisted long without it. The Roman colonies had no legislative authority. It was not till the later period of their republic that the privileges of Roman citizens, among which that of voting in the assemblies of the people at Rome was a principal one, were extended to the inhabitants of Italy. All the laws of the empire were enacted at Rome. Neither their colonies, nor conquered countries had any thing to do with legislation.

The position that we are bound by no laws to which we have not consented, either by ourselves, or our representatives, is a novel position, unsupported by any authorative record of the British constitution, ancient or modern. It is republican in its very nature, and tends to the utter subversion of the English monarchy.

This position has arisen from an artful change of terms. To say that an Englishman is not bound by any laws, but those to which the representatives of the nation have given their consent, is to say what is true: But to say that an Englishman is bound by no laws but those to which *he* hath consented in per-

son, or by *his* representative, is saying what never was true, and never can be true. A great part of the people in England have no vote in the choice of representatives, and therefore are governed by laws to which they never consented either by *themselves* or by *their* representatives.

The right of colonists to exercise a legislative power, is no natural right. They derive it not from nature, but from the indulgence or grant of the parent state, whose subjects they were when the colony was settled, and by whose permission and assistance they made the settlement.

Upon supposition that every English colony enjoyed a legislative power independent of the parliament; and that the parliament has no just authority to make laws to bind them, this absurdity will follow—that there is no power in the British empire, which has authority to make laws for the whole empire; i.e. we have an empire, without government; or which amounts to the same thing, we have a government which has no supreme power. All our colonies are independent of each other: Suppose them independent of the British parliament,—what power do you leave to govern the whole? None at all. You split and divide the empire into a number of petty insignificant states. This is the direct, the necessary tendency of refusing submission to acts of parliament. Every man who can see one inch beyond his nose, must see this consequence. And every man who endeavours to accelerate the independency of the colonies on the British parliament, endeavours to accelerate the ruin of the British empire.

To talk of being liege subjects to King George, while we disavow the authority of parliament is another piece of whiggish nonsense. I love my King as well as any whig in America or England either, and am as ready to yield him all lawful submission: But while I submit to the King, I submit to the authority of the laws of the state, whose guardian the King is. The difference between a good and a bad subject, is only this, that the one obeys, the other transgresses the law. The difference between a loyal subject and a rebel, is, that the one yields obedience to, and faithfully supports the supreme authority of the state, and the other endeavours to overthrow it. If we obey the laws of the King, we obey the laws of the parliament. If we disown the authority of the parliament, we disown the authority of the King. There is no medium without ascribing powers to the King which the constitution knows nothing of:—without making him superior to the laws, and setting him above all restraint. These are some of the ridiculous absurdities of American whiggism. . . .

That you will perceive the force of this reasoning, I pretend not to say. A person diseased with the jaundice sees no colour but yellow. Party heat, the fever of liberty, may for any thing I know, vitiate the mind, as much as the jaundice does the eyes. I flatter myself, however, that all reasonable Americans will feel its force; and will not be led by positive assertions without proof, nor declamatory harangues without argument, into rebellion against the supreme authority of the nation: Nor be beguiled of their present free and happy government, by the loud clamours of unrestrained licentiousness, under the specious name of liberty. Tyranny and slavery must be the consequence of the present system of conduct. If we wantonly throw off that subordination to the British Parliament, which our present state requires, we shall inevitably fall under the dominion of some foreign tyrant, or the more intolerable despotism of a few American demagogues.

If it be said, that admitting the foregoing reasoning and authorities, yet the right of taxation will not follow, let it be considered, that in every government, *legislation* and *taxation,* or the right of raising a revenue, must be conjoined. If you divide them, you weaken, and finally destroy the government; for no government can long subsist without power to raise the supplies necessary for its defence and administration. . . .

If therefore the British Parliament has no power to raise a revenue in the colonies, it has no government over the colonies, i.e. no government can support itself. The burthen of supporting its government over the colonies must lie upon the other parts of the empire. But this is unreasonable. Government implies, not only a power of making and enforcing *laws,* but defence and protection. Now protection implies tribute. Those that share in the protection of any government, are in reason and duty, bound to maintain and support the government that protects them: Otherwise they destroy their own protection; or else they throw an unjust burthen on their fellow-subjects, which they ought to bear in common with them. While therefore the colonies are under the British government, and share in its protection, the British government has a right to raise, and they are in reason and duty bound to pay, a reasonable and proportionable part of the expence of its administration. . . .

Let it be considered, that no scheme of human policy can be so contrived and guarded, but that something must be left to the integrity, prudence, and wisdom of those who govern. We are apt to think, and I believe justly, that the British constitution is the best scheme of government now subsisting: The rights and liberties of the people are better secured by it, than by any other system now subsisting. And yet we find that the rights and liberties of Englishmen may be infringed by wicked and ambitious men. This will ever be the case, even after human sagacity has exerted its utmost ability. This is, however, not argument, that we should not secure ourselves as well as we can. It is rather an argument, that we should use our utmost endeavour to guard against the attempts of ambition or avarice.

A great part of the people in England, a considerable number of people in this province, are bound by laws, and taxed without their consent, or the consent of their representatives: for representatives they have none, unless the absurd position of a *virtual* representation be admitted. These people may object to the present mode of government. They may say, that they have nothing that they can call their own. That if they may be taxed a penny without their consent, they may be taxed a pound, and so on. You will think it a sufficient security to these people, that the representatives of the nation or province cannot hurt *them,* without hurting themselves; because, they cannot tax *them,* without taxing themselves. This security however may not be so effectual as at first may be imagined. The rich are never taxed so much in proportion to their estates as the poor: And even an equal proportion of that tax which a rich man can easily pay, may be a heavy burthen to a poor man. But the same security that these people have against being ruined by the representatives of the nation, or province where they live; the same security have we against being ruined by the British parliament. They cannot hurt us without hurting themselves. The principal profits of our trade center in England. If they lay unnecessary or oppressive burthens on it; or any ways restrain it, so as to injure us, they will soon feel the effect, and very readily remove the cause. If this security is thought insufficient, let us endeavour to obtain a more effectual one. Let it however be remembered, that this security has been thought, and found sufficient till within a short period; and very probably, a prudent management, and a temperate conduct on our part, would have made it permanently effectual.

But the colonies have become so considerable by the increase of their inhabitants and commerce, and by the improvement of their lands, that they seem incapable of being governed in the same lax and precarious manner as formerly. They are arrived to that mature state of manhood which requires a different, and more exact policy of ruling, than was necessary to their infancy and childhood. They want, and are entitled to, a fixed determinate constitution of their own. A constitution which shall unite them firmly with Great-Britain, and with one another;—which shall mark out the line of British supremacy, and colonial dependence, giving on the one hand full force to the supreme authority of the nation over all its dominions, and on the other, securing effectually the rights, liberty, and property of the colonists.—This is an event devoutly to be wished, by all good men; and which all ought to labour to obtain by all prudent, and probable means. Without obtaining this, it is idle to talk of obtaining a redress of the grievances complained of. They naturally, they necessarily result from the relation which we at present stand in to Great-Britain. . . .

Every man who wishes well, either to America or Great-Britain, must wish to see a hearty and firm union subsisting between them, and between every part of the British empire. The first object of his desire will be to heal the unnatural breach that now subsists, and to accomplish a speedy reconciliation. All parties declare the utmost willingness to live in union with Great-Britain. They profess the utmost loyalty to the King; the warmest affection to their fellow-subjects in England, Ireland, and the West-Indies, and their readiness to do every thing to promote their welfare, that can reasonably be expected from them. Even those republicans, who with the destruction of every species and appearance of monarchy in the world, find it necessary to put on a fair face, and make the same declaration.

What steps, Sir, I beseech you, has the Congress taken to accomplish these good purposes? Have they fixed any determined point for us to aim at? they have, and the point marked out by them, is, *absolute* independence on Great-Britain;—a perfect discharge from all subordination to the supreme authority of the British empire.—Have they proposed any method of cementing our union with the mother country? Yes, but a queer one, viz. to break off all dealings and intercourse with her.—Have they done any thing to shew their love and affection to their fellow-subjects in England, Ireland, and the West-Indies?—Undoubtedly they have,—they have endeavoured to starve them all to death.—Is this *"Equity?"* Is this *"Wisdom?"*—Then murder is equity, and folly, wisdom.

I will here, Sir, venture to deliver my sentiments upon the line that ought to be drawn between the supremacy of Great-Britain, and the dependency of the Colonies. And I shall do it with the more boldness, because, I know it to be agreeable to the opinions of many of the warmest advocates for America, both in England and in the colonies, in the time of the stamp-act.—I imagine that if all internal taxation be vested in our own legislatures, and the right of regulating trade by duties, bounties, &c. be left in the power of the Parliament; and also the right of enacting all general laws for the good of all the colonies, that we shall have all the security for our rights, liberties and property, which human policy can give us: The dependence of the colonies on the mother country will be fixed on a firm foundation; the sovereign authority of Parliament, over all the dominions of the empire will be established, and the mother-country and all her colonies will be knit together, in ONE GRAND, FIRM, AND COMPACT BODY.

Daniel Leonard, 1740–1829

Daniel Leonard, one of the most outspoken Loyalist opponents of the American Revolution, was born in Norton, Massachusetts, to a prominent family. In 1652 his ancestors had moved to Taunton, Massachusetts, and established an iron foundry. They were affluent pillars of the community in southern Massachusetts, and Daniel was raised as if he were part of the provincial aristocracy.

Leonard began his political life as a Whig, but was won over to a Loyalist position by Governor Hutchison of Massachusetts. As the controversy widened, Leonard quickly became convinced that the renunciation of Parliament by the colonies would lead to war. Echoing the British philosopher Thomas Hobbes, Leonard argued that revolt would destroy the bonds of civil order, and society would simply revert to the rule of the more powerful.

In order to prevent the return to such a "state of nature," Leonard counselled obedience. He also argued, however, for the inherent justness of the Whig constitution and its superiority as the guarantor of liberty. Dispersing power between "the one, the few, and the many" was a proven means to preserve the liberty of English subjects.

In 1775, Leonard wrote seventeen essays in the *Massachusetts Gazette* under the pen name "Massachusettensis" defending the Crown and Parliament against their American detractors. These essays were answered by another young Massachusetts man, John Adams ("Novanglus"), later the second president of the United States. Adams reprinted their debate in 1812.

Leonard, like most of his adversaries, remained a defender of the mixed Whig Constitution. In this regard, Leonard and Adams shared a great deal in common. Nevertheless, Leonard could not join most American Whigs in their movement toward resistance and finally revolution. While Leonard shared many of the views of most Whigs, he played "Hobbes" to their "Locke."

Simply, like Hobbes, Leonard believed that disobedience to authority inevitably brought ruin, whereas more Lockean Americans believed revolution created the opportunity to begin anew with a fresh and just civil order.

Just before he wrote the "Massachusettensis" essays, Leonard was forced to flee Taunton and seek refuge in British-controlled Boston. When British troops retreated from Boston, Leonard fled to Nova Scotia and then London. His family property was confiscated, and he spent the remainder of his life, first as Chief Justice of Bermuda, and then as a highly respected lawyer in London. He visited Massachusetts twice after the revolution, but he remained what he had always preached—a loyal Englishman.

Daniel Leonard

Massachusettensis (1775)

. . . The security of the people from internal rapacity and violence, and from foreign invasions, is the end and design of government. The simple forms of government are monarchy, aristocracy, and democracy; that is, where the authority of the state is vested in one, a few, or the many. Each of these species of government has advantages peculiar to itself, and would answer the ends of government, were the persons intrusted with the authority of the state always guided, themselves, by unerring wisdom and public virtue; but rulers are not always exempt from the weakness and depravity which make government necessary to society. Thus monarchy is apt to rush headlong into tyranny, aristocracy to beget faction, and multiplied usurpation, and democracy, to degenerate into tumult, violence, and anarchy. A government formed upon these three principles, in due proportion, is the best calculated to answer the ends of government, and to endure. Such a government is the British constitution, consisting of

SOURCE: *Novangulus and Massachusettensis* (Boston: Hews and Goss, 1819).

king, lords and commons, which at once includes the principal excellencies, and excludes the principal defects of the other kinds of government. It is allowed, both by Englishmen and foreigners, to be the most perfect system that the wisdom of ages has produced. The distribution of powers are so just, and the proportions so exact, as at once to support and control each other. An Englishman glories in being subject to, and protected by such a government. The colonies are a part of the British empire. The best writers upon the law of nations tell us, that when a nation takes possession of a distant country, and settles there, that country, though separated from the principal establishment, or mother country, naturally becomes a part of the state, equal with its ancient possessions. Two supreme or independent authorities cannot exist in the same state. It would be what is called *imperium in imperio*, the height of political absurdity. The analogy between the political and human body is great. Two independent authorities in a state would be like two distinct principles of volition and action in the human body, dissenting, opposing, and destroying each other. If, then, we are a part of the British empire, we must be subject to the supreme power of the state, which is vested in the estates of parliament, notwithstanding each of the colonies have legislative and executive powers of their own, delegated, or granted to them for the purposes of regulating their own internal police, which are subordinate to, and must necessarily be subject to the checks, control, and regulation of the supreme authority.

This doctrine is not new, but the denial of it is. It is beyond a doubt, that it was the sense both of the parent country, and our ancestors, that they were to remain subject to parliament. It is evident from the charter itself; and this authority has been exercised by parliament, from time to time, almost ever since the first settlement of the country, and has been expressly acknowledged by our provincial legislatures. It is not less our interest, than our duty, to continue subject to the authority of parliament, which will be more fully considered hereafter. The principal argument against the authority of parliament, is this: the Americans are entitled to all the privileges of an Englishman; it is the privilege of an Englishman to be exempt from all laws, that he does not consent to in person, or by representative. The Americans are not represented in parliament, and therefore are exempt from acts of parliament, or in other words, not subject to its authority. This appears specious; but leads to such absurdities as demonstrate its fallacy. If the colonies are not subject to the authority of parliament, Great Britain and the colonies must be distinct states, as completely so, as England and Scotland were before the union, or as Great Britain and Hanover are now. The colonies in that case will owe no allegiance to the imperial crown, and perhaps not to the person of the king, as the title to the crown is derived from an act of parliament, made since the settlement of this province, which act respects the imperial crown only. Let us waive this difficulty, and

suppose allegiance due from the colonies to the person of the king of Great Britain. He then appears in a new capacity, of king of America, or rather in several new capacities, of king of Massachusetts, king of Rhode-Island, king of Connecticut, &c. &c. For if our connection with Great Britain by the parliament be dissolved, we shall have none among ourselves, but each colony become as distinct from the others, as England was from Scotland, before the union. Some have supposed that each state, having one and the same person for its king, is a sufficient connection. Were he an absolute monarch, it might be; but in a mixed government, it is no union at all. For as the king must govern each state, by its parliament, those several parliaments would pursue the particular interest of its own state; and however well disposed the king might be to pursue a line of interest, that was common to all, the checks and control that he would meet with, would render it impossible. If the king of Great Britain has really these new capacities, they ought to be added to his titles; and another difficulty will arise, the prerogatives of these new crowns have never been defined or limited. Is the monarchical part of the several provincial constitutions to be nearer or more remote from absolute monarchy, in an inverted ratio to each one's approaching to, or receding from a republic? But let us suppose the same prerogatives inherent in the several American crowns, as are in the imperial crown of Great Britain, where shall we find the British constitution, that we all agree we are entitled to? We shall seek for it in vain in our provincial assemblies. They are but faint sketches of the estates of parliament. The houses of representatives, or Burgesses, have not all the powers of the house of commons; in the charter governments they have no more than what is expressly granted by their several charters. The first charters granted to this province did not empower the assembly to tax the people at all. Our council boards are as destitute of the constitutional authority of the house of lords, as their several members are of the noble independence, and splendid appendages of peerage. The house of peers is the bulwark of the British constitution, and through successive ages, has withstood the shocks of monarchy, and the sappings of democracy, and the constitution gained strength by the conflict. Thus the supposition of our being independent states, or exempt from the authority of parliament, destroys the very idea of our having a British constitution. The provincial constitutions, considered as subordinate, are generally well adapted to those purposes of government, for which they were intended; that is, to regulate the internal police of the several colonies; but have no principle of stability within themselves; they may support themselves in moderate times, but would be merged by the violence of turbulent ones, and the several colonies become wholly monarchical, or wholly republican, were it not for the checks, controls, regulations, and supports of the supreme authority of the empire. Thus the argument, that is drawn from their first principle of our being entitled to English liberties, destroys the principle itself, it deprives us of the bill of rights, and all the benefits resulting from the revolution of English laws, and of the British constitution.

Our patriots have been so intent upon building up American rights, that they have overlooked the rights of Great Britain, and our own interest. Instead of proving that we were entitled to privileges, that our fathers knew our situation would not admit us to enjoy, they have been arguing away our most essential rights. If there be any grievance, it does not consist in our being subject to the authority of parliament, but in our not having an actual representation in it. Were it possible for the colonies to have an equal representation in parliament, and were refused it upon proper application, I confess I should think it a grievance; but at present it seems to be allowed, by all parties, to be impracticable, considering the colonies are distant from Great Britain a thousand transmarine leagues. If that be the case, the right or privilege, that we complain of being deprived of, is not withheld by Britain, but the first principles of government, and the immutable laws of nature, render it impossible for us to enjoy it. This is apparently the meaning of that celebrated passage in Governor Hutchinson's letter, that rang through the continent, viz: There must be an abridgment of what is called English liberties. He subjoins, that he had never yet seen the projection, whereby a colony three thousand miles distant from the parent state, might enjoy all the privileges of the parent state, and remain subject to it, or in words to that effect. The obnoxious sentence, taken detached from the letter, appears very unfriendly to the colonies; but considered in connection with the other parts of the letter, is but a necessary result from our situation. Allegiance and protection are reciprocal. It is our highest interest to continue a part of the British empire; and equally our duty to remain subject to the authority of parliament. Our own internal police may generally be regulated by our provincial legislatures, but in national concerns, or where our own assemblies do not answer the ends of government with respect to ourselves, the ordinances or interposition of the great council of the nation is necessary. In this case, the major must rule the minor. After many more centuries shall have rolled away, long after we, who are now bustling upon the stage of life, shall have been received to the bosom of mother earth, and our names are forgotten, the colonies may be so far increased as to have the balance of wealth, numbers and power, in their favor, the good of the empire make it necessary to fix the seat of government here; and some future George, equally the friend of mankind, with him that now sways the British sceptre, may cross the Atlantic, and rule Great Britain, by an American parliament.

Revolution and the Language of Individual Rights

John Adams, 1735–1826

John Adams, like Thomas Jefferson, was part of the founding generation that came to maturity actively resisting British policies in America. A graduate of Harvard College in 1755 and a lawyer by 1758, Adams soon began his public career. In 1765, he joined James Otis in leading Massachusetts opposition to the Stamp Act. He then wrote *Dissertations on the Canon and Feudal Law* (1768), the first of a number of serious works in legal and political theory. *Dissertations* exhibited a Whig interpretation of feudalism that was typical of American thinking.

Adams took an active role in the two Continental Congresses and helped draft the Petition of Rights to the Crown and the Declaration of Independence. He also wrote a series of articles under the pen name "Novanglus," attacking the loyalist writer Daniel Leonard.

Adams then turned from legitimating resistance and revolution to the task of constitution building. In 1780, he became the architect of the Massachusetts constitution and in 1787 and 1788 wrote the *Defenses of the Constitutions of Government of the United States of America*. Again, in 1790, while vice president under George Washington, he wrote a series of public letters called *Discourses on Davila* that drew the anger of many as antirepublican tracts.

Adams was a Whig and remained so all of his life. His moderate attacks on the British and his defense of the Whig Constitution placed him at odds with radicals like Tom Paine. Later in life, even his friend Jefferson found him to be far too aristocratic in his tastes and sentiments. Yet like Jefferson, Adams believed in a natural aristocracy that would emerge over time in a free society. More than Jefferson, however, he believed that government needed to reflect differences in human capabilities and character.

In the articles written under the pen name of "Novanglus," Adams attacked the loyalist logic of Daniel Leonard. However, he still paid lip service to the ideal of the Whig Constitution and hoped to find a compromise solution that would leave the Americans tied to the British in some form of loose confederation. When events moved beyond what Adams had envisioned, he became an avid revolutionary. Nevertheless, he was intellectually and emotionally a Whig, and that separated him from the radical egalitarian individualism of Tom Paine.

John Adams

Novanglus (1775)

. . . if the parliament of Great Britain, had all the natural foundations of authority, wisdom, goodness, justice, power, in as great perfection as they ever existed in any body of men since Adam's fall; and if the English nation was the most virtuous, pure and free, that ever was; would not such an unlimited subjection of three millions of people to that parliament, at three thousand miles distance be real slavery? There are but two sorts of men in the world, freemen and slaves. The very definition of a freeman, is one who is bound by no law to which he has not consented. Americans would have no way of giving or withholding their consent to the acts of this parliament, therefore they would not be freemen. But, when luxury, effeminacy and venality are arrived at such a shocking pitch in England, when both electors and elected, are become one mass of corruption, when the nation is oppressed to death with debts and taxes, owing to their own extravagance, and

SOURCE: *Novanglus and Massachusettensis* (Boston: Hews and Goss, 1819).

want of wisdom, what would be your condition under such an absolute subjection to parliament? You would not only be slaves. But the most abject sort of slaves to the worst sort of masters! at least this is my opinion. Judge for yourselves between Massachusettensis and

NOVANGLUS

Why will not this writer [Massachusettensis] state the question fairly? The whigs allow that from the necessity of a case not provided for by common law, and to supply a defect in the British dominions, which there undoubtedly is, if they are to be governed only by that law, America has all along consented, still consents, and ever will consent, that parliament being the most powerful legislature in the dominions, should regulate the trade of the dominions. This is founding the authority of parliament to regulate our trade, upon *compact* and *consent* of the colonies, not upon any principle of common or statute law, not upon any original principle of the English constitution, not upon the principle that parliament is the supreme and sovereign legislature over them in all cases whatsoever.

The question is not therefore, whether the authority of parliament extends to the colonies in any case; for it is admitted by the whigs that it does in that of commerce: but whether it extends in all cases. . . .

I have said, that the practice of free governments alone can be quoted with propriety, to show the sense of nations. But the sense and practice of nations is not enough. Their practice must be reasonable, just and right, or it will not govern Americans.

Absolute monarchies, whatever their practice may be, are nothing to us. For as Harrington observes, "Absolute monarchy, as that of the Turks, neither plants its people at home nor abroad, otherwise than as tenants for life or at will; wherefore its national and provincial government is all one."

I deny, therefore, that the practice of free nations, or the opinions of the best writers upon the law of nations, will warrant the position of Massachusettensis, that when a nation takes possession of a distant territory, that becomes a part of the state equally with its ancient possessions. The practice of free nations, and the opinions of the best writers, are in general on the contrary.

I agree, that "two supreme and independent authorities cannot exist in the same state," any more than two supreme beings in one universe. And therefore I contend, that our provincial legislatures are the only supreme authorities in our colonies. Parliament, notwithstanding this, may be allowed an authority supreme and sovereign over the ocean, which may be limited by the banks of the ocean, or the bounds of our charters; our charters give us no authority over the high seas. Parliament has our consent to assume a jurisdiction over them. And here is a line fairly drawn between the rights of Britain and the rights of the colonies, viz. the banks of the ocean, or low water mark; the line of division between common law and civil, or maritime law. If

this is not sufficient—if parliament are at a loss for any principle of natural, civil, maritime, moral or common law, on which to ground any authority over the high seas, the Atlantic especially, let the Colonies be treated like reasonable creatures, and they will discover great ingenuity and modesty. . . .

"If then we are a part of the British empire, we must be subject to the supreme power of the state, which is vested in the estates in parliament.". . .

The question should be, whether we are a part of the kingdom of Great Britain: this is the only language, known in English laws. We are not then a part of the British kingdom, realm or state; and therefore the supreme power of the kingdom, realm or state, is not upon these principles, the supreme power of us. That "supreme power over America is vested in the estates in parliament," is an affront to us; for there is not an acre of American land represented there—there are no American estates in parliament. . . .

. . . We think the consequences are, that she has after 150 years, discovered a defect in her government, which ought to be supplied by some just and reasonable means; that is, by the consent of the colonies; for metaphysicians and politicians may dispute forever, but they will never find any other moral principle or foundation of rule or obedience, than the consent of governors and governed. She has found out that the great machine will not go any longer without a new wheel. She will make this herself. We think she is making it of such materials and workmanship as will tear the whole machine to pieces. We are willing if she can convince us of the necessity of such a wheel, to assist with artists and materials, in making it, so that it may answer the end. But she says, we shall have no share in it; and if we will not let her patch it up as she pleases, her Massachusettensis and other advocates tell us, she will tear it to pieces herself, by cutting our throats. To this kind of reasoning we can only answer, that we will not stand still to be butchered. We will defend our lives as long as providence shall enable us. . . .

That the colonies owe "no allegiance" to any imperial crown, provided such a crown involves in it an house of lords and a house of commons, is certain. Indeed, we owe no allegiance to any crown at all. We owe allegiance to the person of his majesty, King George the third, whom God preserve. But allegiance is due universally, both from Britons and Americans to the person of the king, not to his crown: to his natural, not his politic capacity, as I will undertake to prove hereafter, from the highest authorities, and most solemn adjudications, which were ever made within any part of the British dominions.

If his majesty's title to the crown is "derived from an act of parliament, made since the settlement of these colonies," it was not made since the date of our charter. Our charter was granted by King William and Queen Mary, three years after the revolution; and the oaths of allegiance are established by a law of the province. So that our allegiance to his majesty is not due by virtue of any act of a British parliament, but by our own charter and province laws. It ought to be remembered, that there was a revolution here, as well as in England, and that we made an original, express contract with King William, as well as the people of England. . . .

But "where is the British constitution, that we all agree we are entitled to?" I answer, if we enjoy, and are entitled to more liberty than the British constitution allows, where is the harm? Or, if we enjoy the British constitution in greater purity and perfection than they do in England, as is really the case, whose fault is this? Not ours.

We may find all the blessings "of this constitution in our provincial assemblies." Our houses of Representatives have, and ought to exercise, every power of the House of Commons. The first charter to this colony is nothing to the present argument; but it did grant a power of taxing the people, implicitly, though not in express terms. It granted all the rights and liberties of Englishmen, which include the power of taxing the people. . . .

But perhaps it will be said that we are to enjoy the British constitution in our supreme legislature, the parliament, not in our provincial legislatures.

To this I answer, if parliament is to be our supreme legislature, we shall be under a complete oligarchy or aristocracy, not the British constitution, which this writer himself defines a mixture of monarchy, aristocracy, and democracy.—For king, lords and commons will constitute one great oligarchy, as they will stand related to America, as much as the decemvirs did in Rome; with this difference for the worse, that our rulers are to be three thousand miles off.

Samuel Langdon, 1723–1797

Congregationalist minister and twelfth president of Harvard, Samuel Langdon was a typical American Whig. Reared with a love for both the Hebrew prophets and the *ideal* of the British Constitution, Langdon saw a need to return to the purity of "first principles."

In 1775—one year after the battles at Lexington and Concord and with the city of Boston under seige—Langdon delivered an election sermon before the voters of Massachusetts assembled at Watertown. In this sermon, "Government Corrupted by Vice, and Recovered by Righteousness," Langdon demonstrated the typical American Whig reverence for the mixed English Constitution of "King, Lords, and Commons," while at the same time decrying its present corruption.

Langdon sought a return to the purity of the "true spirit of Christianity," and a return to the virtuous principles of British politics. While Langdon used a Lockean theory of natural rights to defend the right of resistance, his primary line of argument was drawn from religious tradition, Whig attitudes about the British Constitution, and a republican emphasis on virtue in government. He counseled resistance and reform but not yet a complete and total separation.

Samuel Langdon

Government Corrupted by Vice, and Recovered by Righteousness (1775)

As a roaring Lion and a ranging Bear, fo is a wicked Ruler over the poor People.

PROV. 28. 15.

AN ELECTION SERMON.

AND I WILL RESTORE THY JUDGES AS AT THE FIRST, AND THY COUNSELLORS AS AT THE BEGINNING; AFTERWARD THOU SHALT BE CALLED THE CITY OF RIGHTEOUSNESS, THE FAITHFUL CITY.

ISAIAH i. 26.

Shall we rejoice, my fathers and brethren, or shall we weep together, on the return of this anniversary, which from the first settlement of this colony has been sacred to liberty, to perpetuate that invaluable privilege of choosing from among ourselves wise men, fearing God and hating covetousness, to be

SOURCE: John Wingate Thornton, *The Pulpit of the American Revolution* (New York: Burt Franklin, 1960 reprint of 1860 edition).

honorable counsellors, to constitute one essential branch of that happy government which was established on the faith of royal charters?

On this day the people have from year to year assembled, from all our towns, in a vast congregation, with gladness and festivity, with every ensign of joy displayed in our metropolis, which now, alas! is made a garrison of mercenary troops, the stronghold of despotism. But how shall I now address you from this desk, remote from the capital, and remind you of the important business which distinguished this day in our calendar, without spreading a gloom over this assembly by exhibiting the melancholy change made in the face of our public affairs?

We have lived to see the time when British liberty is just ready to expire,—when that constitution of government which has so long been the glory and strength of the English nation is deeply undermined and ready to tumble into ruins,—when America is threatened with cruel oppression, and the arm of power is stretched out against New England, and especially against this colony, to compel us to submit to the arbitrary acts of legislators who are not our representatives, and who will not themselves bear the least part of the burdens which, without mercy, they are laying upon us. The most formal and solemn grants of kings to our ancestors are deemed by our oppressors as of little value; and they have mutilated the charter of this colony, in the most essential parts, upon false representations, and new-invented maxims of policy, without the least regard to any legal process. We are no longer permitted to fix our eyes on the faithful of the land, and trust in the wisdom of their counsels and the equity of their judgment; but men in whom we can have no confidence, whose principles are subversive of our liberties, whose aim is to exercise lordship over us, and share among themselves the public wealth,—men who are ready to serve any master, and execute the most unrighteous decrees for high wages,—whose faces we never saw before, and whose interests and connections may be far divided from us by the wide Atlantic,—are to be set over us, as counsellors and judges, at the pleasure of those who have the riches and power of the nation in their hands, and whose noblest plan is to subjugate the colonies, first, and then the whole nation, to their will.

That we might not have it in our power to refuse the most absolute submission to their unlimited claims of authority, they have not only endeavored to terrify us with fleets and armies sent to our capital, and distressed and put an end to our trade,—particularly that important branch of it, the fishery,—but at length attempted, by a sudden march of a body of troops in the night, to seize and destroy one of our magazines, formed by the people merely for their security, if, after such formidable military preparations on the other side, matters should be pushed to an extremity. By this, as might well be expected, a skir-

mish was brought on; and it is most evident, from a variety of concurring circumstances, as well as numerous depositions both of the prisoners·taken by us at that time and our own men then on the spot only as spectators, that the fire began first on the side of the king's troops. At least five or six of our inhabitants were murderously killed by the regulars at Lexington before any man attempted to return the fire, and when they were actually complying with the command to disperse; and two more of our brethren were likewise killed at Concord bridge, by a fire from the king's soldiers, before the engagement began on our side. But, whatever credit falsehoods transmitted to Great Britain from the other side may gain, the matter may be rested entirely on this: that he that arms himself to commit a robbery, and demands the traveller's purse by the terror of instant death, is the first aggressor, though the other should take the advantage of discharging his weapon first, and killing the robber. . . .

That ever-memorable day, the nineteenth of April, is the date of an unhappy war openly begun by the ministers of the king of Great Britain against his good subjects in this colony, and implicitly against all the other colonies. But for what? Because they have made a noble stand for their natural and constitutional rights, in opposition to the machinations of wicked men who are betraying their royal master, establishing Popery in the British dominions, and aiming to enslave and ruin the whole nation, that they may enrich themselves and their vile dependents with the public treasures and the spoils of America. . . .

We must keep our eyes fixed on the supreme government of the Eternal King, as directing all events, setting up or pulling down the kings of the earth at his pleasure, suffering the best forms of human government to degenerate and go to ruin by corruption, or restoring the decayed constitutions of kingdoms and states by reviving public virtue and religion, and granting the favorable interpositions of his providence. To this our text leads us; and, though I hope to be excused on this occasion from a formal discourse on the words in a doctrinal way, yet I must not wholly pass over the religious instruction contained in them.

Let us consider—that for the sins of a people God may suffer the best government to be corrupted or entirely dissolved, and that nothing but a general reformation can give good ground to hope that the public happiness will be restored by the recovery of the strength and perfection of the state, and that Divine Providence will interpose to fill every department with wise and good men.

Isaiah prophesied about the time of the captivity of the Ten Tribes of Israel, and about a century before the captivity of Judah. The kingdom of Israel was brought to destruction because its iniquities were full; its counsellors and judges were wholly taken away because there remained no hope of reformation. But the sceptre did not entirely depart from Judah, nor a lawgiver from between his feet, till the Messiah came; yet greater and greater changes took place in their political affairs: their government degenerated in proportion as their vices increased, till few faithful men were left in any public offices; and at length, when they were delivered up for seventy years into the hands of the king of Babylon, scarce any remains of their original excellent civil polity appeared among them.

The Jewish government, according to the original constitution which was divinely established, if considered merely in a civil view, was a perfect republic. The heads of their tribes and elders of their cities were their counsellors and judges. They called the people together in more general or particular assemblies,—took their opinions, gave advice, and managed the public affairs according to the general voice. Counsellors and judges comprehend all the power of that government; for there was no such thing as legislative authority belonging to it,—their complete code

of laws being given immediately from God by the hand of Moses. And let them who cry up the divine right of kings consider that the only form of government which had a proper claim to a divine establishment was so far from including the idea of a king, that it was a high crime for Israel to ask to be in this respect like other nations; and when they were gratified, it was rather as a just punishment of their folly, that they might feel the burdens of court pageantry, of which they were warned by a very striking description, than as a divine recommendation of kingly authority.

Every nation, when able and agreed, has a right to set up over themselves any form of government which to them may appear most conducive to their common welfare. The civil polity of Israel is doubtless an excellent general model, allowing for some peculiarities; at least, some principal laws and orders of it may be copied to great advantage in more modern establishments.

When a government is in its prime, the public good engages the attention of the whole; the strictest regard is paid to the qualifications of those who hold the offices of the state; virtue prevails; everything is managed with justice, prudence, and frugality; the laws are founded on principles of equity rather than mere policy, and all the people are happy. But vice will increase with the riches and glory of an empire; and this gradually tends to corrupt the constitution, and in time bring on its dissolution. This may be considered not only as the natural effect of vice, but a righteous judgment of Heaven, especially upon a nation which has been favored with the blessings of religion and liberty, and is guilty of undervaluing them, and eagerly going into the gratification of every lust.

In this chapter the prophet describes the very corrupt state of Judah in his day, both as to religion and common morality, and looks forward to that increase of wickedness which would bring on their desolation and captivity. They were "a sinful nation, a people laden with iniquity, a seed of evil-doers, children that were corrupters, who had forsaken the Lord, and provoked the Holy One of Israel to anger." The whole body of the nation, from head to foot, was full of moral and political disorders, without any remaining soundness. Their religion was all mere ceremony and hypocrisy; and even the laws of common justice and humanity were disregarded in their public courts. They had counsellors and judges, but very different from those at the beginning of the commonwealth. Their princes were rebellious against God and the constitution of their country, and companions of thieves,— giving countenance to every artifice for seizing the property of the subjects into their own hands, and robbing the public treasury. . . . The whole body being so corrupted, there could be no rational prospect of any great reformation in the state, but rather of its ruin, which accordingly came on in Jeremiah's time. Yet if a general reformation of religion and morals had taken place, and they had turned to God from all their sins—if they had again recovered the true spirit of their religion,— God, by the gracious interpositions of his providence, would soon have found out methods to restore the former virtue of the state, and again have given them men of wisdom and integrity, according to their utmost wish, to be counsellors and judges. This was verified in fact after the nation had been purged by a long captivity, and returned to their own land humbled and filled with zeal for God and his law.

By all this we may be led to consider the true cause of the present remarkable troubles which are come upon Great Britain and these colonies, and the only effectual remedy.

We have rebelled against God. We have lost the true spirit of Christianity, though we retain the outward profession and form of it. We have neglected and set light by the glorious gospel of our Lord Jesus Christ, and his holy commands and institutions. The worship of many is but mere compliment to the Deity, while their hearts are far from him. By many the gospel is corrupted into a superficial system of moral philosophy, little better than ancient Platonism; and, after all the pretended refinements of moderns in the theory of Christianity, very little of the pure practice of it is to be found among those who once stood foremost in the profession of the gospel. In a general view of the present moral state of Great Britain it may be said, "There is no truth, nor mercy, nor knowledge of God in the land. By swearing, and lying, and killing, and stealing, and committing adultery," their wickedness breaks out, and one murder after another is committed, under the connivance and encouragement even of that authority by which such crimes ought to be punished, that the purposes of oppression and despotism may be answered. As they have increased, so have they sinned; therefore God is changing their glory into shame. The general prevalence of vice has changed the whole face of things in the British government.

The excellency of the constitution has been the boast of Great Britain and the envy of neighboring nations. In former times the great departments of the state, and the various places of trust and authority, were filled with men of wisdom, honesty, and religion, who employed all their powers, and were ready to risk their fortunes and their lives, for the public good. They were faithful counsellors to kings; directed their authority and majesty to the happiness of the nation, and opposed every step by which despotism endeavored to advance. They were fathers of the people, and sought the welfare and prosperity of the whole body. They did not exhaust the national wealth by luxury and bribery, or convert it to their own private benefit or the maintenance of idle, useless officers and dependents, but improved it faithfully for the proper purposes—for the necessary support of government and defence of the kingdom. Their laws were dictated by wisdom and equality, and justice was administered with impartiality. Religion discovered its general influence among all ranks, and kept out great corruptions from places of power.

But in what does the British nation now glory?—In a mere shadow of its ancient political system,—in titles of dignity without virtue,—in vast public treasures continually lavished in corruption till every fund is exhausted, notwithstanding the mighty streams perpetually flowing in,—in the many artifices to stretch the prerogatives of the crown beyond all constitutional bounds, and make the king an absolute monarch, while the people are deluded with a mere phantom of liberty. What idea must we entertain of that great government, if such a one can be found, which pretends to have made an exact counterbalance of power between the sovereign, the nobles and the commons, so that the three branches shall be an effectual check upon each other, and the united wisdom of the whole shall conspire to promote the national felicity, but which, in reality, is reduced to such a situation that it may be managed at the sole will of one court favorite? What difference is there betwixt one man's choosing, at his own pleasure, by his single vote, the majority of those who are to represent the people, and his purchasing in such a majority, according to his own nomination, with money out of the public treasury, or other effectual methods of influencing elections? And what shall we say if, in the same manner, by places, pensions, and other bribes, a minister of the crown can at any time gain over a nobler majority likewise to be entirely subservient to his purposes, and, moreover, persuade his royal master to resign himself up wholly to the direction of his counsels? . . .

The pretence for taxing America has been that the nation contracted an immense debt for the defence of the American colonies, and that, as they are now able to contribute some proportion towards the discharge of this debt, and must be considered as part of the nation, it is reasonable they should be taxed, and the Parliament has a right to tax and govern them, in all cases whatever, by its own supreme authority. . . . Would it not be much superior wisdom, and sounder policy, for a distressed kingdom to retrench the vast unnecessary expenses continually incurred by its enormous vices; to stop the prodigious sums paid in pensions, and to numberless officers, without the least advantage to the public; to reduce the number of devouring servants in the great family; to turn their minds from the pursuit of pleasure and the boundless luxuries of life to the important interests of their country and the salvation of the commonwealth? Would not a reverend regard to the authority of divine revelation, a hearty belief of the gospel of the grace of God, and a general reformation of all those vices which bring misery and ruin upon individuals, families, and kingdoms, and which have provoked Heaven to bring the nation into such perplexed and dangerous circumstances, be the surest way to recover the sinking state, and make it again rich and flourishing? Millions might annually be saved if the kingdom were generally and thoroughly reformed; and the public debt, great as it is, might in a few years to cancelled by a growing revenue, which now amounts to full ten millions per annum, without laying additional burdens on any of the subjects. But the demands of corruption are constantly increasing, and will forever exceed all the resources of wealth which the wit of man can invent or tyranny impose. . . .

But, alas! have not the sins of America, and of New England in particular, had a hand in bringing down upon us the righteous judgments of Heaven? . . . Have we not lost much of that spirit of genuine Christianity which so remarkably appeared in our ancestors, for which God distinguished them with the signal favors of providence when they fled from tyranny and persecution into this western desert? Have we not departed from their virtues? Though I hope and am confident that as much true religion, agreeable to the purity and simplicity of the gospel, remains among us as among any people in the world, yet, in the midst of the present great apostasy of the nations professing Christianity, have not we likewise been guilty of departing from the living God? Have we not made light of the gospel of salvation, and too much affected the cold, formal, fashionable religion of countries grown old in vice, and overspread with infidelity? Do not our follies and iniquities testify against us? Have we not, especially in our seaports, gone much too far into the pride and luxuries of life? . . . Has there been no flattery, no bribery, no artifices practised, to get into places of honor and profit, or carry a vote to serve a particular interest, without regard to right or wrong? Have our statesmen always acted with integrity, and every judge with impartiality, in the fear of God? In short, have all ranks of men showed regard to the divine commands, and joined to promote the Redeemer's kingdom and the public welfare? I wish we could more fully justify ourselves in all these respects. . . .

Let me address you in the words of the prophet? "O Israel! return unto the Lord thy God, for thou hast fallen by thine iniquity." My brethren, let us repent, and implore the divine mercy; let us amend our ways and our doings, reform everything which has been provoking to the Most High, and thus endeavor to obtain the gracious interpositions of Providence for our deliverance.

If true religion is revived by means of these public calamities, and again prevails among us,—if it appears in our religious assemblies, in the conduct of our civil affairs, in our armies, in our families, in all our business and conversation,—we may hope for the direction and blessing of the Most High, while we are using our best endeavors to preserve and restore the civil government of this colony, and defend America from slavery.

Our late happy government is changed into the terrors of military execution. Our firm opposition to the establishment of an arbitrary system is called rebellion, and we are to expect no mercy, but to yield property and life at discretion. This we are resolved at all events not to do, and therefore we have taken up arms in our own defence, and all the colonies are united in the great cause of liberty.

But how shall we live while civil government is disolved? What shall we do without counsellors and judges? A state of absolute anarchy is dreadful. Submission to the tyranny of hundreds of imperious masters, firmly embodied against us, and united in the same cruel design of disposing of our lives and subsistence at their pleasure, and making their own will our law in all cases whatsoever, is the vilest slavery, and worse than death.

Thanks be to God that he has given us, as men, natural rights, independent on all human laws whatever, and that these rights are recognized by the grand charter of British liberties. By the law of nature, any body of people, destitute of order and government, may form themselves into a civil society, according to their best prudence, and so provide for their common safety and advantage. When one form is found by the majority not to answer the grand purpose in any tolerable degree, they may, by common consent, put an end to it and set up another,—only, as all such great changes are attended with difficulty and danger of confusion, they ought not to be attempted without urgent necessity, which will be determined always by the general voice of the wisest and best members of the community.

If the great servants of the public forget their duty, betray their trust, and sell their country, or make war against the most valuable rights and privileges of the people, reason and justice require that they should be discarded, and others appointed in their room, without any regard to formal resignations of their forfeited power. . . .

. . . O, may our camp be free from every accursed thing! May our land be purged from all its sins! May we be truly a holy people, and all our towns cities of righteousness! Then the Lord will be our refuge and strength, a very present help in trouble, and we shall have no reason to be afraid though thousands of enemies set themselves against us round about,—though all nature should be thrown into tumults and convulsions. He can command the stars in their courses to fight his battles, and all the elements to wage war with his enemies. He can destroy them with innumerable plagues, or send faintness into their hearts, so that the men of might shall not find their hands. In a variety of methods he can work salvation for us, as he did for his people in ancient days, and according to the many remarkable deliverances granted in former times to Great Britain and New England when popish machinations threatened both countries with civil and ecclesiastical tyranny.

May the Lord hear us in this day of trouble, and the name of the God of Jacob defend us, send us help from his sanctuary, and strengthen us out of Zion! We will rejoice in his salvation, and in the name of our God we will set up our banners. Let us look to him to fulfil all our petitions.

Thomas Paine, 1737–1809

Thomas Paine represents the most radical side of American republicanism. Born in Thetford, England, the son of a poor Quaker corset maker, Paine lived and worked with the laborers and artisans of London, amongst whom the republican and Dissenter traditions of the English Civil War were very much alive. In 1772, he fell into some difficulty with authorities over what might today be viewed as union activities. Hoping for a new beginning, he emigrated to America in 1774, on the advice of Benjamin Franklin whom he had met in London.

Once here, Paine was naturally attracted to the revolutionary cause and began to edit *The Crisis*, a revolutionary journal. In January of 1776, he wrote *Common Sense*, which electrified the colonies with its sharp break with moderate Whig reasoning.

Paine's commitment to freedom and equality, however, was international. "My country is the world," he wrote, "to do good my religion." He later became an active supporter of the French Revolution and wrote the *Rights of Man* to answer Edmund Burke's conservative attack on that revolution. The work was suppressed and Paine tried for treason. He fled England and took refuge in France where he served in the National Convention, until finally imprisoned by Robespierre.

His release was later arranged by James Monroe as a favor to the United States, and Paine returned to this country. However, Paine had fallen out of favor in America for his defense of the French Revolution, the extreme Deist arguments of the *Age of Reason*, and some of his egalitarian proposals in *Agrarian Justice* (e.g., progressive estate taxes and a quasi-social security program). He died in New York City, a forgotten and lonely man.

Nevertheless, *Common Sense* was one of the most important writings of the independence movement, since it gave Americans a rhetoric they could use to justify a complete break with Britain. The British Constitution had not been corrupted, he argued; it was totally unjust. Americans did not need to restore their rights as Englishmen, they needed to seize their rights as men.

Paine's radical republicanism left him many enemies even within the independence movement. However, his insistence on liberty, equality, and popular government has been shared by many succeeding generations of Americans.

Thomas Paine

Common Sense (1776)

INTRODUCTION

Perhaps the sentiments contained in the following pages, are not *yet* sufficiently fashionable to procure them general favor; a long habit of not thinking a thing *wrong,* gives it a superficial appearance of being *right,* and raises at first a formidable outcry in defence of custom. But the tumult soon subsides. Time makes more converts than reason.

As a long and violent abuse of power is generally the means of calling the right of it in question, (and in matters too which might never have been thought of, had not the sufferers been aggravated into the inquiry,) and as the king of England hath undertaken in his *own right,* to support the Parliament in what he calls *theirs,* and as the good people of this country are grievously oppressed by the combination, they have an undoubted privilege to inquire into the pretensions of both, and equally to reject the usurpation of *either.* . . .

The cause of America is in a great measure

SOURCE: William M. Vander Weyde, ed., *The Life and Works of Thomas Paine,* vol. 2 (New Rochelle, N.Y.: Thomas Paine National Historical Association, 1925).

the cause of all mankind. Many circumstances have, and will arise, which are not local, but universal, and through which the principles of all lovers of mankind are affected, and in the event of which their affections are interested. The laying a country desolate with fire and sword, declaring war against the natural rights of all mankind, and extirpating the defenders thereof from the face of the earth, is the concern of every man to whom nature hath given the power of feeling; of which class, regardless of party censure is

THE AUTHOR

ON THE ORIGIN AND DESIGN OF GOVERNMENT IN GENERAL, WITH CONCISE REMARKS ON THE ENGLISH CONSTITUTION

Some writers have so confounded society with government, as to leave little or no distinction between them; whereas they are not only different, but have different origins. Society is produced by our wants and government by our wickedness; the former promotes our happiness *positively* by uniting our affections, the latter *negatively* by restraining our vices.

The one encourages intercourse, the other creates distinctions. The first is a patron, the last a punisher.

Society in every state is a blessing, but government, even in its best state, is but a necessary evil; in its worst state an intolerable one: for when we suffer, or are exposed to the same miseries *by a government,* which we might expect in a country *without government,* our calamity is heightened by reflecting that we furnish the means by which we suffer. Government, like dress, is the badge of lost innocence; the palaces of kings are built upon the ruins of the bowers of paradise. For were the impulses of conscience clear, uniform and irresistibly obeyed, man would need no other lawgiver; but that not being the case, he finds it necessary to surrender up a part of his property to furnish means for the protection of the rest; and this he is induced to do by the same prudence which in every other case advises him, out of two evils to choose the least. Wherefore, security being the true design and end of government, it unanswerably follows that whatever form thereof appears most likely to ensure it to us, with the least expence and greatest benefit, is preferable to all others.

In order to gain a clear and just idea of the design and end of government, let us suppose a small number of persons settled in some sequestered part of the earth, unconnected with the rest; they will then represent the first peopling of any country, or of the world. In this state of natural liberty, society will be their first thought. A thousand motives will excite them thereto; the strength of one man is so unequal to his wants, and his mind so unfitted for perpetual solitude, that he is soon obliged to seek assistance and relief of another, who in his turn requires the same. Four or five united would be able to raise a tolerable dwelling in the midst of a wilderness, but one man might labor out the common period of life without accomplishing any thing; when he

had felled his timber he could not remove it, nor erect it after it was removed; hunger in the mean time would urge him to quit his work, and every different want would call him a different way. . . .

Thus necessity, like a gravitating power, would soon form our newly arrived emigrants into society, the reciprocal blessings of which would supercede, and render the obligations of law and government unnecessary while they remained perfectly just to each other; but as nothing but Heaven is impregnable to vice, it will unavoidably happen that in proportion as they surmount the first difficulties of emigration, which bound them together in a common cause, they will begin to relax in their duty and attachment to each other: and this remissness will point out the necessity of establishing some form of government to supply the defect of moral virtue.

Some convenient tree will afford them a State House, under the branches of which the whole colony may assemble to deliberate on public matters. It is more than probable that their first laws will have the title only of regulations and be enforced by no other penalty than public disesteem. In this first parliament every man by natural right will have a seat.

But as the colony increases, the public concerns will increase likewise, and the distance at which the members may be separated, will render it too inconvenient for all of them to meet on every occasion as at first, when their number was small, their habitations near, and the public concerns few and trifling. This will point out the convenience of their consenting to leave the legislative part to be managed by a select number chosen from the whole body, who are supposed to have the same concerns at stake which those have who appointed them, and who will act in the same manner as the whole body would act were they present. If the colony continue increasing, it will become necessary to augment the number of representatives, and that the interest of every part of the colony may be attended to, it will be found best to divide the whole into convenient parts, each part sending its proper number: and that the *elected* might never form to themselves an interest separate from the *electors*, prudence will point out the propriety of having elections often: because as the *elected* might by that means return and mix again with the general body of the *electors* in a few months, their fidelity to the public will be secured by the prudent reflection of not making a rod for themselves. And as this frequent interchange will establish a common interest with every part of the community, they will mutually and naturally support each other, and on this, (not on the unmeaning name of king,) depends the *strength of government, and the happiness of the governed.*

Here then is the origin and rise of government; namely, a mode rendered necessary by the inability of moral virtue to govern the world; here too is the design and end of government, viz. freedom and security. And however our eyes may be dazzled with show, or our ears deceived by sound; however prejudice may warp our wills, or interest darken our understanding, the simple voice of nature and reason will say, 'tis right.

I draw my idea of the form of government from a principle in nature which no art can overturn, viz. that the more simple any thing is, the less liable it is to be disordered, and the easier repaired when disordered; and with this maxim in view I offer a few remarks on the so much boasted Constitution of England. That it was noble for the dark and slavish times in which it was erected, is granted. When the world was overrun with tyranny the least remove therefrom was a glorious rescue. But that it is imperfect, subject to convulsions, and incapable of producing what it seems to promise, is easily demonstrated.

Absolute governments, (though the disgrace of human nature) have this advantage with them, they are simple; if the people suffer, they know the head from which their suffering springs; know likewise the remedy; and are not bewildered by a variety of causes and cures. But the Constitution of England is so exceedingly complex, that the nation may suffer for years together without being able to discover in which part the fault lies; some will say in one and some in another, and every political physician will advise a different medicine.

I know it is difficult to get over local or long standing prejudices, yet if we will suffer ourselves to examine the component parts of the English Constitution, we shall find them to be the base remains of two ancient tyrannies, compounded with some new Republican materials.

First—The remains of monarchical tyranny in the person of the king.

Secondly—The remains of aristocratical tyranny in the persons of the peers.

Thirdly—The new Republican materials, in the persons of the Commons, on whose virtue depends the freedom of England.

The two first, by being hereditary, are independent of the people; wherefore in a *constitutional sense* they contribute nothing towards the freedom of the State.

To say that the Constitution of England is an *union* of three powers, reciprocally *checking* each other, is farcical; either the words have no meaning, or they are flat contradictions.

To say that the Commons is a check upon the king, presupposes two things.

First—That the king is not to be trusted without being looked after; or in other words, that a thirst for absolute power is the natural disease of monarchy.

Secondly—That the Commons, by being appointed for that purpose, are either wiser or more worthy of confidence than the crown.

But as the same constitution which gives the Commons a power to check the king by withholding the supplies, gives afterwards the king a power to check the Commons, by empowering him to reject their other bills; it again supposes that the king is wiser than those whom it has already supposed to be wiser than him. A mere absurdity!

There is something exceedingly ridiculous in the composition of monarchy; it first excludes a man from the means of information, yet empowers him to act in cases where the highest judgment is required. The state of a king shuts him from the world, yet the business of a king requires him to know it thoroughly; wherefore the different parts, by unnaturally opposing and destroying each other, prove the whole character to be absurd and useless.

Some writers have explained the English Constitution thus: the king, say they, is one, the people another; the peers are a house in behalf of the king, the Commons in behalf of the people; but this hath all the distinctions of a house divided against itself; and though the expressions be pleasantly arranged, yet when examined they appear idle and ambiguous; and it will always happen, that the nicest construction that words are capable of, when applied to the description of something which either cannot exist, or is too incomprehensible to be within the compass of description, will be words of sound only, and though they may amuse the ear, they cannot inform the mind: for this explanation includes a previous question, viz. *how came the king by a power which the people are afraid to trust, and always obliged to check?* Such a power could not be the gift of a wise people, neither can any power, *which needs checking,* be from God; yet the provision which the Constitution makes supposes such a power to exist.

But the provision is unequal to the task; the means either cannot or will not accomplish the end, and the whole affair is a *Felo de se:* for as the greater weight will always carry up the less, and as all the wheels of a machine are put in motion by one, it only remains to know which power in the constitution has the most weight, for that will govern: and though the others, or a part of them, may clog, or, as the phrase is, check the rapidity of its motion, yet so long as they cannot stop it, their endeavours will be ineffectual: The first moving power will at last have its way, and what it wants in speed is supplied by time.

That the crown is this overbearing part in the English Constitution needs not be mentioned, and that it derives its whole consequence merely from being the giver of places and pensions is self-evident; wherefore, though we have been wise enough to shut and lock a door against absolute Monarchy, we at the same time have been foolish enough to put the crown in possession of the key.

The prejudice of Englishmen, in favor of their own government, by king, lords and Commons, arises as much or more from national pride than reason. Individuals are undoubtedly safer in England than in some other countries: but the will of the king is as much the law of the land in Britain as in France, with this difference, that instead of proceeding directly from his mouth, it is handed to the people under the formidable shape of an act of Parliament. For the fate of Charles the First hath only made kings more subtle—not more just.

Wherefore, laying aside all national pride and prejudice in favor of modes and forms, the plain truth is that *it is wholly owing to the constitution of the people, and not to the constitution of the government* that the crown is not as oppressive in England as in Turkey.

An inquiry into the *constitutional errors* in the English form of government, is at this time highly necessary; for as we are never in a proper condition of doing justice to others, while we continue under the influence of some leading partiality, so neither are we capable of doing it to ourselves while we remain fettered by any obstinate prejudice. And as a man who is attached to a prostitute is unfitted to choose or judge of a wife, so any prepossession in favor of a rotten constitution of government will disable us from discerning a good one.

OF MONARCHY AND HEREDITARY SUCCESSION

. . . If we inquire into the business of a king, we shall find that in some countries they may have none; and after sauntering away their lives without pleasure to themselves or advantage to the nation, withdraw from the scene, and leave their successors to tread the same idle round. In absolute monarchies the whole weight of business civil and military lies on the king; the children of Israel in their request for a king urged this plea, "that he may judge us, and go out before us and fight our battles." But in countries where he is neither a judge nor a general, as in England, a man would be puzzled to know what *is* his business.

The nearer any government approaches to a Republic, the less business there is for a king. It is somewhat difficult to find a proper name for the government of England. Sir William Meredith calls it a Republic; but in its present state it is unworthy of the name, because the corrupt influence of the crown, by having all the places in its disposal, hath so effectually swallowed up the power, and eaten out the virtue of the House of Commons (the republican part in the Constitution) that the government of England is nearly as monarchical as that of France or Spain. Men fall out with names without understanding them. For 'tis the republican and not the monarchical part of the Constitution of England which Englishmen glory in, viz. the liberty of choosing an House of Commons from out of their own body—and it is easy to see that when republican virtues fail, slavery ensues. Why is the Constitution of England sickly, but because monarchy hath poisoned the Republic; the crown has engrossed the Commons.

In England a king hath little more to do than to make war and give away places; which,

in plain terms, is to empoverish the nation and set it together by the ears. A pretty business indeed for a man to be allowed eight hundred thousand sterling a year for, and worshipped into the bargain! Of more worth is one honest man to society, and in the sight of God, than all the crowned ruffians that ever lived.

THOUGHTS ON THE PRESENT STATE OF AMERICAN AFFAIRS

In the following pages I offer nothing more than simple facts, plain arguments, and common sense: and have no other preliminaries to settle with the reader, than that he will divest himself of prejudice and prepossession, and suffer his reason and his feelings to determine for themselves: that he will put on, or rather that he will not put off, the true character of a man, and generously enlarge his views beyond the present day. . . .

I have heard it asserted by some, that as America has flourished under her former connection with Great Britain, the same connection is necessary towards her future happiness, and will always have the same effect. Nothing can be more fallacious than this kind of argument. We may as well assert that because a child has thrived upon milk, that it is never to have meat, or that the first twenty years of our lives is to become a precedent for the next twenty. But even this is admitting more than is true; for I answer roundly, that America would have flourished as much, and probably much more, had no European power taken any notice of her. The commerce by which she hath enriched herself are the necessaries of life, and will always have a market while eating is the custom of Europe.

But she has protected us, say some. That she hath engrossed us is true, and defended the continent at our expense as well as her own, is admitted; and she would have defended Turkey from the same motive, *viz.* for the sake of trade and dominion.

Alas! we have been long led away by ancient prejudices and made large sacrifices to superstition. We have boasted the protection of Great Britain, without considering, that her motive was *interest* not *attachment;* and that she did not protect us from *our enemies* on *our account;* but from *her enemies* on *her own account,* from those who had no quarrel with us on any *other account,* and who will always be our enemies on the *same account.* Let Britain waive her pretensions to the continent, or the continent throw off the dependence, and we should be at peace with France and Spain, were they at war with Britain. The miseries of Hanover's last war ought to warn us against connections.

It hath lately been asserted in Parliament, that the colonies have no relation to each other but through the parent country, *i.e.* that Pennsylvania and the Jerseys, and so on for the rest, are sister colonies by the way of England; this is certainly a very roundabout way of proving relationship, but it is the nearest and only true way of proving enmity (or enemyship, if I may so call it). France and Spain never were, nor perhaps ever will be, our enemies as *Americans,* but as our being the *subjects of Great Britain.*

But Britain is the parent country, say some. Then the more shame upon her conduct. Even brutes do not devour their young, nor savages make war upon their families; wherefore, the assertion, if true, turns to her reproach; but it happens not to be true, or only partly so, and the phrase *parent* or *mother country* hath been jesuitically adopted by the king and his parasites, with a low papistical design of gaining an unfair bias on the credulous weakness of our minds. Europe, and not England, is the parent country of America. This new world hath been the asylum for the persecuted lovers of civil and religious liberty from *every part* of Europe. Hither have they fled, not from the tender embraces of the mother, but from the cruelty of the monster; and it is so far true of England, that the same tyranny which drove the first emigrants from home, pursues their descendants still.

In this extensive quarter of the globe, we forget the narrow limits of three hundred and sixty miles (the extent of England) and carry our friendship on a larger scale; we claim brotherhood with every European Christian, and triumph in the generosity of the sentiment. . . .

But, admitting that we were all of English descent, what does it amount to? Nothing. Britain, being now an open enemy, extinguishes every other name and title: and to say that reconciliation is our duty, is truly farcical. The first king of England, of the present line (William the Conqueror) was a Frenchman, and half the peers of England are descendants from the same country; wherefore, by the same method of reasoning, England ought to be governed by France.

Much hath been said of the united strength of Britain and the colonies, that in conjunction they might bid defiance to the world. But this is mere presumption; the fate of war is uncertain, neither do the expressions mean any thing; for this continent would never suffer itself to be drained of inhabitants, to support the British arms in either Asia, Africa or Europe.

Besides, what have we to do with setting the world at defiance? Our plan is commerce, and that, well attended to, will secure us the peace and friendship of all Europe; because it is the interest of all Europe to have America a free port. Her trade will always be a protection, and her barrenness of gold and silver secure her from invaders.

I challenge the warmest advocate for reconciliation to show a single advantage that this continent can reap by being connected with Great Britain. I repeat the challenge; not a single advantage is derived. Our corn will fetch its price in any market in Europe, and our imported goods must be paid for by them where we will.

But the injuries and disadvantages which

we sustain by that connection, are without number; and our duty to mankind at large, as well as to ourselves, instruct us to renounce the alliance: because, any submission to, or dependence on, Great Britain, tends directly to involve this continent in European wars and quarrels, and set us at variance with nations who would otherwise seek our friendship, and against whom we have neither anger nor complaint. As Europe is our market for trade, we ought to form no partial connection with any part of it. It is the true interest of America to steer clear of European contentions, which she never can do, while, by her dependence on Britain, she is made the makeweight in the scale of British politics. . . .

'Tis repugnant to reason, to the universal order of things, to all examples from former ages, to suppose that this continent can long remain subject to any external power. The most sanguine in Britain doth not think so. The utmost stretch of human wisdom cannot, at this time, compass a plan, short of separation, which can promise the continent even a year's security. Reconciliation is *now* a fallacious dream. Nature has deserted the connection, and art cannot supply her place. For, as Milton wisely expresses, "never can true reconcilement grow where wounds of deadly hate have pierced so deep.". . .

As to government matters, 'tis not in the power of Britain to do this continent justice: the business of it will soon be too weighty and intricate to be managed with any tolerable degree of convenience, by a power so distant from us, and so very ignorant of us; for if they cannot conquer us, they cannot govern us. To be always running three or four thousand miles with a tale or a petition, waiting four or five months for an answer, which, when obtained, requires five or six more to explain it in, will in a few years be looked upon as folly and childishness. There was a time when it was proper, and there is a proper time for it to cease.

Small islands not capable of protecting themselves are the proper objects for government to take under their care; but their is something absurd, in supposing a Continent to be perpetually governed by an island. In no instance hath nature made the satellite larger than its primary planet; and as England and America, with respect to each other, reverse the common order of nature, it is evident that they belong to different systems. England to Europe: America to itself. . . .

OF THE PRESENT ABILITY OF AMERICA WITH SOME MISCELLANEOUS REFLECTIONS

. . . Another reason why the present time is preferable to all others, is, that the fewer our numbers are, the more land there is yet unoccupied, which, instead of being lavished by the king on his worthless dependants, may be hereafter applied, not only to the discharge of the present debt, but to the constant support of government. No nation under heaven hath such an advantage as this.

The infant state of the colonies, as it is called, so far from being against, is an argument in favor of independence. We are sufficiently numerous, and were we more so we might be less united. 'Tis a matter worthy of observation, that the more a country is peopled, the smaller their armies are. In military numbers, the ancients far exceeded the moderns: and the reason is evident, for trade being the consequence of population, men became too much absorbed thereby to attend to any thing else. Commerce diminishes the spirit both of patriotism and military defence. And history sufficiently informs us, that the bravest achievements were always accomplished in the non-age of a nation. With the increase of commerce England hath lost its spirit. The city of London, notwithstanding its numbers, submits to continued insults with the patience of a coward. The more men have to lose, the less willing are they to venture. The rich are in general slaves to fear, and submit to courtly power with the trembling duplicity of a spaniel.

Youth is the seed-time of good habits as well in nations as in individuals. It might be difficult, if not impossible, to form the continent into one government half a century hence.

The present time, likewise, is that peculiar time which never happens to a nation but once, viz. the time of forming itself into a government. Most nations have let slip the opportunity, and by that means have been compelled to receive laws from their conquerors, instead of making laws for themselves. First, they had a king, and then a form of government; whereas the articles or charter of government should be formed first, and men delegated to execute them afterwards: but from the errors of other nations let us learn wisdom, and lay hold of the present opportunity—*to begin government at the right end.*

The Declaration of Independence, July 4, 1776

In June of 1776, the Continental Congress authorized a committee composed of John Adams, Benjamin Franklin, Thomas Jefferson, Robert Livingston, and Roger Sherman to draft a document justifying independence from Great Britain. Nevertheless, the task fell almost completely on Thomas Jefferson, most recently the author of the preamble to the Virginia Declaration of Rights.

Given this trust, Jefferson produced one of the world's most concise and passionate statements of the natural rights philosophy. Borrowing heavily from Lockean imagery, Jefferson argued for the natural right of free and equal individuals to create a government that would protect them in the exercise of their rights to "Life, Liberty and the pursuit of Happiness." Having established the universal right, he went on to argue its particular violation by Great Britain.

As a brilliant defense of the liberty and equality of individuals, the Declaration remains at the core of the American political experience. Most of the democratic reforms of subsequent American history—universal manhood suffrage, abolition of slavery, the civil rights and women's movements—have been a continuation of the Declaration's inherent logic.

In addition to the complete text of the Declaration, two letters of Jefferson discussing his intentions are reprinted below.

The Declaration of Independence
July 4, 1776

When in the course of human events it becomes necessary for one people to dissolve the political bands which have connected them with another, and to assume among the powers of the earth, the separate and equal station to which the Laws of Nature and of Nature's God entitle them, a decent respect to the opinions of mankind requires that they should declare the causes which impel them to the separation.

We hold these truths to be self-evident, that all men are created equal, that they are endowed by their Creator with certain unalienable Rights, that among these are Life, Liberty and the pursuit of Happiness.—That to secure these rights, Governments are instituted among Men, deriving their just powers from the consent of the governed.—That whenever any Form of Government becomes destructive of these ends, it is the Right of the People to alter or to abolish it, and to institute new Government, laying its foundation on such principles, and organizing its powers in such form, as to them shall seem most likely to effect their Safety and Happiness. Prudence, indeed, will dictate that Governments long established should not be changed for light and transient causes; and accordingly all experience hath shewn, that mankind are more disposed to suffer, while evils are sufferable, than to right themselves by abolishing the

forms to which they are accustomed. But when a long train of abuses and usurpations, pursuing invariably the same Object, evinces a design to reduce them under absolute Despotism, it is their right, it is their duty, to throw off such Government, and to provide new Guards for their future security.—Such has been the patient sufferance of these Colonies; and such is now the necessity which constrains them to alter their former Systems of Government. The history of the present King of Great Britain is a history of repeated injuries and usurpations, all having in direct object the establishment of an absolute Tyranny over these States. To prove this, let Facts be submitted to a candid world.

He has refused his Assent to Laws, the most wholesome and necessary for the public good.

He has forbidden his Governors to pass Laws of immediate and pressing importance, unless suspended in their operation till his Assent should be obtained; and when so suspended, he has utterly neglected to attend to them.

He has refused to pass other Laws for the accommodation of large districts of people, unless those people would relinquish the right of Representation in the Legislature, a right inestimable to them and formidable to tyrants only.

He has called together legislative bodies at places unusual, uncomfortable, and distant from the depository of their public Records, for the sole purpose of fatiguing them into compliance with his measures.

SOURCE: Andrew A. Lipcomb, ed., *The Writings of Thomas Jefferson* (Washington, D.C.: Jefferson Memorial Association, 1903).

He has dissolved Representative Houses repeatedly, for opposing with manly firmness his invasions on the rights of the people.

He has refused for a long time, after such dissolutions, to cause others to be elected; whereby the Legislative powers, incapable of Annihilation, have returned to the People at large for their exercise; the State remaining in the mean time exposed to all the dangers of invasion from without, and convulsions within.

He has endeavoured to prevent the population of these States; for that purpose obstructing the Laws for Naturalization of Foreigners; refusing to pass others to encourage their migrations hither, and raising the conditions of new Appropriations of Lands.

He has obstructed the Administration of Justice, by refusing his Assent to Laws for establishing Judiciary powers.

He has made Judges dependent on his Will alone, for the tenure of their offices, and the amount and payment of their salaries.

He has erected a multitude of New Offices, and sent hither swarms of Officers to harrass our people, and eat out their substance.

He has kept among us, in times of peace, Standing Armies without the Consent of our legislatures.

He has affected to render the Military independent of and superior to the Civil power.

He has combined with others to subject us to a jurisdiction foreign to our constitutions, and unacknowledged by our laws; giving his Assent to their Acts of pretended Legislation:

For quartering large bodies of armed troops among us:

For protecting them, by a mock Trial, from punishment for any Murders which they should commit on the Inhabitants of these States:

For cutting off our Trade with all parts of the world:

For imposing Taxes on us without our Consent:

For depriving us in many cases, of the benefits of Trial by Jury:

For transporting us beyond Seas to be tried for pretended offences:

For abolishing the free System of English Laws in a neighbouring Province, establishing therein an Arbitrary government, and enlarging its Boundaries so as to render it at once an example and fit instrument for introducing the same absolute rule into these Colonies:

For taking away our Charters, abolishing our most valuable Laws, and altering fundamentally the Forms of our Governments:

For suspending our own Legislatures, and declaring themselves invested with power to legislate for us in all cases whatsoever.

He has abdicated Government here, by declaring us out of his Protection and waging War against us.

He has plundered our seas, ravaged our Coasts, burnt our towns, and destroyed the lives of our people.

He is at this time transporting large Armies of foreign Mercenaries to compleat the works of death, desolation and tyranny, already begun with circumstances of Cruelty & perfidy scarcely paralleled in the most barbarous ages, and totally unworthy the Head of a civilized nation.

He has constrained our fellow Citizens taken Captive on the high Seas to bear Arms against their Country, to become the executioners of their friends and Brethren, or to fall themselves by their Hands.

He has excited domestic insurrections amongst us, and has endeavoured to bring on the inhabitants of our frontiers; the merciless Indian Savages, whose known rule of warfare, is an undistinguished destruction of all ages, sexes and conditions.

In every stage of these Oppressions We have Petitioned for Redress in the most humble terms: Our repeated Petitions have been answered only by repeated injury. A Prince, whose character is thus marked by every act which may define a Tyrant, is unfit to be the ruler of a free people.

Nor have We been wanting in attentions to our British brethren. We have warned them from time to time of attempts by their legislature to extend an unwarrantable jurisdiction over us. We have reminded them of the circumstances of our emigration and settlement here. We have appealed to their native justice and magnanimity, and we have conjured them by the ties of our common kindred to disavow these usurpations, which would inevitably interrupt our connections and correspondence. They too have been deaf to the voice of justice and of consanguinity. We must, therefore, acquiesce in the necessity, which denounces our Separation, and hold them, as we hold the rest of mankind, Enemies in War, in Peace Friends.

We, therefore, the Representatives of the united States of America, in General Congress, Assembled, appealing to the Supreme Judge of the world for the rectitude of our intentions, do, in the Name, and by Authority of the good People of these Colonies solemnly publish and declare, That these United Colonies are, and of Right ought to be Free and Independent States; that they are Absolved from all Allegiance to the British Crown, and that all political connection between them and the State of Great Britain, is and ought to be totally dissolved; and that as Free and Independent States, they have full Power to levy War, conclude Peace, contract Alliances, establish Commerce, and to do all other Acts and Things which Independent States may of right do.

And for the support of this Declaration, with a firm reliance on the protection of divine Providence, we mutually pledge to each other our Lives, our Fortunes and our sacred Honor.

[handwritten annotations: "God & Providence will be on our side"; "Contract is broken / Trust is broken"]

Thomas Jefferson

Letter to Henry Lee, May 8, 1825

[handwritten annotations: "American exceptionalism / also Biblicalism & Republicanism"]

. . . But with respect to our rights, and the acts of the British government contravening those rights, there was but one opinion on this side of the water. All American Whigs thought alike on these subjects. When forced, therefore, to resort to arms for redress, an appeal to the tribunal of the world was deemed proper for our justification. This was the object of the Declaration of Independence. Not to find out new principles, or new arguments, never before thought of, not merely to say things which had never been said before; but to place before mankind the common sense of the subject, in terms so plain and firm as to command their assent, and to justify ourselves in the independent stand we are compelled to take. Neither aiming at originality of principle or sentiment, nor yet copied from any particular and previous writing, it was intended to be an expression of the American mind, and to give to that expression the proper tone and spirit called for by the occasion. All its authority rests then on the harmonizing sentiments of the day, whether ex-

SOURCE: Andrew A. Lipcomb, ed., *The Writings of Thomas Jefferson* (Washington, D.C.: Jefferson Memorial Association, 1903).

pressed in conversation, in letters, printed essays, or in the elementary books of public right, as Aristotle, Cicero, Locke, Sidney, etc. The historical documents which you mention as in your possession, ought all to be found, and I am persuaded you will find, to be corroborative of the facts and principles advanced in that Declaration. Be pleased to accept assurances of my great esteem and respect.

Thomas Jefferson

Letter to Roger C. Weightman, June 24, 1826

RESPECTED SIR,—The kind invitation I receive from you, on the part of the citizens of the city of Washington, to be present with them at their celebration on the fiftieth anniversary of American Independence, as one of the surviving signers of an instrument pregnant with our own, and the fate of the world, is most flattering to myself, and heightened by the honorable accompaniment proposed for the comfort of such a journey. It adds sensibly to the sufferings of sickness, to be deprived by it of a personal participation in the rejoicings of that day. But acquiescence is a duty, under circumstances not placed among those we are permitted to control. I should, indeed, with peculiar delight, have met and exchanged there congratulations personally with the small band, the remnant of that host of worthies, who joined with us on that day, in the bold and doubtful election we were to make for our country, between submission or the sword; and to have enjoyed with them the consolatory fact, that our fellow citizens, after half a century of experience and prosperity, continue to approve the choice we made. May it be to the world, what I believe it will be, (to some parts sooner, to others later, but finally to all,) the signal of arousing men to burst the chains under which monkish ignorance and superstition had persuaded them to bind themselves, and to assume the blessings and security of self-government. That form which we have substituted, restores the free right to the unbounded exercise of reason and freedom of opinion. All eyes are opened, or opening, to the rights of man. The general spread of the light of science has already laid open to every view the palpable truth, that the mass of mankind has not been born with saddles on their backs, nor a favored few booted and spurred, ready to ride them legitimately, by the grace of God. These are grounds of hope for others. For ourselves, let the annual return of this day forever refresh our recollections of these rights, and an undiminished devotion to them.

I will ask permission here to express the pleasure with which I should have met my ancient neighbors of the city of Washington and its vicinities, with whom I passed so many years of a pleasing social intercourse; an intercourse which so much relieved the anxieties of the public cares, and left impressions so deeply engraved in my affections, as never to be forgotten. With my regret that ill health forbids me the gratification of an acceptance, be pleased to receive for yourself and those for whom you write, the assurance of my highest respect and friendly attachments.

The Voice of Dissent

Jonathan Boucher, 1738–1804

Like Samuel Seabury, an Anglican minister and conservative, Jonathan Boucher was a fierce critic of the political theory of most American revolutionaries.

Born in Blencow, England, Boucher came to Port Royal, Virginia, as a tutor in 1757 and returned to England to receive holy orders in 1762. He came back to Virginia as a schoolmaster and then moved to Maryland in 1770 where he served as a minister and chaplain to the lower house of the state assembly.

As resistance to the British increased, Boucher denounced antiparliamentary protests and preached that individuals had a religious obligation to obey the law. Local opposition to Boucher became so great that he felt compelled to preach with two pistols by his side. He returned to England in 1775, and in 1782 his estate was confiscated by revolutionary forces.

Boucher remained in England, receiving a pension from the British government. In 1797, he published *A View of the Causes and Consequences of the American Revolution*, which he claimed to be thirteen sermons that he had delivered from 1763 through 1775.

In earlier protests against the Stamp Act and the Townshend Acts, Boucher had sided with the colonists. But he feared independence. In his attempt to refute the claims of the American revolutionaries, Boucher took aim at the philosophy of John Locke and ideas such as natural rights, natural equality, the social contract, and the right of revolution. Unlike many Whigs who had ultimately remained loyal to the Crown and Parliament, Boucher returned to the patriarchal ideas of Sir Robert Filmer and argued for the divine right of kings. Boucher, like Filmer, held that the king was natural heir to Adam and had an inherited divine right to rule. Furthermore, he maintained that liberty was in Christ alone and not in the civil polity at all.

One of the few American critics of Lockean individualism, Boucher's attacks on the ideas of a social contract and natural rights left him outside of the American mainstream. Nevertheless, many of his claims were to be repeated almost a century later by those writers who defended the anti-individualist foundation of southern slave society.

Jonathan Boucher

A View of the Causes and Consequences of the American Revolution . . . (1763–1775)

Stand Fast, Therefore, in the Liberty Wherewith Christ Hath Made Us Free.

Galatians, Ch. V. Ver. I.

. . . It has just been observed, that the liberty inculcated in the Scriptures, (and which alone the Apostle had in view in this text,) is wholly of the spiritual or religious kind. This liberty was the natural result of the new religion in which mankind were then instructed; which certainly gave them no new civil privileges. They remained subject to the governments under which they lived, just as they had been before they became Christians, and just as others were who never became Christians; with this difference only, that the duty of submission and obedience to Government was enjoined on the converts to Christianity with new and stronger sanctions. The doctrines of the Gospel make no manner of alteration in the nature or form of Civil Government; but enforce afresh, upon all Christians, that obedience which is due to the respective Constitutions of every nation in which they may happen to live. Be the supreme power lodged in one or in many, be the kind of government established in any country absolute or limited, this is not the concern of the Gospel. Its single object, with respect to these public duties, is to enjoin obedience to the laws of every country, in every kind or form of government.

The only liberty or freedom which converts to Christianity could hope to gain by becoming Christians, was the being exempted from sundry burthensome and servile Jewish ordinances, on the one hand; and, on the other, from Gentile blindness and superstition. They were also in some measure perhaps made more *free* in the *inner man;* by being endowed with greater firmness of mind in the cause of truth, against the terrors and the allurements of the world; and with such additional strength and vigour as enabled them more effectually to resist the natural violence of their lust and passions. On all these accounts it was that our Savior so emphatically told the Jews, that *the truth* (of which himself was now the preacher) would *make them free*. And

SOURCE: Jonathan Boucher, *A View of the Causes and Consequences of the American Revolution in Thirteen Discourses Preached in North America between the Years 1763 and 1775,* (London: G. G. and J. Robinson, 1797).

on the same principle St. James terms the Gospel *the perfect law of liberty.*

In the infancy of Christianity, it would seem that some rumor had spread (probably by Judas of Galilee, who is mentioned in the Acts) that the Gospel was designed to undermine kingdoms and commonwealths; as if the intention of our Saviour's first coming had been the same with that which reserved for the second, viz. to *put down all rule, and all authority, and all power.* On this supposition the apparent solicitude of our Saviour and his Apostles, in their frequent and earnest recommendation of submission to *the higher powers,* is easily and naturally accounted for. Obedience to Government is every man's duty, because it is every man's interest: but it is particularly incumbent on Christians, because (in addition to its moral fitness) it is enjoined by the positive commands of God: and therefore, when Christians are disobedient to human ordinances, they are also disobedient to God. If the form of government under which the good providence of God has been pleased to place us be mild and free, it is our duty to enjoy it with gratitude and with thankfulness; and, in particular, to be careful not to abuse it by licentiousness. If it be less indulgent and less liberal than in reason it ought to be, still it is our duty not to disturb and destroy the peace of the community, by becoming refractory and rebellious subjects, and *resisting the ordinances of God.* However humiliating such acquiescence may seem to men of warm and eager minds, the wisdom of God in having made it our duty is manifest. For, as it is the natural temper and bias of the human mind to be impatient under restraint, it was wise and merciful in the blessed Author of our religion not to add any new impulse to the natural force of this prevailing propensity, but, with the whole weight of his authority, altogether to discountenance every tendency to disobedience. . . .

. . . To respect the laws, is to respect liberty in the only rational sense in which the term can be used; for liberty consists in a subserviency to law. "Where there is no law," says Mr. Locke, "there is no freedom." The mere man of nature (if such an one there ever was) has no freedom: *all his lifetime he is subject to bondage.* It is by being included within the pale of civil polity and government that he takes his rank in society as a free man.

Hence it follows, that we are free, or otherwise, as we are governed by law, or by the mere arbitrary will, or wills, of any individual, or any number of individuals. And liberty is not the setting at nought and despising established laws—much less the making our own wills the rule of our own actions, or the actions of others—and not bearing (whilst yet we dictate to others) the being dictated to, even by the laws of the land; but it is the being governed by law, and by law only. The Greeks described Eleutheria, or Liberty, as the daughter of Jupiter, the supreme fountain of power and law. And the Romans, in like manner, always drew her with the pretor's wand (the emblem of legal power and authority), as well as with the cap. Their idea, no doubt, was that liberty was the fair fruit of just authority and that it consisted in men's being subjected to law. The more carefully well-devised restraints of law are enacted, and the more rigorously they are executed in any country, the greater degree of civil liberty does that country enjoy. To pursue liberty, then, in a manner not warranted by law, whatever the pretense may be, is clearly to be hostile to liberty: and those persons who thus *promise you liberty,* are themselves *the servants of corruption.*

"Civil liberty (says an excellent writer) is a severe and a restrained thing; implies, in the notion of it, authority, settled subordinations, subjection, and obedience; and is altogether as much hurt by too little of this kind, as by too much of it. And the love of liberty, when it is indeed the love of liberty, which carries us to withstand tyranny, will as much carry us to reverence authority, and to support it; for this most obvious reason, that one is as necessary to the being of liberty, as the other is destructive of it. And, therefore, the love of liberty which does not produce this effect, the love of liberty which is not a real principle of dutiful behavior toward authority, is as hypocritical as the religion which is not productive of a good life. Licentiousness is, in truth, such an excess of liberty as is of the same nature with tyranny. For, what is the difference betwixt them, but that one is lawless power exercised under pretense of authority, or by persons vested with it; the other, lawless power exercised under pretense of liberty, or without any pretense at all? A people, then, must always be less free in proportion as they are more licentious, licentiousness being not only different from, liberty but directly contrary to it—a direct breach upon it."

True liberty, then, is a liberty to do everything that is right, and the being restrained from doing anything that is wrong. So far from our having a right to do everything that we please, under a notion of liberty, liberty itself is limited and confined—but limited and confined only by laws which are at the same time both its foundation and its support. It can, however, hardly be necessary to inform you, that ideas and notions respecting liberty, very different from these, are daily suggested in the speeches and the writings of the times; and also that some opinions on the subject of government at large, which appear to me to be particularly loose and dangerous, are advanced in the sermon now under consideration; and that, therefore, you will acknowledge the propriety of my bestowing some farther notice on them both. . . .

* * * * *

This popular notion, that government was originally formed by the consent or by a compact of the people, rests on, and is supported by, another similar notion, not less popular, nor better founded. This other notion is, that the whole human race is born equal; and that no man is naturally inferior, or, in any respect, subjected to another; and that he can be made subject to another only by his own consent. The position is equally ill-founded and false both in its premises and conclusions. In hardly any sense that can be imagined is the position strictly true; but, as applied to the case under consideration, it is demonstrably not true. Man differs from man in everything that can be supposed to lead to supremacy and subjection, *as one star differs from another star in glory.* It was the purpose of the Creator that man should be social: but, without government, there can be no society; nor, without some relative inferiority and superiority, can there be any government. A musical instrument composed of chords, keys, or pipes, all perfectly equal in size and power, might as well be expected to produce harmony, as a society composed of members all perfectly equal to be productive of order and peace. If (according to the idea of the advocates of this chimerical scheme of equality) no man could rightfully *be compelled to come in* and be a member even of a government to be formed by a regular compact, but by his own individual consent; it clearly follows, from the same principles, that neither could he rightfully be made or compelled to submit to the ordinances of any government already formed, to which he has not individually or actually consented. On the principle of equality, neither his parents, not even the vote of a majority of the society (however virtuously and honorably that vote might be obtained,) can have any such authority over any man. Neither can it be maintained that acquiescence implies consent; because acquiescence may have been extorted from impotence or incapacity. Even an explicit consent can bind a man no longer than he chooses to be bound. The same principle of equality that exempts him from being governed without his own consent clearly entitles him to recall and resume that consent whenever he sees fit; and he alone has a right to judge when and for what reasons it may be resumed.

Any attempt, therefore, to introduce this fantastic system into practice would reduce the whole business of social life to the wearisome, confused, and useless task of mankind's first expressing, and then withdrawing, their consent to an endless succession of schemes of government. Governments, though always forming, would never be completely formed: for, the majority today, might be the minority tomorrow; and, of course, that which is now fixed might and would be soon unfixed. Mr. Locke indeed says that, "by consenting with others to make one body-politic under government, a man puts himself under an obligation to every one of that society to submit to the determination of the majority, and to be concluded by it." For the sake of the peace of society, it is undoubtedly reasonable and necessary that this should be the case; but, on the principles of the system now under consideration, before Mr. Locke or any of his followers can have authority to say that it actually is the case, it must be stated and proved that every individual man, on entering into the social compact, did first consent, and declare his consent, to be concluded and bound in all cases by the vote of the majority. In making such a declaration, he would certainly consult both his interest and his duty; but at the same time he would also completely relinquish the principle of equality, and eventually subject himself to the possibility of being governed by ignorant and corrupt tyrants. Mr. Locke himself afterward disproves his own position respecting this supposed obligation to submit to the "determination of the majority," when he argues that a right of resistance still exists in the governed; for, what is resistance but a recalling and resuming the consent heretofore supposed to have been given, and in fact refusing to submit to the "determination of the majority?" It does not clearly appear what Mr. Locke exactly meant by what he calls "the determination of the majority;" but the only rational and practical public manner of declaring "the determination of the majority," is

by law: the laws, therefore, in all countries, even in those that are despotically governed, are to be regarded as the declared "determination of a majority" of the members of that community; because, in such cases, even acquiescence only must be looked upon as equivalent to a declaration. A right of resistance, therefore, for which Mr. Locke contends, is incompatible with the duty of submitting to the determination of "the majority," for which he also contends.

It is indeed impossible to carry into effect any government which, even by compact, might be framed with this reserved right of resistance. Accordingly there is no record that any such government ever was so formed. If there had, it must have carried the seeds of its decay in its very constitution. For, as those men who make a government (certain that they have the power) can have no hesitation to vote that they also have the right to unmake it, and as the people, in all circumstances, but more especially when trained to make and unmake governments, are at least as well disposed to do the latter as the former, it is morally impossible that there should be anything like permanency or stability in a government so formed. Such a system, therefore, can produce only perpetual dissensions and contests, and bring back mankind to a supposed state of nature; arming every man's hand, like Ishmael's, against every man, and rendering the world an *aceldama*, or field of blood.

Such theories of government seem to give something like plausibility to the notions of those other modern theorists who regard all governments as invasions of the natural rights of men, usurpations, and tyranny. On this principle it would follow, and could not be denied, that government was indeed fundamentally, as our people are sedulously taught it still is, an evil. Yet it is to government that mankind owe their having, after their fall and corruption, been again reclaimed, from a state of barbarity and war, to the conveniency and the safety of the social state; and it is by means of government that society is still preserved, the weak protected from the strong, and the artless and innocent from the wrongs of proud oppressors. It was not without reason, then, that Mr. Locke asserted that a greater wrong cannot be done to prince and people than is done by "propagating wrong notions concerning government."

Ashamed of this shallow device, that government originated in superior strength and violence, another party, hardly less numerous, and certainly not less confident than the former, fondly deduce it from some imaginary compact. They suppose that, in the decline perhaps of some fabulous age of old, a multitude of human beings, who, like their brother-beasts, had hitherto ranged the forests, *without guide, overseer, or ruler*—at length convinced, by experience, of the impossibility of living either alone with any degree of comfort or security, or together in society, with peace, without government, had (in some lucid interval of reason and reflection) met together in a spacious plain for the express purpose of framing a government. Their first step must have been the transferring to some individual, or individuals, some of those rights which are supposed to have been inherent in each of them: of these it is essential to government that they should be divested; yet can they not, rightfully, be deprived of them, otherwise than by their own consent. Now, admitting this whole supposed assembly to be perfectly equal as to rights, yet all agreed as to the propriety of ceding some of them, on what principles of equality is it possible to determine, either who shall relinquish such a portion of his rights, or who shall be invested with such new accessory rights? By asking another to exercise jurisdiction over me, I clearly confess that I do not think myself his equal; and by his consenting to exercise such authority, he also virtually declares that he thinks himself superior. And, to establish this hypothesis of a compact, it is farther necessary that the whole assembly should concur in this opinion—a concurrence so extremely improbable, that it seems to be barely possible. The supposition that a large concourse of people, in a rude and imperfect state of society, or even a majority of them, should thus rationally and unanimously concur to subject themselves to various restrictions, many of them irksome and unpleasant, and all of them contrary to all their former habits, is to suppose them possessed of more wisdom and virtue than multitudes in any instance in real life have ever shown. Another difficulty respecting this notion may yet be mentioned. Without a power of life and death, it will, I presume, be readily admitted that there could be no government. Now, admitting it to be possible that men, from motives of public and private utility, may be induced to submit to many heavy penalties, and even to corporal punishment, inflicted by the sentence of the law, there is an insuperable objection to any man's giving to another a power over his life: this objection is, that no man has such a power over his own life; and cannot therefore transfer to another, or to others, be they few or many, on any conditions, a right which he does not himself possess. He only who gave life can give the authority to take it away: and as such authority is essential to government, this argument seems very decidedly to prove, not only that government did not originate in any compact, but also that it was originally from God. . . .

It is from other passages of Scripture, from the nature of the thing, from the practice of Adam, and from the practice of all nations (derived from and founded on this precedent) that we infer that Adam had and exercised sovereign power over all his issue. But the first instance of power exercised by one human being over another is in the subjection of Eve to her husband. This circumstance suggests sundry reflections, of some moment in this argument. In the first place, it shews that power is not a natural right. Adam could not have assumed, nor could Eve have submitted to it, had it not been so ordained of God. It is, therefore, equally an argument against the domineering claims of despotism, and the fantastic notion of a compact. It proves too, that there is a sense in which it may, with truth, be asserted, that government was originally founded in weakness and in guilt: that it may and must be submitted to by a fallen creature, even when exercised by a fallen creature, lost both to wisdom and goodness. The equality of nature (which, merely as it respects an ability to govern, may be admitted, only because God, had he so seen fit, might have ordained that the man should be subjected to the woman) was superseded by the actual interference of the Almighty, to whom alone original underived power can be said to belong.

Even where the Scriptures are silent, they instruct: for, in general, whatever is not therein commanded is actually forbidden. Now, it is certain that mankind are no where in the Scriptures commanded to resist authority; and no less certain that, either by direct injunction, or clear implication, they are commanded to *be subject to the higher powers:* and this subjection is said to be enjoined, not for our sakes only, but also *for the Lord's sake.* The glory of God is much concerned, that there should be good government in the world: it is, therefore, the uniform doctrine of the Scriptures, that it is under the deputation and authority of God alone that *kings reign and princes decree justice.* Kings and princes (which are only other words for supreme magistrates) were doubtless created and appointed, not so much for their own sakes, as for the sake of the people committed to their charge: yet are they not, therefore, the creatures of the people. So far from deriving their authority from any supposed consent or suffrage of men, they receive their commission from Heaven; they receive it from God, the source and original of all power. However obsolete, therefore, either the sentiment or the language may now be deemed, it is with the most perfect propriety that the supreme magistrate, whether consisting of one or of many, and whether denominated an emperor, a king, an archon, a dictator, a consul, or a senate, is to be regarded and venerated as the vicegerent of God. . . .

PART III

Creating an Extended Commercial Republic: The Political Theory of the Constitution

Although most of the Revolutionary generation would have described themselves as republicans, they would not have agreed on any single definition of "republic." As late as 1807, twenty years after the Constitutional Convention and more than thirty years after the Declaration of Independence, John Adams could still write, "I never understood what a republic was and no man ever did, or ever will; a republic may signify anything, everything, or nothing." Adams' difficulty was symptomatic of a change that was taking place in American political language. Many Americans' notions of republican government changed substantially between 1776 and 1787. In fact, the political activists who met in Philadelphia in 1787 to alter the Articles of Confederation, and finally to create a new Constitution, gave a new and different form to the idea of a republic. Moreover, the Constitution's most articulate defenders, the authors of *The Federalist Papers* (James Madison, Alexander Hamilton, and John Jay), produced a startlingly new republican theory of politics.

To most Americans of the Revolutionary generation, a republic brought to mind the classical city-states of Sparta, Athens, and Rome. A republic was self-governing, largely agricultural, and populated by roughly equal land-holders who shared a common class interest. These republican farmers were both citizens and soldiers; they trained in their militias, risked their lives and fortunes in war, and actively participated in government. If the republic was to remain free, according to the republican analysis, its citizens had to remain virtuous—that is, disciplined, frugal, public spirited, and willing to sacrifice for the common good. Their shared economic interests provided a sound basis for sharing a sense of the common good. In many respects this worldview was classical and preliberal, in that it emphasized the public interest and the common good more than individual rights and interests.

The reverse side of the republican analysis was its sense of tragedy, its belief that republics inevitably died as they fell victim to their own forces of decay. Ironically, in this view republican virtue gave rise to wealth and power, which in turn encouraged commerce, plurality of interests, effeminacy, and decay. Simply, the success generated by virtue inevitably gave rise to vice. Republics contained within them the seeds of their own destruction. Thus Americans watched their own republics with a sense of tragic dread.

To the critics of the Articles of Confederation, signs of decay abounded. The inability of the United States under the Articles of Confederation to raise taxes and provide for a stable monetary system indicated to many that the country was plagued by selfishness and vice. Furthermore, the revolt of farmers in western Massachusetts, led by Daniel Shays, provided men of property and status with additional proof. To these reformers—in many respects *conservative* reformers—a new political order was needed if republican government was to survive.

Meeting in Philadelphia in 1787, the Constitutional Convention offered a more powerful central government, directed by a more powerful executive officer, than did the Articles of Confederation. Furthermore, the Constitution provided for a bicameral legislature with a Senate representing the states and a House of Representatives representing the people. It also established an appointed, independent judiciary to adjudicate disputes and interpret the law. In addition, each separate branch of government had the power to check and balance the others to prevent a tyrannical concentration of power in any one branch.

Many of these provisions were criticized by opponents of the Constitution or "Antifederalists." While they were by no means of a common mind on all issues, most Antifederalists had more local orientations and feared the centralizing tendencies of the Federalist system. They preferred a United States that was more a confederation of republics than a single nation-state. In essence the Federalists were nationalists, the Antifederalists decidedly localists. Significantly, any institution that removed political power from a local arena to a distant national body they saw as a threat to the essence of republican self-government. Some found the fact that certain institutions were not elective additionally disturbing since it moved power even further from direct popular control. They also feared that the national government would violate the individual rights already protected by the states. Their vision of politics remained classically republican; they envisioned a political order built upon the virtue of its citizenry, which in turn could only be sustained by agriculture, face-to-face political participation, and service in the militia.

In stark contrast, the supporters of the Constitution offered a new and different republican vision best articulated in James Madison's *Federalist Papers No. 10* and *No. 51*. In these papers, Madison painted the picture of a new extended republic, far too large for simple face-to-face politics. The populace would contain a growing plurality of interests, both economic and social, unlike that of a smaller state which was more likely to be homogeneous or comprised of only a few interests. As a result, in Madison's republic the population would become fragmented into a myriad of competing factions, with none powerful enough to gain despotic control. Competing interests would informally check and balance each other in their respective pursuits of power, just as the system of separation of powers and checks and balances operated within the formal institutions of government.

In this new conception of republican politics, competing self-interest replaced public virtue as the chief barrier to despotism and decay. Whereas excessive self-interest, according to the traditional republican analysis, would have destroyed the republic because a faction would inevitably seek total control, the authors of *The Federalist Papers* saw their republic saved by a multiplication of interests that kept each fragmented and weak. This required a diverse republic that was quite large in size. However, to provide so diverse a political order with coherence or "energy" required a stronger national government with an active executive. Simply, the extended commercial republic required both a more powerful and a more distant government. For the authors of *The Federalist Papers* this meant that the small face-to-face agrarian republic of traditional republican philosophy was obsolete.

It is fair to say that the Federalists, in offering a remedy for old republican ills, created a new science of republican politics. They redefined the essence of republicanism and gave it a far more individualistic and self-interested basis. To be sure, the exact nature of the American republic was not settled once and for all. Disputes over the powers of the central government, the extent of executive power, and the role of the states would continue to characterize American politics up to the present. Moreover, for the remainder of the eighteenth and much of the nineteenth century, the respective roles of commerce, manufacturing, and agriculture in a republican society would continue to be hotly debated. Nevertheless, at its constitutional inception, the new American republic set out in a direction far different from the agrarian model inherited from the past, and far different from that admired by many who had waged the Revolution.

The Old Orthodoxy

Agrarian Republicanism

Thomas Jefferson, 1743–1826

Thomas Jefferson epitomizes that remarkable generation we call our Founding Fathers. Among a group of men who were almost universally individuals both of action and reflection, Jefferson was not only a statesman and prolific writer but also an accomplished lawyer, botanist, and architect. Yet Jefferson was primarily a public man, and his career reads like the history of the emerging nation.

After passing the bar in 1767, he entered the Virginia House of Burgesses in 1769. When conflict between Great Britain and the colonies grew, Jefferson wrote *A Summary View of the Rights of British America* and became a member of the Virginia Committee of Correspondences. He wrote the preamble to the Virginia Declaration of Rights and the Declaration of Independence, and he then took a leading role in forming the new Virginia constitution. During that last project, Jefferson worked hard to ensure freedom of religion, abolish primogeniture and entail, and provide for universal public education. Only in the last endeavor did he fail.

While serving abroad during the Constitutional Convention, Jefferson reluctantly supported the Constitution. However, he demanded that the Bill of Rights be added. He returned to the United States and was named secretary of state in the Washington administration. Later Jefferson helped found the Democratic-Republican party and ultimately became its first successful presidential candidate.

Although mildly approving of the new constitutional framework, Jefferson's political philosophy was different from that of many who participated in its framing, including the authors of *The Federalist Papers*. Jefferson's writings present classic expressions of agrarian republicanism, that is, the belief that a republic can only be built around a class of virtuous yeoman farmers who actively participate in local government. He associated the growth of commercial and manufacturing classes with decay, while he feared a powerful central government would sap the vitality of local republican government.

While America would not remain the decentralized agrarian nation that he envisioned, Jefferson's views were shared by many of the revolutionary generation, most of the Antifederalists, and many members of the later Democratic-Republican party. In a variety of ways, Jefferson's vision has continued as a powerful one in American political thinking.

The following letters of Jefferson are typical examples of the agrarian republican perspective.

Thomas Jefferson

Letter to John Jay (1785)

DEAR SIR,—I shall sometimes ask your permission to write you letters, not official, but private. The present is of this kind, and is occasioned by the question proposed in yours of June the 14th; "whether it would be useful to us, to carry all our own productions, or none?"

Were we perfectly free to decide this question, I should reason as follows. We have now lands enough to employ an infinite number of people in their cultivation. Cultivators of the earth are the most valuable citizens. They are the most vigorous, the most independent, the most virtuous, and they are tied to their country, and wedded to its liberty and interests, by the most lasting bonds. As long, therefore, as they can find employment in this line I would not convert them into mariners, artisans, or anything else. But our citizens will find employment in this line, till their numbers, and of course the productions, become too great for the demand, both internal and foreign. This is not the case as yet, and probably will not be for a considerable time. As soon as it is, the surplus of hands must be turned to something else. I should then, perhaps, wish to turn them to the sea in preference to manufactures; because, comparing the characters of the two classes, I find the former the most valuable citizens. I consider the class of artificers as the panders of vice, and the instruments by which the liberties of a country are generally overturned. However, we are not free to decide this question on principles of theory only. Our people are decided in the opinion, that it is necessary for us to take a share in the occupation of the ocean, and their established habits induce them to require that the sea be kept open to them, and that that line of policy be pursued, which will render the use of that element to them as great as possible. I think it a duty in those entrusted with the administration of their affairs, to conform themselves to the decided choice of their

SOURCE: Andrew A. Lipscomb, ed., *The Writings of Thomas Jefferson* (Washington, D.C.: Thomas Jefferson Memorial Association, 1903).

constituents; and that therefore, we should, in every instance, preserve an equality of right to them in the transportation of commodities, in the right of fishing, and in the other uses of the sea. . . .

Thomas Jefferson

Letter to John Bannister, Jr. (1785)

DEAR SIR,—I should sooner have answered the paragraph in your letter, of September the 19th, respecting the best seminary for the education of youth in Europe, but that it was necessary for me to make inquiries on the subject. The result of these has been, to consider the competition as resting between Geneva and Rome. They are equally cheap, and probably are equal in the course of education pursued. . . .

But why send an American youth to Europe for education? What are the objects of an useful American education? Classical knowledge, modern languages, chiefly French, Spanish, and Italian; Mathematics, Natural philosophy, Natural history, Civil history, and Ethics. In Natural philosophy, I mean to include Chemistry and Agriculture, and in Natural history, to include Botany, as well as the other branches of those departments. It is true that the habit of speaking the modern languages cannot be so well acquired in America; but every other article can be as well acquired at William and Mary college, as at any place in Europe. When college education is done with, and a young man is to prepare himself for public life, he must cast his eyes (for America) either on Law or Physics. For the former, where can he apply so advantageously as to Mr. Wythe? For the latter, he must come to Europe: the medical class of students, therefore, is the only one which need come to Eu-

rope. Let us view the disadvantages of sending a youth to Europe. To enumerate them all, would require a volume. I will select a few. If he goes to England, he learns drinking, horse racing, and boxing. These are the peculiarities of English education. The following circumstances are common to education in that, and the other countries of Europe. He acquires a fondness for European luxury and dissipation, and a contempt for the simplicity of his own country; he is fascinated with the privileges of the European aristocrats, and sees, with abhorrence, the lovely equality which the poor enjoy with the rich, in his own country; he contracts a partiality for aristocracy or monarchy; he forms foreign friendships which will never be useful to him, and loses the seasons of life for forming, in his own country, those friendships which, of all others, are the most faithful and permanent; he is led, by the strongest of all the human passions, into a spirit for female intrigue, destructive of his own and others' happiness, or a passion for whores, destructive of his health, and, in both cases, learns to consider fidelity to the marriage bed as an ungentlemanly practice, and inconsistent with happiness; he recollects the voluptuary dress and arts of the European women, and pities and despises the chaste affections and simplicity of those of his own country; he retains, through life, a fond recollection, and a hankering after those places, which were the scenes of his first pleasures and of his first connections; he returns to his own country, a foreigner, unacquainted with the practices of domestic economy, necessary to preserve him from ruin, speaking and writing his native tongue as a foreigner, and therefore unqualified to obtain those distinctions, which eloquence of the pen and tongue ensures in a free country; for I would observe to you, that what is called style in writing or speaking is formed very early in life, while the imagination is warm, and impressions are permanent. I am of opinion, that there never was an instance of a man's writing or speaking his native tongue with elegance, who passed from fifteen to twenty years of age out of the country where it was spoken. Thus, no instance exists of a person's writing two languages perfectly. That will always appear to be his native language, which was most familiar to him in his youth. It appears to me, then, that an American, coming to Europe for education, loses in his knowledge, in his morals, in his health, in his habits, and in his happiness. I had entertained only doubts on this head before I came to Europe: what I see and hear, since I came here, proves more than I had ever suspected. Cast your eye over America: who are the men of most learning, of most eloquence, most beloved by their countrymen and most trusted and promoted by them? They are those who have been educated among them, and whose manners, morals, and habits, are perfectly homogeneous with those of the country. . . .

Thomas Jefferson

Letter to James Madison (1785)

DEAR SIR,—Seven o'clock, and retired to my fireside, I have determined to enter into conversation with you; this is a village of about 5,000 inhabitants when the court is not here and 20,000 when they are, occupying a valley thro' which runs a brook, and on each side of it a ridge of small mountains most of which are naked rock. The king comes here in the fall always, to hunt. His court attend him, as do also the foreign diplomatic corps. But as this is not indispensably required, and my finances do not admit the expence of a continued residence here, I propose to come occasionally to attend the king's levees, returning again to Paris, distant 40 miles. This being the first trip, I set out yesterday morning to take a view of the place. For this purpose I shaped my course towards the highest of the mountains in sight, to the top of which was about a league. As soon as I had got clear of the town I fell in with a poor woman walking at the same rate with myself and going the same course. Wishing to know the condition of the labouring poor I entered into conversation with her, which I began by enquiries for the path which would lead me into the mountain: and thence proceeded to enquiries into her vocation, condition and circumstance. She told me she was a day labourer, at 8. sous or 4 d. sterling the day; that she had two children to maintain, and to pay a rent of 30 livres for her house (which would consume the hire of 75 days), that often she could get no employment, and of course was without bread. As we had walked together near a mile and she had so far served me as a guide, I gave her, on parting 24 sous. She burst into tears of a gratitude which I could perceive was unfeigned, because she was unable to utter a word. She had probably never before received so great an aid. This little attendrissement, with the solitude of my walk led me into a train of reflections on that unequal division of property which occasions the numberless instances of wretchedness which I had observed in this country and is to be observed all over Europe. The property of this country is absolutely concentrated in a very few hands, having revenues of from half a million of guineas a year downwards. These employ the flower of the country as servants, some of them having as many as 200 domestics, not labouring. They employ also a great number of manufacturers, and tradesmen, and lastly the class of labouring husbandmen. But after all these comes the most numerous of all the classes, that is, the poor who cannot find work. I asked myself what could be the reason that so many should be permitted to beg who are willing to work, in a country where there is a very considerable proportion of uncultivated lands? These lands are kept idle mostly for the sake of game. It should seem then that it must be because of the enormous wealth of the proprietors which places them above attention to the increase of their revenues by permitting these lands to be laboured. I am conscious that an equal division of property

is impracticable. But the consequences of this enormous inequality producing so much misery to the bulk of mankind, legislators cannot invent too many devices for subdividing property, only taking care to let their subdivisions go hand in hand with the natural affections of the human mind. The descent of property of every kind therefore to all the children, or to all the brothers and sisters, or other relations in equal degree is a politic measure, and a practicable one. Another means of silently lessening the inequality of property is to exempt all from taxation below a certain point, and to tax the higher portions of property in geometrical progression as they rise. Whenever there is in any country, uncultivated lands and unemployed poor, it is clear that the laws of property have been so far extended as to violate natural right. The earth is given as a common stock for man to labour and live on. If, for the encouragement of industry we allow it to be appropriated, we must take care that other employment be furnished to those excluded from the appropriation. If we do not the fundamental right to labour the earth returns to the unemployed. It is too soon yet in our country to say that every man who cannot find employment but who can find uncultivated land, shall be at liberty to cultivate it, paying a moderate rent. But it is not too soon to provide by every possible means that as few as possible shall be without a little portion of land. The small landholders are the most precious part of a state. . . .

Thomas Jefferson

Letter to Jean Baptiste Say (1804)

DEAR SIR,—I have to acknowledge the receipt of your obliging letter, and with it, of two very interesting volumes on Political Economy. These found me engaged in giving the leisure moments I rarely find, to the perusal of Malthus' work on population, a work of sound logic, in which some of the opinions of Adam Smith, as well as of the economists, are ably examined. I was pleased, on turning to some chapters where you treat the same questions, to find his opinions corroborated by yours. I shall proceed to the reading of your work with great pleasure. . . .

The differences of circumstance between this and the old countries of Europe, furnish differences of fact whereon to reason, in questions of political economy, and will consequently produce sometimes a difference of result. There, for instance, the quantity of food is fixed, or increasing in a slow and only arithmetical ratio and the proportion is limited by the same ratio. Supernumerary births consequently add only to your mortality. Here the immense extent of uncultivated and fertile lands enables every one who will labor, to marry young, and to raise a family of any size. Our food, then, may increase geometrically with our laborers, and our births, however multiplied, become effective. Again, there the best distribution of labor is supposed to be that which places the manufacturing hands alongside the agricultural; so that the one part shall feed both, and the other part furnish both with clothes and other comforts. Would that be best here? Egoism and first appearances say yes. Or would it be better that all our laborers should be employed in agriculture? In this case a double or treble portion of fertile lands would be brought into culture; a double or treble creation of food be produced, and its surplus go to nourish the now perishing births of Europe, who in return would manufacture and send us in exchange our clothes and other comforts. Morality listens to this, and so invariably do the laws of nature create our duties and interests, that when they seem to be at variance, we ought to suspect some fallacy in our reasonings. In solving this question, too, we should allow its just weight to the moral and physical preference of the agricultural, over the manufacturing, man. My occupations permit me only to ask questions. They deny me the time, if I had the information, to answer them. Perhaps, as worthy the attention of the author of the *Traite d'Economie Politique*, I shall find them answered in that work. If they are not, the reason will have been that you wrote for Europe; while I shall have asked them because I think for America. Accept, Sir, my respectful salutations, and assurances of great consideration.

"The New Science of Politics"

John Adams, 1735–1826

In all of his writings, Adams exhibited a Whig republicanism that was at odds with the more radical and democratic republicanism of a Paine, or even a Jefferson. Far more pessimistic than Jefferson about sustaining a virtuous yeoman republic, Adams believed self-interested ambition and class conflict were inevitable. A well-framed government, he believed, balanced the ambitions of the masses with those of the natural aristocracy. If either ruled by themselves, tyranny would result. Despite his opposition to Great Britain, he was an admirer of the British Constitution, and like many Federalists, he hoped to adopt its best points to the American context.

The following letter to his cousin Samuel Adams summarizes Adams's views on a constitutional republic.

John Adams

Letter to Samuel Adams (1790)

DEAR SIR,—I am thankful to our common friend, as well as to you, for your favor of the fourth, which I received last night. My fears are in unison with yours, that hay, wood, and stubble, will be the materials of the new political buildings in Europe, till men shall be more enlightened and friendly to each other.

You agree, that there are undoubtedly principles of political architecture. But, instead of particularizing any of them, you seem to place all your hopes in the universal, or at least more general, prevalence of knowledge and benevolence. I think with you, that knowledge and benevolence ought to be promoted as much as possible; but, despairing of ever seeing them sufficiently general for the security of society, I am for seeking institutions which may supply in some degree the defect. If there were no ignorance, error, or vice, there would be neither principles nor systems of civil or political government.

I am not often satisfied with the opinions of Hume; but in this he seems well founded, that all projects of government, founded in the supposition or expectation of extraordinary degrees of virtue, are evidently chimerical. Nor do I believe it possible, humanly speaking, that men should ever be greatly improved in knowledge or benevolence, without assistance from the principles and system of government.

I am very willing to agree with you in fancying, that in the greatest improvements of society, government will be in the republican form. It is a fixed principle with me, that all good government is and must be republican. But, at the same time, your candor will agree with me, that there is not in lexicography a more fraudulent word. Whenever I use the word *republic* with approbation, I mean a government in which the people have collectively, or by representation, an essential share in the sovereignty. The republican forms of Poland and Venice are much worse, and those of Holland and Bern very little better, than the monarchical form in France before the late revolution. By the republican form, I know you do not mean the plan of Milton, Nedham, or Turgot. For, after a fair trial of its miseries, the simple monarchical form will ever be, as it has ever been, preferred to it by mankind. Are we not, my friend, in danger of rendering the word *republican* unpopular in this country by an indiscreet, indeterminate, and equivocal use of it? The people of England have been obliged to wean themselves from the use of it, by making it unpopular and unfashionable, because they found it was artfully used by some, and simply understood by others, to mean the government of their interregnum parliament. They found they could not wean themselves from that destructive form of government so entirely, as that a mischievous party would not still remain in favor of it, by any other means than by making the words *republic* and *republican* unpopular. They have

SOURCE: Charles Francis Adams, ed., *The Life and Works of John Adams* (Boston: Little, Brown, 1851).

succeeded to such a degree, that, with a vast majority of that nation, a republican is as unamiable as a witch, a blasphemer, a rebel, or a tyrant. If, in this country, the word *republic* should be generally understood, as it is by some, to mean a form of government inconsistent with a mixture of three powers, forming a mutual balance, we may depend upon it that such mischievous effects will be produced by the use of it as will compel the people of America to renounce, detest, and execrate it as the English do. With these explanations, restrictions, and limitations, I agree with you in your love of republican governments, but in no other sense.

With you, I have also the honor most perfectly to harmonize in your sentiments of the humanity and wisdom of promoting education in knowledge, virtue, and benevolence. But I think that these will confirm mankind in the opinion of the necessity of preserving and strengthening the dikes against the ocean, its tides and storms. Human appetites, passions, prejudices, and self-love will never be conquered by benevolence and knowledge alone, introduced by human means. The millennium itself neither supposes nor implies it. All civil government is then to cease, and the Messiah is to reign. That happy and holy state is therefore wholly out of this question. You and I agree in the utility of universal education; but will nations agree in it as fully and extensively as we do, and be at the expense of it? We know, with as much certainty as attends any human knowledge, that they will not. We cannot, therefore, advise the people to depend for their safety, liberty, and security, upon hopes and blessings which we know will not fall to their lot. If we do our duty then to the people, we shall not deceive them, but advise them to depend upon what is in their power and will relieve them.

Philosophers, ancient and modern, do not appear to me to have studied nature, the whole of nature, and nothing but nature. Lycurgus's principle was war and family pride;

Solon's was what the people would bear, &c. The best writings of antiquity upon government, those, I mean, of Aristotle, Zeno, and Cicero, are lost. We have human nature, society, and universal history to observe and study, and from these we may draw all the real principles which ought to be regarded. Disciples will follow their masters, and interested partisans their chieftains; let us like it or not, we cannot help it. But if the true principles can be discovered, and fairly, fully, and impartially laid before the people, the more light increases, the more the reason of them will be seen, and the more disciples they will have. Prejudice, passion, and private interest, which will always mingle in human inquiries, one would think might be enlisted on the side of truth, at least in the greatest number; for certainly the majority are interested in the truth, if they could see to the end of all its consequences. "Kings have been deposed by aspiring nobles." True, and never by any other. "These" (the nobles, I suppose,) "have waged everlasting war against the common rights of men." True, when they have been possessed of the *summa imperii* in one body, without a check. So have the plebeians; so have the people; so have kings; so has human nature, in every shape and combination, and so it ever will. But, on the other hand, the nobles have been essential parties in the preservation of liberty, whenever and wherever it has existed. In Europe, they alone have preserved it against kings and people, wherever it has been preserved; or, at least, with very little assistance from the people. One hideous despotism, as horrid as that of Turkey, would have been the lot of every nation of Europe, if the nobles had not made stands. By nobles, I mean not peculiarly an hereditary nobility, or any particular modification, but the natural and actual aristocracy among mankind. The existence of this you will not deny. You and I have seen four noble families rise up in Boston,—the CRAFTS, GORES, DAWES, and AUSTINS. These are as really a nobility in our town, as the Howards, Somersets, Berties, &c., in England. Blind, undistinguishing reproaches against the aristocratical part of mankind, a division which nature has made, and we cannot abolish, are neither pious nor benevolent. They are as pernicious as they are false. They serve only to foment prejudice, jealousy, envy, animosity, and malevolence. They serve no ends but those of sophistry, fraud, and the spirit of party. It would not be true, but it would not be more egregiously false, to say that the people have waged everlasting war against the rights of men.

"The love of liberty," you say, "is interwoven in the soul of man." So it is, according to La Fontaine, in that of a wolf; and I doubt whether it be much more rational, generous, or social, in one than in the other, until in man it is enlightened by experience, reflection, education, and civil and political institutions, which are at first produced, and constantly supported and improved by a few; that is, by the nobility. The wolf, in the fable, who preferred running in the forest, lean and hungry, to the sleek, plump, and round sides of the dog, because he found the latter was sometimes restrained, had more love of liberty than most men. The numbers of men in all ages have preferred ease, slumber, and good cheer to liberty, when they have been in competition. We must not then depend alone upon the love of liberty in the soul of man for its preservation. Some political institutions must be prepared, to assist this love against its enemies. Without these, the struggle will ever end only in a change of impostors. When the people, who have no property, feel the power in their own hands to determine all questions by a majority, they ever attack those who have property, till the injured men of property lose all patience, and recur to finesse, trick, and strategem, to outwit those who have too much strength, because they have too many hands to be resisted any other way. Let us be impartial, then, and speak the whole truth. Till we do, we shall never discover all the true princi-

ples that are necessary. The multitude, therefore, as well as nobles, must have a check. This is one principle.

"Were the people of England free, after they had obliged King John to concede to them their ancient rights?" The people never did this. There was no people who pretended to any thing. It was the nobles alone. The people pretended to nothing but to be villains, vassals, and retainers to the king or the nobles. The nobles, I agree, were not free, because all was determined by a majority of their votes, or by arms, not by law. Their feuds deposed their "Henrys, Edwards, and Richards," to gratify lordly ambition, patrician rivalry, and "family pride." But, if they had not been deposed, those kings would have become despots, because the people would not and could not join the nobles in any regular and constitutional opposition to them. They would have become despots, I repeat it, and that by means of the villains, vassals, and retainers aforesaid. It is not family pride, my friend, but family popularity, that does the great mischief, as well as the great good. Pride, in the heart of man, is an evil fruit and concomitant of every advantage; of riches, of knowledge, of genius, of talents, of beauty, of strength, of virtue, and even of piety. It is sometimes ridiculous, and often pernicious. But it is even sometimes, and in some degree, useful. But the pride of families would be always and only ridiculous, if it had not family popularity to work with. The attachment and devotion of the people to some families inspires them with pride. As long as gratitude or interest, ambition or avarice, love, hope, or fear, shall be human motives of action, so long will numbers attach themselves to particular families. When the people will, in spite of all that can be said or done, cry a man or a family up to the skies, exaggerate all his talents and virtues, not hear a word of his weakness or faults, follow implicitly his advice, detest every man he hates, adore every man he loves, and knock down all who will not swim down the stream with them, where is your remedy? When a man or family are thus popular, how can you prevent them from being proud? You and I know of instances in which popularity has been a wind, a tide, a whirlwind. The history of all ages and nations is full of such examples.

Popularity, that has great fortune to dazzle; splendid largesses, to excite warm gratitude; sublime, beautiful, and uncommon genius or talents, to produce deep admiration; or any thing to support high hopes and strong fears, will be proud; and its power will be employed to mortify enemies, gratify friends, procure votes, emoluments, and power. Such family popularity ever did, and ever will govern in every nation, in every climate, hot and cold, wet and dry, among civilized and savage people, Christians and Mahometans, Jews and Heathens. Declamation against family pride is a pretty, juvenile exercise, but unworthy of statesmen. They know the evil and danger is too serious to be sported with. The only way, God knows, is to put these families into a hole by themselves, and set two watches upon them; a superior to them all on one side, and the people on the other.

There are a few popular men in the Massachusetts, my friend, who have, I fear, less honor, sincerity, and virtue, than they ought to have. These, if they are not guarded against, may do another mischief. They may excite a party spirit and a mobbish spirit, instead of the spirit of liberty, and produce another Wat Tyler's rebellion. They can do no more. But I really think their party language ought not to be countenanced, nor their shibboleths pronounced. The miserable stuff that they utter about the *well-born* is as despicable as themselves. . . .

Let us be impartial. There is not more of family pride on one side, than of vulgar malignity and popular envy on the other. Popularity in one family raises envy in others. But the popularity of the least deserving will triumph over envy and malignity; while that which is acquired by real merit, will very often be overborne and oppressed by it.

Let us do justice to the people and to the nobles; for nobles there are, as I have before proved, in Boston as well as in Madrid. But to do justice to both, you must establish an arbitrator between them. This is another principle.

It is time that you and I should have some sweet communion together. I do not believe, that we, who have preserved for more than thirty years an uninterrupted friendship, and have so long thought and acted harmoniously together in the worst of times, are now so far asunder in sentiment as some people pretend; in full confidence of which, I have used this freedom, being ever your warm friend.

The Federalist Papers

In 1787 and 1788, eighty-five essays written by "Publius" appeared in New York newspapers supporting the ratification of the new Constitution. They were soon collected into two volumes and sent to other states in the hope that they would favorably influence ratifying conventions. Although their impact has often been exaggerated, few would disagree that *The Federalist Papers* were especially effective in New York and Virginia.

Even fewer would disagree that *The Federalist Papers* are the best example of a new American science of politics. In a political tradition noteworthy for its lack of theoretical works, *The Federalist Papers* stand as an American contribution to the classics of political thought.

The Federalist Papers were written primarily by Alexander Hamilton (fifty-one essays) and James Madison (twenty-six), with John Jay contributing five essays and five more the joint efforts of Madison and Hamilton.

It would be foolish to contend that Hamilton and Madison shared identical political theories. Madison was closer to Jefferson in his republicanism, and preferred a limited federal government that did not intervene extensively in economic affairs. Hamilton was more the nationalist who favored an active central government—led by a strong executive—which promoted industrial and commercial development. Further, he feared the "Great Beast" of the people and hoped to temper popular participation in government. Yet neither shared Jefferson's enlightenment faith in progress nor his belief that agrarian virtue could sustain the future republic. Hamilton and Madison both envisioned an increasingly commercial society, with a plurality of conflicting interests all vying for power. Like Adams, they hoped to create a strong government that could limit the power of any single group, including the potentially tyrannical majority. A large federal republic, representative government, separation of powers, and an extensive array of checks and balances were all tools to this end.

Federalist No. 1 (Hamilton)

After an unequivocal experience of the inefficacy of the subsisting federal government, you are called upon to deliberate on a new Constitution for the United States of America. The subject speaks its own importance; comprehending in its consequences nothing less than the existence of the UNION, the safety and welfare of the parts of which it is composed, the fate of an empire in many respects the most interesting in the world. It has been frequently remarked that it seems to have been reserved to the people of this country, by their conduct and example, to decide the important question, whether societies of men are really capable or not of establishing good government from reflection and choice, or whether they are forever destined to depend for their political constitutions on accident and force. If there be any truth in the remark, the crisis at which we are arrived may with propriety be regarded as the era in which that decision is to be made; and a wrong election of the part we shall act may, in this view, deserve to be considered as the general misfortune of mankind.

This idea will add the inducements of philanthropy to those of patriotism, to heighten the solicitude which all considerate and good men must feel for the event. Happy will it be if our choice should be directed by a judicious estimate of our true interests, unperplexed and unbiased by considerations not connected with the public good. But this is a thing more ardently to be wished than seri-

SOURCE: Clinton Rossiter, ed., *The Federalist Papers* (New York: New American Library, 1961).

ously to be expected. The plan offered to our deliberations affects too many particular interests, innovates upon too many local institutions, not to involve in its discussion a variety of objects foreign to its merits, and of views, passions, and prejudices little favorable to the discovery of truth.

Among the most formidable of the obstacles which the new Constitution will have to encounter may readily be distinguished the obvious interest of a certain class of men in every State to resist all changes which may hazard a diminution of the power, emolument, and consequence of the offices they hold under the State establishments; and the perverted ambition of another class of men, who will either hope to aggrandize themselves by the confusions of their country, or will flatter themselves with fairer prospects of elevation from the subdivision of the empire into several partial confederacies than from its union under one government.

It is not, however, my design to dwell upon observations of this nature. I am well aware that it would be disingenuous to resolve indiscriminately the opposition of any set of men (merely because their situations might subject them to suspicion) into interested or ambitious views. Candor will oblige us to admit that even such men may be actuated by upright intentions; and it cannot be doubted that much of the opposition which has made its appearance, or may hereafter make its appearance, will spring from sources, blameless at least if not respectable—the honest errors of minds led astray by preconceived jealousies and fears. So numerous indeed and so powerful are the causes which serve to give a false bias to the judgment, that we, upon many occasions, see wise and good men on the wrong as well as on the right side of questions of the first magnitude to society. This circumstance, if duly attended to, would furnish a lesson of moderation to those who are ever so thoroughly persuaded of their being in the right in any controversy. And a further reason

for caution, in this respect, might be drawn from the reflection that we are not always sure that those who advocate the truth are influenced by purer principles than their antagonists. Ambition, avarice, personal animosity, party opposition, and many other motives not more laudable than these, are apt to operate as well upon those who support as those who oppose the right side of a question. Were there not even these inducements to moderation, nothing could be more ill-judged than that intolerant spirit which has at all times characterized political parties. For in politics, as in religion, it is equally absurd to aim at making proselytes by fire and sword. Heresies in either can rarely be cured by persecution.

And yet, however just these sentiments will be allowed to be, we have already sufficient indications that it will happen in this as in all former cases of great national discussion. A torrent of angry and malignant passions will be let loose. To judge from the conduct of the opposite parties, we shall be led to conclude that they will mutually hope to evince the justness of their opinions, and to increase the number of their converts by the loudness of their declamations and by the bitterness of their invectives. An enlightened zeal for the energy and efficiency of government will be stigmatized as the offspring of a temper fond of despotic power and hostile to the principles of liberty. An over-scrupulous jealousy of danger to the rights of the people, which is more commonly the fault of the head than of the heart, will be represented as mere pretense and artifice, the stale bait for popularity at the expense of public good. It will be forgotten, on the one hand, that jealousy is the usual concomitant of violent love, and that the noble enthusiasm of liberty is too apt to be infected with a spirit of narrow and illiberal distrust. On the other hand, it will be equally forgotten that the vigor of government is essential to the security of liberty; that, in the contemplation of a sound and well-informed judgment, their interests can never be separated;

and that a dangerous ambition more often lurks behind the specious mask of zeal for the rights of the people than under the forbidding appearance of zeal for the firmness and efficiency of government. History will teach us that the former has been found a much more certain road to the introduction of despotism than the latter, and that of those men who have overturned the liberties of republics, the greatest number have begun their career by paying an obsequious court to the people, commencing demagogues and ending tyrants. . . .

I am convinced that this is the safest course for your liberty, your dignity, and your happiness. I affect not reserves which I do not feel. I will not amuse you with an appearance of deliberation when I have decided. I frankly acknowledge to you my convictions, and I will freely lay before you the reasons on which they are founded. The consciousness of good intentions disdains ambiguity. I shall not, however, multiply professions on this head. My motives must remain in the depository of my own breast. My arguments will be open to all and may be judged of by all. They shall at least be offered in a spirit which will not disgrace the cause of truth.

I propose, in a series of papers, to discuss the following interesting particulars:—*The utility of the UNION to your political prosperity—The insufficiency of the present Confederation to preserve that Union—The necessity of a government at least equally energetic with the one proposed, to the attainment of this object—The conformity of the proposed Constitution to the true principles of republican government—Its analogy to your own State constitution—*and lastly, *The additional secu-rity, which its adoption will afford to the preservation of that species of government, to liberty, and to property.*

In the progress of this discussion I shall endeavor to give a satisfactory answer to all the objections which shall have made their appearance, that may seem to have any claim to your attention.

It may perhaps be thought superfluous to offer arguments to prove the utility of the UNION, a point, no doubt, deeply engraved on the hearts of the great body of the people in every State, and one which, it may be imagined, has no adversaries. But the fact is that we already hear it whispered in the private circles of those who oppose the new Constitution, that the thirteen States are of too great extent for any general system, and that we must of necessity resort to separate confederacies of distinct portions of the whole.[*] This doctrine will, in all probability, be gradually propagated, till it has votaries enough to countenance an open avowal of it. For nothing can be more evident to those who are able to take an enlarged view of the subject than the alternative of an adoption of the new Constitution or a dismemberment of the Union. It will therefore be of use to begin by examining the advantages of that Union, the certain evils, and the probable dangers, to which every State will be exposed from its dissolution. This shall accordingly constitute the subject of my next address.

PUBLIUS

---

[*] The same idea, tracing the arguments to their consequences, is held out in several of the late publications against the new Constitution.

Federalist No. 10 (Madison)

Among the numerous advantages promised by a well-constructed Union, none deserves to be more accurately developed than its tendency to break and control the violence of faction. The friend of popular governments never finds himself so much alarmed for their character and fate as when he contemplates their propensity to this dangerous vice. He will not fail, therefore, to set a due value on any plan, which, without violating the principles to which he is attached, provides a proper cure for it. The instability, injustice, and confusion introduced into the public councils have, in truth, been the mortal diseases under which popular governments have everywhere perished, as they continue to be the favorite and fruitful topics from which the adversaries to liberty derive their most specious declamations. The valuable improvements made by the American constitutions on the popular models, both ancient and modern, cannot certainly be too much admired; but it would be an unwarrantable partiality to contend that they have as effectually obviated the danger on this side, as was wished and expected. Complaints are everywhere heard from our most considerate and virtuous citizens, equally the friends of public and private faith and of public and personal liberty, that our governments are too unstable, that the public good is disregarded in the conflicts of rival parties, and that measures are too often decided, not according to the rules of justice and the rights of the minor party, but by the superior force of an interested and overbearing majority. However anxiously we may wish that these complaints had no foundation, the evidence of known facts will not permit us to deny that they are in some degree true. It will be found, indeed, on a candid review of our situation, that some of the distresses under which we labor have been erroneously charged on the operation of our governments; but it will be found, at the same time, that other causes will not alone account for many of our heaviest misfortunes; and, particularly, for that prevailing and increasing distrust of public engagements and alarm for private rights which are echoed from one end of the continent to the other. These must be chiefly, if not wholly, effects of the unsteadiness and injustice with which a factious spirit has tainted our public administration.

By a faction I understand a number of citizens, whether amounting to a majority or minority of the whole, who are united and actuated by some common impulse of passion, or of interest, adverse to the rights of other citizens, or to the permanent and aggregate interests of the community.

There are two methods of curing the mischiefs of faction: the one, by removing its causes; the other, by controlling its effects.

There are again two methods of removing the causes of faction: the one, by destroying the liberty which is essential to its existence; the other, by giving to every citizen the same opinions, the same passions, and the same interests.

It could never be more truly said than of the first remedy that it was worse than the disease. Liberty is to faction what air is to fire, an aliment without which it instantly expires. But it could not be a less folly to abolish liberty, which is essential to political life, because it nourishes faction than it would be to wish the annihilation of air, which is essential to animal life, because it imparts to fire its destructive agency.

The second expedient is as impracticable

as the first would be unwise. As long as the reason of man continues fallible, and he is at liberty to exercise it, different opinions will be formed. As long as the connection subsists between his reason and his self-love, his opinions and his passions will have a reciprocal influence on each other; and the former will be objects to which the latter will attach themselves. The diversity in the faculties of men, from which the rights of property originate, is not less an insuperable obstacle to a uniformity of interests. The protection of these faculties is the first object of government. From the protection of different and unequal faculties of acquiring property, the possession of different degrees and kinds of property immediately results; and from the influence of these on the sentiments and views of the respective proprietors ensues a division of the society into different interests and parties.

The latent causes of faction are thus sown in the nature of man; and we see them everywhere brought into different degrees of activity, according to the different circumstances of civil society. A zeal for different opinions concerning religion, concerning government, and many other points, as well of speculation as of practice; an attachment to different leaders ambitiously contending for pre-eminence and power: or to persons of other descriptions whose fortunes have been interesting to the human passions, have, in turn, divided mankind into parties, inflamed them with mutual animosity, and rendered them much more disposed to vex and oppress each other than to co-operate for their common good. So strong is this propensity of mankind to fall into mutual animosities that where no substantial occasion presents itself the most frivolous and fanciful distinctions have been sufficient to kindle their unfriendly passions and excite their most violent conflicts. But the most common and durable source of factions has been the various and unequal distribution of property. Those who hold and those who are without property have ever formed distinct interests in society. Those who are creditors, and those who are debtors, fall under a like discrimination. A landed interest, a manufacturing interest, a mercantile interest, a moneyed interest, with many lesser interests, grow up of necessity in civilized nations, and divide them into different classes, actuated by different sentiments and views. The regulation of these various and interfering interests forms the principal task of modern legislation and involves the spirit of party and faction in the necessary and ordinary operations of government.

No man is allowed to be a judge in his own cause because his interest would certainly bias his judgment, and, not improbably, corrupt his integrity. With equal, nay with greater reason, a body of men are unfit to be both judges and parties at the same time; yet what are many of the most important acts of legislation but so many judicial determinations, not indeed concerning the rights of single persons, but concerning the rights of large bodies of citizens? And what are the different classes of legislators but advocates and parties to the causes which they determine? Is a law proposed concerning private debts? It is a question to which the creditors are parties on one side and the debtors on the other. Justice ought to hold the balance between them. Yet the parties are, and must be, themselves the judges; and the most numerous party, or in other words, the most powerful faction must be expected to prevail. Shall domestic manufacturers be encouraged, and in what degree, by restrictions on foreign manufacturers? are questions which would be differently decided by the landed and the manufacturing classes, and probably by neither with a sole regard to justice and the public good. The apportionment of taxes on the various descriptions of property is an act which seems to require the most exact impartiality; yet there is, perhaps, no legislative act in which greater opportunity and temptation are given to a predominant party to trample on the rules of justice. Every shilling with which they overburden the inferior number is a shilling saved to their own pockets.

It is in vain to say that enlightened statesmen will be able to adjust these clashing interests and render them all subservient to the public good. Enlightened statesmen will not always be at the helm. Nor, in many cases, can such an adjustment be made at all without taking into view indirect and remote considerations, which will rarely prevail over the immediate interest which one party may find in disregarding the rights of another or the good of the whole.

The inference to which we are brought is that the *causes* of faction cannot be removed and that relief is only to be sought in the means of controlling its *effects*.

If a faction consists of less than a majority, relief is supplied by the republican principle, which enables the majority to defeat its sinister views by regular vote. It may clog the administration, it may convulse the society; but it will be unable to execute and mask its violence under the forms of the Constitution. When a majority is included in a faction, the form of popular government, on the other hand, enables it to sacrifice to its ruling passion or interest both the public good and the rights of other citizens. To secure the public good and private rights against the danger of such a faction, and at the same time to preserve the spirit and the form of popular government, is then the great object to which our inquiries are directed. Let me add that it is the great desideratum by which alone this form of government can be rescued from the opprobrium under which it has so long labored and be recommended to the esteem and adoption of mankind.

By what means in this object attainable? Evidently by one of two only. Either the existence of the same passion or interest in a majority at the same time must be prevented, or the majority, having such coexistent passion

or interest, must be rendered, by their number and local situation, unable to concert and carry into effect schemes of oppression. If the impulse and the opportunity be suffered to coincide, we well know that neither moral nor religious motives can be relied on as an adequate control. They are not found to be such on the injustice and violence of individuals, and lose their efficacy in proportion to the number combined together, that is, in proportion as their efficacy becomes needful.

From this view of the subject it may be concluded that a pure democracy, by which I mean a society consisting of a small number of citizens, who assemble and administer the government in person, can admit of no cure for the mischiefs of faction. A common passion or interest will, in almost every case, be felt by a majority of the whole; a communication and concert results from the form of government itself; and there is nothing to check the inducements to sacrifice the weaker party or an obnoxious individual. Hence it is that such democracies have ever been spectacles of turbulence and contention; have ever been found incompatible with personal security or the rights of property; and have in general been as short in their lives as they have been violent in their deaths. Theoretic politicians, who have patronized this species of government, have erroneously supposed that by reducing mankind to a perfect equality in their political rights, they would at the same time be perfectly equalized and assimilated in their possessions, their opinions, and their passions.

A republic, by which I mean a government in which the scheme of representation takes place, opens a different prospect and promises the cure for which we are seeking. Let us examine the points in which it varies from pure democracy, and we shall comprehend both the nature of the cure and the efficacy which it must derive from the Union.

The two great points of difference between a democracy and a republic are: first, the delegation of the government, in the latter, to a small number of citizens elected by the rest: secondly, the greater number of citizens and greater sphere of country over which the latter may be extended.

The effect of the first difference is, on the one hand, to refine and enlarge the public views by passing them through the medium of a chosen body of citizens, whose wisdom may best discern the true interest of their country and whose patriotism and love of justice will be least likely to sacrifice it to temporary or partial considerations. Under such a regulation it may well happen that the public voice, pronounced by the representatives of the people, will be more consonant to the public good than if pronounced by the people themselves, convened for the purpose. On the other hand, the effect may be inverted. Men of factious tempers, of local prejudices, or of sinister designs, may, by intrigue, by corruption, or by other means, first obtain the suffrages, and then betray the interests of the people. The question resulting is, whether small or extensive republics are most favorable to the election of proper guardians of the public weal; and it is clearly decided in favor of the latter by two obvious considerations.

In the first place it is to be remarked that however small the republic may be the representatives must be raised to a certain number in order to guard against the cabals of a few; and that however large it may be they must be limited to a certain number in order to guard against the confusion of a multitude. Hence, the number of representatives in the two cases not being in proportion to that of the constituents, and being proportionally greatest in the small republic, it follows that if the proportion of fit characters be not less in the large than in the small republic, the former will present a greater option, and consequently a greater probability of a fit choice.

In the next place, as each representative will be chosen by a greater number of citizens in the large than in the small republic, it will be more difficult for unworthy candidates to practise with success the vicious arts by which elections are too often carried; and the suffrages of the people being more free, will be more likely to center on men who possess the most attractive merit and the most diffusive and established characters.

It must be confessed that in this, as in most other cases, there is a mean, on both sides of which inconveniences will be found to lie. By enlarging too much the number of electors, you render the representative too little acquainted with all their local circumstances and lesser interests; as by reducing it too much, you render him unduly attached to these, and too little fit to comprehend and pursue great and national objects. The federal Constitution forms a happy combination in this respect; the great and aggregate interests being referred to the national, the local and particular to the State legislatures.

The other point of difference is the greater number of citizens and extent of territory which may be brought within the compass of republican than of democratic government; and it is this circumstance principally which renders factious combinations less to be dreaded in the former than in the latter. The smaller the society, the fewer probably will be the distinct parties and interests composing it; the fewer the distinct parties and interests, the more frequently will a majority be found of the same party; and the smaller the number of individuals composing a majority, and the smaller the compass within which they are placed, the more easily will they concert and execute their plans of oppression. Extend the sphere and you take in a greater variety of parties and interests; you make it less probable that a majority of the whole will have a common motive to invade the rights of other citizens; or if such a common motive exists, it will be more difficult for all who feel it to discover their own strength and to act in unison with each other. Besides other impediments, it may be remarked that, where there is a consciousness of unjust or dishonorable purposes, communication is always checked by distrust in proportion to the number whose concurrence is necessary.

Hence, it clearly appears that the same advantage which a republic has over a democracy in controlling the effects of faction is enjoyed by a large over a small republic—is enjoyed by the Union over the States composing it. Does this advantage consist in the substitution of representatives whose enlightened views and virtuous sentiments render them superior to local prejudices and to schemes of injustice? It will not be denied that the representation of the Union will be most likely to possess these requisite endowments. Does it consist in the greater security afforded by a greater variety of parties, against the event of any one party being able to outnumber and oppress the rest? In an equal degree does the increased variety of parties comprised within the Union increase this security. Does it, in fine, consist in the greater obstacles opposed to the concert accomplishment of the secret wishes of an unjust and interested majority?

Here again the extent of the Union gives it the most palpable advantage.

The influence of factious leaders may kindle a flame within their particular States but will be unable to spread a general conflagration through the other States. A religious sect may degenerate into a political faction in a part of the Confederacy; but the variety of sects dispersed over the entire face of it must secure the national councils against any danger from that source. A rage for paper money, for an abolition of debts, for an equal division of property, or for any other improper or wicked project, will be less apt to pervade the whole body of the Union than a particular member of it, in the same proportion as such a malady is more likely to taint a particular county or district than an entire State.

In the extent and proper structure of the Union, therefore, we behold a republican remedy for the diseases most incident to republican government. And according to the degree of pleasure and pride we feel in being republicans ought to be our zeal in cherishing the spirit and supporting the character of federalists.

PUBLIUS

Federalist No. 15 (Hamilton)

. . . The great and radical vice in the construction of the existing Confederation is in the principle of LEGISLATION for STATES or GOVERNMENTS, in their CORPORATE or COLLECTIVE CAPACITIES, and as contradistinguished from the INDIVIDUALS of whom they consist. Though this principle does not run through all the powers delegated to the Union, yet it pervades and governs those on which the efficacy of the rest depends. Except as to the rule of apportionment, the United States have

an indefinite discretion to make requisitions for men and money; but they have no authority to raise either by regulations extending to the individual citizens of America. The consequence of this is that though in theory their resolutions concerning those objects are laws constitutionally binding on the members of the Union, yet in practice they are mere recommendations which the States observe or disregard at their option.

It is a singular instance of the capriciousness

of the human mind that after all the admonitions we have had from experience on this head, there should still be found men who object to the new Constitution for deviating from a principle which has been found the bane of the old and which is in itself evidently incompatible with the idea of GOVERNMENT; a principle, in short, which, if it is to be executed at all, must substitute the violent and sanguinary agency of the sword to the mild influence of the magistracy.

There is nothing absurd or impracticable in the idea of a league or alliance between independent nations for certain defined purposes precisely stated in a treaty regulating all the details of time, place, circumstance, and quantity, leaving nothing to future discretion, and depending for its execution on the good faith of the parties. Compacts of this kind exist among all civilized nations, subject to the usual vicissitudes of peace and war, of observance and nonobservance, as the interests or passions of the contracting powers dictate. In the early part of the present century there was an epidemical rage in Europe for this species of compacts, from which the politicians of the times fondly hoped for benefits which were never realized. With a view to establishing the equilibrium of power and the peace of that part of the world, all the resources of negotiations were exhausted, and triple and quadruple alliances were formed; but they were scarcely formed before they were broken, giving an instructive but afflicting lesson to mankind how little dependence is to be placed on treaties which have no other sanction than the obligations of good faith, and which oppose general considerations of peace and justice to the impulse of any immediate interest or passion.

If the particular States in this country are disposed to stand in a similar relation to each other, and to drop the project of a general DISCRETIONARY SUPERINTENDENCE, the scheme would indeed be pernicious and would entail upon us all the mischiefs which have been enumerated under the first head; but it would have the merit of being, at least, consistent and practicable. Abandoning all views towards a confederate government, this would bring us to a simple alliance offensive and defensive; and would place us in a situation to be alternate friends and enemies of each other, as our mutual jealousies and rivalships, nourished by the intrigues of foreign nations, should prescribe to us.

But if we are unwilling to be placed in this perilous situation; if we still will adhere to the design of a national government, or, which is the same thing, of a superintending power under the direction of a common council, we must resolve to incorporate into our plan those ingredients which may be considered as forming the characteristic difference between a league and a government; we must extend the authority of the Union to the persons of the citizens—the only proper objects of government.

Government implies the power of making laws. It is essential to the idea of a law that it be attended with a sanction; or, in other words, a penalty or punishment for disobedience. If there be no penalty annexed to disobedience, the resolutions or commands which pretend to be laws will, in fact, amount to nothing more than advice or recommendation. This penalty, whatever it may be, can only be inflicted in two ways: by the agency of the courts and ministers of justice, or by military force; by the COERCION of the magistracy, or by the COERCION of arms. The first kind can evidently apply only to men; the last kind must of necessity be employed against bodies politic, or communities, or States. It is evident that there is no process of a court by which the observance of the laws can in the last resort be enforced. Sentences may be denounced against them for violations of their duty; but these sentences can only be carried into execution by the sword. In an association where the general authority is confined to the collective bodies of the communities that compose it, every breach of the laws must involve a state of war; and military execution must become the only instrument of civil obedience. Such a state of things can certainly not deserve the name of government, nor would any prudent man choose to commit his happiness to it.

There was a time when we were told that breaches by the States of the regulations of the federal authority were not to be expected; that a sense of common interest would preside over the conduct of the respective members, and would beget a full compliance with all the constitutional requisitions of the Union. This language, at the present day, would appear as wild as a great part of what we now hear from the same quarter will be thought, when we shall have received further lessons from that best oracle of wisdom, experience. It at all times betrayed an ignorance of the true springs by which human conduct is actuated, and belied the original inducements to the establishment of civil power. Why has government been instituted at all? Because the passions of men will not conform to the dictates of reason and justice without constraint. Has it been found that bodies of men act with more rectitude or greater disinterestedness than individuals? The contrary of this has been inferred by all accurate observers of the conduct of mankind; and the inference is founded upon obvious reasons. Regard to reputation has a less active influence when the infamy of a bad action is to be divided among a number than when it is to fall singly upon one. A spirit of faction, which is apt to mingle its poison in the deliberations of all bodies of men, will often hurry the persons of whom they are composed into improprieties and excesses for which they would blush in a private capacity. . . .

If, therefore, the measures of the Confederacy cannot be executed without the intervention of the particular administrations, there will be little prospect of their being executed at all. The rulers of the respective members, whether they have a constitutional right to do it or not, will undertake to judge of the propriety of the measures themselves. They will consider the conformity of the thing proposed or required to their immediate interests or aims; the momentary conveniences or inconveniences that would attend its adoption. All this will be done; and in a spirit of interested and suspicious scrutiny, without that knowledge of national circumstances and reasons of state, which is essential to a right judgment, and with that strong predilection in favor of local objects, which can hardly fail to mislead the decision. The same process must be repeated in every member of which the body is constituted: and the execution of the plans, framed by the councils of the whole, will always fluctuate on the discretion of the ill-informed and prejudiced opinion of every part. Those who have been conversant in the proceedings of popular assemblies; who have seen how difficult it often is, when there is no exterior pressure of circumstances, to bring them to harmonious resolutions on important points, will readily conceive how impossible it must be to induce a number of such assemblies, deliberating at a distance from each other, at different times and under different impressions, long to co-operate in the same views and pursuits.

In our case the concurrence of thirteen distinct sovereign wills is requisite under the Confederation to the complete execution of every important measure that proceeds from the Union. It has happened as was to have been forseen. The measures of the Union have not been executed; and the delinquencies of the States have step by step matured themselves to an extreme, which has, at length, arrested all the wheels of the national government and brought them to an awful stand. Congress at this time scarcely possess the means of keeping up the forms of administration, till the States can have time to agree upon a more substantial substitute for the present shadow of a federal government. Things did not come to this desperate extremity at once. The causes which have been specified produced at first only unequal and disproportionate degrees of compliance with the requisitions of the Union. The greater deficiencies of some States furnished the pretext of example and the temptation of interest to the complying, or to the least delinquent States. Why should we do more in proportion than those who are embarked with us in the same political voyage? Why should we consent to bear more than our proper share of the common bur-

den? There were suggestions which human selfishness could not withstand, and which even speculative men, who looked forward to remote consequences, could not without hesitation combat. Each State yielding to the persuasive voice of immediate interest or convenience has successively withdrawn its support, till the frail and tottering edifice seems ready to fall upon our heads and to crush us beneath its ruins.

PUBLIUS

Federalist No. 39 (Madison)

. . . The first question that offers itself is whether the general form and aspect of the government be strictly republican. It is evident that no other form would be reconcilable with the genius of the people of America; with the fundamental principles of the Revolution; or with that honorable determination which animates every votary of freedom to rest all our political experiments on the capacity of mankind for self-government. If the plan of the convention, therefore, be found to depart from the republican character, its advocates must abandon it as no longer defensible.

What, then, are the distinctive characters of the republican form? Were an answer to this question to be sought, not by recurring to principles but in the application of the term by political writers to the constitutions of different States, no satisfactory one would ever be found. Holland, in which no particle of the supreme authority is derived from the people, has passed almost universally under the denomination of a republic. The same title has been bestowed on Venice, where absolute power over the great body of the people is exercised in the most absolute manner by a small body of hereditary nobles. Poland,

which is a mixture of aristocracy and of monarchy in their worst forms, has been dignified with the same appellation. The government of England, which has one republican branch only, combined with an hereditary aristocracy and monarchy, has with equal impropriety been frequently placed on the list of republics. These examples, which are nearly as dissimilar to each other as to a genuine republic, show the extreme inaccuracy with which the term has been used in political disquisitions.

If we resort for a criterion to the different principles on which different forms of government are established, we may define a republic to be, or at least may bestow that name on, a government which derives all its powers directly or indirectly from the great body of the people, and is administered by persons holding their offices during pleasure for a limited period, or during good behavior. It is *essential* to such a government that it be derived from the great body of the society, not from an inconsiderable proportion or a favored class of it; otherwise a handful of tyrannical nobles, exercising their oppressions by a delegation of their powers, might aspire to the rank of republicans and claim for their government the honorable title of republic. It is *sufficient* for such a government that the persons administering it be appointed, either directly or indirectly, by the people; and that they hold their appointments by either of the tenures just specified; otherwise every government in the United States, as well as every other popular government that has been or can be well organized or well executed, would be degraded from the republican character. . . . The House of Representatives, like that of one branch at least of all the State legislatures, is elected immediately by the great body of the people. The Senate, like the present Congress and the Senate of Maryland, derives its appointment indirectly from the people. The President is indirectly derived from the choice of the people, according to the example in most of the States. Even the judges, with all other officers of the Union, will, as in the several States, be the choice, though a remote choice, of the people themselves. The duration of the appointments is equally conformable to the republican standard and to the model of State constitutions. The House of Representatives is periodically elective, as in all the States; and for the period of two years, as in the State of South Carolina. The Senate is elective for the period of six years, which is but one year more than the period of the Senate of Maryland, and but two more than that of the Senates of New York and Virginia. The President is to continue in office for the period of four years; as in New York and Delaware the chief magistrate is elected for three years, and in South Carolina for two years. In the other States the election is annual. In several of the States, however, no explicit provision is made for the impeachment of the chief magistrate. And in Delaware and Virginia he is not impeachable till out of office. The President of the United States is impeachable at any time during his continuance in office. The tenure by which the judges are to hold their places is, as it unquestionably ought to be, that of good behavior. The tenure

of the ministerial offices generally will be a subject of legal regulation, conformably to the reason of the case and the example of the State constitutions.

Could any further proof be required of the republican complexion of this system, the most decisive one might be found in its absolute prohibition of titles of nobility, both under the federal and the State governments; and in its express guaranty of the republican form to each of the latter.

"But it was not sufficient," say the adversaries of the proposed Constitution, "for the convention to adhere to the republican form. They ought with equal care to have preserved the *federal* form, which regards the Union as a *Confederacy* of sovereign states; instead of which they have framed a *national* government, which regards the Union as a *consolidation* of the States." And it is asked by what authority this bold and radical innovation was undertaken? The handle which has been made of this objection requires that it should be examined with some precision. . . .

The next relation is to the sources from which the ordinary powers of government are to be derived. The House of Representatives will derive its powers from the people of America; and the people will be represented in the same proportion and on the same principle as they are in the legislature of a particular State. So far the government is *national*, not *federal*. The Senate, on the other hand, will derive its powers from the States as political and coequal societies; and these will be represented on the principle of equality in the Senate, as they now are in the existing Congress. So far the government is *federal*, not *national*. The executive power will be derived from a very compound source. The immediate election of the President is to be made by the States in their political characters. The votes allotted to them are in a compound ratio, which considers them partly as distinct and coequal societies, partly as unequal members of the same society. The eventual election, again, is to be made by that branch of the legislature which consists of the national representatives; but in this particular act they are to be thrown into the form of individual delegations from so many distinct and coequal bodies politic. From this aspect of the government it appears to be of a mixed character, presenting at least as many *federal* as *national* features.

The difference between a federal and national government, as it relates to the *operation of the government,* is by the adversaries of the plan of the convention supposed to consist in this, that in the former the powers operate on the political bodies composing the Confederacy in their political capacities; in the latter, on the individual citizens composing the nation in their individual capacities. On trying the Constitution by this criterion, it falls under the *national* not the *federal* character; though perhaps not so completely as has been understood. In several cases, and particularly in the trial of controversies to which States may be parties, they must be viewed and proceeded against in their collective and political capacities only. But the operation of the government on the people in their individual capacities, in its ordinary and most essential proceedings, will, in the sense of its opponents, on the whole, designate it, in this relation, a *national* government.

But if the government be national with regard to the *operation* of its powers, it changes its aspect again when we contemplate it in relation to the extent of its powers. The idea of a national government involves in it not only an authority over the individual citizens, but an indefinite supremacy over all persons and things, so far as they are objects of lawful government. Among a people consolidated into one nation, this supremacy is completely vested in the national legislature. Among communities united for particular purposes, it is vested partly in the general and partly in the municipal legislatures. In the former case, all local authorities are subordinate to the su-

preme; and may be controlled, directed, or abolished by it at pleasure. In the latter, the local or municipal authorities form distinct and independent portions of the supremacy, no more subject, within their respective spheres, to the general authority than the general authority is subject to them, within its own sphere. In this relation, then, the proposed government cannot be deemed a *national* one; since its jurisdiction extends to certain enumerated objects only, and leaves to the several States a residuary and inviolable sovereignty over all other objects. It is true that in controversies relating to the boundary between the two jurisdictions, the tribunal which is ultimately to decide is to be established under the general government. But this does not change the principle of the case. The decision is to be impartially made, according to the rules of the Constitution; and all the usual and most effectual precautions are taken to secure this impartiality. Some such tribunal is clearly essential to prevent an appeal to the sword and a dissolution of the compact; and that it ought to be established under the general rather than under the local governments, or, to speak more properly, that it could be safely established under the first alone, is a position not likely to be combated.

If we try the Constitution by its last relation to the authority by which amendments are to be made, we find it neither wholly *national* nor wholly *federal.* Were it wholly national, the supreme and ultimate authority would reside in the *majority* of the people of the Union; and this authority would be competent at all times, like that of a majority of every national society to alter or abolish its established government. Were it wholly federal, on the other hand, the concurrence of each State in the Union would be essential to every alteration that would be binding on all. The mode provided by the plan of the convention is not founded on either of these principles. In requiring more than a majority, and particularly in computing the proportion by *States,* not by *citizens,* it departs from the national and advances towards the *federal* character; in rendering the concurrence of less than the whole number of States sufficient, it loses again the *federal* and partakes of the *national* character.

The proposed Constitution, therefore, even when tested by the rules laid down by its antagonists, is, in strictness, neither a national nor a federal Constitution, but a composition of both. In its foundation it is federal, not national; in the sources from which the ordinary powers of the government are drawn, it is partly federal and partly national; in the operation of these powers, it is national, not federal; in the extent of them, again, it is federal, not national; and, finally in the authoritative mode of introducing amendments, it is neither wholly federal nor wholly national.

PUBLIUS

Federalist No. 51 (Madison)

To what expedient, then, shall we finally resort, for maintaining in practice the necessary partition of power among the several departments as laid down in the Constitution? The only answer that can be given is that as all these exterior provisions are found to be inadequate the defect must be supplied, by so contriving the interior structure of the government as that its several constituent parts may, by their mutual relations, be the means of keeping each other in their proper places. Without presuming to undertake a full development of this important idea I will hazard a few general observations which may perhaps place it in a clearer light, and enable us to form a more correct judgment of the principles and structure of the government planned by the convention.

In order to lay a due foundation for that separate and distinct exercise of the different powers of government, which to a certain extent is admitted on all hands to be essential to the preservation of liberty, it is evident that each department should have a will of its own; and consequently should be so constituted that the members of each should have as little agency as possible in the appointment of the members of the others. Were this principle rigorously adhered to, it would require that all the appointments for the supreme executive, legislative, and judiciary magistracies should be drawn from the same fountain of authority, the people, through channels having no communication whatever with one another. Perhaps such a plan of constructing the several departments would be less difficult in practice than it may in contemplation appear. Some difficulties, however, and some additional expense would attend the execution of it. Some deviations, therefore, from the principle must be admitted. In the constitution of the judiciary department in particular, it might be inexpedient to insist rigorously on the principle: first, because peculiar qualifications being essential in the members, the primary consideration ought to be to select that mode of choice which best secures these qualifications; second, because the permanent tenure by which the appointments are held in that department must soon destroy all sense of dependence on the authority conferring them.

It is equally evident that the members of each department should be as little dependent as possible on those of the others for the emoluments annexed to their offices. Were the executive magistrate, or the judges, not independent of the legislature in this particular, their independence in every other would be merely nominal.

But the great security against a gradual concentration of the several powers in the same department consists in giving to those who administer each department the necessary constitutional means and personal motives to resist encroachments of the others. The provision for defense must in this, as in all other cases, be made commensurate to the danger of attack. Ambition must be made to counteract ambition. The interest of the man must be connected with the constitutional rights of the place. It may be a reflection on human nature that such devices should be necessary to control the abuses of government. But what is government itself but the greatest of all reflections on human nature? If men were angels, no government would be necessary. If angels were to govern men, neither external nor internal controls on government would be necessary. In framing a government which is to be administered by men over men, the great difficulty lies in this: you must first enable the government to control the governed; and in the next place oblige it to control itself. A dependence on the people is, no doubt, the primary control on the government; but experience has taught mankind the necessity of auxiliary precautions.

This policy of supplying, by opposite and rival interests, the defect of better motives, might be traced through the whole system of human affairs, private as well as public. We see it particularly displayed in all the subordinate distributions of power, where the constant aim is to divide and arrange the several offices in such a manner as that each may be a check on the other—that the private interest of every individual may be a sentinel over the public rights. These inventions of prudence cannot be less requisite in the distribution of the supreme powers of the State.

But it is not possible to give to each department an equal power of self-defense. In republican government, the legislative authority necessarily predominates. The remedy for this inconveniency is to divide the legislature into different branches; and to render them, by different modes of election and different principles of action, as little connected with each other as the nature of their common functions and their common dependence on the society will admit. It may even be necessary to guard against dangerous encroachments by still further precautions. As the weight of the legislative authority requires that it should be thus divided, the weakness of the executive may require, on the other hand, that it should be fortified. An absolute negative on the legislature appears, at first view, to be the natural defense with which the executive magistrate should be armed. But perhaps it would be neither altogether safe nor alone sufficient. On ordinary occasions it might not be exerted with the requisite firmness, and on extraordinary occasions it might be perfidiously abused. May not this defect of an absolute negative be supplied by some qualified connection between this weaker department and the weaker branch of the stronger department, by which the latter may be led to support the constitutional rights of the former, without being too much detached from the rights of its own departments?

If the principles on which these observations are founded be just, as I persuade myself they are, and they be applied as a criterion to the several State constitutions, and to the federal Constitution, it will be found that if the latter does not perfectly correspond with them, the former are infinitely less able to bear such a test.

There are, moreover, two considerations particularly applicable to the federal system of America, which place that system in a very interesting point of view.

First. In a single republic, all the power surrendered by the people is submitted to the administration of a single government; and the usurpations are guarded against by a division of the government into distinct and separate departments. In the compound republic of America, the power surrendered by the people is first divided between two distinct governments, and then the portion allotted to each subdivided among distinct and separate departments. Hence a double security arises to the rights of the people. The different governments will control each other, at the same time that each will be controlled by itself.

Second. It is of great importance in a republic not only to guard the society against the oppression of its rulers, but to guard one part of the society against the injustice of the other part. Different interests necessarily exist in different classes of citizens. If a majority be united by a common interest, the rights of the minority will be insecure. There are but two methods of providing against this evil: the one by creating a will in the community independent of the majority—that is, of the society itself; the other, by comprehending in the society so many separate descriptions of citizens as will render an unjust combination of a majority of the whole very improbable, if not impracticable. The first method prevails in all governments possessing an hereditary or self-appointed authority. This, at best, is but a precarious security; because a power independent of the society may as well espouse the unjust views of the major as the rightful interests of the minor party, and may possibly be turned against both parties. The second method will be exemplified in the federal republic of the United States. Whilst all authority in it will be derived from and dependent on the society, the society itself will be broken into so many parts, interests and classes of citizens, that the rights of individuals, or of the minority, will be in little danger from interested combinations of the majority. In a free government the security for civil rights must be the same as that for religious rights. It consists in the one case in the multiplicity of interests, and in the other in the multiplicity of sects. The degree of security in both cases will depend on the number of interests and sects; and this may be presumed to depend on the extent of country and number of people comprehended under the same government. This view of the subject must particularly recommend a proper federal system to all the sincere and considerate friends of republican government, since it shows that in exact proportion as the territory of the Union may be formed into more circumscribed Confederacies, or States, oppressive combinations of a majority will be facilitated; the best security, under the republican forms, for the rights of every class of citizen, will be diminished; and consequently the stability and independence of some member of the government, the only other security, must be proportionally increased. Justice is the end of government. It is the end of civil society. It ever has been and ever will be pursued until it be obtained, or until liberty be lost in the pursuit. In a society under the forms of which the stronger faction can readily unite and oppress the weaker, anarchy may as truly be said to reign as in a state of nature, where the weaker individual is not secured against the violence of the stronger; and as, in the latter state, even the stronger individuals are prompted, by the uncertainty of their condition, to submit to a government which may protect the weak as well as themselves; so, in the former state, will the more powerful factions or parties be gradually induced, by a like motive, to wish for a government which will protect all parties, the weaker as well as the more powerful. It can be little doubted that if the State of Rhode Island was separated from the Confederacy and left to itself, the insecurity of rights under the popular form of government within such narrow limits would be displayed by such reiterated oppressions of factious majorities that some power altogether independent of the people would soon be called for by the voice of the very factions whose misrule had proved the necessity of it. In the extended republic of the United States, and among the great variety of interests, parties, and sects which it embraces, a coalition of a majority of the whole society could seldom take place on any other principles than those of justice and the general good; whilst there being thus less danger to a minor from the will of a major party, there must be less pretext, also, to provide for the security of the former, by introducing into the government a will not dependent on the latter, or, in other words, a will independent of the society itself. It is no less certain than it is important, notwithstanding the contrary opinions which have been entertained, that the larger the society, provided it lie within a practicable sphere, the more duly capable it will be of self-government. And happily for the *republican cause,* the practicable sphere may be carried to a very great extent by a judicious modification and mixture of the *federal principle.*

PUBLIUS

Federalist No. 57 (Madison)

The *third* charge against the House of Representatives is that it will be taken from that class of citizens which will have least sympathy with the mass of the people, and be most likely to aim at an ambitious sacrifice of the many to the aggrandizement of the few.

Of all the objections which have been framed against the federal Constitution, this is perhaps the most extraordinary. Whilst the objection itself is leveled against a pretended oligarchy, the principle of it strikes at the very root of republican government.

The aim of every political constitution is, or ought to be, first to obtain for rulers men who possess most wisdom to discern, and most virtue to pursue, the common good of the society; and in the next place, to take the most effectual precautions for keeping them virtuous whilst they continue to hold their public trust. The elective mode of obtaining rulers is the characteristic policy of republican government. The means relied on in this form of government for preventing their degeneracy are numerous and various. The most effectual one is such a limitation of the term of appointments as will maintain a proper responsibility to the people. . . .

. . . [T]hose ties which bind the representative to his constituents are strengthened by motives of a more selfish nature. His pride and vanity attach him to a form of government which favors his pretensions and gives him a share in its honors and distinctions. Whatever hopes or projects might be entertained by a few aspiring characters, it must generally happen that a great proportion of the men deriving their advancement from their influence with the people would have more to hope from a preservation of the favor than from innovations in the government subversive of the authority of the people.

All these securities, however, would be found very insufficient without the restraint of frequent elections. Hence, in the fourth place, the House of Representatives is so constituted as to support in the members an habitual recollection of their dependence on the people. Before the sentiments impressed on their minds by the mode of their elevation can be effaced by the exercise of power, they will be compelled to anticipate the moment when their power is to cease, when their exercise of it is to be reviewed, and when they must descend to the level from which they were raised; there forever to remain unless a faithful discharge of their trust shall have established their title to a renewal of it.

I will add, as a fifth circumstance in the situation of the House of Representatives, restraining them from oppressive measures, that they can make no law which will not have its full operation on themselves and their friends, as well as on the great mass of the society. This has always been deemed one of the strongest bonds by which human policy can connect the rulers and the people together. It creates between them that communion of interests and sympathy of sentiments of which few governments have furnished examples; but without which every government degenerates into tyranny. If it be asked, what is to restrain the House of Representatives from making legal discriminations in favor of themselves and a particular class of the society? I answer: the genius of the whole system; the nature of just and constitutional laws; and, above all, the vigilant and manly spirit which actuates the people of America— a spirit which nourishes freedom, and in return is nourished by it.

If this spirit shall ever be so far debased as to tolerate a law not obligatory on the legislature, as well as on the people, the people will be prepared to tolerate anything but liberty. . . .

PUBLIUS

Federalist No. 62 (Madison)

Having examined the constitution of the House of Representatives, and answered such of the objections against it as seemed to merit notice, I enter next on the examination of the Senate. The heads into which this member of the government may be considered are: I. The qualifications of senators; II. The appointment of them by the State legislatures; III. The equality of representation in the Senate; IV. The number of senators, and the term for which they are to be elected; V. The powers vested in the Senate.

I. The qualifications proposed for senators, as distinguished from those of representatives, consist in a more advanced age and a longer period of citizenship. A senator must be thirty years of age at least; as a representative must be twenty-five. And the former must have been a citizen nine years; as seven years are required for the latter. The propriety of these distinctions is explained by the nature of the senatorial trust, which, requiring greater extent of information and stability of character, requires at the same time that the senator should have reached a period of life most likely to supply these advantages; and which, participating immediately in transactions with foreign nations, ought to be exercised by none who are not thoroughly weaned from the prepossessions and habits incident to foreign birth and education. The term of nine years appears to be a prudent mediocrity between a total exclusion of adopted citizens, whose merits and talents may claim a share in the public confidence, and an indiscriminate and hasty admission of them, which might create a channel for foreign influence on the national councils.

II. It is equally unnecessary to dilate on the appointment of senators by the State legislatures. Among the various modes which might have been devised for constituting this branch of the government, that which has been proposed by the convention is probably the most congenial with the public opinion. It is recommended by the double advantage of favoring a select appointment, and of giving to the State governments such an agency in the formation of the federal government as must secure the authority of the former, and may form a convenient link between the two systems.

III. The equality of representation in the Senate is another point which, being evidently the result of compromise between the opposite pretensions of the large and the small States, does not call for much discussion. If indeed it be right that among a people thoroughly incorporated into one nation every district ought to have a *proportional* share in the government and that among independent and sovereign States, bound together by a simple league, the parties, however unequal in size, ought to have an *equal* share in the common councils, it does not appear to be without some reason that in a compound republic, partaking both of the national and federal character, the government ought to be founded on a mixture of the principles of proportional and equal representation. But it is superfluous to try, by the standard of theory, a part of the Constitution which is allowed on all hands to be the result, not of theory, but "of a spirit of amity, and that mutual deference and concession which the peculiarity of our political situation rendered indispensable." A common government, with powers equal to its objects, is called for by the voice, and still more loudly by the political situation, of America. A government founded on principles more consonant to the wishes of the larger States is not likely to be obtained from the smaller States. The only option, then, for the former lies between the proposed government and a government still more objectionable. Under this alternative, the advice of prudence must be to embrace the lesser evil; and instead of indulging a fruitless anticipation of the possible mischiefs which may ensue, to contemplate rather the advantageous consequences which may qualify the sacrifice.

In this spirit it may be remarked that the equal vote allowed to each State is at once a constitutional recognition of the portion of sovereignty remaining in the individual States and an instrument for preserving that residuary sovereignty. So far the equality ought to be no less acceptable to the large than to the small States; since they are not less solicitous to guard, by every possible expedient, against an improper consolidation of the States into one simple republic.

Another advantage accruing from this ingredient in the constitution of the Senate is the additional impediment it must prove against improper acts of legislation. No law or resolution can now be passed without the concurrence, first, of a majority of the people, and then of a majority of the States. It must be acknowledged that this complicated check on legislation may in some instances be injurious as well as beneficial; and that the peculiar defense which it involves in favor of the smaller States would be more rational if any interests common to them and distinct from those of the other States would otherwise be exposed to peculiar danger. But as the larger States will always be able, by their power over the supplies, to defeat unreasonable exertions of this prerogative of the lesser States, and as the facility and excess of lawmaking seem to be the diseases to which our governments are most liable, it is not impossible that this part of the Constitution may be more convenient in practice than it appears to many in contemplation.

IV. The number of senators and the duration of their appointment come next to be considered. In order to form an accurate judgment on both these points it will be proper to inquire into the purposes which are to be answered by a senate; and in order to ascertain these it will be necessary to review the inconveniences which a republic must suffer from the want of such an institution.

First. It is a misfortune incident to republican government, though in a less degree than to other governments, that those who administer it may forget their obligations to their constituents and prove unfaithful to their important trust. In this point of view a senate, as a second branch of the legislative assembly distinct from and dividing the power with a first, must be in all cases a salutary check on the government. It doubles the security to the people by requiring the concurrence of two distinct bodies in schemes of usurpation or perfidy, where the ambition or corruption of one would otherwise be sufficient. This is a precaution founded on such clear principles, and now so well understood in the United States, that it would be more than superfluous to enlarge on it. I will barely remark that as the improbability of sinister combinations will be in proportion to the dissimilarity in the genius of the two bodies, it must be politic to distinguish them from each other by every circumstance which will consist with a due harmony in all proper measures, and with the genuine principles of republican government.

Second. The necessity of a senate is not less indicated by the propensity of all single and numerous assemblies to yield to the impulse of sudden and violent passions, and to be seduced by factious leaders into intemperate and pernicious resolutions. Examples on this subject might be cited without number; and from proceedings within the United States, as well as from the history of other nations. But a position that will not be contradicted need not be proved. All that need be remarked is that a body which is to correct this infirmity ought itself to be free from it, and consequently ought to be less numerous. It ought, moreover, to possess great firmness, and consequently ought to hold its authority by a tenure of considerable duration.

Third. Another defect to be supplied by a senate lies in a want of due acquaintance with the objects and principles of legislation. It is not possible that an assembly of men called for the most part from pursuits of a private nature continued in appointment for a short time and led by no permanent motive to devote the intervals of public occupation to a study of the laws, the affairs, and the comprehensive interests of their country, should, if left wholly to themselves, escape a variety of important errors in the exercise of their legislative trust. It may be affirmed, on the best grounds, that no small share of the present embarrassments of America is to be charged on the blunders of our governments; and that these have proceeded from the heads rather than the hearts of most of the authors of them. What indeed are all the repealing, explaining, and amending laws, which fill and disgrace our voluminous codes, but so many monuments of deficient wisdom; so many impeachments exhibited by each succeeding against each preceding session; so many admonitions to the people of the value of those aids which may be expected from a well-constituted senate?

A good government implies two things: first, fidelity to the object of government, which is the happiness of the people; secondly, a knowledge of the means by which that object can be best attained. Some governments are deficient in both these qualities; most governments are deficient in the first. I scruple not to assert that in American governments too little attention has been paid to the last. The federal Constitution avoids this error; and what merits particular notice, it provides for the last in a mode which increases the security for the first.

Fourth. The mutability in the public councils arising from a rapid succession of new members, however qualified they may be, points out, in the strongest manner, the necessity of some stable institution in the government. Every new election in the States is found to change one half of the representatives. From this change of men must proceed a change of opinions; and from a change of opinions, a change of measures. But a continual change even of good measures is inconsistent with every rule of prudence and every prospect of success. The remark is verified in private life, and becomes more just, as well as more important, in national transactions.

To trace the mischievous effects of a mutable government would fill a volume. I will hint a few only, each of which will be perceived to be a source of innumerable others.

In the first place, it forfeits the respect and confidence of other nations, and all the advantages connected with national character. An individual who is observed to be inconstant to his plans, or perhaps to carry on his affairs without any plan at all, is marked at once by all prudent people as a speedy victim to his own unsteadiness and folly. His more friendly neighbors may pity him, but all will decline to connect their fortunes with his; and not a few will seize the opportunity of making their fortunes out of his. . . .

The internal effects of a mutable policy are still more calamitous. It poisons the blessings of liberty itself. It will be of little avail to the people that the laws are made by men of their own choice if the laws be so voluminous that they cannot be read, or so incoherent that they cannot be understood; if they be repealed or revised before they are promulgated, or undergo such incessant changes that no man, who knows what the law is today, can guess what it will be tomorrow. Law is defined to be a rule of action; but how can that be a rule, which is little known, and less fixed?

Another effect of public instability is the unreasonable advantage it gives to the sagacious, the enterprising, and the moneyed few over the industrious and uniformed mass of the people. Every new regulation concerning commerce or revenue, or in any manner affecting the value of the different species of property, presents a new harvest to those who watch the change, and can trace its consequences; a harvest, reared not by themselves, but by the toils and cares of the great body of their fellow-citizens. This is a state of things in which it may be said with some truth that laws are made for the *few*, not for the *many*.

In another point of view, great injury results from an unstable government. The want of confidence in the public councils damps every useful undertaking, the success and profit of which may depend on a continuance of existing arrangements. What prudent merchant will hazard his fortunes in any new branch of commerce when he knows not but that his plans may be rendered unlawful before they can be executed? What farmer or manufacturer will lay himself out for the encouragement given to any particular cultivation or establishment, when he can have no assurance that his preparatory labors and advances will not render him a victim to an inconstant government? In a word, no great improvement or laudable enterprise can go forward which requires the auspices of a steady system of national policy.

But the most deplorable effect of all is that diminution of attachment and reverence which steals into the hearts of the people towards a political system which betrays so many marks of infirmity, and disappoints so many of their flattering hopes. No government, any more than an individual, will long be respected without being truly respectable; nor be truly respectable without possessing a certain portion of order and stability.

PUBLIUS

Federalist No. 70 (Hamilton)

There is an idea, which is not without its advocates, that a vigorous executive is inconsistent with the genius of republican government. The enlightened well-wishers to this species of government must at least hope that the supposition is destitute of foundation; since they can never admit its truth, without at the same time admitting the condemnation of their own principles. Energy in the executive is a leading character in the definition of good government. It is essential to the protection of the community against foreign attacks; it is not less essential to the steady administration of the laws; to the protection of property against those irregular and high-handed combinations which sometimes interrupt the ordinary course of justice; to the security of liberty against the enterprises and assaults of ambition, of faction, and of anarchy. Every man the least conversant in Roman history knows how often that republic was obliged to take refuge in the absolute power of a single man, under the formidable title of dictator, as well against the intrigues of ambitious individuals who aspired to the tyranny, and the seditions of whole classes of the community whose conduct threatened the existence of all government, as against the invasions of external enemies who menaced the conquest and destruction of Rome.

There can be no need, however, to multiply arguments or examples on this head. A feeble executive implies a feeble execution of the government. A feeble execution is but another phrase for a bad execution; and a government ill executed, whatever it may be in theory, must be, in practice, a bad government.

Taking it for granted, therefore, that all men of sense will agree in the necessity of an energetic executive, it will only remain to inquire, what are the ingredients which constitute this energy? How far can they be combined with those other ingredients which constitute safety in the republican sense? And how far does this combination characterize the plan which has been reported by the convention?

The ingredients which constitute energy in the executive are unity; duration; an adequate provision for its support; and competent powers.

The ingredients which constitute safety in the republican sense are a due dependence on the people, and a due responsibility.

Those politicians and statesmen who have been the most celebrated for the soundness of their principles and for the justness of their views have declared in favor of a single executive and a numerous legislature. They have, with great propriety, considered energy as the most necessary qualification of the former, and have regarded this as most applicable to power in a single hand; while they have, with equal propriety, considered the latter as best adapted to deliberation and wisdom, and best calculated to conciliate the confidence of the people and to secure their privileges and interests. . . .

This unity may be destroyed in two ways: either by vesting the power in two or more magistrates of equal dignity and authority, or by vesting it ostensibly in one man, subject in whole or in part to the control and cooperation of others, in the capacity of counselors to him. Of the first, the two consuls of Rome may serve as an example; of the last, we shall find examples in the constitutions of several of the States. New York and New Jersey, if I recollect right, are the only States which have intrusted the executive authority wholly to single men.* Both these methods of destroying the unity of the executive have their partisans; but the votaries of an executive council are the most numerous. They are both liable, if not to equal, to similar objections, and may in most lights be examined in conjunctions.

The experience of other nations will afford little instruction on this head. As far, however, as it teaches anything, it teaches us not to be enamored of plurality in the executive. We have seen that the Archaeans; on an experiment of two Praetors, were induced to abolish one. The Roman history records many instances of mischiefs to the republic from the dissensions between the consuls, and between the military tribunes, who were at times substituted for the consuls. . . .

But quitting the dim light of historical research, and attaching ourselves purely to the dictates of reason and good sense, we shall discover much greater cause to approve the idea of plurality in the executive, under any modification whatever.

Whenever two or more persons are engaged in any common enterprise or pursuit, there is always danger of difference of opinion. If it be a public trust or office in which they are clothed with equal dignity and authority, there is peculiar danger of personal emulation and even animosity. From either, and especially from all these causes, the most bitter dissensions are apt to spring. Whenever these happen, they lessen the respectability, weaken the authority, and distract the plans and operations of those whom they divide. . . . And what is still worse, they might split the community into the most violent and irreconcilable factions, adhering differently to the different individuals who composed the magistracy. . . .

In the legislature, promptitude of decision is oftener an evil than a benefit. The differences of opinion, and the jarring of parties. in that department of the government, though they may sometimes obstruct salutary plans, yet often promote deliberation and circumspection, and serve to check excesses in the majority. When a resolution too is once taken, the opposition must be at an end. That resolution is a law, and resistance to it punishable. But no favorable circumstances palliate or atone for the disadvantages of dissension in the executive department. Here they are pure and unmixed. There is no point at which they cease to operate. They serve to embarrass and weaken the execution of the plan or measure to which they relate, from the first step to the final conclusion of it. They constantly counteract those qualities in the executive which are the most necessary ingredients in its composition—vigor and expedition, and this without any counterbalancing good. In the conduct of war, in which the energy of the executive is the bulwark of the national security, everything would be to be apprehended from its plurality. . . .

In England, the king is a perpetual magistrate; and it is a maxim which has obtained for the sake of the public peace that he is unaccountable for his administration, and his person sacred. Nothing, therefore, can be wiser in that kingdom than to annex to the king a constitutional council, who may be responsible to the nation for the advice they give. Without this, there would be no responsibility whatever in the executive department— an idea inadmissible in a free government. But even there the king is not bound by the resolutions of his council, though they are answerable for the advice they give. He is the absolute master of his own conduct in the exercise of his office and may observe or disre-

---

* New York has no council except for the single purpose of appointing to offices; New Jersey has a council whom the governor may consult. But I think, from the terms of the Constitution, their resolutions do not bind him.

gard the counsel given to him at his sole discretion.

But in a republic where every magistrate ought to be personally responsible for his behavior in office, the reason which in the British Constitution dictates the propriety of a council not only ceases to apply, but turns against the institution. In the monarchy of Great Britain, it furnishes a substitute for the prohibited responsibility of the Chief Magistrate, which serves in some degree as a hostage to the national justice for his good behavior. In the American republic, it would serve to destroy, or would greatly diminish, the intended and necessary responsibility of the Chief Magistrate himself.

The idea of a council to the executive, which has so generally obtained in the State constitutions, has been derived from that maxim of republican jealousy which considers power as safer in the hands of a number of men than of a single man. If the maxim should be admitted to be applicable to the case, I should con-

tend that the advantage on that side would not counterbalance the numerous disadvantages on the opposite side. But I do not think the rule at all applicable to the executive power. I clearly concur in opinion, in this particular, with a writer whom the celebrated Junius pronounces to be "deep, solid, and ingenious," that "the executive power is more easily confined when it is one"; that it is far more safe there should be a single object for the jealousy and watchfulness of the people; and, in a word, that all multiplication of the executive is rather dangerous than friendly to liberty. . . .

I will only add that, prior to the appearance of the Constitution, I rarely met with an intelligent man from any of the States who did not admit, as the result of experience, that the UNITY of the executive of this State was one of the best of the distinguishing features of our Constitution.

PUBLIUS

Alexander Hamilton, 1755–1804

The bastard son of a West Indian-Scottish merchant of very limited means, Alexander Hamilton carries the ironic reputation as the Founding Father least sympathetic to equality and popular government.

Hamilton came to New York in 1773 from the West Indies to attend Kings College. He soon joined the movement to resist British rule by writing a series of pamphlets criticizing Samuel Seabury. He joined the army in 1778 and was Washington's aide-de-camp and a combat officer.

Hamilton became a severe critic of the Articles of Confederation and attended the Annapolis Convention of 1786, and a year later, the Constitutional Convention in Philadelphia. However, he did not assume a leading role until he collaborated in writing *The Federalist Papers* and fought for ratification in New York.

After the Constitution was approved, Hamilton served as secretary of the treasury in George Washington's administration and was largely responsible for establishing a sound currency and the controversial national bank.

In both his writings and actions, Hamilton favored a strong central government, forceful executive leadership, and an active role for government in promoting economic growth through tariffs, credit, and internal improvements.

The following passages are taken from his *Report on Manufactures*, a series of proposals quite at odds with the decentralized, agrarian republic of Jefferson and many Antifederalists.

Alexander Hamilton

Report on Manufactures (1791)

. . . The expediency of encouraging manufactures in the United States, which was not long since deemed very questionable, appears at this time to be pretty generally admitted. The embarrassments which have obstructed the progress of our external trade, have led to serious reflections on the necessity of enlarging the sphere of our domestic commerce. The restrictive regulations, which, in foreign markets, abridge the vent of the increasing surplus of our agricultural produce, serve to beget an earnest desire that a more extensive demand for that surplus may be created at home; and the complete success which has rewarded manufacturing enterprise in some valuable branches, conspiring with the promising symptoms which attend some less mature essays in others, justify a hope that the obstacles to the growth of this species of industry are less formidable than they were apprehended to be, and that it is not difficult to find, in its further extension, a full indemnification for any external disadvantages, which are or may be experienced, as well as an accession of resources, favorable to national independence and safety.

There are still, nevertheless, respectable pa-

SOURCE: Henry Cabot Lodge, ed., *The Works of Alexander Hamilton* (New York: G. Putnam's Sons, 1904).

trons of opinions unfriendly to the encouragement of manufactures. The following are, substantially, the arguments by which these opinions are defended:

"In every country (say those who entertain them) agriculture is the most beneficial and productive object of human industry. This position, generally if not universally true, applies with peculiar emphasis to the United States, on account of their immense tracts of fertile territory, uninhabited and unimproved. Nothing can afford so advantageous an employment for capital and labor, as the conversion of this extensive wilderness into cultivated farms. Nothing, equally with this, can contribute to the population, strength, and real riches of the country.

"To endeavor, by the extraordinary patronage of government, to accelerate the growth of manufactures, is, in fact, to endeavor, by force and art, to transfer the natural current of industry from a more to a less beneficial channel. Whatever has such a tendency, must necessarily be unwise; indeed, it can hardly ever be wise in a government to attempt to give a direction to the industry of its citizens. This, under the quick-sighted guidance of private interest, will, if left to itself, infallibly find its own way to the most profitable employment; and it is by such employment, that the public prosperity will be most effectually promoted. To leave industry to itself, therefore, is, in almost every case, the soundest as well as the simplest policy.

"This policy is not only recommended to the United States, by considerations which affect all nations; it is, in a manner, dictated to them by the imperious force of a very peculiar situation. The smallness of their population compared with their territory; the constant allurements to emigration from the settled to the unsettled parts of the country; the facility with which the less independent condition of an artisan can be exchanged for the more independent condition of a farmer;—these, and similar causes, conspire to produce, and, for a length of time, must continue to occasion, a scarcity of hands for manufacturing occupation, and dearness of labor generally. To these disadvantages for the prosecution of manufactures, a deficiency of pecuniary capital being added, the prospect of a successful competition with the manufactures of Europe, must be regarded as little less than desperate. Extensive manufactures can only be the offspring of a redundant, at least of a full, population. Till the latter shall characterize the situation of this country, 'tis vain to hope for the former.

"If, contrary to the natural course of things, an unseasonable and premature spring can be given to certain fabrics, by heavy duties, prohibitions, bounties, or by other forced expedients, this will only be to sacrifice the interests of the community to those of particular classes. Besides the misdirection of labor, a virtual monopoly will be given to the persons employed on such fabrics; and an enhancement of price, the inevitable consequence of every monopoly, must be defrayed at the expense of the other parts of society. It is far preferable, that those persons should be engaged in the cultivation of the earth, and that we should procure, in exchange for its productions, the commodities with which foreigners are able to supply us in greater perfection and upon better terms."

This mode of reasoning is founded upon facts and principles which have certainly respectable pretensions. If it had governed the conduct of nations more generally than it has done, there is room to suppose that it might have carried them faster to prosperity and greatness than they have attained by the pursuit of maxims too widely opposite. Most general theories, however, admit of numerous exceptions, and there are few, if any, of the political kind, which do not blend a considerable portion of error with the truths they inculcate.

I. In order to make an accurate judgment how far that which has been just stated ought to be deemed liable to a similar imputation, it is necessary to advert carefully to the considerations which plead in favor of manufactures, and which appear to recommend the special and positive encouragement of them in certain cases and under certain reasonable limitations.

It ought readily be conceded that the cultivation of the earth, as the primary and most certain source of national supply, as the immediate and chief source of subsistence to a man, as the principal source of those materials which constitute the nutriment of other kinds of labor, as including a state most favorable to the freedom and independence of the human mind—one, perhaps, most conducive to the multiplication of the human species, has intrinsically a strong claim to pre-eminence over every other kind of industry.

But, that it has a title to any thing like an exclusive predilection, in any country, ought to be admitted with great caution; that it is even more productive than every other branch of industry, requires more evidence than has yet been given in support of the position. That its real interests, precious and important as, without the help of exaggeration, they truly are, will be advanced, rather than injured, by the due encouragement of manufactures, may, it is believed, be satisfactorily demonstrated. And it is also believed that the expediency of such encouragement, in a general view, may be shown to be recommended by the most cogent and persuasive motives of national policy.

It has been maintained that agriculture is not only the most productive, but the only productive, species of industry. The reality of this suggestion in either respect, has, however, not been verified by any accurate detail of facts and calculations; and the general arguments which are adduced to prove it, are rather subtile and paradoxical, than solid or convincing.

Those which maintain its exclusive productiveness are to this effect:

Labor bestowed upon the cultivation of land produces enough not only to replace all the necessary expenses incurred in the business, and to maintain the persons who are employed in it, but to afford, together with the ordinary profit on the stock or capital of the farmer, a net surplus or rent for the landlord or proprietor of the soil. But the labor of artificers does nothing more than to replace the stock which employs them (or which furnishes materials, tools, and wages), and yields the ordinary profit upon that stock. It yields nothing equivalent to the rent of land: neither does it add anything to the total value of the whole annual produce of the land and labor of the country. The additional value given to those parts of the produce of land which are wrought into manufactures, is counterbalanced by the value of those other parts of that produce which are consumed by the manufactures. It can, therefore, only be by saving or parsimony, not by the positive productiveness of their labor, that the classes of artificers can, in any degree, augment the revenue of the society.

To this it has been answered:

1. "That, inasmuch as it is acknowledged that manufacturing labor re-produces a value equal to that which is expended or consumed in carrying it on, and continues in existence the original stock or capital employed, it ought, on that account, alone, to escape being considered as wholly unproductive. That, though it should be admitted, as alleged, that the consumption of the produce of the soil, by the classes of artificers or manufacturers, is exactly equal to the value added by their labor to the materials upon which it is exerted, yet it would not thence follow that it added nothing to the revenue of the society, or to the aggregate value of the annual produce of its land and labor. If the consumption, for any given period, amounted to a given sum, and the increased value of the produce manufactured, in the same period, to a like sum, the total amount of the consumption and production, during that period, would be equal to the two sums, and consequently double the value of the agricultural produce consumed; and though the increment of value produced by the classes of artificers should, at no time, exceed the value of the produce of the land consumed by them, yet there would be, at every moment, in consequence of their labor, a greater value of goods in the market than would exist independent of it."

2. "That the position, that artificers can augment the revenue of a society only by parsimony, is true in no other sense than in one which is equally applicable to husbandmen or cultivators. It may be alike affirmed of all these classes, that the fund acquired by their labor, and destined for their support, is not, in an ordinary way, more than equal to it. And hence it will follow that augmentations of the wealth or capital of the community (except in the instances of some extraordinary dexterity or skill) can only proceed, with respect to any of them, from the savings of the more thrifty and parsimonious."

3. "That the annual produce of the land and labor of a country can only be increased in two ways—by some improvement in the productive powers of the useful labor which actually exists within it, or by some increase in the quantity of such labor. That, with regard to the first, the labor of artificers being capable of greater subdivision and simplicity of operation than that of cultivators, it is susceptible, in a proportionable greater degree of improvement in its productive powers whether to be derived from an accession of skill or from the application of ingenious machinery, in which particular, therefore, the labor employed in the culture of land can pretend to no advantage over that engaged in manufactures. That, with regard to an augmentation of the quantity of useful labor, this, excluding adventitious circumstances, must depend essentially upon an increase of capital, which again must depend upon the savings made out of the revenues of those who furnish or manage that which is at any time employed, whether in agriculture or in manufactures, or in any other way."

But while the exclusive productiveness of agricultural labor has been denied and refuted, the superiority of its productiveness has been conceded without hesitation. As this concession involves a point of considerable magnitude, in relation to maxims of public administration, the grounds on which it rests are worthy of a distinct and particular examination.

One of the arguments made use of in support of the idea may be pronounced both quaint and superficial. It amounts to this: That in the productions of the soil, nature cooperates with man, and that the effect of their joint labor must be greater than that of the labor of man alone.

This, however, is far from being a necessary inference. It is very conceivable that the labor of man alone, laid out upon a work requiring great skill and art to bring it to perfection, may be more productive, in value, than the labor of nature and man combined, when directed towards more simple operations and objects; and when it is recollected to what an extent the agency of nature, in the application of the mechanical powers, is made auxiliary to the prosecution of manufactures, the suggestion which has been noticed loses even the appearance of plausibility.

It might also be observed, with a contrary view, that the labor employed in agriculture is, in a great measure, periodical and occasional, depending on seasons, and liable to various and long intermissions; while that occupied in many manufactures is constant and regular, extending through the year, embracing, in some instances, night as well as day. It is also probable that there are, among the cultivators of land, more examples of remissness than among artificers. The farmer, from the peculiar fertility of his land, or some other favorable circumstance, may frequently obtain a livelihood, even with a considerable degree of carelessness in the mode of cultivation; but the artisan can with difficulty effect the same object, without exerting himself pretty equally with all those who are engaged in the same pursuit. And if it may likewise be assumed as a fact, that manufactures open a wider field to exertions of ingenuity than agriculture, it would not be a strained conjecture, that the labor employed in the former, being at once more constant, more uniform, and more ingenious, than that which is employed in the latter, will be found, at the same time, more productive.

But it is not meant to lay stress on observations of this nature; they ought only to serve as a counterbalance to those of a similar complexion. Circumstances so vague and general, as well as so abstract, can afford little instruction in a matter of this kind.

Another, and that which seems to be the principal argument offered for the superior productiveness of agricultural labor, turns upon the allegation, that labor employed on manufactures yields nothing equivalent to the rent of land, or to that net surplus, as it is called, which accrues to the proprietor of the soil.

But this distinction, important as it has been deemed, appears rather verbal than substantial.

It is easily discernable, that what, in the first instance, is divided into two parts, under the denominations of the ordinary profit of the stock of the farmer and rent to the landlord, is, in the second instance united under the general appellation of the ordinary profit on the stock of the undertaker; and that this formal or verbal distribution constitutes the whole difference in the two cases. It seems to have been overlooked, that the land is itself a stock or capital, advanced or lent by its owner to the occupier or tenant, and that the rent he receives is only the ordinary profit of a certain stock in land, not managed by the proprietor himself, but by another, to whom he lends or lets it, and who, on his part, advances a second capital, to stock and improve the land, upon which he also receives the usual profit. The rent of the landlord and the profit of the farmer are, therefore, nothing more than the ordinary profits of two capitals belonging to two different persons, and united in the cultivation of a farm; as, in the other case, the surplus which arises upon any manufactory, after replacing the expenses of carrying it on, answers to the ordinary profits of one or more capitals engaged in the prosecution of such manufactory. It is said one or more capitals, because, in fact, the same thing which is contemplated in the case of the farm, sometimes happens in that of a manufactory. There is one who furnishes a part of the capital or lends a part of the money by which it is carried on, and another who carries it on with the addition of his own capital. Out of the surplus which remains after defraying expenses, an interest is paid to the moneylender, for the portion of the capital furnished by him, which exactly agrees with the rent paid to the landlord; and the residue of that surplus constitutes the profit of the undertaker or manufacturer, and agrees with what is denom-

inated the ordinary profits on the stock of the farmer. Both together make the ordinary profits of two capitals employed in a manufactory; as, in the other case, the rent of the landlord and the revenue of the farmer compose the ordinary profits of two capitals employed in the cultivation of a farm.

The rent, therefore, accruing to the proprietor of the land, far from being a criterion of exclusive productiveness, as has been argued, is no criterion even of superior productiveness. The question must still be, whether the surplus, after defraying expenses, of a given capital, employed in the purchase and improvement of a piece of land, is greater or less than that of a like capital, employed in the prosecution of a manufactory; or whether the whole value produced from a given capital and a given quantity of labor, employed in one way, be greater or less than the whole value produced from an equal capital and an equal quantity of labor, employed in the other way; or rather, perhaps, whether the business of agriculture, or that of manufactures, will yield the greater product, according to a compound ratio of the quantity of the capital and the quantity of labor which are employed in the one or in the other.

The solution of either of these questions is not easy; it involves numerous and complicated details, depending on an accurate knowledge of the objects to be compared. It is not known that the comparison has ever yet been made upon sufficient data, properly ascertained and analyzed. To be able to make it, on the present occasion, with satisfactory precision, would demand more previous inquiry and investigation than there has been hitherto either leisure or opportunity to accomplish.

Some essays, however, have been made towards acquiring the requisite information, which have rather served to throw doubt upon, than to confirm, the hypothesis under examination. But it ought to be acknowledged that they have been too little diversified, and are too imperfect to authorize a definite conclusion either way; leading rather to probable conjecture than to certain deduction. They render it probable that there are various branches of manufactures, in which a given capital will yield a greater total product, and a considerably greater net product, than an equal capital invested in the purchase and improvement of lands; and that there are also some branches, in which both the gross and the net product will exceed that of the agricultural industry, according to a compound ratio of capital and labor. But it is on this last point that there appears to be the greatest room for doubt. It is far less difficult to infer generally, that the net produce of capital engaged in manufacturing enterprises is greater than that of capital engaged in agriculture.

The foregoing suggestions are not designed to inculcate an opinion that manufacturing industry is more productive than that of agriculture. They are intended rather to show that the reverse of this proposition is not ascertained; that the general arguments which are brought to establish it are not satisfactory; and, consequently, that a supposition of the superior productiveness of tillage ought to be no obstacle to listening to any substantial inducements to the encouragement of manufactures, which may be otherwise perceived to exist, through an apprehension that they may have a tendency to divert labor from a more to a less profitable employment.

It is extremely probable that, on a full and accurate development of the matter, on the ground of fact and calculation, it would be discovered that there is no material difference between the aggregate productiveness of the one and of the other kind of industry; and that the propriety of the encouragements which may, in any case, be proposed to be given to either, ought to be determined upon considerations irrelative to any comparison of that nature.

II. . . . To affirm that the labor of the manufacturer is unproductive, because he consumes as much of the produce of land as he adds value to the raw material which he manufactures, is not better founded than it would be to affirm that the labor of the farmer, which furnishes materials to the manufacturer, is unproductive, because he consumes an equal value of manufactured articles. Each furnishes a certain portion of the produce of his labor to the other, and each destroys a corresponding portion of the produce of the labor of the other. In the meantime, the maintenance of two citizens, instead of one, is going on; the State has two members instead of one; and they, together, consume twice the value of what is produced from the land.

If, instead of a farmer and artificer, there were a farmer only, he would be under the necessity of devoting a part of his labor to the fabrication of clothing and other articles, which he would procure of the artificer, in the case of there being such a person; and of course he would be able to devote less labor to the cultivation of his farm, and would draw from it a proportionately less product. The whole quantity of production, in this state of things, in provisions, raw materials, and manufactures, would certainly not exceed in value the amount of what would be produced in provisions and raw materials only, if there were an artificer as well as a farmer.

Again, if there were both an artificer and a farmer, the latter would be left at liberty to pursue exclusively the cultivation of his farm. A greater quantity of provisions and raw materials would, of course, be produced, equal, at least, as has been already observed, to the whole amount of the provisions, raw materials, and manufactures, which would exist on a contrary supposition. The artificer, at the same time, would be going on in the production of manufactured commodities, to an amount sufficient, not only to repay the farmer, in those commodities, for the provisions and materials which were procured from him, but to furnish the artificer himself with a supply of similar commodities for his own use. Thus, then, there would be two quantities or values in existence, instead of one; and the revenue and consumption would be double, in one case, what it would be in the other.

If, in place of both of these suppositions, there were supposed to be two farmers and no artificer, each of whom applied a part of his labor to the culture of land and another part to the fabrication of manufactures; in this case, the portion of the labor of both, bestowed upon land, would produce the same quantity of provisions and raw materials only, as would be produced by the entire sum of the labor of one, applied in the same manner; and the portion of the labor of both, bestowed upon manufacturers, would produce the same quantity of manufactures only, as would be produced by the entire sum of the labor of one, applied in the same manner. Hence, the produce of the labor of the two farmers would not be greater than the produce of the labor of the farmer and artificer; and hence it results, that the labor of the artificer is as positively productive as that of the farmer, and as positively augments the revenue of the society.

The labor of the artificer replaces to the farmer that portion of his labor with which he provides the materials of exchange with the artificer, and which he would otherwise have been compelled to apply to manufactures; and while the artificer thus enables the farmer to enlarge his stock of agricultural industry, a portion of which he purchases for his own use, he also supplies himself with the manufactured articles of which he stands in need. He does still more. Besides this equivalent, which he gives for the portion of agricultural labor consumed by him, and this supply of manufactured commodities for his own consumption, he furnishes still a surplus which compensates for the use of the capital advanced, either by himself or some other person, for carrying on the business. This is the ordinary profit of the stock employed in the manufactory, and is, in every sense, as effective an addition to the income of the society as the rent of land.

The produce of the labor of the artificer, consequently, may be regarded as composed of three parts: one, by which the provisions for his subsistence and the materials for his work are purchased of the farmer; one, by which he supplies himself with manufactured necessaries; and a third, which constitutes the profit on the stock employed. The two last portions seem to have been overlooked in the system which represents manufacturing industry as barren and unproductive.

In the course of the preceding illustrations, the products of equal quantities of the labor of the farmer and artificer have been treated as if equal to each other. But this is not to be understood as intending to assert any such precise equality. It is merely a manner of expression, adopted for the sake of simplicity and perspicuity. Whether the value of the produce of the labor of the farmer be somewhat more or less than that of the artificer, is not material to the main scope of the argument, which hitherto, has only aimed at showing that the one, as well as the other, occasions a positive argumentation of the total produce and revenue of the society. . . .

Voices of Dissent

Jefferson's Letter to Madison, 1787

In the following letter, Jefferson writes Madison of his support for the Constitution but also notes his objections. He reiterates his ideal of America as an agrarian republic rather at odds with the picture of a plural, extended, commercial republic painted by the authors of *The Federalist Papers*.

Thomas Jefferson

Letter to James Madison (1787)

DEAR SIR,—. . . I like much the general idea of framing a government, which should go on of itself, peaceably, without needing continual recurrence to the State legislatures. I like the organization of the government into legislative, judiciary and executive. I like the power given the legislature to levy taxes, and for that reason solely, I approve of the greater House being chosen by the people directly. For though I think a House so chosen, will be very far inferior to the present Congress, will be very illy qualified to legislate for the Union, for foreign nations, etc., yet this evil does not weigh against the good, of preserving inviolate the fundamental principle, that the people are not to be taxed but by representatives chosen immediately by themselves. I am captivated by the compromise of the opposite

SOURCE: Andrew A. Lipscomb, ed., *The Writings of Thomas Jefferson* (Washington, D.C.: Thomas Jefferson Association, 1903).

claims of the great and little States, of the latter to equal, and the former to proportional influence. I am much pleased, too, with the substitution of the method of voting by person, instead of that of voting by States; and I like the negative given to the Executive, conjointly with a third of either House; though I should have liked it better, had the judiciary been associated for that purpose or invested separately with a similar power. There are other good things of less moment. I will now tell you what I do not like. First, the omission of a bill of rights, providing clearly, and without the aid of sophism, for freedom of religion, freedom of the press, protection against standing armies, restriction of monopolies, the eternal and unremitting force of the habeas corpus laws, and trials by jury in all matters of fact triable by the laws of the land, and not by the laws of nations. To say, as Mr. Wilson does, that a bill of rights was not necessary, because all is reserved in the case of the general government which is not given, while in the particular ones, all is given which is not reserved, might do for the audience to which it was addressed; but it is surely a *gratis dictum,* the reverse of which might just as well be said; and it is opposed by strong inferences from the body of the instrument, as well as from the omission of the cause of our present Confederation, which had made the reservation in express terms. It was hard to conclude, because there has been a want of uniformity among the States as to the cases triable by jury, because some have been so incautious as to dispense with this mode of trial in certain cases, therefore, the more prudent States shall be reduced to the same level of calamity. It would have been more just and wise to have concluded the other way, that as most of the States had preserved with jealousy this sacred palladium of liberty, those who had wandered, should be brought back to it; and to have established general right rather than general wrong. For I consider all the ill as established, which may be established.

I have a right to nothing, which another has a right to take away; and Congress will have a right to take away trials by jury in all civil cases. Let me add, that a bill of rights is what the people are entitled to against every government on earth, general or particular; and what no just government should refuse, or rest on inference.

The second feature I dislike, and strongly dislike, is the abandonment, in every instance, of the principle of rotation in office, and most particularly in the case of the President. Reason and experience tell us, that the first magistrate will always be re-elected if he may be re-elected. He is then an officer for life. This once observed, it becomes of so much consequence to certain nations, to have a friend or a foe at the head of our affairs, that they will interfere with money and with arms. A Galloman, or an Angloman, will be supported by the nation he befriends. If once elected, and at a second or third election outvoted by one or two votes, he will pretend false votes, foul play, hold possession of the reins of government, be supported by the States voting for him, especially if they be the central ones, lying in a compact body themselves and separating their opponents; and they will be aided by one nation in Europe, while the majority are aided by another. . . .

. . . No foreign power, nor domestic party, will waste their blood and money to elect a person, who must go out at the end of a short period. The power of removing every fourth year by the vote of the people, is a power which they will not exercise, and if they were disposed to exercise it, they would not be permitted. . . .

I own, I am not a friend to a very energetic government. It is always oppressive. It places the governors indeed more at their ease, at the expense of the people. The late rebellion in Massachusetts has given more alarm, than I think it should have done. Calculate that one rebellion in thirteen States in the course of eleven years, is but one for each State in a century and a half. No country should be so long without one. Nor will any degree of power in the hands of government, prevent insurrections. In England, where the hand of power is heavier than with us, there are seldom half a dozen years without an insurrection. In France, where it is still heavier, but less despotic, as Montesquieu supposes, than in some other countries, and where there are always two or three hundred thousand men ready to crush insurrections, there have been three in the course of the three years I have been here, in every one of which greater numbers were engaged than in Massachusetts, and a great deal more blood was spilt. In Turkey, where the sole nod of the despot is death, insurrections are the events of every day. Compare again the ferocious depredations of their insurgents, with the order, the moderation and the almost self-extinguishment of ours. And say, finally, whether peace is best preserved by giving energy to the government, or information to the people. This last is the most certain, and the most legitimate engine of government. Educate and inform the whole mass of the people. Enable them to see that it is their interest to preserve peace and order, and they will preserve them. And it requires no very high degree of education to convince them of this. They are the only sure reliance for the preservation of our liberty. After all, it is my principle that the will of the majority should prevail. If they approve the proposed constitution in all its parts I shall concur in it cheerfully, in hopes they will amend it, whenever they shall find it works wrong. This reliance cannot deceive us, as long as we remain virtuous; and I think we shall be so, as long as agriculture is our principal object, which will be the case, while there remains vacant lands in any part of America. When we get piled upon one another in large cities, as in Europe, we shall become corrupt as in Europe, and go to eating one another as they do there. I have tired you by this time with disquisitions which you have already heard repeated by others a thousand and a thousand times; and therefore, shall only add assurances of the esteem and attachment with which I have the honor to be, dear Sir, your affectionate friend and servant.

The Antifederalists

There is no collection of Antifederalist papers that sums up the position of opponents of the federal Constitution. While hundreds of essays and pamphlets appeared throughout the United States urging the defeat of the Constitution, they did not share a single political perspective. These "men of little faith," as historian Cecelia Kenyon called them, disagreed as much among themselves as they did with their Federalist opponents.

Nevertheless, recurrent themes emerge from Antifederalist writings focusing on the fear of a powerful national government that might destroy the liberty of both individuals and states. Antifederalists noted the potential strength of the executive and courts, the absence of a bill of rights, the possibility of regional domination, and the unrepresentative nature of politics in large congressional districts. Often, Antifederalists favored a brand of republicanism that emphasized local government and citizen participation, and abhorred the extending of "the sphere" that Madison had deemed so necessary in Federalist No. 10.

Excerpts from three Antifederalist writers appear below. The first offering is taken from two "Letters of Agrippa," probably the work of James Winthrop, which appeared in the *Massachusetts Gazette*. "Agrippa's" letters are a good example of the local sentiments of many Antifederalists. The second, Samuel Bryan of Pennsylvania's "Letter of Centinel" No. 1, was one of a series of essays he wrote for the *Independent Gazeteer* of Philadelphia in 1787 and 1788. His target was John Adams's *Defense of the Constitutions*. The final tract is Robert Yates' "Letters of Brutus," No. 11, published in the *New York Journal*, and an excellent example of Antifederalist distrust of the judiciary.

James Winthrop

The Letters of Agrippa, No. 4 (1787)

TO THE PEOPLE

Having considered some of the principal advantages of the happy form of government under which it is our peculiar good fortune to live, we find by experience, that it is the best calculated of any form hitherto invented, to secure to us the rights of our persons and of our property, and that the general circumstances of the people shew an advanced state of improvement never before known. We have found the shock given by the war, in a great measure obliterated, and the public debt contracted at that time to be considerably reduced in the nominal sum. The Congress lands are full adequate to the redemption of the principal of their debt, and are selling and populating very fast. The lands of this state, at the west, are, at the moderate price of eighteen pence an acre, worth near half a million pounds in our money. They ought, therefore, to be sold as quick as possible. An application was made lately for a large tract at that price,

and continual applications are made for other lands in the eastern part of the state. Our resources are daily augmenting.

We find, then, that after the experience of near two centuries our separate governments are in full vigor. They discover, for all the purposes of internal regulation, every symptom of strength, and none of decay. The new system is, therefore, for such purposes, useless and burdensome.

Let us now consider how far it is practicable consistent with the happiness of the people and their freedom. It is the opinion of the ablest writers on the subject, that no extensive empire can be governed upon republican principles, and that such a government will degenerate to a despotism, unless it be made up of a confederacy of smaller states, each having the full powers of internal regulation. This is precisely the principle which has hitherto preserved our freedom. No instance can be found of any free government of considerable extent which has been supported upon any other plan. Large and consolidated empires may indeed dazzle the eyes of a distant spectator with their splendour, but if examined more nearly are always found to be full

SOURCE: Paul Leicester Ford, ed., *Essays on the Constitution of the United States* (New York: Burt Franklin, 1892, reprinted 1970).

of misery. The reason is obvious. In large states the same principles of legislation will not apply to all the parts. The inhabitants of warmer climates are more dissolute in their manners, and less industrious, than in colder countries. A degree of severity is, therefore, necessary with one which would cramp the spirit of the other. We accordingly find that the very great empires have always been despotick. They have indeed tried to remedy the inconveniences to which the people were exposed by local regulations; but these contrivances have never answered the end. The laws not being made by the people, who felt the inconveniences, did not suit their circumstances. It is under such tyranny that the Spanish provinces languish, and such would be our misfortune and degradation, if we should submit to have the concerns of the whole empire managed by one legislature. To promote the happiness of the people it is necessary that there should be local laws; and it is necessary that those laws should be made by the representatives of those who are immediately subject to the want of them. By endeavouring to suit both extremes, both are injured.

It is impossible for one code of laws to suit Georgia and Massachusetts. They must, therefore, legislate for themselves. Yet there is, I believe, not one point of legislation that is not surrendered in the proposed plan. Questions of every kind respecting property are determinable in a continental court, and so are all kinds of criminal causes. The continental legislature has, therefore, a right to make rules in all cases by which their judicial courts shall proceed and decide causes. No rights are reserved to the citizens. The laws of Congress are in all cases to be the supreme law of the land, and paramount to the constitutions of the individual states. The Congress may institute what modes of trial they please, and no plea drawn from the constitution of any state can avail. This new system is, therefore, a consolidation of all the states into one large mass, however diverse the parts may be of which it is to be composed. The idea of an uncompounded republick, on an average one thousand miles in length, and eight hundred in breadth, and containing six millions of white inhabitants all reduced to the same standard of morals, of habits, and of laws, is in itself an absurdity, and contrary to the whole experience of mankind. The attempt made by Great Britain to introduce such a system, struck us with horrour, and when it was proposed by some theorist that we should be represented in parliament, we uniformly declared that one legislature could not represent so many different interests for the purposes of legislation and taxation. This was the leading principle of the revolution, and makes an essential article in our creed. All that part, therefore, of the new system, which relates to the internal government of the states, ought at once to be rejected.

James Winthrop

The Letters of Agrippa, No. 13 (1787)

TO THE MASSACHUSETTS CONVENTION

Gentlemen,

. . . By sect. 8 of article 1, Congress are to have the unlimited right to regulate commerce, external and *internal,* and may therefore create monopolies which have been universally injurious to all the subjects of the countries that have adopted them, excepting the monopolists themselves. They have also the unlimited right to imposts and all kinds of taxes, as well to levy as to collect them. They have indeed very nearly the same powers claimed formerly by the British parliament. Can we have so soon forgot our glorious struggle with that power, as to think a moment of surrendering it now? It makes no difference in principle whether the national assembly was elected for seven years or for six. In both cases we should vote to great disadvantage, and therefore ought never to agree to such an article. Let us make provision for the payment of the interest of our part of the debt,

and we shall be fairly acquitted. Let the fund be an impost on our foreign trade, and we shall encourage our manufactures. But if we surrender the unlimited right to regulate trade, and levy taxes, imposts will oppress our foreign trade for the benefit of other states, while excises and taxes will discourage our internal industry. The right to regulate trade, without any limitations, will, as certainly as it is granted, transfer the trade of this state to Pennsylvania. That will be the seat of business and of wealth, while the extremes of the empire will, like Ireland and Scotland, be drained to fatten an overgrown capital. Under our present equal advantages, the citizens of this state come in for their full share of commercial profits. Surrender the rights of taxation and commercial regulation, and the landed states at the southward will all be interested in draining our resources; for whatever can be got by impost on our trade and excises on our manufactures, will be considered as so much saved to a state inhabited by planters. All savings of this sort ought surely to be made in favour of our own state; and we ought never to surrender the unlimited powers of revenue and trade to uncommercial people. If we do, the glory of the state from that moment departs, never to return. . . .

SOURCE: Paul Leicester Ford, ed., *Essays on the Constitution of the United States* (New York: Burt Franklin, 1892, reprinted 1970).

Samuel Bryan

Letter of Centinel, No. 1 (1787)

To the FREEMEN of PENNSYLVANIA.
Friends, Countrymen and Fellow Citizens.

. . . The late Convention have submitted to your consideration a plan of a new federal government. The subject is highly interesting to your future welfare. Whether it be calculated to promote the great ends of civil society, viz., the happiness and prosperity of the community, it behooves you well to consider, uninfluenced by the authority of names. Instead of that frenzy of enthusiasm, that has actuated the citizens of Philadelphia, in their approbation of the proposed plan, before it was possible that it could be the result of a rational investigation into its principles, it ought to be dispassionately and deliberately examined on its own intrinsic merit, the only criterion of your patronage. If ever free and unbiased discussion was proper or necessary, it is on such an occasion. All the blessings of liberty and the dearest privileges of freemen are now at stake and dependent on your present conduct. . . .

The late revolution having effaced in a great measure all former habits, and the present institutions are so recent, that there exists not that great reluctance to innovation, so remarkable in old communities, and which accords with reason, for the most comprehensive mind cannot foresee the full operation of material changes on civil polity; it is the

genius of the common law to resist innovation.

The wealthy and ambitious, who in every community think they have a right to lord it over their fellow creatures, have availed themselves very successfully of this favorable disposition; for the people thus unsettled in their sentiments, have been prepared to accede to any extreme of government. All the distresses and difficulties they experience, proceeding from various causes, have been ascribed to the impotency of the present confederation, and thence they have been led to expect full relief from the adoption of the proposed system of government; and in the other event, immediately ruin and annihilation as a nation.

I am fearful that the principles of government inculcated in Mr. Adams' treatise, and enforced in the numerous essays and paragraphs in the newspapers, have misled some well designing members of the late Convention. But it will appear in the sequel, that the construction of the proposed plan of government is infinitely more extravagant.

I have been anxiously expecting that some enlightened patriot would, ere this, have taken up the pen to expose the futility, and counteract the baneful tendency of such principles. Mr. Adams' *sine qua non* of a good government is three balancing powers; whose repelling qualities are to produce an equilibrium of interests, and thereby promote the happiness of the whole community. He asserts that the administrators of every government, will ever

SOURCE: Cecilia M. Kenyon, ed., *The Antifederalists* (Indianapolis: Bobbs-Merrill Company, 1966).

be actuated by views of private interest and ambition, to the prejudice of the public good; that therefore the only effectual method to secure the rights of the people and promote their welfare, is to create an opposition of interests between the members of two distinct bodies, in the exercise of the powers of government, and balanced by those of a third. This hypothesis supposes human wisdom competent to the task of instituting three co-equal orders in government, and a corresponding weight in the community to enable them respectively to exercise their several parts, and whose views and interests should be so distinct as to prevent a coalition of any two of them for the destruction of the third. Mr. Adams, although he has traced the constitution of every form of government that ever existed, as far as history affords materials, has not been able to adduce a single instance of such a government; he indeed says that the British constitution is such in theory, but this is rather a confirmation that his principles are chimerical and not to be reduced to practice. If such an organization of power were practicable, how long would it continue? Not a day—for there is so great a disparity in the talents, wisdom and industry of mankind, that the scale would presently preponderate to one or the other body, and with every accession of power the means of further increase would be greatly extended. The state of society in England is much more favorable to such a scheme of government than that of America. There they have a powerful hereditary nobility, and real distinctions of rank and interests; but even there, for want of that perfect equality of power and distinction of interests in the three orders of government, they exist but in name; the only operative and efficient check upon the conduct of administration, is the sense of the people at large.

Suppose a government could be formed and supported on such principles, would it answer the great purposes of civil society? If the ad-ministrators of every government are actuated by views of private interest and ambition, how is the welfare and happiness of the community to be the result of such jarring adverse interests?

Therefore, as different orders in government will not produce the good of the whole, we must recur to other principles. I believe it will be found that the form of government, which holds those entrusted with power in the greatest responsibility to their constituents, the best calculated for freemen. A republican, or free government, can only exist where the body of the people are virtuous, and where property is pretty equally divided. In such a government the people are the sovereign and their sense or opinion is the criterion of every public measure; for when this ceases to be the case, the nature of the government is changed, and an aristocracy, monarchy or despotism will rise on its ruin. The highest responsibility is to be attained in a simple structure of government, for the great body of the people never steadily attend to the operations of government, and for want of due information are liable to be imposed on. If you complicate the plan by various orders, the people will be perplexed and divided in their sentiments about the source of abuses or misconduct; some will impute it to the senate, others to the house of representatives, and so on, that the interposition of the people may be rendered imperfect or perhaps wholly abortive. But if, imitating the constitution of Pennsylvania, you vest all the legislative power in one body of men (separating the executive and judicial) elected for a short period, and necessarily excluded by rotation from permanency, and guarded from precipitancy and surprise by delays imposed on its proceedings, you will create the most perfect responsibility; for then, whenever the people feel a grievance, they cannot mistake the authors, and will apply the remedy with certainty and effect, discarding them at the next election. This tie of responsibility will obviate all the dangers apprehended from a single legislature, and will the best secure the rights of the people. . . .

I shall previously consider the extent of the powers intended to be vested in Congress, before I examine the construction of the general government.

It will not be controverted that the legislative is the highest delegated power in government, and that all others are subordinate to it. The celebrated *Montesquieu* establishes it as a maxim, that legislation necessarily follows the power of taxation. By sect. 8, of the first article of the proposed plan of government, "the Congress are to have power to lay and collect taxes, duties, imposts, and excises, to pay the debts and provide for the common defense and *general welfare* of the United States; but all duties, imposts and excises, shall be uniform throughout the United States." Now what can be more comprehensive than these words? Not content by other sections of this plan, to grant all the great executive powers of a confederation, and a STANDING ARMY IN TIME OF PEACE, that grand engine of oppression, and moreover the absolute control over the commerce of the United States and all external objects of revenue, such as unlimited imposts upon imports, etc., they are to be vested with every species of *internal* taxation; whatever taxes, duties and excises that they may deem requisite for the *general welfare,* may be imposed on the citizens of these states, levied by the officers of Congress, distributed through every district in America; and the collection would be enforced by the standing army, however grievous or improper they may be. The Congress may construe every purpose for which the State legislatures now lay taxes, to be for the *general welfare,* and thereby seize upon every object of revenue. . . .

To put the omnipotency of Congress over the State government and judicatories out of all doubt, the 6th article ordains that "this constitution and the laws of the United States which shall be made in pursuance thereof, and all treaties made, or which shall be made under the authority of the United States, shall be the *supreme law of the land,* and the judges in every State shall be bound thereby, anything in the constitution or laws of any State to the contrary notwithstanding."

By these sections the all-prevailing power of taxation, and such extensive legislative and judicial powers are vested in the general government, as must in their operation necessarily absorb the State legislatures and judicatories; and that such was in the contemplation of the framers of it, will appear from the provision made for such event, in another part of it (but that, fearful of alarming the people by so great an innovation, they have suffered the forms of the separate governments to remain, as a blind). By Article 1st sect. 4th, "the times, places and manner of holding elections for senators and representatives, shall be prescribed in each State by the legislature thereof; *but the Congress may at any time, by law, make or alter such regulations, except as to the place of choosing senators."* The plain construction of which is, that when the State legislatures drop out of sight, from the necessary operation of this government, then Congress are to provide for the election and appointment of representatives and senators.

If the foregoing be a just comment, if the United States are to be melted down into one empire, it becomes you to consider whether such a government, however constructed, would be eligible in so extended a territory; and whether it would be practicable, consistent with freedom? It is the opinion of the greatest writers, that a very extensive country cannot be governed on democratical principles, on any other plan than a confederation of a number of small republics, possessing all the powers of internal government, but united in the management of their foreign and general concerns.

It would not be difficult to prove, that anything short of despotism could not bind so great a country under one government; and that whatever plan you might, at the first setting out, establish, it would issue in a despotism.

If one general government could be instituted and maintained on principles of freedom, it would not be so competent to attend to the various local concerns and wants, of every particular district, as well as the peculiar governments, who are nearer the scene, and possessed of superior means of information; besides, if the business of the *whole* union is to be managed by one government, there would not be time. Do we not already see, that the inhabitants in a number of larger States, who are remote from the seat of government, are loudly complaining of the inconveniences and disadvantages they are subjected to on this account, and that, to enjoy the comforts of local government, they are separating into smaller divisions? . . .

The foregoing are the outlines of the plan.

Thus we see, the house of representatives are on the part of the people to balance the senate, who I suppose will be composed of the *better sort,* the *well born,* etc. The number of the representatives (being only one for every 30,000 inhabitants) appears to be too few, either to communicate the requisite information of the wants, local circumstances and sentiments of so extensive an empire, or to prevent corruption and undue influence, in the exercise of such great powers; the term for which they are to be chosen, too long to preserve a due dependence and accountability to their constituents; and the mode and places of their election not sufficiently ascertained,

for as Congress have the control over both, they may govern the choice, by ordering the *representatives* of a *whole* State, to be *elected* in *one* place, and that too may be the most *inconvenient.*

The Senate, the great efficient body in this plan of government, is constituted on the most unequal principles. The smallest State in the Union has equal weight with the great States of Virginia, Massachusetts or Pennsylvania. The senate, besides its legislative functions, has a very considerable share in the executive; none of the principal appointments to office can be made without its advice and consent. The term and mode of its appointment will lead to permanency; the members are chosen for six years, the mode is under the control of Congress, and as there is no exclusion by rotation, they may be continued for life, which, from their extensive means of influence, would follow of course. The President, who would be a mere pageant of State, unless he coincides with the views of the senate, would either become the head of the aristocratic junto in that body, or its minion; besides, their influence being the most predominant, could the best secure his reelection to office. And from his power of granting pardons, he might screen from punishment the most treasonable attempts on the liberties of the people, when instigated by the senate.

From this investigation into the organization of this government, it appears that it is devoid of all responsibility or accountability to the great body of the people, and that so far from being a regular balanced government, it would be in practice a *permanent* ARISTOCRACY. . . .

Robert Yates

Letters of Brutus, No. 11 (1788)

The nature and extent of the judicial power of the United States, proposed to be granted by this constitution, claims our particular attention.

Much has been said and written upon the subject of this new system on both sides, but I have not met with any writer, who has discussed the judicial powers with any degree of accuracy. And yet it is obvious, that we can form but very imperfect ideas of the manner in which this government will work, or the effect it will have in changing the internal police and mode of distributing justice at present subsisting in the respective states, without a thorough investigation of the powers of the judiciary and of the manner in which they will operate. This government is a complete system, not only for making, but for executing laws. And the courts of law, which will be constituted by it, are not only to decide upon the constitution and the laws made in pursuance of it, but by officers subordinate to them to execute all their decisions. The real effect of this system of government, will therefore be brought home to the feelings of the people, through the medium of the judicial power. It is, moreover, of great importance, to examine with care the nature and extent of the judicial power, because those who are to be vested with it, are to be placed in a situation altogether unprecedented in a free country. They are to be rendered totally independent, both of the people and the legislature, both with respect to their offices and salaries. No errors they may commit can be corrected by any power above them, if any such power there be, nor can they be removed from office for making ever so many erroneous adjudications.

The only causes for which they can be displaced, is, conviction of treason, bribery, and high crimes and misdemeanors.

This part of the plan is so modelled, as to authorize the courts, not only to carry into execution the powers expressly given, but where these are wanting or ambiguously expressed, to supply what is wanting by their own decisions. . . .

Though I am not competent to give a perfect explanation of the powers granted to this department of the government, I shall yet attempt to trace some of the leading features of it, from which I presume it will appear, that they will operate to a total subversion of the state judiciaries, if not, to the legislative authority of the states. . . .

The cases arising under the constitution must be different from those arising under the laws, or else the two clauses mean exactly the same thing.

The cases arising under the constitution must include such, as bring into question its meaning, and will require an explanation of the nature and extent of the powers of the different departments under it.

This article, therefore, vests the judicial with a power to resolve all questions that may arise

SOURCE: Cecilia M. Kenyon, ed., *The Antifederalists* (Indianapolis: Bobbs-Merrill, 1966).

on any case on the construction of the constitution, either in law or in equity.

1st. They are authorised to determine all questions that may arise upon the meaning of the constitution in law. This article vests the courts with authority to give the constitution a legal construction, or to explain it according to the rules laid down for construing a law.—These rules give a certain degree of latitude of explanation. According to this mode of construction, the courts are to give such meaning to the constitution as comports best with the common, and generally received acceptation of the words in which it is expressed, regarding their ordinary and popular use, rather than their grammatical propriety. Where words are dubious, they will be explained by the context. The end of the clause will be attended to, and the words will be understood, as having a view to it; and the words will not be so understood as to bear no meaning or a very absurd one.

2d. The judicial are not only to decide questions arising upon the meaning of the constitution in law, but also in equity.

By this they are empowered, to explain the constitution according to the reasoning spirit of it, without being confined to the words or letter.

"From this method of interpreting laws (says Blackstone) by the reason of them, arises what we call equity;" which is thus defined by Grotius, "the correction of that, wherein the law, by reason of its universality, is deficient; for since in laws of all cases cannot be foreseen, or expressed, it is necessary, that when the decrees of the law cannot be applied to particular cases, there should some where be a power vested of defining those circumstances, which had they been foreseen the legislator would have expressed; and these are the cases, which according to Grotius, lex non exacte definit, fed arbitrio boni viri permittet."

The same learned author observes, "That equity, thus depending essentially upon each individual case, there can be no established rules and fixed principles of equity laid down, without destroying its very essence, and reducing it to a positive law."

From these remarks, the authority and business of the courts of law, under this clause, may be understood.

They will give the sense of every article of the constitution, that may from time to time come before them. And in their decisions they will not confine themselves to any fixed or established rules, but will determine, according to what appears to them, the reason and spirit of the constitution. The opinions of the supreme court, whatever they may be, will have the force of law; because there is no power provided in the constitution, that can correct their errors, or controul their adjudications. From this court there is no appeal. And I conceive the legislature themselves, cannot set aside a judgment of this court, because they are authorised by the constitution to decide in the last resort. The legislature must be controuled by the constitution, and not the constitution by them. They have therefore no more right to set aside any judgment pronounced upon the construction of the constitution, than they have to take from the president, the chief command of the army and navy, and commit it to some other person. The reason is plain; the judicial and executive derive their authority from the same source, that the legislature do theirs; and therefore in all cases, where the constitution does not make the one responsible to, or controulable by the other, they are altogether independent of each other.

The judicial power will operate to effect, in the most certain, but yet silent and imperceptible manner, what is evidently the tendency of the constitution:—I mean, an entire subversion of the legislative, executive and judicial powers of the individual states. Every adjudication of the supreme court, on any question that may arise upon the nature and extent of the general government, will affect the limits of the state jurisdiction. In proportion as the former enlarge the exercise of their powers, will that of the latter be restricted.

That the judicial power of the United States, will lean strongly in favour of the general government, and will give such an explanation to the constitution, as will favour an extension of its jurisdiction, is very evident from a variety of considerations.

1st. The constitution itself strongly countenances such a mode of construction. Most of the articles in this system, which convey powers of any considerable importance, are conceived in general and indefinite terms, which are either equivocal, ambiguous, or which require long definitions to unfold the extent of their meaning. The two most important powers committed to any government, those of raising money, and of raising and keeping up troops, have already been considered, and shewn to be unlimited by any thing but the discretion of the legislature. The clause which vests the power to pass all laws which are proper and necessary, to carry the powers given into execution, it has been shewn, leaves the legislature at liberty, to do every thing, which in their judgment is best. It is said, I know, that this clause confers no power on the legislature, which they would not have had without it—though I believe this is not the fact, yet, admitting it to be, it implies that the constitution is not to receive an explanation strictly, according to its letter; but more power is implied than is expressed. And this clause, if it is to be considered, as explanatory of the extent of the powers given, rather than giving a new power, is to be understood as declaring, that in construing any of the articles conveying power, the spirit, intent and design of the clause, should be attended to, as well as the words in their common acceptation.

This constitution gives sufficient colour for adopting an equitable construction, if we consider the great end and design it professedly has in view—this appears from its preamble to be, "to form a more perfect union, establish justice, insure domestic tranquillity, provide for the common defence, promote the general welfare, and secure the blessings of liberty to ourselves and posterity." The design of this system is here expressed, and it is proper to give such a meaning to the various parts, as will best promote the accomplishment of the end; this idea suggests itself naturally upon reading the preamble, and will countenance the court in giving the several articles such a sense, as will the most effectually promote the ends the constitution had in view—how this manner of explaining the constitution will operate in practice, shall be the subject of future enquiry.

2d. Not only will the constitution justify the courts in inclining to this mode of explaining it, but they will be interested in using this latitude of interpretation. Every body of men invested with office are tenacious of power; they feel interested, and hence it has become a kind of maxim, to hand down their offices, with all its rights and privileges, unimpaired to their successors; the same principle will influence them to extend their power, and increase their rights; this of itself will operate strongly upon the courts to give such a meaning to the constitution in all cases where it can possibly be done, as will enlarge the sphere of their own authority. Every extension of the power of the general legislature, as well as of the judicial powers, will increase the powers of the courts; and the dignity and importance of the judges, will be in proportion to the extent and magnitude of the powers they exercise. . . .

This power in the judicial, will enable them to mould the government, into almost any shape they please.

Dissent of the Minority of the Convention of the State of Pennsylvania to Their Constituents, 1787

One of the most common objections to the Constitution was its lack of a Bill of Rights. The tradition of a Bill of Rights or Declaration of Rights went back to Plymouth in 1636, the English Civil War and the Glorious Revolution, and many of the American colonies. During the Revolution, a number of states, including Virginia, Maryland, Pennsylvania, and Massachusetts, wrote Declarations of Rights or Bills of Rights into their state constitutions. In fact, the voters of Massachusetts rejected their state's constitution in 1778 because it lacked a Bill of Rights, and they did not approve it until 1780, when one was added.

At the Constitutional Convention, Charles Pinckney of South Carolina proposed a series of reserved liberties that, in essence, comprised a Bill of Rights. They were sent to a committee, but soon forgotten. A few weeks later, George Mason, one of the authors of the Virginia Bill of Rights, called for a Bill of Rights to be added to the final document. Eldridge Gerry of Massachusetts supported Mason, but his motion was defeated by the state delegates ten votes to none.

Perhaps the delegates felt a Bill of Rights was unnecessary, or that it would infringe on guarantees already preserved by the states. In *Federalist No. 84,* Alexander Hamilton argued that most of the important limitations on government were already in the Constitution. To add more would imply a limitation on powers of the federal government that it did not have in the first place. Bills of Rights were traditionally imposed by nobilities to limit princes, argued Hamilton, and had no place in a republic where all power originated in the people and was exercised by them. "[The] people surrender nothing; and as they retain everything, they have no need of particular reservations."

Thomas Jefferson, to cite one prominent example, found this line of reasoning unacceptable. "[A] bill of rights is what the people are entitled to against every government on earth, general or particular, and what no just government should refuse, or rest on inference." Although five states ratified the Constitution without a Bill of Rights, a movement soon developed to add one. States began ratifying with the condition that a series of amendments would be added to the finished document. In other states, minority factions of Antifederalists withheld approval, citing the absence of a Bill of Rights as one of their chief objections.

One of the most interesting dissents came from the minority faction of the Pennsylvania State Convention, the first ratifying convention. Most of the Antifederalists were poor farmers, many from the western part of the state. They looked upon the Constitution as a tool of the monied eastern interests, and believed that the new federal government would infringe upon state and local authority. Pennsylvania had one of the most democratic and egalitarian of all constitutions, and the Pennsylvania Antifederalists were afraid that the new federal government masked aristocratic ambitions.

The "dissent" is probably the work of Samuel Bryan. Notice that many of the rights are aimed at protecting the states from the national government, while others are aimed at protecting individuals. Many were later incorporated in the Bill of Rights, some in substantially modified form, and others were excluded altogether.

Dissent of the Minority of the Convention of the State of Pennsylvania to Their Constituents (1787)

. . . The proposed system of government for the United States, if adopted, will alter and may annihilate the constitution of Pennsylvania; and therefore the legislature had no authority whatever to recommend the calling a convention for that purpose. This proceeding could not be considered as binding on the people of this commonwealth. The house was formed by violence, some of the members composing it were detained there by force, which alone would have vitiated any proceedings to which they were otherwise competent; but had the legislature been legally formed, this business was absolutely without their power.

In this situation of affairs were the subscribers elected members of the Convention of Pennsylvania—a Convention called by a legislature in direct violation of their duty, and composed in part of members who were compelled to attend for that purpose, to consider of a Constitution proposed by a Convention of the United States, who were not appointed for the purpose of framing a new form of government, but whose powers were

expressly confined to altering and amending the present articles of confederation. Therefore the members of the continental Convention in proposing the plan acted as individuals, and not as deputies from Pennsylvania.[*] The assembly who called the State Convention acted as individuals, and not as the legislature of Pennsylvania; nor could they or the Convention chosen on their recommendation have authority to do any act or thing that can alter or annihilate the Constitution of Pennsylvania (both of which will be done by the new Constitution), nor are their proceedings, in our opinion, at all binding on the people.

The election for members of the Convention was held at so early a period, and the want of information was so great, that some

---

[*] The continental Convention, in direct violation of the 13th article of the confederation, have declared "that the ratification of nine States shall be sufficient for the establishment of this Constitution, between the States so ratifying the same." Thus has the plighted faith of the States been sported with! They had solemnly engaged that the confederation now subsisting should be inviolably preserved by each of them, and the Union thereby formed should be perpetual, unless the same should be altered by mutual consent.

SOURCE: *Pennsylvania Packet and Daily Advertiser*, December 18, 1787.

of us did not know of it until after it was over, and we have reason to believe that great numbers of the people of Pennsylvania have not yet had an opportunity of sufficiently examining the proposed Constitution. We apprehend that no change can take place that will affect the internal government or Constitution of this commonwealth, unless a majority of the people should evidence a wish for such a change; but on examining the number of votes given for members of the present State Convention, we find that of upwards of *seventy thousand* freemen who are entitled to vote in Pennsylvania, the whole convention has been elected by about *thirteen thousand* votes, and though *two-thirds* of the members of the Convention have thought proper to ratify the proposed Constitution, yet those *two-thirds* were elected by the votes of only *six thousand and eight hundred* freemen.

In the city of Philadelphia and some of the eastern counties the junto that took the lead in the business agreed to vote for none but such as would solemnly promise to adopt the system *in toto*, without exercising their judgment. In many of the counties the people did not attend the elections, as they had not an opportunity of judging of the plan. Others did not consider themselves bound by the call of a set of men who assembled at the State-house in Philadelphia and assumed the name of the legislature of Pennsylvania; and some were prevented from voting by the violence of the party who were determined at all events to force down the measure. To such lengths did the tools of despotism carry their outrage, that on the night of the election for members of convention, in the city of Philadelphia, several of the subscribers (being then in the city to transact your business) were grossly abused, ill-treated and insulted while they were quiet in their lodging, though they did not interfere nor had anything to do with the said election, but, as they apprehend, because they were supposed to be adverse to the proposed constitution, and would not tamely surrender those

sacred rights which you had committed to their charge.

The convention met, and the same disposition was soon manifested in considering the proposed constitution, that had been exhibited in every other stage of the business. We were prohibited by an express vote of the convention from taking any questions on the separate articles of the plan, and reduced to the necessity of adopting or rejecting *in toto*. 'Tis true the majority permitted us to debate on each article, but restrained us from proposing amendments. They also determined not to permit us to enter on the minutes our reasons of dissent against any of the articles, nor even on the final question our reasons of dissent against the whole. Thus situated we entered on the examination of the proposed system of government, and found it to be such as we could not adopt, without, as we conceived, surrendering up your dearest rights. We offered our objections to the convention, and opposed those parts of the plan which, in our opinion, would be injurious to you, in the best manner we were able; and closed our arguments by offering the following propositions to the convention.

1. The right of conscience shall be held inviolable; and neither the legislative, executive nor judicial powers of the United States shall have authority to alter, abrogate or infringe any part of the constitution of the several States, which provide for the preservation of liberty in matters of religion.

2. That in controversies respecting property, and in suits between man and man, trial by jury shall remain as heretofore, as well in the federal courts as in those of the several States.

3. That in all capital and criminal prosecutions, a man has a right to demand the cause and nature of his accusation, as well in the federal courts as in those of the several States; to be heard by himself and his counsel; to be confronted with the accusers and witnesses; to call for evidence in his favor, and a speedy trial by an impartial jury of his vicinage, without whose unanimous consent he cannot be found guilty, nor can he be compelled to give evidence against himself; and, that no man be deprived of his liberty, except by the law of the land or the judgment of his peers.

4. That excessive bail ought not to be required, nor excessive fines imposed, nor cruel nor unusual punishments inflicted.

5. That warrants unsupported by evidence, whereby any officer or messenger may be commanded or required to search suspected places; or to seize any person or persons, his or their property not particularly described, are grievous and oppressive, and shall not be granted either by the magistrates of the federal government or others.

6. That the people have a right to the freedom of speech, of writing and publishing their sentiments; therefore the freedom of the press shall not be restrained by any law of the United States.

7. That the people have a right to bear arms for the defence of themselves and their own State or the United States, or for the purpose of killing game; and no law shall be passed for disarming the people or any of them unless for crimes committed, or real danger of public injury from individuals; and as standing armies in the time of peace are dangerous to liberty, they ought not to be kept up; and that the military shall be kept under strict subordination to, and be governed by the civil powers.

8. The inhabitants of the several States shall have liberty to fowl and hunt in seasonable time on the lands they hold, and on all other lands in the United States not inclosed, and in like manner to fish in all navigable waters, and others not private property, without being restrained therein by any laws to be passed by the legislature of the United States.

9. That no law shall be passed to restrain the legislatures of the several States from enacting laws for imposing taxes, except imposts and duties on goods imported or exported, and that no taxes, except imposts and duties upon goods imported and exported, and postage on letters, shall be levied by the authority of Congress.

10. That the house of representatives be properly increased in number; that elections shall remain free; that the several States shall have power to regulate the elections for senators and representatives, without being controlled either directly or indirectly by any interference on the part of the Congress; and that the elections of representatives be annual.

11. That the power of organizing, arming and disciplining the militia (the manner of disciplining the militia to be prescribed by Congress), remain with the individual States, and that Congress shall not have authority to call or march any of the militia out of their own State, without the consent of such State, and for such length of time only as such State shall agree.

That the sovereignty, freedom and independency of the several States shall be retained, and every power, jurisdiction and right which is not by this Constitution expressly delegated to the United States in Congress assembled.

12. That the legislature, executive and judicial powers be kept separate; and to this end that a constitutional council be appointed to advise and assist the President, who shall be responsible for the advice they give—hereby the senators would be relieved from almost constant attendance; and also that the judges be made completely independent.

13. That no treaty which shall be directly opposed to the existing laws of the United States in Congress assembled, shall be valid until such laws shall be repealed or made conformable to such treaty; neither shall any treaties be valid which are in contradiction to the Constitution of the United States, or the constitution of the several States.

14. That the judiciary power of the United States shall be confined to cases affecting ambassadors, other public ministers and consuls, to cases of admiralty and maritime jurisdiction; to controversies to which the United States shall be a party; to controversies between two or more States—between a State and citizens of different States—between citizens claiming lands under grants of different States, and between a State or the citizens thereof and foreign States; and in criminal cases to such only as are expressly enumerated in the constitution; and that the United States in Congress assembled shall not have power to enact laws which shall alter the laws of descent and distribution of the effects of deceased persons, the titles of lands or goods, or the regulation of contracts in the individual States.

After reading these propositions, we declared our willingness to agree to the plan, provided it was so amended as to meet those propositions or something similar to them, and finally moved the convention to adjourn, to give the people of Pennsylvania time to consider the subject and determine for themselves; but these were all rejected and the final vote taken, when our duty to you induced us to vote against the proposed plan and to decline signing the ratification of the same.

During the discussion we met with many insults and some personal abuse. We were not even treated with decency, during the sitting of the convention, by the persons in the gallery of the house. However, we flatter ourselves that in contending for the preservation of those invaluable rights you have thought proper to commit to our charge, we acted with a spirit becoming freemen; and being desirous that you might know the principles which actuated our conduct, and being prohibited from inserting our reasons of dissent on the minutes of the convention, we have subjoined them for your consideration, as to you alone we are accountable. It remains with you whether you will think those inestimable privileges, which you have so ably contended for, should be sacrificed at the shrine of despotism, or whether you mean to contend for them with the same spirit that has so often baffled the attempts of an aristocratic faction to rivet the shackles of slavery on you and your unborn posterity.

Opinion on the Constitutionality of a National Bank, 1791

While not a direct attack on the Constitution, Jefferson's argument against a national bank shares more in common with many Antifederalist views than with the Hamiltonian cast of *The Federalist Papers.* Jefferson's "Opinion" stakes out the position for a strict construction of the Constitution in opposition to the loose interpretation of Hamilton and the emerging Federalist party. Jefferson reiterated his fear of an emerging political order that violated republican principles in his letter to Phillip Mazzei (1796) which follows.

Thomas Jefferson

Opinion on the Constitutionality of a National Bank (1791)

. . . I consider the foundation of the Constitution as laid on this ground: That "all powers not delegated to the United States, by the Constitution, nor prohibited by it to the States, are reserved to the States or to the people." . . . To take a single step beyond the boundaries thus specially drawn around the powers of Congress, is to take possession of a boundless field of power, no longer susceptible of any definition.

The incorporation of a bank, and the powers assumed by this bill, have not, in my opinion, been delegated to the United States by the Constitution.

I. They are not among the powers specially enumerated: for these are: **1st.** A power to lay taxes for the purpose of paying the debts of the United States; but no debt is paid by this bill, nor any tax laid. Were it a bill to raise money, its origination in the Senate would condemn it by the Constitution.

2d. "To borrow money." But this bill neither borrows money nor ensures the borrowing it. The proprietors of the bank will be just as free as any other money holders, to lend or not to lend their money to the public. The operation proposed in the bill, first, to lend them two millions, and then to borrow

them back again, cannot change the nature of the latter act, which will still be a payment, and not a loan, call it by what name you please.

3d. To "regulate commerce with foreign nations, and among the States, and with the Indian tribes." To erect a bank, and to regulate commerce, are very different acts. He who erects a bank, creates a subject of commerce in its bills; so does he who makes a bushel of wheat, or digs a dollar out of the mines; yet neither of these persons regulates commerce thereby. To make a thing which may be bought and sold, is not to prescribe regulations for buying and selling. Besides, if this was an exercise of the power of regulating commerce, it would be void, as extending as much to the internal commerce of every State, as to its external. For the power given to Congress by the Constitution does not extend to the internal regulation of the commerce of a State, (that is to say of the commerce between citizen and citizen,) which remain exclusively with its own legislature; but to its external commerce only, that is to say, its commerce with another State, or with foreign nations, or with the Indian tribes. Accordingly the bill does not propose the measure as a regulation of trade, but as "productive of considerable advantages to trade." Still less are these powers covered by any other of the special enumerations.

II. Nor are they within either of the general phrases, which are the two following:—

SOURCE: Andrew A. Lipscomb, ed., *The Writings of Thomas Jefferson* (Washington, D.C.: Thomas Jefferson Memorial Association, 1903).

1. To lay taxes to provide for the general welfare of the United States, that is to say, "to lay taxes for *the purpose* of providing for the general welfare." For the laying of taxes is the *power,* and the general welfare the *purpose* for which the power is to be exercised. They are not to lay taxes *ad libitum for any purpose they please;* but only *to pay the debts or provide for the welfare of the Union.* In like manner, they are not *to do anything they please* to provide for the general welfare, but only to *lay taxes* for that purpose. To consider the latter phrase, not as describing the purpose of the first, but as giving a distinct and independent power to do any act they please, which might be for the good of the Union, would render all the preceding and subsequent enumerations of power completely useless.

It would reduce the whole instrument to a single phrase, that of instituting a Congress with power to do whatever would be for the good of the United States; and, as they would be the sole judges of the good or evil, it would be also a power to do whatever evil they please.

It is an established rule of construction where a phrase will bear either of two meanings, to give it that which will allow some meaning to the other parts of the instrument, and not that which would render all the others useless. Certainly no such universal power was meant to be given them. It was intended to lace them up straitly within the enumerated powers, and those without which, as means, these powers could not be carried into effect. It is known that the very power now proposed *as a means* was rejected as *an end* by the Convention which formed the Constitution. A proposition was made to them to authorize Congress to open canals, and an amendatory one to empower them to incorporate. But the whole was rejected, and one of the reasons for rejection urged in debate was, that then they would have a power to erect a bank, which would render the great cities, where there

were prejudices and jealousies on the subject, adverse to the reception of the Constitution.

2. The second general phrase is, "to make all laws *necessary* and proper for carrying into execution the enumerated powers." But they can all be carried into execution without a bank. A bank therefore is not *necessary,* and consequently not authorized by this phrase.

It has been urged that a bank will give great facility or convenience in the collection of taxes. Suppose this were true: yet the Constitution allows only the means which are *"necessary,"* not those which are merely "convenient" for effecting the enumerated powers. If such a latitude of construction be allowed to this phrase as to give any non-enumerated power, it will go to every one, for there is not one which ingenuity may not torture into a *convenience* in some instance *or other,* to *some one* of so long a list of enumerated powers. It would swallow up all the delegated powers, and reduce the whole to one power, as before observed. Therefore it was that the Constitution restrained them to the *necessary* means, that is to say, to those means without which the grant of power would be nugatory.

But let us examine this convenience and see what it is. The report on this subject, page 3, states the only *general* convenience to be, the preventing the transportation and retransportation of money between the States and the treasury, (for I pass over the increase of circulating medium, ascribed to it as a want, and which, according to my ideas of paper money, is clearly a demerit.) Every State will have to pay a sum of tax money into the treasury; and the treasury will have to pay, in every State, a part of the interest on the public debt, and salaries to the officers of government resident in that State. In most of the States there will still be a surplus of tax money to come up to the seat of government for the officers residing there. The payments of interest and salary in each State may be made by treasury orders on the State collector. This will take up the greater part of the money he has collected in his State, and consequently prevent the great mass of it from being drawn out of the State. If there be a balance of commerce in favor of that State against the one in which the government resides, the surplus of taxes will be remitted by the bills of exchange drawn for that commercial balance. And so it must be if there was a bank. But if there be no balance of commerce, either direct or circuitous, all the banks in the world could not bring up the surplus of taxes but in the form of money. Treasury orders then, and bills of exchange may prevent the displacement of the main mass of the money collected, without the aid of any bank; and where these fail, it cannot be prevented even with that aid.

Perhaps, indeed, bank bills may be a more *convenient* vehicle than treasury orders. But a little *difference* in the degree of *convenience,* cannot constitute the necessity which the constitution makes the ground for assuming any non-enumerated power.

Besides; the existing banks will, without a doubt, enter into arrangements for lending their agency, and the more favorable, as there will be a competition among them for it, whereas the bill delivers us up bound to the national bank, who are free to refuse all arrangement, but on their own terms, and the public not free, on such refusal, to employ any other bank. That of Philadelphia, I believe, now does this business, by their post-notes, which, by an arrangement with the treasury, are paid by any State collector to whom they are presented. This expedient alone suffices to prevent the existence of that *necessity* which may justify the assumption of a non-enumerated power as a means for carrying into effect an enumerated one. The thing may be done, and has been done, and well done, without this assumption; therefore, it does not stand on that degree of *necessity* which can honestly justify it.

It may be said that a bank whose bills would have a currency all over the States, would be more convenient than one whose currency is limited to a single State. So it would be still more convenient that there should be a bank, whose bills should have a currency all over the world. But it does not follow from this superior conveniency, that there exists anywhere a power to establish such a bank; or that the world may not go on very well without it. . . .

The negative of the President is the shield provided by the constitution to protect against the invasions of the legislature: 1. The right of the Executive. 2. Of the Judiciary. 3. Of the States and State legislatures. The present is the case of a right remaining exclusively with the States, and consequently one of those intended by the Constitution to be placed under its protection.

It must be added, however, that unless the President's mind on a view of everything which is urged for and against this bill, is tolerably clear that it is unauthorized by the Constitution; if the pro and the con hang so even as to balance his judgment, a just respect for the wisdom of the legislature would naturally decide the balance in favor of their opinion. It is chiefly for cases where they are clearly misled by error, ambition, or interest, that the Constitution has placed a check in the negative of the President.

Thomas Jefferson

Letter to Phillip Mazzei (1796)

. . . The aspect of our politics has wonderfully changed since you left us. In place of that noble love of liberty and republican government which carried us triumphantly through the war, an Anglican monarchical aristocratical party has sprung up, whose avowed object is to draw over us the substance, as they have already done the forms, of the British government. The main body of our citizens, however, remain true to their republican principles; the whole landed interest is republican, and so is a great mass of talents. Against us are the Executive, the Judiciary, two out of three branches of the Legislature, all the officers of the government, all who

Source: Andrew A. Lipscomb, ed., *The Writings of Thomas Jefferson* (Washington, D.C.: Thomas Jefferson Memorial Association, 1903).

want to be officers, all timid men who prefer the calm of despotism to the boisterous sea of liberty, British merchants and Americans trading on British capital, speculators and holders in the banks and public funds, a contrivance invented for the purposes of corruption, and for assimilating us in all things to the rotten as well as the sound parts of the English model. It would give you a fever were I to name to you the apostates who have gone over to these heresies, men who were Samsons in the field and Solomons in the council, but who have had their heads shorn by the harlot England. In short, we are likely to preserve the liberty we have obtained only by unremitting labors and perils. But we shall preserve it; and our mass of weight and wealth on the good side is so great, as to leave no danger that force will ever be attempted against us. . . .

Letter to Samuel Kercheval, 1816

In 1816, Jefferson received a pamphlet written by an anonymous western Virginia author calling for a new state constitutional convention. Citizens in the western part of the state believed, correctly, that they were underrepresented in the state legislature and wanted to rewrite important sections of the state's constitution.

Jefferson wrote an affirmative response to the young author, who turned out to be Samuel Kercheval. In the letter, he also laid out many of his basic political ideas, including his commitment to constitutionalism, democracy, and local self-government.

Thomas Jefferson

Letter to Samuel Kercheval (1816)

. . . But inequality of representation in both Houses of our legislature, is not the only republican heresy in this first essay of our revolutionary patriots at forming a constitution. For let it be agreed that a government is republican in proportion as every member composing it has his equal voice in the direction of its concerns (not indeed in person, which would be impracticable beyond the limits of a city, or small township, but) by representatives chosen by himself, and responsible to him at short periods, and let us bring to the test of this canon every branch of our constitution. . . . But it will be said, it is easier to find faults than to amend them. I do not think their amendment so difficult as is pretended. Only lay down true principles, and adhere to them inflexibly. Do not be frightened into their surrender by the alarms of the timid, or the croakings of wealth against the ascendency of the people. If experience be called for, appeal to that of our fifteen or twenty governments for forty years, and show me where the people have done half the mischief in these forty years, that a single despot would have done in a single year; or show half the riots and rebellions, the crimes and the punishments, which have taken place in any single nation, under kingly government, during the same period. The true foundation of republican government is the equal right of every citizen, in his person and property,

SOURCE: Andrew A. Lipscomb, ed., *The Writings of Thomas Jefferson* (Washington, D.C.: Thomas Jefferson Memorial Association, 1903).

and in their management. Try by this, as a tally, every provision of our constitution, and see if it hangs directly on the will of the people. Reduce your legislature to a convenient number for full, but orderly discussion. Let every man who fights or pays, exercise his just and equal right in their election. Submit them to approbation or rejection at short intervals. Let the executive be chosen in the same way, and for the same term, by those whose agent he is to be; and leave no screen of a council behind which to skulk from responsibility. It has been thought that the people are not competent electors of judges *learned in the law*. But I do not know that this is true, and, if doubtful, we should follow principle. In this, as in many other elections, they would be guided by reputation, which would not err oftener, perhaps, than the present mode of appointment. In one State of the Union, at least, it has long been tried, and with the most satisfactory success. The judges of Connecticut have been chosen by the people every six months, for nearly two centuries, and I believe there has hardly ever been an instance of change; so powerful is the curb of incessant responsibility. If prejudice, however, derived from a monarchical institution, is still to prevail against the vital elective principle of our own, and if the existing example among ourselves of periodical election of judges by the people be still mistrusted, let us at least not adopt the evil, and reject the good, of the English precedent; let us retain amovability on the concurrence of the executive and legislative branches, and nomination by the executive alone. Nomination to office is an executive function. To give it to the legislature, as we do, is a violation of the principle of the separation of powers. It swerves the members from correctness, by temptations to intrigue for office themselves, and to a corrupt barter of votes; and destroys responsibility by dividing it among a multitude. By leaving nomination in its proper place, among executive functions, the principle of the distribution of power is preserved, and responsibility weighs with its heaviest force on a single head.

The organization of our county administrations may be thought more difficult. But follow principle, and the knot unties itself. Divide the counties into wards of such size as that every citizen can attend, when called on, and act in person. Ascribe to them the government of their wards in all things relating to themselves exclusively. A justice, chosen by themselves, in each, a constable, a military company, a patrol, a school, the care of their own poor, their own portion of the public roads, the choice of one or more jurors to serve in some court, and the delivery, within their own wards, of their own votes for all elective officers of higher sphere, will relieve the county administration of nearly all its business, will have it better done, and by making every citizen an acting member of the government, and in the offices nearest and most interesting to him, will attach him by his strongest feelings to the independence of his country, and its republican constitution. The justices thus chosen by every ward, would constitute the county court, would do its judiciary business, direct roads and bridges, levy county and poor rates, and administer all the matters of common interest to the whole country. These wards, called townships in New England, are the vital principle of their governments, and have proved themselves the wisest invention ever devised by the wit of man for the perfect exercise of self-government, and for its preservation. We should thus marshal our government

into, 1, the general federal republic, for all concerns foreign and federal; 2, that of the State, for what relates to our own citizens exclusively; 3, the county republics, for the duties and concerns of the county; and 4, the ward republics, for the small, and yet numerous and interesting concerns of the neighborhood; and in government, as well as in every other business of life, it is by division and subdivision of duties alone, that all matters, great and small, can be managed to perfection. And the whole is cemented by giving to every citizen, personally, a part in the administration of the public affairs.

The sum of these amendments is, 1. General Suffrage. 2. Equal representation in the legislature. 3. An executive chosen by the people. 4. Judges elective or amovable. 5. Justices, jurors, and sheriffs elective. 6. Ward divisions. And 7. Periodical amendments of the constitution.

I have thrown out these as loose heads of amendment, for consideration and correction; and their object is to secure self-government by the republicanism of our constitution, as well as by the spirit of the people; and to nourish and perpetuate that spirit. I am not among those who fear the people. They, and not the rich, are our dependence for continued freedom. And to preserve their independence, we must not let our rulers load us with perpetual debt. We must make our election between *economy and liberty*, or *profusion and servitude*. If we run into such debts, as that we must be taxed in our meat and in our drink, in our necessaries and our comforts, in our labors and our amusements, for our callings and our creeds, as the people of England are, our people, like them, must come to labor sixteen hours in the twenty-four, give the earnings of fifteen of these to the government for their debts and daily expenses; and the sixteenth being insufficient to afford us bread, we must live, as they now do, on oatmeal and potatoes; have no time to think, no means of calling the mismanagers to account; but be glad to obtain subsistence by hiring ourselves to rivet their chains on the necks of our fellow-sufferers. Our landholders, too, like theirs, retaining indeed the title and stewardship of estates called theirs, but held really in trust for the treasury, must wander, like theirs, in foreign countries, and be contented with penury, obscurity, exile, and the glory of the nation. This example reads to us the salutary lesson, that private fortunes are destroyed by public as well as by private extravagance. And this is the tendency of all human governments. A departure from principle in one instance becomes a precedent for a second; that second for a third; and so on, till the bulk of the society is reduced to be mere automatons of misery, and to have no sensibilities left but for sinning and suffering. Then begins, indeed, the *bellum omnium in omnia*, which some philosophers observing to be so general in this world, have mistaken it for the natural, instead of the abusive state of man. And the fore horse of this frightful team is public debt. Taxation follows that, and in its train wretchedness and oppression.

Some men look at constitutions with sanctimonious reverence, and deem them like the arc of the covenant, too sacred to be touched. They ascribe to the men of the preceding age a wisdom more than human, and suppose what they did to be beyond amendment. I knew that age well; I belonged to it, and labored with it. It deserved well of its country. It was very like the present, but without the experience of the present; and forty years of experience in government is worth a century of book-reading; and this they would say themselves, were they to rise from the dead. I am certainly not an advocate for frequent and untried changes in laws and constitutions. I think moderate imperfections had better be borne with; because, when once known, we accommodate ourselves to them, and find practical means of correcting their ill effects.

But I know also, that laws and institutions must go hand in hand with the progress of the human mind. As that becomes more developed, more enlightened, as new discoveries are made, new truths disclosed, and manners and opinions change with the change of circumstances, institutions must advance also, and keep pace with the times. We might as well require a man to wear still the coat which fitted him when a boy, as civilized society to remain ever under the regimen of their barbarous ancestors. It is this preposterous idea which has lately deluged Europe in blood. . . .

Each generation is as independent as the one preceding, as that was of all which had gone before. It has then, like them, a right to choose for itself the form of government it believes most promotive of its own happiness; consequently, to accommodate to the circumstances in which it finds itself, that received from its predecessors; and it is for the peace and good of mankind that a solemn opportunity of doing this every nineteen or twenty years, should be provided by the constitution; so that it may be handed on, with periodical repairs, from generation to generation, to the end of time, if anything human can so long endure. It is now forty years since the constitution of Virginia was formed. The same tables inform us, that, within that period, two-thirds of the adults then living are now dead. Have then the remaining third, even if they had the wish, the right to hold in obedience to their will, and to laws heretofore made by them, the other two-thirds, who, with themselves, compose the present mass of adults? If they have not, who has? The dead? But the dead have no rights. They are nothing; and nothing cannot own something.

These, Sir, are my opinions of the governments we see among men, and of the principles by which alone we may prevent our own from falling into the same dreadful track. I have given them at greater length than your letter called for. But I cannot say things by halves; and I confide them to your honor, so to use them as to preserve me from the gridiron of the public papers. If you shall approve and enforce them, as you have done that of equal representation, they may do some good. If not, keep them to yourself as the effusions of withered age and useless time. I shall, with not the less truth, assure you of my great respect and consideration.

Abigail Adams, 1744–1818

Although raised in rural Massachusetts with no formal education, Abigail Adams has become one of America's most famous letter writers.

As a descendant of the Quincy family, wife to John Adams, and mother of John Quincy Adams, she spent her life among the political elite of her colony, state, and nation. Her detailed letters to her husband during the Continental Congresses, the Constitutional Convention, and various assignments abroad provide some of the most interesting pieces of social history from that period.

In the letter below, Abigail Adams writes to her husband at the second Continental Congress and urges him to "remember the ladies." The letter serves as an important reminder that despite the egalitarian rhetoric of the revolutionary and constitutional eras, many in the American polity remained excluded.

Abigail Adams

Letter to John Adams (1776)

. . . I long to hear that you have declared an independancy—and by the way in the new Code of Laws which I suppose it will be necessary for you to make I desire you would Remember the Ladies, and be more generous and favourable to them than your ancestors.

Do not put such unlimited power into the hands of the Husbands. Remember all Men would be tyrants if they could. If perticuliar care and attention is not paid to the Ladies we are determined to foment a Rebelion, and will not hold ourselves bound by any Laws in which we have no voice, or Representation.

That your Sex are Naturally Tyrannical is a Truth so thoroughly established as to admit of no dispute, but such of you as wish to be happy willingly give up the harsh title of Mas-

SOURCE: L. H. Butterfield, Marc Friedlaender, Mary Jo Kline, eds., *The Book of Abigail and John* (Cambridge, Mass.: Belknap Press, 1975).

ter for the more tender and endearing one of Friend. Why then, not put it out of the power of the vicious and the Lawless to use us with cruelty and indignity with impunity. Men of Sense in all Ages abhor those customs which treat us only as the vassals of your Sex. Regard us then as Beings placed by providence under your protection and in immitation of the Supreem Being make use of that power only for our happiness.

PART IV

Extending the Democratic Republic: Liberty, Equality, and the Open Marketplace

Our Founding Fathers strove to ensure individual liberty and republican self-government, yet many of them believed it was equally important to restrain the excesses of democracy. The system of checks and balances, an independent judiciary, the electoral college, indirect election of senators, and various property requirements for voting retained by most states all attempted to curb the power of the majority while tempering their numbers with the excellence of the well-educated and well-born. While not aristocratic in the sense of wishing to perpetuate a class born to its position, many of the founding generation—especially those who later joined the Federalist party—associated individual excellence with economic status. Drawing on authentic agrarian traditions in American thinking, many Federalists and Democratic-Republicans alike felt that owners of land possessed special political virtues that entitled them to special political privileges. Many state constitutions, for example, required landholding as a requisite for voting in state senate elections.

Nevertheless, the drive toward equality and democracy was not easily constrained in the post-Revolution United States. By 1830, egalitarian forces successfully gained passage of universal white manhood suffrage in virtually every state. From 1816 to 1821, six new states entered the Union, and each guaranteed every white male the right to vote regardless of property holdings. Eastern states soon followed with a series of new state constitutional conventions that similarly adopted universal manhood suffrage. The symbol of this movement became President Andrew Jackson (1829–1837), a Tennessee frontiersman, who was swept to power by the votes of farmers and urban workers who belonged to the first mass political party in U.S. history, the Democratic party.

Unlike twentieth-century egalitarians who have supported direct intervention in the marketplace in order to increase opportunity and income for the poor, the egalitarians of the Jacksonian era generally demanded laissez-faire and the free open market. They associated government intervention in the economy with monopoly and privilege, which protected the already rich and established. Laissez-faire rhetoric especially appealed to the young worker or mechanic who hoped soon to possess his own shop or farm.

Jackson in his attacks on the National Bank adeptly combined arguments for laissez-faire, individualism, democracy, and equality with traditional appeals to republican virtue. Attaching new meaning to an old word, Jackson believed "virtue" was available to all who worked for a living, and not simply the yeoman farmer. Virtue came to those who were disciplined in the marketplace and sought self-sufficiency, rather than to those who were rooted in the land and willing to sacrifice self for the public good.

The Jacksonian era produced a tremendous amount of political writing advocating egalitarian and individualist ideals. Robert Dale Owen, Francis Wright, and Horace Mann were eloquent spokesmen for public education. Henry David Thoreau's romantic individualism in *Walden* and "Civil Disobedience" represented individualist themes in the extreme. Walt Whitman, in both poetry and prose, and John O'Sullivan became staunch advocates of limited government, equal rights, and the dignity of labor. In fact, labor as a self-conscious class gained voices in the works of Orestes Brownson, Langdon Byllesby, and Ely Moore.

Most of these egalitarians, like Jackson himself, were staunch nationalists. Using liberal individualist categories of thought, these theorists and activists viewed the nation as an association of equal individuals, rather than an association of property owners or a confederation of states. Despite a desire for limited government, most did not favor near-autonomy for the states. Ours was a nation, they argued, with a strong, if limited, central government. In this sense, Abraham Lincoln himself fit in the liberal individualist and nationalist mold of the Jacksonian era.

The logic of many Jacksonians pushed well beyond the personal values of Andrew Jackson. Abraham Lincoln's magnificent body of speeches all breathed new egalitarian life into the values of the Declaration of Independence. The abolitionist movement began to develop in full force with writers and activists such as William Lloyd Garrison, Frederick Douglass, and the Grimke sisters hoped to extend the egalitarian rights held by the white male population to many who had been left out. Early feminists, many of whom came to political consciousness in the abolition movement, began to demand equality under the law for women. Like the abolitionists, Susan B. Anthony, Elizabeth Cady Stanton, and Angeline Grimke came to criticize Jacksonian society through appeals to the very logic of Jacksonian theory—equality of rights and opportunity.

Despite the primary thrust of this era, serious critics of equality and democracy remained. Alexis de Tocqueville, an aristocratic Frenchman who admired American institutions more than its democratic ideals, pointed out in *Democracy in America* (1835 and 1840) the problems of mindless conformity and tyranny of the majority, which he believed were inherent in democratic societies.

Far more critical of the underlying assumptions of liberal individualism, the writings of brilliant southern reactionaries such as John C. Calhoun and George Fitzhugh appealed to preliberal ideals reminiscent of medieval and patriarchical political theory. Both Fitzhugh and Calhoun argued that every society was inevitably unequal and thus best ordered when each class felt obligated to serve the needs of the other. Calhoun's idea of the nation as a confederation of preexisting, autonomous states further resembled a medieval conception of associated fiefs or estates, rather than a modern nation state rooted in the consent of individuals. While clearly defenders of the slaveholding South, he and Fitzhugh also remain fascinating examples of those few American theorists who have fully rejected Lockean individualism.

Nevertheless, for most Americans during the years 1820 to 1870, equal liberty exercised in an open, expanding commercial society came to represent the requisites for a republican government. American theory had moved out of the classical world of both the early Whigs and the agrarian republicans.

The Republic of Orders

John Adams on Inequality: Letters to James Sullivan and John Taylor

John Adams remained an exponent of traditional Whig notions of "mixed government," adjusted to the special circumstances of America. Throughout his career, he opposed unicameral schemes of legislative government, such as those proposed by Thomas Paine, and proposals for universal manhood suffrage that were to become common in early nineteenth-century America. Although no friend of "artificial aristocracies" decreed by law and perpetuated by birth and property laws such as primogeniture and entail, Adams nonetheless believed that individuals were unequal in talents, ambition, or power and that governments had to be structured to reflect this fact. His arguments were especially useful for those during the Jacksonian era who hoped to stem the tide of universal manhood suffrage, and for those who wanted to keep differential voting requirements for lower and upper chambers in state legislatures.

His letter to James Sullivan written in 1776 is essentially a defense of property requirements for the exercise of the suffrage. His very long letter to John Taylor in 1814 is a response to Taylor's *An Inquiry into the Principles and Policy of the United States* (1814), which was in turn a treatise attacking Adams's three-volume work *A Defense of the Constitutions of Government of the United States of America* (1787–1788). In that work, Adams had praised the idea of a Senate which reflected the power of the aristocracy, and Taylor had taken him to task using militant agrarian and egalitarian language.

John Adams

Letter to James Sullivan (1776)

Our worthy friend, Mr. Gerry, has put into my hands a letter from you, of the sixth of May, in which you consider the principles of representation and legislation, and give us hints of some alterations, which you seem to think necessary, in the qualification of voters.

I wish, Sir, I could possibly find time to accompany you, in your investigation of the principles upon which a representative assembly stands, and ought to stand, and in your examination whether the practice of our colony has been conformable to those principles. But, alas! Sir, my time is so incessantly engrossed by the business before me, that I cannot spare enough to go through so large a field; and as to books, it is not easy to obtain them here; nor could I find a moment to look into them, if I had them.

It is certain, in theory, that the only moral foundation of government is, the consent of the people. But to what an extent shall we carry this principle? Shall we say that every individual of the community, old and young, male and female, as well as rich and poor, must consent, expressly, to every act of legislation? No, you will say, this is impossible. How, then, does the right arise in the majority to govern the minority, against their will? Whence arises the right of the men to govern the women, without their consent? Whence the right of the old to bind the young, without theirs?

But let us first suppose that the whole community, of every age, rank, sex, and condition, has a right to vote. This community is assembled. A motion is made, and carried by a majority of one voice. The minority will not agree to this. Whence arises the right of the majority to govern, and the obligation of the minority to obey?

From necessity, you will say, because there can be no other rule.

But why exclude women?

You will say, because their delicacy renders them unfit for practice and experience in the great businesses of life, and the hardy enterprises of war, as well as the arduous cares of state. Besides, their attention is so much engaged with the necessary nurture of their children, that nature has made them fittest for domestic cares. And children have not judgment or will of their own. True. But will not these reasons apply to others? It is not equally true, that men in general, in every society, who are wholly destitute of property, are also too little acquainted with public affairs to form a right judgment, and too dependent upon other men to have a will of their own? If this is a fact, if you give to every man who has no property, a vote, will you not make a fine encouraging provision for corruption, by your fundamental law? Such is the frailty of the human heart, that very few men who have no property, have any judgment of their own. They talk and vote as they are directed by some man of property, who has attached their minds to his interest.

Upon my word, Sir, I have long thought an army a piece of clock-work, and to be gov-

SOURCE: Charles Francis Adams, ed., *The Life and Works of John Adams* (Boston: Little, Brown, 1851).

erned only by principles and maxims, as fixed as any in mechanics; and, by all that I have read in the history of mankind, and in authors who have speculated upon society and government, I am much inclined to think a government must manage a society in the same manner; and that this is machinery too.

Harrington has shown that power always follows property. This I believe to be as infallible a maxim in politics, as that action and reaction are equal, is in mechanics. Nay, I believe we may advance one step farther, and affirm that the balance of power in a society, accompanies the balance of property in land. The only possible way, then, of preserving the balance of power on the side of equal liberty and public virtue, is to make the acquisition of land easy to every member of society; to make a division of the land into small quantities, so that the multitude may be possessed of landed estates. If the multitude is possessed of the balance of real estate, the multitude will have the balance of power, and in that case the multitude will take care of the liberty, virtue, and interest of the multitude, in all acts of government.

I believe these principles have been felt, if not understood, in the Massachusetts Bay, from the beginning; and therefore I should think that wisdom and policy would dictate in these times to be very cautious of making alterations. Our people have never been very rigid in scrutinizing into the qualifications of voters, and I presume they will not now begin to be so. But I would not advise them to make any alteration in the laws, at present, respecting the qualifications of voters.

Your idea that those laws which affect the lives and personal liberty of all, or which inflict corporal punishment, affect those who are not qualified to vote, as well as those who are, is just. But so they do women, as well as men; children, as well as adults. What reason should there be for excluding a man of twenty years eleven months and twenty-seven days old,

from a vote, when you admit one who is twenty-one? The reason is, you must fix upon some period in life, when the understanding and will of men in general, is fit to be trusted by the public. Will not the same reason justify the state in fixing upon some certain quantity of property, as a qualification?

The same reasoning which will induce you to admit all men who have no property, to vote, with those who have, for those laws which affect the person, will prove that you ought to admit women and children; for, generally speaking, women and children have as good judgments, and as independent minds, as those men who are wholly destitute of property; these last being to all intents and purposes as much dependent upon others, who will please to feed, clothe, and employ them, as women are upon their husbands, or children on their parents.

As to your idea of proportioning the votes of men, in money matters, to the property they hold, it is utterly impracticable. There is no possible way of ascertaining, at any one time, how much every man in a community is worth; and if there was, so fluctuating is trade and property, that this state of it would change in half an hour. The property of the whole community is shifting every hour, and no record can be kept of the changes.

Society can be governed only by general rules. Government cannot accommodate itself to every particular case as it happens, nor to the circumstances of particular persons. It must establish general comprehensive regulations for cases and persons. The only question is, which general rule will accommodate most cases and most persons.

Depend upon it, Sir, it is dangerous to open so fruitful a source of controversy and altercation as would be opened by attempting to alter the qualifications of voters; there will be no end of it. New claims will arise; women will demand a vote; lads from twelve to twenty-one will think their rights not enough attended to; and every man who has not a far-thing, will demand an equal voice with any other, in all acts of state. It tends to confound and destroy all distinctions, and prostrate all ranks to one common level.

John Adams

Letter to John Taylor (1814)

. . . By *natural aristocracy*, in general, may be understood those superiorities of influence in society which grow out of the constitution of human nature. By *artificial aristocracy*, those inequalities of weight and superiorities of influence which are created and established by civil laws. Terms must be defined before we can reason. By aristocracy, I understand all those men who can command, influence, or procure more than an average of votes; by an aristocrat, every man who can and will influence one man to vote besides himself. Few men will deny that there is a natural aristocracy of virtues and talents in every nation and in every party, in every city and village. Inequalities are a part of the natural history of man.

III

I believe that none but Helvetius will affirm, that all children are born with equal genius.

None will pretend, that all are born of dispositions exactly alike,—of equal weight; equal strength; equal length; equal delicacy of nerves; equal elasticity of muscles; equal complexions; equal figure, grace, or beauty.

I have seen, in the Hospital of Foundlings, the *"Enfans Trouvés,"* at Paris, fifty babes in one room;—all under four days old; all in cradles alike; all nursed and attended alike; all dressed alike; all equally neat. I went from one end to the other of the whole row, and attentively observed all their countenances. And I never saw a greater variety, or more striking inequalities, in the streets of Paris or London. Some had every sign of grief, sorrow, and despair; others had joy and gayety in their faces. Some were sinking in the arms of death; others looked as if they might live to fourscore. Some were as ugly and others as beautiful, as children or adults ever are; these were stupid; those sensible. These were all born to equal rights, but to very different fortunes; to very different success and influence in life.

The world would not contain the books, if one should produce all the examples that reading and experience would furnish. One or two permit me to hint.

Will any man say, would Helvetius say, that all men are born equal in strength? Was Hercules no stronger than his neighbors? How many nations, for how many ages, have been governed by his strength, and by the reputation and renown of it by his posterity? If you

SOURCE: Charles Francis Adams, ed., *The Life and Works of John Adams* (Boston: Little, Brown, 1851).

have lately read Hume, Robertson or the Scottish Chiefs, let me ask you, if Sir William Wallace was no more than equal in strength to the average of Scotchmen? and whether Wallace could have done what he did without that extraordinary strength?

Will Helvetius or Rousseau say that all men and women are born equal in beauty? Will any philosopher say, that beauty has no influence in human society? If he does, let him read the histories of Eve, Judith, Helen, the fair Gabrielle, Diana of Poitiers, Pompadour, Du Barry, Susanna, Abigail, Lady Hamilton, Mrs. Clark, and a million others. Are not despots, monarchs, aristocrats, and democrats, equally liable to be seduced by beauty to confer favors and influence suffrages?

Socrates calls beauty a short-lived tyranny; Plato, *the privilege of nature;* Theophrastus, a mute eloquence; Diogenes, the best letter of recommendations; Carneades, a queen without soldiers; Theocritus, a serpent covered with flowers; Bion, a good that does not belong to the possessor, because it is impossible to give ourselves beauty, or to preserve it. Madame du Barry expressed the philosophy of Carneades in more laconic language, when she said, *"La véritable royauté, c'est la beauté,"*— the genuine royalty is beauty. And she might have said with equal truth, that it is genuine aristocracy; for it has as much influence in one form of government as in any other; and produces aristocracy in the deepest democracy that ever was known or imagined, as infallibly as in any other form of government. What shall we say to all these philosophers, male and female? Is not beauty a privilege granted by nature, according to Plato and to truth, often more influential in society, and even upon laws and government, than stars, garters, crosses, eagles, golden fleeces, or any hereditary titles or other distinctions? The grave elders were not proof against the charms of Susanna. The Grecian sages wondered not at the Trojan war when they saw Helen. Holofernes's guards, when they saw Judith, said,

"one such woman let go would deceive the whole earth."

Can you believe, Mr. Taylor, that the brother of such a sister, the father of such a daughter, the husband of such a wife, or even the gallant of such a mistress, would have but one vote in your moral republic? Ingenious— but not historical, philosophical, or political,— learned, classical, poetical Barlow! I mourn over thy life and thy death. Had truth, instead of popularity and party, been thy object, your pamphlet on privileged orders would have been a very different thing!

That all men are born to equal rights is true. Every being has a right to his own, as clear, as moral, as sacred, as any other being has. This is as indubitable as a moral government in the universe. But to teach that all men are born with equal powers and faculties, to equal influence in society, to equal property and advantages through life, is as gross a fraud, as glaring an imposition on the credulity of the people, as ever was practised by monks, by Druids, by Brahmins, by priests of the immortal Lama, or by the self-styled philosophers of the French revolution. For honor's sake, Mr. Taylor, for truth and virtue's sake, let American philosophers and politicians despise it.

Mr. Adams leaves to Homer and Virgil, to Tacitus and Quintilian, to Mahomet and Calvin, to Edwards and Priestly, or, if you will, to Milton's angels reasoning high in pandemonium, all their acute speculations about fate, destiny, foreknowledge absolute, necessity, and predestination. He thinks it problematical, whether there is, or ever will be, more than one Being capable of understanding this vast subject. In his principles of legislation, he has nothing to do with these interminable controversies. He considers men as free, moral, and accountable agents; and he takes men as God has made them. And will Mr. Taylor deny, that God has made some men deaf and some blind, or will he affirm that these will infallibly have as much influence in society, and be able to procure as many votes as any who can see and hear?

Honor the day,* and believe me no enemy.

IV

That aristocracies, both ancient and modern, have been "variable and artificial," as well as natural and unchangeable, Mr. Adams knows as well as Mr. Taylor, and has never denied or doubted. That "they have all proceeded from moral causes," is not so clear, since many of them appear to proceed from physical causes, many from immoral causes, many from pharisaical, jesuitical, and Machiavelian villany; many from sacerdotal and despotic fraud, and as many as all the rest, from democratical dupery, credulity, adulation, corruption, adoration, superstition, and enthusiasm. If all these cannot be regulated by political laws, and controlled, checked, or balanced by constitutional energies, I am willing Mr. Taylor should say of them what bad are infinitely divisible, like matter. Ay! there's the rub! Despots, monarchs, aristocrats, and democrats have, in all ages hit, at times, upon the best men, in the best sense of the word. But, at other times, and much more frequently, they have all chosen the very worst men; the men who have the most devotedly and the most slavishly flattered their vanity, gratified their most extravagant passions, and promoted their selfish and private views. Without searching volumes, Mr. Taylor, I will tell you in a few words what I mean by an aristocrat, and, consequently, what I mean by aristocracy. By an aristocrat, I mean every man who can command or influence TWO VOTES; ONE BESIDE HIS OWN.

Take the first hundred men you meet in the streets of a city, or on a turnpike road in the country, and constitute them a democratical republic. In my next, you may have some conjectures of what will appear in your new democracy.

V

When your new democratical republic meets, you will find half a dozen men of independent fortunes; half a dozen, of more eloquence; half a dozen, with more learning; half a dozen, with eloquence, learning, and fortune.

Let me see. We have now four-and-twenty; to these we may add six more, who will have more art, cunning, and intrigue, than learning, eloquence, or fortune. These will infallibly soon unite with the twenty-four. Thus we make thirty. The remaining seventy are composed of farmers, shopkeepers, merchants, tradesmen, and laborers. Now, if each of these thirty can, by any means, influence one vote besides his own, the whole thirty can carry sixty votes,—a decided and uncontrolled majority of the hundred. These thirty I mean by aristocrats; and they will instantly convert your democracy of ONE HUNDRED into an aristocracy of THIRTY.

Take at random, or select with your utmost prudence, one hundred of your most faithful and capable domestics from your own numerous plantations, and make them a democratical republic. You will immediately perceive the same inequalities, and the same democratical republic. . . . Here will commence the squabble of Danton and Robespierre, of Julius and Pompey, of Anthony and Augustus, of the white rose and the red rose, of Jefferson and Adams, of Burr and Jefferson, of Clinton and Madison, or, if you will, of Napoleon and Alexander.

This, my dear sir, is the history of mankind, past, present, and to come.

---

* 19 April. The anniversary of the action at Lexington.

James Kent, 1763–1847

James Kent was a Federalist and Anglophile in an era that was quickly rejecting these values. As a young man, Kent was befriended by Alexander Hamilton and John Jay and brought to New York City from his law practice in Poughkeepsie, New York. He soon became the first professor of law at Columbia College and later chief justice of the state supreme court.

As a member of the bench, Kent generally supported Federalist positions. He was no friend of laissez-faire, and constantly supported the holders of state monopolies against the claims of hopeful competitors.

Kent is best remembered for his four-volume *Commentaries on American Law* (1826–30), which was the first systematic exposition of Anglo-American law.

In the following speech delivered at the New York State Constitutional Convention in 1821, Kent makes a classic case for franchises based on property.

James Kent

Speech Defending the Freeholders Suffrage for the New York State Senate (1821)

. . . I cannot but think that the considerate men who have studied the history of republics, or are read in lessons of experience, must look with concern upon our apparent disposition to vibrate from a well balanced government, to the extremes of the democratic doctrines. Such a broad proposition as that contained in the report, at the distance of ten years past, would have struck the public mind with astonishment and terror. So rapid has been the career of our vibration.

SOURCE: *Reports of the Proceedings and Debates of the Convention of 1821* (Albany, N.Y.: E. and E. Hosford, 1821).

Let us recall our attention, for a moment, to our past history.

This state has existed for forty-four years under our present constitution, which was formed by those illustrious sages and patriots who adorned the revolution. It has wonderfully fulfilled all the great ends of civil government. During that long period, we have enjoyed in an eminent degree, the blessings of civil and religious liberty. We have had our lives, our privileges, and our property, protected. We have had a succession of wise and temperate legislatures. The code of our statute law has been again and again revised and corrected, and it may proudly bear a comparison with that of any other people. We have had, during that period, (though I am, perhaps, not the fittest person to say it) a regular, stable, honest, and enlightened administration of justice. All the peaceable pursuits of industry, and all the important interests of education and science, have been fostered and encouraged. We have trebled our numbers within the last twenty-five years, have displayed mighty resources, and have made unexampled progress in the career of prosperity and greatness.

Our financial credit stands at an enviable height; and we are now successfully engaged in connecting the great lakes with the ocean by stupendous canals, which excite the admiration of our neighbours, and will make a conspicuous figure even upon the map of the United States.

There are some of the fruits of our present government; and yet we seem to be dissatisfied with our condition, and we are engaged in the bold and hazardous experiment of remodelling the constitution. It is not fit and discreet: I speak as to wise men; it is not fit and proper that we should pause in our career, and reflect well on the immensity of the innovation in contemplation? Discontent in the midst of so much prosperity, and with such abundant means of happiness, looks like ingratitude, and as if we were disposed to arraign the goodness of Providence. Do we not expose ourselves to the danger of being deprived of the blessings we have enjoyed?— When the husbandman has gathered in his harvest, and has filled his barns and his graneries with the fruits of his industry, if he should then become discontented and unthankful, would he not have reason to apprehend, that the Lord of the harvest might come in his wrath, and with his lightning destroy them?

The senate has hitherto been elected by the farmers of the state—by the free and independent lords of the soil, worth at least $250 in freehold estate, over and above all debts charged thereon. The governor has been chosen by the same electors, and we have hitherto elected citizens of elevated rank and character. Our assembly has been chosen by freeholders, possessing a freehold of the value of $50, or by persons renting a tenement of the yearly value of $5, and who have been rated and actually paid taxes to the state. By the report before us, we propose to annihilate, at one stroke, all those property distinctions and to bow before the idol of universal suffrage. That extreme democratic principle, when applied to the legislative and executive departments of government, has been regarded with terror, by the wise men of every age, because in every European republic, ancient and modern, in which it has been tried, it has terminated disastrously, and been productive of corruption, injustice, violence, and tyranny. And dare we flatter ourselves that we are a peculiar people, who can run the career of history, exempted from the passions which have disturbed and corrupted the rest of mankind? If we are like other races of men, with similar follies and vices, then I greatly fear that our posterity will have reason to deplore in sackcloth and ashes, the delusion of the day.

It is not my purpose at present to interfere with the report of the committee, so far as respects the qualifications of electors for governor and members of assembly. I shall feel grateful if we may be permitted to retain the stability and security of a senate, bottomed upon the freehold property of the state. Such a body, so constituted, may prove a sheet anchor amidst the future factions and storms of the republic. The great leading and governing interest of this state, is, at present, the agricultural; and what madness would it be to commit that interest to the winds. The great body of the people, are now the owners and actual cultivators of the soil. With that wholesome population we always expect to find moderation, frugality, order, honesty, and a due sense of independence, liberty, and justice. It is impossible that any people can lose their liberties by internal fraud or violence, so long as the country is parcelled out among freeholders of moderate possessions, and those freeholders have a sure and efficient control in the affairs of the government. Their habits, sympathies, and employments, necessarily inspire them with a correct spirit of freedom and justice; they are the safest guardians of property and the laws: We certainly cannot too highly appreciate the value of the agricultural interest: It is the foundation of national wealth and power. According to the opinion of her ablest political economists, it is the surplus produce of the agriculture of England, that enables her to support her vast body of manufacturers, her formidable fleets and armies, and the crowds of persons engaged in the liberal professions, and the cultivation of the various arts.

Now, sir, I wish to preserve our senate as the representative of the landed interest. I wish those who have an interest in the soil, to retain the exclusive possession of a branch in the legislature, as a strong hold in which they may find safety through all the vicissitudes which the state may be destined, in the course of Providence, to experience. I wish them to be always enabled to say that their freeholds cannot be taxed without their consent. The men of no property, together with the crowds of dependents connected with great manufacturing and commercial establishments, and the motley and undefinable population of crowded ports, may, perhaps, at some future day, under skilful management, predominate in the assembly, and yet we should be perfectly safe if no laws could pass without the free consent of the owners of the soil. That security we at present enjoy; and it is that security which I wish to retain.

The apprehended danger from the experiment of universal suffrage applied to the whole legislative department, is no dream of the imagination. It is too mighty an excitement for the moral constitution of men to endure. The tendency of universal suffrage, is to jeopardize the rights of property, and the principles of liberty. There is a constant tendency in human society, and the history of every age proves it; there is a tendency in the poor to covet and to share the plunder of the rich; in the debtor to relax or avoid the obligation of contracts; in the majority to tyranize over the minority, and trample down their rights; in the indolent and the profligate, to cast the whole burthens of society upon the industrious and the virtuous; and *there is a tendency in ambitious and wicked men, to inflame these combustible materials.* It requires a vigilant government, and a firm administration of justice, to counteract that tendency. Thou shalt not covet; thou shalt not steal; are divine injunctions induced by this miserable depravity of our nature. Who can undertake to calculate with any precision, how many millions of people, this great state will contain in the course of this and the next century, and who can estimate the future extent and magnitude of our commercial ports? The disproportion between the men of property, and the men of no property, will be in every society in a ratio to its commerce, wealth, and population. We are no longer to remain plain and simple republics of farmers, like the New-England colonists, or the Dutch settlements on the Hudson. We are fast becoming a great nation, with great commerce, manufactures, population, wealth, luxuries, and with the vices and miseries that they engender. One seventh of the population of the city of Paris at this day subsists on charity, and one third of the inhabitants of that city die in the hospitals; what would become of such a city with universal suffrage? France has upwards of four, and England upwards of five millions of manufacturing and commercial labourers without property. Could these kingdoms sustain the weight of universal suffrage? The radicals in England, with the force of that mighty engine, would at once sweep away the property, the laws, and the liberties of that island like a deluge.

The growth of the city of New-York is enough to startle and awaken those who are pursuing the *ignis fatuus* of universal suffrage. . . .

It is rapidly swelling into the unwieldly population, and with the burdensome pauperism, of an European metropolis. New-York is destined to become the future London of America; and in less than a century, that city, with the operation of universal suffrage, and under skilful direction, will govern this state.

The notion that every man that works a day on the road, or serves an idle hour in the militia, is entitled as of right to an equal participation in the whole power of the government, is most unreasonable, and has no foundation in justice. We had better at once discard from the report such a nominal test of merit. If such persons have an equal share in one branch of the legislature, it is surely as much as they can in justice or policy demand. Society is an association for the protection of property as well as of life, and the individual who contributes only one cent to the common stock, ought not to have the same power and influence in directing the property concerns of the partnership, as he who contributes his thousands. He will not have the same inducements to care, and diligence, and fidelity. His inducements and his temptation would be to divide the whole capital upon the principles of an agrarian law.

Liberty, rightly understood, is an inestimable blessing, but liberty without wisdom, and without justice, is no better than wild and savage licentiousness. The danger which we have hereafter to apprehend, is not the want, but the abuse, of liberty. We have to apprehend the oppression of minorities, and a disposition to encroach on private right—to disturb chartered privileges—and to weaken, degrade, and overawe the administration of justice; we have

to apprehend the establishment of unequal, and consequently, unjust systems of taxation, and all the mischiefs of a crude and mutable legislation. A stable senate, exempted from the influence of universal suffrage, will powerfully check these dangerous propensities, and such a check becomes the more necessary, since this Convention has already determined to withdraw the watchful eye of the judicial department from the passage of laws.

We are destined to become a great manufacturing as well as commercial state. We have already numerous and prosperous factories of one kind or another, and one master capitalist with his one hundred apprentices, and journeymen, and agents, and dependents, will bear down at the polls, an equal number of farmers of small estates in his vicinity, who cannot safely unite for their common defence. Large manufacturing and mechanical establishments, can act in an instant with the unity and efficacy of disciplined troops. It is against such combinations, among others, that I think we ought to give to the freeholders, or those who have interest in land, one branch of the legislature for their asylum and their comfort. Universal suffrage once granted, is granted forever, and never can be recalled. There is no retrograde step in the rear of democracy. However mischievous the precedent may be in its consequences, or however fatal in its effects, universal suffrage never can be recalled or checked, but by the strength of the bayonet. We stand, therefore, this moment, on the brink of fate, on the very edge of the precipice. If we let go our present hold on the senate, we commit our proudest hopes and our most precious interests to the waves.

It ought further to be observed, that the senate is a court of justice in the last resort. It is the last depository of public and private rights; of civil and criminal justice. This gives the subject an awful consideration, and wonderfully increases the importance of securing that house from the inroads of universal suffrage. Our country freeholders are exclusively our jurors in the administration of justice, and there is equal reason that none but those who have an interest in the soil, should have any concern in the composition of that court. As long as the senate is safe, justice is safe, prop-

erty is safe, and our liberties are safe. But when the wisdom, the integrity, and the independence of that court is lost, we may be certain that the freedom and happiness of this state, are fled forever.

Daniel Webster, 1782–1852

One of the most gifted speakers of his time, Daniel Webster epitomized the Whigs who followed in the demise of the Federalist party. Like Kent, Webster was no friend of an egalitarian suffrage or laissez-faire. Although as a congressman from Massachusetts in 1824 he had voted against the tariff, by 1828 he had become one of its staunchest supporters when manufacturing supplanted shipping as the cornerstone of the New England economy.

Never one to let interest and principle remain long apart, Webster soon became one of the tariff's most eloquent protectors. He was also known as a severe critic of states rights and nullification, a position that he made famous in his debate with Hayne of South Carolina. His nationalist position, however, was shared by most Jacksonians.

Webster ran for president in 1836 as the Whig party candidate but was soundly defeated by Martin Van Buren, Jackson's Democratic successor.

In the following speech, delivered in Philadelphia in 1846, Webster attempted to refute the argument that the tariff—and by association other forms of marketplace intervention—was the tool of a parasitic minority and incompatible with true republican government.

Daniel Webster

Speech in Defense of the Tariff (1846)

. . . Another great subject of public interest at the present time is the recent tariff, which I discussed when it was established, and

SOURCE: *The Works of Daniel Webster*, vol. II (Boston: Little, Brown, 1851).

about which I have nothing new to say. My object is, and has been, in every thing connected with the protective policy, the true policy of the United States, to see that the labor of the country, the industry of the country, is properly provided for. I am looking, not for a law such as will benefit capitalists,—they can take care of themselves,—but for a law that shall induce capitalists to invest their capital in such a manner as to occupy and employ American labor. I am for such laws as shall induce capitalists not to withhold their capital from actual operations, which give employment to thousands of hands. I look to capital, therefore, in no other view than as I wish it drawn out and used for the public good, and the employment of the labor of the country. . . .

I will only say, that I am for protection, ample, permanent, founded on just principles; and that, in my judgment, the principles of the act of 1842 are the true principles,— *specific* duties, and not *ad valorem* assessment; just discrimination, and, in that just discrimination, great care not to tax the raw material so high as to be a bounty to the foreign manufacturer and an oppression on our own. Discrimination and specific duties, and such duties as are full and adequate to the purposes of protection,—these are the principles of the act of 1842. Whenever there is presented to me any proposition, from any quarter, which contains adequate protection, founded on those indispensable principles, I shall take it. My object is to obtain in the best way I can, and when I can, and as I can, full and adequate and thorough protection to the domestic industry of the country, upon just principles.

In the next place, I have to say that I will take no part in any tinkering of the present law, while its vicious principles remain. As far as depends upon me, the administration shall not escape its just responsibility, by any pretended amendments of the recent law with a view to particular political interests. Allow me to say, frankly, ye iron men and ye coal men of Pennsylvania, that I know you are incapable of compromising in such a case; but if you were, and any inducements were held out to you to make your iron a little softer, and your coal burn a little clearer, while

you left the hand-loom weaver—(The vociferous cheering which burst forth drowned the remainder of the sentence.)

I understand there are seven thousand hand-loom weavers in the city and county of Philadelphia; that their wages have hitherto averaged five dollars a week; that the *ad valorem* duty, as applied to cottons, affects them very injuriously, in its tendency to reduce wages and earnings; especially as the wages of a hand-loom weaver in Scotland hardly exceed one dollar and seventy-five cents or two dollars per week. What the precise result may be, remains to be seen. The carpet-weavers, it is said, may find some indemnity in the reduced price of wool. If this be so, it only shows that the loss is shifted from the weaver to the wool-grower. Washington County, Fayette County, and other counties in this State, will probably learn how this is. In the aggregate it has been estimated that the value of manufactures in the city and county of Philadelphia scarcely falls short of the value of those at Lowell; and their production, it is supposed, employs more hands here than are employed in Lowell.

Gentlemen, on the tariff I have spoken so often and so much, that I am sure no gentleman wishes me to utter the word again. There are some things, however, which cannot be too often repeated. Of all countries in the world, England, for centuries, was the most tenacious in adhering to her protective principles, both in matters of commerce and manufacture. She has of late years relaxed, having found that her position could afford somewhat of free trade. She has the skill acquired by long experience, she has vast machinery, and vast capital, she has a dense population; a cheaply working, because a badly fed and badly clothed, population. She can run her career, therefore, in free trade. We cannot, unless willing to become badly fed and badly clothed also. Gentlemen, for the gymnastic exercises, men strip themselves naked and for this strife and competition in free trade, our laborers, it seems, must strip themselves naked also.

It is, after all, an insidious system, in a country of diversified arts and attainments, of varied pursuits of labor, and different occupations of life. If all men in a country were merely agricultural producers, free trade would be very well. But where divers employments and pursuits have sprung up and exist together, it is necessary that they should succor and support one another, and defend all against dangerous foreign competition.

We may see, at this moment, what consequences result from the doctrines of free trade carried to extremes. Ireland is a signal example. The failure of a potato crop half starves a population of eight millions. The people have no employment which enables them to purchase food. Government itself is already absolutely obliged to furnish employment, often on works of little or no value, to keep the people from positive famine. And yet there are able men,—able I admit them to be, but theoretic men I think them to be; distinguished men, nevertheless,—who maintain that Ireland now is no worse off than if all the great landholders owning estates in Ireland, instead of living in England and spending there the rents of their Irish estates, lived in Ireland, and supported Irish labor on their farms, and about their establishments, and in the workshops.

This opinion is maintained by theoretical economists, notwithstanding the cry of Ireland for employment, employment! And has it not come even to that pass, that the government is obliged to employ hundreds and thousands of the people and pay them, and put them on works of very little utility, merely to give them bread? I wish that every Irishman in the State of Pennsylvania could be here to-night, so that I could ask him to remember the condition of the people of his own country, who are starving for the want of employment, and compare that condition with his own, here

in Pennsylvania, where he has good employment and fair wages.

Gentlemen, this notion of free trade, which goes to cut off the employment of large portions and classes of the population, on the ground that it is best to buy where you can buy cheapest, is a folly, in a country like ours. The case of England is not analogous. What is the cry of free trade in England? Why, it is for cheap bread. In England the deficiency is in bread. Labor is limited in its reward. It can earn but so much, and we have Mr. Cobden's authority for saying that there is a disposition to reduce its earnings still lower. It has, accordingly, a vital interest in reducing the price of food. Therefore free trade in England is but another name for cheap bread. It is not so with us. What we desire for our laboring population is employment. We do not expect food to be cheaper in this country; our object is to make it dear; that is to say, our agricultural interests desire to raise the price of grain; and the laboring classes can stand this, if their employments are protected and the price of labor kept up. Our hope, and let all rejoice in it, is, that the price of our agricultural productions may rise for the benefit of the farmer. Manufacturers and operators, so long as they get steady employment and good wages, can buy at any reasonable rate.

These views are confirmed by the practice of most of the civilized governments of the world. Who of all Europe imitates England? Nobody, as far as I know, except Holland and Turkey. Austria, Russia, Spain, and France adhere to what I call the common-sense doctrine of protecting their own labor. M. Dupin, in the French Chamber of Deputies, said, last year, that the instincts of France were in favor of the protection of French labor. Our American instincts from the first have been very much of the same character. Whence arose all those non-importation agreements, soon after the Revolutionary war, but from an instinct, or feeling that the interests of our own industrious population ought to be consulted and promoted? I happen to have a very important document here, which one of your fellow-citizens caused to be copied and printed in a very handsome manner. It is a non-importation agreement, entered into in this city as early as 1765. That was an American instinct! Here are names to be for ever remembered! I perceive amongst them Robert Morris, the financier of the Revolution, Charles Thompson, the Secretary of Congress, and other illustrious names, whose representatives are still amongst us.

There is one imputation that honest men ought to resist, which is, that the protective policy aids capitalists, and is meant to do so, exclusively. We hear every day of the great capitalists and rich corporations of New England. A word dissipates all this. A corporation in New England is a form of partnership. Any body enters into it that chooses. Where individuals invest their property to build a mill, they do it in the form of a corporation, for the sake of convenience in transacting the business of the concern, their private responsibility still remaining in a qualified sense. The talk about rich and exclusive corporations is idle and delusive. There is not one of them into which men of moderate means may not enter, and many such men do enter, and are interested in them to a considerable extent.

Gentlemen, I have already alluded to the great importance of the protective policy, in this State and in other States, to the handicrafts. That was the original specific aim and design of the policy. At the time of the adoption of the Constitution, large manufacturing corporations were not known. No great works existed, though sagacious and far-seeing men perceived that the application of water-power must one day greatly advance the manufacturing interests. At that day, the handicrafts, the mechanics, and artisans in the city were looked upon as those whose labor it was desirable to protect. Will you pardon me, Gentlemen,

for recalling to the recollection of your older fellow-citizens an interesting celebration which took place in this city, on the 4th day of July, 1788. On that day the citizens of Philadelphia celebrated the Declaration of Independence made by the thirteen United States of America on the 4th of July, 1776, and the establishment of the Constitution or frame of government, then recently adopted by ten States. A procession was formed. The military and companies of the various trades and professions united in it. It was organized and commanded by Generals Mifflin and Stewart, and some other well-known personages. The various companies displayed their flags and banners with appropriate devices and mottos. Richard Bache, Esq., on horseback, as a herald, attended by a trumpet, proclaimed a "New Era." The Hon. Peter Muhlenberg carried a blue flag, with the words "17th of September, 1787," in silver letters. Chief Justice McKean, and his associates, in their robes of office, were seated in a lofty car, shaped like an eagle, and drawn by six white horses. The Chief Justice supported a tall staff, on the top of which was the Cap of Liberty; under the cap the "New Constitution," framed and ornamented, and immediately under the Constitution the words "The People," in large gold letters. Next followed various corps and troops and associations, consuls, collectors, judges, and others. Then came the Agricultural Society, with its flag and motto, "Venerate the Plough." Then the Manufacturing Society, with their spinning and carding machines, looms, and other machinery and implements. Mr. Gallaudet carried the flag, the device on which was a Beehive, standing in the beams of the sun, bees issuing from the hive; the flag a blue silk; motto, "In its rays we shall feel new vigor." This was followed by a carriage holding men weaving and printing. A lady and her four daughters sat upon it, pencilling a piece of chintz, all dressed in cotton of their own manufacture, and over them all, on a lofty staff, was a flag with this motto, "May the Union Government protect the Manufactures of America." The federal ship "Union" followed next, and after her, boat-builders, sail-makers, merchants, and others interested in commerce. Then other trades, such as cabinet and chair-makers, with a flag and motto, "By Unity we support Society." Next bricklayers, with a flag on which there was a brickyard and kiln burning; hands at work; and in the distance a federal city building, with this motto, "It was hard in Egypt, but this prospect makes it easy." Then came the porters, bearing on their flag the motto, "May Industry ever be encouraged." After them various trades again, and then whip and cane-makers, with the motto, "Let us encourage our own Manufactures." After them still others, and amongst the last the brewers, with a flag with this motto, "Home-brewed is best."

I now ask you, Gentlemen, whether these sentiments and banners indicated that government was to lay duties only for revenue, and without respect to home industry? Do you believe the doctrines of Mr. Polk, or those of the citizens of Philadelphia in 1788? . . .

The New Orthodoxy

The Republic of Equal Individuals

David Buel, Jr.

The most forceful argument for universal manhood suffrage at the New York State Constitutional Convention of 1821 was delivered by David Buel, Jr., a little-known delegate from Rensselaer County. Despite the eloquence and reputation of James Kent, Buel and his colleagues carried the day.

David Buel, Jr.

Speech in Support of Universal Suffrage Delivered at the New York Constitutional Convention (1821)

. . . The question whether it is safe and proper to extend the right of suffrage to other classes of our citizens, besides the landholders, is decided as I think, by the sober sense and deliberate acts of the great American people.

SOURCE: *Reports of the Proceedings and Debates of the Convention of 1821* (Albany, N.Y.: E. and E. Hosford, 1821).

To this authority I feel willing to bow. An examination of the constitutions of the different states, will show us that those enlightened bodies of statesmen and patriots who have from time to time been assembled for the grave and important purpose of forming and reforming the constitutions of the states have sanctioned and established as a maxim, the opinion that there is no danger in confiding the most extensive right of suffrage to the intelligent population of these United States.

Of the twenty-four states which compose this union, twelve states require only a certain time of residence as a qualification to vote for all their elective officers—eight require in addition to residence the payment of taxes or the performance of militia duty—four states only *require* a freehold qualification, viz. New-York, North-Carolina, Virginia, and Rhode-Island. The distinction which the amendment of the gentleman from Albany proposes to continue, exists only in the constitution of this state, and in that of North-Carolina.

In some of the states, the possession of a freehold, constitutes one of several qualifications, either of which gives the right of suffrage; but in four only, is the exclusive right of voting for any department of the government confined to landholders.

The progressive extension of the right of suffrage by the reformations which have taken place in several of the state constitutions, adds to the force of the authority. By the original constitution of Maryland, (made in 1776,) a considerable property qualification was necessary to constitute an elector. By successive alterations in the years 1802, and 1810, the right has been extended to all the white citizens who have a permanent residence in the state. A similar alteration has been made in the constitution of South-Carolina; and by the recent reformations in the constitutions of Connecticut and Massachusetts, property qualifications in the electors have been abolished; the right is extended in the former almost to universal suffrage, and in the latter to all the citizens who pay taxes. It is not in the smaller states only, that these liberal principles respecting suffrage, have been adopted. The constitution of Pennsylvania, adopted in the year 1790, extends the right of suffrage to all the citizens who pay taxes, and to their sons between the age of twenty-one and twenty-two years.

That constitution was formed by men, distinguished for patriotism and talents. At the head of them, we find the name of Judge [James] Wilson, a distinguished statesman, and one of the founders of the constitution of the United States.

The constitution of Pennsylvania was formed on the broad principle of suffrage, which that distinguished man lays down in his writings. "That every citizen whose circumstances do not render him necessarily dependant on the will of another, should possess a vote in electing those, by whose conduct his property, his reputation, his liberty, and his life may be almost materially affected." This is the correct rule, and it has been adopted into the constitution of every state which has been formed since the government of the United States was organized. So universal an admission of the great principle of general suffrage, by the Conventions of discreet and sober minded men, who have been engaged in forming or amending the different constitutions, produces a strong conviction that the principle is safe and salutary.

It is said by those who contend that the right of voting for senators should be confined to the landholders, that the framers of our constitution were wise and practical men, and that they deemed this distinction essential to the security of the landed property; and that we have not encountered any evils from it during the forty years experience which we have had. To this I answer, that if the restriction of the right of suffrage has produced no positive evil, it cannot be shown to have produced any good results.

The qualifications for assembly voters, under the existing constitution, are as liberal as any which will probably be adopted by this Convention. It is pretended that the assembly, during the forty-three years experience which we have enjoyed under our constitution, has been, in any respect, inferior to the senate? Has the senate, although elected exclusively by freeholders, been composed of men of more talents, or greater probity, than the assembly? Have the rights of property, generally, or of the landed interest in particular, been more vigilantly watched, and more carefully protected by the senate than by the assembly? I might appeal to the journals of the two houses, and to the recollections and information of the members of the committee on this subject; but it is unnecessary, as I understand the gentlemen who support the amendment, distinctly admit, that hitherto the assembly has been as safe a depository of the rights of the landed interest, as the senate. But it is supposed that the framers of our constitution must have had wise and cogent reasons for making such a distinction between the electors of the different branches of the government. May we not, however, without the least derogation from the wisdom and good intentions of the framers of our constitution, ascribe the provision in question to circumstances which then influenced them, but which no longer ought to have weight?

When our constitution was framed, the domain of the state was in the hands of a few. The proprietors of the great manors were almost the only men of great influence; and the landed property was deemed worthy of almost exclusive consideration. Before the revolution, freeholders only were allowed to exercise the right of suffrage. The notions of our ancestors, in regard to real property, were all derived from England. The feudal tenures were universally adopted. The law of primogeniture, by which estates descended to the eldest son, and the rule of descent by which the male branches inherited the paternal estate, to the exclusion of the female, entails, and many other provisions of feudal origin were in force. The tendency of this system, it is well understood, was to keep the lands of the state in few hands. But since that period, by the operation of wiser laws, and by the prevalence of juster principles, an entire revolution has taken place in regard to real property. Our laws for regulating descents, and

for converting entailed estates into fee-simple, have gradually increased the number of landholders: Our territory has been rapidly divided and subdivided: And although the landed interest is no longer controlled by the influence of a few great proprietors, its aggregate importance is vastly increased, and almost the whole community have become interested in its protection. In New-England, the inhabitants, from the earliest period, have enjoyed the system which we are progressively attaining to. There, the property of the soil has always been in the hands of the *many*. The great bulk of the population are farmers and freeholders, yet no provision is incorporated in their constitutions, excluding those who are not freeholders from a full participation in the right of suffrage. May we not trace the notions of the framers of our constitution, respecting the exclusive privilege of the freeholders, to the same source from whence they derived all their ideas of real property?

In England, from the earliest times, the superiority of the landed interest was maintained. To go no farther back than the Norman invasion, we find the domain of England parcelled out in great manors among the followers of the Conqueror. They and their descendants, for many years, were the only legislative and judiciary power in the kingdom. Their baronies gave them the right of legislation. It was a privilege annexed to the land which their vassals cultivated. Their vassals, in process of time, became freeholders, and formed the juries in the manor courts.

It was a long time before any other interests than that of the landholders was attended to. For some hundred years, the great cities and boroughs were not considered worthy of being represented in the great councils of the kingdom. And although numerous great interests have since arisen, the house of peers and the knights of the shire, are still supposed to represent the landed interest exclusively. It was not surprising that the framers of our constitution, though they in the main aimed to establish our government on republican principles, should have adopted some of the notions which they inherited, with their domains, from their ancestors. The force of habit and prejudice which induced those illustrious men to incorporate in the constitution absurd provisions, will manifestly appear by adverting to a single instance of the application of the rule established by them, to determine the right of voting for senators and governor.

A man who is possessed of a piece of land worth $250 for his own life, or the life of another person, is a freeholder, and has the right to vote for governor and senators. But one who has an estate in ever so valuable a farm, for 999 years, or any other definite term, however long, is not a freeholder and cannot vote. The absurdity of the distinction, at this day, is so glaring as to require no comment. Yet there are numerous farmers, in different parts of the state, who are excluded from the right of suffrage on this absurd distinction between freehold and leasehold estates. No person will now pretend that a farmer who holds his land by a thousand years lease is less attached to the soil, or less likely to exercise the privilege of freeman discreetly, than a freeholder. We shall not, I trust, be accused of want of respect to settled institutions, if we expunge such glaring absurdities from our constitution. It is supposed, however, by the honourable member before me (Chancellor Kent) that landed property will become insecure under the proposed extension of the right of suffrage, by the influx of a more dangerous population. That gentleman has drawn a picture from the existing state of society in European kingdoms, which would be indeed appalling, if we could suppose such a state of society could exist here. But are arguments, drawn from the state of society in Europe, applicable to our situation? . . .

It is conceded by my honourable friend, that the great landed estates must be cut up by the operation of our laws of descent; that we have already seen those laws effect a great change; and that it is the inevitable tendency of our rules of descent, to divide up our territory into farms of moderate size. The real property, therefore, will be in the hands of the *many*. But in England, and other European kingdoms, it is the policy of the aristocracy to keep the lands in few hands. The laws of primogeniture, the entailments and family settlements, all tend to give a confined direction to the course of descents. Hence we find in Europe, the landed estates possessed by a few rich men; and the great bulk of the population poor, and without that attachment to the government which is found among the owners of the soil. Hence, also, the poor envy and hate the rich, and mobs and insurrections sometimes render property insecure. Did I believe that our population would degenerate into such a state, I should, with the advocates for the amendment, hesitate in extending the right of suffrage; but I confess I have no such fears. I have heretofore had doubts respecting the safety of adopting the principles of a suffrage as extensive as that now contemplated. I have given to the subject the best reflection of which I am capable; and I have satisfied myself, that there is no danger in adopting those liberal principles which are incorporated in almost all the constitutions of these United States.

There are in my judgment, many circumstances which will forever preserve the people of this state from the vices and the degradation of European population, beside those which I have already taken notice of. The provision already made for the establishment of common schools, will, in a very few years, extend the benefit of education to all our citizens. The universal diffusion of information will forever distinguish our population from that of Europe. Virtue and intelligence are the true basis on which every republican government must rest. When they are lost, freedom will no longer exist. The diffusion of education is the only sure means of establishing these pillars of freedom. I rejoice in this view of the subject, that our common school fund will (if the report on the legislative department be adopted,) be consecrated by a constitutional provision; and I feel no apprehension, for myself, or my posterity, in confiding the right of suffrage to the great mass of such a population as I believe ours will always be. The farmers in this country will always out number all other portions of our population. Admitting that the increase of our cities, and especially of our commercial metropolis, will be as great as it has been hitherto; it is not to be doubted that the agricultural population will increase in the same proportion. The city population will never be able to depress that of the country. New-York has always contained about a tenth part of the population of the state, and will probably always bear a similar proportion. Can she, with such a population, under any circumstances, render the property of the vast population of the country insecure? It may be that mobs will occasionally be collected, and commit depredations in a great city; but, can the mobs traverse our immense territory, and invade the farms, and despoil the property of the landholders? And if such a state of things were possible, would a senate, elected by freeholders, afford any security? It is the regular administration of the laws by an independent judiciary, that renders property secure against private acts of violence. And there will always be a vast majority of our citizens interested in preventing legislative injustice.

But the gentleman who introduced the proposition now before the committee, has predicted dangers of another kind to the landed interest, if their exclusive right of electing the senate shall be taken away. He supposes, that combinations of other interests will be formed to depress the landholders, by charging them exclusively with the burthen of taxation.

I cannot entertain any apprehension that such a state of things will ever exist. Under any probable extension of the right of suffrage, the landed interest will, in my view of the subject, always maintain a vast preponderance of numbers and influence. From what combinations of other interests can danger arise? The mercantile and manufacturing interests are the only ones which can obtain a formidable influence. Are the owners of manufacturing establishments, scattered through the state, as they always must be, likely to enter into a confederacy with the merchants of the great cities, for the purpose of depressing the yeomanry and landholders of this great state? Has our past experience shewn any tendency in those two great interests, to unite in any project, especially for such an one as that which I have mentioned? We usually find the merchants and manufacturers acting as rivals to each other: but both feel a community of interest with the landholders; and it will ever be the interest of the farmers, as it ever has been, to foster and protect both the manufacturing and mercantile interests. The discussions which the tariff has undergone, both in and out of congress, have demonstrated the feelings of rivalship which exist between our manufacturers and our merchants. But who has ever heard, in this or any other country, of a combination of those two classes of men, to destroy the interest of the farmers? No other combination, then, can be imagined, but that of the poor against the rich. Can it be anticipated, that those who have no property can ever so successfully combine their efforts, as to have a majority in both branches of the legislature, unfriendly to the security of property?

One ground of the argument of gentlemen who support the amendment is, that the extension of the right of suffrage will give an undue influence to the rich over the persons who depend upon them for employment; but if the rich control the votes of the poor, the result cannot be unfavourable to the security of property. The supposition that, at some future day, when the poor shall become numerous, they may imitate the radicals of England, or the jacobins of France; that they may rise, in the majesty of their strength, and usurp the property of the landholders, is so unlikely to be realized, that we may dismiss all fear arising from that source. Before that can happen, wealth must lose all its influence; public morals must be destroyed; and the nature of our government changed, and it would be in vain to look to a senate, chosen by landholders, for security in a case of such extremity. I cannot but think, that all the dangers which it is predicted will flow from doing away the exclusive right of the landholders to elect the senators, are groundless.

I contend, that by the true principle of our government, property, as such, is not the basis of representation. Our community is an association of persons—of human beings—not a partnership founded on property. The declared object of the people of this state in associating, was, to "establish such a government as they deemed best calculated to secure the rights and liberties of the good people of the state, and most conducive to their happiness and safety." Property, it is admitted,

is one of the rights to be protected and secured; and although the protection of life and liberty is the highest object of attention, it is certainly true, that the security of property is a most interesting and important object in every free government. Property is essential to our temporal happiness; and is necessarily one of the most interesting subjects of legislation. The desire of acquiring property is a universal passion. I readily give to property the important place which has been assigned to it by the honourable member from Albany (Chancellor Kent). To property we are indebted for most of our comforts, and for much of our temporal happiness. The numerous religious, moral, and benevolent institutions which are every where established, owe their existence to wealth; and it is wealth which enables us to make those great internal improvements which we have undertaken. Property is only one of the incidental rights of the person who possesses it; and, as such, it must be made secure; but it does not follow, that it must therefore be represented specifically in any branch of the government. . . .

Andrew Jackson, 1767–1845

Andrew Jackson was the seventh president of the United States and the symbol of the egalitarian and democratic individualism of his times.

The son of Irish immigrants who were killed in the American Revolution and a man of little formal education, Jackson studied for the bar in North Carolina and then set out to seek his fortune in the frontier of Tennessee. Through trade, speculation, planting, and politics, Jackson achieved his fortune and along the way became a renowned military hero, and finally, the first president to break the dynastic hold of the great families of Virginia and Massachusetts.

In 1796, Jackson helped draft the Tennessee constitution and was elected to serve in the House of Representatives. One year later, he was appointed to the Senate but had to resign because of financial problems. Jackson then embarked on a military career that led to fame during the War of 1812 in the campaign against the Creek Indians and then in the defense of New Orleans. In 1818, he led a brutal and controversial campaign against Indians along the Alabama and Florida borders and was rewarded with the governorship of the new territory of Florida by President Monroe.

In 1823, Jackson returned to the Senate and in 1824 was first in popular votes among four candidates for the presidency. However, supporters of Henry Clay backed John Quincy Adams when the election was decided in the House of Representatives. Jackson's defeat was short lived, and in 1828 he ran against Adams and was elected president.

Jackson's "Farewell Address," parts of which are printed below, shows his skillful use of traditional republican rhetoric to support policies of individualism, limited government, and nationalism. Significantly, Jackson enlarged the scope of the "virtuous" public to encompass all who worked, traded, or invested in the marketplace. He thus successfully grafted the symbols of earlier republicanism onto an increasingly nonagrarian, individualistic society.

Andrew Jackson

Farewell Address (1837)

Being about to retire finally from public life, I beg leave to offer you my grateful thanks for the many proofs of kindness and confidence which I have received at your hands. It has been my fortune, in the discharge of public duties, civil and military, frequently to have found myself in difficult and trying situations where prompt decision and energetic action were necessary and where the interest of the country required that high responsibilities should be fearlessly encountered; and it is with the deepest emotions of gratitude that I acknowledge the continued and unbroken confidence with which you have sustained me in every trial. My public life has been a long one, and I cannot hope that it has, at all times, been free from errors. But I have the consola-

tion of knowing that, if mistakes have been committed, they have not seriously injured the country I so anxiously endeavored to serve; and, at the moment when I surrender my last public trust, I leave this great people prosperous and happy; in the full enjoyment of liberty and peace; and honored and respected by every nation of the world.

If my humble efforts have, in any degree, contributed to preserve to you these blessings, I have been more than rewarded by the honors you have heaped upon me; and, above all, by the generous confidence with which you have supported me in every peril, and with which you have continued to animate and cheer my path to the closing hour of my political life. The time has now come when advanced age and a broken frame warn me to retire from public concerns; but the recollection of the many favors you have bestowed upon me is engraven upon my heart, and I have felt that I could not part from your ser-

SOURCE: "Farewell Address of Andrew Jackson to the People of the United States," and the "Inaugural Address of Martin Van Buren," President of the United States (Washington, 1837).

vice without making this public acknowledgement of the gratitude I owe you. And if I use the occasion to offer to you the counsels of age and experience, you will, I trust, receive them with the same indulgent kindness which you have so often extended to me; and will, at least, see in them an earnest desire to perpetuate, in this favored land, the blessings of liberty and equal laws.

We have now lived almost fifty years under the Constitution framed by the sages and patriots of the Revolution. The conflicts in which the nations of Europe were engaged during a great part of this period; the spirit in which they waged war against each other; and our intimate commercial connections with every part of the civilized world, rendered it a time of much difficulty for the Government of the United States. We have had our seasons of peace and of war, with all the evils which precede or follow a state of hostility with powerful nations. We encountered these trials with our Constitution yet in its infancy, and under the disadvantages which a new and untried Government must always feel when it is called upon to put forth its whole strength, without the lights of experience to guide it or the weight of precedents to justify its measures. But we have passed triumphantly through all these difficulties. Our Constitution is no longer a doubtful experiment; and, at the end of nearly half a century, we find that it has preserved unimpaired the liberties of the people, secured the rights of property, and that our country has improved and is flourishing beyond any former example in the history of nations.

* * * * *

. . . These cheering and grateful prospects and these multiplied favors we owe, under Providence, to the adoption of the Federal Constitution. It is no longer a question whether this great country can remain happily united and flourish under our present form of government. Experience, the unerring test of all human undertakings, has shown the wisdom and foresight of those who formed it; and has proved that in the union of these States there is a sure foundation for the brightest hopes of freedom and for the happiness of the people. At every hazard and by every sacrifice, this Union must be preserved.

The necessity of watching with jealous anxiety for the preservation of the Union was earnestly pressed upon his fellow citizens by the Father of his country in his farewell address. He has there told us that "while experience shall not have demonstrated its impracticability, there will always be reason to distrust the patriotism of those who, in any quarter, may endeavor to weaken its bonds"; and he has cautioned us, in the strongest terms, against the formation of parties on geographical discriminations, as one of the means which might disturb our union, and to which designing men would be likely to resort.

The lessons contained in this invaluable legacy of Washington to his countrymen should be cherished in the heart of every citizen to the latest generation; and, perhaps, at no period of time could they be more usefully remembered than at the present moment. For when we look upon the scenes that are passing around us, and dwell upon the pages of his parting address, his paternal counsels would seem to be not merely the offspring of wisdom and foresight, but the voice of prophecy foretelling events and warning us of the evil to come. Forty years have passed since this imperishable document was given to his countrymen. The Federal Constitution was then regarded by him as an experiment, and he so speaks of it in his address; but an experiment upon the success of which the best hopes of his country depended, and we all know that he was prepared to lay down his life, if necessary, to secure to it a full and a fair trial. The trial has been made. It has succeeded beyond the proudest hopes of those who framed it. Every quarter of this widely extended nation has felt its blessings and shared in the general prosperity produced by its adoption. But amid this general prosperity and splendid success, the dangers of which he warned us are becoming every day more evident and the signs of evil are sufficiently apparent to awaken the deepest anxiety in the bosom of the patriot. We behold systematic efforts publicly made to sow the seeds of discord between different parts of the United States and to place party divisions directly upon geographical distinctions; to excite the *south* against the *north* and the *north* against the *south;* and to force into the controversy the most delicate and exciting topics, topics upon which it is impossible that a large portion of the Union can ever speak without strong emotion. Appeals, too, are constantly made to sectional interests in order to influence the election of the Chief Magistrate, as if it were desired that he should favor a particular quarter of the country instead of fulfilling the duties of his station with impartial justice to all; and the possible dissolution of the Union has at length become an ordinary and familiar subject of discussion. Has the warning voice of Washington been forgotten? or have designs already been formed to sever the Union? Let it not be supposed that I impute to all of those who have taken an active part in these unwise and unprofitable discussions a want of patriotism or of public virtue. The honorable feeling of State pride and local attachments find a place in the bosoms of the most enlightened and pure. But while such men are conscious of their own integrity and honesty of purpose, they ought never to forget that the citizens of other States are their political brethren; and that, however mistaken they may be in their views, the great body of them are equally honest and upright with themselves. Mutual suspicions and reproaches may in time create mutual hostility, and artful and designing men will always be found, who are ready to foment these fatal divisions and to inflame the natural jealousies of different sections of the country. The history of the world is full of such examples and especially the history of republics.

What have you to gain by division and dissension? Delude not yourselves with the belief that a breach once made may be afterwards repaired. If the Union is once severed, the line of separation will grow wider and wider, and the controversies which are now debated and settled in the halls of legislation will then be tried in fields of battle and determined by the sword. Neither should you deceive yourselves with the hope that the first line of separation would be the permanent one, and that nothing but harmony and concord would be found in the new associations formed upon the dissolution of this Union. Local interests would still be found there, and unchastened ambition. And if the recollection of common dangers in which the people of these United States stood side by side against the common foe; the memory of victories won by their united valor; the prosperity and happiness they have enjoyed under the present Constitution; the proud name they bear as citizens of this great republic; if all these recollections and proofs of common interest are not strong enough to bind us together as one people, what tie will hold united the new divisions of empire, when these bonds have been broken and this Union dissevered? The first line of separation would not last for a single generation; new fragments would be torn off; new leaders would spring up; and this great and glorious republic would soon be broken into a multitude of petty states, without commerce, without credit; jealous of one another; armed for mutual aggression; loaded with taxes to pay armies and leaders; seeking aid against each other from foreign powers; insulted and trampled upon by the nations of Europe, until, harassed with conflicts and humbled and debased in spirit, they would be ready to submit to the absolute dominion of any military adventurer and to surrender their liberty for the sake of repose. It is impossible to look on the consequences that would inevitably follow the destruction of this Government and not feel indignant when we hear cold calculations about the value of the Union and have so constantly before us a line of conduct so well calculated to weaken its ties.

There is too much at stake to allow pride or passion to influence your decision. Never for a moment believe that the great body of the citizens of any State of States can deliberately intend to do wrong. They may, under the influence of temporary excitement or misguided opinions, commit mistakes; they may be misled for a time by the suggestions of self-interest; but in a community so enlightened and patriotic as the people of the United States, argument will soon make them sensible of their errors; and, when convinced, they will be ready to repair them. If they have no higher or better motives to govern them, they will at least perceive that their own interest requires them to be just to others as they hope to receive justice at their hands.

But in order to maintain the Union unimpaired, it is absolutely necessary that the laws passed by the constituted authorities should be faithfully executed in every part of the country, and that every good citizen should, at all times, stand ready to put down, with the combined force of the nation, every attempt at unlawful resistance, under whatever pretext it may be made or whatever shape it may assume. Unconstitutional or oppressive laws may no doubt be passed by Congress, either from erroneous views or the want of due consideration; if they are within the reach of judicial authority, the remedy is easy and peaceful; and if, from the character of the law, it is an abuse of power not within the control of the judiciary, then free discussion and calm appeals to reason and to the justice of the people will not fail to redress the wrong. But until the law shall be declared void by the courts or repealed by Congress, no individual or combination of individuals can be justified in forcibly resisting its execution. It is

impossible that any Government can continue to exist upon any other principles. It would cease to be a Government and be unworthy of the name if it had not the power to enforce the execution of its own laws within its own sphere of action.

It is true that cases may be imagined disclosing such a settled purpose of usurpation and oppression on the part of the Government as would justify an appeal to arms. These, however, are extreme cases, which we have no reason to apprehend in a Government where the power is in the hands of a patriotic people; and no citizen who loves his country would in any case whatever resort to forcible resistance, unless he clearly saw that the time had come when a freeman should prefer death to submission; for if such a struggle is once begun and the citizens of one section of the country arrayed in arms against those of another in doubtful conflict, let the battle result as it may, there will be an end of the Union and, with it, an end to the hopes of freedom. The victory of the injured would not secure to them the blessings of liberty; it would avenge their wrongs, but they would themselves share in the common ruin.

But the Constitution cannot be maintained nor the Union preserved in opposition to public feeling by the mere exertion of the coercive powers confided to the General Government. The foundations must be laid in the affections of the people; in the security it gives to life, liberty, character, and property, in every quarter of the country; and in the fraternal attachment which the citizens of the several States bear to one another as members of one political family, mutually contributing to promote the happiness of each other. Hence the citizens of every State should studiously avoid everything calculated to wound the sensibility or offend the just pride of the people of other States; and they should frown upon any proceedings within their own borders likely to disturb the tranquillity of their political brethren in other portions of the Union. In a country so extensive as the United States and with pursuits so varied, the internal regulations of the several States must frequently differ from one another in important particulars; and this difference is unavoidably increased by the varying principles upon which the American colonies were originally planted; principles which had taken deep root in their social relations before the Revolution, and, therefore, of necessity influencing their policy since they became free and independent States. But each State has the unquestionable right to regulate its own internal concerns according to its own pleasure; and while it does not interfere with the rights of the people of other States or the rights of the Union, every State must be the sole judge of the measures proper to secure the safety of its citizens and promote their happiness; and all efforts on the part of people of other States to cast odium upon their institutions, and all measures calculated to disturb their rights of property or to put in jeopardy their peace and internal tranquillity are in direct opposition to the spirit in which the Union was formed, and must endanger its safety. Motives of philanthropy may be assigned for this unwarrantable interference; and weak men may persuade themselves for a moment that they are laboring in the cause of humanity and asserting the rights of the human race; but everyone, upon sober reflection, will see that nothing but mischief can come from these improper assaults upon the feelings and rights of others. Rest assured that the men found busy in this work of discord are not worthy of your confidence and deserve your strongest reprobation.

In the legislation of Congress, also, and in every measure of the General Government, justice to every portion of the United States should be faithfully observed. No free Government can stand without virtue in the people, and a lofty spirit of patriotism; and if the sordid feelings of mere selfishness shall usurp the place which ought to be filled by public spirit, the legislation of Congress will

soon be converted into a scramble for personal and sectional advantages. Under our free institutions, the citizens of every quarter of our country are capable of attaining a high degree of prosperity and happiness without seeking to profit themselves at the expense of others; and every such attempt must in the end fail to succeed, for the people in every part of the United States are too enlightened not to understand their own rights and interests and to detect and defeat every effort to gain undue advantages over them; and when such designs are discovered, it naturally provokes resentments which cannot always be easily allayed. Justice, full and ample justice, to every portion of the United States should be the ruling principle of every freeman and should guide the deliberations of every public body, whether it be State or national.

It is well known that there have always been those amongst us who wish to enlarge the powers of the General Government; and experience would seem to indicate that there is a tendency on the part of this Government to overstep the boundaries marked out for it by the Constitution. Its legitimate authority is abundantly sufficient for all the purposes for which it was created; and its powers being expressly enumerated, there can be no justification for claiming anything beyond them. Every attempt to exercise power beyond these limits should be promptly and firmly opposed. For one evil example will lead to other measures still more mischievous; and if the principle of constructive powers, or supposed advantages, or temporary circumstances, shall ever be permitted to justify the assumption of a power not given by the Constitution, the General Government will before long absorb all the powers of legislation, and you will have, in effect, but one consolidated Government. From the extent of our country, its diversified interests, different pursuits, and different habits, it is too obvious for argument that a single consolidated Government would be wholly inadequate to watch over and protect its interests; and every friend of our free institutions should be always prepared to maintain unimpaired and in full vigor the rights and sovereignty of the States and to confine the action of the General Government strictly to the sphere of its appropriate duties.

There is, perhaps, no one of the powers conferred on the Federal Government so liable to abuse as the taxing power. The most productive and convenient sources of revenue were necessarily given to it, that it might be able to perform the important duties imposed upon it; and the taxes which it lays upon commerce being concealed from the real payer in the price of the article, they do not so readily attract the attention of the people as smaller sums demanded from them directly by the tax gatherer. But the tax imposed on goods enhances by so much the price of the commodity to the consumer; and, as many of these duties are imposed on articles of necessity which are daily used by the great body of the people, the money raised by these imposts is drawn from their pockets. Congress has no right, under the Constitution, to take money from the people unless it is required to execute some one of the specific powers intrusted to the Government; and if they raise more than is necessary for such purposes, it is an abuse of the power of taxation and unjust and oppressive. It may, indeed, happen that the revenue will sometimes exceed the amount anticipated when the taxes were laid. When, however, this is ascertained, it is easy to reduce them; and, in such a case, it is unquestionably the duty of the Government to reduce them, for no circumstances can justify it in assuming a power not given to it by the Constitution nor in taking away the money of the people when it is not needed for the legitimate wants of the Government.

Plain as these principles appear to be, you will yet find that there is a constant effort to induce the General Government to go beyond the limits of its taxing power and to impose unnecessary burdens upon the people. Many powerful interests are continually at work to procure heavy duties on commerce and to swell the revenue beyond the real necessities of the public service; and the country has already felt the injurious effects of their combined influence. They succeeded in obtaining a tariff of duties bearing most oppressively on the agricultural and laboring classes of society and producing a revenue that could not be usefully employed within the range of the powers conferred upon Congress; and, in order to fasten upon the people this unjust and unequal system of taxation, extravagant schemes of internal improvement were got up in various quarters to squander the money and to purchase support. Thus, one unconstitutional measure was intended to be upheld by another, and the abuse of the power of taxation was to be maintained by usurping the power of expending the money in internal improvements. You cannot have forgotten the severe and doubtful struggle through which we passed when the Executive Department of the Government, by its veto, endeavored to arrest this prodigal scheme of injustice, and to bring back the legislation of Congress to the boundaries prescribed by the Constitution. The good sense and practical judgment of the people, when the subject was brought before them, sustained the course of the Executive; and this plan of unconstitutional expenditure for the purpose of corrupt influence is, I trust, finally overthrown.

The result of this decision has been felt in the rapid extinguishment of the public debt and the large accumulation of a surplus in the treasury, notwithstanding the tariff was reduced and is now very far below the amount originally contemplated by its advocates. But, rely upon it, the design to collect an extravagant revenue and to burden you with taxes beyond the economical wants of the Government is not yet abandoned. The various interests which have combined together to impose a heavy tariff and to produce an overflowing treasury are too strong and have too much at stake to surrender the contest. The corporations and wealthy individuals who are engaged in large manufacturing establishments desire a high tariff to increase their gains. Designing politicians will support it to conciliate their favor and to obtain the means of profuse expenditure for the purpose of purchasing influence in other quarters; and since the people have decided that the Federal Government cannot be permitted to employ its income in internal improvements, efforts will be made to seduce and mislead the citizens of the several States by holding out to them the deceitful prospect of benefits to be derived from a surplus revenue collected by the General Government and annually divided among the States. And if, encouraged by these fallacious hopes, the States should disregard the principles of economy which ought to characterize every republican Government and should indulge in lavish expenditures exceeding their resources, they will, before long, find themselves oppressed with debts which they are unable to pay, and the temptation will become irresistible to support a high tariff in order to obtain a surplus for distribution. Do not allow yourselves, my fellow citizens, to be misled on this subject. The Federal Government cannot collect a surplus for such purposes without violating the principles of the Constitution and assuming powers which have not been granted. It is, moreover, a system of injustice, and, if persisted in, will inevitably lead to corruption and must end in ruin. The surplus revenue will be drawn from the pockets of the people, from the farmer, the mechanic, and the laboring classes of society; but who will receive it when distributed among the States, where it is to be disposed of by leading State politicians who have friends to favor and political partisans to gratify? It will certainly not be returned to those who paid it and who have most need of it and are honestly entitled to it. There is but one safe rule, and that is to confine the General Government rigidly within the sphere of its appropriate duties. It has no power to

raise a revenue or impose taxes except for the purposes enumerated in the Constitution; and if its income is found to exceed these wants, it should be forthwith reduced, and the burdens of the people so far lightened.

In reviewing the conflicts which have taken place between different interests in the United States and the policy pursued since the adoption of our present form of government, we find nothing that has produced such deep-seated evil as the course of legislation in relation to the currency. The Constitution of the United States unquestionably intended to secure to the people a circulating medium of gold and silver. But the establishment of a national bank by Congress with the privilege of issuing paper money receivable in the payment of the public dues, and the unfortunate course of legislation in the several States upon the same subject, drove from general circulation the constitutional currency and substituted one of paper in its place. . . .

. . . Some of the evils which arise from this system of paper press with peculiar hardship upon the class of society least able to bear it. A portion of this currency frequently becomes depreciated or worthless, and all of it is easily counterfeited in such a manner as to require peculiar skill and much experience to distinguish the counterfeit from the genuine note. These frauds are most generally perpetrated in the smaller notes, which are used in the daily transactions of ordinary business; and the losses occasioned by them are commonly thrown upon the laboring classes of society whose situation and pursuits put it out of their power to guard themselves from these impositions and whose daily wages are necessary for their subsistence. It is the duty of every Government so to regulate its currency as to protect this numerous class as far as practicable from the impositions of avarice and fraud. It is more especially the duty of the United States where the Government is emphatically the Government of the people, and where this respectable portion of our citizens are so proudly distinguished from the laboring classes of all other nations by their independent spirit, their love of liberty, their intelligence, and their high tone of moral character. Their industry in peace is the source of our wealth; and their bravery in war has covered us with glory; and the Government of the United States will but ill discharge its duties if it leaves them a prey to such dishonest impositions. Yet it is evident that their interests cannot be effectually protected unless silver and gold are restored to circulation.

These views alone of the paper currency are sufficient to call for immediate reform; but there is another consideration which should still more strongly press it upon your attention.

Recent events have proved that the paper money system of this country may be used as an engine to undermine your free institutions; and that those who desire to engross all power in the hands of the few and to govern by corruption or force are aware of its power and prepared to employ it. Your banks now furnish your only circulating medium, and money is plenty or scarce according to the quantity of notes issued by them. While they have capitals not greatly disproportioned to each other, they are competitors in business, and no one of them can exercise dominion over the rest; and although, in the present state of the currency, these banks may and do operate injuriously upon the habits of business, the pecuniary concerns, and the moral tone of society; yet, from their number and dispersed situation, they cannot combine for the purpose of political influence; and whatever may be the dispositions of some of them, their power of mischief must necessarily be confined to a narrow space and felt only in their immediate neighborhoods.

But when the charter for the Bank of the United States was obtained from Congress, it perfected the schemes of the paper system and gave to its advocates the position they have struggled to obtain from the commencement of the Federal Government down to the present hour. The immense capital and peculiar privileges bestowed upon it enabled it to exercise despotic sway over the other banks in every part of the country. From its superior strength it could seriously injure, if not destroy, the business of any one of them which might incur its resentment; and it openly claimed for itself the power of regulating the currency throughout the United States. In other words, it asserted (and it undoubtedly possessed) the power to make money plenty or scarce, at its pleasure, at any time, and in any quarter of the Union, by controlling the issues of other banks and permitting an expansion or compelling a general contraction of the circulating medium according to its own will. The other banking institutions were sensible of its strength, and they soon generally became its obedient instruments, ready, at all times, to execute its mandates; and with the banks necessarily went, also, that numerous class of persons in our commercial cities who depend altogether on bank credits for their solvency and means of business; and who are, therefore, obliged for their own safety to propitiate the favor of the money power by distinguished zeal and devotion in its service. The result of the ill-advised legislation which established this great monopoly was to concentrate the whole moneyed power of the Union, with its boundless means of corruption and its numerous dependents, under the direction and command of one acknowledged head; thus organizing this particular interest as one body and securing to it unity and concert of action throughout the United States and enabling it to bring forward, upon any occasion, its entire and undivided strength to support or defeat any measure of the Government. In the hands of this formidable power, thus perfectly organized, was also placed unlimited dominion over the amount of the circulating medium, giving it the power to regulate the value of property and the fruits of labor in every quarter of the Union and to bestow prosperity or bring ruin upon any city or section of the country as might best comport with its own interest or policy.

We are not left to conjecture how the moneyed power, thus organized and with such a weapon in its hands, would be likely to use it. The distress and alarm which pervaded and agitated the whole country when the Bank of the United States waged war upon the people in order to compel them to submit to its demands cannot yet be forgotten. The ruthless and unsparing temper with which whole cities and communities were oppressed, individuals impoverished and ruined, and a scene of cheerful prosperity suddenly changed into one of gloom and despondency ought to be indelibly impressed on the memory of the people of the United States. . . .

The severe lessons of experience will, I doubt not, be sufficient to prevent Congress from again chartering such a monopoly, even if the Constitution did not present an insuperable objection to it. But you must remember, my fellow citizens, that eternal vigilance by the people is the price of liberty; and that you must pay the price if you wish to secure the blessing. It behooves you, therefore, to be watchful in your States as well as in the Federal Government. The power which the moneyed interest can exercise, when concentrated under a single head, and with our present system of currency, was sufficiently demonstrated in the struggle made by the Bank of the United States. Defeated in the General Government, the same class of intriguers and politicians will now resort to the States and endeavor to obtain there the same organization which they failed to perpetuate in the Union; and with specious and deceitful plans of public advantages and State interests and State pride they will endeavor to establish, in the different States, one moneyed institution with overgrown capital and exclusive privileges sufficient to enable it to control the operations of the other banks. Such an institution will be pregnant with the same evils pro-

duced by the Bank of the United States, although its sphere of action is more confined; and in the State in which it is chartered the money power will be able to embody its whole strength and to move together with undivided force to accomplish any object it may wish to attain. You have already had abundant evidence of its power to inflict injury upon the agricultural, mechanical, and laboring classes of society; and over those whose engagements in trade or speculation render them dependent on bank facilities, the dominion of the State monopoly will be absolute, and their obedience unlimited. With such a bank and a paper currency, the money power would, in a few years, govern the State and control its measures; and if a sufficient number of States can be induced to create such establishments, the time will soon come when it will again take the field against the United States and succeed in perfecting and perpetuating its organization by a charter from Congress.

It is one of the serious evils of our present system of banking that it enables one class of society, and that by no means a numerous one, by its control over the currency to act injuriously upon the interests of all the others and to exercise more than its just proportion of influence in political affairs. The agricultural, the mechanical, and the laboring classes have little or no share in the direction of the great moneyed corporations; and from their habits and the nature of their pursuits, they are incapable of forming extensive combinations to act together with united force. Such concert of action may sometimes be produced in a single city or in a small district of country by means of personal communications with each other; but they have no regular or active correspondence with those who are engaged in similar pursuits in distant places; they have but little patronage to give to the press and exercise but a small share of influence over it; they have no crowd of dependents above them who hope to grow rich without labor by their countenance and favor and who are, therefore, always ready to exercise their wishes. The planter, the farmer, the mechanic, and the laborer all know that their success depends upon their own industry and economy and that they must not expect to become suddenly rich by the fruits of their toil. Yet these classes of society form the great body of the people of the United States; they are the bone and sinew of the country; men who love liberty and desire nothing but equal rights and equal laws and who, moreover, hold the great mass of our national wealth, although it is distributed in moderate amounts among the millions of freemen who possess it. But, with overwhelming numbers and wealth on their side, they are in constant danger of losing their fair influence in the Government and with difficulty maintain their just rights against the incessant efforts daily made to encroach upon them. The mischief springs from the power which the moneyed interest derives from a paper currency which they are able to control; from the multitude of corporations with exclusive privileges which they have succeeded in obtaining in the different States and which are employed altogether for their benefit; and unless you become more watchful in your States and check this spirit of monopoly and thirst for exclusive privileges, you will, in the end, find that the most important powers of Government have been given or bartered away, and the control over your dearest interests has passed into the hands of these corporations.

The paper money system and its natural associates, monopoly and exclusive privileges, have already struck their roots deep in the soil; and it will require all your efforts to check its further growth and to eradicate the evil. The men who profit by the abuses and desire to perpetuate them will continue to besiege the halls of legislation in the General Government as well as in the States and will seek, by every artifice, to mislead and deceive the public servants. It is to yourselves that you must look for safety and the means of guarding and perpetuating your free institutions. In your hands is rightfully placed the sovereignty of the country and to you every one placed in authority is ultimately responsible. It is always in your power to see that the wishes of the people are carried into faithful execution, and their will, when once made known, must sooner or later be obeyed. And while the people remain, as I trust they ever will, uncorrupted and incorruptible and continue watchful and jealous of their rights, the Government is safe, and the cause of freedom will continue to triumph over all its enemies.

But it will require steady and presevering exertions on your part to rid yourselves of the iniquities and mischiefs of the paper system and to check the spirit of monopoly and other abuses which have sprung up with it and of which it is the main support. So many interests are united to resist all reform on this subject that you must not hope the conflict will be a short one nor success easy. My humble efforts have not been spared, during my administration of the Government, to restore the constitutional currency of gold and silver; and something, I trust, has been done towards the accomplishment of this most desirable object. But enough yet remains to require all your energy and preseverance. The power, however, is in your hands, and the remedy must and will be applied, if you determine upon it. . . .

* * * * *

In presenting to you, my fellow citizens, these parting counsels, I have brought before you the leading principles upon which I endeavored to administer the Government in the high office with which you twice honored me. Knowing that the path of freedom is continually beset by enemies who often assume the disguise of friends, I have devoted the last hours of my public life to warn you of the danger. The progress of the United States under our free and happy institutions has surpassed the most sanguine hopes of the founders of the Republic. Our growth has been rapid beyond all former example, in numbers, in wealth, in knowledge, and all the useful arts which contribute to the comforts and convenience of man; and from the earliest ages of history to the present day, there never have been thirteen millions of people associated together in one political body who enjoyed so much freedom and happiness as the people of these United States. You have no longer any cause to fear danger from abroad; your strength and power are well known throughout the civilized world, as well as the high and gallant bearing of your sons. It is from within, among yourselves, from cupidity, from corruption, from disappointed ambition, and inordinate thirst for power, that factions will be formed and liberty endangered. It is against such designs, whatever disguise the actors may assume, that you have especially to guard yourselves. You have the highest of human trusts committed to your care. Providence has showered on this favored land blessings without number and has chosen you as the guardians of freedom to preserve it for the benefit of the human race. May He who holds in his hands the destinies of nations make you worthy of the favors He has bestowed and enabled you, with pure hearts and pure hands and sleepless vigilance, to guard and defend to the end of time the great charge he has committed to your keeping.

My own race is nearly run; advanced age and failing health warn me that before long I must pass beyond the reach of human events and cease to feel the vicissitudes of human affairs. I thank God that my life has been spent in a land of liberty and that He has given me a heart to love my country with the affection of a son. And, filled with gratitude for your constant and unwavering kindness, I bid you a last and affectionate farewell.

Walt Whitman, 1819–1892

Walt Whitman has remained America's foremost democratic poet. For many, he was the authentic but self-conscious voice that Ralph Waldo Emerson had prophesied would soon begin to create an American literature.

Like many later American writers, Whitman apprenticed in his trade by years of newspaper work. He wrote stories and editorials for the *Democratic Review*, the New York *Leader*, the Brooklyn *Standard*, and especially the *Brooklyn Daily Eagle*. While at the *Eagle*, Whitman produced editorials which epitomized the new democratic faith of the Jacksonian era.

Probably Whitman's most famous collection of poems is *Leaves of Grass*. "I hear America Singing," part of that collection, is a tribute to the common people that is the perfect poetic analogue to his prose work, *Democratic Vistas*.

As Whitman's editorials demonstrate, he was a believer in equality, near laissez-faire, limited government, and individual dignity. He opposed the extension of slavery into the territories and was kicked out of the Democratic party for demanding that the party uphold that position as a requisite for membership.

Whitman remained an American nationalist and abhorred the extreme states rights position. After his brother was wounded in battle during the

Civil War, he volunteered for the Union Army and served as a nurse throughout the war.

Excerpts from Whitman's *Brooklyn Daily Eagle* editorials and *Democratic Vistas* appear below.

Walt Whitman

Editorials in the *Brooklyn Daily Eagle*

GOVERNMENT

July 26, 1847

It may seem a tall piece of coolness and presumption, for an humble personage like ourself to put *his* opinions of governments on the same page with those of the wise men of the ancient days; but, as a common engineer, now, could tell Archimedes things to make the latter stare, so the march of improvement has brought to light truths in politics which the wisest sages of Greece and Rome never discovered. And it is, at the same time, painful to yet see the servile regard paid by the more enlightened present to the darker past. The recognized doctrine that the people are *to be governed* by some abstract power, apart from themselves, has not, even at this day in this country, lost its hold—nor that to any thing more than the government must the said people look for their well-doing and the prosperity of the state. In such a form of rule as ours this dogma is particularly inconvenient; because it makes a perpetual and fierce strife between those of opposing views,

to get their notions and doctrines realized in the laws.

In plain truth, "the people expect too much of the government." Under a proper organization, (and even to a great extent as things are,) the wealth and happiness of the citizens could hardly be touched by the government—could neither be retarded nor advanced. *Men* must be "masters unto themselves," and not look to Presidents and legislative bodies for aid. In this wide and naturally rich country, the best government indeed is "that which governs least."

One point, however, must not be forgotten—ought to be put before the eyes of the people every day; and that is, although government can do little *positive* good to the people, it may do an *immense deal of harm*. And here is where the beauty of the Democratic principle comes in. Democracy would prevent all this harm. It would have no man's benefit achieved at the expense of his neighbors. It would have no one's rights infringed upon and that, after all, is pretty much the sum and substance of the prerogatives of government. How beautiful and harmonious a system! How it transcends all other codes, as the golden rule, in its brevity, transcends the ponderous tomes of philosophic lore! While mere politicians, in their narrow minds, are sweating and fuming with their complicated

SOURCE: C. Rogers and J. Black, eds., *The Gathering of Forces*, vol. 1 and 2 (New York: G. P. Putnam's Sons, 1920).

statutes, this one single rule, rationally construed and applied, is enough to form the starting point of all that is necessary in government: *to make no more laws than those useful for preventing a man or body of men from infringing on the rights of other men.*

DUTIES OF GOVERNMENT

April 4, 1846

The end of all governments is the happiness of the whole community; and whenever it does not secure that, it is a bad government, and it is time it *was altered.*—New York *Globe,* March 28, [1846]

We snip out this little paragraph from our New York contemporary because it affords us a chance of nailing a very wide though foolish error. It is only the novice in political, economy who thinks it the duty of government to *make* its citizens happy.—Government has no such office. To protect the weak and the minority from the impositions of the strong and the majority—to prevent any one from positively working to render the people unhappy, (if we may so express it,) to do the labor not of an officious intermeddler in the affairs of men, but of a prudent watchman who prevents outrage—these are rather the proper duties of a government.

Under the specious pretext of effecting "the happiness of the whole community," nearly all the wrongs and intrusions of government have been carried through. The legislature may, and should, when such things fall in its way, lend its potential weight to the cause of virtue and happiness—but to legislate in direct behalf of those objects is never available, and rarely effects any even temporary benefit. Indeed sensible men have long seen that "the best government is that which governs least." And we are surprised that the spirit of this maxim is not oftener and closer to the hearts of our domestic leaders.

YOU CANNOT LEGISLATE MEN INTO VIRTUE!

March 18, 1846

Some winters ago, a wag of a legislator got up in the Capitol at Albany, and moved that from thenceforth, "all licentiousness and immorality be abolished in the State of New York." The immediate cause of the witty fellow's proposition, we believe, was one of those seduction bills which are annually brought before the Legislature, and just as annually laid on the table.

Though the joke was good, we consider the philosophy of our wag to have been better still. It is all folly to expect from *law,* the popular virtues, worth, and self-denial, which must come from entirely different sources—from the influence and example of home, from well-rooted principles, from a habit of morality. We have therefore little faith in laws that interfere with morals. We have no faith at all in the efforts of law to make men *good.* That is not the province of the statute-book at all.

"The Directors of the Fall River Railroad," says the *Mirror* of last evening, "have declared by vote that no ardent spirits shall be transported over their road." Erudite directors! Profound corporation! Sage, grave men! The world owes you statues and portraits, for the new way you have invented to baffle Bacchus! And the sensible Temperance men—*they* must be "transported," with your wisdom, if old Hollands ain't over your road!

It is amazing, in this age of the world—with the past, and all its causes and effects, like beacon lights behind us—that men show such ignorance, not only of the province of law, but of the true way to achieve any great reform. Why, we wouldn't give a snap for the aid of the Legislature, in forwarding a purely moral revolution! It must work its way through individual minds. It must spread from its own beauty, and melt into the hearts of men—not be forced upon them at the point of the sword, or by the stave of the officer.

The license law passed in this State two sessions since gives the citizens of each locality, (except the city of New York, where it was more needed than any other part of the land) the power to decide by ballot whether they will furnish licenses to taverns or not. This we consider a just and equitable law; it is by no means one of those compulsory things that are objectionable both on account of their illegality and bad policy. It leaves the matter with the citizens of every individual district to settle for themselves by ballot—the most radically democratic form of settlement known to human institutions.

The Directors of the Fall River Railroad, State legislators, and all other functionaries, should know that meddlesome laws, directed against even prejudices and superstitions, do more harm than good. Mankind will resist being driven on a road, which they would travel willingly, when persuaded by gentleness, and convinced by reason. Were all the railroads in the United States, to adopt a similar rule with the Fall River one;—were all the States to pass stringent laws against intemperance—would there be any less liquor consumed, or any fewer tipsy people in consequence?

THE UNION NOW AND FOREVER!

February 26, 1847

Does the *Sun* mean really to say that each "united State" *is* a separate sovereign in fact, and in its own right? that it could (for that would follow,) withdraw itself at pleasure from the Union? that it could do *anything at all*, in conflict with the supreme power of the Constitution and Congress? that it is "independent" any farther than that it has full power to manage its own *local* affairs, and supervise its *local* institutions? Nay: we think it time that such

an extreme heresy (appropriately nestling in the extreme sections of Massachusetts and South Carolina,) should be discountenanced by all true Americans. Especially at this juncture, is the potency of the Union to be upheld: for angry voices are already heard even at the capitol, threatening it under certain contingencies. . . . Perhaps, however, the difference between the *Sun* and us involves but the explanation of a word. "Consolidation" (as we suppose) comprises the idea of *compact*, too; and our States are certainly compacted; while just as certainly the greatest and amplest powers of the government are consolidated in Congress and the President. But Congress and the President can't go a step farther than the Constitution allows them—wherein is the palladium of the "states" rights.

"The Union of the States," says the *Sun*, "consists, therefore, in each State maintaining its own sovereignty and independence, passing its own laws, providing for its own local government; and each State by a constitutional compact becomes united within itself." In such talk as this, though it is quite common, there is evidently a misapplication of terms. If each State *really* possesses "sovereignty and independence," each can do what she pleases, irrespective of any limit. But there are so many things which the States cannot do. Among other things they have no right to "nullify" the Union.—"E *pluribus* UNUM" stares such a remark as we have quoted at the commencement of the paragraph, in the face, and puts it down. . . . We, perhaps, are as much a "strict constructionist" as our New York contemporary *can be*—as much in favor of keeping back power from a central point, and having it wielded by the people who are to be directly acted on by it. But we stand by the Constitution, and the Union which stands with *it*—and we say that no dogma or abstraction—no fancied grief or rebellious excitement—no long-drawn inference—shall allow the foundation of a point of danger to that sacred twain.

RIGHTS OF SOUTHERN FREEMEN AS WELL AS NORTHERN FREEMEN.—MR. CALHOUN'S SPEECH

April 27, 1847

In the speech of Mr. Calhoun delivered at Charleston in March last he says:

> Indeed, after all that has occurred during the last twelve months, it would be almost idiotic to doubt, that a large majority of both parties in the non-slaveholding States, have come to a fixed determination to appropriate all the territories of the United States now possessed, or hereafter to be acquired, to themselves, *to the entire exclusion of the slaveholding States.*

Now is it not strange that a man of the conceded ability of Mr. Calhoun, of his reputed precision of logic and accuracy of expression, should use language like this? *"The entire exclusion of the slave-holding states!"* Mr. Calhoun surely cannot mean what he says. He speaks as though the people of the slaveholding States were all slaveholders. This is any thing but true. In every slaveholding State, we believe, except perhaps South Carolina, a majority of the white freemen are non-slaveholders. Will the exclusion of slavery from the new territory deter *them* from going with their axes and their ploughs into its forests, and making their houses upon its unfurrowed surface? Certainly not. They will go with their free brethren from the North and, not deeming labor degrading, will rear States which will prosper and become mighty under the power of *free* arms and stout hearts. The only persons who will be excluded will be the *aristocracy* of the South—the men who work only with other men's hands. If they cannot condescend to labor, to fell the forests and to plough its fields with their own hands, but must have *slaves* to do what the yeomanry of the North and the majority of the white men at the South regard as a proud, virtuous and noble calling—why then they can stay away;

and it is difficult to see where the hardship lies of permitting them to do so. If they are willing to regard labor as honorable and to work like the rest of us, they can go into the new territory and find it open to them as it is to the rest who work for a living. But no— they insist that at the outset *freemen shall be excluded* to enable *them* to monopolize the land and cultivate it by their slaves. Let us see if this is not the true state of the case. From the Northern and Eastern States a constant tide of brave, industrious and energetic *freemen* is flowing to the new territory. Such has been the case for the last fifty years, and such men have founded and matured the great— *nations,* we had almost said—of Ohio, Indiana, Illinois, Michigan, &c. Into those regions have rushed, too, thousands and tens of thousands of freemen from the slaveholding States who have been eager to labor where they could do so without degradation. Tens and hundreds of thousands more like them from the East, North *and South,* will be eager to occupy the new territory which may be acquired from Mexico, if they can go and not find themselves the equals only of negro slaves. Where the land is cultivated by slaves it is *not* also cultivated by freemen. It is not in South Carolina and Virginia and the other slave States, respectable (at any rate it is not so practically regarded) for white men to labor on land.

The voice of the North proclaims that *labor must not be degraded.* The young men of the free States must not be shut out from the new domain (where slavery does not now exist) by the *introduction* of an institution which will render their honorable industry no longer respectable. Slavery must not exact *too much* from the Democracy of the North. That Democracy has been faithful to the "compromise of the Constitution" by protecting the institution of slavery (uncongenial as that institution is to all the instincts and sympathies of Democracy) within the limits that the Constitution found it; and it will be the part of wisdom in its advocates not to weaken its security by further and unreasonable exactions. Instead of a generous recognition of the tolerant spirit with which the North has regarded the institution in the States where it exists, and has conceded almost every thing of power and office and station to the slaveholding States, that spirit is requited much too often by flings and imputations of meanness and of a mercenary spirit, not likely to perpetuate Northern forbearance. Witness the following extract from Mr. Calhoun's speech:

> Fortunately, then, the crusade against our domestic institution does not originate in hostility of interests. If it did, the possibility of arresting the threatened danger, and saving ourselves, short of a disrupture of the Union, would be altogether hopeless; *so predominant is the regard for interest in those States, over all other considerations.*

Was it a mean or mercenary spirit that has induced the Democracy of the North to grant the Presidency, with all its powerful patronage, to the South, ever since the foundation of the government, with the exception of a single term? On the other hand might we not with truth charge faithlessness and utter cupidity to the South? It has monopolized by an *immense* disproportion the offices of the government. It proved faithless to the Democracy of the North in respect to Mr. Van Buren. It is entirely unreliable as to Mr. Wright. Mr. Calhoun is quite right in his conclusion that "it would be almost idiotic to doubt, that a large majority of both parties in the non-slaveholding States have come to a fixed determination" in respect to the new territory—but is wrong in saying that determination is to exclude the people of the slave States. It is to throw the territory open *on equal terms* to the people of the North *and* of the South.

Walt Whitman

Democratic Vistas (1871)

A portion of our pages we might indite with reference toward Europe, especially the British part of it, more than our own land, perhaps not absolutely needed for the home reader. But the whole question hangs together, and fastens and links all peoples. The liberalist of to-day has this advantage over antique or medieval times, that his doctrine seeks not only to individualize but to universalize. The great word Solidarity has arisen. Of all dangers to a nation, as things exist in our day, there can be no greater one than having certain portions of the people set off from the rest by a line drawn—they not privileged as others, but degraded, humiliated, made of no account. Much quackery teems, of course, even on democracy's side, yet does not really affect the orbic quality of the matter. To work in, if we may so term it, and justify God, his divine aggregate, the People, (or, the veritable horn'd and sharp-tail'd Devil, *his* aggregate, if there be who convulsively insist upon it)—this, I say, is what democracy is for; and this is what our America means, and is doing—may I not say, has done? If not, she means nothing more, and does nothing more, than any other land. And as, by virtue of its kosmical, antiseptic power, Nature's stomach is fully strong enough not only to digest the morbific matter always presented, not to be turn'd aside, and perhaps, indeed, intuitively gravitating thither—but even to change such contributions into nutriment for highest use and life—so American democracy's. That is the lesson we, these days, send over to European lands by every western breeze.

And, truly, whatever may be said in the way of abstract argument, for or against the theory of a wider democratizing of institutions in any civilized country, much trouble might well be saved to all European lands by recognizing this palpable fact, (for a palpable fact it is,) that some form of such democratizing is about the only resource now left. *That,* or chronic dissatisfaction continued, mutterings which grow annually louder and louder, till, in due course, and pretty swiftly in most cases, the inevitable crisis, crash, dynastic ruin. Anything worthy to be call'd statesmanship in the Old World, I should say, among the advanced students, adepts, or men of any brains, does not debate to-day whether to hold on, attempting to lean back and monarchize, or to look forward and democratize—but *how,* and in what degree and part, most prudently to democratize.

The eager and often inconsiderate appeals of reformers and revolutionists are indispensable, to counterbalance the inertness and fossilism making so large a part of human institutions. The latter will always take care of themselves—the danger being that they rapidly tend to ossify us. The former is to be treated with indulgence, and even with respect. As circulation to air, so is agitation and a plentiful degree of speculative license to political and moral sanity. Indirectly, but surely, goodness, virtue, law, (of the very best,) follow freedom. These, to democracy, are what the keel is to the ship, or saltness to the ocean.

The true gravitation-hold of liberalism in the United States will be a more universal ownership of property, general homesteads, general comfort—a vast, intertwining reticulation of wealth. As the human frame, or, indeed, any object in this manifold universe, is best kept together by the simple miracle of its own cohesion, and the necessity, exercise and profit thereof, so a great and varied nationality, occupying millions of square miles, were firmest held and knit by the principle of the safety and endurance of the aggregate of its middling property owners. So that, from another point of view, ungracious as it may sound, and a paradox after what we have been saying, democracy looks with suspicious, ill-satisfied eye upon the very poor, the ignorant, and on those out of business. She asks for men and women with occupations, well-off, owners of houses and acres, and with cash in the bank—and with some cravings for literature, too; and must have them, and hastens to make them. Luckily, the seed is already well-sown, and has taken ineradicable root.

Huge and mighty are our days, our republican lands—and most in their rapid shiftings, their changes, all in the interest of the cause. As I write this particular passage, (November, 1868,) the din of disputation rages around me. Acrid the temper of the parties, vital the pending questions. Congress convenes; the President sends his message; reconstruction is still in abeyance; the nomination and the contest for the twenty-first Presidentiad draw close, with loudest threat and bustle. Of these, and all the like of these, the eventuations I know not; but well I know that behind them, and whatever their eventuations, the vital things remain safe and certain, and all the needed work goes on. Time, with soon or later superciliousness, disposes of Presidents, Congressmen, party platforms, and such. Anon, it clears the stage of each and any mortal shred that thinks itself so potent to its day; and at and after which, (with precious, golden exceptions once or twice in a century,) all that relates to sir potency is flung to moulder in a burial-vault, and no one bothers himself the least bit about it afterward. But the People ever remain, tendencies continue, and all the idiocratic transfers in unbroken chain go on.

In a few years the dominion-heart of America will be far inland, toward the West. Our future national capital may not be where the present one is. It is possible, nay likely, that in less than fifty years, it will migrate a thousand or two miles, will be re-founded, and every thing belonging to it made on a different plan, original, far more superb. The main social, political, spine-character of the States will probably run along the Ohio, Missouri and Mississippi rivers, and west and north of them, including Canada. Those regions, with the group of powerful brothers toward the Pacific, (destined to the mastership of that sea and its countless paradises of islands,) will compact and settle the traits of America, with all the old retain'd, but more expanded, grafted on newer, hardier, purely native stock. A giant growth, composite from the rest, getting their contribution, absorbing it, to make it more illustrious. From the north, intellect, the sun of things, also the idea of unswayable justice, anchor amid the last, the wildest tempests. From the south the living soul, the animus of good and bad, haughtily admitting no demonstration but its own. While from the west itself comes solid personality, with blood and brawn, and the deep quality of all-accepting fusion.

Political democracy, as it exists and practically works in America, with all its threatening evils, supplies a training-school for making first-class men. It is life's gymnasium, not of good only, but of all. We try often, though we fall back often. A brave delight, fit for freedom's athletes, fills these arenas, and fully satisfies, out of the action in them, irrespective of success. Whatever we do not attain, we at any rate attain the experiences of the fight, the hardening of the strong campaign, and throb with currents of attempt at least. Time

is ample. Let the victors come after us. Not for nothing does evil play its part among us. Judging from the main portions of the history of the world, so far, justice is always in jeopardy, peace walks amid hourly pitfalls, and of slavery, misery, meanness, the craft of tyrants and the credulity of the populace, in some of their protean forms, no voice can at any time say, They are not. The clouds break a little, and the sun shines out—but soon and certain the lowering darkness falls again, as if to last forever. Yet is there an immortal courage and prophecy in every sane soul that cannot, must not, under any circumstances, capitulate. *Vive,* the attack—the perennial assault! *Vive,* the unpopular cause—the spirit that audaciously aims—the never-abandon'd efforts, pursued the same amid opposing proofs and precedents.

Once, before the war, (Alas! I dare not say how many times the mood has come!) I, too, was fill'd with doubt and gloom. A foreigner, an acute and good man, had impressively said to me, that day—putting in form, indeed, my own observations: "I have travel'd much in the United States, and watch'd their politicians, and listen'd to the speeches of the candidates, and read the journals, and gone into the public houses, and heard the unguarded talk of men. And I have found your vaunted America honeycomb'd from top to toe with infidelism, even to itself and its own programme. I have mark'd the brazen hell-faces of secession and slavery gazing defiantly from all the windows and doorways. I have everywhere found, primarily, thieves and scalliwags arranging the nominations to offices, and sometimes filling the offices themselves. I have found the north just as full of bad stuff as the south. Of the holders of public office in the Nation or the States or their municipalities, I have found that not one in a hundred has been chosen by any spontaneous selection of the outsiders, the people, but all have been nominated and put through by little or large caucuses of the politicians, and have got in by corrupt rings and electioneering, not capacity or desert. I have noticed how the millions of sturdy farmers and mechanics are thus the helpless supple-jacks of comparatively few politicians. And I have noticed more and more, the alarming spectacle of parties usurping the government, and openly and shamelessly wielding it for party purposes."

Sad, serious, deep truths. Yet are there other, still deeper, amply confronting, dominating truths. Over those politicians and great and little rings, and over all their insolence and wiles, and over the powerfulest parties, looms a power, too sluggish maybe, but ever holding decisions and decrees in hand, ready, with stern process, to execute them as soon as plainly needed—and at times, indeed, summarily crushing to atoms the mightiest parties, even in the hour of their pride.

In saner hours far different are the amounts of these things from what, at first sight, they appear. Though it is no doubt important who is elected governor, mayor, or legislator, (and full of dismay when incompetent or vile ones get elected, as they sometimes do,) there are other, quieter contingencies, infinitely more important. Shams, &c., will always be the show, like ocean's scum; enough, if waters deep and clear make up the rest. Enough, that while the piled embroider'd shoddy gaud and fraud spreads to the superficial eye, the hidden warp and weft are genuine, and will wear forever. Enough, in short, that the race, the land which could raise such as the late rebellion, could also put it down.

The average man of a land at last only is important. He, in these States, remains immortal owner and boss, deriving good uses, somehow, out of any sort of servant in office, even the basest; (certain universal requisites, and their settled regularity and protection, being first secured,) a nation like ours, in a sort of geological formation state, trying continually new experiments, choosing new delegations, is not served by the best men only, but sometimes more by those that provoke it—by the combats they arouse. Thus national rage, fury, discussion, &c., better than content. Thus, also, the warning signals, invaluable for after times.

What is more dramatic than the spectacle we have seen repeated, and doubtless long shall see—the popular judgment taking the successful candidates on trial in the offices—standing off, as it were, and observing them and their doings for a while, and always giving, finally, the fit, exactly due reward? I think, after all, the sublimest part of political history, and its culmination, is currently issuing from the American people. I know nothing grander, better exercise, better digestion, more positive proof of the past, the triumphant result of faith in human kind, than a well-contested American national election.

Then still the thought returns, (like the thread-passage in overtures,) giving the key and echo to these pages. When I pass to and fro, different latitudes, different seasons, beholding the crowds of the great cities, New York, Boston, Philadelphia, Cincinnati, Chicago, St. Louis, San Francisco, New Orleans, Baltimore—when I mix with these interminable swarms of alert, turbulent, good-natured, independent citizens, mechanics, clerks, young persons—at the idea of this mass of men, so fresh and free, so loving and so proud, a singular awe falls upon me. I feel, with dejection and amazement, that among our geniuses and talented writers or speakers, few or none have yet really spoken to this people, created a single image-making work for them, or absorb'd the central spirit and the idiosyncrasies which are theirs—and which, thus, in highest ranges, so far remain entirely uncelebrated, unexpress'd.

Dominion strong is the body's; dominion stronger is the mind's. What has fill'd, and fills to-day our intellect, our fancy, furnishing the standards therein, is yet foreign. The great poems, Shakespere included, are poisonous to the idea of the pride and dignity of the common people, the life-blood of democracy. The models of our literature, as we get it from other lands, ultra-marine, have had their birth in courts, and bask'd and grown in castle sunshine; all smells of princes' favors. Of workers of a certain sort, we have, indeed, plenty, contributing after their kind; many elegant, many learn'd, all complacent. But touch'd by the national test, or tried by the standards of democratic personality, they wither to ashes. I say I have not seen a single writer, artist, lecturer, or what not, that has confronted the voiceless but ever erect and active, pervading, underlying will and typic aspiration of the land, in a spirit kindred to itself. Do you call those genteel little creatures American poets? Do you term that perpetual, pistareen, paste-pot work, American art, American drama, taste, verse? I think I hear, echoed as from some mountaintop afar in the west, the scornful laugh of the Genius of these States.

Democracy, in silence, biding its time, ponders its own ideals, not of literature and art only—not of men only, but of women. The idea of the women of America, (extricated from this daze, this fossil and unhealthy air which hangs about the word *lady*,) develop'd, raised to become the robust equals, workers, and, it may be, even practical and political deciders with the men—greater than man, we may admit, through their divine maternity, always their towering, emblematical attribute—but great, at any rate, as man, in all departments; or, rather, capable of being so, soon as they realize it, and can bring themselves to give up toys and fictions, and launch forth, as men do, amid real, independent, stormy life. . . .

Horace Mann, 1796–1859

Horace Mann was a fervent crusader for universal, free public education. Liberty and equality, the key ideals of democratic rhetoric, had no real meaning, Mann felt, unless all children had an equal opportunity to a quality education. The public school was the "great balance wheel" of society which could provide both equality of opportunity and a common set of public values.

Mann himself had little formal schooling. But with the help of an itinerant teacher, he prepared for college entrance into Brown University in a mere six months. He then attended Litchfield Law School in Connecticut and soon after being admitted to the bar began a successful career in Massachusetts state politics. From 1827 to 1837, Mann served in the Massachusetts House of Representatives and then the State Senate.

However in 1837 he resigned his prestigious senate seat and accepted the rather low position of secretary to the newly formed state board of education.

Mann promptly created a revolution in Massachusetts schools that was of great importance throughout the nation. He argued passionately for free public education, created state normal schools (teacher's colleges), and set up county conferences to help create minimum "common" curricula in all

Massachusetts schools. His *Common School Journal* became the leading educational journal of its day.

Mann's lecture, "The Necessity of Education in a Republican Government," excerpted below, demonstrates the crucial role that public education played in middle nineteenth-century egalitarian liberal and republican thought.

Horace Mann

The Necessity of Education in a Republican Government (1839)

. . . I venture, my friends, at this time, to solicit your attention, while I attempt to lay before you some of the relations which we bear to the cause of Education, because we are the citizens of a Republic; and thence to deduce some of the reasons, which, under our political institutions, make the proper training of the rising generation the highest earthly duty of the risen.

It is a truism, that free institutions multiply human energies. A chained body cannot do much harm; a chained mind can do as little. In a despotic government, the human faculties are benumbed and paralyzed; in a Republic, they glow with an intense life, and burst forth with uncontrollable impetuosity. In the former, they are circumscribed and straitened in their range of action; in the latter, they have "ample room and verge enough," and may rise to glory or plunge into ruin. Amidst universal ignorance, there cannot be such wrong notions about right, as there may be in a community partially enlightened; and false conclusions which have been reasoned

SOURCE: Horace Mann, *Lectures on Education* (Boston: William B. Fowle, 1848).

out, are infinitely worse than blind impulses.

To demonstrate the necessity of education in our government, I shall not attempt to derive my proofs from the history of other Republics. Such arguments are becoming stale. Besides, there are so many points of difference between our own political institutions, and those of any other government calling itself free, which has ever existed, that the objector perpetually eludes or denies the force of our reasoning, by showing some want of analogy between the cases presented.

I propose, therefore, on this occasion, not to adduce, as proofs, what has been true only in past times; but what is true, at the present time, and must always continue to be true. I shall rely, not on precedents, but on the nature of things; and draw my arguments less from history than from humanity.

Now it is undeniable that, with the possession of certain higher faculties,—common to all mankind,—whose proper cultivation will bear us upward to hitherto undiscovered regions of prosperity and glory, we possess, also, certain lower faculties or propensities,— equally common,—whose improper indulgence leads, inevitably, to tribulation, and anguish, and ruin. The propensities to which I refer, seem indispensable to our temporal existence, and if restricted within proper limits, they are promotive of our enjoyment; but, beyond those limits, they work dishonor and infatuation, madness and despair. As servants, they are indispensable; as masters, they torture as well as tyrannize. Now despotic and arbitrary governments have dwarfed and crippled the powers of doing evil as much as the powers of doing good; but a republican government, from the very fact of its freedom, un-reins their speed, and lets loose their strength. It is justly alleged against despotisms, that they fetter, mutilate, almost extinguish the noblest powers of the human soul; but there is a *per contra* to this, for which we have not given them credit;—they circumscribe the ability to do the greatest evil, as well as to do the greatest good.

My proposition, therefore, is simply this:— If republican institutions do wake up unexampled energies in the whole mass of a people, and give them implements of unexampled power wherewith to work out their will; then these same institutions ought also to confer upon that people unexampled wisdom and rectitude. If these institutions give greater scope and impulse to the lower order of faculties belonging to the human mind, then, they must also give more authoritative control, and more skilful guidance to the higher ones. If they multiply temptations, they must fortify against them. If they quicken the activity and enlarge the sphere of the appetites and passions, they must, at least in an equal ration, establish the authority and extend the jurisdiction of reason and conscience. In a word, we must not add to the impulsive, without also adding to the regulating forces.

If we maintain institutions, which bring us within the action of new and unheard-of powers, without taking any corresponding measures for the government of those powers, we shall perish by the very instruments prepared for our happiness.

The truth has been so often asserted, that there is no security for a republic but in morality and intelligence, that a repetition of it seems hardly in good taste. But all permanent blessings being founded on permanent truths, a continued observance of the truth is the condition of a continued enjoyment of the blessing. I know we are often admonished that, without intelligence and virtue, as a chart and a compass, to direct us in our untried political voyage, we shall perish in the first storm; but I venture to add that, without these qualities, we shall not wait for a storm—we cannot weather a calm. If the sea is as smooth as glass we shall founder, for we are in a stoneboat. Unless these qualities pervade the general head and the general heart, not only will republican institutions vanish from amongst us, but the words *prosperity* and *happiness* will become obsolete. And all this may be affirmed, not from historical examples merely, but from the very constitution of our nature. We are created and brought into life with a set of innate, organic dispositions or propensities, which a free government rouses and invigorates, and which, if not bridled and tamed, by our actually seeing the eternal laws of justice, as plainly as we can see the sun in the heavens,—and by our actually feeling the sovereign sentiment of duty, as plainly as we feel the earth beneath our feet,—will hurry us forward into regions populous with every form of evil.

. . . From the accursed thirst for gold have come the felon frauds of the marketplace, and the more wicked pious frauds of the church, the robber's blow, the burglar's stealthy step around the midnight couch, the pirate's murders, the rapine of cities, the plundering and captivity of nations. Even now, in self-styled Christian communities, are there not men who, under the sharp goadings of this impulse, equip vessels to cross the ocean,—not to carry the glad tidings of the gospel to heathen lands, but to descend upon defenceless villages in a whirlwind of fire and ruin, to kidnap men, women and children, and to transport them through all the horrors of the middle passage, where their cries of agony and despair outvoice the storm, that the wretched victims may at last be sold into remorseless bondage, to wear chains, and to bequeath chains;—and all this is perpetrated and suffered because a little gold can be transmuted, by such fiery alchemy, from human tears and blood! Such is the inexorable power of cupidity, in self-styled Christian lands, in sight of the spires of God's temples pointing upward to heaven, which, if Truth had its appropriate emblems, would be reversed and point downward to hell.

Startle not, my friends, at these far-off enormities. Are there not monsters amongst ourselves, who sell their own children into bondage for the money they can earn? who coin not only the health of their own offspring, but their immortal capacities of intelligence and virtue, into pelf? Are there not others, who, at home, at the town meeting, and at the school meeting, win all the victories of ignorance by the cry of expense? Are there not men amongst us, possessed of superfluous wealth, who will vote against a blackboard for a schoolroom, because the scantling costs a shilling and the paint sixpence! . . .

Let the lover of wealth seek wealth by all honest means, and with earnestness, if he will;—let him surround himself with the comforts and the embellishments of life, and add the pleasures of beauty to the pleasures of utility. Let every honorable man indulge a quick and sustaining confidence in his own worthiness, whenever disparaged or maligned; and let him count upon the affections of his friends, and the benedictions of his race, as a part of the solid rewards of virtue. These, and kindred feelings, are not to be crushed, extinguished. Let them rouse themselves in presence of their objects, and rush out to seize them, and neigh, like a war-horse for the battle,—only let them know that they have a rider, to whose eye no mist can dim the severe line

they are never to pass, and whose arm can bend every neck of them, like the twig of an osier.

But I must pass to the next topic for consideration,—the stimulus which, in this country, is applied to the propensities; and the free, unbarred, unbounded career, which is here opened for their activity. In every other nation that has ever existed,—not even excepting Greece and Rome,—the mind of the masses has been obstructed in its development. Amongst millions of men, only some half dozen of individuals,—often only a single individual,—have been able to pour out the lava of their passions, with full, volcanic force. These few men have made the Pharaohs, the Neros, the Napoleons of the race. The rest have usually been subjected to a systematic course of blinding, deafening, crippling. As an inevitable consequence of this, the minds of men have never yet put forth one thousandth part of their tremendous energies. Bad men have swarmed upon the earth, it is true, but they have been weak men. Another consequence is, that we, by deriving our impressions from history, have formed too low an estimate of the marvellous powers and capacities of the human being for evil as well as for good. The general estimate is altogether inadequate to what the common mind will be able to effect, when apt instruments are put into its hands, and the wide world is opened for its sphere of operations. . . .

Amongst ourselves it is, that this spirit is now walking forth, full of its new-found life, wantoning in freshly-discovered energies, surrounded by all the objects which can inflame its boundless appetites, and, as yet, too purblind, from the long darkness of its prison-house, to discern clearly between its blessing and its bane. That unconquerable force of the human soul, which all the arts and power of despotism,—which all the enginery borrowed from both worlds,—could not subdue, is here, amongst ourselves, to do its sovereign will. . . .

. . . Through the right,—almost universal,—of suffrage, we have established a community of power; and no proposition is more plain and self-evident, than that nothing but mere popular inclination lies between a community of power and a community in every thing else. And though, in the long-run, and when other things are equal, a righteous cause always has a decisive advantage over an evil one, yet, in the first onset between right and wrong, bad men possess one advantage over the good. They have double resources,—two armories. The arts of guilt are as welcome to them as the practices of justice. They can use poisoned weapons as well as those approved by the usages of war.

Again; has it been sufficiently considered, that all which has been said,—and truly said,—of the excellence of our institutions, if administered by an upright people, must be reversed and read backwards, if administered by a corrupt one? I am aware that some will be ready to say, "we have been unwise and infatuated to confide all the constituents of our social and political welfare, to such irresponsible keeping." But let me ask of such,—of what avail is their lamentation? The irresistible movement in the diffusion of power is still progressive, not retrograde. Every year puts more of social strength into the hands of physical strength. The arithmetic of numbers is more and more excluding all estimate of moral forces, in the administration of government. And this, whether for good or for evil, will continue to be. Human beings cannot be remanded to the dungeons of imbecility, if they are to those of ignorance. . . .

. . . And let me ask, further, have those who believe our institutions to be too free, and who, therefore, would go back to less liberal ones,—have they settled the question, how far back they will go? Will they go back to the dark ages, and recall an eclipse which lasted centuries long? or will they ascend a little higher for their models,—to a time when our ancestors wore undressed skins, and burrowed in holes of the earth? or will they strike at once for the institutions of Egypt, where, though the monkey was a god, there was still a sufficient distance between him and his human worshipper? But all such discussions are vain. The oak will as soon go back into the acorn, or the bird into its shell, as we return to the monarchical or aristocratic forms of by-gone ages.

Nor let it be forgotten, in contemplating our condition, that the human passions, as unfolded and invigorated by our institutions, are not only possessed of all the prerogatives, and equipped with all the implements of sovereignty; but that they are forever roused and spurred to the most vehement efforts. It is a law of the passions, that they exert strength in proportion to the causes which excite them,—a law which holds true in cases of sanity, as well as in the terrible strength of insanity. And with what endless excitements are the passions of men here plied! . . .

All objects which stimulate the passions of men, are made to pass before the eyes of all, as in a circling panorama. In very truth we are hung upon the same electrical wire, and if the ignorant and vicious get possession of the apparatus, the intelligent and the virtuous must take such shocks as the stupid or profligate experimenters may choose to administer.

So the inordinate love of office will present the spectacle of gladiatorial contests,—of men struggling for station as for life, and using against each other the poisonous weapons of calumny and vituperation;—while the abiding welfare, the true greatness and prosperity of the people will be like the soil of some neutral Flanders, over which the hostile bands of partisans will march and countermarch, and convert it into battlefields;—so that, whichever side may triumph, the people will be ruined. And even after one cause or one party has prevailed, the conquered land will not be wide enough to settle a tithe of the conquerors upon. Hence must come new rallyings; new banners must be unfurled, and the repose of the land be again broken by the convulsions of party strife. Hence, too, the death-grapple between the defenders of institutions which ought to be abolished, and the assailants of institutions which ought to be preserved. Laocoön cries, "My life and my children are mine." The hissing and enwreathing serpents respond, "They are ours." If each party espouses and supports whatever is wrong on its own side, because such a course is deemed necessary to union and strength; and denounces whatever is right in the plans of its antagonists, because such are the approved tactics of opposition; if each party sounds the loudest alarms, when the most trivial danger from its opponents is apprehended, and sings the gentlest lullabies over perils of its own producing, can seer or prophet foretell but one catastrophe?

Again; we hear good men, every day, bemoaning the *ignorance* of certain portions of our country, and of individuals in all parts of it. . . .

With exceptions comparatively few, we have but two classes of ignorant persons amongst us, and they are harmless. Infants and idiots are ignorant; few others are so. Those whom we are accustomed to call ignorant, are full of false notions, as much worse than ignorance as wisdom is better. A merely ignorant man has no skill in adapting means to ends, whereby to jeopard the welfare of great interests or great numbers. Ignorance is blankness; or, at most, a lifeless, inert mass, which can, indeed, be moved and placed where you please, but will stay where it is placed. In Europe, there are multitudes of ignorant men,— men into whose minds no idea ever entered respecting the duties of society or of government, or the conditions of human prosperity. They, like their work-fellows, the cattle, are obedient to their masters; and the range of their ideas on political or social questions, is hardly more extensive than that of the brutes. But with our institutions, this state of things,

to any great extent, is impossible. The very atmosphere we breathe is freighted with the ideas of property, of acquisition and transmission; of wages, labor and capital; of political and social rights; of the appointment to, and tenure of offices; of the reciprocal relations between the great departments of government—executive, legislative, and judicial. Every native-born child amongst us imbibes notions, either false or true, on these subjects. Let these notions be false; let an individual grow up, with false ideas of his own nature and destiny as an immortal being, with false views respecting what government, laws, customs, should be; with no knowledge of the works, or the opinions of those great men who framed our government, and adjusted its various parts to each other;—and when such an individual is invested with the political rights of citizenship, with power to give an authoritative voice and vote upon the affairs of his country, he will look upon all existing things as rubbish which it is his duty to sweep away, that he may have room for the erection of other structures, planned after the model of his own false ideas. No man that ever lived could, by mere intuition or instinct, form just opinions upon a thousand questions, pertaining to civil society, to its jurisprudence, its local, national and international duties. Many truths, vital to the welfare of the people, differ in their reality, as much from the appearances which they present to uninstructed minds, as the apparent size of the sun differs from its real size, which, in truth, is so many thousand times larger than the earth, while to the untaught eye it appears to be so many thousand times smaller. And if the human propensities are here to manifest themselves through the enlarged means of false knowledge which our institutions, unaided by special instruction, will furnish; if they are to possess all the instruments and furtherances which our doctrine of political equality confers; then the result must be, a power to do evil almost infinitely greater than ever existed before, instigated by impulses proportionately strong. Hence our dangers are to be, not those of ignorance, which would be comparatively tolerable, but those of false knowledge, which transcend the powers of mortal imagination to portray. Would you appreciate the amazing difference between ignorance and false knowledge, look at France, before and during her great revolution. Before the revolution, her people were merely ignorant; during the revolution, they acted under the lights of false knowledge. An idiot is ignorant, and does little harm; a maniac has false ideas, and destroys, burns and murders. . . .

Such, then, is our condition. The minds that are to regulate all things and govern all things, in this country, are innately strong; they are intensely stimulated; they are supplied with the most formidable artillery of means; and each one is authorized to form its own working-plan, its own ground-scheme, according to which, when the social edifice has been taken to pieces, it is to be reconstructed;—some are for going back a thousand or two thousand years for their model; others, for introducing what they consider the millennium, at once, by force of law, or by force without law.

And now, my friends, I ask, with the deepest anxiety, what institutions exist amongst us, which at once possess the power and are administered with the efficiency, requisite to save us from the dangers that spring up in our own bosoms? That the propensities, which each generation brings into the world, possess terrific power, and are capable of inflicting the completest ruin, none can deny. Nor will it be questioned that amongst *us*, they have an open career, and a command of means, such as never before coëxisted. What antagonist power have we provided against them? By what exorcism can we lay the spirits we have raised? Once, brute force, directed by a few men, trampled upon the many. Here, the many are the possessors of that very force, and have almost abolished its use as a means

of government. The French *gendarmerie,* the British horse-guards, the dreadful punishment of the Siberian mines, will never be copied here. Should the government resort to a standing army, that army would consist of the very forces they dread, organized, equipped and officered. Can laws save us? With us, the very idea of legislation is reversed. Once, the law prescribed the actions and shaped the wills of the multitude; here, the wills of the multitude prescribe and shape the law. With us, legislators study the will of the multitude, just as natural philosophers study a volcano,—not with any expectation of doing aught to the volcano, but to see what the volcano is about to do to them. While the law was clothed with majesty and power, and the mind of the multitude was weak, then, as in all cases of a conflict between unequal forces, the law prevailed. But now, when the law is weak, and the passions of the multitude have gathered irresistible strength, it is fallacious and insane to look for security in the moral force of the law. . . .

But perhaps others may look for security to the public Press, which has now taken its place amongst the organized forces of modern civilization. Probably its political department supplies more than half the reading of the mass of our people. But, bating the point, whether, in times of public excitement, when the sobriety and thoughtfulness of wisdom, when severe and exact truth are, more than ever else, necessary,—whether, at such times, the press is not itself liable to be inflamed by the heats it should allay, and to be perverted by the obliquities it should rectify;—bating this point, it is still obvious that its principal efforts are expended upon one department only of all our social duties. The very existence of the newspaper press, for any useful purpose, presupposes that the people are already supplied with the elements of knowledge and inspired with the love of right; and are therefore prepared to decide, with intelligence and honesty, those complicated and conflicting claims, which the tide of events is constantly presenting, and which, by the myriad messengers of the press, are carried to every man's fireside for his adjudication. For, of what value is it, that we have the most wisely-framed government on earth; to what end is it, that the wisest schemes which a philanthropic statesmanship can devise, are propounded to the people, if this people has not the intelligence to understand, or the integrity to espouse them? Each of two things is equally necessary to our political prosperity; namely, just principles of government and administration, on one side, and a people able to understand and resolute to uphold them, on the other. Of what use is the most exquisite music ever composed by the greatest masters of the art, until you have orchestra or choir that can perform the pieces? Pupils must thoroughly master the vocal elements, musical language must be learned, voices must be long and severely trained, or the divinest compositions of Haydn or Mozart would only set the teeth of an auditory on edge. And so must it be with our government and laws;—the best will be useless, unless we have a people who will appreciate and uphold them.

. . . The same Almighty power which implants in our nature the germs of these terrible propensities, has endowed us also, with reason and conscience and a sense of responsibility to Him; and, in his providence, he has opened a way by which these nobler faculties can be elevated into dominion and supremacy over the appetites and passions. But if this is ever done, it must be mainly done, during the docile and teachable years of childhood. I repeat it, my friends, *if this is ever done, it must be mainly done, during the docile and teachable years of childhood.* Wretched, incorrigible, demoniac, as any human being may ever have become, there was a time when he took the first step in error and in crime; when, for the first time,

he just nodded to his fall, on the brink of ruin. Then, ere he was irrecoverably lost, ere he plunged into the abyss of infamy and guilt, he might have been recalled, as it were by the waving of the hand. Fathers, mothers, patriots, Christians! it is this very hour of peril through which our children are now passing. They know it not, but we know it; and where the knowledge is, there rests the responsibility. Society is responsible;—not society considered as an abstraction, but society as it consists of living members, which members we are. Clergymen are responsible;—all men who have enjoyed the opportunities of a higher education in colleges and universities are responsible, for they can convert their means, whether of time or of talent, into instruments for elevating the masses of the people. The conductors of the public press are responsible, for they have daily access to the public ear, and can infuse just notions of this high duty into the public mind. Legislators and rulers are responsible. In our country, and in our times, no man is worthy the honored name of a statesman, who does not include the highest practicable education of the people in all his plans of administration. He may have eloquence, he may have a knowledge of all history, diplomacy, jurisprudence, and by these he might claim, in other countries, the elevated rank of a statesman; but, unless he speaks, plans, labors, at all times and in all places, for the culture and edification of the whole people, he is not, he cannot be, an American statesman.

If this dread responsibility for the fate of our children be disregarded, how, when called upon, in the great eventful day, to give an account of the manner in which our earthly duties have been discharged, can we expect to escape the condemnation: "Inasmuch as ye have not done it to one of the least of these, ye have not done it unto me?"

Abraham Lincoln, 1809–1865

Abraham Lincoln's rise from a log cabin in Hardin County, Kentucky, to the White House is one of the great examples of America's egalitarian ideal made reality. As one might suspect, Lincoln was a believer in the Lockean values of individualism and equal opportunity.

Abraham Lincoln served as a Whig in the Illinois state legislature from 1837 to 1841. From 1847 to 1849, he was the lone Whig in the Illinois delegation to the U.S. House of Representatives. During that period, he supported the Wilmot Proviso and introduced a bill calling for the abolition of slavery in Washington D.C., with compensation to be paid to slave owners. Throughout this period, and during Lincoln's later political career as well, he did not argue for abolition but rather an end to the extension of slavery into new territories. Lincoln's commitment was to maintaining the Union and to providing opportunity and land for his primary constituency, the free white man.

In 1856, Lincoln became the Republican party's leader in Illinois, and in 1858, he ran a famous unsuccessful race for the Senate against Stephen Douglas. In accepting the Republican nomination, Lincoln declared that "a house divided against itself cannot stand . . . this government cannot endure permanently, half slave and half free." Although he lost, his debates with Douglas made him a widely known national figure.

In 1860, however, Lincoln defeated Douglas and two other candidates to become president of the United States. Although he claimed "my paramount object is to save the Union and not either to save or destroy slavery," by the time he had been inaugurated, seven southern states had seceded. Lincoln was left with no choice but to save the Union by war.

Lincoln was not as prolific a writer as a Thomas Jefferson, nor as serious a political theorist as John Adams. Yet he was the master of the short political speech that self-consciously echoed themes from an earlier political theory tradition. Lincoln believed that his job was to salvage and renew the ideals of the founding generation rather than to create new ones. Thus, his words called Americans back to the principles of the Declaration of Independence and the individualism of the Jacksonians:

> All honor to Jefferson—to the man who in the concrete pressure of a struggle for national independence by a single people, had the coolness, forecast, and capacity to introduce into a merely revolutionary document, an abstract truth, applicable to all men and all times, and so to embalm it there, that to-day, and in all coming days, it shall be a rebuke and a stumbling-block to the very harbingers of reappearing tyranny and oppression.

Four examples of Lincoln's speeches that follow are his "Address before the Young Man's Lyceum" (1838), "Speech on the Dred Scott Decision" (1857), the "First Inaugural Address" (1861), and "The Gettysburg Address" (1863).

Abraham Lincoln

Address before the Young Man's Lyceum of Springfield, Illinois (1838)

THE PERPETUATION OF OUR POLITICAL INSTITUTIONS

As a subject for the remarks of the evening, *the perpetuation of our political institutions,* is selected.

In the great journal of things happening under the sun, we, the American People, find our account running, under date of the nineteenth century of the Christian era. We find ourselves in the peaceful possession, of the fairest portion of the earth, as regards extent of territory, fertility of soil, and salubrity of climate. We find ourselves under the government of a system of political institutions, conducing more essentially to the ends of civil and religious liberty, than any of which the history of former times tells us. We, when mounting the stage of existence, found ourselves the legal inheritors of these fundamental blessings. We toiled not in the acquirement or establishment of them—they are a legacy bequeathed us, by a *once* hardy, brave, and patriotic, but *now* lamented and departed race of ancestors. Their's was the task (and nobly they performed it) to possess themselves, and through themselves, us, of this goodly land; and to uprear upon its hills and its valleys, a political edifice of liberty and equal rights; 'tis ours only, to transmit these, the former,

unprofaned by the foot of an invader; the latter, undecayed by the lapse of time. . . .

How, then, shall we perform it? At what point shall we expect the approach of danger? By what means shall we fortify against it? Shall we expect some transatlantic military giant, to step the Ocean, and crush us at a blow? Never! All the armies of Europe, Asia and Africa combined, with all the treasure of the earth (our own excepted) in their military chest; with a Buonaparte for a commander, could not by force, take a drink from the Ohio, or make a track on the Blue Ridge, in a trial of a thousand years.

At what point then is the approach of danger to be expected? I answer, if it ever reach us, it must spring up amongst us. It cannot come from abroad. If destruction be our lot, we must ourselves be its author and finisher. As a nation of freemen, we must live through all time, or die by suicide.

I hope I am over wary; but if I am not, there is, even now, something of ill-omen amongst us. I mean the increasing disregard for law which pervades the country; the growing disposition to substitute the wild and furious passions, in lieu of the sober judgement of Courts; and the worse than savage mobs, for the executive ministers of justice. This disposition is awfully fearful in any community; and that it now exists in ours, though grating to our feelings to admit, it would be a violation of truth, and an insult to our intelligence, to deny. Accounts of outrages committed by

SOURCE: Roy P. Basler, ed., *The Collected Works of Abraham Lincoln,* (New Brunswick, N.J.: Rutgers University Press, 1953).

mobs, form the every-day news of the times. They have pervaded the country, from New England to Louisiana;—they are neither peculiar to the eternal snows of the former, nor the burning suns of the latter;—they are not the creature of climate—neither are they confined to the slaveholding, or the non-slaveholding States. Alike, they spring up among the pleasure hunting masters of Southern slaves, and the order loving citizens of the land of steady habits. Whatever, then, their cause may be, it is common to the whole country. . . .

Turn, then, to that horror-striking scene at St. Louis. A single victim was only sacrificed there. His story is very short; and is, perhaps, the most highly tragic, of any thing of its length, that has ever been witnessed in real life. A mulatto man, by the name of McIntosh, was seized in the street, dragged to the suburbs of the city, chained to a tree, and actually burned to death; and all within a single hour from the time he had been a freeman, attending to his own business, and at peace with the world.

Such are the effects of mob law; and such are the scenes, becoming more and more frequent in this land so lately famed for love of law and order; and the stories of which, have even now grown too familiar, to attract any thing more, than an idle remark.

But you are, perhaps, ready to ask, "What has this to do with the perpetuation of our political institutions?" I answer, it has much to do with it. . . .

By such examples, by instances of the perpetrators of such acts going unpunished, the lawless in spirit, are encouraged to become lawless in practice; and having been used to no restraint, but dread of punishment, they thus become, absolutely unrestrained. Having ever regarded Government as their deadliest bane, they make a jubilee of the suspension of its operations; and pray for nothing so much, as its total annihilation. While, on the other hand, good men, men who love tranquility, who desire to abide by the laws, and enjoy their benefits, who would gladly spill their blood in the defence of their country; seeing their property destroyed; their families insulted, and their lives endangered; their persons injured; and seeing nothing in prospect that forebodes a change for the better; become tired of, and disgusted with, a Government that offers them no protection; and are not much averse to a change in which they imagine they have nothing to lose. Thus, then, by the operation of this mobocratic spirit, which all must admit, is now abroad in the land, the strongest bulwark of any Government, and particularly of those constituted like ours, may effectually be broken down and destroyed—I mean the *attachment* of the People. Whenever this effect shall be produced among us; whenever the vicious portion of population shall be permitted to gather in bands of hundreds and thousands, and burn churches, ravage and rob provision stores, throw printing presses into rivers, shoot editors, and hang and burn obnoxious persons at pleasure, and with impunity; depend on it, this Government cannot last. By such things, the feelings of the best citizens will become more or less alienated from it; and thus it will be left without friends, or with too few, and those few too weak, to make their friendship effectual. At such a time and under such circumstances, men of sufficient tal[ent and ambition will not be want]ing to seize [the opportunity, strike the blow, and overturn that fair fabric], which for the last half century, has been the fondest hope, of the lovers of freedom, throughout the world.

I know the American People are *much* attached to their Government;—I know they would suffer *much* for its sake;—I know they would endure evils long and patiently, before they would ever think of exchanging it for another. Yet, notwithstanding all this, if the laws be continually despised and disregarded, if their rights to be secure in their persons and property, are held by no better tenure than the caprice of a mob, the alienation of their affections from the Government is the natural consequence; and to that, sooner or later, it must come.

Here then, is one point at which danger may be expected.

The question recurs "how shall we fortify against it?" The answer is simple. Let every American, every lover of liberty, every well wisher to his posterity, swear by the blood of the Revolution, never to violate in the least particular, the laws of the country; and never to tolerate their violation by others. As the patriots of seventy-six did to the support of the Declaration of Independence, so to the support of the Constitution and Laws, let every American pledge his life, his property, and his sacred honor;—let every man remember that to violate the law, is to trample on the blood of his father, and to tear the character [charter?] of his own, and his children's liberty. Let reverence for the laws, be breathed by every American mother, to the lisping babe, that prattles on her lap—let it be taught in schools, in seminaries, and in colleges;—let it be written in Primmers, spelling books, and in Almanacs;—let it be preached from the pulpit, proclaimed in legislative halls, and enforced in courts of justice. And, in short, let it become the *political religion* of the nation; and let the old and the young, the rich and the poor, the grave and the gay, of all sexes and tongues, and colors and conditions, sacrifice unceasingly upon its altars.

While ever a state of feeling, such as this, shall universally, or even, very generally prevail throughout the nation, vain will be every effort, and fruitless every attempt, to subvert our national freedom.

When I so pressingly urge a strict observance of all the laws, let me not be understood as saying there are no bad laws, nor that grievances may not arise, for the redress of which, no legal provisions have been made. I mean to say no such thing. But I do mean to say, that, although bad laws, if they exist, should

be repealed as soon as possible, still while they continue in force, for the sake of example, they should be religiously observed. So also in unprovided cases. If such arise, let proper legal provisions be made for them with the least possible delay; but, till then, let them if not too intolerable, be borne with.

. . . That our government should have been maintained in its original form from its establishment until now, is not much to be wondered at. It had many props to support it through that period, which now are decayed, and crumbled away. Through that period, it was felt by all, to be an undecided experiment; now, it is understood to be a successful one. Then, all that sought celebrity and fame, and distinction, expected to find them in the success of that experiment. Their *all* was staked upon it;—their destiny was *inseparably* linked with it. Their ambition aspired to display before an admiring world, a practical demonstration of the truth of a proposition, which had hitherto been considered, at best no better, than problematical; namely, *the capability of a people to govern themselves*. If they succeeded, they were to be immortalized; their names were to be transferred to counties and cities, and rivers and mountains; and to be revered and sung, and toasted through all time. If they failed, they were to be called knaves and fools, and fanatics for a fleeting hour; then to sink and be forgotten. They succeeded. The experiment is successful; and thousands have won their deathless names in making it so. But the game is caught; and I believe it is true, that with the catching, end the pleasures of the chase. This field of glory is harvested, and the crop is already appropriated. But new reapers will arise, and *they*, too, will seek a field. It is to deny, what the history of the world tells us is true, to suppose that men of ambition and talents will not continue to spring up amongst us. And, when they do, they will as naturally seek the gratification of their ruling passion, as others have *so* done before them. The question then, is, can that gratification be found in supporting and maintaining an edifice that has been erected by others? Most certainly it cannot. Many great and good men sufficiently qualified for any task they should undertake, may ever be found, whose ambition would aspire to nothing beyond a seat in Congress, a gubernatorial or a presidential chair; *but such belong not to the family of the lion, or the tribe of the eagle,*[.] What! think you these places would satisfy an Alexander, a Caesar, or a Napoleon? Never! Towering genius disdains a beaten path. It seeks regions hitherto unexplored. It sees *no distinction* in adding story to story, upon the monuments of fame, erected to the memory of others. It *denies* that it is glory enough to serve under any chief. It *scorns* to tread in the footsteps of *any* predecessor, however illustrious. It thirsts and burns for distinction; and, if possible, it will have it, whether at the expense of emancipating slaves, or enslaving freemen. Is it unreasonable then to expect, that some man possessed of the loftiest genius, coupled with ambition sufficient to push it to its utmost stretch, will at some time, spring up among us? And when such a one does, it will require the people to be united with each other, attached to the government and laws, and generally intelligent, to successfully frustrate his designs.

Distinction will be his paramount object; and although he would as willingly, perhaps more so, acquire it by doing good as harm; yet, that opportunity being past, and nothing left to be done in the way of building up, he would set boldly to the task of pulling down. . . .

I do not mean to say, that the scenes of the revolution *are now* or *ever will be* entirely forgotten; but that like every thing else, they must fade upon the memory of the world, and grow more and more dim by the lapse of time. In history, we hope, they will be read of, and recounted, so long as the bible shall be read;—but even granting that they will, their influence *cannot be* what it heretofore has been. Even then, they *cannot be* so universally known, nor so vividly felt, as they were by the generation just gone to rest. At the close of that struggle, nearly every adult male had been a participator in some of its scenes. The consequence was, that of those scenes, in the form of a husband, a father, a son or a brother, a *living history was* to be found in every family—a history bearing the indubitable testimonies of its own authenticity, in the limbs mangled, in the scars of wounds received, in the midst of the very scenes related—a history, too, that could be read and understood alike by all, the wise and the ignorant, the learned and the unlearned. But *those* histories are gone. They *can* be read no more forever. They *were* a fortress of strength; but, what invading foemen could *never do,* the silent artillery of time *has done;* the levelling of its walls. They are gone. They *were* a forest of giant oaks; but the all-resistless hurricane has swept over them, and left only, here and there, a lonely trunk, despoiled of its verdure, shorn of its foliage; unshading and unshaded, to murmur in a few more gentle breezes, and to combat with its mutilated limbs, a few more ruder storms, then to sink, and be no more.

They *were* the pillars of the temple of liberty; and now, that they have crumbled away, that temple must fall, unless we, their descendants, supply their places with other pillars, hewn from the solid quarry of sober reason. Passion has helped us; but can do so no more. It will in future be our enemy. Reason, cold, calculating, unimpassioned reason, must furnish all the materials for our future support and defence. Let those [materials] be moulded into *general intelligence, [sound] morality* and, in particular, *a reverence for the constitution and laws;* and, that we improved to the last; that we remained free to the last; that we revered his name to the last; [tha]t, during his long sleep, we permitted no hostile foot to pass over or desecrate [his] resting place; shall be that which to le[arn the last] trump shall awaken our Wash[ington.

Upon these] let the proud fabric of freedom r[est, as the] rock of its basis; and as truly as

has been said of the only greater institution, *"the gates of hell shall not prevail against it."*

Abraham Lincoln

Speech on the Dred Scott Decision (1857)

FELLOW CITIZENS:—I am here to-night, partly by the invitation of some of you, and partly by my own inclination. Two weeks ago Judge Douglas spoke here on the several subjects of Kansas, the Dred Scott decision, and Utah. I listened to the speech at the time, and have read the report of it since. It was intended to controvert opinions which I think just, and to assail (politically, not personally,) those men who, in common with me, entertain those opinions. For this reason I wished then, and still wish, to make some answer to it, which I now take the opportunity of doing. . . .

I have said, in substance, that the Dred Scott decision was, in part, based on assumed historical facts which were not really true; and I ought not to leave the subject without giving some reasons for saying this; I therefore give an instance or two, which I think fully sustain me. Chief Justice Taney, in delivering the opinion of the majority of the Court, insists at great length that negroes were no part of the people who made, or for whom was made, the Declaration of Independence, or the Constitution of the United States.

On the contrary, Judge Curtis, in his dissenting opinion, shows that in five of the then thirteen states, to wit. New Hampshire, Massachusetts, New York, New Jersey and North

Carolina, free negroes were voters, and, in proportion to their numbers, had the same part in making the Constitution that the white people had. He shows this with so much particularity as to leave no doubt of its truth; and, as a sort of conclusion on that point, holds the following language:

"The Constitution was ordained and established by the people of the United States, through the action, in each State, of those persons who were qualified by its laws to act thereon in behalf of themselves and all other citizens of the State. In some of the States, as we have seen, colored persons were among those qualified by law to act on the subject. These colored persons were not only included in the body of 'the people of the United States,' by whom the Constitution was ordained and established; but in at least five of the States they had the power to act, and, doubtless, did act, by their suffrages, upon the question of its adoption."

Again, Chief Justice Taney says: "It is difficult, at this day to realize the state of public opinion in relation to that unfortunate race, which prevailed in the civilized and enlightened portions of the world at the time of the Declaration of Independence, and when the Constitution of the United States was framed and adopted." And again, after quoting from the Declaration, he says: "The general words above quoted would seem to include the whole human family, and if they were used in a

SOURCE: Roy P. Basler, ed., *The Collected Works of Abraham Lincoln* (New Brunswick, N.J.: Rutgers University Press, 1953).

similar instrument at this day, would be so understood."

In these the Chief Justice does not directly assert, but plainly assumes, as a fact, that the public estimate of the black man is more favorable *now* than it was in the days of the Revolution. This assumption is a mistake. In some trifling particulars, the condition of that race has been ameliorated; but, as a whole, in this country, the change between then and now is decidedly the other way; and their ultimate destiny has never appeared so hopeless as in the last three or four years. In two of the five States—New Jersey and North Carolina—that then gave the free negro the right of voting, the right has since been taken away; and in a third—New York—it has been greatly abridged; while it has not been extended, so far as I know, to a single additional State, though the number of the States has more than doubled. In those days, as I understand, masters could, at their own pleasure, emancipate their slaves; but since then, such legal restraints have been made upon emancipation, as to amount almost to prohibition. In those days, Legislatures held the unquestioned power to abolish slavery in their respective States; but now it is becoming quite fashionable for State Constitutions to withhold that power from the Legislatures. In those days, by common consent, the spread of the black man's bondage to new countries was prohibited; but now, Congress decides that it *will* not continue the prohibition, and the Supreme Court decides that it *could* not if it would. In those days, our Declaration of Independence was held sacred by all, and thought to include all; but now, to aid in making the bondage of the negro universal and eternal, it is assailed, and sneered at, and construed, and hawked at, and torn, till, if its framers could rise from their graves, they could not at all recognize it. All the powers of earth seem rapidly combining against him. Mammon is after him; ambition follows, and philosophy follows, and the Theology of the day is fast joining the cry. They have him in his prison house; they have searched his person, and left no prying instrument with him. One after another they have closed the heavy iron doors upon him, and now they have him, as it were, bolted in with a lock of a hundred keys, which can never be unlocked without the concurrence of every key; the keys in the hands of a hundred different men, and they scattered to a hundred different and distant places; and they stand musing as to what invention, in all the dominions of mind and matter, can be produced to make the impossibility of his escape more complete than it is.

It is grossly incorrect to say or assume, that the public estimate of the negro is more favorable now than it was at the origin of the government. . . .

There is a natural disgust in the minds of nearly all white people, to the idea of an indiscriminate amalgamation of the white and black races; and Judge Douglas evidently is basing his chief hope, upon the chances of being able to appropriate the benefit of this disgust to himself. If he can, by much drumming and repeating, fasten the odium of that idea upon his adversaries, he thinks he can struggle through the storm. He therefore clings to this hope, as a drowning man to the last plank. He makes an occasion for lugging it in from the opposition to the Dred Scott decision. He finds the Republicans insisting that the Declaration of Independence includes ALL men, black as well as white; and forthwith he boldly denies that it includes negroes at all, and proceeds to argue gravely that all who contend it does, do so only because they want to vote, and eat, and sleep, and marry with negroes! He will have it that they cannot be consistent else. Now I protest against that counterfeit logic which concludes that, because I do not want a black woman for a *slave* I must necessarily want her for a *wife*. I need not have her for either, I can just leave her alone. In some respects she certainly is not my equal; but in her natural right to eat the bread she earns with her own hands without asking leave of any one else, she is my equal, and the equal of all others.

Chief Justice Taney, in his opinion in the Dred Scott case, admits that the language of the Declaration is broad enough to include the whole human family, but he and Judge Douglas argue that the authors of that instrument did not intend to include negroes, by the fact that they did not at once, actually place them on an equality with the whites. Now this grave argument comes to just nothing at all, by the other fact, that they did not at once, *or ever afterwards,* actually place all white people on an equality with one or another. And this is the staple argument of both the Chief Justice and the Senator, for doing this obvious violence to the plain unmistakable language of the Declaration. I think the authors of that notable instrument intended to include *all* men, but they did not intend to declare all men equal *in all respects.* They did not mean to say all were equal in color, size, intellect, moral developments, or social capacity. They defined with tolerable distinctness, in what respects they did consider all men created equal—equal in "certain inalienable rights, among which are life, liberty, and the pursuit of happiness." This they said, and this meant. They did not mean to assert the obvious untruth, that all were then actually enjoying that equality, nor yet, that they were about to confer it immediately upon them. In fact they had no power to confer such a boon. They meant simply to declare the *right,* so that the *enforcement* of it might follow as fast as circumstances should permit. They meant to set up a standard maxim for free society, which should be familiar to all, and revered by all; constantly looked to, constantly labored for, and even though never perfectly attained, constantly approximated, and thereby constantly spreading and deepening its influence, and augmenting the happiness and value of life to all people of all colors everywhere. The assertion that "all men are created equal" was

of no practical use in effecting our separation from Great Britain; and it was placed in the Declaration, not for that, but for future use. Its authors meant it to be, thank God, it is now proving itself, a stumbling block to those who in after times might seek to turn a free people back into the hateful paths of despotism. They knew the proneness of prosperity to breed tyrants, and they meant when such should re-appear in this fair land and commence their vocation they should find left for them at least one hard nut to crack.

I have now briefly expressed my view of the *meaning* and *objects* of that part of the Declaration of Independence which declares that "all men are created equal."

Now let us hear Judge Douglas' view of the same subject, as I find it in the printed report of his late speech. Here it is:

"No man can vindicate the character, motives and conduct of the signers of the Declaration of Independence, except upon the hypothesis that they referred to the white race alone, and not to the African, when they declared all men to have been created equal—that they were speaking of British subjects on this continent being equal to British subjects born and residing in Great Britain—that they were entitled to the same inalienable rights, and among them were enumerated life, liberty and the pursuit of happiness. The Declaration was adopted for the purpose of justifying the colonists in the eyes of the civilized world in withdrawing their allegiance from the British crown, and dissolving their connection with the mother country."

My good friends, read that carefully over some leisure hour, and ponder well upon it—see what a mere wreck—mangled ruin—it makes of our once glorious Declaration.

"They were speaking of British subjects on this continent being equal to British subjects born and residing in Great Britain!" Why, according to this, not only negroes but white people outside of Great Britain and America are not spoken of in that instrument. The

English, Irish and Scotch, along with white Americans, were included to be sure, but the French, Germans and other white people of the world are all gone to pot along with the Judge's inferior races.

I had thought the Declaration promised something better than the condition of British subjects; but no, it only meant that we should be *equal* to them in their own oppressed and *unequal* condition. According to that, it gave no promise that having kicked off the King and Lords of Great Britain, we should not at once be saddled with a King and Lords of our own.

I had thought the Declaration contemplated the progressive improvement in the condition of all men everywhere; but no, it merely "was adopted for the purpose of justifying the colonists in the eyes of the civilized world in withdrawing their allegiance from the British crown, and dissolving their connection with the mother country." Why, that object having been effected some eighty years ago, the Declaration is of no practical use now—mere rubbish—old wadding left to rot on the battlefield after the victory is won.

I understand you are preparing to celebrate the "Fourth," tomorrow week. What for? The doings of that day had no reference to the present; and quite half of you are not even descendants of those who were referred to at that day. But I suppose you will celebrate; and will even go so far as to read the Declaration. Suppose after you read it once in the old fashioned way, you read it once more with Judge Douglas' version. It will then run thus: "We hold these truths to be self-evident that all British subjects who were on this continent eighty-one years ago, were created equal to all British subjects born and *then* residing in Great Britain."

And now I appeal to all—to Democrats as well as others,—are you really willing that the Declaration shall be thus frittered away?—thus left no more at most, than an interesting memorial of the dead past? thus shorn of its vitality, and practical value; and left without the *germ* or even the *suggestion* of the individual rights of man in it?

But Judge Douglas is especially horrified at the thought of the mixing blood by the white and black races: agreed for once—a thousand times agreed. There are white men enough to marry all the white women, and black men enough to marry all the black women; and so let them be married. On this point we fully agree with the Judge; and when he shall show that his policy is better adapted to prevent amalgamation than ours we shall drop ours, and adopt his. Let us see. In 1850 there were in the United States, 405,751, mulattoes. Very few of these are the offspring of whites and *free* blacks; nearly all have sprung from black *slaves* and white masters. A separation of the races is the only perfect preventive of amalgamation but as an immediate separation is impossible the next best thing is to *keep* them apart *where* they are not already together. If white and black people never get together in Kansas, they will never mix blood in Kansas. That is at least one self-evident truth. A few free colored persons may get into the free States, in any event; but their number is too insignificant to amount to much in the way of mixing blood. In 1850 there were in the free states, 56,649 mulattoes; but for the most part they were not born there—they came from the slave States, ready made up. In the same year the slave States had 348,874 mulattoes all of home production. The proportion of free mulattoes to free blacks—the only colored classes in the free states—is much greater in the slave than in the free states. It is worthy of note too, that among the free states those which make the colored man the nearest to equal the white, have, proportionably the fewest mulattoes the least of amalgamation. In New Hampshire, the State which goes farthest towards equality between the races, there are just 184 mulattoes while there are in Virginia—how many do you think? 79,775, being 23,126 more than in all the free States together.

These statistics show that slavery is the

greatest source of amalgamation; and next to it, not the elevation, but the degeneration of the free blacks. Yet Judge Douglas dreads the slightest restraints on the spread of slavery, and the slightest human recognition of the negro, as tending horribly to amalgamation.

I have said that the separation of the races is the only perfect preventive of amalgamation. I have no right to say all the members of the Republican party are in favor of this, nor to say that as a party they are in favor of it. There is nothing in their platform directly on the subject. But I can say a very large proportion of its members are for it, and that the chief plank in their platform—opposition to the spread of slavery—is most favorable to that separation.

Such separation, if ever effected at all, must be effected by colonization; and no political party, as such, is now doing anything directly for colonization. Party operations at present only favor or retard colonization incidentally. The enterprise is a difficult one; but "when there is a will there is a way;" and what colonization needs most is a hearty will. Will springs from the two elements of moral sense and self-interest. Let us be brought to believe it is morally right, and, at the same time, favorable to, or, at least, not against, our interest, to transfer the African to his native clime, and we shall find a way to do it, however great the task may be. The children of Israel, to such numbers as to include four hundred thousand fighting men, went out of Egyptian bondage in a body.

How differently the respective courses of the Democratic and Republican parties incidentally bear on the question of forming a will—a public sentiment—for colonization, is easy to see. The Republicans inculcate, with whatever of ability they can, that the negro is a man; that his bondage is cruelly wrong, and that the field of his oppression ought not to be enlarged. The Democrats deny his manhood; deny, or dwarf to insignificance, the wrong of his bondage; so far as possible, crush all sympathy for him, and cultivate and excite hatred and disgust against him; compliment themselves as Union-savers for doing so; and call the indefinite outspreading of his bondage "a sacred right of self-government."

The plainest print cannot be read through a gold eagle; and it will be ever hard to find many men who will send a slave to Liberia, and pay his passage while they can send him to a new country, Kansas for instance, and sell him for fifteen hundred dollars, and the rise.

Abraham Lincoln

First Inaugural Address (1861)

<small>FELLOW CITIZENS OF THE UNITED STATES:</small>
In compliance with a custom as old as the

SOURCE: Roy P. Basler, ed., *The Collected Works of Abraham Lincoln* (New Brunswick, N.J.: Rutgers University Press, 1953).

government itself, I appear before you to address you briefly, and to take, in your presence, the oath prescribed by the Constitution of the United States, to be taken by the President "before he enters on the execution of his office."

I do not consider it necessary, at present, for me to discuss those matters of administration about which there is no special anxiety, or excitement.

Apprehension seems to exist among the people of the Southern States, that by the accession of a Republican Administration, their property, and their peace, and personal security, are to be endangered. There has never been any reasonable cause for such apprehension. Indeed, the most ample evidence to the contrary has all the while existed, and been open to their inspection. It is found in nearly all the published speeches of him who now addresses you. I do but quote from one of those speeches when I declare that "I have no purpose, directly or indirectly, to interfere with the institution of slavery in the States where it exists. I believe I have no lawful right to do so, and I have no inclination to do so." Those who nominated and elected me did so with full knowledge that I had made this, and many similar declarations, and had never recanted them. And more than this, they placed in the platform, for my acceptance, and as a law to themselves, and to me, the clear and emphatic resolution which I now read:

"*Resolved,* That the maintenance inviolate of the rights of the States, and especially the right of each State to order and control its own domestic institutions according to its own judgment exclusively, is essential to that balance of power on which the perfection and endurance of our political fabric depend; and we denounce the lawless invasion by armed force of the soil of any State or Territory, no matter under what pretext, as among the gravest of crimes."

I now reiterate these sentiments: and in doing so, I only press upon the public attention the most conclusive evidence of which the case is susceptible, that the property, peace and security of no section are to be in anywise endangered by the now incoming Administration. I add too, that all the protection which, consistently with the Constitution and the laws, can be given, will be cheerfully given to all the States when lawfully demanded, for whatever cause—as cheerfully to one section, as to another.

There is much controversy about the delivering up of fugitives from service or labor. The clause I now read is as plainly written in the Constitution as any other of its provisions:

"No person held to service or labor in one State, under the laws thereof, escaping into another, shall, in consequence of any law or regulation therein, be discharged from such service or labor, but shall be delivered up on claim of the party to whom such service or labor may be due."

It is scarcely questioned that this provision was intended by those who made it, for the reclaiming of what we call fugitive slaves; and the intention of the law-giver is the law. All members of Congress swear their support to the whole Constitution—to this provision as much as to any other. To the proposition, then, that slaves whose cases come within the terms of this clause, "shall be delivered up," their oaths are unanimous. Now, if they would make the effort in good temper, could they not, with nearly equal unanimity, frame and pass a law, by means of which to keep good that unanimous oath?

There is some difference of opinion whether this clause should be enforced by national or by state authority; but surely that difference is not a very material one. If the slave is to be surrendered, it can be of but little consequence to him, or to others, by which authority it is done. And should any one, in any case, be content that his oath shall go unkept, on a merely unsubstantial controversy as to *how* it shall be kept?

Again, in any law upon this subject, ought not all the safeguards of liberty known in civilized and humane jurisprudence to be introduced, so that a free man be not, in any case, surrendered as a slave? And might it not be well, at the same time, to provide by law for the enforcement of that clause in the Constitution which guarranties that "The citizens of each State shall be entitled to all privileges and immunities of citizens in the several States?"

I take the official oath to-day, with no mental reservations, and with no purpose to construe the Constitution or laws, by any hypercritical rules. And while I do not choose now to specify particular acts of Congress as proper to be enforced, I do suggest, that it will be much safer for all, both in official and private stations, to conform to, and abide by, all those acts which stand unrepealed, than to violate any of them, trusting to find impunity in having them held to be unconstitutional.

It is seventy-two years since the first inauguration of a President under our national Constitution. During that period fifteen different and greatly distinguished citizens, have, in succession, administered the executive branch of the government. They have conducted it through many perils; and, generally, with great success. Yet, with all this scope for precedent, I now enter upon the same task for the brief constitutional term of four years, under great and peculiar difficulty. A disruption of the Federal Union heretofore only menaced, is now formidably attempted.

I hold, that in contemplation of universal law, and of the Constitution, the Union of these States is perpetual. Perpetuity is implied, if not expressed, in the fundamental law of all national governments. It is safe to assert that no government proper, ever had a provision in its organic law for its own termination. Continue to execute all the express provisions of our national Constitution, and the Union will endure forever—it being impossible to destroy it, except by some action not provided for in the instrument itself.

Again, if the United States be not a government proper, but an association of States in the nature of contract merely, can it, as a contract, be peaceably unmade, by less than all

the parties who made it? One party to a contract may violate it—break it, so to speak; but does it not require all to lawfully rescind it?

Descending from these general principles, we find the proposition that, in legal contemplation, the Union is perpetual, confirmed by the history of the Union itself. The Union is much older than the Constitution. It was formed in fact, by the Articles of Association in 1774. It was matured and continued by the Declaration of Independence in 1776. It was further matured and the faith of all the then thirteen States expressly plighted and engaged that it should be perpetual, by the Articles of Confederation in 1778. And finally, in 1787, one of the declared objects for ordaining and establishing the Constitution, was *"to form a more perfect union."*

But if destruction of the Union, by one, or by a part only, of the States, be lawfully possible, the Union is *less* perfect than before the Constitution, having lost the vital element of perpetuity.

It follows from these views that no State, upon its own mere motion, can lawfully get out of the Union,—that *resolves* and *ordinances* to that effect are legally void; and that acts of violence, within any State or States, against the authority of the United States, are insurrectionary or revolutionary, according to circumstances.

I therefore consider that, in view of the Constitution and the laws, the Union is unbroken; and, to the extent of my ability, I shall take care, as the Constitution itself expressly enjoins upon me, that the laws of the Union be faithfully executed in all the States. Doing this I deem to be only a simple duty on my part; and I shall perform it, so far as practicable, unless my rightful masters, the American people, shall withhold the requisite means, or, in some authoritative manner, direct the contrary. I trust this will not be regarded as a menace, but only as the declared purpose of the Union that it *will* constitutionally defend, and maintain itself. . . .

That there are persons in one section, or another who seek to destroy the Union at all events, and are glad of any pretext to do it, I will neither affirm or deny; but if there be such, I need address no word to them. To those, however, who really love the Union, may I not speak?

Before entering upon so grave a matter as the destruction of our national fabric, with all its benefits, its memories, and its hopes, would it not be wise to ascertain precisely why we do it? Will you hazard so desperate a step, while there is any possibility that any portion of the ills you fly from, have no real existence? Will you, while the certain ills you fly to, are greater than all the real ones you fly from? Will you risk the commission of so fearful a mistake?

All profess to be content in the Union, if all constitutional rights can be maintained. Is it true, then, that any right, plainly written in the Constitution, has been denied? I think not. Happily the human mind is so constituted, that no party can reach to the audacity of doing this. Think, if you can, of a single instance in which a plainly written provision of the Constitution has ever been denied. If, by the mere force of numbers, a majority should deprive a minority of any clearly written constitutional right, it might, in a moral point of view, justify revolution—certainly would, if such right were a vital one. But such is not our case. All the vital rights of minorities, and of individuals, are so plainly assured to them, by affirmations and negations, guarranties and prohibitions, in the Constitution, that controversies never arise concerning them. But no organic law can ever be framed with a provision specifically applicable to every question which may occur in practical administration. No foresight can anticipate, nor any document of reasonable length contain express provisions for all possible questions. Shall fugitives from labor be surrendered by national or by State authority? The Constitution does not expressly say. *May* Congress pro-

hibit slavery in the territories? The Constitution does not expressly say. *Must* Congress protect slavery in the territories? The Constitution does not expressly say.

From questions of this class spring all our constitutional controversies, and we divide upon them into majorities and minorities. If the minority will not acquiesce, the majority must, or the government must cease. There is no other alternative; for continuing the government, is acquiescence on one side or the other. If a minority, in such case, will secede rather than acquiesce, they make a precedent which, in turn, will divide and ruin them; for a minority of their own will secede from them, whenever a majority refuses to be controlled by such minority. For instance, why may not any portion of a new confederacy, a year or two hence, arbitrarily secede again, precisely as portions of the present Union now claim to secede from it. All who cherish disunion sentiments, are now being educated to the exact temper of doing this. Is there such perfect identity of interests among the States to compose a new Union, as to produce harmony only, and prevent renewed secession?

Plainly, the central idea of secession, is the essence of anarchy. A majority, held in restraint by constitutional checks, and limitations, and always changing easily, with deliberate changes of popular opinions and sentiments, is the only true sovereign of a free people. Whoever rejects it, does, of necessity, fly to anarchy or to despotism. Unanimity is impossible; the rule of a minority, as a permanent arrangement, is wholly inadmissible; so that, rejecting the majority principle, anarchy, or despotism in some form, is all that is left.

I do not forget the position assumed by some, that constitutional questions are to be decided by the Supreme Court; nor do I deny that such decisions must be binding in any case, upon the parties to a suit, as to the object of that suit, while they are also entitled to very high respect and consideration, in all parallel cases, by all other departments of the government. And while it is obviously possible that such decision may be erroneous in any given case, still the evil effect following it, being limited to that particular case, with the chance that it may be over-ruled, and never become a precedent for other cases, can better be borne than could the evils of a different practice. At the same time the candid citizen must confess that if the policy of the government, upon vital questions, affecting the whole people, is to be irrevocably fixed by decisions of the Supreme Court, the instant they are made, in ordinary litigation between parties, in personal actions, the people will have ceased, to be their own rulers, having, to that extent, practically resigned their government, into the hands of that eminent tribunal. Nor is there, in this view, any assault upon the court, or the judges. It is a duty, from which they may not shrink, to decide cases properly brought before them; and it is no fault of theirs, if others seek to turn their decisions to political purposes.

One section of our country believes slavery is *right,* and ought to be extended, while the other believes it is *wrong,* and ought not to be extended. This is the only substantial dispute. The fugitive slave clause of the Constitution, and the law for the suppression of the foreign slave trade, are each as well enforced, perhaps, as any law can ever be in a community where the moral sense of the people imperfectly supports the law itself. The great body of the people abide by the dry legal obligation in both cases, and a few break over in each. This, I think, cannot be perfectly cured; and it would be worse in both cases *after* the separation of the sections, than before. The foreign slave trade, now imperfectly suppressed, would be ultimately revived without restriction, in one section; while fugitive slaves, now only partially surrendered, would not be surrendered at all, by the other.

Physically speaking, we cannot separate. We cannot remove our respective sections from each other, nor build an impassable wall between them. A husband and wife may be divorced, and go out of the presence, and beyond the reach of each other; but the different parts of our country cannot do this. They cannot but remain face to face; and intercourse, either amicable or hostile, must continue between them. It is possible then to make that intercourse more advantageous, or more satisfactory, *after* separation than *before*? Can aliens make treaties easier than friends can make laws? Can treaties be more faithfully enforced between aliens, than laws can among friends? Suppose you go to war, you cannot fight always; and when, after much loss on both sides, and no gain on either, you cease fighting, the identical old questions, as to terms of intercourse, are again upon you.

This country, with its institutions, belongs to the people who inhabit it. Whenever they shall grow weary of the existing government, they can exercise their *constitutional* right of amending it, or their *revolutionary* right to dismember, or overthrow it. I can not be ignorant of the fact that many worthy, and patriotic citizens are desirous of having the national constitution amended. While I make no recommendation of amendments, I fully recognize the rightful authority of the people over the whole subject, to be exercised in either of the modes prescribed in the instrument itself; and I should, under existing circumstances, favor, rather than oppose, a fair opportunity being afforded the people to act upon it.

I will venture to add that, to me, the convention mode seems preferable, in that it allows amendments to originate with the people themselves, instead of only permitting them to take, or reject, propositions, originated by others, not especially chosen for the purpose, and which might not be precisely such, as they would wish to either accept or refuse. I understand a proposed amendment: to the Constitution—which amendment, however, I have not seen, has passed Congress, to the effect that the federal government, shall never interfere with the domestic institutions of the States, including that of persons held to service. To avoid misconstruction of what I have said, I depart from my purpose not to speak of particular amendments, so far as to say that, holding such a provision to now be implied constitutional law, I have no objection to its being made express, and irrevocable.

The Chief Magistrate derives all his authority from the people, and they have conferred none upon him to fix terms for the separation of the States. The people themselves can do this also if they choose; but the executive, as such, has nothing to do with it. His duty is to administer the present government, as it came to his hands, and to transmit it, unimpaired by him, to his successor.

Why should there not be a patient confidence in the ultimate justice of the people? Is there any better, or equal hope, in the world? In our present differences, is either party without faith of being in the right? If the Almighty Ruler of nations, with his eternal truth and justice, be on your side of the North, or on yours of the South, that truth, and that justice, will surely prevail, by the judgment of this great tribunal, the American people.

By the frame of the government under which we live, this same people have wisely given their public servants but little power for mischief; and have, with equal wisdom, provided for the return of that little to their own hands at very short intervals.

While the people retain their virtue, and vigilence, no administration, by any extreme of wickedness or folly, can very seriously injure the government, in the short space of four years.

My countrymen, one and all, think calmly and *well,* upon this whole subject. Nothing valuable can be lost by taking time. If there be an object to *hurry* any of you, in hot haste, to a step which you would never take *deliberately,* that object will be frustrated by taking time; but no good object can be frustrated by it. Such of you as are now dissatisfied, still have the old Constitution unimpaired, and, on the sensitive point, the laws of your own framing under it; while the new administration will have no immediate power, if it would, to change either. If it were admitted that you who are dissatisfied, hold the right side in the dispute, there still is no single good reason for precipitate action. Intelligence, patriotism, Christianity, and a firm reliance on Him, who has never yet forsaken this favored land, are still competent to adjust, in the best way, all our present difficulty.

In *your* hands, my dissatisfied fellow countrymen, and not in *mine,* is the momentous issue of civil war. The government will not assail *you.* You can have no conflict, without being yourselves the aggressors. *You* have no oath registered in Heaven to destroy the government, while *I* shall have the most solemn one to "preserve, protect and defend" it.

I am loath to close. We are not enemies, but friends. We must not be enemies. Though passion may have strained, it must not break our bonds of affection. The mystic chords of memory, stretching from every battle-field, and patriot grave, to every living heart and hearthstone, all over this broad land, will yet swell the chorus of the Union, when again touched, as surely they will be, by the better angels of our nature.

Abraham Lincoln

The Gettysburg Address (1863)

Four score and seven years ago our fathers brought forth on this continent, a new nation, conceived in Liberty, and dedicated to the proposition that all men are created equal.

Now we are engaged in a great civil war, testing whether that nation, or any nation so conceived and so dedicated, can long endure. We are met on a great battle-field of that war. We have come to dedicate a portion of that field, as a final resting place for those who here gave their lives that that nation might live. It is altogether fitting and proper that we should do this.

But, in a larger sense, we can not dedicate—

SOURCE: Roy P. Basler, ed., *The Collected Works of Abraham Lincoln* (New Brunswick, N.J.: Rutgers University Press, 1953).

we can not consecrate—we can not hallow—this ground. The brave men, living and dead, who struggled here, have consecrated it, far above our poor power to add or detract. The world will little note, nor long remember what we say here, but it can never forget what they did here. It is for us the living, rather, to be dedicated here to the unfinished work which they who fought here have thus far so nobly advanced. It is rather for us to be here dedicated to the great task remaining before us—that from these honored dead we take increased devotion to that cause for which they gave the last full measure of devotion—that we here highly resolve that these dead shall not have died in vain—that this nation, under God, shall have a new birth of freedom—and that government of the people, by the people, for the people, shall not perish from the earth.

Affirmative Dissent: For Greater Equality

Frances Wright, 1795–1852

Frances Wright, an unusual free-thinker and radical for nineteenth century America, was born in Scotland. Her father, a wealthy man, was a devoted reader of Thomas Paine who distributed Paine's *Rights of Man* throughout his region of the country. Both of Wright's parents died before she was three years old, but she had her own money and an enlightened mind like her father's.

In her early twenties, Wright decided to travel through the United States, rather than Europe, as a way to complete her education. This unusual step led to a life-long attachment to the United States, and ultimately a permanent move to this country.

Frances Wright was committed to many causes, almost all of them connected with increased equality. She was an impassioned champion of emancipation for slaves, equal rights for women, and free public education for all children. Yet she usually went beyond the agenda of most reformers of her time. For example, Wright delighted in attacks on conventional morality and religion and advocated abolishing all legal marriage in favor of mere pledges of commitment. She was also an early advocate of labor unions, and even a labor party, but her influence among workers was quite limited due to her views on religion and morality.

In 1828, Wright joined Robert Dale Owen, the son of English utopian socialist Robert Owen, in editing the *New Harmony Gazette*. Later Wright revived the paper as the *Free Enquirer*. In her writings in these journals, Wright strongly advocated free public education for all school-age children. However, unlike Horace Mann, who argued that the newly enfranchised working class needed educational leavening if republican government were to survive, Wright demanded equal education so that each child would receive an equal start in the race of life. Typical of her radicalism, Wright pushed for public boarding schools so that each child would be equal, without any additional influence from his or her family.

Needless to say, Wright's radical views were out of step with other Americans, even in the egalitarian atmosphere of Jacksonian America.

Frances Wright

On Existing Evils and Their Remedy (1829)

The result of my observation has been the conviction that the reform commenced at the Revolution of '76 has been but little improved through the term of years which have succeeded; that the national policy of the country was then indeed changed, but that its social economy has remained such as it was in the days of its European vassalage.

In confirmation of this I will request you to observe that your religion is the same as that of monarchical England, taught from the same books, and promulgated and sustained by similar means—viz., a salaried priesthood set apart from the people; sectarian churches in whose property the people have no share, and over whose use and occupancy the people have no control; expensive missions, treasury funds, association; and, above all, a compulsory power, compounded at once of accumulated wealth, established custom, extensive correspondence, and a system of education imbued with its spirit and all pervaded by its influence.

SOURCE: Frances Wright, *A Course of Popular Lectures* (New York: Office of the Free Enquirer, 1829).

Again, in proof of the similarity between your internal policy and that of monarchical England, I will request you to observe that *her law is your law*. Every part and parcel of that absurd, cruel, ignorant, inconsistent, incomprehensible jumble styled the common law of England—every part and parcel of it, I say, not abrogated or altered expressly by legislative statutes, which has been very rarely done—is at this hour the law of revolutionized America.

Further, in proof of the identity of your fabric of civil polity with that of aristocratical England, I will request you to observe that the system of education pursued in both countries is, with little variation, one and the same. There you have endowed universities, privileged by custom, enriched by ancient royal favor, protected by parliamentary statutes, and devoted to the upholding, perpetuating, and strengthening the power and privilege to which they owe their origin. There, too, you have parish schools under the control of the parish priest, and a press everywhere coerced by law, swayed, bribed, or silenced by ascendant parties or tyrannous authority. And *here*, have we not colleges with endowments still held by the royal charters which first bestowed them; and colleges with lands and money granted by American legislatures, not for the advantage of the American people, but for that of their rulers, for the children of privileged professions upon whom is thus entailed the privilege of their fathers, and that as certainly as the son of a duke is born to a dukedom in England? *Here,* have we not also schools controlled by the clergy; nay, have we not all our public institutions, scientific, literary, judicial, or humane, ridden by the spirit of orthodoxy and invaded, perverted, vitiated, and tormented by opiniative distinctions? And *here,* have we not a press paralyzed by fear, disgraced by party, and ruled by loud tongued fanaticism, or aspiring and threatening sectarian ambition? And more, my friends: see we not, in this nation of confederated freemen, as many distinctions of class as afflict the aristocracies of Britain or the despotism of the Russias, and more distinctions of sect than ever cursed all the nations of Europe together, from the preaching of Peter the hermit to the trances of Madame Krudner or the miracles of Prince Hohenlohe?

Surely all these are singular anomalies in a republic. Sparta, when she conceived her democracy, commenced with educational equality; when she aimed at national union, she cemented that union in childhood at the public board, in the gymnasium, in the temple, in the common habits, common feelings, common duties, and common condition. And so, notwithstanding all the errors with which her institutions were fraught and all the vices which arose out of those errors, did she present for ages a wondrous sample of democratic union and consequently of national prosperity.

What, then, is wanted here? What Sparta had: *a national education.* And what Sparta, in many respects, had not: *a rational education.*

Hitherto, my friends, in government as in every branch of morals, we have but too much mistaken words for truths and forms for principles. To render men free, it sufficeth not to proclaim their liberty; to make them equal, it sufficeth not to call them so. True, the Fourth of July, '76, commenced a new era for our race. True, the sun of promise then rose upon the world. But let us not mistake for the fulness of light what was but its harbinger. Let us not conceive that man, in signing the declaration of his rights, secured their possession; that having framed the theory he had not, and hath not still, the practice to seek. . . .

Who speaks of liberty while the human mind is in chains? Who of equality while the thousands are in squalid wretchedness, the millions harassed with health-destroying labor, the few afflicted with health-destroying idleness, and all tormented by health-destroying solicitude? Look abroad on the misery which is gaining on the land! Mark the strife and the discord and the jealousies, the shock of interests and opinions, the hatreds of sect, the estrangements of class, the pride of wealth, the debasement of poverty, the helplessness of youth unprotected, of age uncomforted, of industry unrewarded, of ignorance unenlightened, of vice unreclaimed, of misery unpitied, of sickness, hunger, and nakedness unsatisfied, unalleviated, and unheeded. Go! mark all the wrongs and the wretchedness with which the eye and the ear and the heart are familiar, and then echo in triumph and celebrate in jubilee the insulting declaration: *all men are free and equal.*

. . . I had occasion formerly to observe, in allusion to the efforts already made and yet making, in the cause of popular instruction, more or less throughout the Union, that as yet the true principle has not been hit, and that until it be hit all reform must be slow and inefficient.

The noble example of New England has been imitated by other States until all not possessed of common schools blush for the popular remissness. But, after all, how can *common schools,* under their best form and in fullest supply, effect even the purpose which they have in view?

The object proposed by common schools—if I rightly understand it—is to impart to the whole population those means for the acquirement of knowledge which are in common use: reading and writing. To these are added arithmetic and, occasionally perhaps, some imperfect lessons in the simpler sciences. But, I would ask, supposing these institutions should even be made to embrace all the branches of intellectual knowledge, and thus science offered gratis to all the children of the land, how are the children of the very class for whom we suppose the schools instituted to be supplied with food and raiment, or instructed in the trade necessary to their future subsistence, while they are following these studies? How are they, I ask, to be fed and clothed, when, as all facts show, the labor of the parents is often insufficient for their own sustenance and, almost universally, inadequate to the provision of the family without the united efforts of all its members? In your manufacturing districts you have children worked for twelve hours a day; and, in the rapid and certain progress of the existing system, you will soon have them, as in England, *worked to death,* and yet unable, through the period of their miserable existence, to earn a pittance sufficient to satisfy the cravings of hunger. At this present time, what leisure or what spirit, think you, have the children of the miserable widows of Philadelphia, realizing, according to the most favorable estimate of your city and county committee, sixteen dollars per annum for food and clothing; what leisure or what spirit may their children find for visiting a school, although the same should be open to them from sunrise to sunset? Or what leisure have usually the children of your most thriving mechanics, after their strength is sufficiently developed to spin, sew, weave, or wield a tool? It seems to me, my friends, that to build schoolhouses nowadays is something like building churches. When you have

them, you need some measure to ensure their being occupied. . . .

In lieu of all common schools, high schools, colleges, seminaries, houses of refuge, or any other juvenile institution, instructional or protective, I would suggest that the state legislatures be directed (after laying off the whole in townships or hundreds) to organize, at suitable distances and in convenient and healthy situations, establishments for the general reception of all the children resident within the said school district. These establishments to be devoted, severally, to children between a certain age. Say, the first to infants between two and four, or two and six, according to the density of the population, and such other local circumstances as might render a greater or less number of establishments necessary or practicable. The next to receive children from four to eight, or six to twelve years. The next from twelve to sixteen, or to an older age, if found desirable. Each establishment to be furnished with instructors in every branch of knowledge, intellectual and operative, with all the apparatus, land, and conveniences necessary for the best development of all knowledge; the same, whether operative or intellectual, being always calculated to the age and strength of the pupils.

To obviate, in the commencement, every evil result possible from the first mixture of a young population, so variously raised in error or neglect, a due separation should be made in each establishment, by which means those entering with bad habits would be kept apart from the others until corrected. How rapidly reform may be effected on the plastic disposition of childhood has been sufficiently proved in your houses of refuge, more especially when such establishments have been under *liberal* superintendence, as was formerly the case in New York. Under their orthodox directors, those asylums of youth have been converted into jails.

It will be understood that, in the proposed establishments, the children would pass from one to the other in regular succession; and that the parents, who would necessarily be resident in their close neighborhood, could visit the children at suitable hours but in no case interfere with or interrupt the rules of the institution.

In the older establishments, the well-directed and well-protected labor of the pupil would, in time, suffice for and then exceed their own support, when the surplus might be devoted to the maintenance of the infant establishments.

In the beginning, and until all debt was cleared off and so long as the same should be found favorable to the promotion of these best palladiums of a nation's happiness, a double tax might be at once expedient and politic.

First, a moderate tax per head for every child, to be laid upon its parents conjointly or divided between them, due attention being always paid to the varying strength of the two sexes and to the undue depreciation which now rests on female labor. The more effectually to correct the latter injustice, as well as to consult the convenience of the industrious classes generally, this parental tax might be rendered payable either in money or in labor, produce, or domestic manufactures; and should be continued for each child until the age when juvenile labor should be found, on the average, equivalent to the educational expenses, which, I have reason to believe, would be at twelve years.

This first tax on parents to embrace equally the whole population, as, however moderate, it would inculcate a certain forethought in all the human family, more especially where it is most wanted: in young persons who, before they assumed the responsibility of parents, would estimate their fitness to meet it.

The second tax to be on property, increasing in percentage with the wealth of the individual. In this manner I conceive the rich would contribute, according to their riches, to the relief of the poor and to the support of the state, by raising up its best bulwark: an enlightened and united generation.

Preparatory to or connected with such measures, a registry should be opened by the state, with offices through all the townships, where, on the birth of every child, or within a certain time appointed, the same should be entered, together with the names of its parents. When two years old, the parental tax should be payable and the juvenile institution open for the child's reception, from which time forward it would be under the protective care and guardianship of the state, while it need never be removed from the daily, weekly, or frequent inspection of the parents.

Orphans, of course, would find here an open asylum. If possessed of property, a contribution would be paid from its revenue to the common educational fund; if unprovided, they would be sustained out of the same.

In these nurseries of a free nation, no inequality must be allowed to enter. Fed at a common board; clothed in a common garb, uniting neatness with simplicity and convenience; raised in the exercise of common duties, in the acquirement of the same knowledge and practice of the same industry, varied only according to individual taste and capabilities, in the exercise of the same virtues, in the enjoyment of the same pleasures, in the study of the same nature, in pursuit of the same object—their own and each other's happiness—say! would not such a race, when arrived at manhood and womanhood, work out the reform of society, perfect the free institutions of America?

I have drawn but a sketch; nor could I presume to draw the picture of that which the mind's eye hath seen alone, and which it is for the people of this land to realize. . . .

To develop further my views on this all-important subject at the present time would be to fatigue your attention and exhaust my own strength. I shall prosecute this subject in the periodical of which I am editor, which, in common with my public discourses, have been and will ever be devoted to the common cause of human improvement and addressed to humankind without distinction of nation, class, or sect. May you, my fellow beings, unite in the same cause, in the same spirit! May you learn to seek truth without fear! May you further learn to advocate truth as you distinguish it; to be valiant in its defense, and peaceful while valiant; to meet all things, bear all things, and dare all things for the correction of abuses and the effecting, in private and in public, in your own minds, through the minds of your children, friends, and companions, and, above all, *through your legislature*, a radical reform in all your measures, whether as citizens or as men!

Orestes A. Brownson, 1803–1876

Orestes Brownson's life was one of political, social, and religious searching. Although he had little formal education, Brownson was a powerful writer and an editor of tremendous influence in nineteenth-century America. In religion, Brownson was a Presbyterian, Universalist, Unitarian, and finally, a Roman Catholic. In politics, he was a Chartist, a Jacksonian Democrat, a member of the Workingman's party, and finally, an unaffiliated political philosopher more concerned with duty and authority than with rights. As with his religion, Brownson's politics had gone full circle.

In 1836, Brownson founded the *Boston Quarterly Review* and later merged it with the magnificent Jacksonian journal the *Democratic Review*. As Brownson grew more conservative, he was asked to resign from the *Democratic Review*. He did, converted to Catholicism, and in 1844 began to edit the *Brownson Quarterly Review* until 1865 and then again from 1872 to 1875.

The following piece, "The Laboring Classes," is taken from Brownson's most democratic and egalitarian period. Here, Brownson espouses a most radical version of Jacksonian egalitarianism, but in so doing, attacks the institution of inherited wealth. Since even most Jacksonians were liberal individualists who cherished private property, this smacked of heresy. In fact, Brownson was removed from the Democratic party as a result of its publication.

Orestes A. Brownson

The Laboring Classes (1840)

No one can observe the signs of the times with much care without perceiving that a crisis as to the relation of wealth and labor is approaching. It is useless to shut our eyes to the fact, and like the ostrich fancy ourselves secure because we have so concealed our heads that we see not the danger. We or our children will have to meet this crisis. The old war between the King and the Barons is well nigh ended, and so is that between the Barons and the Merchants and Manufacturers, landed capital and commercial capital. The businessman has become the peer of my Lord. And now commences the new struggle between the operative and his employer, between wealth and labor. Every day does this struggle extend further and wax stronger and fiercer; what or when the end will be God only knows.

In this coming contest there is a deeper question at issue than is commonly imagined, a question which is but remotely touched in your controversies about United States banks and sub-treasuries, chartered banking and free banking, free trade and corporations, although these controversies may be paving the way for it to come up. We have discovered no presentiment of it in any king's or queen's speech, nor in any President's message. It is embraced in no popular political creed of the day, whether christened Whig or Tory, *Justemilieu* or Democratic. No popular Senator or deputy or peer seems to have any glimpse

SOURCE: Orestes A. Brownson, "The Laboring Classes," *Boston Quarterly Review*, 3, no. 3, (1840).

of it; but it is working in the hearts of the million, is struggling to shape itself, and one day it will be uttered, and in thunder tones. Well will it be for him who, on that day, shall be found ready to answer it.

What we would ask is, throughout the Christian world, the actual condition of the laboring classes, viewed simply and exclusively in their capacity of laborers? They constitute at least a moiety of the human race. We exclude the nobility, we exclude also the middle class, and include only actual laborers, who are laborers and not proprietors, owners of none of the funds of production, neither houses, shops, nor lands, nor implements of labor, being therefore solely dependent on their hands. We have no means of ascertaining their precise proportion to the whole number of the race, but we think we may estimate them at one half. In any contest they will be as two to one, because the large class of proprietors who are not employers but laborers on their own lands or in their own shops will make common cause with them.

Now we will not so belie our acquaintance with political economy as to allege that these alone perform all that is necessary to the production of wealth. We are not ignorant of the fact that the merchant, who is literally the common carrier and exchange dealer, performs a useful service and is therefore entitled to a portion of the proceeds of labor. But make all necessary deductions on his account, and then ask what portion of the remainder is retained, either in kind or in its equivalent, in the hands of the original producer, the workingman? All over the world this fact stares us in the face: the workingman is poor and depressed, while a large portion of the nonworkingmen, in the sense we now use the term, are wealthy. It may be laid down as a general rule, with but few exceptions, that men are rewarded in an inverse ratio to the amount of actual service they perform. Under every government on earth the largest salaries are annexed to those offices which demand of their incumbents the least amount of actual labor either mental or manual. And this is in perfect harmony with the whole system of repartition of the fruits of industry which obtains in every department of society. Now here is the system which prevails, and here is its result. The whole class of simple laborers are poor and in general unable to procure any thing beyond the bare necessaries of life.

In regard to labor two systems obtain: one that of slave labor, the other that of free labor. Of the two, the first is, in our judgment, except so far as the feelings are concerned, decidedly the least oppressive. If the slave has never been a free man, we think, as a general rule, his sufferings are less than those of the free laborer at wages. As to actual freedom one has just about as much as the other. The laborer at wages has all the disadvantages of freedom and none of its blessings, while the slave, if denied the blessings, is freed from the disadvantages. We are no advocates of slavery; we are as heartily opposed to it as any modern abolitionist can be; but we say frankly that, if there must always be a laboring population distinct from proprietors and employers, we regard the slave system as decidedly preferable to the system at wages. It is no pleasant thing to go days without food, to lie idle for weeks, seeking work and finding none, to rise in the morning with a wife and children you love, and know not where to procure them a breakfast, and to see constantly before you no brighter prospect than the almshouse. Yet these are no unfrequent incidents in the lives of our laboring popula-

tion. Even in seasons of general prosperity, when there was only the ordinary cry of "hard times," we have seen hundreds of people in a not very populous village, in a wealthy portion of our common country, suffering for the want of the necessaries of life, willing to work, and yet finding no work to do. Many and many is the application of a poor man for work, merely for his food, we have seen rejected. These things are little thought of, for the applicants are poor; they fill no conspicuous place in society, and they have no biographers. But their wrongs are chronicled in heaven. It is said there is no want in this country. There may be less than in some other countries. But death by actual starvation in this country is, we apprehend, no uncommon occurrence. The sufferings of a quiet, unassuming but useful class of females in our cities, in general sempstresses, too proud to beg or to apply to the almshouse, are not easily told. They are industrious; they do all that they can find to do, but yet the little there is for them to do, and the miserable pittance they receive for it is hardly sufficient to keep soul and body together. And yet there is a man who employs them to make shirts, trousers, etc., and grows rich on their labors. He is one of our respectable citizens, perhaps is praised in the newspapers for his liberal donations to some charitable institution. He passes among us as a pattern of morality and is honored as a worthy Christian. And why should he not be, since our *Christian* community is made up of such as he, and since our clergy would not dare question his piety lest they should incur the reproach of infidelity and lose their standing and their salaries? Nay, since our clergy are raised up, educated, fashioned, and sustained by such as he? Not a few of our churches rest on Mammon for their foundation. The basement is a trader's shop.

We pass through our manufacturing villages; most of them appear neat and flourishing. The operatives are well dressed and, we are told, well paid. They are said to be healthy, contented, and happy. This is the fair side of the picture; the side exhibited to distinguished visitors. There is a dark side, moral as well as physical. Of the common operatives, few, if any, by their wages, acquire a competence. A few of what Carlyle terms not inaptly the "body-servants" are well paid, and now and then an agent or an overseer rides in his coach. But the great mass wear out their health, spirits, and morals without becoming one whit better off than when they commenced labor. The bills of mortality in these factory villages are not striking, we admit, for the poor girls when they can toil no longer go home to die. The average life—working life, we mean—of the girls that come to Lowell, for instance, from Maine, New Hampshire, and Vermont, we have been assured, is only about three years. What becomes of them then? Few of them ever marry; fewer still ever return to their native places with reputations unimpaired. "She has worked in a factory," is almost enough to damn to infamy the most worthy and virtuous girl. We know no sadder sight on earth than one of our factory villages presents when the bell, at break of day, or at the hour of breakfast or dinner, calls out its hundreds or thousands of operatives. We stand and look at these hard-working men and women hurrying in all directions and ask ourselves where go the proceeds of their labors? The man who employs them and for whom they are toiling as so many slaves is one of our city nabobs, reveling in luxury; or he is a member of our legislature, enacting laws to put money in his own pocket; or he is a member of Congress, contending for a high tariff to tax the poor for the benefit of the rich; or in these times he is shedding crocodile tears over the deplorable condition of the poor laborer, while he docks his wages twenty-five per cent; building miniature log cabins, shouting Harrison and "hard cider." And this man too would fain pass for a Christian and a republican. He shouts for liberty, stickles for equality, and is horrified at a Southern planter who keeps slaves.

One thing is certain: that, of the amount actually produced by the operative, he retains a less proportion than it costs the master to feed, clothe, and lodge his slave. Wages is a cunning device of the devil for the benefit of tender consciences who would retain all the advantages of the slave system without the expense, trouble, and odium of being slaveholders. . . .

The slave system, however, in name and form, is gradually disappearing from Christendom. It will not subsist much longer. But its place is taken by the system of labor at wages, and this system, we hold, is no improvement upon the one it supplants. Nevertheless the system of wages will triumph. It is the system which in name sounds honester than slavery and in substance is more profitable to the master. It yields the wages of iniquity, without its opprobrium. It will therefore supplant slavery and be sustained, for a time.

Now, what is the prospect of those who fall under the operation of this system? We ask, is there a reasonable chance that any considerable portion of the present generation of laborers shall ever become owners of a sufficient portion of the funds of production to be able to sustain themselves by laboring on their own capital—that is, as independent laborers? We need not ask this question, for everybody knows there is not. Well, is the condition of a laborer at wages the best that the great mass of the working people ought to be able to aspire to? Is it a condition—nay, can it be made a condition—with which a man should be satisfied, in which he should be contented to live and die?

In our own country this condition has existed under its most favorable aspects and has been made as good as it can be. It has reached all the excellence of which it is susceptible. It is now not improving but growing worse. The actual condition of the workingman today, viewed in all its bearings, is not so good as it was fifty years ago. If we have not been altogether misinformed, fifty years ago, health and industrious habits constituted no mean stock in trade, and with them almost any man might aspire to competence and independence. But it is so no longer. The wilderness has receded, and already the new lands are beyond the reach of the mere laborer, and the employer has him at his mercy. If the present relation subsist, we see nothing better for him in reserve than what he now possesses, but something altogether worse. . . .

Now the great work for this age and the coming is to raise up the laborer, and to realize in our own social arrangements and in the actual condition of all men that equality between man and man which God has established between the rights of one and those of another. In other words, our business is to emancipate the proletaries as the past has emancipated the slaves. This is our work. There must be no class of our fellow men doomed to toil through life as mere workmen at wages. If wages are tolerated it must be, in the case of the individual operative, only under such conditions that, by the time he is of a proper age to settle in life, he shall have accumulated enough to be an independent laborer on his own capital, on his own farm or in his own shop. Here is our work. How is it to be done?

Reformers in general answer this question, or what they deem its equivalent, in a manner which we cannot but regard as very unsatisfactory. They would have all men wise, good, and happy; but in order to make them so, they tell us that we want not external changes, but internal. And therefore, instead of declaiming against society and seeking to disturb existing social arrangements, we should confine ourselves to the individual reason and conscience, seek merely to lead the individual to repentance and to reformation of life, make the individual a practical, a truly religious

man; and all evils will either disappear, or be sanctified to the spiritual growth of the soul. . . .

The truth is the evil we have pointed out is not merely individual in its character. . . . What is purely individual in its nature, efforts of individuals to perfect themselves may remove. But the evil we speak of is inherent in all our social arrangements, and cannot be cured without a radical change of those arrangements. Could we convert all men to Christianity in both theory and practice, as held by the most enlightened sect of Christians among us, the evils of the social state would remain untouched. Continue our present system of trade, and all its present evil consequences will follow, whether it be carried on by your best men or your worst. . . . The only way to get rid of its evils is to change the system, not its managers. The evils of slavery do not result from the personal characters of slave masters. They are inseparable from the system, let who will be masters. Make all your rich men good Christians, and you have lessened not the evils of existing inequality in wealth. The mischievous effects of this inequality do not result from the personal characters of either rich or poor, but from itself, and they will continue just so long as there are rich men and poor men in the same community. You must abolish the system or accept its consequences. No man can serve both God and Mammon. If you will serve the devil, you must look to the devil for your wages; we know no other way. . . .

* * * * *

The next step in this work of elevating the working classes will be to resuscitate the Christianity of Christ. The Christianity of the Church has done its work. We have had enough of that Christianity. It is powerless for good, but by no means powerless for evil. It now unmans us and hinders the growth of God's kingdom. The moral energy which is awakened it misdirects, and makes its deluded disciples believe that they have done their duty to God when they have joined the Church, offered a prayer, sung a Psalm, and contributed of their means to send out a missionary to preach unintelligible dogmas enough already, and more than enough. All this must be abandoned, and Christianity, as it came from Christ, be taken up and preached, and preached in simplicity and power.

According to the Christianity of Christ, no man can enter the kingdom of God who does not labor with all zeal and diligence to establish the kingdom of God on the earth—who does not labor to bring down the high and bring up the low; to break the fetters of the bound and set the captive free; to destroy all oppression, establish the reign of justice, which is the reign of equality, between man and man; to introduce new heavens and a new earth; wherein dwelleth righteousness, wherein all shall be as brothers, loving one another, and no one possessing what another lacketh. No man can be a Christian who does not labor to reform society, to mold it according to the will of God and the nature of man, so that free scope shall be given to every man to unfold himself in all beauty and power, and to grow up into the stature of a perfect man in Christ Jesus. No man can be a Christian who does not refrain from all practices by which the rich grow richer and the poor poorer, and who does not do all in his power to elevate the laboring classes, so that one man shall not be doomed to toil while another enjoys the fruits; so that each man shall be free and independent, sitting under "his own vine and fig tree with none to molest or to make afraid." We grant the power of Christianity in working out the reform we demand; we agree that one of the most efficient means of elevating the workingmen is to Christianize the community. But you must Christianize it. It is the gospel of Jesus you must preach, and not the gospel of the priests. Preach the gospel of Jesus, and that will turn every man's attention to the crying evil we have designated, and will arm every Christian with power to effect those changes in social arrangements which shall secure to all men the equality of position and condition which it is already acknowledged they possess in relation to their rights. But let it be the genuine gospel that you preach, and not that pseudo-gospel which lulls the conscience asleep and permits men to feel that they may be servants of God while they are slaves to the world, the flesh, and the devil, and while they ride roughshod over the hearts of their prostrate brethren. We must preach no gospel that permits men to feel that they are honorable men and good Christians, although rich and with eyes standing out with fatness, while the great mass of their brethren are suffering from iniquitous laws, from mischievous social arrangements, and pining away for the want of the refinements and even the necessaries of life. . . .

* * * * *

Having, by breaking down the power of the priesthood and the Christianity of the priests, obtained an open field and freedom for our operations, and by preaching the true Gospel of Jesus, directed all minds to the great social reform needed, and quickened in all souls the moral power to live for it or to die for it, our next resort must be to government, to legislative enactments. Government is instituted to be the agent of society, or more properly the organ through which society may perform its legitimate functions. It is not the master of society; its business is not to control society, but to be the organ through which society effects its will. Society has never to petition government; government is its servant and subject to its commands.

Now the evils of which we have complained are of a social nature. That is, they have their root in the constitution of society as it is; and they have attained to their present growth by means of social influences, the action of government, of laws, and of systems and institutions upheld by society, and of which individuals are the slaves. This being the case, it is evident that they are to be removed only by the action of society, that is, by government, for the action of society is government.

But what shall government do? Its first doing must be an *un*doing. There has been thus far quite too much government, as well as government of the wrong kind. The first act of government we want is a still further limitation of itself. It must begin by circumscribing within narrower limits its powers. And then it must proceed to repeal all laws which bear against the laboring classes, and then to enact such laws as are necessary to enable them to maintain their equality. We have no faith in those systems of elevating the working classes which propose to elevate them without calling in the aid of government. We must have government and legislation expressly directed to this end.

But again what legislation do we want so far as this country is concerned? We want first the legislation which shall free the Government, whether State or Federal, from the control of the banks. The banks represent the interest of the employer, and therefore of necessity interests adverse to those of the employed; that is, they represent the interests of the business community in opposition to the laboring community. So long as the Government remains under the control of the banks, so long it must be in the hands of the natural enemies of the laboring classes, and may be made, nay, will be made, an instrument of depressing them yet lower. It is obvious then that, if our object be the elevation of the laboring classes, we must destroy the power of the banks over the Government and place the Government in the hands of the laboring classes themselves or in the hands of those, if such there be, who have an identity of interest with them. But this cannot be done

so long as the banks exist. Such is the subtle influence of credit and such the power of capital that a banking system like ours, if sustained, necessarily and inevitably becomes the real and efficient government of the country. We have been struggling for ten years in this country against the power of the banks, struggling to free merely the Federal Government from their grasp, but with humiliating success. At this moment, the contest is almost doubtful, not indeed in our mind, but in the minds of no small portion of our countrymen. The partisans of the banks count on certain victory. The banks discount freely to build "log cabins," to purchase "hard cider," and to defray the expense of manufacturing enthusiasm for a cause which is at war with the interests of the people. That they will succeed, we do not for one moment believe; but that they could maintain the struggle so long and be as strong as they now are at the end of ten years' constant hostility proves but all too well the power of the banks and their fatal influence on the political action of the community. The present character, standing, and resources of the bank party prove to a demonstration that the banks must be destroyed or the laborer not elevated. Uncompromising hostility to the whole banking system should therefore be the motto of every workingman and of every friend of humanity. The system must be destroyed. On this point there must be no misgiving, no subterfuge, no palliation. The system is at war with the rights and interest of labor, and it must go. Every friend of the system must be marked as an enemy to his race, to his country, and especially to the laborer. No matter who he is, in what party he is found, or what name he bears, he is, in our judgment, no true democrat, as he can be no true Christian.

Following the destruction of the banks, must come that of all monopolies, of all privilege. There are many of these. We cannot specify them all; we therefore select only one, the greatest of them all, the privilege which some have of being born rich while others are born poor. It will be seen at once that we allude to the hereditary descent of property, an anomaly in our American system, which must be removed or the system itself will be destroyed. We cannot now go into a discussion of this subject, but we promise to resume it at our earliest opportunity. We only say now that as we have abolished hereditary monarchy and hereditary nobility we must complete the work by abolishing hereditary property. A man shall have all he honestly acquires, so long as he himself belongs to the world in which he acquires it. But his power over his property must cease with his life, and his property must then become the property of the State, to be disposed of by some equitable law for the use of the generation which takes his place. Here is the principle without any of its details, and this is the grand legislative measure to which we look forward. We see no means of elevating the laboring classes which can be effectual without this. And is this a measure to be easily carried? Not at all. It will cost infinitely more than it cost to abolish either hereditary monarchy or hereditary nobility. It is a great measure, and a startling. The rich, the business community, will never voluntarily consent to it, and we think we know too much of human nature to believe that it will ever be effected peaceably. It will be effected only by the strong arm of physical force. It will come, if it ever come at all, only at the conclusion of war, the like of which the world as yet has never witnessed, and from which, however inevitable it may seem to the eye of philosophy, the heart of Humanity recoils with horror.

We are not ready for this measure yet. There is much previous work to be done, and we should be the last to bring it before the legislature. The time, however, has come for its free and full discussion. It must be canvassed in the public mind, and society prepared for acting on it. No doubt they who broach it, and especially they who support it, will experience a due share of contumely and abuse. They will be regarded by the part of the community they oppose or may be thought to oppose as "graceless varlets," against whom every man of substance should set his face. But this is not, after all, a thing to disturb a wise man nor to deter a true man from telling his whole thought. He who is worthy of the name of man speaks what he honestly believes the interests of his race demand and seldom disquiets himself about what may be the consequences to himself. Men have, for what they believed the cause of God or man, endured the dungeon, the scaffold, the stake, the cross; and they can do it again, if need be. This subject must be freely, boldly, and fully discussed, whatever may be the fate of those who discuss it.

Henry David Thoreau, 1817–1862

Henry David Thoreau was a leading Transcendentalist thinker most known for his two years of solitude at Walden Pond, his writings on civil disobedience, and his opposition to the Mexican War and the institution of slavery.

Thoreau was born in the Massachusetts town of Concord—also home to Emerson, Hawthorne, Alcott, and Channing—and lived there most of his life. He attended Harvard College (class of 1837) and returned to Concord to teach school and write. Thoreau authored thirty-nine manuscript volumes, but only two were published during his lifetime. Most of his writings, including *Walden* and *A Week on the Concord and Merrimack Rivers,* were buried in extensive journals, which he dutifully kept.

In 1841, Thoreau went to live in the house of the leading Transcendentalist, Ralph Waldo Emerson, and managed his older mentor's practical affairs. He wrote for *The Dial,* the voice of Transcendentalist thought, and working within Transcendentalist tradition began to develop his own ideas about human beings' relation to nature. In general, Transcendentalists were not systematic philosophers, but rather romantics who believed in the power of personal inspiration. Transcendentalists believed that mankind and material were the totality of God, and that we worshipped Him by living in harmony with nature and nature's laws.

In pursuit of the innocence that might put him in harmony with the natural order, Thoreau retreated to a cabin on Walden Pond in 1845. He grew contemptuous of ordinary men and women who made daily compromises with other individuals and institutions for the sake of wealth or social acceptance. It was during and after this period that Thoreau refused to pay his poll tax to a government that supported slavery, and began his active commitment to the abolitionist movement.

Civil Disobedience was printed in 1849 and marks Thoreau as the father of a school of thought later put into practice by Mahatma Ghandi and Martin Luther King, Jr. It is an eloquent statement on behalf of individual conscience, at times calling for a political movement to bring the gears of government to a grinding halt, at other times simply stressing the need for each individual's clear conscience and clean hands.

In stressing the supreme sanctity of the individual, Thoreau takes a standard theme of classical liberalism to a logical, near anarchist conclusion.

Henry David Thoreau

Civil Disobedience (1849)

I heartily accept the motto,—"That government is best which governs least;" and I should like to see it acted up to more rapidly and systematically. Carried out, it finally amounts

to this, which also I believe,—"That government is best which governs not at all;" and when men are prepared for it, that will be the kind of government which they will have. Government is at best but an expedient; but most governments are usually, and all governments are sometimes, inexpedient. The objec-

---

SOURCE: Henry David Thoreau, *Works,* ed. Henry Seidel Canby (Boston: Houghton-Mifflin, 1937).

tions which have been brought against a standing army, and they are many and weighty, and deserve to prevail, may also at last be brought against a standing government. The standing army is only an arm of the standing government. The government itself, which is only the mode which the people have chosen to execute their will, is equally liable to be abused and perverted before the people can act through it. Witness the present Mexican war, the work of comparatively a few individuals using the standing government as their tool; for, in the outset, the people would not have consented to this measure.

This American government,—what is it but a tradition, though a recent one, endeavoring to transmit itself unimpaired to posterity, but each instant losing some of its integrity? It has not the vitality and force of a single living man; for a single man can bend it to his will. It is a sort of wooden gun to the people themselves. But it is not the less necessary for this; for the people must have some complicated machinery or other, and hear its din, to satisfy that idea of government which they have. Governments show thus how successfully men can be imposed on, even impose on themselves, for their own advantage. It is excellent, we must all allow. Yet this government never of itself furthered any enterprise, but by the alacrity with which it got out of its way. *It* does not keep the country free. *It* does not settle the West. *It* does not educate. The character inherent in the American people has done all that has been accomplished; and it would have done somewhat more, if the government had not sometimes got in its way. For government is an expedient by which men would fain succeed in letting one another alone; and, as has been said, when it is most expedient, the governed are most let alone by it. Trade and commerce, if they were not made of India-rubber, would never manage to bounce over the obstacles which legislators are continually putting in their way; and, if one were to judge these men wholly by the

effects of their actions and not partly by their intentions, they would deserve to be classed and punished with those mischievous persons who put obstructions on the railroads.

But, to speak practically and as a citizen, unlike those who call themselves no-government men, I ask for, not at once no government, but *at once* a better government. Let every man make known what kind of government would command his respect, and that will be one step toward obtaining it.

After all, the practical reason why, when the power is once in the hands of the people, a majority are permitted, and for a long period continue, to rule is not because they are most likely to be in the right, nor because this seems fairest to the minority, but because they are physically the strongest. But a government in which the majority rule in all cases cannot be based on justice, even as far as men understand it. Can there not be a government in which majorities do not virtually decide right and wrong, but conscience?—in which majorities decide only those questions to which the rule of expediency is applicable? Must the citizen ever for a moment, or in the least degree, resign his conscience to the legislator? Why has every man a conscience then? I think that we should be men first, and subjects afterward. It is not desirable to cultivate a respect for the law, so much as for the right. The only obligation which I have a right to assume is to do at any time what I think right. It is truly enough said, that a corporation has no conscience; but a corporation of conscientious men is a corporation *with* a conscience. Law never made men a whit more just; and, by means of their respect for it, even the well-disposed are daily made the agents of injustice. A common and natural result of an undue respect for law is, that you may see a file of soldiers, colonel, captain, corporal, privates, powdermonkeys, and all, marching in admirable order over hill and dale to the wars, against their wills, ay, against their common sense and consciences, which makes it very steep marching indeed, and produces a palpitation of the heart. They have no doubt that it is a damnable business in which they are concerned; they are all peaceably inclined. Now, what are they? Men at all? or small movable forts and magazines, at the service of some unscrupulous man in power? Visit the Navy-Yard, and behold a marine, such a man as an American government can make, or such as it can make a man with its black arts,—a mere shadow and reminiscence of humanity, a man laid out alive and standing, and already, as one may say, buried under arms with funeral accompaniments, though it may be,—

> "Not a drum was heard, not a funeral
> note,
>   As his corse to the rampart we
> hurried;
> Not a soldier discharged his farewell
> shot
>   O'er the grave where our hero we
> buried."

The mass of men serve the state thus, not as men mainly, but as machines, with their bodies. They are the standing army, and the militia, jailors, constables, posse comitatus, etc. In most cases there is no free exercise whatever of the judgment or of the moral sense; but they put themselves on a level with wood and earth and stones; and wooden men can perhaps be manufactured that will serve the purpose as well. Such command no more respect than men of straw or a lump of dirt. They have the same sort of worth only as horses and dogs. Yet such as these even are commonly esteemed good citizens. Others—as most legislators, politicians, lawyers, ministers, and office-holders—serve the state chiefly with their heads; and, as they rarely make any moral distinctions, they are as likely to serve the Devil, without *intending* it, as God. A very few, as heroes, patriots, martyrs, reformers in the great sense, and *men,* serve the state with their consciences also, and so necessarily resist it for the most part; and they are commonly treated as enemies by it. A wise

man will only be useful as a man, and will not submit to be "clay," and "stop a hole to keep the wind away," but leave that office to his dust at least:—

> "I am too high-born to be propertied,
>   To be a secondary at control,
>   Or useful serving-man and
> instrument
>   To any sovereign state throughout the
> world."

He who gives himself entirely to his fellow-men appears to them useless and selfish; but he who gives himself partially to them is pronounced a benefactor and philanthropist.

How does it become a man to behave toward this American government to-day? I answer, that he cannot without disgrace be associated with it. I cannot for an instant recognize that political organization as *my* government which is the *slave's* government also.

All men recognize the right of revolution; that is, the right to refuse allegiance to, and to resist, the government, when its tyranny or its inefficiency are great and unendurable. But almost all say that such is not the case now. But such was the case, they think, in the Revolution of '75. If one were to tell me that this was a bad government because it taxed certain foreign commodities brought to its ports, it is most probable that I should not make an ado about it, for I can do without them. All machines have their friction; and possibly this does enough good to counterbalance the evil. At any rate, it is a great evil to make a stir about it. But when the friction comes to have its machine, and oppression and robbery are organized, I say, let us not have such a machine any longer. In other words, when a sixth of the population of a nation which has undertaken to be the refuge of liberty are slaves, and a whole country is unjustly overrun and conquered by a foreign army, and subjected to military law, I think that it is not too soon for honest men to rebel and revolutionize. What makes this duty the more urgent is the fact that the country so overrun is not our own, but ours is the invading army.

Paley, a common authority with many on moral questions, in his chapter on the "Duty of Submission to Civil Government," resolves all civil obligation into expediency; and he proceeds to say, "that so long as the interest of the whole society requires it, that is, so long as the established government cannot be resisted or changed without public inconveniency, it is the will of God that the established government be obeyed, and no longer. . . . This principle being admitted, the justice of every particular case of resistance is reduced to a computation of the quantity of the danger and grievance on the one side, and of the probability and expense of redressing it on the other." Of this, he says, every man shall judge for himself. But Paley appears never to have contemplated those cases to which the rule of expediency does not apply, in which a people, as well as an individual, must do justice, cost what it may. If I have unjustly wrested a plank from a drowning man, I must restore it to him though I drown myself. This, according to Paley, would be inconvenient. But he that would save his life, in such a case, shall lose it. This people must cease to hold slaves, and to make war on Mexico, though it cost them their existence as a people.

. . . Practically speaking, the opponents to a reform in Massachusetts are not a hundred thousand politicians at the South, but a hundred thousand merchants and farmers here, who are more interested in commerce and agriculture than they are in humanity, and are not prepared to do justice to the slave and to Mexico, *cost what it may*. I quarrel not with far-off foes, but with those who, near at home, coöperate with, and do the bidding of, those far away, and without whom the latter would be harmless. We are accustomed to say, that the mass of men are unprepared; but improvement is slow, because the few are not materially wiser or better than the many.

It is not so important that many should be as good as you, as that there be some absolute goodness somewhere; for that will leaven the whole lump. There are thousands who are *in opinion* opposed to slavery and to the war, who yet in effect do nothing to put an end to them; who, esteeming themselves children of Washington and Franklin, sit down with their hands in their pockets, and say that they know not what to do, and do nothing; who even postpone the question of freedom to the question of free-trade, and quietly read the prices-current along with the latest advices from Mexico, after dinner, and, it may be, fall asleep over them both. What is the price-current of an honest man and patriot to-day? They hesitate, and they regret, and sometimes they petition; but they do nothing in earnest and with effect. They will wait, well disposed, for others to remedy the evil, that they may no longer have it to regret. At most, they give only a cheap vote, and a feeble countenance and God-speed, to the right, as it goes by them. There are nine hundred and ninety-nine patrons of virtue to one virtuous man. But it is easier to deal with the real possessor of a thing than with the temporary guardian of it.

All voting is a sort of gaming, like checkers or backgammon, with a slight moral tinge to it, a playing with right and wrong, with moral questions; and betting naturally accompanies it. The character of the voters is not staked. I cast my vote, perchance, as I think right; but I am not vitally concerned that that right should prevail. I am willing to leave it to the majority. Its obligation, therefore, never exceeds that of expediency. Even voting *for the right* is *doing* nothing for it. It is only expressing to men feebly your desire that it should prevail. A wise man will not leave the right to the mercy of chance, nor wish it to prevail through the power of the majority. There is but little virtue in the action of masses of men. When the majority shall at length vote for the abolition of slavery, it will be because they are indifferent to slavery, or because there is but little slavery left to be abolished by their vote. *They* will then be the only slaves. Only *his* vote can hasten the abolition of slavery who asserts his own freedom by his vote.

. . . It is not a man's duty, as a matter of course, to devote himself to the eradication of any, even the most enormous wrong; he may still properly have other concerns to engage him; but it is his duty, at least, to wash his hands of it, and, if he gives it no thought longer, not to give it practically his support. If I devote myself to other pursuits and contemplations, I must first see, at least, that I do not pursue them sitting upon another man's shoulders. I must get off him first, that he may pursue his contemplations too. See what gross inconsistency is tolerated. I have heard some of my townsmen say, "I should like to have them order me out to help put down an insurrection of the slaves, or to march to Mexico;—see if I would go;" and yet these very men have each, directly by their allegiance, and so indirectly, at least, by their money, furnished a substitute. The soldier is applauded who refuses to serve in an unjust war by those who do not refuse to sustain the unjust government which makes the war; is applauded by those whose own act and authority he disregards and sets at naught; as if the state were penitent to that degree that it hired one to scourge it while it sinned, but not to that degree that it left off sinning for a moment. Thus, under the name of Order and Civil Government, we are all made at last to pay homage to and support our own meanness. After the first blush of sin comes its indifference; and from immoral it becomes, as it were, *un*moral, and not quite unnecessary to that life which we have made.

The broadest and most prevalent error requires the most disinterested virtue to sustain it. The slight reproach to which the virtue of patriotism is commonly liable, the noble are most likely to incur. Those who, while they disapprove of the character and measures of a government, yield to it their allegiance and support are undoubtedly its most conscientious supporters, and so frequently the most serious obstacles to reform. Some are petitioning the state to dissolve the Union, to disregard the requisitions of the President. Why do they not dissolve it themselves,—the union between themselves and the state,—and refuse to pay their quota into its treasury? Do not they stand in the same relation to the state that the state does to the Union? And have not the same reasons prevented the state from resisting the Union which have prevented them from resisting the state?

. . . Unjust laws exist; shall we be content to obey them, or shall we endeavor to amend them, and obey them until we have succeeded, or shall we transgress them at once? Men generally, under such a government as this, think that they ought to wait until they have persuaded the majority to alter them. They think that, if they should resist, the remedy would be worse than the evil. But it is the fault of the government itself that the remedy *is* worse than the evil. *It* makes it worse. Why is it not more apt to anticipate and provide for reform? Why does it not cherish its wise minority? Why does it cry and resist before it is hurt? Why does it not encourage its citizens to be on the alert to point out its faults, and *do* better than it would have them? Why does it always crucify Christ, and excommunicate Copernicus and Luther, and pronounce Washington and Franklin rebels?

One would think, that a deliberate and practical denial of its authority was the only offense never contemplated by government; else, why has it not assigned its definite, its suitable and proportionate penalty? If a man who has no property refuses but once to earn nine shillings for the state, he is put in prison for a period unlimited by any law that I know, and determined only by the discretion of those who placed him there; but if he should steal ninety times nine shillings from the state, he is soon permitted to go at large again.

If the injustice is part of the necessary friction of the machine of government, let it go, let it go: perchance it will wear smooth,—certainly the machine will wear out. If the injustice has a spring, or a pulley, or a rope, or a crank, exclusively for itself, then perhaps you may consider whether the remedy will not be worse than the evil; but if it is of such a nature that it requires you to be the agent of injustice to another, then, I say, break the law. Let your life be a counter friction to stop the machine. What I have to do is to see, at any rate, that I do not lend myself to the wrong which I condemn.

As for adopting the ways which the state has provided for remedying the evil, I know not of such ways. They take too much time, and a man's life will be gone. I have other affairs to attend to. I came into this world, not chiefly to make this a good place to live in, but to live in it, be it good or bad. A man has not everything to do, but something; and because he cannot do *everything,* it is not necessary that he should do *something* wrong. It is not my business to be petitioning the Governor or the Legislature any more than it is theirs to petition me; and if they should not hear my petition, what should I do then? But in this case the state has provided no way: its very Constitution is the evil. This may seem to be harsh and stubborn and unconciliatory; but it is to treat with the utmost kindness and consideration the only spirit that can appreciate or deserves it. So is all change for the better, like birth and death, which convulse the body.

. . . I meet this American government, or its representative, the state government, directly, and face to face, once a year—no more—in the person of its tax-gatherer; this is the only mode in which a man situated as I am necessarily meets it; and it then says distinctly, Recognize me; and the simplest, most effectual, and, in the present posture of affairs, the indispensablest mode of treating with it on this head, of expressing your little satisfaction with and love for it, is to deny it

then. My civil neighbor, the tax-gatherer, is the very man I have to deal with,—for it is, after all, with men and not with parchment that I quarrel,—and he has voluntarily chosen to be an agent of the government. How shall he ever know well what he is and does as an officer of the government, or as a man, until he is obliged to consider whether he shall treat me, his neighbor, for whom he has respect, as a neighbor and well-disposed man, or as a maniac and disturber of the peace, and see if he can get over this obstruction to his neighborliness without a ruder and more impetuous thought or speech corresponding with his action. I know this well, that if one thousand, if one hundred, if ten men whom I could name,—if ten *honest* men only,—ay, if *one* HONEST man, in this State of Massachusetts, *ceasing to hold slaves,* were actually to-withdraw from this copartnership, and be locked up in the county jail therefor, it would be the abolition of slavery in America. For it matters not how small the beginning may seem to be: what is once well done is done forever. But we love better to talk about it: that we say is our mission. Reform keeps many scores of newspapers in its service, but not one man. If my esteemed neighbor, the State's ambassador, who will devote his days to the settlement of the question of human rights in the Council Chamber, instead of being threatened with the prisons of Carolina, were to sit down the prisoner of Massachusetts, that State which is so anxious to foist the sin of slavery upon her sister,—though at present she can discover only an act of inhospitality to be the ground of a quarrel with her,—the Legislature would not wholly waive the subject the following winter.

Under a government which imprisons any unjustly, the true place for a just man is also a prison. The proper place to-day, the only place which Massachusetts has provided for her freer and less desponding spirits, is in her prisons, to be put out and locked out of the State by her own act, as they have already put themselves out by their principles. It is there that the fugitive slave, and the Mexican prisoner on parole, and the Indian come to plead the wrongs of his race should find them; on that separate, but more free and honorable ground, where the State places those who are not *with* her, but *against* her,—the only house in a slave State in which a free man can abide with honor. If any think that their influence would be lost there, and their voices no longer afflict the ear of the State, that they would not be as an enemy within its walls, they do not know by how much truth is stronger than error, nor how much more eloquently and effectively he can combat injustice who has experienced a little in his own person. Cast your whole vote, not a strip of paper merely, but your whole influence. A minority is powerless while it conforms to the majority; it is not even a minority then; but it is irresistible when it clogs by its whole weight. If the alternative is to keep all just men in prison, or give up war and slavery, the State will not hesitate which to choose. If a thousand men were not to pay their tax-bills this year, that would not be a violent and bloody measure, as it would be to pay them, and enable the State to commit violence and shed innocent blood. This is, in fact, the definition of a peaceable revolution, if any such is possible. If the tax-gatherer, or any other public officer, asks me, as one has done, "But what shall I do?" my answer is, "If you really wish to do anything, resign your office." When the subject has refused allegiance, and the officer has resigned his office, then the revolution is accomplished. But even suppose blood should flow. Is there not a sort of blood shed when the conscience is wounded? Through this wound a man's real manhood and immortality flow out, and he bleeds to an everlasting death. I see this blood flowing now.

. . . I have paid no poll-tax for six years. I was put into a jail once on this account, for one night; and, as I stood considering the walls of solid stone, two or three feet thick, the door of wood and iron, a foot thick, and the iron grating which strained the light, I could not help being struck with the foolishness of that institution which treated me as if I were mere flesh and blood and bones, to be locked up. I wondered that it should have concluded at length that this was the best use it could put me to, and had never thought to avail itself of my services in some way. I saw that, if there was a wall of stone between me and my townsmen, there was a still more difficult one to climb or break through before they could get to be as free as I was. I did not for a moment feel confined, and the walls seemed a great waste of stone and mortar. I felt as if I alone of all my townsmen had paid my tax. They plainly did not know how to treat me, but behaved like persons who are underbred. In every threat and in every compliment there was a blunder; for they thought that my chief desire was to stand the other side of that stone wall. I could not but smile to see how industriously they locked the door on my meditations, which followed them out again without let or hindrance, and *they* were really all that was dangerous. As they could not reach me, they had resolved to punish my body; just as boys, if they cannot come at some person against whom they have a spite, will abuse his dog. I saw that the State was half-witted, that it was timid as a lone woman with her silver spoons, and that it did not know its friends from its foes, and I lost all my remaining respect for it, and pitied it.

Thus the State never intentionally confronts a man's sense, intellectual or moral, but only his body, his senses. It is not armed with superior wit or honesty, but with superior physical strength. I was not born to be forced. I will breathe after my own fashion. Let us see who is the strongest. What force has a multitude? They only can force me who obey a higher law than I. They force me to become like themselves. I do not hear of *men* being *forced* to live this way or that by masses of men. What sort of life were that to live? When I meet a government which says to me, "Your money or your life," why should I be in haste to give it my money? It may be in a great strait, and not know what to do: I cannot help that. It must help itself; do as I do. It is not worth the while to snivel about it. I am not responsible for the successful working of the machinery of society. I am not the son of the engineer. I perceive that, when an acorn and a chestnut fall side by side, the one does not remain inert to make way for the other, but both obey their own laws, and spring and grow and flourish as best they can, till one, perchance, overshadows and destroys the other. If a plant cannot live according to its nature, it dies; and so a man.

The night in prison was novel and interesting enough. The prisoners in their shirtsleeves were enjoying a chat and the evening air in the doorway, when I entered. But the jailer said, "Come, boys, it is time to lock up;" and so they dispersed, and I heard the sound of their steps returning into the hollow apartments. My room-mate was introduced to me by the jailer as "a first-rate fellow and a clever man." When the door was locked, he showed me where to hang my hat, and how he managed matters there. The rooms were whitewashed once a month; and this one, at least, was the whitest, most simply furnished, and probably the neatest apartment in the town. He naturally wanted to know where I came from, and what brought me there; and, when I had told him, I asked him in my turn how he came there, presuming him to be an honest man, of course; and, as the world goes, I believe he was. "Why," said he, "they accuse me of burning a barn; but I never did it." As near as I could discover, he had probably gone to bed in a barn when drunk, and smoked his pipe there; and so a barn was burnt. He had the reputation of being a clever man, had been there some three months waiting for his trial to come on, and would have to wait as much longer; but he was quite domesticated and contented, since he got his board for nothing, and thought that he was well treated.

He occupied one window, and I the other; and I saw that if one stayed there long, his principal business would be to look out the window. I had soon read all the tracts that were left there, and examined where former prisoners had broken out, and where a grate had been sawed off, and heard the history of the various occupants of that room; for I found that even here there was a history and a gossip which never circulated beyond the walls of the jail. Probably this is the only house in the town where verses are composed, which are afterward printed in a circular form, but not published. I was shown quite a long list of verses which were composed by some young men who had been detected in an attempt to escape, who avenged themselves by singing them.

I pumped my fellow-prisoner as dry as I could, for fear I should never see him again; but at length he showed me which was my bed, and left me to blow out the lamp.

It was like traveling into a far country, such as I had never expected to behold, to lie there for one night. It seemed to me that I never had heard the town-clock strike before, nor the evening sounds of the village; for we slept with the windows open, which were inside the grating. It was to see my native village in the light of the Middle Ages, and our Concord was turned into a Rhine stream, and visions of knights and castles passed before me. They were the voices of old burghers that I heard in the streets. I was an involuntary spectator and auditor of whatever was done and said in the kitchen of the adjacent village-inn,—a wholly new and rare experience to me. It was a closer view of my native town. I was fairly inside of it. I never had seen its institutions before. This is one of its peculiar institutions; for it is a shire town. I began to comprehend what its inhabitants were about.

In the morning, our breakfasts were put through the hole in the door, in small oblong-square tin pans, made to fit, and holding a pint of chocolate, with brown bread, and an iron spoon. When they called for the vessels again, I was green enough to return what bread I had left; but my comrade seized it, and said that I should lay that up for lunch or dinner. Soon after he was let out to work at haying in a neighboring field, whither he went every day, and would not be back till noon; so he bade me good-day, saying that he doubted if he should see me again.

When I came out of prison,—for some one interfered, and paid that tax,—I did not perceive that great changes had taken place on the common, such as he observed who went in a youth and emerged a tottering and gray-headed man; and yet a change had to my eyes come over the scene,—the town, and State, and country,—greater than any that mere time could effect. I saw yet more distinctly the State in which I lived. I saw to what extent the people among whom I lived could be trusted as good neighbors and friends; that their friendship was for summer weather only; that they did not greatly propose to do right; that they were a distinct race from me by their prejudices and superstitions, as the Chinamen and Malays are; that in their sacrifices to humanity they ran no risks, not even to their property; that after all they were not so noble but they treated the thief as he had treated them, and hoped, by a certain outward observance and a few prayers, and by walking in a particular straight though useless path from time to time, to save their souls. This may be to judge my neighbors harshly; for I believe that many of them are not aware that they have such an institution as the jail in their village.

It was formerly the custom in our village, when a poor debtor came out of jail, for his acquaintances to salute him, looking through their fingers, which were crossed to represent the grating of a jail window, "How do ye do?" My neighbors did not thus salute me, but first looked at me, and then at one another, as if I had returned from a long journey. I was put into jail as I was going to the shoemaker's to get a shoe which was mended. When I was let out the next morning, I proceeded to finish my errand, and, having put on my mended shoe, joined a huckleberry party, who were impatient to put themselves under my conduct; and in half an hour,—for the horse was soon tackled,—was in the midst of a huckleberry field, on one of our highest hills, two miles off, and then the State was nowhere to be seen.

This is the whole history of "My Prisons."

I have never declined paying the highway tax, because I am as desirous of being a good neighbor as I am of being a bad subject; and as for supporting schools, I am doing my part to educate my fellow-countrymen now. It is for no particular item in the tax-bill that I refuse to pay it. I simply wish to refuse allegiance to the State, to withdraw and stand aloof from it effectually. I do not care to trace the course of my dollar, if I could, till it buys a man or a musket to shoot with,—the dollar is innocent,—but I am concerned to trace the effects of my allegiance. In fact, I quietly declare war with the State, after my fashion, though I will still make what use and get what advantage of her I can, as is usual in such cases.

If others pay the tax which is demanded of me, from a sympathy with the State, they do but what they have already done in their own case, or rather they abet injustice to a greater extent than the State requires. If they pay the tax from a mistaken interest in the individual taxed, to save his property, or prevent his going to jail, it is because they have not considered wisely how far they let their private feelings interfere with the public good.

This, then, is my position at present. But one cannot be too much on his guard in such a case, lest his action be biased by obstinacy or an undue regard for the opinions of men. Let him see that he does only what belongs to himself and to the hour.

I think sometimes, Why, this people mean well, they are only ignorant; they would do better if they knew how: why give your neighbors this pain to treat you as they are not inclined to? But I think again, This is no reason why I should do as they do, or permit others to suffer much greater pain of a different kind. Again, I sometimes say to myself, When many millions of men, without heat, without ill will, without personal feeling of any kind, demand of you a few shillings only, without the possibility, such is their constitution, of retracting or altering their present demand, and without the possibility, on your side, of appeal to any other millions, why expose yourself to this overwhelming brute force? You do not resist cold and hunger, the winds and the waves, thus obstinately; you quietly submit to a thousand similar necessities. You do not put your head into the fire. But just in proportion as I regard this as not wholly a brute force, but partly a human force, and consider that I have relations to those millions as to so many millions of men, and not of mere brute or inanimate things, I see that appeal is possible, first and instantaneously, from them to the Maker of them, and, secondly, from them to themselves. But if I put my head deliberately into the fire, there is no appeal to fire or to the Maker of fire, and I have only myself to blame. If I could convince myself that I have any right to be satisfied with men as they are, and to treat them accordingly, and not according, in some respects, to my requisitions and expectations of what they and I ought to be, then, like a good Mussulman and fatalist, I should endeavor to be satisfied with things as they are, and say it is the will of God. And, above all, there is this difference between resisting this and a purely brute or natural force, that I can resist this with some effect; but I cannot expect, like Orpheus, to change the nature of the rocks and trees and beasts.

I do not wish to quarrel with any man or nation. I do not wish to split hairs, to make fine distinctions, or set myself up as better than my neighbors. I seek rather, I may say, even an excuse for conforming to the laws of the land. I am but too ready to conform to them. Indeed, I have reason to suspect myself on this head; and each year, as the tax-gatherer comes round, I find myself disposed to review the acts and position of the general and State governments, and the spirit of the people, to discover a pretext for conformity.

> "We must affect our country as our
> parents,
> And if at any time we alienate
> Our love or industry from doing it
> honor,
> We must respect effects and teach the
> soul
> Matter of conscience and religion,
> And not desire of rule or benefit."

I believe that the State will soon be able to take all my work of this sort out of my hands, and then I shall be no better a patriot than my fellow-countrymen. Seen from a lower point of view, the Constitution, with all its faults, is very good; the law and the courts are very respectable; even this State and this American government are, in many respects, very admirable, and rare things, to be thankful for, such as a great many have described them; but seen from a point of view a little higher, they are what I have described them; seen from a higher still, and the highest, who shall say what they are, or that they are worth looking at or thinking of at all?

However, the government does not concern me much, and I shall bestow the fewest possible thoughts on it. It is not many moments that I live under a government, even in this world. If a man is thought-free, fancy-free, imagination-free, that which *is not* never for a long time appearing *to be* to him, unwise rulers or reformers cannot fatally interrupt him.

I know that most men think differently from myself; but those whose lives are by profession devoted to the study of these or kindred subjects content me as little as any. Statesmen and legislators, standing so completely within the institution, never distinctly and nakedly behold it. They speak of moving society, but have no resting-place without it. They may be men of a certain experience and discrimination, and have no doubt invented ingenious and even useful systems, for which we sincerely thank them; but all their wit and usefulness lie within certain not very wide limits. They are wont to forget that the world is not governed by policy and expediency. Webster never goes behind government, and so cannot speak with authority about it. His words are wisdom to those legislators who contemplate no essential reform in the existing government; but for thinkers, and those who legislate for all time, he never once glances at the subject. I know of those whose serene and wise speculations on this theme would soon reveal the limits of his mind's range and hospitality. Yet, compared with the cheap professions of most reformers, and the still cheaper wisdom and eloquence of politicians in general, his are almost the only sensible and valuable words, and we thank Heaven for him. Comparatively, he is always strong, original, and, above all, practical. Still, his quality is not wisdom, but prudence. The lawyer's truth is not Truth, but consistency or a consistent expediency. Truth is always in harmony with herself, and is not concerned chiefly to reveal the justice that may consist with wrong-doing. He well deserves to be called, as he has been called, the Defender of the Constitution. There are really no blows to be given by him but defensive ones. He is not a leader, but a follower. His leaders are the men of '87. "I have never made an effort," he says, "and never propose to make an effort; I have never countenanced an effort, and never mean to countenance an effort, to disturb the arrangement as originally made, by which the various States came into the Union." Still thinking of the sanction which the Constitution gives

to slavery, he says, "Because it was a part of the original compact,—let it stand." Notwithstanding his special acuteness and ability, he is unable to take a fact out of its merely political relations, and behold it as it lies absolutely to be disposed of by the intellect,—what, for instance, it behooves a man to do here in America to-day with regard to slavery,—but ventures, or is driven, to make some such desperate answer as the following, while professing to speak absolutely, and as a private man,—from which what new and singular code of social duties might be inferred? "The manner," says he, "in which the governments of those States where slavery exists are to regulate it is for their own consideration, under their responsibility to their constituents, to the general laws of propriety, humanity, and justice, and to God. Associations formed elsewhere, springing from a feeling of humanity, or other cause, have nothing whatever to do with it. They have never received any encouragement from me, and they never will."

They who know of no purer sources of truth, who have traced up its stream no higher, stand, and wisely stand, by the Bible and the Constitution, and drink at it there with reverence and humility; but they who behold where it comes trickling into this lake or that pool, gird up their loins once more, and continue their pilgrimage toward its fountainhead.

No man with a genius for legislation has appeared in America. They are rare in the history of the world. There are orators, politicians, and eloquent men, by the thousand; but the speaker has not yet opened his mouth to speak who is capable of settling the much-vexed questions of the day. We love eloquence for its own sake, and not for any truth which it may utter, or any heroism it may inspire. Our legislators have not yet learned the comparative value of free-trade and of freedom, of union, and of rectitude, to a nation. They have no genius or talent for comparatively humble questions of taxation and finance, commerce and manufactures and agriculture. If we were left solely to the wordy wit of legislators in Congress for our guidance, uncorrected by the seasonable experience and the effectual complaints of the people, America would not long retain her rank among the nations. For eighteen hundred years, though perchance I have no right to say it, the New Testament has been written; yet where is the legislator who has wisdom and practical talent enough to avail himself of the light which it sheds on the science of legislation?

The authority of government, even such as I am willing to submit to,—for I will cheerfully obey those who know and can do better than I, and in many things even those who neither know nor can do so well,—is still an impure one: to be strictly just, it must have the sanction and consent of the governed. It can have no pure right over my person and property but what I concede to it. The progress from an absolute to a limited monarchy, from a limited monarchy to a democracy, is a progress toward a true respect for the individual. Even the Chinese philosopher was wise enough to regard the individual as the basis of the empire. Is a democracy, such as we know it, the last improvement possible in government? Is it not possible to take a step further towards recognizing and organizing the rights of man? There will never be a really free and enlightened State until the State comes to recognize the individual as a higher and independent power, from which all its own power and authority are derived, and treats him accordingly. I please myself with imagining a State at last which can afford to be just to all men, and to treat the individual with respect as a neighbor; which even would not think it inconsistent with its own repose if a few were to live aloof from it, not meddling with it, nor embraced by it, who fulfilled all the duties of neighbors and fellow-men. A State which bore this kind of fruit, and suffered it to drop off as fast as it ripened, would prepare the way for a still more perfect and glorious State, which also I have imagined, but not yet anywhere seen.

Susan B. Anthony, 1820–1906

Along with that of Elizabeth Cady Stanton, no other name is more closely associated with early American feminism than that of Susan B. Anthony. Stanton and Anthony are best remembered for their fierce advocacy of women's suffrage. However, their egalitarian commitment actually had a far greater scope. Both were ardent abolitionists and, after the Civil War, believers in voting rights for blacks as well as for women. Anthony was also a leader in the temperance movement and was vitally concerned with the women's labor movement.

Anthony was raised a Quaker and grew up believing the Quaker teaching that women were equal to men in the eyes of God. She began to work as a teacher but left to participate in the temperance movement. She experienced discrimination because of her sex and helped form a separate group, the Women's State Temperance Society of New York. She soon began to struggle against slavery as well and organized the American Anti-Slavery Society.

Susan B. Anthony's partnership with Elizabeth Cady Stanton lasted a lifetime, and the two women left a monumental work, *The History of Women's Suffrage*, as a testimony to their shared struggles.

Susan B. Anthony

Speech in Defense of Equal Suffrage (1873)

Friends and fellow-citizens: I stand before you tonight under indictment for the alleged crime of having voted at the last Presidential election, without having a lawful right to vote. It shall be my work this evening to prove to you that in thus voting, I not only committed no crime, but, instead, simply exercised my citizen's rights, guaranteed to me and all United States citizens by the National Constitution, beyond the power of any State to deny.

The preamble of the Federal Constitution says:

"We, the people of the United States, in order to form a more perfect union, establish justice, insure domestic tranquillity, provide for the common defense, promote the general welfare, and secure the blessings of liberty to ourselves and our posterity, do ordain and establish this Constitution for the United States of America."

It was we, the people; not we, the white male citizens; nor yet we, the male citizens; but we, the whole people, who formed the Union. And we formed it, not to give the blessings of liberty, but to secure them; not to the half of ourselves and the half of our posterity, but to the whole people—women as well as men. And it is a downright mockery to talk to women of their enjoyment of the blessings of liberty while they are denied the use of the only means of securing them provided by this democratic-republican government—the ballot.

For any State to make sex a qualification that must ever result in the disfranchisement of one entire half of the people is to pass a bill of attainder, or an *ex post facto* law, and is therefore a violation of the supreme law of the land. By it the blessings of liberty are forever withheld from women and their female posterity. To them this government has no just powers derived from the consent of the governed. To them this government is not a democracy. It is not a republic. It is an odious aristocracy; a hateful oligarchy of sex; the most hateful aristocracy ever established on the face of the globe; an oligarchy of wealth, where the rich govern the poor. An oligarchy of learning, where the educated govern the ignorant, or even an oligarchy of race, where the Saxon rules the African, might be endured; but this oligarchy of sex, which makes father, brothers, husband, sons, the oligarchs over the mother and sisters, the wife and daughters of every household—which ordains all men sovereigns, all women subjects, carries dissension, discord and rebellion into every home of the nation.

Webster, Worcester and Bouvier all define a citizen to be a person in the United States, entitled to vote and hold office.

The only question left to be settled now

SOURCE: Charles Hurd, ed., *Great American Speeches* (New York: Hawthorne Books, 1957).

is: Are women persons? And I hardly believe any of our opponents will have the hardihood to say they are not. Being persons, then, women are citizens; and no State has a right to make any law, or to enforce any old law, that shall abridge their privileges or immunities. Hence, every discrimination against women in the constitutions and laws of the several States is today null and void, precisely as is every one against Negroes.

Angelina Grimke, 1792–1872

Angelina Grimke and her sister Sarah Grimke were unique in the abolitionist movement. They were the only activist writers and lecturers who were white southern women.

Born in Charleston, South Carolina, the daughters of a French Huguenot who had fought in the American Revolution, both sisters became restless in the formal surroundings in which they were raised. Sarah had become incensed at an early age by the inferiority of her own education as compared with that of her brothers and soon began to demand more equal instruction. Impressed by the Quakers on a family trip to Philadelphia, she decided to remain there as a church member and join the abolitionist movement. She was soon joined by her younger sister Angelina.

The younger Grimke soon outshone her elder sister and in 1836 wrote *An Appeal to the Christian Women of the South.* Sarah followed with an *Epistle to the Clergy of the Southern States,* but she remained in the background as Angelina became a well-known lecturer for the antislavery cause.

When Angelina was criticized by some congregationalist clergy for her "unwomanly" behavior, she came to embrace the women's movement and see the common ground that it shared with the antislavery struggle. In 1838, Sarah and Angelina wrote *Letters on the Equality of the Sexes.*

Angelina Grimke's *Letters to Catherine E. Beecher,* selections printed below, describe her experiences with the abolitionist movement and how they came to illuminate to her the second-class status of women. Like Anthony, Grimke's dissent nevertheless affirms the liberal egalitarian values of Jacksonian America and asks only that they be expanded.

Angelina Grimke

Human Rights Not Founded on Sex (1837)

DEAR FRIEND—The investigation of the rights of the slave has led me to a better understanding of my own. I have found the Anti-Slavery cause to be the high school of morals in our land—the school in which *human rights* are more fully investigated, and better understood and taught, than in any other. Here a great fundamental principle is uplifted and illuminated, and from this central light, rays innumerable stream all around. Human beings have *rights*, because they are *moral* beings: the rights of *all* men grow out of their moral nature; and as all men have the same moral nature, they have essentially the same rights. These rights may be wrested from the slave, but they cannot be alienated: his title to himself is as perfect *now*, as is that of Lyman Beecher: it is stamped on his moral being, and is, like it, imperishable. Now if rights are founded in the nature of our moral being, then the *mere circumstance of sex* does not give to man higher rights and responsibilities, than to woman. To suppose that it does, would be to deny the self-evident truth, that the "physical constitution is the mere instrument of the moral nature." To suppose that it does, would be to break up utterly the relations, of the two natures, and to reverse their functions, exalting the animal nature into a monarch, and humbling the moral into a slave; making the former a proprietor, and the latter its property. When human beings are re-

garded as *moral* beings, *sex,* instead of being enthroned upon the summit, administering upon rights and responsibilities, sinks into insignificance and nothingness. My doctrine then is, that whatever it is morally right for man to do, it is morally right for women to do. Our duties originate, not from difference of sex, but from the diversity of our relations in life, the various gifts and talents committed to our care, and the different eras in which we live.

This regulation of duty by the mere circumstance of sex, rather than by the fundamental principle of moral being, has led to all that multifarious train of evils flowing out of the anti-christian doctrine of masculine and feminine virtues. By this doctrine, man has been converted into the warrior, and clothed with sternness, and those other kindred qualities, which in common estimation belong to his character as a *man;* whilst woman has been taught to lean upon an arm of flesh, to sit as a doll arrayed in "gold, and pearls, and costly array," to be admired for her personal charms, and caressed and humored like a spoiled child, or converted into a mere drudge to suit the convenience of her lord and master. Thus have all the diversified relations of life been filled with "confusion and every evil work." This principle has given to man a charter for the exercise of tyranny and selfishness, pride and arrogance, lust and brutal violence. It has robbed woman of essential rights, the right to think and speak and act on all great moral questions, just as men think and speak and act; the right to share their responsibili-

---

SOURCE: Angelina Grimke, *Letters to Catherine E. Beecher,* "Letter XII" (Boston: Isaac Knapp, 1838).

ties, perils and toils; the right to fulfil the great end of her being, as a moral, intellectual and immortal creature, and of glorifying God in her body and her spirit which are His. Hitherto, instead of being a help meet to man, in the highest, noblest sense of the term, as a companion, a co-worker, an equal; she has been a mere appendage of his being, an instrument of his convenience and pleasure, the pretty toy with which he wiled away his leisure moments, or the pet animal whom he humored into playfulness and submission. Woman, instead of being regarded as the equal of man, has uniformly been looked down upon as his inferior, a mere gift to fill up the measure of his happiness. In "the poetry of romantic gallantry," it is true, she has been called "the last *best gift* of God to man;" but I believe I speak forth the words of truth and soberness when I affirm, that woman never was given to man. She was created, like him, in the image of God, and crowned with glory and honor; created only a little lower than the angels—not, as is almost universally assumed, a little lower than man; on her brow, as well as on his, was placed the "diadem of beauty," and in her hands the sceptre of universal dominion. Gen: i. 27, 28. "The last *best gift* of God to man!" Where is the scripture warrant for this "rhetorical flourish, this splendid absurdity?" Let us examine the account of her creation. "And the rib which the Lord God had taken from man, made he a woman, and brought her unto the man." Not as a gift—for Adam immediately recognized her *as a part of himself*—("this is now bone of my bone, and flesh of my flesh")—a companion and equal, not one hair's breadth beneath him in the majesty and glory of her moral being; not placed under his authority as a *subject*, but by his side, on the same platform of human rights, under the government of God only. This idea of woman's being "the last best gift of God to man," however pretty it may sound to the ears of those who love to discourse

upon "the poetry of romantic gallantry, and the generous promptings of chivalry," has nevertheless been the means of sinking her from an *end* into a mere *means*—of turning her into an *appendage* to man, instead of recognizing her as *a part of man*—of destroying her individuality, and rights, and responsibilities, and merging her moral being in that of man. Instead of *Jehovah* being *her* king, *her* lawgiver, and *her* judge, she has been taken out of the exalted scale of existence in which He placed her, and subjected to the despotic control of man.

I have often been amused at the vain efforts made to define the rights and responsibilities of immortal beings as *men* and *women*. No one has yet found out just *where* the line of separation between them should be drawn, and for this simple reason, that no one knows just how far below man woman is, whether she be a head shorter in her moral responsibilities, or head and shoulders, or the full length of his noble stature, below him, i.e., under his feet. Confusion, uncertainty, and great inconsistencies, must exist on this point, so long as woman is regarded in the least degree inferior to man; but place her where her Maker placed her, on the same high level of human rights with man, side by side with him, and difficulties vanish, the mountains of perplexity flow down at the pressence of this grand equalizing principle. Measure her rights and duties by the unerring standard of *moral being*, not by the false weights and measures of a mere circumstance of her human existence, and then the truth will be self-evident, that whatever it is *morally* right for a man to do, it is *morally* right for a woman to do. I recognize no rights but *human* rights—I know nothing of men's rights and women's rights; for in Christ Jesus, there is neither male nor female. It is my solemn conviction, that, until this principle of equality is recognised and embodied in practice, the church can do nothing effectual for the permanent reformation of the world. Woman was the first transgressor, and the first victim of power. In all heathen nations, she has been the slave of man, and Christian nations have never acknowledged her rights. Nay more, no Christian denomination or Society has ever acknowledged them on the broad basis of humanity. I know that in some denominations, she is permitted to preach the gospel; not from a conviction of her rights, nor upon the ground of her equality as a *human being,* but of her equality in spiritual gifts—for we find that woman, even in these Societies, is allowed no voice in framing the Discipline by which she is to be governed. Now, I believe it is woman's right to have a voice in all the laws and regulations by which she is to be *governed,* whether in Church or State; and that the present arrangements of society, on these points, are *a violation of human rights, a rank usurpation of power,* a violent seizure and confiscation of what is sacredly and inalienably hers—thus inflicting upon woman outrageous wrongs, working mischief incalculable in the social circle, and in its influence on the world producing only evil, and that continually. *If* Ecclesiastical and Civil governments are ordained of God, *then* I contend that woman has just as much right to sit in solemn counsel in Conventions, Conferences, Associations and General Assemblies, as man—just as much right to sit upon the throne of England, or in the Presidential chair of the United States.

Dost thou ask me, if I would wish to see woman engaged in the contention and strife of sectarian controversy, or in the intrigues of political partizans? I say no! never—never. I rejoice that she does not stand on the same platform which man now occupies in these respects; but I mourn, also, that he should thus prostitute his higher nature, and vilely cast away his birthright. I prize the purity of *his* character as highly as I do that of hers. As a moral being, *whatever it is morally wrong for her to do, it is morally wrong for him to do.* The fallacious doctrine of male and female virtues has well nigh ruined all that is morally great and lovely in his character: he has been quite as deep a sufferer by it as woman, though mostly in different respects and by other processes. As my time is engrossed by the pressing responsibilities of daily public duty, I have no leisure for that minute detail which would be required for the illustration and defence of those principles. Thou wilt find a wide field opened before thee, in the investigation of which, I doubt not, thou wilt be instructed. Enter this field, and explore it: thou wilt find in it a hid treasure, more precious than rubies—a fund, a mine of principles, as new as they are great and glorious. . . .

Frederick Douglass, 1817–1895

Frederick Douglass was born Frederick W. Bailey, a slave on the eastern shore of Maryland. At the age of seven, he was sent to Baltimore as a house servant and while there learned to read and write. He was trained and worked in Baltimore as a ship caulker and in 1838 escaped to New York. He soon left for New Bedford, Massachusetts, and changed his name to Douglass.

In 1841, Douglass attended a lecture of the Massachusetts Anti-Slavery Society and delivered an inspiring extemporaneous speech. He was asked to become a lecturer for the society and thus began his career as an activist for black equality.

In 1845, he wrote his famous *Narrative of the Life of Frederick Douglass* and in 1847 began to publish the *North Star,* which became, along with William Lloyd Garrison's *The Liberator,* the leading abolitionist journal.

Unlike Garrison, Douglass began to take an active interest in electoral politics. Garrison viewed slavery as a moral and religious problem and felt the Constitution was a proslavery document, a "Covenant with Death." Douglass argued that properly understood, the Constitution outlawed slavery; and he began to associate with political parties, eventually supporting the Free Soil party and later, reluctantly, the Republican party.

After the Civil War, Douglass remained a passionate spokesman for black rights and a believer that the problems of blacks were political and capable of political solutions.

The "Fourth of July Oration," reprinted below, is a good example of Douglass's egalitarian passion and commitment to individual rights.

Frederick Douglass

Fourth of July Oration (1852)

MR. PRESIDENT, FRIENDS AND FELLOW CITIZENS: . . . This, for the purpose of this celebration, is the Fourth of July. It is the birthday of your National Independence, and of your political freedom. This, to you, is what the Passover was to the emancipated people of God. It carries your minds back to the day, and to the act of your great deliverance; and to the signs, and to the wonders, associated with that act, and that day. This celebration also marks the beginning of another year of your national life; and reminds you that the Republic of America is now 76 years old. I am glad, fellow-citizens, that your nation is so young. Seventy-six years, though a good

old age for a man, is but a mere speck in the life of a nation. Three score years and ten is the allotted time for individual men; but nations number their years by thousands. According to this fact, you are, even now, only in the beginning of your national career, still lingering in the period of childhood. I repeat, I am glad this is so. There is hope in the thought, and hope is much needed, under the dark clouds which lower above the horizon. The eye of the reformer is met with angry flashes, portending disastrous times; but his heart may well beat lighter at the thought that America is young, and that she is still in the impressible stage of her existence. May he not hope that high lessons of wisdom, of justice and of truth, will yet give direction to her destiny? Were the nation older, the patriot's heart might be sadder, and the reformer's

SOURCE: Philip S. Foner, ed., *The Life and Writings of Frederick Douglass* (New York: International Publishers, 1950).

brow heavier. Its future might be shrouded in gloom, and the hope of its prophets go out in sorrow. There is consolation in the thought that America is young—Great streams are not easily turned from channels, worn deep in the course of ages. They may sometimes rise in quiet and stately majesty, and inundate the land, refreshing and fertilizing the earth with their mysterious properties. They may also rise in wrath and fury, and bear away, on their angry waves, the accumulated wealth of years of toil and hardship. They, however, gradually flow back to the same old channel, and flow on as serenely as ever. But, while the river may not be turned aside, it may dry up, and leave nothing behind but the withered branch, and the unsightly rock, to howl in the abyss-sweeping wind, the sad tale of departed glory. As with rivers so with nations.

Fellow-citizens, I shall not presume to dwell at length on the associations that cluster about this day. The simple story of it is, that, 76 years ago, the people of this country were British subjects. The style and title of your "sovereign people" (in which you now glory) was not then born. You were under the British Crown. Your fathers esteemed the English Government as the home government; and England as the fatherland. This home government, you know, although a considerable distance from your home, did, in the exercise of its parental prerogatives, impose upon its colonial children, such restraints, burdens and limitations, as, in its mature judgment, it deemed wise, right and proper.

But your fathers, who had not adopted the fashionable idea of this day, of the infallibility of government, and the absolute character of its acts, presumed to differ from the home government in respect to the wisdom and the justice of some of those burdens and restraints. They went so far in their excitement as to pronounce the measures of government unjust, unreasonable, and oppressive, and altogether such as ought not to be quietly submitted to. I scarcely need say, fellow-citizens, that my opinion of those measures fully accords with that of your fathers. Such a declaration of agreement on my part would not be worth much to anybody. It would certainly prove nothing as to what part I might have taken had I lived during the great controversy of 1776. To say now that America was right, and England wrong, is exceedingly easy. Everybody can say it; the dastard, not less than the noble brave, can flippantly discant on the tyranny of England towards the American Colonies. It is fashionable to do so; but there was a time when, to pronounce against England, and in favor of the cause of the colonies, tried men's souls. They who did so were accounted in their day plotters of mischief, agitators and rebels, dangerous men. To side with the right against the wrong, with the weak against the strong, and with the oppressed against the oppressor! here lies the merit, and the one which, of all others, seems unfashionable in our day. The cause of liberty may be stabbed by the men who glory in the deeds of your fathers. But, to proceed.

Feeling themselves harshly and unjustly treated, by the home government, your fathers, like men of honesty, and men of spirit, earnestly sought redress. They petitioned and remonstrated; they did so in a decorous, respectful, and loyal manner. Their conduct was wholly unexceptionable. This, however, did not answer the purpose. They saw themselves treated with sovereign indifference, coldness and scorn. Yet they persevered. They were not the men to look back.

As the sheet anchor takes a firmer hold, when the ship is tossed by the storm, so did the cause of your fathers grow stronger as it breasted the chilling blasts of kingly displeasure. The greatest and best of British statesmen admitted its justice, and the loftiest eloquence of the British Senate came to its support. But, with that blindness which seems to be the unvarying characteristic of tyrants, since Pharaoh and his hosts were drowned in the Red Sea, the British Government persisted in the exactions complained of.

The madness of this course, we believe, is admitted now, even by England; but we fear the lesson is wholly lost on our present rulers.

Oppression makes a wise man mad. Your fathers were wise men, and if they did not go mad, they became restive under this treatment. They felt themselves the victims of grievous wrongs, wholly incurable in their colonial capacity. With brave men there is always a remedy for oppression. Just here, the idea of a total separation of the colonies from the crown was born! It was a startling idea, much more so than we, at this distance of time, regard it. The timid and the prudent (as has been intimated) of that day were, of course, shocked and alarmed by it.

Such people lived then, have lived before, and will, probably, ever have a place on this planet; and their course, in respect to any great change (no matter how great the good to be attained, or the wrong to be redressed by it), may be calculated with as much precision as can be the course of the stars. They hate all changes, but silver, gold and copper change! Of this sort of change they are always strongly in favor.

These people were called Tories in the days of your fathers; and the appellation, probably, conveyed the same idea that is meant by a more modern, though a somewhat less euphonious term, which we often find in our papers, applied to some of our old politicians.

Their opposition to the then dangerous thought was earnest and powerful; but, amid all their terror and affrighted vociferations against it, the alarming and revolutionary idea moved on, and the country with it.

On the 2d of July, 1776, the old Continental Congress, to the dismay of the lovers of ease, and the worshipers of property, clothed that dreadful idea with all the authority of national sanction. They did so in the form of a resolution; and as we seldom hit upon resolutions, drawn up in our day, whose transparency is at all equal to this, it may refresh your minds and help my story if I read it.

"Resolved, That these united colonies are, and of right, ought to be free and Independent States; that they are absolved from all allegiance to the British Crown; and that all political connection between them and the State of Great Britain is, and ought to be, dissolved."

Citizens, your fathers made good that resolution. They succeeded; and to-day you reap the fruits of their success. The freedom gained is yours; and you, therefore, may properly celebrate this anniversary. The 4th of July is the first great fact in your nation's history—the very ringbolt in the chain of your yet undeveloped destiny.

Pride and patriotism, not less than gratitude, prompt you to celebrate and to hold it in perpetual remembrance. I have said that the Declaration of Independence is the ringbolt to the chain of your nation's destiny; so, indeed, I regard it. The principles contained in that instrument are saving principles. Stand by those principles, be true to them on all occasions, in all places, against all foes, and at whatever cost. . . .

Fellow-citizens, pardon me, allow me to ask, why am I called upon to speak here today? What have I, or those I represent, to do with your national independence? Are the great principles of political freedom and of natural justice, embodied in that Declaration of Independence, extended to us? and am I, therefore, called upon to bring our humble offering to the national altar, and to confess the benefits and express devout gratitude for the blessings resulting from your independence to us?

Would to God, both for your sakes and ours, that an affirmative answer could be truthfully returned to these questions! Then would my task be light, and my burden easy and delightful. For *who* is there so cold, that a nation's sympathy could not warm him? Who so obdurate and dead to the claims of gratitude, that would not thankfully acknowledge such priceless benefits? Who so stolid and selfish, that would not give his voice to swell the hallelujahs of a nation's jubilee, when the chains of servitude had been torn from his limbs? I am not that man. In a case like that, the dumb might eloquently speak, and the "lame man leap as an hart."

But such is not the state of the case. I say it with a sad sense of the disparity between us. I am not included within the pale of this glorious anniversary! Your high independence only reveals the immeasurable distance between us. The blessings in which you, this day, rejoice, are not enjoyed in common.— The rich inheritance of justice, liberty, prosperity and independence, bequeathed by your fathers, is shared by you, not by me. The sunlight that brought light and healing to you, has brought stripes and death to me. This Fourth July is *yours*, not *mine. You* may *rejoice, I* must mourn. To drag a man in fetters into the grand illuminated temple of liberty, and call upon him to join you in joyous anthems, were inhuman mockery and sacrilegious irony. Do you mean, citizens, to mock me, by asking me to speak to-day? If so, there is a parallel to your conduct. And let me warn you that it is dangerous to copy the example of a nation whose crimes, towering up to heaven, were thrown down by the breath of the Almighty, burying that nation in irrevocable ruin! I can to-day take up the plaintive lament of a peeled and woe-smitten people!

"By the rivers of Babylon, there we sat down. Yea! we wept when we remembered Zion. We hanged our harps upon the willows in the midst thereof. For there, they that carried us away captive, required of us a song; and they who wasted us required of us mirth, saying, Sing us one of the songs of Zion. How can we sing the Lord's song in a strange land? If I forget thee, O Jerusalem, let my right hand forget her cunning. If I do not remember thee, let my tongue cleave to the roof of my mouth."

Fellow-citizens, above your national, tumultuous joy, I hear the mournful wail of millions! whose chains, heavy and grievous yesterday, are, to-day, rendered more intolerable by the jubilee shouts that reach them. If I do forget, if I do not faithfully remember those bleeding children of sorrow this day, "may my right hand forget her cunning, and may my tongue cleave to the roof of my mouth!" To forget them, to pass lightly over their wrongs, and to chime in with the popular theme, would be treason most scandalous and shocking, and would make me a reproach before God and the world. My subject, then, fellow-citizens, is American slavery. I shall see this day and its popular characteristics from the slave's point of view. Standing there identified with the American bondman, making his wrongs mine, I do not hesitate to declare, with all my soul, that the character and conduct of this nation never looked blacker to me than on this 4th of July! Whether we turn to the declarations of the past, or to the professions of the present, the conduct of the nation seems equally hideous and revolting. America is false to the past, false to the present, and solemnly binds herself to be false to the future. Standing with God and the crushed and bleeding slave on this occasion, I will, in the name of humanity which is outraged, in the name of liberty which is fettered, in the name of the constitution and the Bible which are disregarded and trampled upon, dare to call in question and to denounce, with all the emphasis I can command, everything that serves to perpetuate slavery—the great sin and shame of America! "I will not equivocate; I will not excuse"; I will use the severest language I can command; and yet not one word shall escape me that any man, whose judgment is not blinded by prejudice, or who is not at heart a slaveholder, shall not confess to be right and just.

But I fancy I hear some one of my audience say, "It is just in this circumstance that you and your brother abolitionists fail to make a favorable impression on the public mind. Would you argue more, and denounce less;

would you persuade more, and rebuke less; your cause would be much more likely to succeed." But, I submit, where all is plain there is nothing to be argued. What point in the antislavery creed would you have me argue? On what branch of the subject do the people of this country need light? Must I undertake to prove that the slave is a man? That point is conceded already. Nobody doubts it. The slaveholders themselves acknowledge it in the enactment of laws for their government. They acknowledge it when then punish disobedience on the part of the slave. There are seventy-two crimes in the State of Virginia which, if committed by a black man (no matter how ignorant he be), subject him to the punishment of death; while only two of the same crimes will subject a white man to the like punishment. What is this but the acknowledgment that the slave is a moral, intellectual, and responsible being? The manhood of the slave is conceded. It is admitted in the fact that Southern statute books are covered with enactments forbidding, under severe fines and penalties, the teaching of the slave to read or to write. When you can point to any such laws in reference to the beasts of the field, then I may consent to argue the manhood of the slave. When the dogs in your streets, when the fowls of the air, when the cattle on your hills, when the fish of the sea, and the reptiles that crawl, shall be unable to distinguish the slave from a brute, *then* will I argue with you that the slave is a man!

For the present, it is enough to affirm the equal manhood of the Negro race. It is not astonishing that, while we are ploughing, planting, and reaping, using all kinds of mechanical tools, erecting houses, constructing bridges, building ships, working in metals of brass, iron, copper, silver and gold; that, while we are reading, writing and ciphering, acting as clerks, merchants and secretaries, having among us lawyers, doctors, ministers, poets, authors, editors, orators and teachers; that, while we are engaged in all manner of enter-

prises common to other men, digging gold in California, capturing the whale in the Pacific, feeding sheep and cattle on the hillside, living, moving, acting, thinking, planning, living in families as husbands, wives and children, and, above all, confessing and worshipping the Christian's God, and looking hopefully for life and immortality beyond the grave, we are called upon to prove that we are men!

Would you have me argue that man is entitled to liberty? that he is the rightful owner of his own body? You have already declared it. Must I argue the wrongfulness of slavery? Is that a question for Republicans? Is it to be settled by the rules of logic and argumentation, as a matter beset with great difficulty, involving a doubtful application of the principle of justice, hard to be understood? How should I look to-day, in the presence of Americans, dividing, and subdividing a discourse, to show that men have a natural right to freedom? speaking of it relatively and positively, negatively and affirmatively. To do so, would be to make myself ridiculous, and to offer an insult to your understanding.—There is not a man beneath the canopy of heaven that does not know that slavery is wrong *for him*.

What, am I to argue that it is wrong to make men brutes, to rob them of their liberty, to work them without wages, to keep them ignorant of their relations to their fellow men, to beat them with sticks, to flay their flesh with the lash, to load their limbs with irons, to hunt them with dogs, to sell them at auction, to sunder their families, to knock out their teeth, to burn their flesh, to starve them into obedience and submission to their masters? Must I argue that a system thus marked with blood, and stained with pollution, is *wrong*? No! I will not. I have better employment for my time and strength than such arguments would imply.

What, then, remains to be argued? Is it that slavery is not divine; that God did not establish it; that our doctors of divinity are mistaken?

There is blasphemy in the thought. That which is inhuman, cannot be divine! *Who* can reason on such a proposition? They that can, may; I cannot. The time for such argument is passed. . . .

What, to the American slave, is your 4th of July? I answer; a day that reveals to him, more than all other days in the year, the gross injustice and cruelty to which he is the constant victim. To him, your celebration is a sham; your boasted liberty, an unholy license; your national greatness, swelling vanity; your sounds of rejoicing are empty and heartless; your denunciation of tyrants, brass fronted impudence; your shouts of liberty and equality, hollow mockery; your prayers and hymns, your sermons and thanksgivings, with all your religious parade and solemnity, are, to Him, mere bombast, fraud, deception, impiety, and hypocrisy—a thin veil to cover up crimes which would disgrace a nation of savages. There is not a nation on the earth guilty of practices more shocking and bloody than are the people of the United States, at this very hour. . . .

Behold the practical operation of this internal slave-trade, the American slave-trade, sustained by American politics and American religion. Here you will see men and women reared like swine for the market. You know what is a swine-drover? I will show you a man-drover. They inhabit all our Southern States. They perambulate the country, and crowd the highways of the nation, with droves of human stock. You will see one of these human flesh jobbers, armed with pistol, whip, and bowie-knife, driving a company of a hundred men, women, and children, from the Potomac to the slave market at New Orleans. These wretched people are to be sold singly, or in lots, to suit purchasers. They are food for the cotton-field and the deadly sugar-mill. Mark the sad procession, as it moves wearily along, and the inhuman wretch who drives them. Hear his savage yells and his blood-curdling oaths, as he hurries on his affrighted

captives! There, see the old man with locks thinned and gray. Cast one glance, if you please, upon that young mother, whose shoulders are bare to the scorching sun, her briny tears falling on the brow of the babe in her arms. See, too, that girl of thirteen, weeping, *yes!* weeping, as she thinks of the mother from whom she has been torn! The drove moves tardily. Heat and sorrow have nearly consumed their strength; suddenly you hear a quick snap, like the discharge of a rifle; the fetters clank, and the chain rattles simultaneously; your ears are saluted with a scream, that seems to have torn its way to the centre of your soul! The crack you heard was the sound of the slave-whip; the scream you heard was from the woman you saw with the babe. Her speed had faltered under the weight of her child and her chains! that gash on her shoulder tells her to move on. Follow this drove to New Orleans. Attend the auction; see men examined like horses; see the forms of women rudely and brutally exposed to the shocking gaze of American slave-buyers. See this drove sold and separated forever; and never forget the deep, sad sobs that arose from that scattered multitude. Tell me, citizens, where, under the sun, you can witness a spectacle more fiendish and shocking. Yet this is but a glance at the American slave-trade, as it exists, at this moment, in the ruling part of the United States.

I was born amid such sights and scenes. To me the American slave-trade is a terrible reality. When a child, my soul was often pierced with a sense of its horrors. I lived on Philpot Street, Fell's Point, Baltimore, and have watched from the wharves the slave ships in the Basin, anchored from the shore, with their cargoes of human flesh, waiting for favorable winds to waft them down the Chesapeake. There was, at that time, a grand slave mart kept at the head of Pratt Street, by Austin Woldfolk. His agents were sent into every town and county in Maryland, announcing their arrival, through the papers, and on flaming *"hand-bills,"* headed cash for Negroes. These men were generally well dressed men, and very captivating in their manners; ever ready to drink, to treat, and to gamble. The fate of many a slave has depended upon the turn of a single card; and many a child has been snatched from the arms of its mother by bargains arranged in a state of brutal drunkenness.

The flesh-mongers gather up their victims by dozens, and drive them, chained, to the general depot at Baltimore. When a sufficient number has been collected here, a ship is chartered for the purpose of conveying the forlorn crew to Mobile, or to New Orleans. From the slave prison to the ship, they are usually driven in the darkness of night; for since the anti-slavery agitation, a certain caution is observed.

In the deep, still darkness of midnight, I have been often aroused by the dead, heavy footsteps, and the piteous cries of the chained gangs that passed our door. The anguish of my boyish heart was intense; and I was often consoled, when speaking to my mistress in the morning, to hear her say that the custom was very wicked; that she hated to hear the rattle of the chains and the heart-rending cries. I was glad to find one who sympathized with me in my horror. . . .

* * * * *

For black men there is neither law nor justice, humanity nor religion. The Fugitive Slave *Law* makes mercy to them a crime; and bribes the judge who tries them. An American judge gets ten dollars for every victim he consigns to slavery, and five, when he fails to do so. The oath of any two villains is sufficient, under this hell-black enactment, to send the most pious and exemplary black man into the remorseless jaws of slavery! His own testimony is nothing. He can bring no witnesses for himself. The minister of American justice is bound by the law to hear but *one* side; and *that* side is the side of the oppressor. Let this damning

fact be perpetually told. Let it be thundered around the world that in tyrant-killing, king-hating, people-loving, democratic, Christian America the seats of justice are filled with judges who hold their offices under an open and palpable *bribe*, and are bound, in deciding the case of a man's liberty, *to hear only his accusers!*

In glaring violation of justice, in shameless disregard of the forms of administering law, in cunning arrangement to entrap the defenceless, and in diabolical intent this Fugitive Slave Law stands alone in the annals of tyrannical legislation. I doubt if there be another nation on the globe having the brass and the baseness to put such a law on the statute-book. If any man in this assembly thinks differently from me in this matter, and feels able to disprove my statements, I will gladly confront him at any suitable time and place he may select.

I take this law to be one of the grossest infringements of Christian Liberty, and, if the churches and ministers of our country were not stupidly blind, or most wickedly indifferent, they, too, would so regard it.

At the very moment that they are thanking God for the enjoyment of civil and religious liberty, and for the right to worship God according to the dictates of their own consciences, they are utterly silent in respect to a law which robs religion of its chief significance and makes it utterly worthless to a world lying in wickedness. Did this law concern the *"mint, anise, and cummin"*—abridge the right to sing psalms, to partake of the sacrament, or to engage in any of the ceremonies of religion, it would be smitten by the thunder of a thousand pulpits. . . . The fact that the church of our country (with fractional exceptions) does not esteem "the Fugitive Slave Law" as a declaration of war against religious liberty, implies that that church regards religion simply as a form of worship, an empty ceremony, and *not* a vital principle, requiring active benevolence, justice, love, and good will towards man. It esteems sacrifice above mercy; psalm-singing above right doing; solemn meetings above practical righteousness. A worship that can be conducted by persons who refuse to give shelter to the houseless, to give bread to the hungry, clothing to the naked, and who enjoin obedience to a law forbidding these acts of mercy is a curse, not a blessing to mankind. The Bible addresses all such persons as "scribes, pharisees, hypocrites, who pay tithe of *mint, anise,* and *cummin,* and have omitted the weightier matters of the law, judgment, mercy, and faith."

But the church of this country is not only indifferent to the wrongs of the slave, it actually takes sides with the oppressors. It has made itself the bulwark of American slavery, and the shield of American slave-hunters. Many of its most eloquent Divines, who stand as the very lights of the church, have shamelessly given the sanction of religion and the Bible to the whole slave system. They have taught that man may, properly, be a slave; that the relation of master and slave is ordained of God; that to send back an escaped bondman to his master is clearly the duty of all the followers of the Lord Jesus Christ; and this horrible blasphemy is palmed off upon the world for Christianity.

For my part, I would say, welcome infidelity! welcome atheism! welcome anything! in preference to the gospel, *as preached by those Divines!* They convert the very name of religion into an engine of tyranny and barbarous cruelty, and serve to confirm more infidels, in this age, than all the infidel writings of Thomas Paine, Voltaire, and Bolingbroke put together have done! These ministers make religion a cold and flinty-hearted thing, having neither principles of right action nor bowels of compassion. They strip the love of God of its beauty and leave the throne of religion a huge, horrible, repulsive form. It is a religion for oppressors, tyrants, man-stealers, and *thugs.* It is not that *"pure and undefiled religion"* which is from above, and which is *"first pure,*

then peaceable, easy to be entreated, full of mercy and good fruits, *without partiality, and without hypocrisy."* But a religion which favors the rich against the poor; which exalts the proud above the humble; which divides mankind into two classes, tyrants and slaves; which says to the man in chains, *stay there;* and to the oppressor, *oppress on;* it is a religion which may be professed and enjoyed by all the robbers and enslavers of mankind; it makes God a respecter of persons, denies his fatherhood of the race, and tramples in the dust the great truth of the brotherhood of man. All this we affirm to be true of the popular church, and the popular worship of our land and nation—a religion, a church, and a worship which, on the authority of inspired wisdom, we pronounce to be an abomination in the sight of God. In the language of Isaiah, the American church might be well addressed. "Bring no more vain oblations; incense is an abomination unto me: the new moons and Sabbaths, the calling of assemblies, I cannot away with; it is iniquity, even the solemn meeting. Your new moons, and your appointed feasts my soul hateth. They are a trouble to me; I am weary to bear them; and when ye spread forth your hands I will hide mine eyes from you. Yea! when ye make many prayers, I will not hear. Your hands are full of blood; cease to do evil, learn to do well; seek judgment; relieve the oppressed; judge for the fatherless; plead for the widow.". . .

Americans! your republican politics, not less than your republican religion, are flagrantly inconsistent. You boast of your love of liberty, your superior civilization, and your pure Christianity, while the whole political power of the nation (as embodied in the two great political parties) is solemnly pledged to support and perpetuate the enslavement of three millions of your countrymen. You hurl your anathemas at the crowned headed tyrants of Russia and Austria and pride yourselves on your Democratic institutions, while you yourselves consent to be the mere *tools* and *body-*

guards of the tyrants of Virginia and Carolina. You invite to your shores fugitives of oppression from abroad, honor them with banquets, greet them with ovations, cheer them, toast them, salute them, protect them, and pour out your money to them like water; but the fugitives from your own land you advertise, hunt, arrest, shoot, and kill. You glory in your refinement and your universal education; yet you maintain a system as barbarous and dreadful as ever stained the character of a nation— a system begun in avarice, supported in pride, and perpetuated in cruelty. You shed tears over fallen Hungary, and make the sad story of her wrongs the theme of your poets, statesmen, and orators, till your gallant sons are ready to fly to arms to vindicate her cause against the oppressor: but, in regard to the ten thousand wrongs of the American slave, you would enforce the strictest silence, and would hail him as an enemy of the nation who dares to make those wrongs the subject of public discourse! You are all on fire at the mention of liberty for France or for Ireland; but are as cold as an iceberg at the thought of liberty for the enslaved of America. You discourse eloquently on the dignity of labor; yet, you sustain a system which, in its very essence, casts a stigma upon labor. You can bare your bosom to the storm of British artillery to throw off a three-penny tax on tea; and yet wring the last hard earned farthing from the grasp of the black laborers of your country. You profess to believe "that, of one blood, God made all nations of men to dwell on the face of all the earth," and hath commanded all men, everywhere, to love one another; yet you notoriously hate (and glory in your hatred) all men whose skins are not colored like your own. You declare before the world, and are understood by the world to declare that you *"hold these truths to be self-evident, that all men are created equal; and are endowed by their Creator with certain inalienable rights; and that among these are, life, liberty, and the pursuit of happiness;"* and yet, you hold securely, in a bondage which, according to your own Thomas Jefferson, *"is worse than ages of that which your fathers rose in rebellion to oppose,"* a *seventh part* of the inhabitants of your country.

Fellow-citizens, I will not enlarge further on your national inconsistencies. The existence of slavery in this country brands your republicanism as a sham, your humanity as a base pretense, and your Christianity as a lie. It destroys your moral power abroad: it corrupts your politicians at home. It saps the foundation of religion; it makes your name a hissing and a bye-word to a mocking earth. It is the antagonistic force in your government, the only thing that seriously disturbs and endangers your *Union*. It fetters your progress; it is the enemy of improvement; the deadly foe of education; it fosters pride; it breeds insolence; it promotes vice; it shelters crime; it is a curse to the earth that supports it; and yet you cling to it as if it were the sheet anchor of all your hopes. Oh! be warned! be warned! a horrible reptile is coiled up in your nation's bosom; the venomous creature is nursing at the tender breast of your youthful republic; *for the love of God, tear away,* and fling from you the hideous monster, and *let the weight of twenty millions crush and destroy it forever!*

But it is answered in reply to all this, that precisely what I have now denounced is, in fact, guaranteed and sanctioned by the Constitution of the United States; that, the right to hold, and to hunt slaves is a part of that Constitution framed by the illustrious Fathers of this Republic. . . .

Now, take the Constitution according to its plain reading, and I defy the presentation of a single pro-slavery clause in it. On the other hand, it will be found to contain principles and purposes, entirely hostile to the existence of slavery.

I have detained my audience entirely too

long already. At some future period I will gladly avail myself of an opportunity to give this subject a full and fair discussion.

Allow me to say, in conclusion, notwithstanding the dark picture I have this day presented, of the state of the nation, I do not despair of this country. There are forces in operation which must inevitably work the downfall of slavery. "The arm of the Lord is not shortened," and the doom of slavery is certain. I, therefore, leave off where I began, with hope. While drawing encouragement from "the Declaration of Independence," the great principles it contains, and the genius of American Institutions, my spirit is also cheered by the obvious tendencies of the age. Nations do not now stand in the same relation to each other that they did ages ago. No nation can now shut itself up from the surrounding world and trot round in the same old path of its fathers without interference. The time was when such could be done. Long established customs of hurtful character could formerly fence themselves in, and do their evil work with social impunity. Knowledge was then confined and enjoyed by the privileged few, and the multitude walked on in mental darkness. But a change has now come over the affairs of mankind. Walled cities and empires have become unfashionable. The arm of commerce has borne away the gates of the strong city. Intelligence is penetrating the darkest corners of the globe. It makes its pathway over and under the sea, as well as on the earth. Wind, steam, and lightning are its chartered agents. Oceans no longer divide, but link nations together. From Boston to London is now a holiday excursion. Space is comparatively annihilated.—Thoughts expressed on one side of the Atlantic are distinctly heard on the other.

The far off and almost fabulous Pacific rolls in grandeur at our feet. The Celestial Empire, the mystery of ages, is being solved. The fiat of the Almighty, "Let there be Light," has not yet spent its force. No abuse, no outrage whether in taste, sport or avarice, can now hide itself from the all-pervading light. . . .

Restrained Dissent: The Fear of Equality's Excesses

Alexis de Tocqueville, 1805–1859

Tocqueville was not an American writer at all, but a Frenchman writing about the American experiment with democracy for French audiences. Nevertheless, *Democracy in America* has become a classic for American readers who have valued the keen insight of the foreigner who looked at the New World with fresh eyes.

Alexis de Tocqueville was born during the Napoleonic era to a landed family that had been supporters of the deposed Bourbon monarchy. He came of age, however, during the restored monarchy of Louis XVIII and valued that regime's combination of constitutional government and restricted political participation.

Tocqueville and his friend Gustave de Beaumont visited the United States in the 1830s, during the height of the Jacksonian era, with the nominal intention of studying the U.S. prison system for the French government. Although they produced a volume on this subject—*The Penitentiary System in the United States*—Tocquevilles's real project became that of explaining democratic government and society to European readers. *Democracy in America* was published in two volumes in 1835 and 1840.

Tocqueville was an aristocrat by temperament and feared that democracy inherently led to tyranny of the majority and to an overbearing, stifling conformity. "Intellectually I have an inclination for democratic institutions," he wrote in his diary, "but I am an aristocrat by instinct—that is to say I despise and fear the mass." Thus, Tocqueville was a critic of democracy and a critic of certain democratic characteristics that he found in America.

Nevertheless, Tocqueville was an admiring critic who felt that Americans had avoided democracy's worst pitfalls. He praised the spirit of voluntary association and local government that he found here and felt that these institutions had helped moderate some of the inherent difficulties of an egalitarian democratic system. It was these lessons that Tocqueville hoped to bring to European readers, whom he felt inevitably would be faced with democratic governments of their own in the near future.

All of the following selections are taken from *Democracy in America.*

Alexis de Tocqueville

Democracy in America (1835, 1840)

AUTHOR'S INTRODUCTION*

No novelty in the United States struck me more vividly during my stay there than the equality of conditions. It was easy to see the immense influence of this basic fact on the whole course of society. It gives a particular turn to public opinion and a particular twist to the laws, new maxims to those who govern and particular habits to the governed.

I soon realized that the influence of this fact extends far beyond political mores and laws, exercising dominion over civil society as much as over the government; it creates opinions, gives birth to feelings, suggests customs, and modifies whatever it does not create.

So the more I studied American society, the more clearly I saw equality of conditions as the creative element from which each particular fact derived, and all my observations constantly returned to this nodal point.

Later, when I came to consider our own

* Volume 1.

SOURCE: J. P. Mayer, ed., *Democracy in America*, trans. George Lawrence (Garden City, N.Y.: Anchor Books, 1969).

side of the Atlantic, I thought I could detect something analogous to what I had noticed in the New World. I saw an equality of conditions which, though it had not reached the extreme limits found in the United States, was daily drawing closer thereto; and that same democracy which prevailed over the societies of America seemed to me to be advancing rapidly toward power in Europe.

It was at that moment that I conceived the idea of this book.

A great democratic revolution is taking place in our midst; everybody sees it, but by no means everybody judges it in the same way. Some think it a new thing and, supposing it an accident, hope that they can still check it; others think it irresistible, because it seems to them the most continuous, ancient, and permanent tendency known to history.

I should like for a moment to consider the state of France seven hundred years ago; at that time it was divided up between a few families who owned the land and ruled the inhabitants. At that time the right to give orders descended, like real property, from generation to generation; the only means by which men controlled each other was force;

there was only one source of power, namely, landed property.

But then the political power of the clergy began to take shape and soon to extend. The ranks of the clergy were open to all, poor or rich, commoner or noble; through the church, equality began to insinuate itself into the heart of government, and a man who would have vegetated as a serf in eternal servitude could, as a priest, take his place among the nobles and often take precedence over kings.

As society became more stable and civilized, men's relations with one another became more numerous and complicated. Hence the need for civil laws was vividly felt, and the lawyers soon left their obscure tribunals and dusty chambers to appear at the king's court side by side with feudal barons dressed in chain mail and ermine.

While kings were ruining themselves in great enterprises and nobles wearing each other out in private wars, the commoners were growing rich by trade. The power of money began to be felt in affairs of state. Trade became a new way of gaining power and financiers became a political force, despised but flattered.

Gradually enlightenment spread, and a taste for literature and the arts awoke. The mind became an element in success; knowledge became a tool of government and intellect a social force; educated men played a part in affairs of state.

In proportion as new roads to power were found, the value of birth decreased. In the eleventh century, nobility was something of inestimable worth; in the thirteenth it could be bought; the first ennoblement took place in 1270, and equality was finally introduced into the government through the aristocracy itself.

During the last seven hundred years it has sometimes happened that, to combat the royal authority or dislodge rivals from power, nobles have given the people some political weight.

Even more often we find kings giving the lower classes in the state a share in government in order to humble the aristocracy.

In France the kings proved the most active and consistent of levelers. When they were strong and ambitious they tried to raise the people to the level of the nobles, and when they were weak and diffident they allowed the people to push past them. The former monarchs helped democracy by their talents, the latter by their vices. Louis XI and Louis XIV were at pains to level everyone below the throne, and finally Louis XV with all his court descended into the dust.

As soon as citizens began to hold land otherwise than by feudal tenure, and the newly discovered possibilities of personal property could also lead to influence and power, every invention in the arts and every improvement in trade and industry created fresh elements tending toward equality among men. Henceforward every new invention, every new need occasioned thereby, and every new desire craving satisfaction were steps towards a general leveling. The taste for luxury, the love of war, the dominion of fashion, all the most superficial and profound passions of the human heart, seemed to work together to impoverish the rich and enrich the poor.

Once the work of the mind had become a source of power and wealth, every addition to knowledge, every fresh discovery, and every new idea became a germ of power within reach of the people. Poetry, eloquence, memory, the graces of the mind, the fires of the imagination and profundity of thought, all things scattered broadcast by heaven, were a profit to democracy, and even when it was the adversaries of democracy who possessed these things, they still served its cause by throwing into relief the natural greatness of man. Thus its conquests spread along with those of civilization and enlightenment, and literature was an arsenal from which all, including the weak and poor, daily chose their weapons.

Running through the pages of our history,

there is hardly an important event in the last seven hundred years which has not turned out to be advantageous for equality.

The Crusades and the English wars decimated the nobles and divided up their lands. Municipal institutions introduced democratic liberty into the heart of the feudal monarchy; the invention of firearms made villein and noble equal on the field of battle; printing offered equal resources to their minds; the post brought enlightenment to hovel and palace alike; Protestantism maintained that all men are equally able to find the path to heaven. America, once discovered, opened a thousand new roads to fortune and gave any obscure adventurer the chance of wealth and power.

If, beginning at the eleventh century, one takes stock of what was happening in France at fifty-year intervals, one finds each time that a double revolution has taken place in the state of society. The noble has gone down in the social scale, and the commoner gone up; as the one falls, the other rises. Each half century brings them closer, and soon they will touch.

And that is not something peculiar to France. Wherever one looks one finds the same revolution taking place throughout the Christian world.

Everywhere the diverse happenings in the lives of peoples have turned to democracy's profit; all men's efforts have aided it, both those who intended this and those who had no such intention, those who fought for democracy and those who were the declared enemies thereof; all have been driven pell-mell along the same road, and all have worked together, some against their will and some unconsciously, blind instruments in the hands of God.

Therefore the gradual progress of equality is something fated. The main features of this progress are the following: it is universal and permanent, it is daily passing beyond human control, and every event and every man helps it along. Is it wise to suppose that a movement which has been so long in train could be halted by one generation? Does anyone imagine that democracy, which has destroyed the feudal system and vanquished kings, will fall back before the middle classes and the rich? Will it stop now, when it has grown so strong and its adversaries so weak?

Whither, then, are we going? No one can tell, for already terms of comparison are lacking; in Christian lands now conditions are nearer equality than they have ever been before at any time or in any place; hence the magnitude of present achievement makes it impossible to forecast what may still be done.

This whole book has been written under the impulse of a kind of religious dread inspired by contemplation of this irresistible revolution advancing century by century over every obstacle and even now going forward amid the ruins it has itself created.

God does not Himself need to speak for us to find sure signs of His will; it is enough to observe the customary progress of nature and the continuous tendency of events; I know, without special revelation, that the stars follow orbits in space traced by His finger.

If patient observation and sincere mediation have led men of the present day to recognize that both the past and the future of their history consist in the gradual and measured advance of equality, that discovery in itself gives this progress that sacred character of the will of the Sovereign Master. In that case effort to halt democracy appears as a fight against God Himself, and nations have no alternative but to acquiesce in the social state imposed by Providence.

To me the Christian nations of our day present an alarming spectacle; the movement which carries them along is already too strong to be halted, but it is not yet so swift that we must despair of directing it; our fate is in our hands, but soon it may pass beyond control.

The first duty imposed on those who now

direct society is to educate democracy; to put, if possible, new life into its beliefs; to purify its mores; to control its actions; gradually to substitute understanding of statecraft for present inexperience and knowledge of its true interests for blind instincts; to adapt government to the needs of time and place; and to modify it as men and circumstances require.

A new political science is needed for a world itself quite new.

But it is just that to which we give least attention. Carried away by a rapid current, we obstinately keep our eyes fixed on the ruins still in sight on the bank, while the stream whirls us backward—facing toward the abyss.

This great social revolution has made more rapid progress with us than with any other nation of Europe, but the progress has always been haphazard.

The leaders of the state have never thought of making any preparation by anticipation for it. The progress has been against their will or without their knowledge. The most powerful, intelligent, and moral classes of the nation have never sought to gain control of it in order to direct it. Hence democracy has been left to its wild instincts; it has grown up like those children deprived of parental care who school themselves in our town streets and know nothing of society but its vices and wretchedness. Men would seem still unaware of its existence, when suddenly it has seized power. Then all submit like slaves to its least desires; it is worshiped as the idol of strength; thereafter, when it has been weakened by its own excesses, the lawgivers conceive the imprudent project of abolishing it instead of trying to educate and correct it, and without any wish to teach it how to rule, they only strive to drive it out of the government.

As a result the democratic revolution has taken place in the body of society without those changes in laws, ideas, customs, and mores which were needed to make that revolution profitable. Hence we have our democracy without those elements which might have mitigated its vices and brought out its natural good points. While we can already see the ills it entails, we are as yet unaware of the benefits it might bring.

When royal power supported by aristocracies governed the nations of Europe in peace, society, despite all its wretchedness, enjoyed several types of happiness which are difficult to appreciate or conceive today.

The power of some subjects raised insuperable obstacles to the tyranny of the prince. The kings, feeling that in the eyes of the crowd they were clothed in almost divine majesty, derived, from the very extent of the respect they inspired, a motive for not abusing their power.

The nobles, placed so high above the people, could take the calm and benevolent interest in their welfare which a shepherd takes in his flock. Without regarding the poor as equals, they took thought for their fate as a trust confided to them by Providence.

Having never conceived the possibility of a social state other than the one they knew, and never expecting to become equal to their leaders, the people accepted benefits from their hands and did not question their rights. They loved them when they were just and merciful and felt neither repugnance nor degradation in submitting to their severities, which seemed inevitable ills sent by God. Furthermore, custom and mores had set some limits to tyranny and established a sort of law in the very midst of force.

Because it never entered the noble's head that anyone wanted to snatch away privileges which he regarded as legitimate, and since the serf considered his inferiority as an effect of the immutable order of nature, one can see that a sort of goodwill could be established between these two classes so differently favored by fortune. At that time one found inequality and wretchedness in society, but men's souls were not degraded thereby.

It is not exercise of power or habits of obedience which deprave men, but the exercise of a power which they consider illegitimate and obedience to a power which they think usurped and oppressive.

On the one side were wealth, strength, and leisure combined with farfetched luxuries, refinements of taste, the pleasures of the mind, and the cultivation of the arts; on the other, work, coarseness, and ignorance.

But among this coarse and ignorant crowd lively passions, generous feelings, deep beliefs, and untamed virtues were found.

The body social thus ordered could lay claim to stability, strength, and above all, glory.

But distinctions of rank began to get confused, and the barriers separating men to get lower. Great estates were broken up, power shared, education spread, and intellectual capacities became more equal. The social state became democratic, and the sway of democracy was finally peacefully established in institutions and in mores.

At that stage one can imagine a society in which all men, regarding the law as their common work, would love it and submit to it without difficulty; the authority of the government would be respected as necessary, not as sacred; the love felt toward the head of the state would be not a passion but a calm and rational feeling. Each man having some rights and being sure of the enjoyment of those rights, there would be established between all classes a manly confidence and a sort of reciprocal courtesy, as far removed from pride as from servility.

Understanding its own interests, the people would appreciate that in order to enjoy the benefits of society one must shoulder its obligations. Free association of the citizens could then take the place of the individual authority of the nobles, and the state would be protected both from tyranny and from license.

I appreciate that in a democracy so constituted society would not be at all immobile; but the movements inside the body social could be orderly and progressive; one might find less glory there than in an aristocracy, but there would be less wretchedness; pleasures would be less extreme, but well-being more general; the heights of knowledge might not be scaled, but ignorance would be less common; feelings would be less passionate, and manners gentler; there would be more vices and fewer crimes.

Without enthusiasm or the zeal of belief, education and experience would sometimes induce the citizens to make great sacrifices; each man being equally weak would feel a like need for the help of his companions, and knowing that he would not get their support without supplying his, he would easily appreciate that for him private interest was mixed up with public interest.

The nation as a body would be less brilliant, less glorious, and perhaps less strong, but the majority of the citizens would enjoy a more prosperous lot, and the people would be pacific not from despair of anything better but from knowing itself to be well-off.

Though all would not be good and useful in such a system of things, society would at least have appropriated all that it could of the good and useful; and men, by giving up forever the social advantages offered by aristocracy, would have taken from democracy all the good things that it can provide.

But in abandoning our ancestors' social state and throwing their institutions, ideas, and mores pell-mell behind us, what have we put in their place?

The prestige of the royal power has vanished but has not been replaced by the majesty of the law; nowadays the people despise authority but fear it, and more is dragged from them by fear than was formerly granted through respect and love.

I notice that we have destroyed those individual powers which were able singlehanded to cope with tyranny, but I see that it is the government alone which has inherited all the prerogatives snatched from families, corporations, and individuals; so the sometimes oppressive but often conservative strength of a small number of citizens has been succeeded by the weakness of all.

The breakup of fortunes has diminished the distance between rich and poor, but while bringing them closer, it seems to have provided them with new reasons for hating each other, so that with mutual fear and envy they rebuff each other's claims to power. Neither has any conception of rights, and for both force is the only argument in the present or guarantee for the future.

The poor have kept most of the prejudices of their fathers without their beliefs, their ignorance without their virtues; they accept the doctrine of self-interest as motive for action without understanding that doctrine; and their egotism is now as unenlightened as their devotion was formerly.

Society is tranquil, but the reason for that is not that it knows its strength and its good fortune, but rather that it thinks itself weak and feeble; it fears that a single effort may cost its life; each man feels what is wrong, but none has the courage or energy needed to seek something better; men have desires, regrets, sorrows, and joys which produce no visible or durable result, like old men's passions ending in impotence.

Thus we have abandoned whatever good things the old order of society could provide but have not profited from what our present state can offer; we have destroyed an aristocratic society, and settling down complacently among the ruins of the old building, we seem to want to stay there like that forever.

What is now taking place in the world of the mind is just as deplorable.

French democracy, sometimes hindered in its progress and at others left uncontrolled to its disorderly passions, has overthrown everything it found in its path, shaking all that it did not destroy. It has not slowly gained control of society in order peacefully to establish its sway; on the contrary, its progress has ever been amid the disorders and agitations of conflict. In the heat of the struggle each partisan is driven beyond the natural limits of his own views by the views and the excesses of his adversaries, loses sight of the very aim he was pursuing, and uses language which ill corresponds to his real feelings and to his secret instincts.

Hence arises that strange confusion which we are forced to witness.

I search my memory in vain, and find nothing sadder or more pitiable than that which happens before our eyes; it would seem that we have nowadays broken the natural link between opinions and tastes, acts and beliefs; that harmony which has been observed throughout history between the feelings and the ideas of men seems to have been destroyed, and one might suppose that all the laws of moral analogy had been abolished.

There are still zealous Christians among us who draw spiritual nourishment from the truths of the other life and who no doubt will readily espouse the cause of human liberty as the source of all moral greatness. Christianity, which has declared all men equal in the sight of God, cannot hesitate to acknowledge all citizens equal before the law. But by a strange concatenation of events, religion for the moment has become entangled with those institutions which democracy overthrows, and so it is often brought to rebuff the equality which it loves and to abuse freedom as its adversary, whereas by taking it by the hand it could sanctify its striving.

Alongside these religious men I find others whose eyes are turned more to the earth than to heaven; partisans of freedom, not only because they see in it the origin of the most noble virtues, but even more because they think it the source of the greatest benefits, they sincerely wish to assure its sway and allow men to taste its blessings. I think these latter should hasten to call religion to their aid, for they must know that one cannot establish the reign of liberty without that of mores, and mores cannot be firmly founded without beliefs. But they have seen religion in the ranks of their adversaries, and that is enough for them; some of them openly attack it, and the others do not dare to defend it.

In past ages we have seen low, venal minds advocating slavery, while independent, generous hearts struggled hopelessly to defend human freedom. But now one often meets naturally proud and noble men whose opinions are in direct opposition to their tastes and who vaunt that servility and baseness which they themselves have never known. Others, on the contrary, speak of freedom as if they could feel its great and sacred quality and noisily claim for humanity rights which they themselves have always scorned.

I also see gentle and virtuous men whose pure mores, quiet habits, opulence, and talents fit them to be leaders of those who dwell around them. Full of sincere patriotism, they would make great sacrifices for their country; nonetheless they are often adversaries of civilization; they confound its abuses with its benefits; and in their minds the idea of evil is indissolubly linked with that of novelty.

Besides these, there are others whose object is to make men materialists, to find out what is useful without concern for justice, to have science quite without belief and prosperity without virtue. Such men are called champions of modern civilization, and they insolently put themselves at its head, usurping a place which has been abandoned to them, though they are utterly unworthy of it.

Where are we, then?

Men of religion fight against freedom, and lovers of liberty attack religions; noble and generous spirits praise slavery, while low, servile minds preach independence; honest and enlightened citizens are the enemies of all progress, while men without patriotism or morals make themselves the apostles of civilization and enlightenment!

Have all ages been like ours? And have men always dwelt in a world in which nothing is connected? Where virtue is without genius, and genius without honor? Where love of order is confused with a tyrant's tastes, and the sacred cult of freedom is taken as scorn of law? Where conscience sheds but doubtful light on human actions? Where nothing any longer seems either forbidden or permitted, honest or dishonorable, true or false?

Am I to believe that the Creator made man in order to let him struggle endlessly through the intellectual squalor now surrounding us? I cannot believe that; God intends a calmer and more stable future for the peoples of Europe; I do not know His designs but shall not give up believing therein because I cannot fathom them, and should prefer to doubt my own understanding rather than His justice.

There is one country in the world in which this great social revolution seems almost to have reached its natural limits; it took place in a simple, easy fashion, or rather one might say that that country sees the results of the democratic revolution taking place among us, without experiencing the revolution itself.

The emigrants who colonized America at the beginning of the seventeenth century in some way separated the principle of democracy from all those other principles against which they contended when living in the heart of the old European societies, and transplanted that principle only on the shores of the New World. It could there grow in freedom, and, progressing in conformity with mores, develop peacefully within the law.

It seems to me beyond doubt that sooner or later we, like the Americans, will attain almost complete equality of conditions. But I certainly do not draw from that the conclusion that we are necessarily destined one day to derive the same political consequences as the Americans from the similar social state. I am very far from believing that they have found the only form possible for democratic government; it is enough that the creative source of laws and mores is the same in the two countries, for each of us to have a profound interest in knowing what the other is doing.

So I did not study America just to satisfy curiosity, however legitimate; I sought there lessons from which we might profit. Anyone who supposes that I intend to write a panegyric is strangely mistaken; any who read this book will see that that was not my intention at all; nor have I aimed to advocate such a form of government in general, for I am one of those who think that there is hardly ever absolute right in any laws; I have not even claimed to judge whether the progress of the social revolution, which I consider irresistible, is profitable or prejudicial for mankind. I accept that revolution as an accomplished fact, or a fact that soon will be accomplished, and I selected of all the peoples experiencing it that nation in which it has come to the fullest and most peaceful completion, in order to see its natural consequences clearly, and if possible, to turn it to the profit of mankind. I admit that I saw in America more than America; it was the shape of democracy itself which I sought, its inclinations, character, prejudices, and passions; I wanted to understand it so as at least to know what we have to fear or hope therefrom. . . .

Therefore, in the first part of this book I have endeavored to show the natural turn given to the laws by democracy when left in America to its own inclinations with hardly any restraint on its instincts, and to show its stamp on the government and its influence on affairs in general. I wanted to know what blessings and what ills it brings forth. I have inquired into the precautions taken by the Americans to direct it, and noticed those others which they have neglected, and I have aimed to point out the factors which enable it to govern society.

I had intended in a second part to describe the influence in America of equality of conditions and government by democracy upon civil society, customs, ideas, and mores, but my urge to carry out this plan has cooled off. Before I could finish this self-imposed task, it would have become almost useless. Another author is soon to portray the main characteristics of the American people and, casting a thin veil over the seriousness of his purpose, give to truth charms I could not rival.[1]

I do not know if I have succeeded in making what I saw in America intelligible, but I am sure that I sincerely wished to do so and that I never, unless unconsciously, fitted the facts to opinions instead of subjecting opinions to the facts.

Wherever there were documents to establish facts, I have been at pains to refer to the original texts or the most authentic and reputable works.[2] I have cited my authorities in the notes, so those who wish can check them. Where opinions, political customs, and mores were concerned, I have tried to consult the best-informed people. In important or doubtful cases I was not content with the testimony of one witness, but based my opinions on that of several.

The reader must necessarily take my word for that. I could often have supported my

_____

[1] At the time when the first edition of this work was being published, M. Gustave de Beaumont, my traveling companion in America, was still working on his book *Marie, or Slavery in the United States,* which has since been published. M. de Beaumont's main object was to draw emphatic attention to the condition of the Negroes in Anglo-American society. His book threw new and vivid light on the question of slavery, a vital question for the united republics. I may be mistaken, but I think M. de Beaumont's book, after arousing the vivid interest of those who sought emotions and descriptions therein, should have a more solid and permanent success with those readers who seek, above all, true appreciations and profound truths.

[2] I shall always remember with gratitude the kindness with which I was furnished with legislative and administrative documents. Among the American officials who aided my researchers I would especially mention. Mr. Edward Livingston, at that time Secretary of State and subsequently Minister Plenipotentiary in Paris. During my stay in Washington he kindly provided me with most of the documents I possess concerning the federal government. Mr. Livingston is one of those rare men whose writings inspire affection, so that we admire and respect them even before we know them, and we are glad to owe them a debt of gratitude.

views with the authority of names he knows, or which at least are worth knowing, but I have abstained from doing so. A stranger often hears important truths at his host's fireside, truths which he might not divulge to his friends; it is a relief to break a constrained silence with a stranger whose short stay guarantees his discretion. I noted down all such confidences as soon as I heard them, but they will never leave my notebooks; I would rather let my comments suffer than add my name to the list of those travelers who repay generous hospitality with worries and embarrassments.

I realize that despite the trouble taken, nothing will be easier than to criticize this book, if anyone thinks of doing so.

Those who look closely into the whole work will, I think, find one pregnant thought which binds all its parts together. But the diversity of subjects treated is very great, and whoever chooses can easily cite an isolated fact to contradict the facts I have assembled, or an isolated opinion against my opinions. I would therefore ask for my book to be read in the spirit in which it was written and would wish it to be judged by the general impression it leaves, just as I have formed my own judgments not for any one particular reason but in conformity with a mass of evidence.

It must not be forgotten that an author who wishes to be understood is bound to derive all the theoretical consequences from each of his ideas and must go to the verge of the false and impracticable, for while it is sometimes necessary to brush rules of logic aside in action, one cannot do so in the same way in conversation, and a man finds it almost as difficult to be inconsequent in speech as he generally finds it to be consistent in action.

To conclude, I will myself point out what many readers will consider the worst defect of this work. This book is not precisely suited to anybody's taste; in writing it I did not intend to serve or to combat any party; I have tried to see not differently but further than any party; while they are busy with tomorrow, I have wished to consider the whole future.

CHAPTER 4: POLITICAL ASSOCIATION IN THE UNITED STATES

Everyday use that the Anglo-Americans make of the right of association. Three types of political associations. How the Americans apply the representative system to associations. Dangers resulting therefrom to the state. Great convention of 1831 concerned with tariffs. Legislative character of that convention. Why the unlimited exercise of the right of association is not as dangerous in the United States as elsewhere. Why it may be considered necessary. Utility of associations in democratic nations.

Better use has been made of association and this powerful instrument of action has been applied to more varied aims in America than anywhere else in the world.

Apart from permanent associations such as townships, cities, and counties created by law, there are a quantity of others whose existence and growth are solely due to the initiative of individuals.

The inhabitant of the United States learns from birth that he must rely on himself to combat the ills and trials of life; he is restless and defiant in his outlook toward the authority of society and appeals to its power only when he cannot do without it. The beginnings of this attitude first appear at school, where the children, even in their games, submit to rules settled by themselves and punish offenses which they have defined themselves. The same attitude turns up again in all the affairs of social life. If some obstacle blocks the public road halting the circulation of traffic, the neighbors at once form a deliberative body; this improvised assembly produces an executive authority which remedies the trouble before anyone has thought of the possibility of some previously constituted authority beyond that of those concerned. Where enjoyment is concerned, people associate to make festivities grander and more orderly. Finally, associations are formed to combat exclusively moral troubles: intemperance is fought in common. Public security, trade and industry, and morals and religion all provide the aims for associations in the United States. There is no end which the human will despairs of attaining by the free action of the collective power of individuals.

Later I shall have occasion to speak of the effects of association on civil life. For the moment I must stick to the world of politics.

The right of association being recognized, citizens can use it in different ways. An association simply consists in the public and formal support of specific doctrines by a certain number of individuals who have undertaken to cooperate in a stated way in order to make these doctrines prevail. Thus the right of association can almost be identified with freedom to write, but already associations are more powerful than the press. When some view is represented by an association, it must take clearer and more precise shape. It counts its supporters and involves them in its cause; these supporters get to know one another, and numbers increase zeal. An association unites the energies of divergent minds and vigorously directs them toward a clearly indicated goal.

Freedom of assembly marks the second stage in the use made of the right of association. When a political association is allowed to form centers of action at certain important places in the country, its activity becomes greater and its influence more widespread. There men meet, active measures are planned, and opinions are expressed with that strength and warmth which the written word can never attain.

But the final stage is the use of association in the sphere of politics. The supporters of an agreed view may meet in electoral colleges and appoint mandatories to represent them in a central assembly. That is, properly speaking, the application of the representative system to one party.

So, in the first of these cases, men sharing one opinion are held together by a purely intellectual tie; in the second case, they meet together in small assemblies representing only a fraction of the party; finally, in the third case, they form something like a separate nation within the nation and a government within the government. Their mandatories, like those of the majority, represent by themselves all the collective power of their supporters, and, like them in this too, they appear as national representatives with all the moral prestige derived therefrom. It is true that, unlike the others, they have no right to make laws, but they do have the power to attack existing laws and to formulate, by anticipation, laws which should take the place of the present ones.

Imagine some people not perfectly accustomed to the use of freedom, or one in which profound political passions are seething. Suppose that, besides the majority that makes the laws, there is a minority which only deliberates and which gets laws ready for adoption; I cannot help but think that then public order would be exposed to great risks.

There is certainly a great gap between proving that one law is in itself better than another and establishing that it ought to be substituted for it. But where trained minds may still see a wide gap, the hasty imagination of the crowd may be unaware of this. Moreover, there are times when the nation is divided into two almost equal parties, each claiming to represent the majority. If, besides the ruling power, another power is established with almost equal moral authority, can one suppose that in the long run it will just talk and not act?

Will it always stop short in front of the metaphysical consideration that the object of associations is to direct opinions and not to constrain them, and to give advice about the law but not to make it?

The more I observe the main effects of a free press, the more convinced am I that, in the modern world, freedom of the press is the principal and, so to say, the constitutive element in freedom. A nation bent on remaining free is therefore right to insist, at whatever cost, on respect for this freedom. But *unlimited* freedom of association must not be entirely identified with freedom to write. The former is both less necessary and more dangerous than the latter. A nation may set limits there without ceasing to be its own master; indeed, in order to remain its own master, it is sometimes necessary to do so.

In America there is no limit to freedom of association for political ends.

One example will show better than anything I could say just how far it is tolerated.

One remembers how excited the Americans were by the free-trade-tariff controversy. Not opinions only, but very powerful material interests stood to gain or lose by a tariff. The North thought that some of its prosperity was due thereto, while the South blamed it for almost all its woes. One may say that over a long period the tariff question gave rise to the only political passions disturbing the Union.

In 1831, when the quarrel was most envenomed, an obscure citizen of Massachusetts thought of suggesting through the newspapers that all opponents of the tariff should send deputies to Philadelphia to concert together measures to make trade free. Thanks to the invention of printing, this suggestion passed in but a few days from Maine to New Orleans. The opponents of the tariff took it up ardently. They assembled from all sides and appointed deputies. Most of the latter were known men, and some of them had risen to celebrity. South Carolina, which was later to take up arms in this cause, sent sixty-three people as its delegates. On October 1, 1831, the assembly, which in American fashion styled itself a convention, was constituted at Philadelphia; it counted more than two hundred members. The discussions were public, and from the very first day it took on an altogether legislative character; discussion covered the extent of the powers of Congress, theories of free trade, and finally the various provisions of the tariff. After ten days the assembly broke up, having issued an address to the American people. In that address it declared first that Congress had not the right to impose a tariff and that the existing tariff was unconstitutional, and second that it was against the interest of any people, in particular the American people, that trade should not be free.

It must be admitted that unlimited freedom of association in the political sphere has not yet produced in America the fatal results that one might anticipate from it elsewhere. The right of association is of English origin and always existed in America. Use of this right is now an accepted part of customs and of mores.

In our own day freedom of association has become a necessary guarantee against the tyranny of the majority. In the United States, once a party has become predominant, all public power passes into its hands; its close supporters occupy all offices and have control of all organized forces. The most distinguished men of the opposite party, unable to cross the barrier keeping them from power, must be able to establish themselves outside it; the minority must use the whole of its moral authority to oppose the physical power oppressing it. Thus the one danger has to be balanced against a more formidable one.

The omnipotence of the majority seems to me such a danger to the American republics that the dangerous expedient used to curb it is actually something good.

Here I would repeat something which I have put in other words when speaking of municipal freedom: no countries need associations more—to prevent either despotism of parties or the arbitrary rule of a prince—than those with a democratic social state. In aristocratic nations secondary bodies form natural associations which hold abuses of power in check. In countries where such associations do not exist, if private people did not artificially and temporarily create something like them, I see no other dike to hold back tyranny of whatever sort, and a great nation might with impunity be oppressed by some tiny faction or by a single man.

The meeting of a great political convention (for conventions are of all kinds), though it may often be a necessary measure, is always, even in America, a serious event and one that good patriots cannot envisage without alarm.

That came out clearly during the convention of 1831, when all the men of distinction taking part therein tried to moderate its language and limit its objective. Probably the convention of 1831 did greatly influence the attitude of the malcontents and prepared them for the open revolt of 1832 against the commercial laws of the Union.

One must not shut one's eyes to the fact that unlimited freedom of association for political ends is, of all forms of liberty, the last that a nation can sustain. While it may not actually lead it into anarchy, it does constantly bring it to the verge thereof. But this form of freedom, howsoever dangerous, does provide guarantees in one direction; in countries where associations are free, secret societies are unknown. There are factions in America, but no conspirators.

CHAPTER 5: GOVERNMENT BY DEMOCRACY IN AMERICA

I know that I am now treading on live cinders. Every word in this chapter must in some respect offend the various parties dividing my country. Nevertheless, I shall say all I think.

In Europe it is hard for us to judge the true character and permanent instincts of democracy, for in Europe two contrary principles are contending, and one cannot precisely know what is due to the principles themselves and what to the passions engendered by the fight.

That is not the case in America. There the people prevail without impediment; there are neither dangers to fear nor injuries to revenge.

Therefore in America democracy follows its own inclinations. Its features are natural and its movements free. It is there that it must be judged. And such a study should be interesting and profitable for nobody more than ourselves, for we are being daily carried along by an irresistible movement, walking like blind men toward—what? Despotism perhaps, perhaps a republic, but certainly toward a democratic social state.

Universal Suffrage

I have previously mentioned that all the states of the Union have adopted universal suffrage; consequently it functions among communities at very different stages on the social ladder. I have had the chance to see its effects in diverse places and among men who by race, language, religion, or mores are almost total strangers one to another, in Louisiana as well as New England and in Georgia as well as Canada. I noted that in America universal suffrage was far from producing all the blessings or all the ills expected from it in Europe and that, generally speaking, its effects are other than is supposed.

The People's Choice and the Instincts of American Democracy in Such Choices

In the United States the most outstanding men are seldom called on to direct public affairs. Reasons therefor. The envy of the lower classes toward their superiors in France is not a specifically French feeling, but a democratic one. Why, in America, men of distinction often deliberately avoid a political career.

In Europe many people either believe without saying or say without believing that one of the great advantages of universal suffrage is to summon men worthy of public confidence to the direction of affairs. The people, men say, do not know how themselves to rule but always sincerely desire the good of the state, and their instinct unfailingly tells them who are filled with the same desire and most capable of wielding power.

For my part, I am bound to say that what I saw in America gives me no cause to think that so. When I arrived in the United States I discovered with astonishment that good qualities were common among the governed but rare among the rulers. In our day it is a constant fact that the most outstanding Americans are seldom summoned to public office, and it must be recognized that this tendency has increased as democracy has gone beyond its previous limits. It is clear that during the last fifty years the race of American statesmen has strangely shrunk.

One can point to several reasons for this phenomenon.

Whatever one does, it is impossible to raise the standard of enlightenment in a nation above a certain level. Whatever facilities are made available for acquiring information and whatever improvements in teaching technique make knowledge available cheaply, men will never educate and develop their intelligence without devoting time to the matter.

Therefore the greater or less ease with which people can live without working sets inevitable limits to their intellectual progress. That limit is further off in some countries and closer in others, but for it not to exist at all, the people would have to have no more trouble with the material cares of life and so would no longer be "the people." It is therefore as difficult to conceive a society in which all men are very enlightened as one in which all are rich; these two difficulties are correlative. I freely admit that the mass of the citizens very sincerely desires the country's good; I would go further and say that the lower classes of society generally confuse their personal interests with this desire less than the upper classes do; but what they always lack to some extent is skill to judge the means to attain this sincerely desired end. Consider the manifold considerations and the prolonged study involved in forming an exact notion of the character of a single man. There, where the greatest geniuses go astray, are the masses to succeed? The people never can find time or means to devote themselves to such work. They are bound always to make hasty judgments and to seize on the most prominent characteristics. That is why charlatans of every sort so well understand the secret of pleasing them, whereas for the most part their real friends fail in this.

Furthermore, it is not always ability to choose men of merit which democracy lacks; sometimes it has neither desire nor taste to do so.

One must not blind oneself to the fact that democratic institutions most successfully develop sentiments of envy in the human heart. This is not because they provide the means for everybody to rise to the level of everybody else but because these means are constantly proving inadequate in the hands of those using them. Democratic institutions awaken and flatter the passion for equality without ever being able to satisfy it entirely. This complete equality is always slipping through the people's fingers at the moment when they think to grasp it, fleeing, as Pascal says, in an eternal flight; the people grow heated in search of this blessing, all the more precious because it is near enough to be seen but too far off to be tasted. They are excited by the chance and irritated by the uncertainty of success; the excitement is followed by weariness and then by bitterness. In that state anything which in any way transcends the people seems an obstacle to their desires, and they are tired by the sight of any superiority, however legitimate.

Many people suppose that this secret instinct leading the lower classes to keep their superiors as far as possible from the direction of affairs is found only in France; that is a mistake; the instinct of which I speak is not French, but democratic; political circumstances may give it a particularly bitter taste, but they do not create it.

In the United States the people have no hatred toward the higher classes of society; but they have little goodwill toward them and are careful to keep them from power; they are not afraid of great talents but have little taste for them. In general one notices that anyone who has risen without the people's support has difficulty in winning their favor.

While the natural instincts of democracy lead the people to keep men of distinction from power, an equally strong instinct diverts the latter from a political career, in which it would be difficult to remain completely themselves or to make any progress without cheapening themselves. Chancellor Kent gives very ingenuous expression to this feeling. For this famous author, after singing the praises of the part of the Constitution which gives the executive the right to appoint the judges, adds: "The fittest men would probably have too much reservedness of manners and severity of morals to secure an election resting on universal suffrage." (Kent's *Commentaries*, Vol. I, p. 273.) That was printed, and not contradicted, in America in the year 1830.

I take it as proved that those who consider universal suffrage as a guarantee of the excellence of the resulting choice suffer under a complete delusion. Universal suffrage has other advantages, but not that one. . . .

* * * * *

PART II, CHAPTER 7

. . . Tyranny of the Majority

How the principle of the sovereignty of the people should be understood. Impossibility of conceiving a mixed government. Sovereign power must be placed somewhere. Precautions which one should take to moderate its action. These precautions have not been taken in the United States. Result thereof.

I regard it as an impious and detestable maxim that in matters of government the majority of a people has the right to do everything, and nevertheless I place the origin of all powers in the will of the majority. Am I in contradiction with myself?

There is one law which has been made, or at least adopted, not by the majority of this or that people, but by the majority of all men. That law is justice.

Justice therefore forms the boundary to each people's right.

A nation is like a jury entrusted to represent universal society and to apply the justice which is its law. Should the jury representing society have greater power than that very society whose laws it applies?

Consequently, when I refuse to obey an unjust law, I by no means deny the majority's right to give orders; I only appeal from the sovereignty of the people to the sovereignty of the human race.

There are those not afraid to say that in matters which only concern itself a nation cannot go completely beyond the bounds of justice and reason and that there is therefore no need to fear giving total power to the majority representing it. But that is the language of a slave.

What is a majority, in its collective capacity, if not an individual with opinions, and usually with interests, contrary to those of another individual, called the minority? Now, if you admit that a man vested with omnipotence can abuse it against his adversaries, why not admit the same concerning a majority? Have men, by joining together, changed their character? By becoming stronger, have they become more patient of obstacles? For my part, I cannot believe that, and I will never grant to several that power to do everything which I refuse to a single man. . . .

Omnipotence in itself seems a bad and dangerous thing. I think that its exercise is beyond man's strength, whoever he be, and that only God can be omnipotent without danger because His wisdom and justice are always equal to His power. So there is no power on earth in itself so worthy of respect or vested with such a sacred right that I would wish to let it act without control and dominate without obstacles. So when I see the right and capacity to do all given to any authority whatsoever, whether it be called people or king, democracy or aristocracy, and whether the scene of action is a monarchy or a republic, I say: the germ of tyranny is there, and I will go look for other laws under which to live.

My greatest complaint against democratic government as organized in the United States is not, as many Europeans make out, its weakness, but rather its irresistible strength. What I find most repulsive in America is not the extreme freedom reigning there but the shortage of guarantees against tyranny.

When a man or a party suffers an injustice in the United States, to whom can he turn? To public opinion? That is what forms the majority. To the legislative body? It represents the majority and obeys it blindly. To the executive power? It is appointed by the majority and serves as its passive instrument. To the police? They are nothing but the majority under arms. A jury? The jury is the majority vested with the right to pronounce judgment; even the judges in certain states are elected by the majority. So, however iniquitous or unreasonable the measure which hurts you, you must submit.[3]

---

[3] At Baltimore during the War of 1812 there was a striking example of the excesses to which despotism of the majority may lead. At that time the war was very popular at Baltimore. A newspaper which came out in strong opposition to it aroused the indignation of the inhabitants. The people assembled, broke the presses, and attacked the house of the editors. An attempt was made to summon the militia, but it did not answer the appeal. Finally, to save the lives of these wretched men

But suppose you were to have a legislative body so composed that it represented the majority without being necessarily the slave of its passions, an executive power having a strength of its own, and a judicial power independent of the other two authorities; then you would still have a democratic government, but there would be hardly any remaining risk of tyranny.

I am not asserting that at the present time in America there are frequent acts of tyranny. I do say that one can find no guarantee against it there and that the reasons for the government's gentleness must be sought in circumstances and in mores rather than in the laws. . . .

The Power Exercised by the Majority in America over Thought

In the United States, when the majority has irrevocably decided about any question, it is no longer discussed. Why? Moral authority exercised by the majority over thought. Democratic republics have turned despotism into something immaterial.

It is when one comes to look into the use made of thought in the United States that one most clearly sees how far the power of the majority goes beyond all powers known to us in Europe.

Thought is an invisible power and one almost impossible to lay hands on, which makes sport of all tyrannies. In our day the most absolute sovereigns in Europe cannot prevent certain thoughts hostile to their power from silently circulating in their states and even in their own courts. It is not like that in America; while the majority is in doubt, one talks; but when it has irrevocably pronounced, everyone

---

threatened by the fury of the public, they were taken to prison like criminals. This precaution was useless. During the night the people assembled again; the magistrates having failed to bring up the militia, the prison was broken open; one of the journalists was killed on the spot and the others left for dead; the guilty were brought before a jury and acquitted. . . .

is silent, and friends and enemies alike seem to make for its bandwagon. The reason is simple: no monarch is so absolute that he can hold all the forces of society in his hands, and overcome all resistance, as a majority invested with the right to make the laws and to execute them, can do.

Moreover, a king's power is physical only, controlling actions but not influencing desires, whereas the majority is invested with both physical and moral authority, which acts as much upon the will as upon behavior and at the same moment prevents both the act and the desire to do it.

I know no country in which, speaking generally, there is less independence of mind and true freedom of discussion than in America.

There is no religious or political theory which one cannot preach freely in the constitutional states of Europe or which does not penetrate into the others, for there is no country in Europe so subject to a single power that he who wishes to speak the truth cannot find support enough to protect him against the consequences of his independence. If he is unlucky enough to live under an absolute government, he often has the people with him; if he lives in a free country, he may at need find shelter behind the royal authority. In democratic countries the aristocracy may support him, and in other lands the democracy. But in a democracy organized on the model of the United States there is only one authority, one source of strength and of success, and nothing outside it.

In America the majority has enclosed thought within a formidable fence. A writer is free inside that area, but woe to the man who goes beyond it. Not that he stands in fear of an *auto-da-fé*, but he must face all kinds of unpleasantness and everyday persecution. A career in politics is closed to him, for he has offended the only power that holds the keys. He is denied everything, including renown. Before he goes into print, he believes he has supporters; but he feels that he has

them no more once he stands revealed to all, for those who condemn him express their views loudly, while those who think as he does, but without his courage, retreat into silence as if ashamed of having told the truth.

Formerly tyranny used the clumsy weapons of chains and hangmen; nowadays even despotism, though it seemed to have nothing more to learn, has been perfected by civilization.

Princes made violence a physical thing, but our contemporary democratic republics have turned it into something as intellectual as the human will it is intended to constrain. Under the absolute government of a single man, despotism, to reach the soul, clumsily struck at the body, and the soul, escaping from such blows, rose gloriously above it; but in democratic republics that is not at all how tyranny behaves; it leaves the body alone and goes straight for the soul. The master no longer says: "Think like me or you die." He does say: "You are free not to think as I do; you can keep your life and property and all; but from this day you are a stranger among us. You can keep your privileges in the township, but they will be useless to you, for if you solicit your fellow citizens' votes, they will not give them to you, and if you only ask for their esteem, they will make excuses for refusing that. You will remain among men, but you will lose your rights to count as one. When you approach your fellows, they will shun you as an impure being, and even those who believe in your innocence will abandon you too, lest they in turn be shunned. Go in peace. I have given you your life, but it is a life worse than death.". . .

We need seek no other reason for the absence of great writers in America so far; literary genius cannot exist without freedom of the spirit, and there is no freedom of the spirit in America.

In Spain the Inquisition was never able to prevent the circulation of books contrary to the majority religion. The American majority's sway extends further and has rid itself even of the thought of publishing such books. One finds unbelievers in America, but unbelief has, so to say, no organ.

One finds governments striving to protect mores by condemning the authors of licentious books. No one in the United States is condemned for works of that sort, but no one is tempted to write them. Not that all the citizens are chaste in their mores, but those of the majority are regular.

In this, no doubt, power is well used, but my point is the nature of the power in itself. This irresistible power is a continuous fact and its good use only an accident. . . .

CHAPTER 9: THE MAIN CAUSES TENDING TO MAINTAIN A DEMOCRATIC REPUBLIC IN THE UNITED STATES. . .

Accidental or Providential Causes Helping to Maintain a Democratic Republic in the United States

The Union has no neighbors. No great capital. The chances of birth have favored the Americans. America is an empty land. How this circumstance is a great help toward maintaining a democratic republic. How the wildernesses of America are peopled. Avidity with which the Anglo-Americans take possession of the solitudes of the New World. Influence of material prosperity on the political opinions of the Americans.

There are very many circumstances unconnected with human volition which make things easy for a democratic republic in the United States. Some are well known and the others are easily pointed out. I will confine myself to the main ones.

The Americans have no neighbors and consequently no great wars, financial crises, invasions, or conquests to fear; they need neither heavy taxes nor a numerous army nor great generals; they have also hardly anything to

fear from something else which is a greater scourge for democratic republics than all these others put together, namely, military glory.

How can one deny the incredible influence military glory has over a nation's spirit? General Jackson, whom the Americans have for the second time chosen to be at their head, is a man of violent character and middling capacities; nothing in the whole of his career indicated him to have the qualities needed for governing a free people; moreover, a majority of the enlightened classes in the Union have always been against him. Who, then, put him on the President's chair and keeps him there still? Is it all due to the memory of a victory he won twenty years ago under the walls of New Orleans. But that New Orleans victory was a very commonplace feat of arms which could attract prolonged attention only in a country where there are no battles; and the nation who thus let itself be carried away by the prestige of glory is, most assuredly, the coldest, most calculating, the least militaristic, and if one may put it so, the most prosaic in all the world.

America has not yet any great capital[4] whose

---

[4] There is not yet any great capital in America, but there are already very large towns. In 1830 the population of Philadelphia was 160,000 and of New York, 202,000. The lowest classes in these vast cities are a rabble more dangerous even than that of European towns. The very lowest are the freed Negroes condemned by law and opinion to a hereditary state of degradation and wretchedness. Then, there is a crowd of Europeans driven by misfortune or misbehavior to the shores of the New World; such men carry our worst vices to the United States without any of those interests which might counteract their influence. Living in the land without being citizens, they are ready to profit from all the passions that agitate it; thus quite recently there have been serious riots in Philadelphia and New York. Such disorders are unknown in the rest of the country, which does not get excited because the populations of the towns do not at present exercise any authority or influence over the country people.

Nevertheless, I regard the size of some American cities and especially the nature of their inhabitants as a real danger threatening the future of the democratic republics direct or indirect influence is felt through the length and breadth of the land, and I believe that that is one of the primary reasons why republican institutions are maintained in the United States. In towns it is impossible to prevent men assembling, getting excited together, and forming sudden passionate resolves. Towns are like great meeting houses with all the inhabitants as members. In them the people wield immense influence over their magistrates and often carry their desires into execution without intermediaries.

Therefore, to subject the provinces to the capital is to place the destinies of the whole empire not only into the hands of a section of the people, which is unfair, but also into the hands of the people acting on their own, which is very dangerous. Therefore the preponderance of capitals is a great threat to the representative system; it makes modern republics share this defect with those of antiquity, all of which perished because they did not know this system.

I could easily enumerate here a large number of secondary causes favoring the establishment and assuring the maintenance of the democratic republic in the United States. But among this mass of lucky circumstances there are two main features which I am anxious to point out now. . . .

I have said before that I regarded the origin of the Americans, what I have called their point of departure, as the first and most effective of all elements leading to their present prosperity. The chances of birth favored the Americans; their fathers of old brought to the land in which they live that equality both of conditions and of mental endowments from which, as from its natural source, a democratic republic was one day to arise. But that is not

all; with a republican social state they bequeathed to their descendants the habits, ideas, and mores best fitted to make a republic flourish. When I consider all that has resulted from this first fact, I think I can see the whole destiny of America contained in the first Puritan who landed on those shores, as that of the whole human race in the first man.

Among the lucky circumstances that favored the establishment and assured the maintenance of a democratic republic in the United States, the most important was the choice of the land itself in which the Americans live. Their fathers gave them a love of equality and liberty, but it was God who, by handing a limitless continent over to them, gave them the means of long remaining equal and free.

General prosperity favors stability in all governments, but particularly in a democratic one, for it depends on the moods of the greatest number, and especially on the moods of those most exposed to want. When the people rule, they must be happy, if they are not to overthrow the state. With them wretchedness has the same effect as ambition has on kings. Now, the physical causes, unconnected with laws, which can lead to prosperity are more numerous in America than in any other country at any other time in history.

In the United States not legislation alone is democratic, for Nature herself seems to work for the people.

Where, among all that man can remember, can we find anything like what is taking place before our eyes in North America?

The famous societies of antiquity were all founded in the midst of enemy peoples who had to be conquered in order to take their place. Modern nations have found in some parts of South America vast lands inhabited by peoples less enlightened than themselves, but those people had already taken possession of the soil and were cultivating it. The newcomers, to found their states, had to destroy or enslave numerous populations, and civilization blushes at their triumphs.

But North America was only inhabited by

---

of the New World, and I should not hesitate to predict that it is through them that they will perish, unless their government succeeds in creating an armed force which, while remaining subject to the wishes of the national majority, is independent of the peoples of the towns and capable of suppressing their excesses.

wandering tribes who had not thought of exploiting the natural wealth of the soil. One could still properly call North America an empty continent, a deserted land waiting for inhabitants.

Everything about the Americans, from their social condition to their laws, is extraordinary; but the most extraordinary thing of all is the land that supports them.

When the Creator handed the earth over to men, it was young and inexhaustible, but they were weak and ignorant; and by the time that they had learned to take advantage of the treasures it contained, they already covered its face, and soon they were having to fight for the right to an asylum where they could rest in freedom.

It was then that North America was discovered, as if God had held it in reserve and it had only just arisen above the waters of the flood.

There, there are still, as on the first days of creation, rivers whose founts never run dry, green and watery solitudes, and limitless fields never yet turned by the plowshare. In this condition it offers itself not to the isolated, ignorant, and barbarous man of the first ages, but to man who has already mastered the most important secrets of nature, united to his fellows, and taught by the experience of fifty centuries.

Now, at the time of writing, thirteen million civilized Europeans are quietly spreading over these fertile wildernesses whose exact resources and extent they themselves do not yet know. Three or four thousand soldiers drive the wandering native tribes before them; behind the armed men woodcutters advance, penetrating the forests, scaring off the wild beasts, exploring the course of rivers, and preparing the triumphal progress of civilization across the wilderness.

In the course of this book I have often mentioned the material prosperity enjoyed by the Americans and have pointed it out as one of the great reasons for the success of their laws. . . .

American legislation favors the division of property as much as possible, but something more powerful than legislation prevents it being divided up to excess.[5] The states which are at last beginning to be filled up illustrate this clearly. Massachusetts, the most densely populated part of the Union, has eighty inhabitants to the square mile, which is much less than the one hundred and sixty-two found in France.

But already it is a rare occurrence in Massachusetts for small properties to be divided up; generally the eldest keeps the land, while the younger sons go to seek their fortunes in the wilds.

The law has abolished primogeniture, but one may say that Providence has reestablished it without complaint from anybody, and just for once it does not offend equity.

A single fact will give an idea of the vast number of individuals who leave New England to make homes in the wilds. I am told that in 1830 thirty-six of the members of Congress had been born in the small state of Connecticut. Therefore Connecticut, with one forty-third of the population of the United States, furnished one eighth of the representatives.

But Connecticut itself only sends five members to Congress, while the other thirty-one came in the capacity of representatives of the new states to the west. In those thirty-one had stayed in Connecticut, in all probability they would have remained humble laborers, not rich landowners, and would have passed their lives in obscurity, not able to venture on a political career, and instead of becoming useful legislators, they would have been dangerous citizens. . . .

In Europe we habitually regard a restless spirit, immoderate desire for wealth, and an extreme love of independence as great social dangers. But precisely those things assure a

---

[5] In New England the land is divided up into very small holdings, but it is not being further subdivided.

long and peaceful future for the American republics. Without such restless passions the population would be concentrated around a few places and would soon experience, as we do, needs which are hard to satisfy. What a happy land the New World is, where man's vices are almost as useful to society as his virtues!

This exercises a great influence over the way human actions are judged in the two hemispheres. What we call love of gain is praiseworthy industry to the Americans, and they see something of a cowardly spirit in what we consider moderation of desires.

In France we regard simple tastes, quiet mores, family feeling, and love of one's birthplace as great guarantees for the tranquillity and happiness of the state. But in America nothing seems more prejudicial to society than virtues of that sort. The French of Canada, who loyally preserve the tradition of their ancient mores, are already finding it difficult to live on their land, and this small nation which has only just come to birth will soon be a prey to all the afflictions of old nations. The most enlightened, patriotic, and humane men in Canada make extraordinary efforts to render people dissatisfied with the simple happiness that still contents them. They extol the advantages of wealth in much the same way as, perhaps, in France they would have praised the charms of a moderate competence, and are at greater pains to goad human passions than others elsewhere to calm them. To change the pure and quiet pleasures which his homeland offers even to the poor man for the sterile enjoyments of prosperity under an alien sky, to flee from the paternal hearth and the fields where his ancestors rest, and to leave both living and dead to chase after fortune are all things most praiseworthy in their eyes.

In our day no human industry could fully exploit all the vast opportunities America offers.

In America there cannot be enough of knowledge, for all knowledge benefits both those who possess it and those who do not. New wants are not to be feared, for there all wants can easily be satisfied; there is no need to dread the growth of excessive passions, for there is healthy food easily available to feed them all; men there cannot have too much freedom, for they are hardly ever tempted to make ill use thereof.

The present-day American republics are like companies of merchants formed to exploit the empty lands of the New World, and prosperous commerce is their occupation.

The passions that stir the Americans most deeply are commercial and not political ones, or rather they carry a trader's habits over into the business of politics. They like order, without which affairs do not prosper, and they set an especial value on regularity of mores, which are the foundation of a sound business; they prefer the good sense which creates fortunes to the genius which often dissipates them; their minds, accustomed to definite calculations, are frightened by general ideas; and they hold practice in greater honor than theory.

One must go to America to understand the power of material prosperity over political behavior, and even over opinions too, though those should be subject to reason alone. It is the foreigners who best illustrate the truth of this. Most European immigrants carry over to the New World that fierce love of independence and of change which often breeds amid our afflictions. Occasionally in the United States I met some of those Europeans who had been forced to leave their country on account of their political opinions. The conversation of all of them astonished me, but one most of all. As I was passing through one of the remotest parts of Pennsylvania, I was overtaken by night and went to ask for hospitality at the house of a rich planter. He was French. He welcomed me to his fireside, and we began to talk with the freedom suitable to people meeting in the depths of the forest two thousand leagues from their native land. I was aware that my host had been a great leveler and an ardent demagogue forty years before, for his name had left a mark on history.

It was therefore strange and astonishing to hear him talk like an economist—I almost said a landowner—about the rights of property; he spoke of the necessary hierarchy that wealth establishes among men, of obedience to the established law, of the influence of good mores in republics, and of the support to order and freedom afforded by religious ideas; and it even happened that he inadvertently quoted the authority of Jesus Christ in support of one of his political opinions.

I listened and marveled at the feebleness of human reason. A thing is true or false; but how can one find out amid the uncertainties of knowledge and the diverse lessons of experience? A new fact may come and remove all my doubts. I was poor, and now, look, I am rich; if only prosperity, while affecting my conduct, would leave my judgment free! In fact, my opinions do change with my fortune, and the lucky circumstances of which I take advantage really do provide that decisive argument I could not find before.

Prosperity's influence operates even more freely over Americans than over foreigners. The American has always seen order and public prosperity linked together and marching in step; it never strikes him that they could be separate; consequently he has nothing to forget and has no need to unlearn, as Europeans must, the lessons of his early education. . . .

Indirect Influence of Religious Beliefs upon Political Society in the United States

Christian morality common to all sects. Influence of religion on American mores. Respect for the marriage tie. How religion keeps the imagination of the Americans within certain limits and moderates their passion for innovation. Opinion of the Americans con-

cerning the political value of religion. Their efforts to extend and assure its sway.

I have just pointed out the direct action of religion on politics in the United States. Its indirect action seems to me much greater still, and it is just when it is not speaking of freedom at all that it best teaches the Americans the art of being free.

There is an innumerable multitude of sects in the United States. They are all different in the worship they offer to the Creator, but all agree concerning the duties of men to one another. Each sect worships God in its own fashion, but all preach the same morality in the name of God. Though it is very important for man as an individual that his religion should be true, that is not the case for society. Society has nothing to fear or hope from another life; what is most important for it is not that all citizens should profess the true religion but that they should profess religion. Moreover, all the sects in the United States belong to the great unity of Christendom, and Christian morality is everywhere the same.

One may suppose that a certain number of Americans, in the worship they offer to God, are following their habits rather than their convictions. Besides, in the United States the sovereign authority is religious, and consequently hypocrisy should be common. Nonetheless, America is still the place where the Christian religion has kept the greatest real power over men's souls; and nothing better demonstrates how useful and natural it is to man, since the country where it now has widest sway is both the most enlightened and the freest.

I have said that American priests proclaim themselves in general terms in favor of civil liberties without excepting even those who do not admit religious freedom; but none of them lend their support to any particular political system. They are at pains to keep out of affairs and not mix in the combinations of parties. One cannot therefore say that in the United States religion influences the laws or political opinions in detail, but it does direct mores, and by regulating domestic life it helps to regulate the state.

I do not doubt for an instant that the great severity of mores which one notices in the United States has its primary origin in beliefs. There religion is often powerless to restrain men in the midst of innumerable temptations which fortune offers. It cannot moderate their eagerness to enrich themselves, which everything contributes to arouse, but it reigns supreme in the souls of the women, and it is women who shape mores. Certainly of all countries in the world America is the one in which the marriage tie is most respected and where the highest and truest conception of conjugal happiness has been conceived.

In Europe almost all the disorders of society are born around the domestic hearth and not far from the nuptial bed. It is there that men come to feel scorn for natural ties and legitimate pleasures and develop a taste for disorder, restlessness of spirit, and instability of desires. Shaken by the tumultuous passions which have often troubled his own house, the European finds it hard to submit to the authority of the state's legislators. When the American returns from the turmoil of politics to the bosom of the family, he immediately finds a perfect picture of order and peace. There all his pleasures are simple and natural and his joys innocent and quiet and as the regularity of life brings him happiness, he easily forms the habit of regulating his opinions as well as his tastes.

Whereas the European tries to escape his sorrows at home by troubling society, the American derives from his home that love of order which he carries over into affairs of state.

In the United States it is not only mores that are controlled by religion, but its sway extends even over reason.

Among the Anglo-Americans there are some who profess Christian dogmas because they believe them and others who do so because they are afraid to look as though they did not believe in them. So Christianity reigns without obstacles, by universal consent; consequently, as I have said elsewhere, everything in the moral field is certain and fixed, although the world of politics seems given over to argument and experiment. So the human spirit never sees an unlimited field before itself; however bold it is, from time to time it feels that it must halt before insurmountable barriers. Before innovating, it is forced to accept certain primary assumptions and to submit its boldest conceptions to certain formalities which retard and check it.

The imagination of the Americans, therefore, even in its greatest aberrations, is circumspect and hesitant; it is embarrassed from the start and leaves its work unfinished. These habits of restraint are found again in political society and singularly favor the tranquillity of the people as well as the durability of the institutions they have adopted. Nature and circumstances have made the inhabitant of the United States a bold man, as is sufficiently attested by the enterprising spirit with which he seeks his fortune. If the spirit of the Americans were free of all impediment, one would soon find among them the boldest innovators and the most implacable logicians in the world. But American revolutionaries are obliged ostensibly to profess a certain respect for Christian morality and equity, and that does not allow them easily to break the laws when those are opposed to the executions of their designs; nor would they find it easy to surmount the scruples of their partisans even if they were able to get over their own. Up till now no one in the United States has dared to profess the maxim that everything is allowed in the interests of society, an impious maxim apparently invented in an age of freedom in order to legitimatize every future tyrant.

Thus, while the law allows the American people to do everything, there are things which religion prevents them from imagining and forbids them to dare.

Religion, which never intervenes directly in the government of American society, should therefore be considered as the first of their political institutions, for although it did not give them the taste for liberty, it singularly facilitates their use thereof.

The inhabitants of the United States themselves consider religious beliefs from this angle. I do not know if all Americans have faith in their religion—for who can read the secrets of the heart?—but I am sure that they think it necessary to the maintenance of republican institutions. That is not the view of one class or party among the citizens, but of the whole nation; it is found in all ranks.

In the United States, if a politician attacks a sect, that is no reason why the supporters of that very sect should not support him; but if he attacks all sects together, everyone shuns him, and he remains alone.

While I was in America, a witness called at assizes of the county of Chester (state of New York) declared that he did not believe in the existence of God and the immortality of the soul. The judge refused to allow him to be sworn in, on the ground that the witness had destroyed before hand all possible confidence in his testimony.[6] Newspapers reported the fact without comment.

For the Americans the ideas of Christianity and liberty are so completely mingled that it is almost impossible to get them to conceive of the one without the other; it is not a question with them of sterile beliefs bequeathed by the past and vegetating rather than living in the depths of the soul.

---

[6] This is how the New York *Spectator* of August 23, 1831, reported the matter: "The court of common pleas of Chester county (New York) a few days since, rejected a witness who declared his disbelief in the existence of God. The presiding judge remarked that he was not before aware that there was a man living who did not believe in the existence of God; that this belief constituted the sanction of all testimony in a court of justice; and that he knew of no cause in a Christian country, where a witness has been permitted to testify without such belief."

I have known Americans to form associations to send priests out into the new states of the West and establish schools and churches there; they fear that religion might be lost in the depths of the forest and that the people growing up there might be less fitted for freedom than those from whom they sprang. I have met rich New Englanders who left their native land in order to establish the fundamentals of Christianity and of liberty by the banks of the Missouri or on the prairies of Illinois. In this way, in the United States, patriotism continually adds fuel to the fires of religious zeal. You will be mistaken if you think that such men are guided only by thoughts of the future life; eternity is only one of the things that concern them. If you talk to these missionaries of Christian civilization you will be surprised to hear them so often speaking of the goods of this world and to meet a politician where you expected to find a priest. "There is a solidarity between all the American republics," they will tell you; "if the republics of the West were to fall into anarchy or to be mastered by a despot, the republican institutions now flourishing on the Atlantic coast would be in great danger; we therefore have an interest in seeing that the new states are religious so that they may allow us to remain free."

That is what the Americans think, but our pedants find it an obvious mistake; constantly they prove to me that all is fine in America except just that religious spirit which I admire; I am informed that on the other side of the ocean freedom and human happiness lack nothing but Spinoza's belief in the eternity of the world and Cabanis' contention that thought is a secretion of the brain. To that I have really no answer to give, except that those who talk like that have never been in America and have never seen either religious peoples or free ones. So I shall wait till they come back from a visit to America.

There are people in France who look on republican institutions as a temporary expedient for their own aggrandizement. They mentally measure the immense gap separating their vices and their poverty from power and wealth, and they would like to fill this abyss with ruins in an attempt to bridge it. Such people stand toward liberty much as the medieval *condottieri* stood toward the kings; they make war on their own account, no matter whose colors they wear: the republic, they calculate, will at least last long enough to lift them from their present degradation. It is not to such as they that I speak, but there are others who look forward to a republican form of government as a permanent and tranquil state and as the required aim to which ideas and mores are constantly steering modern societies. Such men sincerely wish to prepare mankind for liberty. When such as these attack religious beliefs, they obey the dictates of their passions, not their interests. Despotism may be able to do without faith, but freedom cannot. Religion is much more needed in the republic they advocate than in the monarchy they attack, and in democratic republics most of all. How could society escape destruction if, when political ties are relaxed, moral ties are not tightened? And what can be done with a people master of itself if it is not subject to God?

VOLUME II, CHAPTER 2 OF INDIVIDUALISM IN DEMOCRACIES

I have shown how, in ages of equality, every man finds his beliefs within himself, and I shall now go on to show that all his feelings are turned in on himself.

"Individualism" is a word recently coined to express a new idea. Our fathers only knew about egoism.

Egoism, is a passionate and exaggerated love of self which leads a man to think of all things in terms of himself and to prefer himself to all.

Individualism is a calm and considered feeling which disposes each citizen to isolate himself from the mass of his fellows and withdraw into the circle of family and friends; with this little society formed to his taste, he gladly leaves the greater society to look after itself.

Egoism springs from a blind instinct; individualism is based on misguided judgment rather than depraved feeling. It is due more to inadequate understanding than to perversity of heart.

Egoism sterilizes the seeds of every virtue; individualism at first only dams the spring of public virtues, but in the long run it attacks and destroys all the others too and finally merges in egoism.

Egoism is a vice as old as the world. It is not peculiar to one form of society more than another.

Individualism is of democratic origin and threatens to grow as conditions get more equal.

Among aristocratic nations families maintain the same station for centuries and often live in the same place. So there is a sense in which all the generations are contemporaneous. A man almost always knows about his ancestors and respects them; his imagination extends to his great-grandchildren, and he loves them. He freely does his duty by both ancestors and descendants and often sacrifices personal pleasures for the sake of beings who are no longer alive or are not yet born.

Moreover, aristocratic institutions have the effect of linking each man closely with several of his fellows.

Each class in an aristocratic society, being clearly and permanently limited, forms, in a sense, a little fatherland for all its members, to which they are attached by more obvious and more precious ties than those linking them to the fatherland itself.

Each citizen of an aristocratic society has his fixed station, one above another, so that there is always someone above him whose protection he needs and someone below him whose help he may require.

So people living in an aristocratic age are almost always closely involved with something outside themselves, and they are often inclined to forget about themselves. It is true that in these ages the general conception of *human fellowship* is dim and that men hardly ever think of devoting themselves to the cause of humanity, but men do often make sacrifices for the sake of certain other men.

In democratic ages, on the contrary, the duties of each to all are much clearer but devoted service to any individual much rarer. The bonds of human affection are wider but more relaxed.

Among democratic peoples new families continually rise from nothing while others fall, and nobody's position is quite stable. The woof of time is ever being broken and the track of past generations lost. Those who have gone before are easily forgotten, and no one gives a thought to those who will follow. All a man's interests are limited to those near himself.

As each class catches up with the next and gets mixed with it, its members do not care about one another and treat one another as strangers. Aristocracy links everybody, from peasant to king, in one long chain. Democracy breaks the chain and frees each link.

As social equality spreads there are more and more people who, though neither rich nor powerful enough to have much hold over others, have gained or kept enough wealth and enough understanding to look after their own needs. Such folk owe no man anything and hardly expect anything from anybody. They form the habit of thinking of themselves in isolation and imagine that their whole destiny is in their own hands.

Thus, not only does democracy make men forget their ancestors, but also clouds their view of their descendants and isolates them from their contemporaries. Each man is forever thrown back on himself alone, and there is danger that he may be shut up in the solitude of his own heart.

CHAPTER 3: HOW INDIVIDUALISM IS MORE PRONOUNCED AT THE END OF A DEMOCRATIC REVOLUTION THAN AT ANY OTHER TIME

It is just at the moment when a democratic society is establishing itself on the ruins of an aristocracy that this isolation of each man from the rest and the egoism resulting therefrom stand out clearest.

Not only are there many independent people in such a society, but their number is constantly increasing with more and more of those who have just attained independence and are drunk with their new power. These latter have a presumptuous confidence in their strength, and never imagining that they could ever need another's help again, they have no inhibition about showing that they care for nobody but themselves.

There is usually a prolonged struggle before an aristocracy gives way, and in the course of that struggle implacable hatreds have been engendered between the classes. Such passions last after victory, and one can see traces of them in the ensuing democratic confusion.

Those who once held the highest ranks in the subverted hierarchy cannot forget their ancient greatness at once and for a long time feel themselves strangers in the new society. They regard all those whom society now makes their equals as oppressors whose fate could not concern them; they have lost sight of their former equals and no longer feel tied by common interests to their lot; each of them, in his separate retreat, feels reduced to taking care of himself alone. But those formerly at the bottom of the social scale and now brought up to the common level by a sudden revolution cannot enjoy their newfound independence without some secret uneasiness: there is a look of fear mixed with triumph in their eyes if they do meet one of their former superiors, and they avoid them.

↳ isolation which can lead to apathy + despotism

Therefore it is usually at the time when democratic societies are taking root that men are most disposed to isolate themselves.

There is a tendency in democracy not to draw men together, but democratic revolutions make them run away from each other and perpetuate, in the midst of equality, hatreds originating in inequality.

The Americans have this great advantage, that they attained democracy without the sufferings of a democratic revolution and that they were born equal instead of becoming so.

CHAPTER 4: HOW THE AMERICANS COMBAT THE EFFECTS OF INDIVIDUALISM BY FREE INSTITUTIONS

Despotism, by its very nature suspicious, sees the isolation of men as the best guarantee of its own permanence. So it usually does all it can to isolate them. Of all the vices of the human heart egoism is that which suits it best. A despot will lightly forgive his subjects for not loving him, provided they do not love one another. He does not ask them to help him guide the state; it is enough if they do not claim to manage it themselves. He calls those who try to unite their efforts to create a general prosperity "turbulent and restless spirits," and twisting natural meaning of words, he calls those "good citizens" who care for none but themselves.

Thus vices originating in despotism are precisely those favored by equality. The two opposites fatally complete and support each other.

Equality puts men side by side without a common link to hold them firm. Despotism raises barriers to keep them apart. It disposes them not to think of their fellows and turns indifference into a sort of public virtue.

Despotism, dangerous at all times, is therefore particularly to be feared in ages of democracy.

It is easy to see that in such ages men have a peculiar need for freedom.

Citizens who are bound to take part in public affairs must turn from the private interests and occasionally take a look at something other than themselves.

As soon as common affairs are treated in common, each man notices that he is not as independent of his fellows as he used to suppose and that to get their help he must often offer his aid to them.

When the public governs, all men feel the value of public goodwill and all try to win it by gaining the esteem and affection of those among whom they must live.

Those frigid passions that keep hearts asunder must then retreat and hide at the back of consciousness. Pride must be disguised; contempt must not be seen. Egoism is afraid of itself.

Under a free government most public officials are elected, so men whose great gifts and aspirations are too closely circumscribed in private life daily feel that they cannot do without the people around them.

It thus happens that ambition makes a man care for his fellows, and, in a sense, he often finds his self-interest in forgetting about himself. I know that one can point to all the intrigues caused by an election, the dishonorable means often used by candidates, and the calumnies spread by their enemies. These do give rise to feelings of hatred, and the more frequent the elections, the worse they are.

Those are great ills, no doubt, but passing ones, whereas the benefits that attend them remain.

Eagerness to be elected may, for the moment, make particular men fight each other, but in the long run this same aspiration induces mutual helpfulness on the part of all; and while it may happen that the accident of an election estranges two friends, the electoral system forges permanent links between a great number of citizens who might otherwise have remained forever strangers to one another. Liberty engenders particular hatreds, but despotism is responsible for general indifference.

The Americans have used liberty to combat the individualism born of equality, and they have won.

The lawgivers of America did not suppose that general representation of the whole nation would suffice to ward off a disorder at once so natural to the body social of a democracy and so fatal. They thought it also right to give each part of the land its own political life so that there should be an infinite number of occasions for the citizens to act together and so that every day they should feel that they depended on one another.

That was wise conduct.

The general business of a country keeps only the leading citizens occupied. It is only occasionally that they come together in the same places, and since they often lose sight of one another, no lasting bonds form between them. But when the people who live there have to look after the particular affairs of a district, the same people are always meeting, and they are forced, in a manner, to know and adapt themselves to one another.

It is difficult to force a man out of himself and get him to take an interest in the affairs of the whole state, for he has little understanding of the way in which the fate of the state can influence his own lot. But if it is a question of taking a road past his property, he sees at once that this small public matter has a bearing on his greatest private interests, and there is no need to point out to him the close connection between his private profit and the general interest.

Thus, far more may be done by entrusting citizens with the management of minor affairs than by handing over control of great matters, toward interesting them in the public welfare and convincing them that they constantly stand in need of one another in order to provide for it.

Some brilliant achievement may win a people's favor at one stroke. But to gain the affection and respect of your immediate neighbors, a long succession of little services rendered and of obscure good deeds, a constant habit of kindness and an established reputation for disinterestedness, are required.

Local liberties, then, which induce a great number of citizens to value the affection of their kindred and neighbors, bring men constantly into contact, despite the instincts which separate them, and force them to help one another.

In the United States the most opulent citizens are at pains not to get isolated from the people. On the contrary, they keep in constant contact, gladly listen and themselves talk any and every day. They know that the rich in democracies always need the poor and that good manners will draw them to them more than benefits conferred. For benefits by their very greatness spotlight the difference in conditions and arouse a secret annoyance in those who profit from them. But the charm of simple good manners is almost irresistible. Their affability carries men away, and even their vulgarity is not always unpleasant.

The rich do not immediately appreciate this truth. They generally stand out against it as long as a democratic revolution is in progress and do not admit it at once even after the revolution is accomplished. They will gladly do good to the people, but they still want carefully to keep their distance from them. They think that that is enough, but they are wrong. They could ruin themselves in that fashion without warming their neighbors' hearts. What is wanted is not the sacrifice of their money but of their pride.

It would seem as if in the United States every man's power of invention was on the stretch to find new ways of increasing the wealth and satisfying the needs of the public. The best brains in every neighborhood are constantly employed in searching for new secrets to increase the general prosperity, and any that they find are at once at the service of the crowd.

If one takes a close look at the weaknesses and vices of many of those who bear sway in America, one is surprised at the growing prosperity of the people, but it is a mistake to be surprised. It is certainly not the elected magistrate who makes the American democracy prosper, but the fact that the magistrates are elected.

It would not be fair to assume that American patriotism and the universal zeal for the common good have no solid basis. Though private interest, in the United States as elsewhere, is the driving force behind most of men's actions, it does not regulate them all.

I have often seen Americans make really great sacrifices for the common good, and I have noticed a hundred cases in which, when help was needed, they hardly ever failed to give each other trusty support.

The free institutions of the United States and the political rights enjoyed there provide a thousand continual reminders to every citizen that he lives in society. At every moment they bring his mind back to this idea, that it is the duty as well as the interest of men to be useful to their fellows. Having no particular reason to hate others, since he is neither their slave nor their master, the American's heart easily inclines toward benevolence. At first it is of necessity that men attend to the public interest, afterward by choice. What had been calculation becomes instinct. By dint of working for the good of his fellow citizens, he in the end acquires a habit and taste for serving them.

There are many men in France who regard equality of conditions as the first of evils and political liberty as the second. When forced to submit to the former, they strive at least to escape the latter. But for my part, I maintain that there is only one effective remedy against the evils which equality may cause, and that is political liberty.

CHAPTER 5: ON THE USE WHICH THE AMERICANS MAKE OF ASSOCIATIONS IN CIVIL LIFE

I do not propose to speak of those political associations by means of which men seek to defend themselves against the despotic action of the majority or the encroachments of royal power. I have treated that subject elsewhere. It is clear that unless each citizen learned to combine with his fellows to preserve his freedom at a time when he individually is becoming weaker and so less able in isolation to defend it, tyranny would be bound to increase with equality. But here I am only concerned with those associations in civil life which have no political object.

In the United States, political associations are only one small part of the immense number of different types of associations found there.

Americans of all ages, all stations in life, and all types of disposition are forever forming associations. There are not only commercial and industrial associations in which all take part, but others of a thousand different types—religious, moral, serious, futile, very general and very limited, immensely large and very minute. Americans combine to give fêtes, found seminaries, build churches, distribute books, and send missionaries to the antipodes. Hospitals, prisons, and schools take shape in that way. Finally, if they want to proclaim a truth or propagate some feeling by the encouragement of a great example, they form an association. In every case, at the head of any new undertaking, where in France you would find the government or in England some territorial magnate, in the United States you are sure to find an association.

I have come across several types of association in America of which, I confess, I had not previously the slightest conception, and I have often admired the extreme skill they show in proposing a common object for the exertions of very many and in inducing them voluntarily to pursue it.

Since that time I have traveled in England, a country from which the Americans took some of their laws and many of their customs, but it seemed to me that the principle of association was not used nearly so constantly or so adroitly there.

A single Englishman will often carry through some great undertaking, whereas Americans form associations for no matter how small a matter. Clearly the former regard association as a powerful means of action, but the latter seem to think of it as the only one.

Thus the most democratic country in the world now is that in which men have in our time carried to the highest perfection the art of pursuing in common the objects of common desires and have applied this new technique to the greatest number of purposes. Is that just an accident, or is there really some necessary connection between associations and equality?

In aristocratic societies, while there is a multitude of individuals who can do nothing on their own, there is also a small number of very rich and powerful men, each of whom can carry out great undertakings on his own.

In aristocratic societies men have no need to unite for action, since they are held firmly together.

Every rich and powerful citizen is in practice the head of a permanent and enforced association composed of all those whom he makes help in the execution of his designs.

But among democratic peoples all the citizens are independent and weak. They can do hardly anything for themselves, and none of them is in a position to force his fellows to help him. They would all therefore find themselves helpless if they did not learn to help each other voluntarily.

If the inhabitants of democratic countries had neither the right nor the taste for uniting for political objects, their independence would

run great risks, but they could keep both their wealth and their knowledge for a long time. But if they did not learn some habits of acting together in the affairs of daily life, civilization itself would be in peril. A people in which individuals had lost the power of carrying through great enterprises by themselves, without acquiring the faculty of doing them together, would soon fall back into barbarism.

Unhappily, the same social conditions that render associations so necessary to democratic nations also make their formation more difficult there than elsewhere.

When several aristocrats want to form an association, they can easily do so. As each of them carries great weight in society, a very small number of associates may be enough. So, being few, it is easy to get to know and understand one another and agree on rules.

But that is not so easy in democratic nations, where, if the association is to have any power, the associates must be very numerous.

I know that many of my contemporaries are not the least embarrassed by this difficulty. They claim that as the citizens become weaker and more helpless, the government must become proportionately more skillful and active, so that society should do what is no longer possible for individuals. They think that answers the whole problem, but I think they are mistaken.

A government could take the place of some of the largest associations in America, and some particular states of the Union have already attempted that. But what political power could ever carry on the vast multitude of lesser undertakings which associations daily enable American citizens to control?

It is easy to see the time coming in which men will be less and less able to produce, by each alone, the commonest bare necessities of life. The tasks of government must therefore perpetually increase, and its efforts to cope with them must spread its net ever wider. The more government takes the place of associations, the more will individuals lose the idea of forming associations and need the government to come to their help. That is a vicious circle of cause and effect. Must the public administration cope with every industrial undertaking beyond the competence of one individual citizen? And if ultimately, as a result of the minute subdivision of landed property, the land itself is so infinitely parceled out that it can only be cultivated by associations of laborers, must the head of the government leave the helm of state to guide the plow?

The morals and intelligence of a democratic people would be in as much danger as its commerce and industry if ever a government wholly usurped the place of private associations.

Feelings and ideas are renewed, the heart enlarged, and the understanding developed only by the reciprocal action of men one upon another.

I have shown how these influences are reduced almost to nothing in democratic countries; they must therefore be artificially created, and only associations can do that.

When aristocrats adopt a new idea or conceive a new sentiment, they lend it something of the conspicuous station they themselves occupy, and so the mass is bound to take notice of them, and they easily influence the minds and hearts of all around.

In democratic countries only the governing power is naturally in a position so to act, but it is easy to see that its action is always inadequate and often dangerous.

A government, by itself, is equally incapable of refreshing the circulation of feelings and ideas among a great people, as it is of controlling every industrial undertaking. Once it leaves the sphere of politics to launch out on this new track, it will, even without intending this, exercise an intolerable tyranny. For a government can only dictate precise rules. It imposes the sentiments and ideas which it favors, and it is never easy to tell the difference between its advice and its commands.

Things will be even worse if the government supposes that its real interest is to prevent the circulation of ideas. It will then stand motionless and let the weight of its deliberate somnolence lie heavy on all.

It is therefore necessary that it should not act alone.

Among democratic peoples associations must take the place of the powerful private persons whom equality of conditions has eliminated.

As soon as several Americans have conceived a sentiment or an idea that they want to produce before the world, they seek each other out, and when found, they unite. Thenceforth they are no longer isolated individuals, but a power conspicuous from the distance whose actions serve as an example; when it speaks, men listen.

The first time that I heard in America that one hundred thousand men had publicly promised never to drink alcoholic liquor, I thought it more of a joke than a serious matter and for the moment did not see why these very abstemious citizens could not content themselves with drinking water by their own firesides.

In the end I came to understand that these hundred thousand Americans, frightened by the progress of drunkenness around them, wanted to support sobriety by their patronage. They were acting in just the same way as some great territorial magnate who dresses very plainly to encourage a contempt of luxury among simple citizens. One may fancy that if they had lived in France each of these hundred thousand would have made individual representations to the government asking it to supervise all the public houses throughout the realm.

Nothing, in my view, more deserves attention than the intellectual and moral associations in America. American political and industrial associations easily catch our eyes, but the others tend not to be noticed. And even if we do notice them we tend to misunderstand them, hardly ever having seen anything similar before. However, we should recognize that the latter are as necessary as the former to the American people; perhaps more so.

In democratic countries knowledge of how to combine is the mother of all other forms of knowledge; on its progress depends that of all the others.

Among laws controlling human societies there is one more precise and clearer, it seems to me, than all the others. If men are to remain civilized or to become civilized, the art of association must develop and improve among them at the same speed as equality of conditions spreads. . . .

CHAPTER 8: HOW THE AMERICANS COMBAT INDIVIDUALISM BY THE DOCTRINE OF SELF-INTEREST PROPERLY UNDERSTOOD

When the world was under the control of a few rich and powerful men, they liked to entertain a sublime conception of the duties of man. It gratified them to make out that it is a glorious thing to forget oneself and that one should do good without self-interest, as God himself does. That was the official doctrine of morality at that time.

I doubt whether men were better in times of aristocracy than at other times, but certainly they talked continually about the beauties of virtue. Only in secret did they study its utility. But since imagination has been taking less lofty flights, and every man's thoughts are centered on himself, moralists take fright at this idea of sacrifice and no longer venture to suggest it for consideration. So they are reduced to inquiring whether it is not to the individual advantage of each to work for the good of all, and when they have found one of those points where private advantage does meet and coincide with the general interest, they eagerly call attention thereto. Thus what was an isolated observation becomes a general doctrine, and in the end one comes to believe

that one sees that by serving his fellows man serves himself and that doing good is to his private advantage.

I have already shown elsewhere in several places in this book how the inhabitants of the United States almost always know how to combine their own advantage with that of their fellow citizens. What I want to point out now is the general theory which helps them to this result.

In the United States there is hardly any talk of the beauty of virtue. But they maintain that virtue is useful and prove it every day. American moralists do not pretend that one must sacrifice himself for his fellows because it is a fine thing to do so. But they boldly assert that such sacrifice is as necessary for the man who makes it as for the beneficiaries.

They have seen that in their time and place the forces driving man in on himself are irresistible, and despairing of holding such forces back, they only consider how to control them.

They therefore do not raise objections to men pursuing their interests, but they do all they can to prove that it is in each man's interest to be good.

I do not want to follow their arguments in detail here, as that would lead too far from my subject. It is enough for my purpose to note that they have convinced their fellow citizens.

Montaigne said long ago: "If I did not follow the straight road for the sake of its straightness, I should follow it having found by experience that, all things considered, it is the happiest and the most convenient."

So the doctrine of self-interest properly understood is not new, but it is among the Americans of our time that it has come to be universally accepted. It has become popular. One finds it at the root of all actions. It is interwoven in all they say. You hear it as much from the poor as from the rich.

The version of this doctrine current in Europe is much grosser but at the same time less widespread and, especially, less advertised. Every day men profess a zeal they no longer feel.

The Americans, on the other hand, enjoy explaining almost every act of their lives on the principle of self-interest properly understood. It gives them pleasure to point out how an enlightened self-love continually leads them to help one another and disposes them freely to give part of their time and wealth for the good of the state. I think that in this they often do themselves less than justice, for sometimes in the United States, as elsewhere, one sees people carried away by the disinterested, spontaneous impulses natural to man. But the Americans are hardly prepared to admit that they do give way to emotions of this sort. They prefer to give the credit to their philosophy rather than to themselves.

I might drop the argument at this point without attempting to pass judgment on what I have described. The extreme difficulty of the subject would be my excuse. But I do not want to plead that. I would rather that my readers, seeing clearly what I mean, refuse to agree with me than that I should leave them in suspense.

Self-interest properly understood is not at all a sublime, doctrine, but it is clear and definite. It does not attempt to reach great aims, but it does, without too much trouble, achieve all it sets out to do. Being within the scope of everybody's understanding, everyone grasps it and has no trouble in bearing it in mind. It is wonderfully agreeable to human weaknesses, and so easily wins great sway. It has no difficulty in keeping its power, for it turns private interest against itself and uses the same goad which excites them to direct passions.

The doctrine of self-interest properly understood does not inspire great sacrifices, but every day it prompts some small ones; by itself it cannot make a man virtuous, but its discipline shapes a lot of orderly, temperate, moderate, careful, and self-controlled citizens. If it does not lead the will directly to virtue, it establishes habits which unconsciously turn it that way.

If the doctrine of self-interest properly understood ever came to dominate all thought about morality, no doubt extraordinary virtues would be rarer. But I think that gross depravity would also be less common. Such teaching may stop some men from rising far above the common level of humanity, but many of those who fall below this standard grasp it and are restrained by it. Some individuals it lowers, but mankind it raises.

I am not afraid to say that the doctrine of self-interest properly understood appears to me the best suited of all philosophical theories to the wants of men in our time and that I see it as their strongest remaining guarantee against themselves. Contemporary moralists therefore should give most of their attention to it. Though they may well think it incomplete, they must nonetheless adopt it as necessary.

I do not think, by and large, that there is more egoism among us than in America; the only difference is that there it is enlightened, while here it is not. Every American has the sense to sacrifice some of his private interests to save the rest. We want to keep, and often lose, the lot.

I see around nothing but people bent publicly on proving, by word and deed, that what is useful is never wrong. Is there no chance of finding some who will make the public understand that what is right may be useful?

No power on earth can prevent increasing equality from turning men's minds to look for the useful or disposing each citizen to get wrapped up in himself.

One must therefore expect that private interest will more than ever become the chief if not the only driving force behind all behavior. But we have yet to see how each man will interpret his private interest.

If citizens, attaining equality, were to remain ignorant and coarse, it would be difficult to foresee any limit to the stupid excesses into which their selfishness might lead them, and no one could foretell into what shameful troubles they might plunge themselves for fear of sacrificing some of their own well-being for the prosperity of their fellow men.

I do not think that the doctrine of self-interest as preached in America is in all respects self-evident. But it does contain many truths so clear that for men to see them it is enough to educate them. Hence it is all-important for them to be educated, for the age of blind sacrifice and instinctive virtues is already long past, and I see a time approaching in which freedom, public peace, and social stability will not be able to last without education.

Reactionary Dissent: The South's Attack on Egalitarian Individualism

John C. Calhoun, 1782–1850

A congressman, vice president, senator, secretary of war, and secretary of state, John C. Calhoun was also one of the most original of American political thinkers. As a theorist, Calhoun is usually remembered as a defender of sectionalism and states' rights. His theories are interesting for the modern reader, moreover, because they show a sophisticated analysis of class conflict— Richard Hofstadter called Calhoun the "Marx of the master class"—and a special sensitivity to the problems of group rights in a majoritarian democracy.

Calhoun's defense of sectionalism and states' rights is ironic in that earlier he had been an ardent nationalist. He favored a strong army and navy and positive governmental action to encourage industrial development. However, by 1828, Calhoun saw clearly that the South would remain an agricultural section for the forseeable future, and he began to actively oppose the tariff. He wrote the "South Carolina Exposition and Protest" in 1828 claiming that the tariff was unconstitutional and that states had the right to nullify unconstitutional legislation. This contention formed the basis of Calhoun's novel theory of "concurrent majority" which he developed at some length in his *Disquisition on Government* and *Discourse on the Constitution and Government of the United States,* both published posthumously in 1853.

Calhoun, along with fellow Southerner George Fitzhugh, presented fascinating if reactionary attacks on the Lockean assumptions of Jacksonian America. The polity was not the product of a social contract made by equal individuals but a contingent association of preexistent semisovereign, corporate units, that is, the states. Furthermore, he argued that a society of equal individuals free to buy and sell labor and capital in the marketplace was not the essence of justice but rather a formula for cruelty. Since exploitation and inequality were inevitable, it was better to create formal classes and bind them together through a sense of mutual obligation that extended throughout a lifetime. In short, the lot of the slave treated with paternalistic care was superior to that of the northern wage earner left to fend in a brutally competitive labor market.

Two selections are presented below that give an example of Calhoun's thought. One, a speech delivered on the floor of the Senate in 1837, offers a fascinating theory of class conflict as well as a defense of slavery. The second, the Fort Hill Address of 1831, is an example of Calhoun's anti-individualist conception of the political order.

John C. Calhoun

Speech on the Reception of Abolition Petitions (delivered in the U.S. Senate, February 6, 1837)

The peculiar institution of the South—that, on the maintenance of which the very existence of the slaveholding States depends, is pronounced to be sinful and odious, in the sight of God and man; and this with a systematic design of rendering us hateful in the eyes of the world—with a view to a general crusade against us and our institutions. This, too, in the legislative halls of the Union; created by these confederated States, for the better protection of their peace, their safety, and their respective institutions;—and yet, we, the representatives of twelve of these sovereign States against whom this deadly war is waged, are expected to sit here in silence, hearing ourselves and our constituents day after day denounced, without uttering a word; for if we but open our lips, the charge of agitation is

Source: Richard K. Crallé, ed., *The Works of John C. Calhoun* (New York: Russell & Russell, 1968).

resounded on all sides, and we are held up as seeking to aggravate the evil which we resist. Every reflecting mind must see in all this a state of things deeply and dangerously diseased.

I do not belong . . . to the school which holds that aggression is to be met by concession. Mine is the opposite creed, which teaches that encroachments must be met at the beginning, and that those who act on the opposite principle are prepared to become slaves. In this case, in particular, I hold concession or compromise to be fatal. If we concede an inch, concession would follow concession—compromise would follow compromise, until our ranks would be so broken that effectual resistance would be impossible. We must meet the enemy on the frontier, with a fixed determination of maintaining our position at every hazard. Consent to receive these insulting petitions, and the next demand will be that they be referred to a committee in order that they may be deliberated and acted upon. . . .

As widely as this incendiary spirit has spread, it has not yet infected this body, or the great mass of the intelligent and business portion of the North; but unless it be speedily stopped, it will spread and work upwards till it brings the two great sections of the Union into deadly conflict. This is not a new impression with me. Several years since, in a discussion with one of the Senators from Massachusetts (Mr. Webster), before this fell spirit had showed itself, I then predicted that the doctrine of the proclamation and the Force Bill—that this Government had a right, in the last resort, to determine the extent of its own powers, and enforce its decision at the point of the bayonet, which was so warmly maintained by that Senator, would at no distant day arouse the dormant spirit of abolitionism. I told him that the doctrine was tantamount to the assumption of unlimited power on the part of the Government, and that such would be the impression on the public mind in a large portion of the Union. The consequence would be inevitable. A large portion of the Northern States believed slavery to be a sin, and would consider it as an obligation of conscience to abolish it if they should feel themselves in any degree responsible for its continuance—and that this doctrine would necessarily lead to the belief of such responsibility. I then predicted that it would commence as it has with this fanatical portion of society, and that they would begin their operations on the ignorant, the weak, the young, and the thoughtless—and gradually extend upwards till they would become strong enough to obtain political control, when he and others holding the highest stations in society, would, however reluctant, be compelled to yield to their doctrines, or be driven into obscurity. But four years have since elapsed, and all this is already in a course of regular fulfilment.

Standing at the point of time at which we have now arrived, it will not be more difficult to trace the course of future events now than it was then. They who imagine that the spirit now abroad in the North, will die away of itself without a shock or convulsion, have formed a very inadequate conception of its real character; it will continue to rise and spread, unless prompt and efficient measures to stay its progress be adopted. Already it has taken possession of the pulpit, of the schools, and, to a considerable extent, of the press; those great instruments by which the mind of the rising generation will be formed.

However sound the great body of the non-slaveholding States are at present, in the course of a few years they will be succeeded by those who will have been taught to hate the people and institutions of nearly one-half of this Union, with a hatred more deadly than one hostile nation ever entertained towards another. It is easy to see the end. By the necessary course of events, if left to themselves, we must become, finally, two people. It is impossible under the deadly hatred which must spring up between the two great sections, if the present causes are permitted to operate unchecked, that we should continue under the same political system. The conflicting elements would burst the Union asunder, powerful as are the links which hold it together. Abolition and the Union cannot coexist. As the friend of the Union I openly proclaim it,—and the sooner it is known the better. . . .

* * * * *

. . . I appeal to facts. Never before has the black race of Central Africa, from the dawn of history to the present day, attained a condition so civilized and so improved, not only physically, but morally and intellectually. It came among us in a low, degraded, and savage condition, and in the course of a few generations it has grown up under the fostering care of our institutions, reviled as they have been, to its present comparatively civilized condition. This, with the rapid increase of numbers, is conclusive proof of the general happiness of the race, in spite of all the exaggerated tales to the contrary.

In the mean time, the white or European race has not degenerated. It has kept pace with its brethren in other sections of the Union where slavery does not exist. It is odious to make comparison; but I appeal to all sides whether the South is not equal in virtue, intelligence, patriotism, courage, disinterestedness, and all the high qualities which adorn our nature. I ask whether we have not contributed our full share of talents and political wisdom in forming and sustaining this political fabric; and whether we have not constantly inclined most strongly to the side of liberty, and been the first to see and first to resist the encroachments of power.

In one thing only are we inferior—the arts of gain; we acknowledge that we are less wealthy than the Northern section of this Union, but I trace this mainly to the fiscal action of this Government, which has extracted much from and spent little among us. Had it been the reverse—if the exaction had been from the other section, and the expenditure with us, this point of superiority would not be against us now, as it was not at the formation of this Government.

But I take higher ground. I hold that in the present state of civilization, where two races of different origin, and distinguished by color, and other physical differences, as well as intellectual, are brought together, the relation now existing in the slaveholding States between the two, is, instead of an evil, a good—a positive good. I feel myself called upon to speak freely upon the subject where the honor and interests of those I represent are involved. I hold then that there never has yet existed a wealthy and civilized society in which one portion of the community did not, in point of fact, live on the labor of the other. Broad and general as is this assertion, it is fully borne out by history. This is not the proper occasion, but if it were, it would not

be difficult to trace the various devices by which the wealth of all civilized communities has been so unequally divided, and to show by what means so small a share has been allotted to those by whose labor it was produced, and so large a share given to the non-producing classes. The devices are almost innumerable, from the brute force and gross superstition of ancient times, to the subtle and artful fiscal contrivances of modern. I might well challenge a comparison between them and the more direct, simple, and patriarchal mode by which the labor of the African race is, among us, commanded by the European. I may say with truth, that in few countries so much is left to the share of the laborer, and so little exacted from him, or where there is more kind attention paid to him in sickness or infirmities of age. Compare his condition with the tenants of the poor houses in the more civilized portions of Europe—look at the sick, and the old and infirm slave, on one hand, in the midst of his family and friends, under the kind superintending care of his master and mistress, and compare it with the forlorn and wretched condition of the pauper in the poor house. But I will not dwell on this aspect of the question; I turn to the political; and here I fearlessly assert that the existing relation between the two races in the South, against which these blind fanatics are waging war, forms the most solid and durable foundation on which to rear free and stable political institutions. It is useless to disguise the fact. There is and always has been in an advanced stage of wealth and civilization, a conflict between labor and capital. The condition of society in the South exempts us from the disorders and dangers resulting from this conflict; and which explains why it is that the political condition of the slaveholding States has been so much more stable and quiet than that of the North. The advantages of the former, in this respect, will become more and more manifest if left undisturbed by interference from without, as the country advances in wealth and numbers. We have, in fact, but just entered that condition of society where the strength and durability of our political institutions are to be tested; and I venture nothing in predicting that the experience of the next generation will fully test how vastly more favorable our condition of society is to that of other sections for free and stable institutions, provided we are not disturbed by the interference of others, or shall have sufficient intelligence and spirit to resist promptly and successfully such interference. It rests with ourselves to meet and repel them. I look not for aid to this Government, or to the other States; not but there are kind feelings towards us on the part of the great body of the non-slaveholding States; but as kind as their feelings may be, we may rest assured that no political party in those States will risk their ascendency for our safety. If we do not defend ourselves none will defend us; if we yield we will be more and more pressed as we recede; and if we submit we will be trampled under foot. Be assured that emancipation itself would not satisfy these fanatics—that gained, the next step would be to raise the negroes to a social and political equality with the whites; and that being effected, we would soon find the present condition of the two races reversed. They and their northern allies would be the masters, and we the slaves; the condition of the white race in the British West India Islands, bad as it is, would be happiness to ours. There the mother country is interested in sustaining the supremacy of the European race. It is true that the authority of the former master is destroyed, but the African will there still be a slave, not to individuals but to the community,—forced to labor, not by the authority of the overseer, but by the bayonet of the soldiery and the rod of the civil magistrate.

Surrounded as the slaveholding States are with such imminent perils, I rejoice to think that our means of defence are ample, if we shall prove to have the intelligence and spirit to see and apply them before it is too late. All we want is concert, to lay aside all party differences, and unite with zeal and energy in repelling approaching dangers. Let there be concert of action, and we shall find ample means of security without resorting to secession or disunion. I speak with full knowledge and a thorough examination of the subject, and for one, see my way clearly. One thing alarms me—the eager pursuit of gain which overspreads the land, and which absorbs every faculty of the mind and every feeling of the heart. Of all passions avarice is the most blind and compromising—the last to see and the first to yield to danger. I dare not hope that any thing I can say will arouse the South to a due sense of danger; I fear it is beyond the power of mortal voice to awaken it in time from the fatal security into which it has fallen.

John C. Calhoun

Fort Hill Address on the Relation Which the States and General Government Bear to Each Other (1831)

The question of the relation which the States and General Government bear to each other is not one of recent origin. From the commencement of our system, it has divided public sentiment. Even in the Convention, while the Constitution was struggling into existence, there were two parties as to what this relation should be, whose different sentiments constituted no small impediment in forming that instrument. After the General Government went into operation, experience soon proved that the question had not terminated with the labors of the Convention. The great struggle that preceded the political revolution of 1801, which brought Mr. Jefferson into power, turned essentially on it, and the doctrines and arguments on both sides were embodied and ably sustained—on the one, in the Virginia and Kentucky Resolutions, and the Report to the Virginia Legislature;—and on the other, in the replies of the Legislature of Massachusetts and some of the other States. These Resolutions and this Report, with the decision of the Supreme Court of Pennsylvania about the same time (particularly in the case of Cobbett, delivered by Chief Justice M'Kean, and concurred in by the whole bench), contain what I believe to be the true doctrine on this important subject. I refer to them in order to avoid the necessity of presenting my views, with the reasons in support of them, in detail. . . .

The great and leading principle is, that the General Government emanated from the people of the several States, forming distinct political communities, and acting in their separate and sovereign capacity, and not from all of the people forming one aggregate political community; that the Constitution of the United States is, in fact, a compact, to which each State is a party, in the character already described; and that the several States, or parties, have a right to judge of its infractions; and in case of a deliberate, palpable, and dangerous exercise of power not delegated, they have the right, in the last resort, to use the language of the Virginia Resolutions, *"to interpose for arresting the progress of the evil, and for maintaining, within their respective limits, the authorities, rights, and liberties appertaining to them."* This right of interposition, thus solemnly asserted by the State of Virginia, be it called what it may,—State-right, veto, nullification, or by any other name,—I conceive to be the fundamental principle of our system, resting on facts historically as certain as our revolution itself, and deductions as simple and demonstrative as that of any political or moral truth whatever; and I firmly believe that on its recognition, depend the stability and safety of our political institutions.

I am not ignorant that those opposed to the doctrine have always, now and formerly, regarded it in a very different light, as anarchi-

SOURCE: Richard K. Crallé, ed., *The Works of John C. Calhoun* (New York: Russell and Russell, 1968).

cal and revolutionary. Could I believe such, in fact, to be its tendency, to me it would be no recommendation. I yield to none, I trust, in a deep and sincere attachment to our political institutions and the union of these States. I never breathed an opposite sentiment; but, on the contrary, I have ever considered them the great instruments of preserving our liberty, and promoting the happiness of ourselves and our posterity; the next to these I have ever held them most dear. Nearly half my life has been passed in the service of the Union, and whatever public reputation I have acquired is indissolubly identified with it. To be too national has, indeed, been considered by many, even of my friends, my greatest political fault. With these strong feelings of attachment, I have examined, with the utmost care, the bearing of the doctrine in question; and, so far from anarchical or revolutionary, I solemnly believe it to be the only solid foundation of our system, and of the Union itself; and that the opposite doctrine, which denies to the States the right of protecting their reserved powers, and which would vest in the General Government (it matters not through what department) the right of determining, exclusively and finally, the powers delegated to it, is incompatible with the sovereignty of the States, and of the Constitution itself, considered as the basis of a Federal Union. As strong as this language is, it is not stronger than that used by the illustrious Jefferson, who said, to give to the General Government the final and exclusive right to judge of its powers, is to make *"its discretion, and not the Constitution, the measure of its powers;"* and that, *"in all cases of compact between parties having no common judge, each party has an equal right to judge for itself, as well of the infraction as of the mode and measure of redress."* Language cannot be more explicit, nor can higher authority be adduced. . . . It has been well said by one of the most sagacious men of antiquity, that the object of a constitution is, *to restrain the government, as that of laws* is to restrain *individu-*

als. The remark is correct; nor is it less true where the government is vested in a majority, than where it is in a single or a few individuals—in a republic, than a monarchy or aristocracy. No one can have a higher respect for the maxim that the majority ought to govern that I have, taken in its proper sense, subject to the restrictions imposed by the Constitution, and confined to objects in which every portion of the community have similar interests; but it is a great error to suppose, as many do, that the right of a majority to govern is a natural and not a conventional right, and therefore absolute and unlimited. By nature, every individual has the right to govern himself; and governments, whether founded on majorities or minorities, must derive their right from the assent, expressed or implied, of the governed, and be subject to such limitations as they may impose. Where the interests are the same, that is, where the laws that may benefit one will benefit all, or the reverse, it is just and proper to place them under the control of the majority; but where they are dissimilar, so that the law that may benefit one portion may be ruinous to another, it would be, on the contrary, unjust and absurd to subject them to its will; and such I conceive to be the theory on which our Constitution rests.

That such dissimilarity of interests may exist, it is impossible to doubt. They are to be found in every community, in a greater or less degree, however small or homogeneous; and they constitute every where the great difficulty of forming and preserving free institutions. To guard against the unequal action of the laws, when applied to dissimilar and opposing interests, is, in fact, what mainly renders a constitution indispensable; to overlook which, in reasoning on our Constitution, would be to omit the principal element by which to determine its character. Were there no contrariety of interests, nothing would be more simple and easy than to form and preserve free institutions. The right of suffrage alone would be a sufficient guarantee. It is the conflict of opposing interests which renders it the most difficult work of man.

Where the diversity of interests exists in separate and distinct classes of the community, as is the case in England, and was formerly the case in Sparta, Rome, and most of the free States of antiquity, the rational constitutional provision is, that each should be represented in the government, as a separate estate, with a distinct voice, and a negative on the acts of its co-estates, in order to check their encroachments. In England, the Constitution has assumed expressly this form, while in the governments of Sparta and Rome, the same thing was effected under different, but not much less efficacious forms. The perfection of their organization, in this particular, was that which gave to the constitutions of these renowned States all their celebrity, which secured their liberty for so many centuries, and raised them to so great a height of power and prosperity. Indeed, a constitutional provision giving to the great and separate interests of the community the right of self-protection, must appear, to those who will duly reflect on the subject, not less essential to the preservation of liberty than the right of suffrage itself. They, in fact, have a common object, to effect which the one is as necessary as the other to secure *responsibility; that is, that those who make and execute the laws should be accountable to those on whom the laws in reality operate— the only solid and durable foundation of liberty.* If, without the right of suffrage, our rulers would oppress us, so, without the right of self-protection, the major would equally oppress the minor interests of the community. The absence of the former would make the governed the slaves of the rulers; and of the latter, the feebler interests, the victim of the stronger.

Happily for us, we have no artificial and separate classes of society. We have wisely exploded all such distinctions; but we are not, on that account, exempt from all contrariety of interests, as the present distracted and dangerous condition of our country, unfortunately, but too clearly proves. With us they are almost exclusively geographical, resulting mainly from difference of climate, soil, situation, industry, and production; but are not, therefore, less necessary to be protected by an adequate constitutional provision, than where the distinct interests exist in separate classes. The necessity is, in truth, greater, as such separate and dissimilar geographical interests are more liable to come into conflict, and more dangerous, when in that state, than those of any other description: so much so, that *ours is the first instance on record where they have not formed, in an extensive territory, separate and independent* communities, *or subjected the whole to despotic sway.* That such may not be our unhappy fate also, must be the sincere prayer of every lover of his country.

So numerous and diversified are the interests of our country, that they could not be fairly represented in a single government, organized so as to give to each great and leading interest a separate and distinct voice, as in governments to which I have referred. A plan was adopted better suited to our situation, but perfectly novel in its character. The powers of government were divided, not, as heretofore, in reference to classes, but geographically. One General Government was formed for the whole, to which were delegated all the powers supposed to be necessary to regulate the interests common to all the States, leaving others subject to the separate control of the States, being, from their local and peculiar character, such that they could not be subject to the will of a majority of the whole Union, without the certain hazard of injustice and oppression. It was thus that the interests of the whole were subjected, as they ought to be, to the will of the whole, while the peculiar and local interests were left under the control of the States separately, to whose custody only they could be safely confided. This distribution of power, settled solemnly by a constitutional compact, to which all the States are parties, constitutes the peculiar character and excellence of our political system. It is truly and emphatically *American, without example or parallel*. . . .

To realize its perfection, we must view the General Government and those of the States as a whole, each in its proper sphere independent; each perfectly adapted to its respective objects; the States acting separately, representing and protecting the local and peculiar interests; and acting jointly through one General Government, with the weight respectively assigned to each by the Constitution, representing and protecting the interest of the whole; and thus perfecting, by an admirable but simple arrangement, the great principle of representation and responsibility, without which no government can be free or just. To preserve this sacred distribution as originally settled, by coercing each to move in its prescribed orbit, is the great and difficult problem, on the solution of which the duration of our Constitution, of our Union, and, in all probability, our liberty depends. How is this to be effected?

The question is new, when applied to our peculiar political organization, where the separate and conflicting interests of society are represented by distinct but connected governments; but it is, in reality, an old question under a new form, long since perfectly solved. Whenever separate and dissimilar interests have been separately represented in any government; whenever the sovereign power has been divided in its exercise, the experience and wisdom of ages have devised but one mode by which such political organization can be preserved,—the mode adopted in England, and by all governments, ancient and modern, blessed with constitutions deserving to be called free—to give to each coestate the right to judge of its powers, with a negative or veto on the acts of the others, in order to protect against encroachments the interests it particularly represents: a principle which all of our

constitutions recognize in the distribution of power among their respective departments, as essential to maintain the independence of each; but which, to all who will duly reflect on the subject, must appear far more essential, for the same object, in that great and fundamental distribution of powers between the General and State Governments. So essential is the principle, that, to withhold the right from either, where the sovereign power is divided, is, in fact, *to annul the division* itself, and to *consolidate*, in the one left in the exclusive possession of the right, *all* powers of government; for it is not possible to distinguish, practically, between a government having all power, and one having the right to take what powers it pleases. Nor does it in the least vary the principle, whether the distribution of power be between co-estates, as in England, or between distinctly organized but connected governments, as with us. The reason is the same in both cases, while the necessity is greater in our case, as the danger of conflict is greater where the interests of a society are divided geographically than in any other, as has already been shown.

These truths do seem to me to be incontrovertible; and I am at a loss to understand how any one, who has maturely reflected on the nature of our institutions, or who has read history or studied the principles of free government to any purpose, can call them in question. The explanation must, it appears to me, be sought in the fact that, in every free State there are those who look more to the necessity of maintaining power than guarding against its abuses. I do not intend reproach, but simply to state a fact apparently necessary to explain the contrariety of opinions among the intelligent, where the abstract consideration of the subject would seem scarcely to admit of doubt. If such be the true cause, I must think the fear of weakening the government too much, in this case, to be in a great measure unfounded, or, at least, that the danger is much less from that than the opposite side. I do not deny that a power of so high a nature may be abused by a State; but when I reflect that the States unanimously called the General Government into existence with all its powers, which they freely delegated on their part, under the conviction that their common peace, safety, and prosperity required it; that they are bound together by a common origin, and the recollection of common suffering and common triumph in the great and splendid achievement of their independence; and that the strongest feelings of our nature, and among them the love of national power and distinction, are on the side of the Union, it does seem to me that the fear which would strip the States of their sovereignty, and degrade them, in fact, to mere dependent corporations, lest they should abuse a right indispensable to the peaceable protection of those interests which they reserved under their own peculiar guardianship when they created the General Government, is unnatural and unreasonable. If those who voluntarily created the system cannot be trusted to preserve it, who can?

So far from extreme danger, I hold that there never was a free State in which this great conservative principle, undispensable to all, was ever so safely lodged. In others, when the co-estates representing the dissimilar and conflicting interests of the community came into contact, the only alternative was compromise, submission, or force. Not so in ours. Should the General Government and a State come into conflict, we have a higher remedy: the power which called the General Government into existence, which gave it all its authority, and can enlarge, contract, or abolish its powers at its pleasure, may be invoked. The States themselves may be appealed to— three fourths of which, in fact, for a power, whose decrees are the Constitution itself, and whose voice can silence all discontent. The utmost extent, then, of the power is, that a State, acting in its sovereign capacity as one of the parties to the constitutional compact, may compel the Government, created by that compact, to submit a question touching its infraction, to the parties who created it: to avoid the supposed dangers of which, it is proposed to resort to the novel, the hazardous, and, I must add, fatal project of giving to the General Government the sole and final right of interpreting the Constitution:— thereby reversing the whole system, making that instrument the creature of its will, instead of a rule of action impressed on it at its creation, and annihilating, in fact, the authority which imposed it, and from which the Government itself derives its existence.

. . . The Tariff itself is a strong case in point; and the reason applies equally *to all others where Congress perverts a power from an object intended, to one not intended, the most insidious and dangerous of all infractions; and which may be extended to all of its powers, more especially to the taxing and appropriating.* But, supposing it competent to take cognizance of all infractions of every description, the insuperable objection still remains, that it would not be a safe tribunal to exercise the power in question.

It is a universal and fundamental political principle, that the power to protect can safely be confided only to those interested in protecting, or their responsible agents,—a maxim not less true in private than in public affairs. The danger in our system is, that the General Government, which represents the interests of the whole, may encroach on the States, which represent the peculiar and local interests, or that the latter may encroach on the former.

In examining this point, we ought not to forget that the Government, through all its departments, judicial as well as others, is administered by delegated and responsible agents; and that the *power which really controls, ultimately, all the movements, is not in the agents, but those who elect or appoint them.* To understand, then, its real character, and what would be the action of the system in any supposable case, we must raise our view from the mere agents to this high controlling power, which finally impels every movement of the machine. By doing so, we shall find all under the control of the will of a majority, compounded of the majority of the States, taken as political bodies, and the majority of the people of the States, estimated in federal numbers. These, united, constitute the real and final power which impels and directs the movements of the General Government. The majority of the States elect the majority of the Senate; of the people of the States, that of the House of Representatives; the two united, the President; and the President and a majority of the Senate appoint the judges: a majority of whom, and a majority of the Senate and House, with the President, really exercise all the powers of the Government, with the exception of the cases where the Constitution requires a greater number than a majority. The judges are, in fact, as truly the judicial representatives of this united majority, as the majority of Congress itself, or the President, is its legislative or executive representative; and to confide the power to the Judiciary to determine finally and conclusively what powers are delegated and what reserved, would be, in reality, to confide it to the majority, whose agents they are, and by whom they can be controlled in various ways; and, of course, to subject (against the fundamental principle of our system and all sound political reasoning) the reserved powers of the States, with all the local and peculiar interests they were intended to protect, to the will of the very majority against which the protection was intended. Nor will the tenure by which the judges hold their office, however valuable the provision in many other respects, materially vary the case. Its highest possible effect would be to *retard*, and not *finally* to *resist*, the will of a dominant majority.

But it is useless to multiply arguments. . . .

. . . Stripped of all its covering, the naked question is, whether ours is a federal or a consolidated government; a constitutional or absolute one; a government resting ultimately on the solid basis of the sovereignty of the States or on the unrestrained will of a majority; a form of government, as in all other unlimited ones, in which injustice and violence, and force must finally prevail. *Let it never be forgotten that, where the majority rules without restriction, the minority is the subject;* and that, if we should absurdly attribute to the former the exclusive right of construing the Constitution, there would be, in fact, between the sovereign and subject, under such a government, no Constitution, or, at least, nothing deserving the name, or serving the legitimate object of so sacred an instrument.

How the States are to exercise this high power of interposition, which constitutes so essential a portion of their reserved rights that it *cannot be delegated without an entire surrender of their sovereignty,* and converting our system from a *federal* into a *consolidated* Government, is a question that the States only are competent to determine. The arguments which prove that they possess the power, equally prove that they are, in the language of Jefferson, *"the rightful judges of the mode and measure of redress."* But the spirit of forbearance, as well as the nature of the right itself, forbids a recourse to it, except in cases of dangerous infractions of the Constitution; and then only in the last resort, when all reasonable hope of relief from the ordinary action of the Government has failed; when, if the right to interpose did not exist, the alternative would be submission and oppression on one side, or resistance by force on the other. That our system should afford, in such extreme cases, an intermediate point between these dire alternatives, by which the Government may be brought to a pause, and thereby an interval obtained to compromise differences, or, if impracticable, be compelled to submit the question to a constitutional adjustment, through an appeal to the States themselves, is an evidence of its high wisdom: an element not, as is supposed by some, of weakness, but of strength; not of anarchy or revolution, but of peace and safety. *Its general recognition would of itself, in a great measure, if not altogether, supersede the necessity of its exercise, by impressing on the movements of the Government that moderation and justice so essential to harmony and peace, in a country of such vast extent and diversity of interests as ours;* and would, if controversy should come, turn the resentment of the aggrieved from the system to those who had abused its powers (a point all-important), and cause them to seek redress, *not in revolution or overthrow, but in reformation.* It is, in fact, properly understood, *a substitute,—where the alternative would be force—tending to prevent, and, if that fails, to correct peaceably the aberrations to which all systems are liable, and which, if permitted to accumulate without correction, must finally end in a general catastrophe. . . .*

PART V

The Republic as Industrial Capitalism: Social Darwinism and the New Inequality

In the last decades of the nineteenth century, after the Civil War, the United States began a rapid transformation from a predominantly agrarian to an industrial nation. With industry came also huge new corporations, especially in railroads, iron, and steel; fabulously wealthy businessmen such as Jay Gould, Commodore Vanderbilt, Andrew Carnegie, and J. P. Morgan; and a propertyless urban working class with little economic security. From the perspective of traditional American republican theory, these developments should have brought the end of the republic.

Republican theory had always assumed that self-government required rough equality and a wide dispersion of property. In its classical form, for example in the writings of Jefferson and many Antifederalists, republicanism exhibited an agrarian bias that persisted in American thinking throughout much of the nineteenth and even twentieth centuries. For many, a nation dominated by commerce and manufacturing and populated with a large propertyless working class smacked of dependence and decay. Even those who held a Jacksonian faith in laissez-faire feared the rise of a new class of capitalists who concentrated so much capital and power in so few hands. Whereas the previous generation had seen the open, competitive market as a leveling device that helped to keep liberty and equality compatible, many now saw the unhampered marketplace as a race that only a few could win. In a twist, open markets and laissez-faire economics seemed to allow the rich to get richer while everyone else fell behind.

Ironically, as laissez-faire ceased to satisfy egalitarians, it found a new set of adherents among those who praised the unique contributions of the very wealthy. Unlike Whig or Federalist defenders of wealth, these new conservatives opposed any state interference with the market or the sanctity of the contract. Many turned to the Manchester school of economics and the writings of English classical liberals such as Jeremy Bentham, David Ricardo, Richard Cobden, and Herbert Spencer for support.

Spencer, especially, provided a useful rationale for inequality in his contention that survival of the fittest provided the only basis for social progress and evolution. In *Social Statics,* written in 1850, nine years before Darwin's *Origin of the Species* (1859), and in *Man versus the State* (1884), which incorporated a pseudo-Darwinian biological argument into his theory of social evolution, Spencer held to the belief that ruthless competition helped society weed out the weak and advance (and reproduce) the strong. In this view, social welfare programs, and even charity, impeded progress by perpetuating the unfit and hampering the superior.

Spencer found his most faithful and articulate follower in an American, William Graham Sumner. From his faculty position at Yale, Sumner attacked all attempts to interfere with individuals in the market. His alternatives were stark: "liberty, inequality, survival of the fittest; non-liberty, equality, survival of the unfittest." Similar views were offered by steel magnate Andrew Carnegie, a premier symbol of the new order, who nevertheless urged the wealthy to offer philanthropic aid to educational institutions and libraries.

Religious writers, as well, began to praise the new wealth and attempt to demonstrate the compatibility of Christian and marketplace behavior. Russell Conwell, a Baptist minister and president of Temple College (later Temple University), made a fortune delivering his "Acres of Diamonds" speech extolling the virtue of economic success. Consistent with the times, many black leaders, led by Booker T. Washington, were willing to postpone the dream of equal rights articulated by the previous generation for the immediate promise of economic development for blacks.

However, the new inequality had more than a few detractors. Many with egalitarian sentiments attempted to revive Jacksonian liberalism in ways they felt were compatible with new economic conditions. Blacks such as Monroe Trotter and W. E. B. Du Bois staunchly maintained that social and political equality were prerequisites for blacks' economic progress. For many other reformers, the desire to revive the competition of smaller economic units and the sense of equal opportunity that had existed earlier led them to advocate the Sherman Antitrust Act of 1890 and the later antitrust "New Freedom" agenda of Louis Brandeis and Woodrow Wilson. Late in the nineteenth century, many agrarian Populists tried to build a political and economic order that could sustain small farmers, who were losing their land. Henry George's arguments for a "single tax" symbolized the feeling of many that the America of the new industrial age no longer included them as full and equal participants. George argued that the masses of Americans had created our tremendous wealth, but only a few truly shared in it.

Many Populist and, later, Progressive proposals attempted to break up corporate monopolies. These proposals often led theorists to revive Lockean individualist themes, and therefore required little in the way of a new political consciousness. However, many Populists also advocated nationalizing railroads and sought government aid for cooperative banks, mills, and storage facilities. Furthermore, their view of honest labor being exploited by capitalists and financiers indicated an awareness of class conflict that departed from much of the liberal individualist tradition in America.

Even more conscious of class were socialist activists and writers such as Eugene V. Debs, Victor Berger, Laurence Grounlund, and Morris Hilquit. Many of these socialists appealed to older republican notions of virtue and self-sufficiency, but argued they could not be achieved in a capitalist market system. In fact, socialist politics probably reached its zenith in American politics during this period.

As America entered the twentieth century, a subtle ideological transformation had begun. Defenders of exceptional wealth had appropriated the rhetoric and outlook of laissez-faire, stripped of its egalitarian content. Advocates of greater equality, on the other hand, began to look elsewhere for philosophical support, and often in directions that deviated radically from traditional Lockean individualism.

The New Orthodoxy:

Inequality as Progress

William Graham Sumner, 1840–1910

A social scientist and theologian, William Graham Sumner is the American most associated with the doctrine of social Darwinism, that is, the belief that nature ordained the "survival of the fittest."

Sumner was born in Paterson, New Jersey, and grew up in Hartford, Connecticut. He graduated from Yale in 1863 with an interest in religion and left to study in Geneva, Gottingen, and Oxford in the hope of entering the ministry. From 1866 to 1869, he returned to Yale as a tutor, and in 1869, he became a minister for a Protestant Episcopal Church in Morristown, New Jersey. However, in 1872, he left the ministry and returned to Yale as a professor of political and social science.

Sumner was greatly influenced by Herbert Spencer and believed that fierce social and economic competition produced both material progress and the improvement of the race. Social welfare legislation was simply misguided sentimentalism that hindered the rise of the most capable and perpetuated those who were least capable. As an economist, Sumner favored free trade, sound money, and laissez-faire. Unlike the Jacksonians who also advocated laissez-faire, however, Sumner had nothing but praise for inequality and social stratification.

The combination of laissez-faire and inequality found favor with the newly rich industrialists of the United States. Sumner's doctrines offered social legitimacy for their success. Ironically, Sumner feared plutocracy and lionized "the forgotten man," that is, the independent, middle class, head of the household who asked little of anyone. Nevertheless, it was among the very rich that he found his most appreciative audience.

William Graham Sumner was the author of many collections of essays

322

and lectures and also wrote a classic work on mores and customs, *Folkways*, in 1906. In 1927, a posthumous edition of his unfinished grand sociological work was published under the title of *The Science of Society*.

The selection that follows is taken from the famous 1883 book *What Social Classes Owe to Each Other*, which expresses clearly Sumner's views on individualism and political economy.

William Graham Sumner

What Social Classes Owe to Each Other (1883)

INTRODUCTION

We are told every day that great social problems stand before us and demand a solution, and we are assailed by oracles, threats, and warnings in reference to those problems. There is a school of writers who are playing quite a *rôle* as the heralds of the coming duty and the coming woe. They assume to speak for a large, but vague and undefined, constituency, who set the task, exact a fulfilment, and threaten punishment for default. The task or problem is not specifically defined. Part of the task which devolves on those who are subject to the duty is to define the problem. They are told only that something is the matter: that it behooves them to find out what it is, and how to correct it, and then to work out the cure. All this is more or less truculently set forth.

After reading and listening to a great deal of this sort of assertion I find that the question forms itself with more and more distinctness in my mind: Who are those who assume to put hard questions to other people and to demand a solution of them? How did they

SOURCE: William Graham Sumner, *What Social Classes Owe to Each Other* (New York: Harper and Brothers, 1883).

acquire the right to demand that others should solve their world-problems for them? Who are they who are held to consider and solve all questions, and how did they fall under this duty?

So far as I can find out what the classes are who are respectively endowed with the rights and duties of posing and solving social problems, they are as follows: Those who are bound to solve the problems are the rich, comfortable, prosperous, virtuous, respectable, educated, and healthy; those whose right it is to set the problems are those who have been less fortunate or less successful in the struggle for existence. The problem itself seems to be, How shall the latter be made as comfortable as the former? To solve this problem, and make us all equally well off, is assumed to be the duty of the former class; the penalty, if they fail of this, is to be bloodshed and destruction. If they cannot make everybody else as well off as themselves, they are to be brought down to the same misery as others.

During the last ten years I have read a great many books and articles, especially by German writers, in which an attempt has been made to set up "the State" as an entity having conscience, power, and will sublimated above human limitations, and as constituting a tutelary genius over us all. I have never been able to find in history or experience anything to fit this concept. I once lived in Germany for two years, but I certainly saw nothing of it there then. Whether the State which Bismarck is moulding will fit the notion is at best a matter of faith and hope. My notion of the State has dwindled with growing experience of life. As an abstraction, the State is to me only All-of-us. In practice—that is, when it exercises will or adopts a line of action—it is only a little group of men chosen in a very hap-hazard way by the majority of us to perform certain services for all of us. The majority do not go about their selection very rationally, and they are almost always disappointed by the results of their own operation. Hence "the State," instead of offering resources of wisdom, right reason, and pure moral sense beyond what the average of us possess, generally offers much less of all those things. Furthermore, it often turns out in practice that "the State" is not even the known and accredited servants of the State, but, as has been well said, is only some obscure clerk, hidden in the recesses of a Government bureau, into whose power the chance has fallen for the moment to pull one of the stops which control the Government machine. In former days it often happened that "the State" was a barber, a fiddler, or a bad woman. In our day it often happens that "the State" is a little functionary on whom a big functionary is forced to depend. . . .

If anybody is to benefit from the action of the State it must be Some-of-us. If, then, the question is raised, What ought the State to do for labor, for trade, for manufactures, for the poor, for the learned professions? etc., etc.—that is, for a class or an interest—it is really the question, What ought All-of-us to do for Some-of-us? But Some-of-us are included in All-of-us, and, so far as they get the benefit of their own efforts, it is the same as if they worked for themselves, and they

may be cancelled out of All-of-us. Then the question which remains is, What ought Some-of-us to do for Others-of-us? or, What do social classes owe to each other?

I now propose to try to find out whether there is any class in society which lies under the duty and burden of fighting the battles of life for any other class, or of solving social problems for the satisfaction of any other class; also, whether there is any class which has the right to formulate demands on "society"—that is, on other classes; also, whether there is anything but a fallacy and a superstition in the notion that "the State" owes anything to anybody except peace, order, and the guarantees of rights.

I have in view, throughout the discussion, the economic, social, and political circumstances which exist in the United States.

I.

ON A NEW PHILOSOPHY: THAT POVERTY IS THE BEST POLICY.

It is commonly asserted that there are in the United States no classes, and any allusion to classes is resented. On the other hand, we constantly read and hear discussions of social topics in which the existence of social classes is assumed as a simple fact. "The poor," "the weak," "the laborers," are expressions which are used as if they had exact and well-understood definition. Discussions are made to bear upon the assumed rights, wrongs, and misfortunes of certain social classes; and all public speaking and writing consists, in a large measure, of the discussion of general plans for meeting the wishes of classes of people who have not been able to satisfy their own desires. These classes are sometimes discontented, and sometimes not. Sometimes they do not know that anything is amiss with them until the "friends of humanity" come to them with offers of aid. Sometimes they are discontented and envious. They do not take their achievements as a fair measure of their rights. They do not blame themselves or their parents for their lot, as compared with that of other people. Sometimes they claim that they have a right to everything of which they feel the need for their happiness on earth. To make such a claim against God or Nature would, of course, be only to say that we claim a right to live on earth if we can. But God and Nature have ordained the chances and conditions of life on earth once for all. The case cannot be reopened. We cannot get a revision of the laws of human life. We are absolutely shut up to the need and duty, if we would learn how to live happily, of investigating the laws of Nature, and deducing the rules of right living in the world as it is. These are very wearisome and commonplace tasks. They consist in labor and self-denial repeated over and over again in learning and doing. When the people whose claims we are considering are told to apply themselves to these tasks they become irritated and feel almost insulted. They formulate their claims as rights against society—that is, against some other men. In their view they have a right, not only to *pursue* happiness, but to *get* it; and if they fail to get it, they think they have a claim to the aid of other men—that is, to the labor and self-denial of other men—to get it for them. They find orators and poets who tell them that they have grievances, so long as they have unsatisfied desires.

Now, if there are groups of people who have a claim to other people's labor and self-denial, and if there are other people whose labor and self-denial are liable to be claimed by the first groups, then there certainly are "classes," and classes of the oldest and most vicious type. For a man who can command another man's labor and self-denial for the support of his own existence is a privileged person of the highest species conceivable on earth. Princes and paupers meet on this plane, and no other men are on it at all. On the

other hand, a man whose labor and self-denial may be diverted from his maintenance to that of some other man is not a free man, and approaches more or less toward the position of a slave. Therefore we shall find that, in all the notions which we are to discuss, this elementary contradiction, that there are classes and that there are not classes, will produce repeated confusion and absurdity. We shall find that, in our efforts to eliminate the old vices of class government, we are impeded and defeated by new products of the worst class theory. We shall find that all the schemes for producing equality and obliterating the organization of society produce a new differentiation based on the worst possible distinction—the right to claim and the duty to give one man's effort for another man's satisfaction. We shall find that every effort to realize equality necessitates a sacrifice of liberty. . . .

Certain ills belong to the hardships of human life. They are natural. They are part of the struggle with Nature for existence. We cannot blame our fellow-men for our share of these. My neighbor and I are both struggling to free ourselves from these ills. The fact that my neighbor has succeeded in this struggle better than I constitutes no grievance for me. Certain other ills are due to the malice of men, and to the imperfections or errors of civil institutions. These ills are an object of agitation, and a subject of discussion. The former class of ills is to be met only by manly effort and energy; the latter may be corrected by associated effort. The former class of ills is constantly grouped and generalized, and made the object of social schemes. We shall see, as we go on, what that means. The second class of ills may fall on certain social classes, and reform will take the form of interference by other classes in favor of that one. The last fact is, no doubt, the reason why people have been led, not noticing distinctions, to believe that the same method was applicable to the other class of ills. The distinction here made between the ills which belong to the struggle for existence and those which are due to the faults of human institutions is of prime importance. . . .

There is no possible definition of "a poor man." A pauper is a person who cannot earn his living; whose producing powers have fallen positively below his necessary consumption; who cannot, therefore, pay his way. A human society needs the active co-operation and productive energy of every person in it. A man who is present as a consumer, yet who does not contribute either by land, labor, or capital to the work of society, is a burden. On no sound political theory ought such a person to share in the political power of the State. He drops out of the ranks of workers and producers. Society must support him. It accepts the burden, but he must be cancelled from the ranks of the rulers likewise. So much for the pauper. About him no more need be said. But he is not the "poor man." The "poor man" is an elastic term, under which any number of social fallacies may be hidden.

Neither is there any possible definition of "the weak." Some are weak in one way, and some in another; and those who are weak in one sense are strong in another. In general, however, it may be said that those whom humanitarians and philanthropists call the weak are the ones through whom the productive and conservative forces of society are wasted. They constantly neutralize and destroy the finest efforts of the wise and industrious, and are a dead-weight on the society in all its struggles to realize any better things. Whether the people who mean no harm, but are weak in the essential powers necessary to the performance of one's duties in life, or those who are malicious and vicious, do the more mischief, is a question not easy to answer.

Under the names of the poor and the weak, the negligent, shiftless, inefficient, silly, and imprudent are fastened upon the industrious and prudent as a responsibility and a duty. On the one side, the terms are extended to cover the idle, intemperate, and vicious, who,

by the combination, gain credit which they do not deserve, and which they could not get if they stood alone. On the other hand, the terms are extended to include wage-receivers of the humblest rank, who are degraded by the combination. The reader who desires to guard himself against fallacies should always scrutinize the terms "poor" and "weak" as used, so as to see which or how many of these classes they are made to cover. . . .

In all these schemes and projects the organized intervention of society through the State is either planned or hoped for, and the State is thus made to become the protector and guardian of certain classes. The agents who are to direct the State action are, of course, the reformers and philanthropists. Their schemes, therefore, may always be reduced to this type—that A and B decide what C shall do for D. It will be interesting to inquire, at a later period of our discussion, who C is, and what the effect is upon him of all these arrangements. In all the discussions attention is concentrated on A and B, the noble social reformers, and on D, the "poor man." I call C the Forgotten Man, because I have never seen that any notice was taken of him in any of the discussions. When we have disposed of A, B, and D we can better appreciate the case of C, and I think that we shall find that he deserves our attention, for the worth of his character and the magnitude of his unmerited burdens. Here it may suffice to observe that, on the theories of the social philosophers to whom I have referred, we should get a new maxim of judicious living: Poverty is the best policy. If you get wealth, you will have to support other people; if you do not get wealth, it will be the duty of other people to support you.

No doubt one chief reason for the unclear and contradictory theories of class relations lies in the fact that our society, largely controlled in all its organization by one set of doctrines, still contains survivals of old social theories which are totally inconsistent with the former. In the Middle Ages men were united by custom and prescription into associations, ranks, guilds, and communities of various kinds. These ties endured as long as life lasted. Consequently society was dependent, throughout all its details, on status, and the tie, or bond, was sentimental. In our modern state, and in the United States more than anywhere else, the social structure is based on contract, and status is of the least importance. Contract, however, is rational—even rationalistic. It is also realistic, cold, and matter-of-fact. A contract relation is based on a sufficient reason, not on custom or prescription. It is not permanent. It endures only so long as the reason for it endures. In a state based on contract sentiment is out of place in any public or common affairs. It is relegated to the sphere of private and personal relations, where it depends not at all on class types, but on personal acquaintance and personal estimates. The sentimentalists among us always seize upon the survivals of the old order. They want to save them and restore them. Much of the loose thinking also which troubles us in our social discussions arises from the fact that men do not distinguish the elements of status and of contract which may be found in our society.

Whether social philosophers think it desirable or not, it is out of the question to go back to status or to the sentimental relations which once united baron and retainer, master and servant, teacher and pupil, comrade and comrade. That we have lost some grace and elegance is undeniable. That life once held more poetry and romance is true enough. But it seems impossible that any one who has studied the matter should doubt that we have gained immeasurably, and that our farther gains lie in going forward, not in going backward. The feudal ties can never be restored. If they could be restored they would bring back personal caprice, favoritism, sycophancy, and intrigue. A society based on contract is a society of free and independent men, who form ties without

favor or obligation, and cooperate without cringing or intrigue. A society based on contract, therefore, gives the utmost room and chance for individual development, and for all the self-reliance and dignity of a free man. That a society of free men, co-operating under contract, is by far the strongest society which has ever yet existed; that no such society has ever yet developed the full measure of strength of which it is capable; and that the only social improvements which are now conceivable lie in the direction of more complete realization of a society of free men united by contract, are points which cannot be controverted. It follows, however, that one man, in a free state, cannot claim help from, and cannot be charged to give help to, another. To understand the full meaning of this assertion it will be worth while to see what a free democracy is.

X.

THE CASE OF THE FORGOTTEN MAN FURTHER CONSIDERED.

. . . It is plain that the Forgotten Man and the Forgotten Woman are the real productive strength of the country. The Forgotten Man works and votes—generally he prays—but his chief business in life is to pay. His name never gets into the newspapers except when he marries or dies. He is an obscure man. He may grumble sometimes to his wife, but he does not frequent the grocery, and he does not talk politics at the tavern. So he is forgotten. Yet who is there whom the statesman, economist, and social philosopher ought to think of before this man? If any student of social science comes to appreciate the case of the Forgotten Man, he will become an unflinching advocate of strict scientific thinking in sociology, and a hard-hearted sceptic as regards any scheme of social amelioration. He will always want to know, Who and where is the

Forgotten Man in this case, who will have to pay for it all?

The Forgotten Man is not a pauper. It belongs to his character to save something. Hence he is a capitalist, though never a great one. He is a "poor" man in the popular sense of the word, but not in a correct sense. In fact, one of the most constant and trustworthy signs that the Forgotten Man is in danger of a new assault is, that "the poor man" is brought into the discussion. Since the Forgotten Man has some capital, any one who cares for his interest will try to make capital secure by securing the inviolability of contracts, the stability of currency, and the firmness of credit. Any one, therefore, who cares for the Forgotten Man will be sure to be considered a friend of the capitalist and an enemy of the poor man.

It is the Forgotten Man who is threatened by every extension of the paternal theory of government. It is he who must work and pay. When, therefore, the statesmen and social philosophers sit down to think what the State can do or ought to do, they really mean to decide what the Forgotten Man shall do. What the Forgotten Man wants, therefore, is a fuller realization of constitutional liberty. He is suffering from the fact that there are yet mixed in our institutions mediaeval theories of protection, regulation, and authority, and modern theories of independence and individual liberty and responsibility. The consequence of this mixed state of things is, that those who are clever enough to get into control use the paternal theory by which to measure their own rights—that is, they assume privileges; and they use the theory of liberty to measure their own duties—that is, when it comes to the duties, they want to be "let alone." The Forgotten Man never gets into control. He has to pay both ways. His rights are measured to him by the theory of liberty—that is, he has only such as he can conquer; his duties are measured to him on the paternal theory—that is, he must discharge all which are laid

upon him, as is the fortune of parents. In a paternal relation there are always two parties, a father and a child; and when we use the paternal relation metaphorically, it is of the first importance to know who is to be father and who is to be child. The *rôle* of parent falls always to the Forgotten Man. What he wants, therefore, is that ambiguities in our institutions be cleared up, and that liberty be more fully realized.

It behooves any economist or social philosopher, whatever be the grade of his orthodoxy, who proposes to enlarge the sphere of the "State," or to take any steps whatever having to view the welfare of any class whatever, to pursue the analysis of the social effects of his proposition until he finds that other group whose interests must be curtailed or whose energies must be placed under contribution by the course of action which he proposes; and he cannot maintain his proposition until he has demonstrated that it will be more advantageous, *both quantitatively and qualitatively,* to those who must bear the weight of it than complete non-interference by the State with the relations of the parties in question.

XI.

WHEREFORE WE SHOULD LOVE ONE ANOTHER.

. . . We each owe it to the other to guarantee rights. Rights do not pertain to *results,* but only to *chances.* They pertain to the *conditions* of the struggle for existence, not to any of the results of it; to the *pursuit* of happiness, not to the possession of happiness. It cannot be said that each one has a right to have some property, because if one man had such a right some other man or men would be under a corresponding obligation to provide him with some property. Each has a right to acquire and possess property if he can. It is plain what fallacies are developed when we overlook this distinction. Those fallacies run through *all* socialistic schemes and theories. If we take rights to pertain to results, and then say that rights must be equal, we come to say that men have a right to be equally happy, and so on in all the details. Rights should be equal, because they pertain to chances, and all ought to have equal chances so far as chances are provided or limited by the action of society. This, however, will not produce equal results, but it is right just because it will produce unequal results—that is, results which shall be proportioned to the merits of individuals. We each owe it to the other to guarantee mutually the chance to earn, to possess, to learn, to marry, etc., etc., against any interference which would prevent the exercise of those rights by a person who wishes to prosecute and enjoy them in peace for the pursuit of happiness. If we generalize this, it means that All-of-us ought to guarantee rights to each of us. But our modern free, constitutional States are constructed entirely on the notion of rights, and we regard them as performing their functions more and more perfectly according as they guarantee rights in consonance with the constantly corrected and expanded notions of rights from one generation to another. Therefore, when we say that we owe it to each other to guarantee rights we only say that we ought to prosecute and improve our political science.

If we have in mind the value of chances to earn, learn, possess, etc., for a man of independent energy, we can go on one step farther in our deductions about help. The only help which is generally expedient, even within the limits of the private and personal relations of two persons to each other, is that which consists in helping a man to help himself. This always consists in opening the chances. A man of assured position can, by an effort which is of no appreciable importance to him, give aid which is of incalculable value to a man who is all ready to make his own career if he can only get a chance. The truest and deepest pathos in this world is not that of suffering but that of brave struggling. The truest sympathy is not compassion, but a fellow-feeling with courage and fortitude in the midst of noble effort.

Now, the aid which helps a man to help himself is not in the least akin to the aid which is given in charity. If alms are given, or if we "make work" for a man, or "give him employment," or "protect" him, we simply take a product from one and give it to another. If we help a man to help himself, by opening the chances around him, we put him in a position to add to the wealth of the community by putting new powers in operation to produce. It would seem that the difference between getting something already in existence from the one who has it, and producing a new thing by applying new labor to natural materials, would be so plain as never to be forgotten; but the fallacy of confusing the two is one of the commonest in all social discussions. . . .

The class distinctions simply result from the different degrees of success with which men have availed themselves of the chances which were presented to them. Instead of endeavoring to redistribute the acquisitions which have been made between the existing classes, our aim should be to *increase, multiply, and extend the chances*. Such is the work of civilization. Every old error or abuse which is removed opens new chances of development to all the new energy of society. Every improvement in education, science, art, or government expands the chances of man on earth. Such expansion is no guarantee of equality. On the contrary, if there be liberty, some will profit by the chances eagerly and some will neglect them altogether. Therefore, the greater the chances the more unequal will be the fortune of these two sets of men. So it ought to be, in all justice and right reason. The yearning after equality is the offspring of envy and covetousness, and there is no possible plan for satisfying that yearning which can do aught else than rob A to give to B; consequently all such plans nourish some of the meanest vices of human nature, waste capital, and overthrow civilization. But if we can expand the chances we can count on a general and steady growth of civilization and advancement of society by and through its best members. In the prosecution of these chances we all owe to each other good-will, mutual respect, and mutual guarantees of liberty and security. Beyond this nothing can be affirmed as a duty of one group to another in a free state.

Andrew Carnegie, 1835–1909

Andrew Carnegie is remembered as one of the leading businessmen of the so-called Gilded Age and as a tremendously generous philanthropist. Unlike most of his business contemporaries, he was also a popular and influential essayist.

As a young boy, Carnegie, came to the United States with his family from Scotland. His parents had been involved in the radical Chartist movement, and despite all of Andrew's later wealth and his hostility to labor unions, he retained a fierce commitment to the ideal of equality of opportunity throughout his life. As a youth, Carnegie had lived in poverty. He had no more than a grammar school education, and by the age of ten was hard at work as a bobbin boy in a cotton mill. He later became a telegraph office messenger boy and soon moved up the ladder to positions of greater responsibility within the Pennsylvania Railroad. Carnegie rose rapidly through the ranks, but by 1865, he had set out on his own with his first firm, the Keystone Bridge Company.

By 1873, Carnegie had begun to invest heavily in the Bessemer steel process, and after weathering the panic of 1893, emerged with the top firm in the steel industry. With the help of Henry C. Frick, he violently suppressed the Homestead steel strike of 1894. In 1901, Carnegie sold his steel interests to J. P. Morgan and U.S. Steel.

Carnegie then began to change his course and devoted his energies to writing and philanthropy. In 1889, he published a famous article "Wealth" (later called the "Gospel of Wealth") in the *North American Review*. In this and other works, he argued for the obligation of the wealthy to give generously to charities and civic and educational institutions. He also called for the elimination of all inherited wealth.

During this period, Carnegie gave generously of his own money, especially to libraries, universities, and research institutions.

The following writings of Andrew Carnegie are taken from the 1889 essay "Wealth."

Andrew Carnegie

Wealth (1889)

The problem of our age is the proper administration of wealth, so that the ties of brotherhood may still bind together the rich and poor in harmonious relationship. The conditions of human life have not only been changed, but revolutionized, within the past few hundred years. In former days there was little difference between the dwelling, dress, food, and environment of the chief and those of his retainers. The Indians are to-day where civilized man then was. When visiting the Sioux, I was led to the wigwam of the chief. It was just like the others in external appearance, and even within the difference was trifling between it and those of the poorest of his braves. The contrast between the palace of the millionaire and the cottage of the laborer with us to-day measures the change which has come with civilization.

This change, however, is not to be deplored, but welcomed as highly beneficial. It is well, nay, essential for the progress of the race, that the houses of some should be homes for all that is highest and best in literature and the arts, and for all the refinements of civilization, rather than that none should be so. Much better this great irregularity than universal squalor. Without wealth there can be no Maecenas. The "good old times" were not good old times. Neither master nor servant was as well situated then as to-day. A relapse to old conditions would be disastrous to both—not the least so to him who serves—and would

SOURCE: *North American Review* 148, no. 391 (June 1889).

sweep away civilization with it. But whether the change be for good or ill, it is upon us, beyond our power to alter, and therefore to be accepted and made the best of. It is a waste of time to criticise the inevitable.

It is easy to see how the change has come. One illustration will serve for almost every phase of the cause. In the manufacture of products we have the whole story. It applies to all combinations of human industry, as stimulated and enlarged by the inventions of this scientific age. Formerly articles were manufactured at the domestic hearth or in small shops which formed part of the household. The master and his apprentices worked side by side, the latter living with the master, and therefore subject to the same conditions. When these apprentices rose to be masters, there was little or no change in their mode of life, and they, in turn, educated in the same routine succeeding apprentices. There was, substantially, social equality, and even political equality, for those engaged in industrial pursuits had then little or no political voice in the State.

But the inevitable result of such a mode of manufacture was crude articles at high prices. To-day the world obtains commodities of excellent quality at prices which even the generation preceding this would have deemed incredible. In the commercial world similar causes have produced similar results, and the race is benefited thereby. The poor enjoy what the rich could not before afford. What were the luxuries have become the necessaries of life. The laborer has now more comforts than the farmer had a few generations ago. The farmer has more luxuries than the landlord had, and is more richly clad and better housed. The landlord has books and pictures rarer, and appointments more artistic, than the King could then obtain.

The price we pay for this salutary change is, no doubt, great. We assemble thousands of operatives in the factory, in the mine, and in the counting-house, of whom the employer can know little or nothing, and to whom the employer is little better than a myth. All intercourse between them is at an end. Rigid Castes are formed, and, as usual, mutual ignorance breeds mutual distrust. Each Caste is without sympathy for the other, and ready to credit anything disparaging in regard to it. Under the law of competition, the employer of thousands is forced into the strictest economies, among which the rates paid to labor figure prominently, and often there is friction between the employer and the employed, between capital and labor, between rich and poor. Human society loses homogeneity.

The price which society pays for the law of competition, like the price it pays for cheap comforts and luxuries, is also great; but the advantages of this law are also greater still, for it is to this law that we owe our wonderful material development, which brings improved conditions in its train. But, whether the law be benign or not, we must say of it, as we say of the change in the conditions of men to which we have referred: It is here; we cannot evade it; no substitutes for it have been found; and while the law may be sometimes hard for the individual, it is best for the race, because it insures the survival of the fittest in every department. We accept and welcome, therefore, as conditions to which we must accommodate ourselves, great inequality of environment, the concentration of business, industrial and commercial, in the hands of a few, and the law of competition between these, as being not only beneficial, but essential for the future progress of the race. Having accepted these, it follows that there must be great scope for the exercise of special ability in the merchant and in the manufacturer who has to conduct affairs upon a great scale. That this talent for organization and management is rare among men is proved by the fact that it invariably secures for its possessor enormous rewards, no matter where or under what laws or conditions. The experienced in affairs always rate the MAN whose services can be obtained as a partner as not only the first consideration, but such as to render the question of his capital scarcely worth considering, for such men soon create capital; while, without the special talent required, capital soon takes wings. Such men become interested in firms or corporations using millions; and estimating only simple interest to be made upon the capital invested, it is inevitable that their income must exceed their expenditures, and that they must accumulate wealth. Nor is there any middle ground which such men can occupy, because the great manufacturing or commercial concern which does not earn at least interest upon its capital soon becomes bankrupt. It must either go forward or fall behind: to stand still is impossible. It is a condition essential for its successful operation that it should be thus far profitable, and even that, in addition to interest on capital, it should make profit. It is a law, as certain as any of the others named, that men possessed of this peculiar talent for affairs, under the free play of economic forces, must, of necessity, soon be in receipt of more revenue than can be judiciously expended upon themselves; and this law is as beneficial for the race as the others.

Objections to the foundations upon which society is based are not in order, because the condition of the race is better with these than it has been with any others which have been tried. Of the effect of any new substitutes proposed we cannot be sure. The Socialist or Anarchist who seeks to overturn present conditions is to be regarded as attacking the foundation upon which civilization itself rests, for civilization took its start from the day that the capable, industrious workman said to his incompetent and lazy fellow, "If thou dost not sow, thou shalt not reap," and thus ended primitive Communism by separating the drones from the bees. One who studies this subject will soon be brought face to face with the conclusion that upon the sacredness of property civilization itself depends—the right of the laborer to his hundred dollars in the savings bank, and equally the legal right of the millionaire to his millions. To those who propose to substitute Communism for this intense Individualism the answer, therefore, is: The race has tried that. All progress from that barbarous day to the present time has resulted from its displacement. Not evil, but good, has come to the race from the accumulation of wealth by those who have the ability and energy that produce it. . . . We might as well urge the destruction of the highest existing type of man because he failed to reach our ideal as to favor the destruction of Individualism, Private Property, the Law of Accumulation of Wealth, and the Law of Competition; for these are the highest results of human experience, the soil in which society so far has produced the best fruit. Unequally or unjustly, perhaps, as these laws sometimes operate, and imperfect as they appear to the Idealist, they are, nevertheless, like the highest type of man, the best and most valuable of all that humanity has yet accomplished.

We start, then, with a condition of affairs under which the best interests of the race are promoted, but which inevitably gives wealth to the few. Thus far, accepting conditions as they exist, the situation can be surveyed and pronounced good. The question then arises, —and, if the foregoing be correct, it is the only question with which we have to deal,— What is the proper mode of administering wealth after the laws upon which civilization is founded have thrown it into the hands of the few? And it is of this great question that I believe I offer the true solution. It will be understood that *fortunes* are here spoken of,

not moderate sums saved by many years of effort, the returns from which are required for the comfortable maintenance and education of families. This is not *wealth*, but only *competence*, which it should be the aim of all to acquire.

There are but three modes in which surplus wealth can be disposed of. It can be left to the families of the decedents; or it can be bequeathed for public purposes; or, finally, it can be administered during their lives by its possessors. Under the first and second modes most of the wealth of the world that has reached the few has hitherto been applied. Let us in turn consider each of these modes. The first is the most injudicious. In monarchical countries, the estates and the greatest portion of the wealth are left to the first son, that the vanity of the parent may be gratified by the thought that his name and title are to descend to succeeding generations unimpaired. The condition of this class in Europe to-day teaches the futility of such hopes or ambitions. The successors have become impoverished through their follies or from the fall in the value of land. . . .

Why should men leave great fortunes to their children? If this is done from affection, is it not misguided affection? Observation teaches that, generally speaking, it is not well for the children that they should be so burdened. Neither is it well for the state. Beyond providing for the wife and daughters moderate sources of income, and very moderate allowances indeed, if any, for the sons, men may well hesitate, for it is no longer questionable that great sums bequeathed oftener work more for the injury than for the good of the recipients. Wise men will soon conclude that, for the best interests of the members of their families and of the state, such bequests are an improper use of their means.

It is not suggested that men who have failed to educate their sons to earn a livelihood shall cast them adrift in poverty. If any man has seen fit to rear his sons with a view to their living idle lives, or, what is highly commendable, has instilled in them the sentiment that they are in a position to labor for public ends without reference to pecuniary considerations, then, of course, the duty of the parent is to see that such are provided for *in moderation*. There are instances of millionaires' sons unspoiled by wealth, who, being rich, still perform great services in the community. Such are the very salt of the earth, as valuable as, unfortunately, they are rare; still it is not the exception, but the rule, that men must regard, and, looking at the usual result of enormous sums conferred upon legatees, the thoughtful man must shortly say, "I would as soon leave to my son a curse as the almighty dollar," and admit to himself that it is not the welfare of the children, but family pride, which inspires these enormous legacies.

The growing disposition to tax more and more heavily large estates left at death is a cheering indication of the growth of a salutary change in public opinion. The State of Pennsylvania now takes—subject to some exceptions—one-tenth of the property left by its citizens. The budget presented in the British Parliament the other day proposes to increase the death-duties; and, most significant of all, the new tax is to be a graduated one. Of all forms of taxation, this seems the wisest. Men who continue hoarding great sums all their lives, the proper use of which for public ends would work good to the community, should be made to feel that the community, in the form of the state, cannot thus be deprived of its proper share. By taxing estates heavily at death the state marks its condemnation of the selfish millionaire's unworthy life.

It is desirable that nations should go much further in this direction. Indeed, it is difficult to set bounds to the share of a rich man's estate which should go at his death to the public through the agency of the state, and by all means such taxes should be graduated, beginning at nothing upon moderate sums to dependents, and increasing rapidly as the amounts swell, until of the millionaire's hoard, as of Shylock's, at least

———The other half
Comes to the privy coffer of the state.

This policy would work powerfully to induce the rich man to attend to the administration of wealth during his life, which is the end that society should always have in view, as being that by far most fruitful for the people. Nor need it be feared that this policy would sap the root of enterprise and render men less anxious to accumulate, for to the class whose ambition it is to leave great fortunes and be talked about after their death, it will attract even more attention, and, indeed, be a somewhat nobler ambition to have enormous sums paid over to the state from their fortunes.

There remains, then, only one mode of using great fortunes; but in this we have the true antidote for the temporary unequal distribution of wealth, the reconciliation of the rich and the poor—a reign of harmony—another ideal, differing, indeed, from that of the Communist in requiring only the further evolution of existing conditions, not the total overthrow of our civilization. It is founded upon the present most intense individualism, and the race is prepared to put it in practice by degrees whenever it pleases. Under its sway we shall have an ideal state, in which the surplus wealth of the few will become, in the best sense, the property of the many, because administered for the common good, and this wealth, passing through the hands of the few, can be made a much more potent force for the elevation of our race than if it had been distributed in small sums to the people themselves. Even the poorest can be made to see this, and to agree that great sums gathered by some of their fellow-citizens and spent for public purposes, from which the masses reap the principal benefit, are more valuable to them than if scattered among them through the course of many years in trifling amounts.

If we consider what results flow from the Cooper Institute, for instance, to the best portion of the race in New York not possessed of means, and compare these with those which would have arisen for the good of the masses from an equal sum distributed by Mr. Cooper in his lifetime in the form of wages, which is the highest form of distribution, being for work done and not for charity, we can form some estimate of the possibilities for the improvement of the race which lie embedded in the present law of the accumulation of wealth. Much of this sum, if distributed in small quantities among the people, would have been wasted in the indulgence of appetite, some of it in excess, and it may be doubted whether even the part put to the best use, that of adding to the comforts of the home, would have yielded results for the race, as a race, at all comparable to those which are flowing and are to flow from the Cooper Institute from generation to generation. Let the advocate of violent or radical change ponder well this thought.

We might even go so far as to take another instance, that of Mr. Tilden's bequest of five millions of dollars for a free library in the city of New York, but in referring to this one cannot help saying involuntarily. How much better if Mr. Tilden had devoted the last years of his own life to the proper administration of this immense sum; in which case neither legal contest nor any other cause of delay could have interfered with his aims. But let us assume that Mr. Tilden's millions finally become the means of giving to this city a noble public library, where the treasures of the world contained in books will be open to all forever, without money and without price. Considering the good of that part of the race which congregates in and around Manhattan Island, would its permanent benefit have been better promoted had these millions been allowed to circulate in small sums through the hands of the masses? Even the most strenuous advocate of Communism must entertain a doubt upon this subject. Most of those who think will probably entertain no doubt whatever. . . .

This, then, is held to be the duty of the man of Wealth: First, to set an example of modest, unostentatious living, shunning display or extravagance; to provide moderately for the legitimate wants of those dependent upon him; and after doing so to consider all surplus revenues which come to him simply as trust funds, which he is called upon to administer, and strictly bound as a matter of duty to administer in the manner which, in his judgment, is best calculated to produce the most beneficial results for the community—the man of wealth thus becoming the mere agent and trustee for his poorer brethren, bringing to their service his superior wisdom, experience, and ability to administer, doing for them better than they would or could do for themselves. . . .

The best uses to which surplus wealth can be put have already been indicated. Those who would administer wisely must, indeed, be wise, for one of the serious obstacles to the improvement of our race is indiscriminate charity. It were better for mankind that the millions of the rich were thrown into the sea than so spent as to encourage the slothful, the drunken, the unworthy. Of every thousand dollars spent in so called charity to-day, it is probable that $950 is unwisely spent; so spent, indeed, as to produce the very evils which it proposes to mitigate or cure. A well-known writer of philosophic books admitted the other day that he had given a quarter of a dollar to a man who approached him as he was coming to visit the house of his friend. He knew nothing of the habits of this beggar; knew not the use that would be made of this money, although he had every reason to suspect that it would be spent improperly. This man professed to be a disciple of Herbert Spencer; yet the quarter-dollar given that night will probably work more injury than all the money which its thoughtless donor will ever be able to give in true charity will do good. He only gratified his own feelings, saved himself from annoyance—and this was probably one of the most selfish and very worst actions of his life, for in all respects he is most worthy.

In bestowing charity, the main consideration should be to help those who will help themselves; to provide part of the means by which those who desire to improve may do so; to give those who desire to rise the aids by which they may rise; to assist, but rarely or never to do all. Neither the individual nor the race is improved by alms-giving. Those worthy of assistance, except in rare cases, seldom require assistance. The really valuable men of the race never do, except in cases of accident or sudden change. Every one has, of course, cases of individuals brought to his own knowledge where temporary assistance can do genuine good, and these he will not overlook. But the amount which can be wisely given by the individual for individuals is necessarily limited by his lack of knowledge of the circumstances connected with each. He is the only true reformer who is as careful and as anxious not to aid the unworthy as he is to aid the worthy, and, perhaps, even more so, for in alms-giving more injury is probably done by rewarding vice than by relieving virtue. . . .

Thus is the problem of Rich and Poor to be solved. The laws of accumulation will be left free; the laws of distribution free. Individualism will continue, but the millionaire will be but a trustee for the poor; intrusted for a season with a great part of the increased wealth of the community, but administering it for the community far better than it could or would have done for itself. The best minds will thus have reached a stage in the development of the race in which it is clearly seen that there is no mode of disposing of surplus wealth creditable to thoughtful and earnest men into whose hands it flows save by using it year by year for the general good. This day already dawns. But a little while, and although, without incurring the pity of their fellows, men may die sharers in great business enterprises from which their capital cannot be or has not been withdrawn, and is left chiefly at death for public uses, yet the man who dies leaving behind him millions of available wealth, which was his to administer during life, will pass away "unwept, unhonored, and unsung," no matter to what uses he leaves the dross which he cannot take with him. Of such as these the public verdict will then be: "The man who dies thus rich dies disgraced."

Such, in my opinion, is the true Gospel concerning Wealth, obedience to which is destined some day to solve the problem of the Rich and the Poor, and to bring "Peace on earth, among men Good-Will."

Russell Conwell, 1843–1925

Russell Conwell was a lawyer, lecturer, and clergyman whose mixture of capitalist enterprise and religion made him one of America's most sought-after public speakers.

Conwell grew up on a Massachusetts farm that was a stopping point on the Underground Railroad. He attended Yale until the Civil War, when he joined the Union Army and rose to the rank of lieutenant colonel. After the war, Conwell became a lawyer, moved to Minnesota, and began a career as a journalist. He returned to Massachusetts, however, and after another stint as a journalist became a minister in a Baptist church in Lexington in 1879. By 1882, he had taken a job with Grace Baptist Church in Philadelphia. He began to build a large number of church institutions, including hospitals, night schools, and finally Temple College (later University), which he served as its first president.

Conwell was most famous for his "Acres of Diamonds" speech that he delivered over 6,000 times and that earned him over $8 million. In its deprecation of public life in favor of the joys of a successful private life, "Acres of Diamonds," is a prime example of the antipolitical as well as anti-egalitarian character of late nineteenth-century American individualism.

Russell H. Conwell

Acres of Diamonds Speech (1915)

. . . I say that you ought to get rich, and it is your duty to get rich. How many of my pious brethren say to me, "Do you, a Christian minister, spend your time going up and down the country advising young people to get rich, to get money?" "Yes, of course I do." They say, "Isn't that awful! Why don't you preach the gospel instead of preaching about man's making money?" "Because to make money honestly is to preach the gospel." That is the reason. The men who get rich may be the most honest men you find in the community.

"Oh," but says some young man here to-night, "I have been told all my life that if a person has money he is very dishonest and dishonorable and mean and contemptible." My friend, that is the reason why you have none, because you have that idea of people. The foundation of your faith is altogether false. Let me say here clearly, and say it briefly, though subject to discussion which I have not time for here, ninety-eight out of one-hun-

dred of the rich men of America are honest. That is why they are rich. That is why they are trusted with money. That is why they carry on great enterprises and find plenty of people to work with them. It is because they are honest men.

Says another young man, "I hear sometimes of men that get millions of dollars dishonestly." Yes, of course you do, and so do I. But they are so rare a thing in fact that the newspapers talk about them all the time as a matter of news until you get the idea that all the other rich men got rich dishonestly.

My friend, you take and drive me—if you furnish the auto—out into the suburbs of Philadelphia, and introduce me to the people who own their homes around this great city, those beautiful homes with gardens and flowers, those magnificent homes so lovely in their art, and I will introduce you to the very best people in character as well as in enterprise in our city, and you know I will. A man is not really a true man until he owns his own home, and they that own their homes are made more honorable and honest and pure,

SOURCE: Russell H. Conwell, *Acres of Diamonds* (New York: Harper & Row, 1915).

and true and economical and careful, by owning the home.

For a man to have money, even in large sums, is not an inconsistent thing. We preach against covetousness, and you know we do, in the pulpit, and oftentimes preach against it so long and use the terms about "filthy lucre" so extremely that Christians get the idea that when we stand in the pulpit we believe it is wicked for any man to have money—until the collection-basket goes around, and then we almost swear at the people because they don't give more money. Oh, the inconsistency of such doctrines as that!

Money is power, and you ought to be reasonably ambitious to have it. You ought because you can do more good with it than you could without it. Money printed your Bible, money builds your churches, money sends your missionaries, and money pays your preachers, and you would not have many of them, either, if you did not pay them. I am always willing that my church should raise my salary, because the church that pays the largest salary always raises it the easiest. You never knew an exception to it in your life. The man who gets the largest salary can do the most good with the power that is furnished to him. Of course he can if his spirit be right to use it for what it is given to him.

I say, then, you ought to have money. If you can honestly attain unto riches in Philadelphia, it is your Christian and godly duty to do so. It is an awful mistake of these pious people to think you must be awfully poor in order to be pious.

Some men say, "Don't you sympathize with the poor people?" Of course I do, or else I would not have been lecturing these years. I won't give in but what I sympathize with the poor, but the number of poor who are to be sympathized with is very small. To sympathize with a man whom God has punished for his sins, thus to help him when God would still continue a just punishment, is to do wrong, no doubt about it, and we do that more than

we help those who are deserving. While we should sympathize with God's poor—that is, those who cannot help themselves—let us remember there is not a poor person in the United States who was not made poor by his own shortcomings, or by the shortcomings of some one else. It is all wrong to be poor, anyhow. Let us give in to that argument and pass that to one side. . . .

Yet the age is prejudiced against advising a Christian man (or, as a Jew would say, a godly man) from attaining unto wealth. The prejudice is so universal and the years are far enough back, I think, for me to safely mention that years ago up at Temple University there was a young man in our theological school who thought he was the only pious student in that department. He came into my office one evening and sat down by my desk, and said to me: "Mr. President, I think it is my duty sir, to come in and labor with you." "What has happened now?" Said he, "I heard you say at the Academy, at the Peirce School commencement, that you thought it was an honorable ambition for a young man to desire to have wealth, and that you thought it made him temperate, made him anxious to have a good name, and made him industrious. You spoke about man's ambition to have money helping to make him a good man. Sir, I have come to tell you the Holy Bible says that 'money is the root of all evil.'"

I told him I had never seen it in the Bible, and advised him to go out into the chapel and get the Bible, and show me the place. So out he went for the Bible, and soon he stalked into my office with the Bible open, with all the bigoted pride of the narrow sectarian, or of one who founds his Christianity on some misinterpretation of Scripture. He flung the Bible down on my desk, and fairly squealed into my ear: "There it is, Mr. President; you can read it for yourself." I said to him: "Well, young man, you will learn when you get a little older that you cannot trust another denomination to read the Bible for you. You belong to another denomination. You are taught in the theological school, however, that emphasis is exegesis. Now, will you take that Bible and read it yourself, and give the proper emphasis to it?"

He took the Bible, and proudly read, " 'The love of money is the root of all evil.' "

Then he had it right, and when one does quote aright from that same old Book he quotes the absolute truth. . . .

So I say that when he quoted right, of course he quoted the absolute truth. "The love of money is the root of all evil." He who tries to attain unto it too quickly, or dishonestly, will fall into many snares, no doubt about that. The love of money. What is that? It is making an idol of money, and idolatry pure and simple everywhere is condemned by the Holy Scriptures and by man's common sense. The man that worships the dollar instead of thinking of the purposes for which it ought to be used, the man who idolizes simply money, the miser that hordes his money in the cellar, or hides it in his stocking, or refuses to invest it where it will do the world good, that man who hugs the dollar until the eagle squeals has in him the root of all evil.

I think I will leave that behind me now and answer the question of nearly all of you who are asking, "Is there opportunity to get rich in Philadelphia?" Well, now, how simple a thing it is to see where it is, and the instant you see where it is it is yours. Some old gentleman gets up back there and says, "Mr. Conwell, have you lived in Philadelphia for thirty-one years and don't know that the time has gone by when you can make anything in this city?" "No, I don't think it is." "Yes, it is; I have tried it." "What business are you in?" "I kept a store here for twenty years, and never made over a thousand dollars in the whole twenty years."

"Well, then, you can measure the good you have been to this city by what this city has paid you, because a man can judge very well what he is worth by what he receives; that

is, in what he is to the world at this time. If you have not made over a thousand dollars in twenty years in Philadelphia, it would have been better for Philadelphia if they had kicked you out of the city nineteen years and nine months ago. A man has no right to keep a store in Philadelphia twenty years and not make at least five hundred thousand dollars, even though it be a corner grocery up-town." You say, "You cannot make five thousand dollars in a store now." Oh, my friends, if you will just take only four blocks around you, and find out what the people want and what you ought to supply and set them down with your pencil, and figure up the profits you would make if you did supply them, you would very soon see it. There is wealth right within the sound of your voice. . . .

There are some over-pious Christian people who think if you take any profit on anything you sell that you are an unrighteous man. On the contrary, you would be a criminal to sell goods for less than they cost. You have no right to do that. You cannot trust a man with your money who cannot take care of his own. You cannot trust a man in your family that is not true to his own wife. You cannot trust a man in the world that does not begin with his own heart, his own character, and his own life. It would have been my duty to have furnished a jack-knife to the third man, or the second, and to have sold it to him and actually profited myself. I have no more right to sell goods without making a profit on them than I have to overcharge him dishonestly beyond what they are worth. But I should so sell each bill of goods that the person to whom I sell shall make as much as I make.

To live and let live is the principle of the gospel, and the principle of every-day common sense. Oh, young man, hear me; live as you go along. Do not wait until you have reached my years before you begin to enjoy anything of this life. If I had the millions back, or fifty cents of it, which I have tried to earn in these years, it would not do me anything like the good that it does me now in this almost sacred presence tonight. Oh, yes, I am paid over and over a hundredfold to-night for dividing as I have tried to do in some measure as I went along through the years. I ought not speak that way, it sounds egotistic, but I am old enough now to be excused for that. I should have helped my fellow-men, which I have tried to do, and every one should try to do, and get the happiness of it. The man who goes home with the sense that he has stolen a dollar that day, that he has robbed a man of what was his honest due, is not going to sweet rest. He arises tired in the morning, and goes with an unclean conscience to his work the next day. He is not a successful man at all, although he may have laid up millions. But the man who has gone through life dividing always with his fellow-men, making and demanding his own rights and his own profits, and giving to every other man his rights and profits, lives every day, and not only that, but it is the royal road to great wealth. The history of the thousands of millionaires shows that to be the case. . . .

Arise, ye millions of Philadelphians, trust in God and man, and believe in the great opportunities that are right here—not over in New York or Boston, but here—for business, for everything that is worth living for on earth. There was never an opportunity greater. Let us talk up our own city.

But there are two other young men here to-night, and that is all I will venture to say, because it is too late. One over there gets up and says, "There is going to be a great man in Philadelphia, but never was one." "Oh, is that so? When are you going to be great?" "When I am elected to some political office." Young man, won't you learn a lesson in the primer of politics that it is a *prima facie* evidence of littleness to hold office under our form of government? Great men get into office sometimes, but what this country needs is men that will do what we tell them to do. This nation—where the people rule—is governed by the people, for the people, and so long as it is, then the office-holder is but the servant of the people, and the Bible says the servant cannot be greater than the master. The Bible says, "He that is sent cannot be greater than Him who sent Him." The people rule, or should rule, and if they do, we do not need the greater men in office. If the great men in America took our offices, we would change to an empire in the next ten years.

I know of a great many young women, now that woman's suffrage is coming, who say, "I am going to be President of the United States some day." I believe in woman's suffrage, and there is no doubt but what it is coming, and I am getting out of the way, anyhow. I may want an office by and by myself; but if the ambition for an office influences the women in their desire to vote I want to say right here what I say to the young men, that if you only get the privilege of casting one vote, you don't get anything that is worth while. Unless you can control more than one vote, you will be unknown, and your influence so dissipated as practically not to be felt. This country is not run by votes. Do you think it is? It is governed by influence. It is governed by the ambitions and the enterprises which control votes. The young woman that thinks she is going to vote for the sake of holding an office is making an awful blunder. . . .

We ought not to so teach history. We ought to teach that, however humble a man's station may be, if he does his full duty in that place he is just as much entitled to the American people's honor as is the king upon his throne. But we do not so teach. We are now teaching everywhere that the generals do all the fighting. . . .

Oh, I learned the lesson then that I will never forget so long as the tongue of the bell of time continues to swing for me. Greatness consists not in the holding of some future office, but really consists in doing great deeds with little means and the accomplishment of vast purposes from the private ranks of life. To be great at all one must be great here, now, in Philadelphia. He who can give to this city better streets and better sidewalks, better schools and more colleges, more happiness and more civilization, more of God, he will be great anywhere. Let every man or woman here, if you never hear me again, remember this, that if you wish to be great at all, you must begin where you are and what you are, in Philadelphia, now. He that can give to his city any blessing, he who can be a good citizen while he lives here, he that can make better homes, he that can be a blessing whether he works in the shop or sits behind the counter or keeps house, whatever be his life, he who would be great anywhere must first be great in his own Philadelphia.

Booker T. Washington, 1856–1915

Booker T. Washington was an educator and social reformer, adviser to presidents, and the most famous black leader of his times. In the spirit of those times, however, Washington counseled a retreat from the hard-line egalitarianism of a Frederick Douglass and suggested instead that blacks accept temporary social and political inequality in return for economic and educational opportunity. For this, he was severely criticized by black leaders such as W. E. B. Du Bois. To this day, Washington's career continues to be a source of controversy among contemporary scholars and theorists of the civil rights movement.

Washington was born a slave in Franklin County, Virginia, and moved with his family to West Virginia after emancipation. At the age of nine, he went to work in a salt furnace and then in the coal mines. Once he attended school for newly freed blacks, his lifelong passion for education began.

In 1872, Washington attended Hampton Institute and studied there for three years while he also worked as a janitor to support himself and pay for his schooling. Upon leaving Hampton, he went to work as a schoolteacher, studied to become a Baptist minister, and then returned to Hampton to teach in a program for American Indians.

In 1881, Washington was named the first principal of Tuskegee Institute in Alabama, a position that he held until his death. He began with two spare buildings, little equipment, and 40 local farm boys as students. When he died, 34 years later, he had 100 buildings, 1,500 students, a faculty of 200, and an endowment of over $2 million.

Washington accomplished this task by currying the favor of white philanthropists in the North and South. He rejected the goal of a liberal arts education for blacks and downplayed the cause of equality. For this, he was praised by most American leaders in business and government, but he drew criticism from some blacks such as Du Bois and Monroe Trotter of the *Boston Guardian*.

Washington's writings include *Up from Slavery* (1901) and *My Larger Education* (1911). The following selection is from Washington's famous "Atlanta

Exposition Address" of 1895, which he delivered at the Atlanta Cotton Exposition.

Booker T. Washington

The Atlanta Exposition Address (1895)

MR. PRESIDENT AND GENTLEMEN OF THE BOARD OF DIRECTORS AND CITIZENS—One-third of the population of the South is of the Negro race. No enterprise seeking the material, civil, or moral welfare of this section can disregard this element of our population and reach the highest success. I but convey to you, Mr. President and Directors, the sentiment of the masses of my race when I say that in no way have the value and manhood of the American Negro been more fittingly and generously recognized than by the managers of this magnificent Exposition at every stage of its progress. It is a recognition that will do more to cement the friendship of the two races than any occurrence since the dawn of our freedom.

Not only this, but the opportunity here afforded will awaken among us a new era of industrial progress. Ignorant and inexperienced, it is not strange that in the first years of our new life we began at the top instead of at the bottom; that a seat in Congress or the state legislature was more sought than real estate or industrial skill; that the political convention or stump speaking had more attractions than starting a dairy farm or truck garden.

A ship lost at sea for many days suddenly sighted a friendly vessel. From the mast of

SOURCE: Booker T. Washington, *Up From Slavery! An Autobiography* (New York: Doubleday Page, 1901).

the unfortunate vessel was seen a signal, "Water, water; we die of thirst!" The answer from the friendly vessel at once came back, "Cast down your bucket where you are." A second time the signal, "Water, water; send us water!" ran up from the distressed vessel, and was answered, "Cast down your bucket where you are." And a third and fourth signal for water was answered, "Cast down your bucket where you are." The captain of the distressed vessel, at last heeding the injunction, cast down his bucket, and it came up full of fresh, sparkling water from the mouth of the Amazon River. To those of my race who depend on bettering their condition in a foreign land or who underestimate the importance of cultivating friendly relations with the Southern white man, who is there next-door neighbour, I would say: "Cast down your bucket where you are"—cast it down in making friends in every manly way of the people of all races by whom we are surrounded.

Cast it down in agriculture, mechanics, in commerce, in domestic service, and in the professions. And in this connection it is well to bear in mind that whatever other sins the South may be called to bear, when it comes to business, pure and simple, it is in the South that the Negro is given a man's chance in the commercial world, and in nothing is this Exposition more eloquent than in emphasizing this chance. Our greatest danger is that in the great leap from slavery to freedom we may overlook the fact that the masses of us are to live by the productions of our hands, and fail to keep in mind that we shall prosper in proportion as we learn to dignify and glorify common labour and put brains and skill into the common occupations of life; shall prosper in proportion as we learn to draw the line between the superficial and the substantial, the ornamental gewgaws of life and the useful. No race can prosper till it learns that there is as much dignity in tilling a field as in writing a poem. It is at the bottom of life we must begin, and not at the top. Nor should we permit our grievances to overshadow our opportunities.

To those of the white race who look to the incoming of those of foreign birth and strange tongue and habits for the prosperity of the South, were I permitted I would repeat what I say to my own race, "Cast down your bucket where you are." Cast it down among the eight millions of Negroes whose habits you know, whose fidelity and love you have tested in days when to have proved treacherous meant the ruin of your firesides. Cast down your bucket among these people who have, without strikes and labour wars, tilled your fields, cleared your forests, builded your railroads and cities, and brought forth treasures from the bowels of the earth, and helped make possible this magnificent representation of the progress of the South. Casting down your bucket among my people, helping and encouraging them as you are doing on these grounds, and to education of head, hand, and heart, you will find that they will buy your surplus land, make blossom the waste places in your fields, and run your factories. While doing this, you can be sure in the future, as in the past, that you and your families will be surrounded by the most patient, faithful, law abiding, and unresentful people that the world has seen. As we have proved our loyalty to you in the past, in nursing your children, watching by the sickbed of your mothers and fathers, and often following them with tear-dimmed eyes to their graves, so in the future, in our humble way, we shall stand by you with a devotion that no foreigner can approach, ready to lay down our lives, if need be, in defence of yours, interlacing our industrial, commercial, civil, and religious life with yours in a way that shall make the interests of both races one. In all things that are purely social we can be as separate as the fingers, yet one as the hand in all things essential to mutual progress.

There is no defence or security for any of us except in the highest intelligence and development of all. If anywhere there are efforts tending to curtail the fullest growth of the Negro, let these efforts be turned into stimulating, encouraging, and making him the most useful and intelligent citizen. Effort or means so invested will pay a thousand per cent interest. These efforts will be twice blessed—"blessing him that gives and him that takes."

There is no escape through law of man or God from the inevitable:—

> The laws of changeless justice bind
>   Oppressor with oppressed;
> And close as sin and suffering joined
>   We march to fate abreast.

Nearly sixteen millions of hands will aid you in pulling the load upward, or they will pull against you the load downward. We shall constitute one-third and more of the ignorance and crime of the South, or one-third its intelligence and progress; we shall contribute one-third to the business and industrial prosperity of the South, or we shall prove a veritable body of death, stagnating, depressing, retarding every effort to advance the body politic.

Gentlemen of the Exposition, as we present to you our humble effort at an exhibition of our progress, you must not expect overmuch. Starting thirty years ago with ownership here and there in a few quilts and pumpkins and chickens (gathered from miscellaneous sources), remember the path that has led from these to the inventions and production of agricultural implements, buggies, steam-engines, newspapers, books, statuary, carving, paintings, the management of drugstores and banks, has not been trodden without contact with thorns and thistles. While we take pride in what we exhibit as a result of our independent efforts, we do not for a moment forget that our part in this exhibition would fall far short of your expectations but for the constant help that has come to our educational life, not only from the Southern states, but especially from Northern philanthropists, who have made their gifts a constant stream of blessing and encouragement.

The wisest among my race understand that the agitation of questions of social equality is the extremest folly, and that progress in the enjoyment of all the privileges that will come to us must be the result of severe and constant struggle rather than of artificial forcing. No race that has anything to contribute to the markets of the world is long in any degree ostracized. It is important and right that all privileges of the law be ours, but it is vastly more important that we be prepared for the exercises of these privileges. The opportunity to earn a dollar in a factory just now is worth infinitely more than the opportunity to spend a dollar in an opera-house.

In conclusion, may I repeat that nothing in thirty years has given us more hope and encouragement, and drawn us so near to you of the white race, as this opportunity offered by the Exposition; and here bending, as it were, over the altar that represents the results of the struggles of your race and mine, both starting practically empty-handed three decades ago, I pledge that in your effort to work out the great and intricate problem which God has laid at the doors of the South, you shall have at all times the patient, sympathetic help of my race; only let this be constantly in mind, that, while from representations in these buildings of the product of field, of forest, of mine, of factory, letters, and art, much good will come, yet far above and beyond material benefits will be that higher good, that, let us pray God, will come, in a blotting out of sectional differences and racial animosities and suspicions, in a determination to administer absolute justice, in a willing obedience among all classes to the mandates of law. This, coupled with our material prosperity, will bring into our beloved South a new heaven and a new earth.

Voices of Dissent

Richard T. Ely, 1854–1953

Richard T. Ely was a social scientist, economist, historian, and lifelong political reformer. He received degrees from Dartmouth and Columbia, and earned a Ph.D. in political economy from Heidelberg. In 1881, he took a position at Johns Hopkins University and helped create its first Ph.D. program in economics.

In 1885, Ely helped found the American Economic Association and spearheaded a revolt against the classical economic tradition of Adam Smith and David Ricardo that had dominated U.S. schools. He also became an active social reformer and a leading member of the reformist Christian Social Union.

In 1892, Ely became a professor of political science, economics, and history at the University of Wisconsin, where he remained for thirty-three years. Along with John R. Commons and the president of the university, Charles R. Van Hise, Ely helped make the school an active participant in Wisconsin's progressive politics.

Ely's many books include works on French and German Socialism and a classic text, *Introduction to Political Economy.* His speech before the first meeting of the American Economic Association in 1886 is a good example of the growing opposition to laissez-faire that would later come to fruition in the Progressive Era and again in the New Deal.

Richard T. Ely

Report of the Organization of the American Economic Association (1886)

OBJECTS OF THIS ASSOCIATION.

I. The encouragement of economic research.

II. The publication of economic monographs.

III. The encouragement of perfect freedom in all economic discussion.

IV. The establishment of a bureau of information designed to aid all members with friendly counsels in their economic studies.

PLATFORM.

1. We regard the state as an educational and ethical agency whose positive aid is an indispensable condition of human progress. While we recognize the necessity of individual initiative in industrial life, we hold that the doctrine of *laissez-faire* is unsafe in politics and unsound in morals; and that it suggests an inadequate explanation of the relations between the state and the citizens.

2. We do not accept the final statements which characterized the political economy of a past generation; for we believe that political economy is still in the first stages of its scientific development, and we look not so much to speculation as to an impartial study of actual conditions of economic life for the satisfactory accomplishment of that development. We seek the aid of statistics in the present, and of history in the past.

3. We hold that the conflict of labor and capital has brought to the front a vast number of social problems whose solution is impossible without the united efforts of Church, state and science.

4. In the study of the policy of government, especially with respect to restrictions on trade and to protection of domestic manufactures, we take no partisan attitude. We are convinced that one of the chief reasons why greater harmony has not been attained, is because economists have been too ready to assert themselves as advocates. We believe in a progressive development of economic conditions which must be met by corresponding changes of policy. . . .

Statement of Dr. Richard T. Ely.

. . . One aim of our association should be the education of public opinion in regard to economic questions and economic literature. In no other science is there so much quackery and it must be our province to expose it and bring it into merited contempt. A review at each of our meetings of the economic works of the past year, if published in our proceedings, might help in the formation of enlightened judgment.

Coming to the platform, a position is first of all taken in regard to the state, because it is thought necessary precisely at this time to emphasize its proper province. No one invited

SOURCE: *Publications of the American Economic Association* 1, no. 1, 1887.

to join this association, certainly no one who has been active in calling this meeting, contemplates a form of pure socialism. "We recognize the necessity of individual initiative." We would do nothing to weaken individual activity, but we hold that there are certain spheres of activity which do not belong to the individual, certain functions which the great co-operative society, called the state—must perform to keep the avenues open for those who would gain a livelihood by their own exertions. The avenues to wealth and preferment are continually blocked by the greed of combinations of men and by monopolists, and individual effort and initiative are thus discouraged. Two examples will suffice—You know that in the Western grazing regions water is often scarce, and those who control the streams virtually own the country. Now it is a notorious fact that unlawful combinations seize upon these streams and, keeping others from them, retain exclusive privileges which shut off effectually individual exertions on the part of those not in the ring. A second example is found in unjust discriminations in freight charges which have built up the fortunes of the favored, and ruined competitors. In looking over the field of economic life, it is evident that there is a wide feeling of discouragement, repressing the activities of the individual, because the avenues to material well-being are so often blocked. Then there are things which individuals ought not to perform because the functions concerned are public; and in certain places the wastes of private competition are too enormous. There are, likewise, important things which individual effort is powerless to effect, e.g., the education of the masses.

We hold that the doctrine of *laissez-faire* is unsafe in politics and unsound in morals, and that it suggests an inadequate explanation of the relations between the state and the citizens. In other words we believe in the existence of a system of social ethics; we do not believe that any man lives for himself alone, nor yet do we believe social classes are devoid

of mutual obligations corresponding to their infinitely varied inter-relations. All have duties as well as rights, and, as Emerson said several years ago, it is time we heard more about duties and less about rights. We who have resolved to form an American Economic Association hope to do something towards the development of a system of social ethics.

It is asked: what is meant by *laissez-faire?* It is difficult to define *laissez-faire* categorically, because it is so absurd that its defenders can never be induced to say precisely what they mean. Yet it stands for a well-known, though rather vague set of ideas, to which appeal is made every day in the year by the bench, the bar, the newspapers and our legislative bodies. It means that government, the state, the people in their collective capacity, ought not to interfere in industrial life; that, on the contrary, free contract should regulate all the economic relations of life and public authority should simply enforce this, punish crime and preserve peace. It means that the laws of economic life are natural laws like those of physics and chemistry, and that this life must be left to the free play of natural forces. One adherent uses these words: "This industrial world is governed by natural laws. . . . These laws are superior to man. Respect this providential order—let alone the work of God."

The platform then emphasizes the mission of the State and the mission of the individual in that State. *To distinguish between the proper functions of the two must be one of the purposes of our association.*

The mission of the Church is likewise emphasized, and for this there is good reason which cannot, perhaps, be better stated than in the words of Professor Macy of Iowa College. I quote from a letter recently received from him:

"The preacher, in an important sense, is to be the originator of true social science; his work is to render possible such a science.

"The physical scientist needs no preacher. There is an external material thing which compels belief. For the most part, men have no selfish interest in believing other than the truth in regard to the material world. Those who devote themselves to the study of matter are led naturally into a truth-loving and truth-telling spirit, and they can laugh at the preacher. But those who devote themselves to the study of the conflicting interests of men, have on their hands altogether a different task. There is no external material thing to solve their doubts, and men prefer to believe that which is not true; and when they believe the truth they often think it best to pretend to believe the false. Falsehood, deception, lying, and above all an honest and dogged belief in error—these are athwart the path which might lead to a real social science. And who can tackle these better than the preacher?"

In addition to these words of Professor Macy, it may be said that we wish to accomplish certain practical results in the social and financial world, and believing that our work lies in the direction of practical Christianity, we appeal to the church, the chief of the social forces in this country, to help us, to support us, and to make our work a complete success, which it can by no possibility be without her assistance.

The religious press of the country can aid us greatly in our task, and it will not, I believe, refuse its co-operation. Its influence is enormous, and notwithstanding all that has been said against it to the contrary, I believe that to-day it is the fairest, purest and most liberal press in the country. The fourth paragraph in the platform seems to me to be imperatively necessary. We want to proclaim to the world that political economy is something much broader than partisan controversies about free-trade and protection, that we are in fact neither free-traders nor protectionists in the partisan sense of those words. . . .

Our platform is very broad and will include nearly all those who can co-operate advantageously with us. It advocates simply certain methods of study and the accomplishment of reforms by certain means which alone seem to us to promise valuable results. We believe in historical and statistical inquiries and examinations into actual conditions, and should we include those who do not, there would be division at the start. If two people are journeying together to a certain goal and come to a fork in the road, it is evident that they must part company if each insists on believing that their common destination lies in a different direction. That is our case. We have little faith that the methods advocated by certain economists will ever lead to any valuable results. They may take their own way, and far be it from us to hinder them, but we must part company.

Again, it is not easy to arouse interest in an association which professes nothing. This proposed economic association has been greeted with enthusiasm precisely because it is not colorless, precisely because it stands for something.

Finally, it is of the utmost importance to us to emphasize certain fundamental views in order to bring them prominently before the public. It is essential that intelligent men and women should distinguish between us and certain economists in whom there is little faith. The respect for political economy, as it has been hitherto taught, is very slight. I think it has been kept alive largely by ignorance on the one hand—on the other by the cloak it affords to wrong-doing and the balm it offers to still the voice of outraged conscience. On every side we find intelligent people dissatisfied with it, throwing all political economy to the winds, while John Stuart Mill repudiated his own economic system, and one of the most careful students of economic facts, Thorold Rogers, finds its conclusions so at variance with the results of his investigations, that he rejects it with scorn, and believes it necessary to build up a new political economy by a long and careful process, piecemeal, as he himself expresses it.[1] We of this association must come before the public with the unequivocal assertion that we, also, refuse to accept as final "the statements which characterize the political economy of a past generation, and that we believe our science is in the first stages of its scientific development."

Our attitude is a modest one, and must, I think, appeal to the best intelligence of the country. We acknowledge our ignorance, and if we claim superiority to others it is largely on the very humble ground that we know better what we do not know. We confess our ignorance, but are determined to do our best to remedy it, and we call upon those who are willing to go to work in this spirit to come forward and help us.

[1] It does not follow that the work of men like Adam Smith, Malthus and Ricardo was not valuable, nor that its conclusions were altogether erroneous. They and other thinkers of their day occupy a brilliant place in the history of political economy. The chief fault to be found with those who have attempted to build up a standard of orthodoxy on the basis afforded by these great thinkers is that they hinder progress, that they pervert the spirit of their masters, and fail to recognize that political economy must grow with the growth of society. A political economy written before the introduction of railroads can hardly be sufficient in the year 1885. Adam Smith would have been the first one to recognize this, and I think that the latest developments in economic science are in some respects a return to the spirit and methods of the "Wealth of Nations," as was suggested by Professor Henry C. Adams in the discussion of the "platform" at Saratoga.

Woodrow Wilson, 1856–1921

Woodrow Wilson was most famous, of course, as president of the United States. In addition to a remarkably successful career in politics, he was also one of America's best-known political scientists and historians.

Wilson, the son of a Presbyterian minister, was born in Virginia and grew up in Georgia and the Carolinas. He graduated from Princeton (College of New Jersey) and then the University of Virginia Law School in 1879. He passed the bar in 1882 and practiced law briefly, but soon entered Johns Hopkins University to study politics, history, and economics. His dissertation *Congressional Government* (1885) became a minor classic. In it, Wilson complained about the overwhelming power of congressional committees in American politics and argued for a parliamentary system along the lines of the British. Wilson became one of the early pioneers in the field of public administration, teaching in a number of universities and colleges, and contributing to the theory of administration in his writings. Wilson was also the author of *The State* (1889)—one of the first modern texts in comparative government—and *Constitutional Government in the United States* (1908). A common theme in his writings was an attack on laissez-faire and a defense of positive political action in regulating the economy.

Wilson became president of Princeton University in 1902 and in 1910 successfully ran for governor of New Jersey. During his brief term in office, he helped pass bills establishing workers' compensation, direct primaries, regulation of public utilities, and school reform.

In 1912, he ran for president as the democratic candidate against both Theodore Roosevelt and William Howard Taft. Wilson organized his campaign around the theme of "The New Freedom," that is, the need for far-reaching antitrust legislation to restore a competitive economy and enlarge individual opportunity.

In office, Wilson helped create the Federal Trade Commission and pass the Clayton Act. He took a leading role in promoting tariff reform and labor and social welfare legislation. Wilson also became the leading spokesman for a set of foreign policy values that have since come to be known as "Wilsonian"—the commitment to further democracy and national self-determination, and to oppose all forms of colonial domination. Despite these beliefs, however, he was quick to send American troops to intervene in the Mexican Revolution in order to protect U.S. interests. Nevertheless, Wilson led the United States through World War I espousing internationalist ideals and tried desperately—ultimately bringing about his own physical demise—to bring his own country into the League of Nations.

The following article, "Freemen Need No Guardians," was written in 1913 by the president-elect. It is a good example of Wilson's fear that the end result of laissez-faire had been a new set of monopolies and a new elite—both foreign to the democratic aspirations and traditions of America. Note how Wilson borrowed the egalitarian and democratic rhetoric of Jacksonian America in justifying the positive role for the state.

Woodrow Wilson

Freemen Need No Guardians (1913)

There are two theories of government that have been contending with each other ever since government began. One of them is the theory which in America is associated with the name of a very great man, Alexander Hamilton. A great man, but, in my judgment, not a great American. He did not think in terms of American life. Hamilton believed that the only people who could understand government, and therefore the only people who were qualified to conduct it, were the men who had the biggest financial stake in the commercial and industrial enterprises of our country.

That theory, though few have now the hardihood to profess it openly, has been the working theory upon which our government has lately been conducted. It is astonishing how persistent it is. It is amazing how quickly the political party which had Lincoln for its

SOURCE: *Fortnightly Review* 93, February 1913.

first leader—Lincoln, who not only denied, but in his own person so completely disproved, the aristocratic theory—it is amazing how quickly that party founded on faith in the people forgot the precepts of Lincoln and fell under the delusion that the "masses" needed the guardianship of "men of affairs."

For indeed, if you stop to think about it, nothing could be a further departure from original Americanism, from faith in the ability of a confident, resourceful, and independent people, than the discouraging doctrine that somebody has got to provide prosperity for the rest of us. And yet that is exactly the doctrine on which the government of the United States has been conducted lately. Who have been consulted when important measures of government, like tariff acts, and currency acts, and railroad acts, were under consideration? The people whom the tariff chiefly affects, the people for whom the currency is supposed to exist, the people who pay the duties and ride on the railroads? Oh! no. What do they know about such matters! The gentlemen whose ideas have been sought are the big manufacturers, the bankers, and the heads of the great railroad combinations. The masters of the government of the United States are the combined capitalists and manufacturers of the United States. It is written over every intimate page of the records of Congress; it is written all through the history of conferences at the White House, that the suggestions of economic policy in this country have come from one source, not from many sources; the benevolent guardians, the kindhearted trustees who have taken the troubles of government off our hands have become so conspicuous that almost anybody can write out a list of them. They have become so conspicuous that their names are mentioned upon almost every political platform. The men who have undertaken the interesting job of taking care of us do not force us to requite them with anonymously directed gratitude. We know them by name.

Suppose you go to Washington and try to get at your government. You will always find that while you are politely listened to, the men really consulted are the men who have the biggest stake—the big bankers, the big manufacturers, the big masters of commerce, the heads of railroad corporations and of steamship corporations. I have no objection to these men being consulted, because they also, though they do not themselves seem to admit it, are part of the people of the United States. But I do very seriously object to these gentlemen being *chiefly* consulted, and particularly to their being exclusively consulted, and if the government of the United States is to do the right thing by the people of the United States it has got to do it directly and not through the intermediation of these gentlemen. Every time it has come to a critical question, these gentlemen have been yielded to, and their demands have been treated as the demands that should be followed as a matter of course.

The government of the United States at present is a foster-child of the special interests. It is not allowed to have a will of its own. It is told at every move, "Don't do that; you will interfere with our prosperity." And when we ask, "Where is our prosperity lodged?" a certain group of gentlemen say, "With us." The government of the United States in recent years has not been administered by the common people of the United States. You know just as well as I do—it is not an indictment against anybody, it is a mere statement of the facts—that the people have stood outside and looked on at their own government and that all they have had to determine in past years has been which crowd they would look on at; whether they would look on at this little group or that little group who had managed to get the control of affairs in its hands. Have you ever heard, for example, of any hearing before any great committee of the Congress in which the people of the country as a whole were represented, except it may be by the Congressmen themselves? The men who appear at those meetings in order to argue for this schedule in the tariff, for this measure or against that measure, are men who represent special interests. They may represent them very honestly; they may intend no wrong to their fellow-citizens, but they are speaking from the point of view always of a small portion of the population. I have sometimes wondered why men, particularly men of means, men who didn't have to work for their living, shouldn't constitute themselves attorneys for the people, and every time a hearing is held before a committee of Congress should not go and ask, "Gentle-men, in considering these things suppose you consider the whole country? Suppose you consider the citizens of the United States?"

Now I don't want a smug lot of experts to sit down behind closed doors in Washington and play Providence to me. There is a Providence to which I am perfectly willing to submit. But as for other men setting up as Providence over myself, I seriously object. I have never met a political saviour in the flesh, and I never expect to meet one. I am reminded of Gillet Burgess' verses:—

> I never saw a purple cow,
>   I never hope to see one,
> But this I'll tell you anyhow,
>   I'd rather see than be one.

That is the way I feel about this saving of my fellow-countrymen. I'd rather see a saviour of the United States than set up to be one; because I have found out, I have actually found out, that men I consult with know more than I do—especially if I consult with enough of them. I never came out of a committee meeting or a conference without seeing more of the question that was under discussion than I had seen when I went in. And that to my mind is an image of government. I am not willing to be under the patronage of the trusts, no matter how providential a government presides over the process of their control of my life.

I am one of those who absolutely reject the trustee theory, the guardianship theory. I have never found a man who knew how to take care of me, and, reasoning from that point out, I conjecture that there isn't any man who knows how to take care of all the people of the United States. I suspect that the people of the United States understand their own interests better than any group of men in the confines of the country understand them. The men who are sweating blood to get their foothold in the world of endeavour understand the conditions of business in the United States very much better than the men who have arrived and are at the top. They know what the thing is that they are struggling against. They know how difficult it is to start a new enterprise. They know how far they have to search for credit that will put them upon an even footing with the men who have already built up industry in this country. They know that somewhere by somebody the development of industry in this country is being controlled.

I do not say this with the slightest desire to create any prejudice against wealth; on the contrary, I should be ashamed of myself if I excited class feeling of any kind. But I do mean to suggest this: that the wealth of the country has, in recent years, come from particular sources; it has come from those sources which have built up monopoly. Its point of view is a special point of view. It is the point of view of those men who do not wish that the people should determine their own affairs, because they do not believe that the people's judgment is sound. They want to be commissioned to take care of the United States and of the people of the United States, because they believe that they, better than anybody else, understand the interests of the United States. I do not challenge their character; I challenge their point of view. We cannot afford to be governed as we have been governed in the last generation, by men who occupy so narrow, so prejudiced, so limited a point of view.

The government of our country cannot be

lodged in any special class. The policy of a great nation cannot be tied up with any particular set of interests. I want to say, again and again, that my arguments do not touch the character of the men to whom I am opposed. I believe that the very wealthy men who have got their money by certain kinds of corporate enterprises have closed in their horizon, and that they do not see and do not understand the rank and file of the people. It is for that reason that I want to break up the little coterie that has determined what the government of the nation should do. The list of the men who used to determine what New Jersey should and should not do did not exceed half a dozen, and they were always the same men. These very men now are, some of them, frank enough to admit that New Jersey has finer energy in her because more men are consulted and the whole field of action is widened and liberalised.

We have got to relieve our government from the domination of special classes, not because these special classes are bad, necessarily, but because no special class can understand the interests of a great community. . . .

If any part of our people want to be wards, if they want to have guardians put over them, if they want to be taken care of, if they want to be children, patronised by the government, why, I am sorry, because it will sap the manhood of America. But I don't believe they do. I believe they want to stand on the firm foundation of law and right and take care of themselves. I, for my part, don't want to belong to a nation, I believe that I do not belong to a nation, that needs to be taken care of by guardians. I want to belong to a nation, and I am proud that I do belong to a nation, that knows how to take care of itself. If I thought that the American people were reckless, were ignorant, were vindictive, I might shrink from putting the government into their hands. But the beauty of democracy is that when you are reckless you destroy your own established conditions of life; when you are vindictive, you wreck vengeance upon your-

self; the whole stability of democratic polity rests upon the fact that every interest is every man's interest.

The theory that the men of biggest affairs, whose field of operation is the widest, are the proper men to advise the government is, I am willing to admit, rather a plausible theory. If my business covers the United States not only, but covers the world, it is to be presumed that I have a pretty wide scope in my vision of business. But the flaw is that it is my own business that I have a vision of, and not the business of the men who lie outside of the scope of the plans I have made for a profit out of the particular transactions I am connected with. And you can't, by putting together a large number of men who understand their own business, no matter how large it is, make up a body of men who will understand the business of the nation as contrasted with their own interest.

In a former generation, half a century ago, there were a great many men associated with the government whose patriotism we are not privileged to deny nor to question, who intended to serve the people, but had become so saturated with the point of view of a governing class, that it was impossible for them to see America as the people of America themselves saw it. Then there arose that interesting figure, the immortal figure of the great Lincoln, who stood up declaring that the politicians, the men who had governed this country, did not see from the point of view of the people. When I think of that tall, gaunt figure rising in Illinois, I have a picture of a man free, unentangled, unassociated with the governing influences of the country, ready to see things with an open eye, to see them steadily, to see them whole, to see them as the men he rubbed shoulders with and associated with saw them. What the country needed in 1860 was a leader who understood and represented the thought of the whole people, as contrasted with that of a special class which imagined itself the guardian of the country's welfare.

Now, likewise, the trouble with our present

political condition is that we need some man who has not been associated with the governing classes and the governing influences of this country to stand up and speak for us; we need to hear a voice from the outside calling upon the American people to assert again their rights and prerogatives in the possession of their own government. . . .

I sometimes think that the men who are now governing us are unconscious of the chains in which they are held. I do not believe that men such as we know, among our public men at least—most of them—have deliberately put us into leading strings to the special interests. The special interests have grown up. They have grown up by processes which at last, happily, we are beginning to understand. And, having grown up, having occupied the seats of greatest advantage nearest the ear of those who are conducting government, having contributed the money which was necessary to the elections, and therefore having been kindly thought of after elections, there has closed around the government of the United States a very interesting, a very able, a very aggressive coterie of gentlemen who are most definite and explicit in their ideas as to what they want.

They don't have to consult us as to what they want. They don't have to resort to anybody. They know their plans, and therefore they know what will be convenient for them. It may be that they have really thought what they have said they thought; it may be that they know so little of the history of economic development and of the interests of the United States as to believe that their leadership is indispensable for our prosperity and development. I don't have to prove that they believe that, because they themselves admit it. I have heard them admit it on many occasions.

I want to say to you very frankly that I do not feel vindictive about it. Some of the men who have exercised this control are excellent fellows; they really believe that the prosperity of the country depends upon them. They re-

ally believe that if the leadership of economic development in this country dropped from their hands, the rest of us are too muddle-headed to undertake the task. They not only comprehend the power of the United States within their grasp, but they comprehend it within their imagination. They are honest men, they have just as much right to express their views as I have to express mine or you to express yours, but it is just about time that we examined their views and determined their validity.

As a matter of fact, their thought does not cover the processes of their own undertakings. As a university president, I learned that the men who dominate our manufacturing processes could not conduct their business for twenty-four hours without the assistance of the experts with whom the universities were supplying them. Modern industry depends upon technical knowledge; and all that these gentlemen did was to manage the external features of great combinations and their financial operation, which had very little to do with the intimate skill with which the enterprises were conducted. I know men not catalogued in the public prints, men not spoken of in public discussion, are the very bone and sinew of the industry of the United States.

Do our masters of industry speak in the spirits and interest even of those whom they employ? When men ask me what I think about the labour question and labouring men, I feel that I am being asked what I know about the vast majority of the people, and I feel as if I were being asked to separate myself, as belonging to a particular class, from that great body of my fellow-citizens who sustain and conduct the enterprises of the country. Until we get away from that point of view it will be impossible to have a free government. . . .

I tell you the men I am interested in are the men who, under the conditions we have had, never had their voices heard, who never got a line in the newspapers, who never got a moment on the platform, who never had access to the ears of Governors or Presidents or of anybody who was responsible for the conduct of public affairs, but who went silently and patiently to their work every day carrying the burden of the world. How are they to be understood by the masters of finance, if only the masters of finance are consulted.

That is what I mean when I say, "Bring the government back to the people." I do not mean anything demagogic; I do not mean to talk as if we wanted a great mass of men to rush in and destroy something. That is not the idea. I want the people to come in and take possession of their own premises; for I hold that the government belongs to the people, and that they have a right to that intimate access to it which will determine every turn of its policy.

America is never going to submit to guardianship. America is never going to choose thralldom instead of freedom. Look what there is to decide! There is the tariff question. Can the tariff question be decided in favour of the people so long as the monopolies are the chief counsellors at Washington? There is the currency question. Are we going to settle the currency question so long as the government listens only to the counsel of those who command the banking situation?

Then there is the question of conservation. What is our fear about conservation? The hands that are being stretched out to monopolise our forests, to prevent the use of our great power-producing streams, the hands that are being stretched into the bowels of the earth to take possession of the great riches that lie hidden in Alaska and elsewhere in the incomparable domain of the United States, are the hands of monopoly. Are these men to continue to stand at the elbow of government and tell us how we are to save ourselves—from themselves? You cannot settle the question of conservation while monopoly is close to the ears of those who govern. And the question of conservation is a great deal bigger than the question of saving our forests and our mineral resources and our waters; it is as big as the life and happiness and strength and elasticity and hope of our people.

There are tasks awaiting the government of the United States which it cannot perform until every pulse of that government beats in unison with the needs and the desires of the whole body of the American people. Shall we not give the people access of sympathy, access of authority, to the instrumentalities which are to be indispensable to their lives?

The Populist Party, 1892–1896

The People's or Populist party was the culmination of a series of late-nineteenth-century agrarian organizations that together created the most significant native American radical movement. The Populist movement was a reaction to two decades of falling agricultural prices and a precipitous decline in the number of family-owned farms. Throughout the West and South, farmers were forced to mortgage their lands or sell out to absentee landlords and become tenant farmers. The targets of much of their anger were the railroads—whose power over rates for shipping products to market was critical—and the banks whose ability to offer or withhold credit was often the key to survival.

The roots of the Populist party can be found in the Patrons of Husbandry

injustice, and poverty shall eventually cease in the land.

While our sympathies as a party of reform are naturally upon the side of every proposition which will tend to make men intelligent, virtuous, and temperate, we nevertheless regard these questions, important as they are, as secondary to the great issues now pressing for solution, and upon which not only our individual prosperity but the very existence of free institutions depend; and we ask all men to first help us to determine whether we are to have a republic to administer before we differ as to the conditions upon which it is to be administered, believing that the forces of reform this day organized will never cease to move forward until every wrong is righted and equal rights and equal privileges securely established for all the men and women of this country.

PLATFORM

We declare, therefore—

First—That the union of the labor forces of the United States this day consummated shall be permanent and perpetual; may its spirit enter into all hearts for the salvation of the Republic and the uplifting of mankind.

Second—Wealth belongs to him who creates it, and every dollar taken from industry without an equivalent is robbery. "If any will not work, neither shall he eat." The interests of rural and civil labor are the same; their enemies are identical.

Third—We believe that the time has come when the railroad corporations will either own the people or the people must own the railroads; and should the government enter upon the work of owning and managing all railroads, we should favor an amendment to the constitution by which all persons engaged in the government service shall be placed under a civil-service regulation of the most rigid character, so as to prevent the increase of the power of the national administration by the use of such additional government employes.

Finance. We demand a national currency, safe, sound, and flexible issued by the general government only, a full legal tender for all debts, public and private, and that without the use of banking corporations; a just, equitable, and efficient means of distribution direct to the people; at a tax not to exceed 2 per cent, per annum, to be provided as set forth in the sub-treasury plan of the Farmers' Alliance, or a better system; also by payments in discharge of its obligations for public improvements.

1. We demand free and unlimited coinage of silver and gold at the present legal ratio of 16 to 1.

2. We demand that the amount of circulating medium be speedily increased to not less than $50 per capita.

3. We demand a graduated income tax.

4. We believe that the money of the country should be kept as much as possible in the hands of the people, and hence we demand that all State and national revenues shall be limited to the necessary expenses of the government, economically and honestly administered.

5. We demand that postal savings banks be established by the government for the safe deposit of the earnings of the people and to facilitate exchange.

Transportation. Transportation being a means of exchange and a public necessity, the government should own and operate the railroads in the interest of the people. The telegraph and telephone, like the post-office system, being a necessity for the transmission of news, should be owned and operated by the government in the interest of the people.

Land. The land, including all the natural sources of wealth, is the heritage of the people, and should not be monopolized for speculative purposes, and alien ownership of land should be prohibited. All land now held by railroads and other corporations in excess of their actual needs, and all lands now owned by aliens should be reclaimed by the government and held for actual settlers only.

EXPRESSION OF SENTIMENTS

Your Committee on Platform and Resolutions beg leave unanimously to report the following:

Whereas, Other questions have been presented for our consideration, we hereby submit the following, not as a part of the Platform of the People's Party, but as resolutions expressive of the sentiment of this Convention.

1. RESOLVED, That we demand a free ballot and a fair count in all elections, and pledge ourselves to secure it to every legal voter without Federal intervention, through the adoption by the States of the unperverted Australian or secret ballot system.

2. RESOLVED, That the revenue derived from a graduated income tax should be applied to the reduction of the burden of taxation now levied upon the domestic industries of this country.

3. RESOLVED, That we pledge our support to fair and liberal pensions to ex-Union soldiers and sailors.

4. RESOLVED, That we condemn the fallacy of protecting American labor under the present system, which opens our ports to the pauper and criminal classes of the world and crowds out our wage-earners; and we denounce the present ineffective laws against contract labor, and demand the further restriction of undesirable emigration.

5. RESOLVED, That we cordially sympathize with the efforts of organized workingmen to shorten the hours of labor, and demand a rigid enforcement of the existing eight-hour law on Government work, and ask that a penalty clause be added to the said law.

6. RESOLVED, That we regard the maintenance of a large standing army of mercenaries, known as the Pinkerton system, as a menace to our liberties, and we demand its abolition; and we condemn the recent invasion of the Territory of Wyoming by the hired assassins of plutocracy, assisted by Federal officers.

7. RESOLVED, That we commend to the favorable consideration of the people and the reform press the legislative system known as the initiative and referendum.

8. RESOLVED, That we favor a constitutional provision limiting the office of President and Vice-President to one term, and providing for the election of Senators of the United States by a direct vote of the people.

9. RESOLVED, That we oppose any subsidy or national aid to any private corporation for any purpose.

10. RESOLVED, That this convention sympathizes with the Knights of Labor and their righteous contest with the tyrannical combine of clothing manufacturers of Rochester, and declare it to be a duty of all who hate tyranny and oppression to refuse to purchase the goods made by the said manufacturers, or to patronize any merchant who sells such goods.

Henry George, 1839–1897

Henry George was an economist and reformer whose writings captured the discontent of many late nineteenth-century Americans with the transformation of their society. His most famous work, *Progress and Poverty,* was written in 1879. After its publication, he became well known both in the United States and in Europe.

George had little formal education. He left school before his fourteenth birthday and, by the age of sixteen, had signed on as a deckhand on a ship bound for Calcutta and Melbourne. He kept a journal on this trip and commented on the "shocking contrast between monstrous wealth and debasing want" that he saw in India.

He returned to the United States and, upon hearing of high-paying work in Oregon, headed for the West Coast. He was unsuccessful in his search for fortune in California and Oregon—including a stint in the gold mines—but stayed in California working as a printer and then reporter on a number of small newspapers.

After the Civil War, George became a staunch advocate of free trade in opposition to the growing protectionism advocated by eastern and midwestern industrialists. On a trip back to New York late in 1868, George was again struck by contrasts between rich and poor, even in the midst of industrial progress. He concluded that the western United States was a land of opportunity because its landed wealth had not yet been monopolized by a wealthy few. Like many early American agrarian republicans, George blamed monopoly power for all of our political and social ills and sought ways to prevent it.

Upon returning to California, George witnessed wild land speculation wherever the railroad opened new lands for settlement. He arrived at the startling conclusion that land values skyrocketed largely because of the march of civilization. Yet, this led to anomolous results. Those who already had the money to speculate in land became wealthier, but those who did not were locked out of the market. Land simply became too expensive to buy and cultivate. He developed this insight in a pamphlet titled *Our Land and Land Policy (1871)* and again in his famous *Progress and Poverty.*

George argued that all people had the natural right to apply their labor to the land. At the same time, however, private ownership of land limited this right for some, and the high costs of rent and taxes inhibited it for others. To help solve the problem, George advocated a "single tax" on land to regain for the community the added value that the community (not the specific landowner) had created. At the same time, the single tax would ease the tax burden for everyone else.

Progress and Poverty made George a celebrity. "Land and Labor Clubs" espousing George's ideas sprang up throughout the nation and even in Scotland and Ireland.

In 1880, George moved to New York. He ran for Mayor of New York in 1886 and lost in a close race. With the support of labor organizations and social reformers, George came in second, ahead of Theodore Roosevelt.

George's insights were firmly rooted in traditions of national rights and the labor theory of value. His arguments found favor with populist farmers and workers throughout the country. Although he never won office and his ideas did not become law, his insights influenced public debate on the legitimacy of large-scale wealth in the midst of economic want.

Henry George

Progress and Poverty (1879)

THE PERSISTENCE OF POVERTY AMID ADVANCING WEALTH.

The great problem, of which these recurring seasons of industrial depression are but peculiar manifestations, is now, I think, fully solved, and the social phenomena which all over the civilized world appall the philanthropist and perplex the statesman, which hang with clouds the future of the most advanced races, and suggest doubts of the reality and ultimate goal of what we have fondly called progress, are now explained.

> *The reason why, in spite of the increase of productive power, wages constantly tend to a minimum which will give but a bare living, is that, with increase in productive power, rent tends to even greater increase, thus producing a constant tendency to the forcing down of wages.*

In every direction, the direct tendency of advancing civilization is to increase the power of human labor to satisfy human desires—to

SOURCE: *Progress and Poverty* (New York: Henry George and Co., 1887).

extirpate poverty, and to banish want and the fear of want. All the things in which progress consists, all the conditions which progressive communities are striving for, have for their direct and natural result the improvement of the material (and consequently the intellectual and moral) condition of all within their influence. The growth of population, the increase and extension of exchanges, the discoveries of science, the march of invention, the spread of education, the improvement of government, and the amelioration of manners, considered as material forces, have all a direct tendency to increase the productive power of labor—not of some labor, but of all labor; not in some departments of industry, but in all departments of industry; for the law of the production of wealth in society is the law of "each for all, and all for each."

But labor cannot reap the benefits which advancing civilization thus brings, because they are intercepted. Land being necessary to labor, and being reduced to private ownership, every increase in the productive power of labor but increases rent—the price that labor must pay for the opportunity to utilize its powers; and thus all the advantages gained by the march of progress go to the owners of land, and wages do not increase. Wages cannot increase; for the greater the earnings of labor the greater the price that labor must pay out of its earnings for the opportunity to make any earnings at all. The mere laborer has thus no more interest in the general advance of productive power than the Cuban slave has in advance in the price of sugar. And just as an advance in the price of sugar may make the condition of the slave worse, by inducing the master to drive him harder, so may the condition of the free laborer be positively, as well as relatively, changed for the worse by the increase in the productive power of his labor. For, begotten of the continuous advance of rents, arises a speculative tendency which discounts the effect of future improvements by a still further advance of rent, and thus tends, where this has not occurred from the normal advance of rent, to drive wages down to the slave point—the point at which the laborer can just live.

And thus robbed of all the benefits of the increase in productive power, labor is exposed to certain effects of advancing civilization which, without the advantages that naturally accompany them, are positive evils, and of themselves tend to reduce the free laborer to the helpless and degraded condition of the slave.

For all the improvements which add to productive power as civilization advances, consist in, or necessitate, a still further subdivision of labor, and the efficiency of the whole body of laborers is increased at the expense of the independence of the constituents. The individual laborer acquires knowledge of, and skill in, but an infinitesimal part of the varied processes which are required to supply even the commonest wants. The aggregate produce of the labor of a savage tribe is small, but each member is capable of an independent life. He can build his own habitation, hew out or stitch together his own canoe, make his own clothing, manufacture his own weapons, snares, tools and ornaments. He has all the knowledge of nature possessed by his tribe—knows what vegetable productions are fit for food, and where they may be found; knows the habits and resorts of beasts, birds, fishes, and insects; can pilot himself by the sun or the stars, by the turning of blossoms or the mosses on the trees; is, in short, capable of supplying all his wants. He may be cut off from his fellows and still live; and thus possesses an independent power which makes him a free contracting party in his relations to the community of which he is a member.

Compare with this savage the laborer in the lowest ranks of civilized society, whose life is spent in producing but one thing, or oftener but the infinitesimal part of one thing, out of the multiplicity of things that constitute the wealth of society and go to supply even the most primitive wants; who not only cannot make even the tools required for his work, but often works with tools that he does not own, and can never hope to own. Compelled to even closer and more continuous labor than the savage, and gaining by it no more than the savage gets—the mere necessaries of life—he loses the independence of the savage. He is not only unable to apply his own powers to the direct satisfaction of his own wants, but, without the concurrence of many others, he is unable to apply them indirectly to the satisfaction of his wants. He is a mere link in an enormous chain of producers and consumers, helpless to separate himself, and helpless to move, except as they move. The worse his position in society, the more dependent is he on society; the more utterly unable does he become to do anything for himself. The very power of exerting his labor for the satisfaction of his wants passes from his own control, and may be taken away or restored by the actions of others, or by general causes over which he has no more influence than he has over the motions of the solar system.

The primeval curse comes to be looked upon as a boon, and men think, and talk, and clamor, and legislate as though monotonous manual labor in itself were a good and not an evil, an end and not a means. Under such circumstances, the man loses the essential quality of manhood—the godlike power of modifying and controlling conditions. He becomes a slave, a machine, a commodity—a thing, in some respects, lower than the animal.

I am no sentimental admirer of the savage state. I do not get my ideas of the untutored children of nature from Rousseau, or Chateaubriand or Cooper. I am conscious of its material and mental poverty, and its low and narrow range. I believe that civilization is not only the natural destiny of man, but the enfranchisement, elevation, and refinement of all his powers, and think that it is only in such moods as may lead him to envy the cud-chewing cattle, that a man who is free to the advantages of civilization could look with regret upon the savage state. But, nevertheless, I think no one who will open his eyes to the facts, can resist the conclusion that there are in the heart of our civilization large classes with whom the veriest savage could not afford to exchange. It is my deliberate opinion that if, standing on the threshold of being, one were given the choice of entering life as a Terra del Fuegan, a black fellow of Australia, an Esquimaux in the Arctic Circle, or among the lowest classes in such a highly civilized country as Great Britain, he would make infinitely the better choice in selecting the lot of the savage. For those classes who in the midst of wealth are condemned to want, suffer all the privations of the savage, without his sense of personal freedom; they are condemned to more than his narrowness and littleness, without opportunity for the growth of his rude virtues; if their horizon is wider, it is but to reveal blessings that they cannot enjoy.

There are some to whom this may seem like exaggeration, but it is only because they have never suffered themselves to realize the true condition of those classes upon whom the iron heel of modern civilization presses with full force. As De Tocqueville observes, in one of his letters to Mme. Swetchine, "we so soon become used to the thought of want that we do not feel, that an evil which grows greater to the sufferer the longer it lasts becomes less to the observer by the very fact of its duration;" and perhaps the best proof of the justice of this observation is that in cities where there exists a pauper class and a criminal class, where young girls shiver as they sew for bread, and tattered and barefooted children make a home in the streets, money is regularly raised to send missionaries to the heathen! Send missionaries to the heathen! it would be laughable if it were not so sad. Baal no longer stretches forth his hideous, sloping arms; but in Christian lands mothers slay their infants for a burial fee! And I challenge the production from any authentic accounts of savage life of such descriptions of degradation as are to be found in official documents of highly civilized countries—in reports of Sanitary Commissioners and of inquiries into the condition of the laboring poor.

The simple theory which I have outlined (if indeed it can be called a theory which is but the recognition of the most obvious relations) explains this conjunction of poverty with wealth, of low wages with high productive power, of degradation amid enlightenment, of virtual slavery in political liberty. It harmonizes, as results flowing from a general and inexorable law, facts otherwise most perplexing, and exhibits the sequence and relation between phenomena that without reference to it are diverse and contradictory. It explains why interest and wages are higher in new than in older communities, though the average, as well as the aggregate, production of wealth is less. It explains why improvements which increase the productive power of labor and capital, increase the reward of neither. It explains what is commonly called the conflict between labor and capital, while proving the real harmony of interest between them. It cuts the last inch of ground from under the fallacies of protection, while showing why free trade fails to permanently benefit the working classes. It explains why want increases with abundance, and wealth tends to greater and greater aggregations. It explains the periodically recurring depressions of industry without recourse either to the absurdity of "over-production" or the absurdity of "over-consumption." It explains the enforced idleness of large numbers of would-be producers, which wastes the productive force of advanced communities, without the absurd assumption that there is too little work to do, or that there are too many to do it. It explains the ill effects upon the laboring classes which often follow the introduction of machinery, without denying the natural advantages which the use of machinery gives. It explains the vice and misery which show themselves amid dense population, without attributing to the laws of the All-Wise and All-Beneficent defects which belong only to the short-sighted and selfish enactments of men. . . .

THE INJUSTICE OF PRIVATE PROPERTY IN LAND.

When it is proposed to abolish private property in land the first question that will arise is that of justice. Though often warped by habit, superstition, and selfishness into the most distorted forms, the sentiment of justice is yet fundamental to the human mind, and whatever dispute arouses the passions of men, the conflict is sure to rage, not so much as to the question "Is it wise?" as to the question "Is it right?"

This tendency of popular discussions to take an ethical form has a cause. It springs from a law of the human mind; it rests upon a vague and instinctive recognition of what is probably the deepest truth we can grasp. That

alone is wise which is just; that alone is enduring which is right. In the narrow scale of individual actions and individual life this truth may be often obscured, but in the wider field of national life it everywhere stands out.

I bow to this arbitrament, and accept this te t. If our inquiry into the cause which makes low wages and pauperism the accompaniments of material progress has led us to a correct conclusion, it will bear translation from terms of political economy into terms of ethics, and as the source of social evils show a wrong. If it will not do this, it is disproved. If it will do this, it is proved by the final decision. If private property in land be just, then is the remedy I propose a false one; if, on the contrary, private property in land be unjust, then is this remedy the true one.

What constitutes the rightful basis of property? What is it that enables a man to justly say of a thing, "It is mine!" From what springs the sentiment which acknowledges his exclusive right as against all the world? Is it not, primarily, the right of a man to himself, to the use of his own powers, to the enjoyment of the fruits of his own exertions? Is it not this individual right, which springs from and is testified to by the natural facts of individual organization—the fact that each particular pair of hands obey a particular brain and are related to a particular stomach; the fact that each man is a definite, coherent, independent whole—which alone justifies individual ownership? As a man belongs to himself, so his labor when put in concrete form belongs to him.

And for this reason, that which a man makes or produces is his own, as against all the world—to enjoy or to destroy, to use, to exchange, or to give. No one else can rightfully claim it, and his exclusive right to it involves no wrong to any one else. Thus there is to everything produced by human exertion a clear and indisputable title to exclusive possession and enjoyment, which is perfectly consistent with justice, as it descends from the original producer, in whom it vested by natural law. The pen with which I am writing is justly mine. No other human being can rightfully lay claim to it, for in me is the title of the producers who made it. It has become mine, because transferred to me by the stationer, to whom it was transferred by the importer, who obtained the exclusive right to it by transfer from the manufacturer, in whom, by the same process of purchase, vested the rights of those who dug the material from the ground and shaped it into a pen. Thus, my exclusive right of ownership in the pen springs from the natural right of the individual to the use of his own faculties. . . .

There is no escape from this position. To affirm that a man can rightfully claim exclusive ownership in his own labor when embodied in material things, is to deny that any one can rightfully claim exclusive ownership in land. To affirm the rightfulness of property in land, is to affirm a claim which has no warrant in nature, as against a claim founded in the organization of man and the laws of the material universe.

What most prevents the realization of the injustice of private property in land is the habit of including all the things that are made the subject of ownership in one category, as property, or, if any distinction is made, drawing the line, according to the unphilosophical distinction of the lawyers, between personal property and real estate, or things movable and things immovable. The real and natural distinction is between things which are the produce of labor and things which are the gratuitous offerings of nature; or, to adopt the terms of political economy, between wealth and land.

These two classes of things are in essence and relations widely different, and to class them together as property is to confuse all thought when we come to consider the justice or the injustice, the right or the wrong of property.

A house and the lot on which it stands are alike property, as being the subject of ownership, and are alike classed by the lawyers as real estate. Yet in nature and relations they differ widely. The one is produced by human labor, and belongs to the class in political economy styled wealth. The other is a part of nature, and belongs to the class in political economy styled land.

The essential character of the one class of things is that they embody labor, are brought into being by human exertion, their existence or non-existence, their increase or diminution, depending on man. The essential character of the other class of things is that they do not embody labor, and exist irrespective of human exertion and irrespective of man; they are the field or environment in which man finds himself; the storehouse from which his needs must be supplied, the raw material upon which, and the forces with which alone his labor can act.

The moment this distinction is realized, that moment is it seen that the sanction which natural justice gives to one species of property is denied to the other; that the rightfulness which attaches to individual property in the produce of labor implies the wrongfulness of individual property in land; that, whereas the recognition of the one places all men upon equal terms, securing to each the due reward of his labor, the recognition of the other is the denial of the equal rights of men, permitting those who do not labor to take the natural reward of those who do.

Whatever may be said for the institution of private property in land, it is therefore plain that it cannot be defended on the score of justice.

The equal right of all men to the use of land is as clear as their equal right to breathe the air—it is a right proclaimed by the fact of their existence. For we cannot suppose that some men have a right to be in this world and others no right.

If we are all here by the equal permission of the Creator, we are all here with an equal title to the enjoyment of his bounty—with an equal right to the use of all that nature so impartially offers. This is a right which is natural and inalienable; it is a right which vests in every human being as he enters the world, and which during his continuance in the world can be limited only by the equal rights of others. There is in nature no such thing as a fee simple in land. There is on earth no power which can rightfully make a grant of exclusive ownership in land. If all existing men were to unite to grant away their equal rights, they could not grant away the right of those who follow them. For what are we but tenants for a day? Have we made the earth, that we should determine the rights of those who after us shall tenant it in their turn? The Almighty, who created the earth for man and man for the earth, has entailed it upon all the generations of the children of men by a decree written upon the constitution of all things—a decree which no human action can bar and no prescription determine. Let the parchments be ever so many, or possession ever so long, natural justice can recognize no right in one man to the possession and enjoyment of land that is not equally the right of all his fellows. . . .

Our previous conclusions, irresistible in themselves, thus stand approved by the highest and final test. Translated from terms of political economy into terms of ethics they show a wrong as the source of the evils which increase as material progress goes on.

The masses of men, who in the midst of abundance suffer want; who, clothed with political freedom, are condemned to the wages of slavery; to whose toil labor-saving inventions bring no relief, but rather seem to rob them of a privilege, instinctively feel that "there is something wrong." And they are right.

The wide-spreading social evils which everywhere oppress men amid an advancing civilization, spring from a great primary wrong—the appropriation, as the exclusive property of some men, of the land on which and from which all must live. From this fundamental injustice flow all the injustices which distort and endanger modern development, which condemn the producer of wealth to poverty and pamper the non-producer in luxury, which rear the tenement house with the palace, plant the brothel behind the church, and compel us to build prisons as we open new schools. . . .

What is necessary for the use of land is not its private ownership, but the security of improvements. It is not necessary to say to a man, "this land is yours," in order to induce him to cultivate or improve it. It is only necessary to say to him, "whatever your labor or capital produces on this land shall be yours." Give a man security that he may reap, and he will sow; assure him of the possession of the house he wants to build, and he will build it. These are the natural rewards of labor. It is for the sake of the reaping that men sow; it is for the sake of possessing houses that men build. The ownership of land has nothing to do with it.

It was for the sake of obtaining this security, that in the beginning of the feudal period so many of the smaller landholders surrendered the ownership of their lands to a military chieftain, receiving back the use of them in fief or trust, and kneeling bareheaded before the lord, with their hands between his hands, swore to serve him with life, and limb, and worldly honor. Similar instances of the giving up of ownership in land for the sake of security in its enjoyment are to be seen in Turkey, where a peculiar exemption from taxation and extortion attaches to *vakouf*, or church lands, and where it is a common thing for a land owner to sell his land to a mosque for a nominal price, with the understanding that he may remain as tenant upon it at a fixed rent.

It is not the magic of property, as Arthur Young said, that has turned Flemish sands into fruitful fields. It is the magic of security to labor. This can be secured in other ways than making land private property, just as the heat necessary to roast a pig can be secured in other ways than by burning down houses. The mere pledge of an Irish landlord that for twenty years he would not claim in rent any share in their cultivation induced Irish peasants to turn a barren mountain into gardens; on the mere security of a fixed ground rent for a term of years the most costly buildings of such cities as London and New York are erected on leased ground. If we give improvers such security, we may safely abolish private property in land.

The complete recognition of common rights to land need in no way interfere with the complete recognition of individual right to improvements or produce. Two men may own a ship without sawing her in half. The ownership of a railway may be divided into a hundred thousand shares, and yet trains be run with as much system and precision as if there were but a single owner. In London, joint stock companies have been formed to hold and manage real estate. Everything could go on as now, and yet the common right to land be fully recognized by appropriating rent to the common benefit. There is a lot in the center of San Francisco to which the common rights of the people of that city are yet legally recognized. This lot is not cut up into infinitesimal pieces nor yet is it an unused waste. It is covered with fine buildings, the property of private individuals, that stand there in perfect security. The only difference between this lot and those around it, is that the rent of the one goes into the Common School Fund, the rent of the others into private pockets. What is to prevent the land of a whole country being held by the people of the country in this way? . . .

So far from the recognition of private property in land being necessary to the proper use of land, the contrary is the case. Treating land as private property stands in the way of its proper use. Were land treated as public property it would be used and improved as soon as there was need for its use or improvement, but being treated as private property, the individual owner is permitted to prevent others from using or improving what he cannot or will not use or improve himself. When the title is in dispute, the most valuable land lies unimproved for years; in many parts of England improvement is stopped because, the estates being entailed, no security to improvers can be given; and large tracts of ground which, were they treated as public property, would be covered with buildings and crops, are kept idle to gratify the caprice of the owner. In the thickly settled parts of the United States there is enough land to maintain three or four times our present population, lying unused, because its owners are holding it for higher prices, and immigrants are forced past this unused land to seek homes where their labor will be far less productive. In every city, valuable lots may be seen lying vacant for the same reason. If the best use of land be the test, then private property in land is condemned, as it is condemned by every other consideration. It is as wasteful and uncertain a mode of securing the proper use of land, as the burning down of houses is of roasting pigs. . . .

I do not propose either to purchase or to confiscate private property in land. The first would be unjust; the second, needless. Let the individuals who now hold it still retain, if they want to, possession of what they are pleased to call *their* land. Let them continue to call it *their* land. Let them buy and sell, and bequeath and devise it. We may safely leave them the shell, if we take the kernel. *It is not necessary to confiscate land; it is only necessary to confiscate rent.*

Nor to take rent for public uses is it necessary that the State should bother with the letting of lands, and assume the chances of the favoritism, collusion, and corruption this might involve. It is not necessary that any new machinery should be created. The machinery already exists. Instead of extending it, all we have to do is to simplify and reduce it. By leaving to land owners a percentage of rent which would probably be much less than the cost and loss involved in attempting to rent lands through State agency, and by making use of this existing machinery, we may, without jar or shock, assert the common right to land by taking rent for public uses.

We already take some rent in taxation. We have only to make some changes in our modes of taxation to take it all.

What I, therefore, propose, as the simple yet sovereign remedy, which will raise wages, increase the earnings of capital, extirpate pauperism, abolish poverty, give remunerative employment to whoever wishes it, afford free scope to human powers, lessen crime, elevate morals, and taste, and intelligence, purify government and carry civilization to yet nobler hights, is—*to appropriate rent by taxation.*

In this way, the State may become the universal landlord without calling herself so, and without assuming a single new function. In form, the ownership of land would remain just as now. No owner of land need be dispossessed, and no restriction need be placed upon the amount of land any one could hold. For, rent being taken by the State in taxes, land, no matter in whose name it stood, or in what parcels it was held, would be really common property, and every member of the community would participate in the advantages of its ownership.

Now, insomuch as the taxation of rent, or land values, must necessarily be increased just as we abolish other taxes, we may put the proposition into practical form by proposing—

To Abolish All Taxation Save That upon Land Values.

As we have seen, the value of land is at the beginning of society nothing, but as society develops by the increase of population and the advance of the arts, it becomes greater and greater. In every civilized country, even the newest, the value of the land taken as a whole is sufficient to bear the entire expenses of government. In the better developed countries it is much more than sufficient. Hence it will not be enough merely to place all taxes upon the value of land. It will be necessary, where rent exceeds the present governmental revenues, to commensurately increase the amount demanded in taxation, and to continue this increase as society progresses and rent advances. But this is so natural and easy a matter, that it may be considered as involved, or at least understood, in the proposition to put all taxes on the value of land. That is the first step, upon which the practical struggle must be made. When the hare is once caught and killed, cooking him will follow as a matter of course. When the common right to land is so far appreciated that all taxes are abolished save those which fall upon rent, there is no danger of much more than is necessary to induce them to collect the public revenues being left to individual landholders.

Experience has taught me (for I have been for some years endeavoring to popularize this proposition) that wherever the idea of concentrating all taxation upon land values finds lodgment sufficient to induce consideration, it invariably makes way, but that there are few of the classes most to be benefitted by it, who at first, or even for a long time afterwards, see its full significance and power. It is difficult for workingmen to get over the idea that there is a real antagonism between capital and labor. It is difficult for small farmers and homestead owners to get over the idea that to put all taxes on the value of land would be to unduly tax them. It is difficult for both classes to get over the idea that to exempt capital from taxation would be to make the rich richer, and the poor poorer. These ideas spring from confused thought. But behind ignorance and prejudice there is a powerful interest, which has hitherto dominated literature, education, and opinion. A great wrong always dies hard, and the great wrong which in every civilized country condemns the masses of men to poverty and want, will not die without a bitter struggle.

Charlotte Perkins Gilman, 1860–1935

Charlotte Perkins Gilman was an early feminist writer whose works both reflected changes in American society and pointed to changes yet to come. Writing at the turn of the century, Gilman witnessed growing numbers of American women entering a labor market outside of the family home. Responding to what she saw, she called for changes in child-rearing and household organization in order to ease women's burdens. In one of her best-known works, *Women and Economics* (1898), Gilman discussed institutional adjustments in family life that remind the reader of the feminist writers of the 1960s and after.

Called the "militant madonna" because of her crusading spirit combined with her gentle personality, Gilman was a popular lecturer and speaker. Nevertheless, her writings were essentially forgotten after World War I until contemporary feminists "rediscovered" her. Unlike many early feminists who concentrated on individual political rights, Gilman sought to move beyond discussions of liberal "rights" to study the roots of human personality and possibility. This led her to analyze, and attempt to alter, relationships in the family, church, and workplace. She always viewed herself as a sociologist rather than a political activist, and she probed the interaction between physical nature and culture in the development of the individual personality. By looking at the social roots of individual personality, Gilman was pushing her analysis beyond traditional liberal individualism, which respected the split between the political and social realms. While classical liberals argued that individual freedom was secure if the state stayed out of private lives, Gilman implied that it was the so-called private lives of women that kept them in chains. Although she did not advocate the state as the primary agent of change, Gilman's analysis took her beyond the more comfortable liberal language of women's rights.

The following excerpt is from *His Religion and Hers*. Like many nineteenth-century writers, Gilman believed in the inevitability of progress, that is, that history was a series of stages that would lead to greater equality and fuller development. In this work, Gilman examined the biological origins of women's roles and the way that social institutions—including religion—further developed and altered the biological formation. She concluded that our inherited institutions no longer encouraged "normal social evolution" and thus needed to be reformed.

Charlotte Perkins Gilman

His Religion and Hers (1923)

. . . The major position taken in this book—that religion, our greatest help in conscious progress, has been injured by coming through the minds of men alone—leads to the natural question of why the male of our species should so be blamed while the males of other species are harmless and useful.

Here we reach the biological basis for that "innate perversity," for the peculiar behavior of the species which has so opposed and retarded its natural progress. This lies, not in any essential fault in the male of our race, but in his unnatural relation to the female. By the early and universal subjection of the female to the male, by her segregation to the lowest form of service and to an exaggerated sex-development, we have made ourselves a crippled race, a race whose whole development was left to be carried on by one half of it.

It is the strange, lonely, unnatural position of the human male, accentuated beyond all reason by his cumulative over-development in sex, which quite easily accounts for that "perversity." It is not the natural male in a natural relation who works evil, to religion or anything else, but our human speciality, the male of the species carrying on all the social activities as best he can, while served and catered to by the other half of the race.

That these conditions have begun to change is the most hopeful fact in our present life, but it will be many generations before we can

SOURCE: Charlotte Perkins Gilman, *His Religion and Hers* (New York: The Century Co., 1923).

show the equally human pair capable of carrying on the smooth and happy development of society. In hastening so desirable a movement it is more than necessary for us to understand the precise nature of the previous morbid condition, with its unavoidable evil results.

The bitterness and antagonism aroused by the recent struggle of women to reach normal human development, was enhanced by their not unnatural blame of men for their unjust treatment. "Tyrant man" was treated as an opponent, condemned and berated for his cruelty. Such a position was well warranted at the time, but it has no bearing on the initial problem of how this great misplacement started.

Just as early religions were animistic, and natural objects and forces personified, so women sought to explain the new charge of "original sin" by assuming a man with a club who suddenly rose up against his female and subjugated her by main force. Being ignorant of biological processes they did not realize how absurd it was to imagine a relation as old as sex itself to have been instantaneously changed and inverted by one man—or one generation of men.

The freedom and power of the female were unbroken after the male appeared, up to and well into the human race. In the earliest known stages of our savage state the female was still free, useful, and honored. Between that time and the beginnings of history, a period of enormous length, the change took place. It appears to have occurred at about the same stage of primitive culture, in widely separated races, in various parts of the earth. Reasons for such a change must be looked for in the race itself; it must be due to some inherent distinction peculiar to the human animal, and manifesting itself at a certain stage of development.

Such inherent distinction is not far to seek.

The human race is characterized by the prolongation of infancy, this prolongation increasing with human development.

The prolongation of infancy involved an extension of motherhood; not only in length, as the period of infancy grew longer, but in breadth, as the mother was called upon to serve more than one child at the same time, of different ages, having different wants.

The extension of motherhood, in the human animal, with its skillful hand, its thinking brain, manifested itself not only in the nurture and defense given by lower mothers but in the beginnings of industry. Within their limits we see the same force working in lower creatures. All the endless labor and care, all the complex organization and varied products of the bees and ants and other insects are the efforts of motherhood. Motherhood is the great developer, throughout nature. With us it poured out its rising flood of love in service, in work, in the making of things, in the securing, storing, and preparing of food. Note this last.

The mother was the first worker. Her mate was still only a hunter and fighter. The initial steps in all the primitive industries were taken by women alone.

Work is a human distinction; the human distinction par excellence. Through work alone have we developed our special race capacities. The female as the race type naturally developed along racial lines. The fact that her labors were for the child gives them no character of sex. As was earlier shown, the variation in the reproductive process is a race distinction, manifested before sex was introduced. This prolongation of infancy was a race-improvement, and its attendant development of

mother-power was also a race distinction, having no bearing upon the natural sex relation. Nevertheless it is precisely her increased capacity for human service which lies at the root of our great race tragedy, the subjugation of the female. This came about not by any act of cruelty on the part of man but by the increasing desirability of woman's services.

In all other races the female is desirable to the male merely as a female; she has no further value to him. In our race, by the industrial development of woman, the female assumed a new attraction, not that of sex, but that of service. As she increased in usefulness, as her children grew older and larger, yet still profited by her intelligent care, as she learned to prepare food for them, why should not he partake of it? He was not much older than his oldest son, for primitive life was short; her motherliness to this day extends to her husband; it so extended then. Of course he liked it; he does yet. Easily and unconsciously he slipped into more and more dependence on her services. She was of economic value to him, as is no other female to a male. It is motherhood of which he first took advantage, not sex. In some low cultures we still find women slaves in economics but free and respected in sex.

There is a distinction between industry, in all its wide specialization,—with the resultant distribution and exchange of products which form the economic base of social life,—and service, which is a personal relation. Personal service is necessary to infancy; it is normal and right. Personal service of the female to the adult male is abnormal and wrong. It is no more right that a healthy man should be waited on like a baby by a woman than that a healthy woman should be fed and clothed by a man.

This grown baby, enjoying a mother's care and service long after it was normal, grew to depend on it. There must have been some advantage in the absurd relation, in those dark old days, to account for its wide development.

Obviously a fighting male, served and mothered by a working female, was a more competent warrior than one who had to stop fighting and take care of himself. The Mexican soldiery still take their women with them to wait on them.

The economic value of the female is quite sufficient to account for an increasing demand for her possession; the more women a man had to work for him, the more rich and comfortable he was. But extensive polygamy and the sex slavery resultant could not appear until cattle-keeping and, in time, a settled agriculture gave at last the house, and the housekeeper. It is the economic value of the woman which makes men so sure that "A woman's place is the home."

Our persistent misunderstanding in the matter is due to our general confusion of sex and service. Yet it is clear to any fair observer that the woman whose place is in the home is first of all the serving mother (the man never ceases to dwell lovingly on her service); and after that, may be, the wife, the sister, the daughter, the aunt—any sort of female relative who does not have to be paid—or, at worst, a "hired girl." The main idea is that the man must be served by women.

. . . So we find the simple, natural, unavoidable extension of motherhood into service, taken advantage of by the adult male by slow degrees, becoming a settled custom, and inevitably developing into slavery.

In following out the results of such extension, we must first note the immense difference between the survival and development of humanity, which is a progressive form of social relationship, and the mere persistence of the human animal.

The reason our species can go wrong more widely than any other and not die of it, is because of our social economic functions. While we lived by hunting and fishing, our existence was precarious, our progress slow, and any marked error in behavior met the same prompt death sentence so clearly seen in lower races. Even the pastoral tribes were limited by almost similar economic restrictions. If the grass failed, or the cattle failed, they failed too.

But when agriculture was reached, man conquered his food supply; and that by the exertion of only a portion of his powers. The labor of some could now feed others, an increasing proportion of others as the processes of cultivation of food improved.

Given a basis of physical existence like this, and given women sufficiently well treated to produce more people, the persistence of the human species was secured. But no more. Social progress was now possible, but not by any means assured. We find in Africa low cultures based on agriculture, with woman-slavery, which have apparently stayed at that level for uncounted ages.

Where progress did appear, it was open to any amount of error which did not cut off the source of supply, motherhood plus agriculture. This primal source has kept the human race alive on earth through ages of unnecessary evils which would have long since extinguished any other species. One early tribe has given way to another; one far higher people has been destroyed by another; and one culture after another has died of self-made diseases and follies, but the race survives and has developed in various places and distributed far and wide those inventions and discoveries, arts and sciences which make us harder to kill than early man.

Before any religion worthy of the name was developed we find the race already established on the basis of woman-slavery, and, later, its inevitable consequence—man-slavery as well. Our culture, for all historic time up to a few centuries ago, was a slave culture, we in America, to our shame, being the last civilized people to abolish this primitive evil.

The male, master of the female, carrying on his mastership to other men, developing industry by force, as a tribute, a degradation, brought his prejudices to bear on every early religion in its formative period, and kept them in action through all later years.

We who have passed it, can now see the essential evils of slavery. It acts upon the slave, with well-known weakening results. It acts upon the master, tending to produce pride, laziness, and self-indulgence, cruelty, injustice, and, from its dim beginnings to its glaring end, licentiousness. Where the slave was of a different race and color, this last result was evidenced beyond any possible dispute.

When characteristics like these have formed the minds of men for ages, the influence of those minds upon religion is sadly evident. Facing the evils in behavior inevitably developed by his position as master, man vainly sought, by stern commandments, to prohibit the behavior, while maintaining the cause. The master himself becoming, through long slaveholding, proud, lazy, selfish, cruel, and unjust, it is no wonder that his early gods were all of these together.

The habit of mastership, growing as improved conditions made larger the group of subject workers, stretched out and on, unchecked by any truer concept of social life, and gave us kings. The son of a slave was a slave, the son of a master was a master. Here is the philosophic base for "the divine right of kings," and all those pursuant customs of inheritance and primogeniture, the forcing of a trade from father to son, and a number of like collateral errors.

. . . In a normal social evolution we should have seen the gradual differentiation of our varied gifts, the products of our varied abilities, the distribution of those products so as best to promote social progress, and the careful cultivation of all children so as to secure the maximum of social efficiency. A normal development of religion meanwhile, seeing the broad road of progress as the line to be followed in right doing, would have strength-

ened our joy in good workmanship, exhorted us to mutual appreciation and interservice, kept before us the splendid hope of race-improvement.

But man, master of women and of slaves, had quite other habits of mind. Recognizing clearly enough the deadly results of iniquity, he summoned, to account for his behavior, theories of fate and the devil; and to prevent wrong-doing, used the only power he knew—command—with threat of punishment and promise of reward.

Our man-modified religions have never recognized the basic evils of subject womanhood, and its resultant, slavery. Within a lifetime we heard the preachers of our South—yes, and many in the North as well—defending slavery on the ground that Jesus had not objected to it, and that St. Paul told Onesimus to obey his master. Yet they might have found one text, Exodus xxi, 16, which certainly had an adverse bearing on the slave-trade:

> And he that stealeth a man, and selleth him, or if he be found in his hand, he shall surely be put to death.

As to the subjection of woman, the key to the whole position, none of the old religions objected to that as wrong. On the contrary, they one and all assumed her to be the natural inferior of man and to be endured only for his use and convenience, because, forsooth, it was "not good that the man should be alone." In view of what we now know as to his relative origin, this becomes charmingly funny.

The man's mind influenced the religion, and the religion, petrified and immovable, influenced the man's mind, and so, inevitably, the woman's. Because of its heavy injunctions as to the woman's duty of submission to him, that submission has been enforced long after changed conditions would have led to freedom.

We can see in actual fact women working

with men in many peasantries, and even in domestic industry, showing racial abilities, with some approach to recognition. Wherever freedom of choice was allowed, they manifested human capacities in several trades. As life moved on, changing and broadening, so would women have grown had they been free. But religion did not move, change, grow. Religion was supposed to be final, to be "the truth," all the truth there was.

Our belief in salvation rests on a previous damnation; damnation rests on "original sin,"—the eating of forbidden fruit,—and that requires belief in the story of Eden. If the ancient Hebrew religion accepted the still more ancient Assyrian legend, stating that woman was made out of Adam's rib, for his personal accommodation, and that her subsequent interest in apples was responsible for the loss of that horticultural paradise, it is not remarkable that the pious modern Hebrew still mutters his daily prayer of masculine superiority, thanking God that he was not born a woman.

One religion after another has accepted and perpetuated man's original mistake in making a private servant of the mother of the race.

W. E. B. Du Bois, 1868–1963

A civil rights activist, Pan-Africanist, sociologist, and historian, Du Bois was the model of the intellectual political activist. He is best remembered for his critical attacks on Booker T. Washington. Social and political inequality were totally unacceptable to Du Bois. In the tradition of Frederick Douglass, he argued that black men and women were entitled to every right granted to their white counterparts. Furthermore, Du Bois believed that Washington's commitment to agricultural and industrial education for young blacks would destroy the black community's opportunity to build a strong leadership. The "talented tenth" of black youth needed a rigorous liberal arts education, Du Bois argued, if blacks were to develop any political strength whatsoever.

Du Bois received a B.A. from Fisk in 1888 and another B.A. degree from Harvard (in philosophy) in 1890. In 1895, he received his Ph.D. in history and wrote a famous dissertation "The Suppression of the African Slave Trade in the U.S. 1638–1870," which was soon published by the Harvard Historical Series. He taught at Wilberforce in Ohio and then the University of Pennsylvania. From 1897 to 1910, he taught at Atlanta University and organized the famous Annual Conferences on the Negro, whose proceedings were regularly published.

Du Bois's academic life was always closely tied to his political activities. From 1905 to 1909, he was a leader in the Niagara movement that culminated in the formation of the National Association for the Advancement of Colored People (NAACP). From 1909 to 1934, Du Bois served as the NAACP's director of publicity and research, and editor of its monthly paper *The Crisis*. He left in 1934 in a disagreement over how to respond to the depression but returned as director of special research from 1944 to 1948, when he retired at the age of 80.

Late in life, Du Bois began to move rapidly to the left. In 1950, he ran unsuccessfully for the U.S. Senate as a candidate of the American Labor Party, and in 1951 was arrested but acquitted on charges of acting as an agent for a foreign power. In 1961, he joined the American Communist party and then moved to Ghana to live out his life as editor in chief of the *Encyclopedia Africana.*

Du Bois was the author of twenty-one books and novels including *The Philadelphia Negro* (1899), *The Souls of Black Folk* (1903), *Black Reconstruction* (1935), and *The World and Africa* (1943).

The following selection is from a speech Du Bois delivered at the National Negro Conference in 1909 and is an excellent example of early twentieth-century critiques of social Darwinism.

W. E. B. Du Bois

The Evolution of the Race Problem (1909)

Those who complain that the Negro problem is always with us and apparently insoluble must not forget that under this vague and general designation are gathered many social problems and many phases of the same problem; that these problems and phases have passed through a great evolutionary circle and that today especially one may clearly see a repetition, vaster but similar, of the great cycle of the past.

That problem of the past, so far as the black American was concerned, began with caste—a definite place preordained in custom, law, and religion where all men of black blood must be thrust. To be sure, this caste idea as applied to blacks was no sudden, full-grown conception, for the enslavement of the workers was an idea which America inherited from Europe and was not synonymous for many years with the enslavement of the blacks, al-

though the blacks were the chief workers. Men came to the idea of exclusive black slavery by gradually enslaving the workers, as was the world's long custom, and then gradually conceiving certain sorts of work and certain colors of men as necessarily connected. It was, when once set up definitely in the southern slave system, a logically cohering whole which the simplest social philosopher could easily grasp and state. The difficulty was it was too simple to be either just or true. Human nature is not simple and any classification that roughly divides men into good and bad, superior and inferior, slave and free, is and must ever be ludicrously untrue and universally dangerous as a permanent exhaustive classification. So in the southern slave system the thing that from the first damned it was the free Negro—the Negro legally free, the Negro economically free and the Negro spiritually free.

How was the Negro to be treated and conceived of who was legally free? At first with

SOURCE: *Proceedings of the National Negro Conference,* New York, 1909.

perfect naturalness he was treated as a man—he voted in Massachusetts and in South Carolina, in New York and Virginia; he intermarried with black and white, he claimed and received his civil rights—all this until the caste of color was so turned as to correspond with the caste of work and enslave not only slaves but black men who were not slaves. Even this system, however, was unable to ensure complete economic dependence on the part of all black men; there were continually artisans, foremen and skilled servants who became economically too valuable to be slaves. In vain were laws hurled at Negro intelligence and responsibility; black men continued to hire their time and to steal some smattering of knowledge, and it was this fact that became the gravest menace to the slave system. But even legal and economic freedom was not so dangerous to slavery as the free spirit which continually cropped out among men fated to be slaves: they thought, they dreamed, they aspired, they resisted. In vain were they beaten, sold south and killed, the ranks were continually filled with others and they either led revolt at home or ran away to the North, and these by showing their human qualities continually gave the lie to the slave assumption. Thus it was the free Negro in these manifold phases of his appearance who hastened the economic crisis which killed slavery and who made it impossible to make the caste of work and the caste of color correspond, and who became at once the promise and excuse of those who forced the critical revolution.

Today in larger cycle and more intricate detail we are passing through certain phases of a similar evolution. Today we have the caste idea—again not a sudden full-grown conception but one being insidiously but consciously and persistently pressed upon the nation. The steps toward it which are being taken are: first, political disfranchisement, then vocational education with the distinct idea of narrowing to the uttermost of the vocations in view, and finally a curtailment of civil freedom of travel, association, and entertainment, in systematic effort to instill contempt and kill self-respect.

Here then is the new slavery of black men in America—a new attempt to make degradation of social condition correspond with certain physical characteristics—not to be sure fully realized as yet, and probably unable for reasons of social development ever to become as systematized as the economic and physical slavery of the past—and yet realized to an extent almost unbelievable by those who have not taken the pains to study the facts—to an extent which makes the lives of thinking black men in this land a perpetual martyrdom.

But right here, as in the past, stands in the path of this idea the figure of this same thinking black man—this new freedman. This freedman again, as in the past, presents himself as free in varying phases: there is the free black voter of the North and border states whose power is far more tremendous than even he dare think so that he is afraid to use it; there is the black man who has accomplished economic freedom and who by working himself into the vast industrial development of the nation is today accumulating property at a rate that is simply astounding. And finally there is the small but growing number of black men emerging into spiritual freedom and becoming participators and freemen of the kingdom of culture around which it is so singularly difficult to set metes and bounds, and who in art, science and literature are making their modest but ineffaceable mark.

The question is what is the significance of this group of men for the future of the caste program and for the future social development of America? In order to answer this question intelligently let us retrace our steps and follow more carefully the details of the proposed program of renewed caste in America. This program when one comes to define and state it is elusive. There are even those who deny its existence as a definite consciously conceived plan of action. But, certain it is, there is growing unanimity of a peculiar sort on certain matters. And this unanimity is centering about three propositions:

1. That it was a mistake to give Negroes the ballot.

2. That Negroes are essentially an inferior race.

3. That the only permanent settlement of the race problem will be open and legal recognition of this inferiority.

When now a modern nation condemns 10 million of its fellows to such a fate it would be supposed that this conclusion has been reluctantly forced upon them after a careful study and weighing of the facts. This, however, is not the case in the Negro problem. On the contrary there has been manifest a singular reluctance and indisposition carefully to study the Negro problem. Ask the average American: why should the ballot have been withheld from the Negro, and he will answer: "Because he wasn't fit for it." But that is not a sufficient answer: first, because few newly enfranchised groups of the most successful democracies have been fit for the ballot when it was first given, and secondly, because there were Negroes in the United States fit for the ballot in 1870.

Moreover the political philosophy that condemns out of hand the Fifteenth Amendment does not often stop to think that the problem before the American nation 1865–1870 was not a simple problem of fixing the qualifications of voters. It was, on the contrary, the immensely more complicated problem of enforcing a vast social and economic revolution on a people determined not to submit to it. Whenever a moral reform is forced on a people from without there ensue complicated and tremendous problems, whether that reform is the correction of the abuse of alcohol, the abolition of child labor or the emancipation of slaves. The enforcement of such a reform will strain every nerve of the nation and the real question is not: is it a good thing to strain the framework of the nation but rather: is slavery so dangerous a thing that sudden enfranchisement of the ex-slaves is too great a price to pay for its abolition?

To be sure there are those who profess to think that the white South of its own initiative after the war, with the whole of the wealth, intelligence and lawmaking power in its hands, would have freely emancipated its slaves in obedience to a decree from Washington, just as there are those who would entrust the regulation of the whiskey traffic to saloon keepers and the bettering of the conditions of child labor to the employers. It is no attack on the South or on saloon keepers or on employers to say that such a reform from such a source is unthinkable. It is simply human nature that men trained to a social system or condition should be the last to be entirely entrusted with its reformation.

It was, then, not the Emancipation Proclamation but the Fifteenth Amendment that made slavery impossible in the United States and those that object to the Fifteenth Amendment have simply this question to answer: which was best, slavery or ignorant Negro voters? The answer is clear as day: Negro voters never did anything as bad as slavery. If they were guilty of all the crimes charged to them by the wildest enemies, even then what they did was less dangerous, less evil, and less cruel than the system of slavery whose death knell they struck. And when in addition to this we remember that the black voters of the South established the public schools, gave the poor whites the ballot, modernized the penal code, and put on the statute books of the South page after page of legislation that still stands today—when we remember this, we have a right to conclude that the Fifteenth Amendment was a wise and far-sighted piece of statesmanship.

But today the men who oppose the right of Negroes to vote are no longer doing so on the ground of ignorance, and with good reason, for today a majority and an appreciable majority of the black men of the South twenty-one years of age and over can read and write. In other words, the bottom has been clean knocked out of their ignorance argument and yet the fact has elicited scarcely a loud remark. . . .

But no sooner do facts like these come to the fore than again the ground of opposition subtly shifts and this last shifting has been so gradual and so insidious that the Negro and his friends are still answering arguments that are no longer being pushed. The most subtle enemies of democracy and the most persistent advocates of the color line admit almost contemptuously most that their forebears strenuously denied: the Negroes have progressed since slavery, they are accumulating some property, some of them work readily and they are susceptible of elementary training; but, they say, all thought of treating black men like white men must be abandoned. They are an inferior stock of men, limited in attainment by nature. You cannot legislate against nature, and philanthropy is powerless against deficient cerebral development.

To realize the full weight of this argument recall to mind a character like John Brown and contrast his attitude with the attitude of today. John Brown loved his neighbor as himself. He could not endure, therefore, to see his neighbor poor, unfortunate or oppressed. This natural sympathy was strengthened by a saturation in Hebrew religion which stressed the personal responsibility of every man's soul to a just God. To this religion of equality and sympathy with misfortune was added the strong influence of the social doctrines of the French Revolution with its emphasis on freedom and power in political life. And on all this was built John Brown's own inchoate but growing belief in a juster and more equal distribution of property. From all this John Brown concluded—and acted on that conclusion—that all men were created free and equal and that the cost of liberty was less than the price of repression.

Up to the time of John Brown's death this doctrine was a growing, conquering social thing. Since then there has come a change and many would rightly find reason for that change in the coincidence that the year John Brown suffered martyrdom was the year that first published the *Origin of Species*. Since that tremendous scientific and economic advance has been accompanied by distinct signs of moral change in social philosophy; strong arguments have been made for the fostering of war, the social utility of human degradation and disease, and the inevitable and known inferiority of certain classes and races of men. While such arguments have not stopped the efforts of the advocates of peace, the workers of social uplift and the believers in human brotherhood, they have, it must be confessed, often made their voices falter and tinged their arguments with apology.

Why is this? It is because the splendid scientific work of Darwin, Weissman, Galton and others has been widely and popularly interpreted as meaning that there is such essential and inevitable inequality among men and races of men as no philanthropy can or ought to eliminate; that civilization is a struggle for existence whereby the weaker nations and individuals will gradually succumb and the strong will inherit the earth. With this interpretation has gone the silent assumption that the white European stock represents the strong surviving peoples and that the swarthy, yellow and black people are the ones rightly doomed to eventual extinction.

One can easily see what influence such a doctrine would have on the nation. Those that stepped into the pathway marked by the early abolitionists faltered and large numbers turned back. They said: they were good men—even great, but they have no message for us today—John Brown was a "belated covenanter," William Lloyd Garrison was an anachronism in the age of Darwin—men who gave their lives to lift not the unlifted but the unliftable. We have, consequently, the present reaction—a reaction which says in effect: keep these black people in their places, and do not attempt to treat a Negro simply as a white man with a black face; to do this would mean moral deterioration of the race and nation—a fate against which a divine racial prejudice is successfully fighting. This is the attitude of the larger portion of the thinking nation today. . . .

To meet this difficulty in racial philosophy a step has been taken in America fraught with the gravest social consequences to the world and threatening not simply the political but the moral integrity of the nation: that step is to deny in the case of black men the validity of those evidences of culture, ability and decency which are accepted unquestionably in the case of other people, and by vague assertion, unprovable assumption, unjust emphasis, and now and then by deliberate untruth, to secure not only the continued proscription of these people, but by caste distinction to shut in the faces of their rising classes many of the paths to further advance.

When a social policy based on a supposed scientific sanction leads to such a moral anomaly it is time to examine rather carefully the logical foundations of the argument. And so soon as we do this many things are clear. First, assuming that there are certain stocks of human beings whose elimination the best welfare of the world demands; it is certainly questionable if these stocks include the majority of mankind and it is indefensible and monstrous to pretend that we know today with any reasonable certainty which these stocks are. We can point to degenerate individuals and families here and there among all races, but there is not the slightest warrant for assuming that there do not exist among the Chinese and Hindus, the African Bantus and American-Indians as lofty possibilities of human culture as any European race has ever exhibited. It is, to be sure, puzzling to know why the Sudan should linger a thousand years in culture behind the valley of the Seine, but it is no more

puzzling than the fact that the valley of the Thames was miserably backward as compared with the banks of the Tiber. Climate, human contact, facilities of communication, and what we call accident have played greater part in the rise of culture among nations: to ignore these and to assert dogmatically that the present distribution of culture is a fair index of the distribution of human ability and desert is to make an assertion for which there is not the slightest scientific warrant.

What the age of Darwin has done is to add to the eighteenth-century idea of individual worth the complementary idea of physical immortality of the human race. And this, far from annulling or contracting the idea of human freedom, rather emphasizes its necessity and eternal possibility—the boundlessness and endlessness of possible human achievement. Freedom has come to mean not individual caprice or aberration but social self-realization in an endless chain of selves, and freedom for such development is not the denial but the central assertion of the revolutionary theory. So, too, the doctrine of human equality passed through the fire of scientific inquiry not obliterated but transfigured; not equality of present attainment but equality of opportunity for unbounded future attainment is the rightful demand of mankind.

What now does the present hegemony of the white races threaten? It threatens by the means of brute force a survival of some of the worst stocks of mankind. It attempts to people the best part of the earth and put in absolute authority over the rest not only, and indeed not mainly, the culture of Europe, but its greed and degradation—not only some representatives of the best stocks of the West End of London, upper New York and the Champs Elysées but also, and in as large, if not larger, numbers, the worst stocks of Whitechapel, the East Side and Montmartre; and it attempts to make the slums of white society in all cases and under all circumstances the superior of any colored group, no matter what its ability or culture; it attempts to put the intelligent, property-holding, efficient Negroes of the South under the heels and at the absolute mercy of such constituencies as Tillman, Vardaman and Jeff Davis represent. . . .

This movement gathered force and strength during the latter half of the nineteenth century and reached its culmination when France, Germany and England, and Russia began the partition of China and the East. With the sudden self-assertion of Japan its wildest dreams collapsed, but it is still today a living, virile, potent force and motive, and the most subtle and dangerous enemy of world peace and the dream of human brotherhood. It has a whole vocabulary of its own: the strong races, superior peoples, race preservation, the struggle for survival and a peculiar use of the word "white." And by this it means the right of white men of any kind to club blacks into submission, to make them surrender their wealth and the use of their women, and to submit to the dictation of white men without murmur, for the sake of being swept off the fairest portions of the earth or held there in perpetual serfdom or guardianship. Ignoring the fact that the era of physical struggle for survival has passed away among human beings and that there is plenty of room accessible on earth for all, this theory makes the possession of Krupp guns the main criterion of mental stamina and moral fitness.

Even armed with this morality of the club and every advantage of modern culture, the white races have been unable to possess the earth; many signs of degeneracy have appeared among them; their birthrate is falling, their average ability is not increasing, their physical stamina is impaired, their social condition is not reassuring, and their religion is a growing mass of transparent and self-confessed hypocrisy. Lacking the physical ability to take possession of the world, they are today fencing in America, Australia, and South Africa and declaring that no dark race shall occupy or develop the land which they themselves are unable to use. And all this on the plea that their stock is threatened with deterioration from without, when in fact its most dangerous fate is deterioration from within.

We are in fact today repeating in our intercourse between races all the former evils of class injustice, unequal taxation and rigid caste. Individual nations outgrew these fatal things by breaking down the horizontal barriers between classes. We are bringing them back by seeking to erect vertical barriers between races. Men were told that abolition of compulsory class distinction meant leveling down, degradation, disappearance of culture and genius, and the triumph of the mob. As a matter of fact, it has been the salvation of European civilization. Some deterioration and leveling there was, but it was more than balanced by the discovery of new reservoirs of ability and strength. So today, we are told that free racial contact—or "social equality" as southern *patois* has it—means contamination of blood and lowering of ability and culture. It need mean nothing of the sort. Abolition of class distinction does not mean universal intermarriage of stocks, but rather the survival of the fittest by peaceful personal and social selection, a selection all the more effective because free democracy and equality of opportunity allow the best to rise to their rightful place. . . .

* * * * *

. . . Not only is the cost of repression today large—it is a continually increasing cost, because of the fact that furnished the fatal moral anomaly against which physical slavery could not stand—the free Negro—the Negro who in spite of contempt, discouragement, caste and poverty has put himself on a plane where it is simply impossible to deny that he is by every legitimate measurement the equal of his average white neighbor. The former argument was as I have mentioned that no such class existed. This assertion was persisted in until it became ludicrous. Today the fashion is come to regard this class as exceptional so far as the logic of the Negro problem is concerned, dangerous so far as social peace is concerned, and its existence more than offset by an abnormal number of criminals, degenerates and defectives.

Right here, then, comes the center of the present problem, namely: What is the *truth* about this? What are the real facts? How far is Negro crime due to inherited and growing viciousness and how far to poverty, degradation, and systematic oppression?

How far is Negro labor lazy and how far is it the listless victim of systematic theft?

How far is the Negro woman lewd and how far the helpless victim of social custom?

How far are Negro children being educated today in the public schools of the South and how far is the effort to curtail that training increasingly successful?

How far are Negroes leaving the farms and rushing to the cities to escape work and how far to escape slavery?

How far is this race designated as Negroes the descendants of African slaves and how far is it descended from the most efficient white blood of the nation?

What does actual physical and social measurement prove as to the status of these descendants of black men?

All these are fundamental questions. Not a single valid conclusion as to the future can be absolutely insisted upon without definite skillful scientific answers to these questions and yet not a single systematic effort to answer these questions on an adequate scale has been made in these United States from 1619 to 1909. Not only this but on all sides opposition ranging from indifference and reluctance to actual force is almost universal when any attempt to study the Negro problem adequately is proposed. Yet in spite of this universal and deliberate ignorance the demand is made that one line of solution, which a number of good men have assumed is safe and sane, shall be accepted by everybody and particularly by thinking black men. The penalty for not accepting this program is to be dubbed a radical, a busybody, an impatient dreamer and a dangerous agitator. Yet this program involves justification of disfranchisement, the personal humiliation of Jim Crowism, a curtailed and purposely limited system of education and a virtual acknowledgement of the inevitable and universal inferiority of black men. And then in the face of this we are asked to look pleasant and do our very best. I think it is the most cowardly dilemma that a strong people ever thrust upon the weak. And I for one have protested and do protest and shall protest that in my humble opinion the assumption is an outrageous falsehood dictated by selfishness, cowardice and greed and for the righteousness of my cause and the proof of my assertions, I appeal to one arbitrament and one alone and that is: *the truth*.

W. E. B. Du Bois

Of Mr. Booker T. Washington and Others (1903)

Easily the most striking thing in the history of the American Negro since 1876 is the ascendancy of Mr. Booker T. Washington. It began at the time when war memories and ideals were rapidly passing; a day of astonishing commercial development was dawning; a sense of doubt and hesitation overtook the freedmen's sons,—then it was that his leading began. Mr. Washington came, with a simple definite programme, at the psychological moment when the nation was a little ashamed of having bestowed so much sentiment on Negroes, and was concentrating its energies on Dollars. His programme of industrial education, conciliation of the South, and submission and silence as to civil and political rights, was not wholly original; the Free Negroes from 1830 up to war-time had striven to build industrial schools, and the American Missionary Association had from the first taught various trades; and Price and others had sought a way of honorable alliance with the best of the Southerners. But Mr. Washington first indissolubly linked these things; he put enthusiasm, unlimited energy, and perfect faith into this programme, and changed it from a by-path into a veritable Way of Life. And the tale of the methods by which he did this is a fascinating study of human life.

It startled the nation to hear a Negro advocating such a programme after many decades of bitter complaint; it startled and won the applause of the South, it interested and won the admiration of the North; and after a confused murmur of protest, it silenced if it did not convert the Negroes themselves.

To gain the sympathy and cooperation of the various elements comprising the white South was Mr. Washington's first task; and this, at the time Tuskegee was founded, seemed, for a black man, well-nigh impossible. And yet ten years later it was done in the word spoken at Atlanta: "In all things purely social we can be as separate as the five fingers, and yet one as the hand in all things essential to mutual progress." This "Atlanta Compromise" is by all odds the most notable thing in Mr. Washington's career. The South interpreted it in different ways: the radicals received it as a complete surrender of the demand for civil and political equality; the conservatives, as a generously conceived working basis for mutual understanding. So both approved it, and to-day its author is certainly the most distinguished Southerner since Jefferson Davis, and the one with the largest personal following.

Next to this achievement comes Mr. Washington's work in gaining place and consideration in the North. Others less shrewd and tactful had formerly essayed to sit on these two stools and had fallen between them; but as Mr. Washington knew the heart of the South from birth and training, so by singular insight he intuitively grasped the spirit of the age which was dominating the North. And so thoroughly did he learn the speech and thought of triumphant commercialism, and the ideals of material prosperity, that the pic-

SOURCE: *The Souls of Black Folk* (Chicago: A. C. McClurg & Co., 1903).

ture of a lone black boy poring over a French grammar amid the weeds and dirt of a neglected home soon seemed to him the acme of absurdities. One wonders what Socrates and St. Francis of Assisi would say to this.

And yet this very singleness of vision and thorough oneness with his age is a mark of the successful man. It is as though Nature must needs make men narrow in order to give them force. So Mr. Washington's cult has gained unquestioning followers, his work has wonderfully prospered, his friends are legion, and his enemies are confounded. To-day he stands as the one recognized spokesman of his ten million fellows, and one of the most notable figures in a nation of seventy millions. One hesitates, therefore, to criticise a life which, beginning with so little, has done so much. And yet the time is come when one may speak in all sincerity and utter courtesy of the mistakes and shortcomings of Mr. Washington's career, as well as of his triumphs, without being thought captious or envious, and without forgetting that it is easier to do ill than well in the world. . . .

Mr. Washington represents in Negro thought the old attitude of adjustment and submission; but adjustment at such a peculiar time as to make his programme unique. This is an age of unusual economic development, and Mr. Washington's programme naturally takes an economic cast, becoming a gospel of Work and Money to such an extent as apparently almost completely to overshadow the higher aims of life. Moreover, this is an age when the more advanced races are coming in closer contact with the less developed races, and the race-feeling is therefore intensified; and Mr. Washington's programme practically accepts the alleged inferiority of the Negro races. Again, in our own land, the reaction from the sentiment of war time has given impetus to race-prejudice against Negroes, and Mr. Washington withdraws many of the high demands of Negroes as men and American citizens. In other periods of intensified preju-

dice all the Negro's tendency to self-assertion has been called forth; at this period a policy of submission is advocated. In the history of nearly all other races and peoples the doctrine preached at such crises has been that manly self-respect is worth more than lands and houses, and that a people who voluntarily surrender such respect, or cease striving for it, are not worth civilizing.

In answer to this, it has been claimed that the Negro can survive only through submission. Mr. Washington distinctly asks that black people give up, at least for the present, three things,—

First, political power.

Second, insistence on civil rights,

Third, higher education of Negro youth,— and concentrate all their energies on industrial education, the accumulation of wealth, and the conciliation of the South. This policy has been courageously and insistently advocated for over fifteen years, and has been triumphant for perhaps ten years. As a result of this tender of the palm-branch, what has been the return? In these years there have occurred:

1. The disfranchisement of the Negro.
2. The legal creation of a distinct status of civil inferiority for the Negro.
3. The steady withdrawal of aid from institutions for the higher training of the Negro.

These movements are not, to be sure, direct results of Mr. Washington's teachings; but his propaganda has, without a shadow of doubt, helped their speedier accomplishment. The question then comes: Is it possible, and probable, that nine millions of men can make effective progress in economic lines if they are deprived of political rights, made a servile caste, and allowed only the most meagre chance for developing their exceptional men? If history and reason give any distinct answer to these questions, it is an emphatic *No.* And Mr. Washington thus faces the triple paradox of his career:

1. He is striving nobly to make Negro artisans business men and property-owners; but it is utterly impossible, under modern competitive methods, for workingmen and property-owners to defend their rights and exist without the right of suffrage.

2. He insists on thrift and self-respect, but at the same time counsels a silent submission to civic inferiority such as is bound to sap the manhood of any race in the long run.

3. He advocates common-school and industrial training, and depreciates institutions of higher learning; but neither the Negro common-schools, nor Tuskegee itself, could remain open a day were it not for teachers trained in Negro colleges, or trained by their graduates.

This triple paradox in Mr. Washington's position is the object of criticism by two classes of colored Americans. One class is spiritually descended from Toussaint the Savior, through Gabriel, Vesey, and Turner, and they represent the attitude of revolt and revenge; they hate the white South blindly and distrust the white race generally, and so far as they agree on definite action, think that the Negro's only hope lies in emigration beyond the borders of the United States. And yet, by the irony of fate, nothing has more effectually made this programme seem hopeless than the recent course of the United States toward weaker and darker peoples in the West Indies, Hawaii, and the Philippines,—for where in the world may we go and be safe from lying and brute force?

The other class of Negroes who cannot agree with Mr. Washington has hitherto said little aloud. They deprecate the sight of scattered counsels, of internal disagreement; and especially they dislike making their just criticism of a useful and earnest man an excuse for a general discharge of venom from small-minded opponents. Nevertheless, the questions involved are so fundamental and serious that it is difficult to see how men like the Grimkes, Kelly Miller, J. W. E. Bowen, and other representatives of this group, can much longer be silent. Such men feel in conscience bound to ask of this nation three things:

1. The right to vote.
2. Civic equality.
3. The education of youth according to ability.

They acknowledge Mr. Washington's invaluable service in counselling patience and courtesy in such demands; they do not ask that ignorant black men vote when ignorant whites are debarred, or that any reasonable restrictions in the suffrage should not be applied; they know that the low social level of the mass of the race is responsible for much discrimination against it, but they also know, and the nation knows, that relentless color-prejudice is more often a cause than a result of the Negro's degradation; they seek the abatement of this relic of barbarism, and not its systematic encouragement and pampering by all agencies of social power from the Associated Press to the Church of Christ. They advocate, with Mr. Washington, a broad system of Negro common schools supplemented by thorough industrial training; but they are surprised that a man of Mr. Washington's insight cannot see that no such educational system ever has rested or can rest on any other basis than that of the well-equipped college and university, and they insist that there is a demand for a few such institutions throughout the South to train the best of the Negro youth as teachers, professional men, and leaders.

This group of men honor Mr. Washington for his attitude of conciliation toward the white South; they accept the "Atlanta Compromise" in its broadest interpretation; they recognize, with him, many signs of promise, many men of high purpose and fair judgment, in this section; they know that no easy task has been laid upon a region already tottering under heavy burdens. But, nevertheless, they insist that the way to truth and right lies in straightforward honesty, not in indiscriminate flattery; in praising those of the South who do well and criticising uncompromisingly those who do ill; in taking advantage of the opportunities at hand and urging their fellows to do the same, but at the same time in remembering that only a firm adherence to their higher ideals and aspirations will ever keep those ideals within the realm of possibility. They do not expect that the free right to vote, to enjoy civic rights, and to be educated, will come in a moment; they do not expect to see the bias and prejudices of years disappear at the blast of a trumpet; but they are absolutely certain that the way for a people to gain their reasonable rights is not by voluntarily throwing them away and insisting that they do not want them; that the way for a people to gain respect is not by continually belittling and ridiculing themselves; that, on the contrary, Negroes must insist continually, in season and out of season, that voting is necessary to modern manhood, that color discrimination is barbarism, and that black boys need education as well as white boys.

In failing thus to state plainly and unequivocally the legitimate demands of their people, even at the cost of opposing an honored leader, the thinking classes of American Negroes would shirk a heavy responsibility,—a responsibility to themselves, a responsibility to the struggling masses, a responsibility to the darker races of men whose future depends so largely on this American experiment, but especially a responsibility to this nation,—this common Fatherland. It is wrong to encourage a man or a people in evil-doing; it is wrong to aid and abet a national crime simply because it is unpopular not to do so. The growing spirit of kindliness and reconciliation between the North and South after the frightful differences of a generation ago ought to be a source of deep congratulation to all, and especially to those whose mistreatment caused the war; but if that reconciliation is to be marked by the industrial slavery and civic death of those same black men, with permanent legislation into a position of inferiority, then those black men, if they are really men, are called upon by every consideration of patriotism and loyalty to oppose such a course by all civilized methods, even though such opposition involves disagreement with Mr. Booker T. Washington. We have no right to sit silently by while the inevitable seeds are sown for a harvest of disaster to our children, black and white. . . .

The black men of America have a duty to perform, a duty stern and delicate,—a forward movement to oppose a part of the work of their greatest leader. So far as Mr. Washington preaches Thrift, Patience, and Industrial Training for the masses, we must hold up his hands and strive with him, rejoicing in his honors and glorying in the strength of this Joshua called of God and of man to lead the headless host. But so far as Mr. Washington apologizes for injustice, North or South, does not rightly value the privilege and duty of voting, belittles the emasculating effects of caste distinctions, and opposes the higher training and ambition of our brighter minds,—so far as he, the South, or the Nation, does this,—we must unceasingly and firmly oppose them. By every civilized and peaceful method we must strive for the rights which the world accords to men, clinging unwaveringly to those great words which the sons of the Fathers would fain forget: "We hold these truths to be self-evident: That all men are created equal; that they are endowed by their Creator with certain unalienable rights; that among these are life, liberty, and the pursuit of happiness."

Eugene V. Debs, 1855–1926

Eugene Victor Debs was a militant union organizer, a founder of the Socialist Party of America, and a five-time candidate for the U.S. presidency. He is probably the best known Socialist leader in the history of the United States, a nation where the Socialist tradition has had difficulty taking root.

Debs was born in Terre Haute, Indiana, the son of Alsatian immigrant shopkeepers. He began to work on the railroad at the age of fourteen and after a time became active in the Brotherhood of Locomotive Firemen. At first, Debs was a very conservative unionist, and he opposed strikes as an organizing or bargaining tactic. Soon he became more militant, however, and resigned in order to help form the American Railway Union.

Debs believed that craft unions helped only skilled workers and thus allowed employers to pit one group of workers against another. He felt broader industrial unions, organizing the skilled and unskilled alike, were essential if progress was to be made. He committed himself to class solidarity and soon began to move in socialist directions.

After Debs was imprisoned for six months on a contempt of court charge following the violent Pullman strike of 1894, he turned to political action. In 1896 he supported William Jennings Bryan on the Populist ticket. In the wake of Bryan's defeat and failure to reconstruct the Democratic party along lines favorable to the old Populist coalition, Debs, along with Victor L. Berger, set about organizing the Social Democratic party. He also helped organize the Industrial Workers of the World (IWW) although he became less active because he was discouraged by the union's constant internal disputes.

Unlike many socialists reared in the European tradition, Debs' commitment to socialism was more the result of experience than theory or doctrine. Each confrontation with recalcitrant employers, strike-breaking police, or anti-labor courts pushed him to adopt a more consciously leftist position.

During World War I, Debs was an outspoken opponent of the war. He was charged with sedition, and after a highly publicized trial, he was sentenced to ten years in jail. In 1920, while still in jail, he received the largest vote ever by any Socialist candidate for the presidency. He was released by President Warren G. Harding in 1921 and returned to active organizing until his death in 1926.

Eugene V. Debs

Acceptance Speech as Socialist Party Candidate for President (1912)

It is with a full sense of the responsibility it imposes and the service it exacts that I accept the nomination for president tendered to me by the Socialist party of the United States. Personally I did not wish the nomination. It came to me unsought. It came as summons to service and not as a personal honor.

Every true member of the Socialist party is at the party's service. The confidence of his comrades is to him a sacred trust and their collective will the party's law.

My chief concern as a presidential candidate is that I shall serve well the party, and the class and the cause the party represents.

SOCIALIST PARTY DIFFERENT

The Socialist party is fundamentally different from all other parties. It came in the process of evolution and grows with the growth of the forces which created it. Its spirit is militant and its aim revolutionary. It expresses in political terms the aspiration of the working class to freedom and to a larger and fuller life than they have yet known.

The world's workers have always been and still are the world's slaves. They have borne all the burdens of the race and built all the monuments along the track of civilization;

they have produced all the world's wealth and supported all the world's governments. They have conquered all things but their own freedom. They are still the subject class in every nation on earth and the chief function of every government is to keep them at the mercy of their masters.

The workers in the mills and factories, in the mines and on the farms and railways never had a party of their own until the Socialist party was organized. They divided their votes between the parties of their masters. They did not realize that they were using their ballots to forge their own fetters.

But the awakening came. It was bound to come. Class rule became more and more oppressive and wage slavery more and more galling. The eyes of the workers began to open. They began to see the cause of the misery they had dumbly suffered so many years. It dawned upon them that society was divided into two classes—capitalists and workers, exploiters and producers; that the capitalists, while comparatively few, owned the nation and controlled the government; that the courts and the soldiers were at their command, and that the workers, while in a great majority, were in slavish subjection.

When they ventured to protest they were discharged and found themselves blacklisted; when they went out on strike they were suppressed by the soldiers and sent to jail.

They looked about them and saw a land

SOURCE: *International Socialist Review*, 1912. Reprinted in *Debs*, ed. Ronald Radosh (Englewood Cliffs, N.J.: Prentice-Hall, 1971).

of wonderful resources; they saw the productive machinery made by their own hands and the vast wealth produced by their own labor, in the shadow of which their wives and children were perishing in the skeleton clutch of famine.

BEGAN TO THINK

The very suffering they were forced to endure quickened their senses. They began to think. A new light dawned upon their dark skies. They rubbed the age-long sleep from their eyes. They had long felt the brutalizing effect of class rule; now they saw the cause of it. Slowly but steadily they became class conscious. They said, "We are brothers, we are comrades," and they saw themselves multiplied by millions. They caught the prophetic battle cry of Karl Marx, the world's greatest labor leader, the inspired evangel of working-class emancipation, "Workers of all countries, unite!"

And now, behold! The international Socialist movement spreads out over all the nations of the earth. The world's workers are aroused at last. They are no longer on their knees; their bowed bodies are now erect. Despair has given way to hope, weakness to strength, fear to courage. They no longer cringe and supplicate; they hold up their heads and command. They have ceased to fear their masters and have learned to trust themselves.

And this is how the Socialist party came to be born. It was quickened into life in the bitter struggle of the world's enslaved workers. It expresses their collective determination to break their fetters and emancipate themselves and the race.

Is it strange that the workers are loyal to such a party, that they proudly stand beneath its blazing banners and fearlessly proclaim its conquering principles? It is the one party of their class, born of their agony and baptized in the blood of their countless brethren who perished in the struggle to give it birth.

Hail to this great party of the toiling millions whose battle cry is heard around the world!

DOESN'T PLEAD FOR VOTES

We do not plead for votes; the workers give them freely the hour they understand.

But we need to destroy the prejudice that still exists and dispel the darkness that still prevails in the working-class world. We need the clear light of sound education and the conquering power of economic and political organization.

Before the unified hosts of labor all the despotic governments on earth are powerless and all resistance vain. Before their onward march all ruling classes disappear and all slavery vanishes forever.

The appeal of the Socialist party is to all the useful people of the nation, all who work with brain and muscle to produce the nation's wealth and who promote its progress and conserve its civilization.

Only they who bear its burdens may rightfully enjoy the blessings of civilized society.

There are no boundary lines to separate race from race, sex from sex, or creed from creed in the Socialist party. The common rights of all are equally recognized.

Every human being is entitled to sunlight and air, to what his labor produces, and to an equal chance with every other human being to unfold and ripen and give to the world the riches of his mind and soul.

Economic slavery is the world's greatest curse today. Poverty and misery, prostitution, insanity, and crime are its inevitable results.

The Socialist party is the one party which stands squarely and uncompromisingly for the abolition of industrial slavery; the one party pledged in every fiber of its being to the economic freedom of all the people.

So long as the nation's resources and productive and distributive machinery are the private property of a privileged class the masses will be at their mercy, poverty will be their lot and life will be shorn of all that raises it above the brute level.

NEW PROGRESSIVE PARTY

The infallible test of a political party is the private ownership of the sources of wealth and the means of life. Apply that test to the Republican, Democratic, and Progressive parties and upon that basic, fundamental issue you will find them essentially one and the same. They differ according to the conflicting interests of the privileged classes, but at bottom they are alike and stand for capitalist class rule and working-class slavery.

The new Progressive party is a party of progressive capitalism. It is lavishly financed and shrewdly advertised. But it stands for the rule of capitalism all the same.

When the owners of the trusts finance a party to put themselves out of business; when they turn over their wealth to the people from whom they stole it and go to work for a living, it will be time enough to consider the merits of the Roosevelt Progressive party.

One question is sufficient to determine the true status of all these parties. Do they want the workers to own the tools they work with, control their own jobs, and secure to themselves the wealth they produce? Certainly not. That is utterly ridiculous and impossible from their point of view.

The Republican, Democratic, and Progressive parties all stand for the private ownership by the capitalists of the productive machinery used by the workers, so that the capitalists can continue to filch the wealth produced by the workers.

The Socialist party is the only party which declares that the tools of labor belong to labor and that the wealth produced by the working class belongs to the working class.

Intelligent workingmen are no longer deceived. They know that the struggle in which the world is engaged today is a class struggle and that in this struggle the workers can never win by giving their votes to capitalist parties. They have tried this for many years and it has always produced the same result to them.

The class of privilege and pelf has had the world by the throat and the working class beneath its iron-shod hoofs long enough. The magic word of freedom is ringing through the nation and the spirit of intelligent revolt is finding expression in every land beneath the sun.

The solidarity of the working class is the salient force in the social transformation of which we behold the signs upon every hand. Nearer and nearer they are being drawn together in the bonds of unionism; clearer and clearer becomes their collective vision; greater and greater the power that throbs within them.

HOSTS OF FREEDOM

They are the twentieth-century hosts of freedom who are to destroy all despotisms, topple over all thrones, seize all sceptres of authority and hold them in their own strong hands, tear up all privilege by the roots, and consecrate the earth and all its fullness to the joy and service of all humanity.

It is vain to hope for material relief upon the prevailing system of capitalism. All the reforms that are proposed by the three capitalist parties, even if carried out in good faith, would still leave the working class in industrial slavery.

The working class will never be emancipated by the grace of the capitalists class, but only by overthrowing that class.

The power to emancipate itself is inherent in the working class, and this power must be developed through sound education and applied through sound organization.

It is as foolish and self-destructive for workingmen to turn to Republican, Democratic, and Progressive parties on election day as it would be for them to turn to the Manufacturers' Association and the Citizens' Alliance when they are striking against starvation wages.

The capitalist class is organized economically and politically to keep the working class in subjection and perpetuate its power as a ruling class. They do not support a working-class union nor a working-class party. They are not so foolish. They wisely look out for themselves.

The capitalist class despise a working-class party. Why should the working class give their support to a capitalist-class party?

Capitalist misrule under which workingmen suffer slavery and the most galling injustice exists only because it has workingmen's support. Withdraw that support and capitalism is dead.

The capitalists can enslave and rob the workers only by the consent of the workers when they cast their ballots on election day.

Every vote cast for a capitalist party, whatever its name, is a vote for wage-slavery, for poverty and degradation.

Every vote cast for the Socialist party, the workers' own party, is a vote for emancipation.

We appeal to the workers and to all who sympathize with them to make their power felt in this campaign. Never before has there been so great an opportunity to strike an effective blow for freedom.

CAPITALISM DOOMED

Capitalism is rushing blindly to its impending doom. All the signs portend the inevitable breakdown of the existing order. Deep-seated discontent has seized upon the masses. They must indeed be deaf who do not hear the mutterings of the approaching storm.

Poverty, high prices, unemployment, child slavery, widespread misery and haggard want in a land bursting with abundance; prostitution and insanity, suicide and crime, these in solemn numbers tell the tragic story of capitalism's saturnalia of blood and tears and shame as its end draws near.

It is to abolish this monstrous system and the misery and crime which flow from it in a direful and threatening stream that the Socialist party was organized and now makes its appeal to the intelligence and conscience of the people. Social reorganization is the imperative demand of this world-wide revolutionary movement.

The Socialist party's emission is not only to destroy capitalist despotism but to establish industrial and social democracy. To this end the workers are steadily organizing and fitting themselves for the day when they shall take control of the people's industries and when the right to work shall be as inviolate as the right to breathe the breath of life.

Standing as it does for the emancipation of the working class from wage-slavery, for the equal rights and opportunities of all men and all women, for the abolition of child labor and the conservation of all childhood, for social self-rule and the equal freedom of all, the Socialist party is the party of progress, the party of the future, and its triumph will signalize the birth of a new civilization and the dawn of a happier day for all humanity.

PART VI

The Republic as Social Democracy: Reining in the Market

With the rapid development of industrial capitalism, serious social strains began to create problems for American society and politics. A seemingly permanent industrial working class, non-English-speaking immigrants, and native-born Americans unable to survive on the land began to swell American cities. Economic insecurity was rampant, and many industrial workers suffered declines in their standards of living even as the nation's industrial wealth grew. Even many engaged in business and commerce began to question the benefits of laissez-faire economics in the face of unstable markets, declining profits, and cutthroat competition.

Massive strikes and demands for higher wages and better working conditions often pitted recalcitrant management against militant workers, not uncommonly with violent results. Public attention became especially aroused after the Haymarket riot in Chicago (1886), which left a number of striking workers and policemen dead and led to the hysterical conviction of eight anarchists on rather flimsy evidence. As labor groups and socialists began to gather strength and populist organizations made tremendous headway in the rural South and West, middle-class reformers looked for ways to make the new industrial system more compatible with their own vision of a rational and humane society.

The early reformers, or "Progressives," hoped to find a middle ground between laissez-faire capitalism and state socialism. They often split into two different wings of the reform movement that can be usefully characterized by Woodrow Wilson's "New Freedom" and Theodore Roosevelt's "New Nationalism." In general, the former hoped to restore competition by abolishing monopolies or trusts while the latter sought to regulate their behavior with the guiding intelligence of government.

In time, most reformers also accepted a public role in setting minimum labor, health, and safety standards that could not be sacrificed to the demands of competition. Many also supported social insurance programs such as unemployment and disability compensation. All of these goals sought to soften the hard edges of industrial life and to stabilize the precarious marketplace. Most reformers were also sympathetic to the moderate claims of trade unions and hoped that the recognition of collective bargaining rights would help institutionalize class conflict and thus reduce violent confrontations.

In order to make these claims in a coherent fashion, political activists required a new approach to political theory, one which could envision the state as something more than the guarantor of individual rights and the umpire for unlimited competition. This, however, required a departure from the dominant tradition of liberal individualism.

Many academic reformers, such as Richard T. Ely and Henry Carter Adams, studied in Germany and were influenced by philosophers such as Hegel and economists such as Schmoller who saw the state as a natural part of the larger social organism. As the organism changed, so must the state; thus its functions could not be universally limited, nor frozen in time. Others, such as Herbert Croly, who greatly influenced Theodore Roosevelt's "New Nationalism," resurrected the Hamiltonian tradition in American political thought. Croly wanted the state to play an active role, along with capital and labor, in guiding economic development and social welfare. Through government, he hoped to restore the "promise of American life" that had earlier been available in the marketplace and frontier.

John R. Commons, economist and historian, emphasized that property rights were creatures of an evolving legal structure. Property laws were created by an organic state, he argued, and were quite mutable. Thus the claims of property were by no means absolute, and new rights specifically to protect the working class were appropriate for an evolving industrial society.

That government had a legitimate role to play in the economy was finally established by Franklin Roosevelt and the New Deal. Undertaken as a desperate response to the Depression that followed the stock market crash of 1929, Roosevelt's New Deal drew the basic outlines of the modern welfare state. For the president and his "brain trusters" such as Adolph Berle and Sumner Slicter, individuals had substantive as well as procedural rights that government had an obligation to protect. Not only did individuals have the right to speak or vote, they had the right to work and to economic opportunity. When the market could not provide these, government had to respond. Thus Roosevelt helped articulate a new individualism and a new liberalism, which required a greatly enhanced role for the state.

The individual who best expressed this new liberalism in a coherent fashion was John Dewey, the foremost philosopher of American pragmatism. Martin Luther King, Jr., and many other civil rights leaders have given additional weight to the new liberalism's use of the state, urging the federal government to guarantee equal rights and equal opportunity for minorities who have been excluded or left behind.

Modern liberalism and its offspring, the welfare state, have dominated American politics since the 1930s. To be sure, both have received a great deal of criticism, from both the left and right. For many conservatives, the welfare state violates the rights of property, deprives people of their liberty, is inefficient, unfairly favors certain organized interests, and creates a dangerous dependency on the state. Critics from the left have argued that the welfare state is dependent on the success of capitalist firms and thus remains captive to the investment decisions of a narrow group of corporate executives and their shareholders.

New Left critics such as Herbert Marcuse have argued further that the material plenty of contemporary capitalism has deadened us to its repressive effects. Capitalist enterprises, sustained by the welfare state, have created a culture of consumption that is necessary to their success, but that enslaves us to a set of artificial needs. Other New Left thinkers, especially the early theorists for Students for a Democratic Society such as Tom Hayden, believed that the welfare state placed too much power in the central government and a military-industrial complex. In its place they urged a decentralized participatory democracy that combined the localism of many conservatives with the social welfare aims of many liberals.

Nevertheless, welfare-state capitalism remains the political economy of the United States, and some variant of the new liberalism its dominant political ideology. To be sure, in the late 1970s and early 1980s the most successful critics of New Deal liberalism have been conservatives (often traditional liberal individualists) or neoconservatives (often former liberals such as Irving Kristol and Michael Novak), who have called for a return to the marketplace and a greater reliance on traditional "mediating structures" such as the family and church. Yet even most conservatives have been willing to retain the basic outlines of the welfare state and have been unable to frame a distinctly new political philosophy.

As has been common in the rhetoric of American political life, liberals have emphasized greater equality and conservatives (liberal individualists) greater liberty. However, there is little consensus within either camp. American liberals and conservatives both share variants of neoliberal thought that accept the tension between the welfare state and the private marketplace. Events in recent years have strengthened, not reduced, these similarities.

The Old Orthodoxy:

The Republic of Voluntary Exchange Revisited

Herbert Hoover, 1874–1964

Herbert Hoover was the thirty-first president of the United States. His name is associated—often unfairly—with a rigid adherence to laissez-faire principles in the face of the economic disaster of the Depression. In fact, Hoover put his faith neither in individualistic laissez-faire economics nor in extensive government regulation. He believed that voluntary cooperation between capital and labor and among companies in the same field of industrial production would enable the economy to stabilize and return to a prosperity "just around the corner." Government's role was to facilitate voluntary efforts but not to coerce them. When this strategy failed, Hoover was soundly defeated in the election of 1932 by Franklin D. Roosevelt.

Hoover's belief in private-sector voluntarism was a result of his early training in both business and government. After graduating from Stanford in 1895, Hoover began to work for a variety of companies as a mining engineer. His work as an engineer and businessman took him to Australia, China, Burma, and Russia. During World War I he served as chairman of the commission for relief in Belgium and then the Food Administration Board in Washington, D.C. After the war he directed tremendously successful efforts to provide food relief for war-torn Europe. In all of these jobs, Hoover had succeeded in encouraging voluntary conservation of food in the United States and in securing contributions of money and food to help those abroad.

In 1921, Warren G. Harding appointed Hoover secretary of commerce, and he used that post to encourage the formation of voluntary trade associations to exchange information and discuss prices and costs within respective industries.

When Hoover was elected president in 1928, he continued to favor voluntarism. After the stock market crash of 1929, he hoped that private-sector groups could buoy the economy by keeping wages and prices high while curtailing any excessive production that might create a glut. Furthermore, he believed that private charities could provide a great deal of the necessary relief. Hoover encouraged state and local governments to offer relief programs, but he resisted giving federal funds to those same governments. However, in 1932 he proposed that the federal government create the Reconstruction Finance Corporation to make loans to banks, railroads, and insurance companies, believing that such seed money would soon pay dividends.

Despite his failure, Hoover remained an opponent of extensive federal government interference in economic life and in the affairs of states. His views on foreign policy mirrored his views on political economy; he argued that the United States ought to avoid involvement in problems abroad as much as possible.

The following address by Hoover in 1931 reiterates certain nineteenth-century themes that were still very much alive in the twentieth century.

Herbert Hoover

Statement to the Press in Defense of "Mutual Self-Help through Voluntary Giving" (1931)

Certain senators have issued a public statement to the effect that unless the President and the House of Representatives agree to appropriations from the Federal Treasury for charitable purposes they will force an extra session of Congress.

I do not wish to add acrimony to a discussion, but would rather state this case as I see its fundamentals.

This is not an issue as to whether people shall go hungry or cold in the United States. It is solely a question of the best method by which hunger and cold shall be prevented.

SOURCE: William Starr Myers, ed., *The State Papers and Other Public Writings of Herbert Hoover* (New York: Doubleday, Doran and Company, 1934).

It is a question as to whether the American people on one hand will maintain the spirit of charity and mutual self help through voluntary giving and the responsibility of local government as distinguished on the other hand from appropriations out of the Federal Treasury for such purposes. My own conviction is strongly that if we break down this sense of responsibility of individual generosity to individual and mutual self help in the country in times of national difficulty and if we start appropriations of this character we have not only impaired something infinitely valuable in the life of the American people but have struck at the roots of self-government. Once this has happened it is not the cost of a few score millions but we are faced with the abyss of reliance in future upon Government charity in some form or other. The money involved is indeed the least of the costs to American ideals and American institutions.

President Cleveland, in 1887, confronted with a similar issue stated in part:

A prevalent tendency to disregard the limited mission of this power and duty should, I think, be steadfastly resisted, to the end that the lesson should be constantly enforced that though the people support the Government, the Government should not support the people.

The friendliness and charity of our countrymen can always be relied upon to relieve their fellow-citizens in misfortune. This has been repeatedly and quite lately demonstrated. Federal aid in such cases encourages the expectation of paternal care on the part of the Government and weakens the sturdiness of our national character, while it prevents the indulgence among our people of that kindly sentiment and conduct which strengthens the bonds of a common brotherhood.

And there is a practical problem in all this. The help being daily extended by neighbors, by local and national agencies, by municipalities, by industry and a great multitude of organizations throughout the country today is many times any appropriation yet proposed. The opening of the doors of the Federal Treasury is likely to stifle this giving and thus destroy far more resources than the proposed charity from the Federal Government.

The basis of successful relief in national distress is to mobilize and organize the infinite number of agencies of self help in the community. That has been the American way of relieving distress among our own people and the country is successfully meeting its problem in the American way today.

We have two entirely separate and distinct situations in the country; the first is the drought area; the second is the unemployment in our large industrial centers—for both of which these appropriations attempt to make charitable contributions. . . .

Immediately upon the appearance of the drought last August, I convoked a meeting of the governors, the Red Cross and the railways, the bankers and other agencies in the country and laid the foundations of organization and the resources to stimulate every degree of self help to meet the situation which it was then obvious would develop. The result of this action was to attack the drought problem in a number of directions. The Red Cross established committees in every drought country, comprising the leading citizens of those countries, with instructions to them that they were to prevent starvation among their neighbors and, if the problem went beyond local resources, the Red Cross would support them.

The organization has stretched throughout the area of suffering, the people are being cared for today through the hands and with sympathetic understanding and upon the responsibility of their neighbors who are being supported in turn by the fine spirit of mutual assistance of the American people. The Red Cross officials whose long devoted service and experience are unchallenged, inform me this morning that except for the minor incidents of any emergency organization, no one is going hungry and no one need go hungry or cold.

To reinforce this work at the opening of Congress I recommended large appropriations for loans to rehabilitate agriculture from the drought and provision of further large sums for public works and construction in the drought territory which would give employment in further relief to the whole situation. These Federal activities provide for an expenditure of upward of $100 million in this area and it is in progress today.

The Red Cross has always met the situations which it has undertaken. After careful survey and after actual experience of several months with their part of the problem they have announced firmly that they can command the resources with which to meet any call for human relief in prevention of hunger and suffering in drought areas and that they accept this responsibility. They have refused to accept Federal appropriations as not being consonant either with the need or the character of their organization. The Government Departments have given and are giving them every assistance. We possibly need to strengthen the public health service in matters of sanitation and to strengthen the credit facilities of that area through the method approved by the Government departments to divert some existing appropriations to strengthen agricultural credit corporations.

In the matter of unemployment outside of the drought areas important economic measures of mutual self help have been developed such as those to maintain wages, to distribute employment equitably, to increase construction work by industry, to increase Federal construction work from a rate of about $275 million a year prior to the depression to a rate now of over $750 million a year; to expand state and municipal construction—all upon a scale never before provided or even attempted in any depression. But beyond this to assure that there shall be no suffering, in every town and county voluntary agencies in relief of distress have been strengthened and

created and generous funds have been placed at their disposal. They are carrying on their work efficiently and sympathetically.

But after and coincidently with voluntary relief, our American system requires that municipal, county and state governments shall use their own resources and credit before seeking such assistance from the Federal Treasury.

I have indeed spent much of my life in fighting hardship and starvation both abroad and in the southern states. I do not feel that I should be charged with lack of human sympathy for those who suffer but I recall that in all the organizations with which I have been connected over these many years, the foundation has been to summon the maximum of self help. I am proud to have sought the help of Congress in the past for nations who were so disorganized by war and anarchy that self help was impossible. But even these appropriations were but a tithe of that which was coincidently mobilized from the public charity of the United States and foreign countries. There is no such paralysis in the United States and I am confident that our people have the resources, the initiative, the courage, the stamina and kindliness of spirit to meet this situation in the way they have met their problems over generations.

The New Orthodoxy:
The New Liberalism

Henry Carter Adams, 1851–1921

Henry Carter Adams was one of the early, German-educated, American economists who began to lay the intellectual foundations for the neoliberal or welfare state.

A graduate of Iowa College (Grinnell) in 1874 and Johns Hopkins in 1878, where he was that university's first doctorate in social sciences, Adams also studied at Oxford, Heidelberg, Berlin, and Bonn. He taught briefly at Cornell; but after some difficulty over remarks supportive of striking rail workers, Adams left to become a professor of economics and finance at the University of Michigan. He remained there until his death.

Along with Richard T. Ely, Adams was one of the prime movers in forming the American Economic Association and in leading the repudiation of doctrinaire laissez-faire. Adams believed that government must regulate the competition between corporations to prevent the behavior of the least ethical firm from becoming the norm. Furthermore, he believed that natural monopolies needed to be strictly regulated if the public benefits were to be realized.

Adams was not at all a socialist. He believed property was necessary for liberty but also that property needed to be more broadly defined. He defended trade unions and collective bargaining as new property rights that were equally necessary to freedom in modern industrial economies. Some of Adams works include "The Relation of the State to Industrial Action" (1887), "Economics and Jurisprudence" (1897), and *American Railway Accounting* (1918).

The following excerpts are taken from "The Relation of the State to Industrial Action."

Henry Carter Adams

The State and Industrial Action (1887)

. . . The fundamental error of English political philosophy lies in regarding the state as a necessary evil: the fundamental error of German political philosophy lies in its conception of the state as an organism complete within itself. Neither the one nor the other of these views is correct. *Society* is the organic entity about which all our reasoning should center. Both state action and the industrial activity of individuals are functions of the complete social organism. The state is not made out of the chips and blocks left over after framing industrial society, nor does industrial society serve its full purpose in furnishing a means of existence for the poor unfortunates who are thrust out of the civil or the military service. Society, as a living and growing organism, is the ultimate thing disclosed by an analysis of human relations; and because this is true it is not right to speak of a presumption in favor of individual initiative or of state control, as though these stood like contestants opposed to each other. It is not proper to consider individual activity as supplementary to state powers, or to look upon the functions of the state as supplementary to personal activity. It is futile to expect sound principles for the guidance of intricate legislation so long as we over-estimate either public or private duties; the true principle must recognize society as a unity, subject only to the laws of its own development.

SOURCE: Joseph Dorfman, ed., *The Relation of the State to Industrial Action* (New York: Columbia University Press, 1954).

PRINCIPLES THAT SHOULD CONTROL INDUSTRIAL LEGISLATION

There are two classes of thinkers with whom I have not the fullest intellectual sympathy; the one comprises those who rest satisfied with criticism, the other those whose critical analysis leads only to exhortation. Though each is useful in its way, neither renders to society the highest service of which scholarship is capable. For the end of criticism is construction, and its service should be to point out the way in which men may avoid the recurrence of mistakes disclosed. Applying this thought to the subject in hand, it now becomes our difficult task to search for those principles to which industrial legislation should conform, for there can be no greater misfortune than this, that legislation should proceed blindly, controlled only by what practical men call expediency.

Much of the confusion that now surrounds the question of the appropriate duties of government, so far as the people in this country are concerned, is due to the failure to distinguish between *laissez-faire* as a dogma and free competition as a principle. The former is a rule or maxim intended for the guidance of public administration; the latter is a convenient expression for bringing to mind certain conditions of industrial society. Thus when one speaks of the benefits of free competition, one means the benefits conferred by industrial freedom. And when one argues for free competition, one is called upon to show that the best possible results may be expected for society, as a whole, and for each member of it, when labor is free and independent, when the right to acquire and enjoy property is guaranteed, when contracts are defended, and when every man is obliged to stand on his own legs, enjoying to the full the fruits of his own labor and suffering to the full the barren harvest of idleness. It seems that there should be no reasonable doubt respecting the benefits that must flow from such an organization of society, and I for one have no quarrel with those who urge its realization as a worthy object of endeavor. But I do take serious issue (and this is the important point to be observed), with those who hold that the rule of *laissez-faire* indicates the way by means of which such a state of affairs may be established and maintained. The claim that laborers should be free and independent is readily admitted, but at the same time it is denied that the language of public law, which makes all men equal before it, is a guarantee of freedom and independence; the right to acquire property is heartily endorsed, but it is also urged that property should not be acquired in such a manner, or to such a degree, as to defeat the purpose for which the right was granted; the necessity of maintaining contracts is conceded, but it must not be forgotten that the liberty of contract is a mere corollary of personal liberty. It cannot then be said that they who deny the sufficiency of the dogma of *laissez-faire* do so because they fail to appreciate the advantages of competitive action. It is true that some are open to this charge, but, on the other hand, many who believe the theory of individualism no longer applicable to modern relations, are quite willing to recognize competition as a beneficent social principle. They do, however, say that the benefits of this principle can never be realized through the uncontrolled play of private interests, carried on in harmony with existing property right.

It is unfortunate, though it is a natural consequence of the proneness in human nature to establish parties, that discussion upon this question has led to the formation of opposing schools of thought. Individualists and socialists maintain extremes of opinion respecting the nature and working of competition.[1] The former hold it to be necessarily a benevolent principle; the latter regard it as inherently a malevolent principle. Individualists, therefore, would grant it the freest play, and on this account advocate *laissez-faire;* socialists would exclude it from the society which they propose to establish, at least as a directing and controlling agency, and to this end propose a socialistic state. Upon one point only do these leaders of opposing opinions agree, and that is in the opinion that the denial of one view involves the acceptance of the other. There is no peace for an economic mugwump.

Nevertheless I venture to suggest that the question here involved is not one of excluded middle. Competition is neither malevolent nor beneficent, but will work malevolence or beneficence according to the conditions under which it is permitted to act. If this very reason-

---

[1] There is little need of testimony to this statement respecting individualism, but the claims of socialism may not be as familiar to my readers. I know of no better characterization of socialism as a scheme of economic thought than may be found in the six propositions upon which Louis Blanc [French socialist leader in the Revolution of 1848] based his system. I give them as summarized by Dr. Heinrich Contzen:

1. The deep and daily growing misery of the masses *(du peuple)* is the greatest misfortune.
2. The cause of the misery wherein the masses live is competition.
3. Competition is likewise for the property owners *(la bourgeoisie)* the cause of their ruin.
4. Government is the highest orderer of production and as such must be clothed with greater power.
5. The state as the greatest capitalist has this duty to perform, that through its competition private competition should be made to disappear. To this end national workshops must be established at the cost of the state.
6. Such wages must be paid as in every case to richly provide for the existence of the laborers. *(Geschichte der Socialen Frage von den ältesten Zeiten bis zur Gegenwart,* von Dr. Heinrich Contzen [Berlin, 1877], p. 128.)

able view of the case be admitted, it follows that we may escape the practical conclusions of both socialists and individualists; or at least, so far as we accept their proposals, we may rest our decisions upon some sound analysis of social relations. We may admit with Louis Blanc, that great evils follow the unbridled passion of accumulation, and recognize with Adam Smith, that personal interest in work done is the life of healthy industry; yet at the same time we may deny that the state should crush out all private control in business, and refuse assent to the doctrine that police duties exhaust the proper functions of government.

This presentation of the problem suggests the general principle according to which the relation of governmental agency to industrial affairs should be adjusted. It should be the purpose of all laws, touching matters of business, to maintain the beneficent results of competitive action while guarding society from the evil consequences of unrestrained competition. This may seem a truism, but its statement is necessary as the starting point for constructive study. It is at least sufficiently distinct from either the English or the German rule, as above stated, to warrant the belief that it may serve as the basis of a wholly different system of thought. For, according to this view of the case, neither governmental activity nor private enterprise exists by sufferance. There is no presumption for or against either the one or the other in itself considered, for both are essential to the development of a highly organized society, and the purpose of constructive thought should be to maintain them in harmonious relations.

But what are the beneficial workings of competition? Modern industrial society is built upon four legal facts: Private property in land, private property in labor, private property in capital, and the right of contract for all alike. The development of these rights, which required centuries for its accomplishment, portrays the growth of individualism and the de-

cay of communalism and no one who fully appreciates the opportunities thus offered, as compared with the opportunities offered by an industrial society based on slavery, or on undeveloped or general proprietary rights, can seriously advocate a return to the conditions of the past. The peculiar claims urged in favor of a society organized on the competitive basis are familiar to all. Perhaps the most important of these is that men are in this manner guaranteed full enjoyment in the fruits of their labor, and on this account will be jealous in its application. Competitive society also provides for ease of movement from one grade of labor to another, or from one business to another, and thus ensures elasticity in thought and expansion of purpose as the result of the manner in which motives are applied to individual conduct. Under such conditions, it is the future and not the past that claims the attention of men. It is hope and ambition, rather than fear and apprehension, that move the energies of men. We should not forget that the material progress of the nineteenth century is in large measure due to the mobility of action which the idea of equal rights before the law brought into modern life. It may, however, be remarked in passing that the energy displayed in modern society is due to the openness of opportunity in all forms of industry. Each competitor imagines himself the successful runner for the prize he seeks; but should the practical difficulties of attaining success ever come to be so great as to restrict the number of contestants, the healthful activity which now follows high anticipations would be replaced by the lethargy of hopelessness. It is a mistake to conclude that equal opportunities are surely maintained by granting equality before the law.

Again, wherever the conditions for competitive action are maintained, society has a guarantee that goods will be produced at the lowest possible cost; for the hope of personal gain leads to the best disposal of labor, to invention, and to the adoption of the best machinery. Assuming the same premise, society has also a guarantee that the goods produced will be placed upon the market at fair prices. It is unnecessary to enter upon any explanation of the manner in which this guarantee works, for popular economic philosophy devotes much of its attention to an elaboration of the reasoning here suggested; and our only quarrel with popular economic philosophy is that it arrests its analysis of industrial relations after discovering the advantages which might accrue to society, could the conditions for competitive action be maintained. It refuses to inquire what is necessary on the part of the state to ensure the maintenance of such conditions, or to proceed in its study to the consideration of the evils that flow from individualism in industrial life. But assuming the dogma of *laissez-faire* to be the most practical method of establishing competitive action, it shuts itself up to a sort of fatalism and witnesses with a stolid countenance the fruitless efforts to men to realize a rational existence.

But what are the evils of unrestrained competition; or, more accurately stated, what are the pernicious results of the attempted realization of competitive action under the direction of the doctrine of *laissez-faire*? I cannot hope to present a complete answer to this question, but must rest content with certain suggestions that may lead to a clear understanding of such rules for governmental action as will be proposed. The important evils of unrestrained competition are of three sorts.

First. The free play of individual interests tends to force the moral sentiment pervading any trade down to the level of that which characterizes the worst man who can maintain himself in it. So far as morals are concerned, it is the character of the worst men and not of the best men that gives color to business society.

Second. The application of the rule of non-interference renders it impossible for men to realize the benefits that arise, in certain lines of business, from organization in the form of a monopoly. The theory of *laissez-faire* sees clearly the beneficent principle in free competition, but fails wholly to recognize a beneficent principle in monopoly.

Third. The policy of restricting public powers within the narrowest possible limits tends to render government weak and inefficient, and a weak government placed in the midst of a society controlled by the commercial spirit will quickly become a corrupt government; this in its turn reacts upon commercial society by encouraging private corporations to adopt bold measures for gaining control of government machinery. Thus the doctrine of *laissez-faire* overreaches itself; for the application of the rule which it lays down will surely destroy that harmony between public and private duties essential to the best results in either domain of action.

Herbert D. Croly, 1869–1930

Croly was a journalist and political theorist, best known for his book *The Promise of American Life* and for his pioneering editorial work at the *New Republic*.

Despite his enduring fame, Croly's career was a rather sketchy one. After studying at the City College of New York and at Harvard, Croly left school without a degree and took a number of different jobs editing real estate and architectural reviews. He resigned as editor of the *Architectural Record* in 1906 to write *The Promise of American Life* (1909), which he later followed with another work *Progressive Democracy* (1914). The former work influenced Theodore Roosevelt's "New Nationalism" and to a lesser extent Woodrow Wilson's "New Freedom."

In *The Promise of American Life*, Croly argued that the conditions which had characterized the American democracy of the past—an open frontier and extensive individual opportunity—had been altered by the more structured institutions of industrial society. Big labor and big business required an equally powerful government to balance the two and provide for the common good through active regulation. In essence, Croly suggested a neo-Hamiltonian, nationalist solution to the problems of industrial life, in contrast to the extreme Jeffersonian individualism which had characterized the age.

Realizing the potential abuses of such a state, Croly's later work *Progressive Democracy* emphasized the importance of democratic reforms such as referendum, recall, and initiative to the continued health of the American system.

In 1924, Croly actively supported Robert LaFollette's Progressive party candidacy, but afterwards he retreated from political affairs and devoted his time to religious and philosophical questions.

The following selections are from Croly's most famous work *The Promise of American Life.*

Herbert Croly

The Promise of American Life (1909)

CHAPTER I

I

What Is the Promise of American Life?

The average American is nothing if not patriotic. "The Americans are filled," says Mr. Emil Reich in his "Success among the Nations," "with such an implicit and absolute confidence in their Union and in their future success that any remark other than laudatory is inacceptable to the majority of them. We

SOURCE: Arthur Schlesinger, Jr., ed., *The Promise of American Life* (Cambridge, Mass.: Belknap Press, 1965).

have had many opportunities of hearing public speakers in America cast doubts upon the very existence of God and of Providence, question the historic nature or veracity of the whole fabric of Christianity; but never has it been our fortune to catch the slightest whisper of doubt, the slightest want of faith, in the chief God of America—unlimited belief in the future of America." Mr. Reich's method of emphasis may not be very happy, but the substance of what he says is true. The faith of Americans in their own country is religious, if not in its intensity, at any rate in its almost absolute and universal authority. It pervades the air we breathe. As children we hear it asserted or implied in the conversation of our

404

elders. Every new stage of our educational training provides some additional testimony on its behalf. Newspapers and novelists, orators and playwrights, even if they are little else, are at least loyal preachers of the Truth. The skeptic is not controverted; he is overlooked. It constitutes the kind of faith which is the implication, rather than the object, of thought, and consciously or unconsciously it enters largely into our personal lives as a formative influence. We may distrust and dislike much that is done in the name of our country by our fellow-countrymen; but our country itself, its democratic system, and its prosperous future are above suspicion. . . .

The higher American patriotism . . . combines loyalty to historical tradition and precedent with the imaginative projection of an ideal national Promise. The Land of Democracy has always appealed to its more enthusiastic children chiefly as a land of wonderful and more than national possibilities. "Neither race nor tradition," says Professor Hugo Münsterberg in his volume on "The Americans," "nor the actual past, binds the American to his countrymen, but rather the future which together they are building." This vision of a better future is not, perhaps, as unclouded for the present generation of Americans as it was for certain former generations; but in spite of a more friendly acquaintance with all sorts of obstacles and pitfalls, our country is still figured in the imagination of its citizens as the Land of Promise. They still believe that somehow and sometime something better will happen to good Americans than has happened to men in any other country; and this belief, vague, innocent, and uninformed though it be, is the expression of an essential constituent in our national ideal. The past should mean less to a European than it does to an American, and the future should mean more. To be sure, American life cannot with impunity be wrenched violently from its moorings any more than the life of a European country can; but our American past,

compared to that of any European country, has a character all its own. Its peculiarity consists, not merely in its brevity, but in the fact that from the beginning it has been informed by an idea. From the beginning Americans have been anticipating and projecting a better future. From the beginning the Land of Democracy has been figured as the Land of Promise. Thus the American's loyalty to the national tradition rather affirms than denies the imaginative projection of a better future. An America which was not the Land of Promise, which was not informed by a prophetic outlook and a more or less constructive ideal, would not be the America bequeathed to us by our forefathers. In cherishing the Promise of a better national future the American is fulfilling rather than imperiling the substance of the national tradition. . . .

The great majority of Americans would expect a book written about "The Promise of American Life" to contain chiefly a fanciful description of the glorious American future—a sort of Utopia up-to-date, situated in the land of Good-Enough, and flying the Stars and Stripes. They might admit in words that the achievement of this glorious future implied certain responsibilities, but they would not regard the admission either as startling or novel. Such responsibilities were met by our predecessors; they will be met by our followers. Inasmuch as it is the honorable American past which prophesies on behalf of the better American future, our national responsibility consists fundamentally in remaining true to traditional ways of behavior, standards, and ideals. What we Americans have to do in order to fulfill our national Promise is to keep up the good work—to continue resolutely and cheerfully along the appointed path.

The reader who expects this book to contain a collection of patriotic prophecies will be disappointed. I am not a prophet in any sense of the word, and I entertain an active and intense dislike of the foregoing mixture of optimism, fatalism, and conservatism. To conceive the better American future as a consummation which will take care of itself,—as the necessary result of our customary conditions, institutions, and ideas,—persistence in such a conception is admirably designed to deprive American life of any promise at all. The better future which Americans propose to build is nothing if not an idea which must in certain essential respects emancipate them from their past. American history contains much matter for pride and congratulation, and much matter for regret and humiliation. On the whole, it is a past of which the loyal American has no reason to feel ashamed, chiefly because it has throughout been made better than it was by the vision of a better future; and the American of to-day and to-morrow must remain true to that traditional vision. He must be prepared to sacrifice to that traditional vision even the traditional American ways of realizing it. Such a sacrifice is, I believe, coming to be demanded; and unless it is made, American life will gradually cease to have any specific Promise. . . .

No doubt Americans have in some measure always conceived their national future as an ideal to be fulfilled. Their anticipations have been uplifting as well as confident and vainglorious. They have been prophesying not merely a safe and triumphant, but also a better, future. The ideal demand for some sort of individual and social amelioration has always accompanied even their vainest flights of patriotic prophecy. They may never have sufficiently realized that this better future, just in so far as it is better, will have to be planned and constructed rather than fulfilled of its own momentum; but at any rate, in seeking to disentangle and emphasize the ideal implications of the American national Promise, I am not wholly false to the accepted American tradition. Even if Americans have neglected these ideal implications, even if they have conceived the better future as containing chiefly a larger portion of familiar benefits, the ideal

demand, nevertheless, has always been palpably present; and if it can be established as the dominant aspect of the American tradition, that tradition may be transformed, but it will not be violated.

Furthermore, much as we may dislike the American disposition to take the fulfillment of our national Promise for granted, the fact that such a disposition exists in its present volume and vigor demands respectful consideration. It has its roots in the salient conditions of American life, and in the actual experience of the American people. The national Promise, as it is popularly understood, has in a way been fulfilling itself. If the underlying conditions were to remain much as they have been, the prevalent mixture of optimism, fatalism, and conservatism might retain a formidable measure of justification; and the changes which are taking place in the underlying conditions and in the scope of American national experience afford the most reasonable expectation that this state of mind will undergo a radical alteration. It is new conditions which are forcing Americans to choose between the conception of their national Promise as a process and an ideal. Before, however, the nature of these novel conditions and their significance can be considered, we must examine with more care the relation between the earlier American economic and social conditions and the ideas and institutions associated with them. Only by a better understanding of the popular tradition, only by an analysis of its merits and its difficulties, can we reach a more consistent and edifying conception of the Promise of American life.

II

How the Promise Has Been Realized

. . . No more explicit expression has ever been given to the way in which the Land of Promise was first conceived by its children than in the "Letters of an American Farmer." This book was written by a French immigrant,

Hector St. John de Crèvecoeur before the Revolution, and is informed by an intense consciousness of the difference between conditions in the Old and in the New World. "What, then, is an American, this new man?" asks the Pennsylvanian farmer. "He is either a European or the descendant of a European; hence the strange mixture of blood, which you will find in no other country. . . .

"He becomes an American by being received in the broad lap of our great *Alma Mater.* Here individuals of all nations are melted into a new race of men, whose labors and prosperity will one day cause great changes in the world. Here the rewards of his industry follow with equal steps the progress of his labor; this labor is founded on the basis of *self-interest;* can it want a stronger allurement? Wives and children, who before in vain demanded a morsel of bread, now fat and frolicsome, gladly help their father to clear those fields, whence exuberant crops are to arise to feed them all; without any part being claimed either by a despotic prince, a rich abbot, or a mighty lord. . . . The American is a new man, who acts upon new principles; he must therefore entertain new ideas and form new opinions. From involuntary idleness, servile dependence, penury, and useless labor, he has passed to toils of a very different nature rewarded by ample subsistence. This is an American."

Although the foregoing is one of the first, it is also one of the most explicit descriptions of the fundamental American; and it deserves to be analyzed with some care. According to this French convert the American is a man, or the descendant of a man, who has emigrated from Europe chiefly because he expects to be better able in the New World to enjoy the fruits of his own labor. The conception implies, consequently, an Old World, in which the ordinary man cannot become independent and prosperous, and, on the other hand, a New World in which economic opportunities are much more abundant and accessible.

America has been peopled by Europeans primarily because they expected in that country to make more money more easily. To the European immigrant—that is, to the aliens who have been converted into Americans by the advantages of American life—the Promise of America has consisted largely in the opportunity which it offered of economic independence and prosperity. Whatever else the better future, of which Europeans anticipate the enjoyment in America, may contain, these converts will consider themselves cheated unless they are in a measure relieved of the curse of poverty.

This conception of American life and its Promise is as much alive to-day as it was in 1780. Its expression has no doubt been modified during four generations of democratic political independence, but the modification has consisted of an expansion and a development rather than of a transposition. The native American, like the alien immigrant, conceives the better future which awaits himself and other men in America as fundamentally a future in which economic prosperity will be still more abundant and still more accessible than it has yet been either here or abroad. No alteration or attenuation of this demand has been permitted. With all their professions of Christianity their national idea remains thoroughly worldly. They do not want either for themselves or for their descendants an indefinite future of poverty and deprivation in this world, redeemed by beatitude in the next. The Promise, which bulks so large in their patriotic outlook, is a promise of comfort and prosperity for an ever increasing majority of good Americans. . . .

Let it be immediately added, however, that this economic independence and prosperity has always been absolutely associated in the American mind with free political institutions. The "American Farmer" traced the good fortune of the European immigrant in America, not merely to the abundance of economic opportunity, but to the fact that a ruling class of abbots and lords had no prior claim to a large share of the products of the soil. He did not attach the name of democracy to the improved political and social institutions of America, and when the political differences between Great Britain and her American colonies culminated in the Revolutionary War, the converted "American Farmer" was filled with anguish at this violent assertion of the "New Americanism." Nevertheless he was fully alive to the benefits which the immigrant enjoyed from a larger dose of political and social freedom; and so, of course, have been all the more intelligent of the European converts to Americanism. A certain number of them, particularly during the early years, came over less for the purpose of making money than for that of escaping from European political and religious persecution. America has always been conventionally conceived, not merely as a land of abundant and accessible economic opportunities, but also as a refuge for the oppressed; and the immigrant ships are crowded both during times of European famine during times of political revolution and persecution. . . .

Such are the claims advanced on behalf of the American system; and within certain limits this system has made good. Americans have been more than usually prosperous. They have been more than usually free. They have, on the whole, made their freedom and prosperity contribute to a higher level of individual and social excellence. Most assuredly the average Americanized American is neither a more intelligent, a wiser, nor a better man than the average European; but he is likely to be a more energetic and hopeful one. Out of a million well-established Americans, taken indiscriminately from all occupations and conditions, compared to a corresponding assortment of Europeans, a larger proportion of the former will be leading alert, active, and useful lives. Within a given social area there will be a smaller amount of social wreckage and a larger amount of wholesome and profit-

able achievement. The mass of the American people is, on the whole, more deeply stirred, more thoroughly awake, more assertive in their personal demands, and more confident of satisfying them. In a word, they are more alive, and they must be credited with the moral and social benefit attaching to a larger amount of vitality.

Furthermore, this greater individual vitality, although intimately connected with the superior agricultural and industrial opportunities of a new country, has not been due exclusively to such advantages. Undoubtedly the vast areas of cheap and fertile land which have been continuously available for settlement have contributed, not only to the abundance of American prosperity, but also to the formation of American character and institutions; and undoubtedly many of the economic and political evils which are now becoming offensively obtrusive are directly or indirectly derived from the gradual monopolization of certain important economic opportunities. Nevertheless, these opportunities could never have been converted so quickly into substantial benefits had it not been for our more democratic political and social forms. A privileged class does not secure itself in the enjoyment of its advantages merely by legal intrenchments. It depends quite as much upon disqualifying the "lower classes" from utilizing their opportunities by a species of social inhibition. The rail-splitter can be so easily encouraged to believe that rail-splitting is his vocation. . . .

III

How the Promise Is to Be Realized

In the preceding section I have been seeking to render justice to the actual achievements of the American nation. A work of manifest individual and social value has been wrought; and this work, not only explains the expectant popular outlook towards the future, but it partially determines the character as distinguished from the continued fulfillment of the American national Promise. The better future, whatever else it may bring, must bring at any rate a continuation of the good things of the past. The drama of its fulfillment must find an appropriate setting in the familiar American social and economic scenery. No matter how remote the end may be, no matter what unfamiliar sacrifices may eventually be required on its behalf, the substance of the existing achievement must constitute a veritable beginning, because on no other condition can the attribution of a peculiar Promise to American life find a specific warrant. On no other condition would our national Promise constitute more than an admirable but irrelevant moral and social aspiration.

The moral and social aspiration proper to American life is, of course, the aspiration vaguely described by the word democratic; and the actual achievement of the American nation points towards an adequate and fruitful definition of the democratic ideal. Americans are usually satisfied by a most inadequate verbal description of democracy, but their national achievement implies one which is much more comprehensive and formative. In order to be true to their past, the increasing comfort and economic independence of an ever increasing proportion of the population must be secured, and it must be secured by a combination of individual effort and proper political organization. Above all, however, this economic and political system must be made to secure results of moral and social value. It is the seeking of such results which converts democracy from a political system into a constructive social ideal; and the more the ideal significance of the American national Promise is asserted and emphasized, the greater will become the importance of securing these moral and social benefits.

The fault in the vision of our national future possessed by the ordinary American does not consist in the expectation of some continuity of achievement. It consists rather in the expectation that the familiar benefits will continue to accumulate automatically. In his mind the ideal Promise is identified with the processes and conditions which hitherto have very much simplified its fulfillment, and he fails sufficiently to realize that the conditions and processes are one thing and the ideal Promise quite another. Moreover, these underlying social and economic conditions are themselves changing, in such wise that hereafter the ideal Promise, instead of being automatically fulfilled, may well be automatically stifled. For two generations and more the American people were, from the economic point of view, most happily situated. They were able, in a sense, to slide down hill into the valley of fulfillment. Economic conditions were such that, given a fair start, they could scarcely avoid reaching a desirable goal. But such is no longer the case. Economic conditions have been profoundly modified, and American political and social problems have been modified with them. The Promise of American life must depend less than it did upon the virgin wilderness and the Atlantic Ocean, for the virgin wilderness has disappeared, and the Atlantic Ocean has become merely a big channel. The same results can no longer be achieved by the same easy methods. Ugly obstacles have jumped into view, and ugly obstacles are peculiarly dangerous to a person who is sliding down hill. The man who is clambering up hill is in a much better position to evade or overcome them. Americans will possess a safer as well as a worthier vision of their national Promise as soon as they give it a house on a hill-top rather than in a valley. . . .

The transformation of the old sense of a glorious national destiny into the sense of a serious national purpose will inevitably tend to make the popular realization of the Promise of American life both more explicit and more serious. As long as Americans believed they were able to fulfill a noble national Promise merely by virtue of maintaining intact a set of political institutions and by the vigorous individual pursuit of private ends, their allegiance to their national fulfillment remained more a matter of words than of deeds; but now that they are being aroused from their patriotic slumber, the effect is inevitably to disentangle the national idea and to give it more dignity. The redemption of the national Promise has become a cause for which the good American must fight, and the cause for which a man fights is a cause which he more than ever values. The American idea is no longer to be propagated merely by multiplying the children of the West and by granting ignorant aliens permission to vote. Like all sacred causes, it must be propagated by the Word and by that right arm of the Word, which is the Sword.

The more enlightened reformers are conscious of the additional dignity and value which the popularity of reform has bestowed upon the American idea, but they still fail to realize the deeper implications of their own programme. In abandoning the older conception of an automatic fulfillment of our national destiny, they have abandoned more of the traditional American point of view than they are aware. The traditional American optimistic fatalism was not of accidental origin, and it cannot be abandoned without involving in its fall some other important ingredients in the accepted American tradition. Not only was it dependent on economic conditions which prevailed until comparatively recent times, but it has been associated with certain erroneous but highly cherished political theories. It has been wrought into the fabric of our popular economic and political ideas to such an extent that its overthrow necessitates a partial revision of some of the most important articles in the traditional American creed.

The extent and the character of this revision may be inferred from a brief consideration of the effect upon the substance of our national Promise of an alteration in its proposed method of fulfillment. The substance of our national Promise has consisted, as we have seen, of an improving popular economic condition, guaranteed by democratic political institutions, and resulting in moral and social amelioration. These manifold benefits were to be obtained merely by liberating the enlightened self-interest of the American people. The beneficent result followed inevitably from the action of wholly selfish motives—provided, of course, the democratic political system of equal rights was maintained in its integrity. The fulfillment of the American Promise was considered inevitable because it was based upon a combination of self-interest and the natural goodness of human nature. On the other hand, if the fulfillment of our national Promise can no longer be considered inevitable, if it must be considered as equivalent to a conscious national purpose instead of an inexorable national destiny, the implication necessarily is that the trust reposed in individual self-interest has been in some measure betrayed. No preestablished harmony can then exist between the free and abundant satisfaction of private needs and the accomplishment of a morally and socially desirable result. The Promise of American life is to be fulfilled—not merely by a maximum amount of economic freedom, but by a certain measure of discipline; not merely by the abundant satisfaction of individual desires, but by a large measure of individual subordination and self-denial. And this necessity of subordinating the satisfaction of individual desires to the fulfillment of a national purpose is attached particularly to the absorbing occupation of the American people,—the occupation, viz.: of accumulating wealth. The automatic fulfillment of the American national Promise is to be abandoned, if at all, precisely because the traditional American confidence in individual freedom has resulted in a morally and socially undesirable distribution of wealth.

In making the concluding statement of the last paragraph I am venturing, of course, upon very debatable ground. Neither can I attempt in this immediate connection to offer any justification for the statement which might or should be sufficient to satisfy a stubborn skeptic. I must be content for the present with the bare assertion that the prevailing abuses and sins, which have made reform necessary, are all of them associated with the prodigious concentration of wealth, and of the power exercised by wealth, in the hands of a few men. I am far from believing that this concentration of economic power is wholly an undesirable thing, and I am also far from believing that the men in whose hands this power is concentrated deserve, on the whole, any exceptional moral reprobation for the manner in which it has been used. In certain respects they have served their country well, and in almost every respect their moral or immoral standards are those of the great majority of their fellow-countrymen. But it is none the less true that the political corruption, the unwise economic organization, and the legal support afforded to certain economic privileges are all under existing conditions due to the malevolent social influence of individual and incorporated American wealth; and it is equally true that these abuses, and the excessive "money power" with which they are associated, have originated in the peculiar freedom which the American tradition and organization have granted to the individual. Up to a certain point that freedom has been and still is beneficial. Beyond that point it is not merely harmful; it is by way of being fatal. Efficient regulation there must be; and it must be regulation which will strike, not at the symptoms of the evil, but at its roots. The existing concentration of wealth and financial power in the hands of a few irresponsible men is the inevitable outcome of the chaotic individualism of our political and economic organization, while at the same time it is inimical to democracy, because it tends to erect political abuses and social inequalities into a system. The inference which follows may be disagreeable, but it is not to be escaped. In becoming responsible for the subordination of the individual to the demand of a dominant and constructive national purpose, the American state will in effect be making itself responsible for a morally and socially desirable distribution of wealth.

John Dewey, 1859–1952

John Dewey is probably America's most influential and widely read philosopher. Like many influential neoliberals, Dewey received his Ph.D. at Johns Hopkins University. He was a pragmatist, broadly speaking, who followed in the footsteps of William James in demanding that philosophy be rooted in experience and be measured by its accomplishments in the world.

Dewey is often remembered primarily as a philosopher of education. He wrote widely on the problems of education and was vitally concerned about the role of the school in a democratic society. While head of the department of philosophy, psychology, and pedagogy at the University of Chicago, Dewey created the Laboratory School which became the center of the progressive school movement in the United States. Dewey believed that children needed to learn by doing and that traditional barriers between vocational and liberal arts educations were obsolete. In fact, Dewey believed that all of life was learning through doing, and that philosophy was reflection upon that experience. All philosophy was involved with education and the compartmentalizing of various areas of philosophy, or for that matter psychology and politics, was artificial.

Dewey was always vitally concerned with politics. He considered himself to be a liberal, but felt it important to constantly adapt older liberal values to new and changing circumstances. He was active in founding the Liberal party in 1946 and supported the American Civil Liberties Union and the NAACP. Dewey was criticized by many as a dangerous leftist for his early willingness to maintain an open mind about the Soviet Union, and was later branded a reactionary by many on the left for his criticism of the Soviet state. In 1937 Dewey headed an international commission which investigated Joseph Stalin's charges against Leon Trotsky, and he found them groundless.

Dewey's writings are too numerous to be listed here. Nonetheless some of his more notable works include *The School and Society* (1899), *Democracy and Education* (1916), *Art as Experience* (1934), *Freedom and Culture* (1939), *The Public and Its Problem* (1927), and *Liberalism and Social Action* (1935).

The following selection is taken from *Liberalism and Social Action* and shows Dewey's insistence on adapting values to the needs of current experience.

John Dewey

Liberalism and Social Action (1935)

The net effect of the struggle of early liberals to emancipate individuals from restrictions imposed upon them by the inherited type of social organization was to pose a problem, that of a new social organization. The ideas of liberals set forth in the first third of the nineteenth century were potent in criticism and in analysis. They released forces that had been held in check. But analysis is not construction, and release of force does not of itself give direction to the force that is set free. Victorian optimism concealed for a time

SOURCE: John Dewey, "The Crisis in Liberalism," in *Liberalism and Social Action* (New York: G. P. Putnam's Sons, 1935). Reprinted by permission of G. P. Putnam's Sons. Copyright © 1935; renewed copyright 1962 by John Dewey.

the crisis at which liberalism had arrived. But when that optimism vanished amid the conflict of nations, classes and races characteristic of the latter part of the nineteenth century— a conflict that has grown more intense with the passing years—the crisis could no longer be covered up. The beliefs and methods of earlier liberalism were ineffective when faced with the problems of social organization and integration. Their inadequacy is a large part of belief now so current that all liberalism is an outmoded doctrine. At the same time, insecurity and uncertainty in belief and purpose are powerful factors in generating dogmatic faiths that are profoundly hostile to everything to which liberalism in any possible formulation is devoted. . . .

The demand for a form of social organization that should include economic activities but yet should convert them into servants of the development of the higher capacities of individuals, is one that earlier liberalism did not meet. If we strip its creed from adventitious elements, there are, however, enduring values for which earlier liberalism stood. These values are liberty; the development of the inherent capacities of individuals made possible through liberty, and the central rôle of free intelligence in inquiry, discussion and expression. But elements that were adventitious to these values colored every one of these ideals in ways that rendered them either impotent or perverse when the new problem of social organization arose.

Before considering the three values, it is advisable to note one adventitious idea that played a large rôle in the later incapacitation of liberalism. The earlier liberals lacked historic sense and interest. For a while this lack had an immediate pragmatic value. It gave liberals a powerful weapon in their fight with reactionaries. For it enabled them to undercut the appeal to origin, precedent and past history by which the opponents of social change gave sacrosanct quality to existing inequities and abuses. But disregard of history took its revenge. It blinded the eyes of liberals to the fact that their own special interpretations of liberty, individuality and intelligence were themselves historically conditioned, and were relevant only to their own time. They put forward their ideas as immutable truths good at all times and places; they had no idea of historic relativity, either in general or in its application to themselves.

When their ideas and plans were projected they were an attack upon the interests that were vested in established institutions and that had the sanction of custom. The new forces for which liberals sought an entrance were incipient; the *status quo* was arrayed against their release. By the middle of the nineteenth century the contemporary scene had radically altered. The economic and political changes for which they strove were so largely accomplished that they had become in turn the vested interest, and their doctrines, especially in the form of *laissez faire* liberalism, now provided the intellectual justification for the *status quo*. This creed is still powerful in this country. The earlier doctrine of "natural rights," superior to legislative action, has been given a definitely economic meaning by the courts, and used by judges to destroy social legislation passed in the interest of a real, instead of purely formal, liberty of contract. Under the caption of "rugged individualism" it inveighs against all new social policies. Beneficiaries of the established economic régime band themselves together in what they call Liberty Leagues to perpetuate the harsh regimentation of millions of their fellows. I do not imply that resistance to change would not have appeared if it had not been for the doctrines of earlier liberals. But had the early liberals appreciated the historic relativity of their own interpretation of the meaning of liberty, the later resistance would certainly have been deprived of its chief intellectual and moral support. The tragedy is that although these liberals were the sworn foes of political absolutism, they were themselves absolutists in the social creed they formulated. . . .

If the early liberals had put forth their special interpretation of liberty as something subject to historic relativity they would not have frozen it into a doctrine to be applied at all times under all social circumstances. Specifically, they would have recognized that effective liberty is a function of the social conditions existing at any time. If they had done this, they would have known that as economic relations became dominantly controlling forces in setting the pattern of human relations, the necessity of liberty for individuals which they proclaimed will require social control of economic forces in the interest of the great mass of individuals. Because the liberals failed to make a distinction between purely formal or legal liberty and effective liberty of thought and action, the history of the last one hundred years is the history of nonfulfillment of their predictions. It was prophesied that a régime of economic liberty would bring about interdependence among nations and consequently peace. The actual scene has been marked by wars of increasing scope and destructiveness. Even Karl Marx shared the idea that the new economic forces would destroy economic nationalism and usher in an era of internationalism. The display of exacerbated nationalism now characterizing the world is a sufficient comment. Struggle for raw materials and markets in backward countries, combined with foreign financial control of their domestic industrial development, has been accompanied by all kinds of devices to prevent access of other advanced nations to the national marketplace.

The basic doctrine of early economic liberals was that the régime of economic liberty as they conceived it, would almost automatically direct production through competition into channels that would provide, as effectively as possible, socially needed commodities and services. Desire for personal gain early learned that it could better further the satisfaction of that desire by stifling competition and substituting great combinations of noncompeting capital. The liberals supposed the motive of individual self-interest would so release productive energies as to produce ever-increasing abundance. They overlooked the fact that in many cases personal profit can be better served by maintaining artificial scarcity and by what Veblen called systematic sabotage of production. Above all, in identifying the extension of liberty in all of its modes with extension of their particular brand of economic liberty, they completely failed to anticipate the bearing of private control of the means of production and distribution upon the effective liberty of the masses in industry as well as in cultural goods. An era of power possessed by the few took the place of the era of liberty for all envisaged by the liberals of the early nineteenth century.

These statements do not imply that these liberals should or could have foreseen the changes that would occur, due to the impact of new forces of production. The point is that their failure to grasp the historic position of the interpretation of liberty they put forth served later to solidify a social régime that was a chief obstacle to attainment of the ends they professed. One aspect of this failure is worth especial mention. No one has ever seen more clearly than the Benthamites that the political self-interest of rulers, if not socially checked and controlled, leads to actions that destroy liberty for the mass of people. Their perception of this fact was a chief ground for their advocacy of representative government, for they saw in this measure a means by which the self-interest of the rulers would be forced into conformity with the interests of their subjects. But they had no glimpse of the fact that private control of the new forces of production, forces which affect the life of every one, would operate in the same way as private unchecked control of political power. They saw the need of new legal institutions, and of different political conditions as a means to political liberty. But they failed to perceive that social control of economic forces is equally necessary if anything approaching economic equality and liberty is to be realized. . . .

When it became evident that disparity, not equality, was the actual consequence of *laissez faire* liberalism, defenders of the latter developed a double system of justifying apologetics. Upon one front, they fell back upon the natural inequalities of individuals in psychological and moral make-up, asserting that inequality of fortune and economic status is the "natural" and justifiable consequence of the free play of these inherent differences. Herbert Spencer even erected this idea into a principle of cosmic justice, based upon the idea of the proportionate relation existing between cause and effect. I fancy that today there are but few who are hardy enough, even admitting the principal of natural inequalities, to assert that the disparities of property and income bear any commensurate ratio to inequalities in the native constitution of individuals. If we suppose that there is in fact such a ratio, the consequences are so intolerable that the practical inference to be drawn is that organized social effort should intervene to prevent the alleged natural law from taking full effect.

The other line of defense is unceasing glorification of the virtues of initiative, independence, choice and responsibility, virtues that center in and proceed from individuals as such. I am one who believes that we need more, not fewer, "rugged individuals" and it is in the name of rugged individualism that I challenge the argument. Instead of independence, there exists parasitical dependence on a wide scale—witness the present need for the exercise of charity, private and public, on a vast scale. The current argument against the public dole on the ground that it pauperizes and demoralizes those who receive it has an ironical sound when it comes from those who would leave intact the conditions that cause the necessity for recourse to the method of support of millions at public expense. Servility and regimentation are the result of control by the few of access to means of productive labor on the part of the many. An even more serious objection to the argument is that it conceives of initiative, vigor, independence exclusively in terms of their least significant manifestation. They are limited to exercise in the economic area. The meaning of their exercise in connection with the cultural resources of civilization, in such matters as companionship, science and art, is all but ignored. It is at this last point in particular that the crisis of liberalism and the need for a reconsideration of it in terms of the genuine liberation of individuals are most evident. The enormous exaggeration of material and materialistic economics that now prevails at the expense of cultural values, is not itself the result of earlier liberalism. But, as was illustrated in the personal crisis through which Mill passed, it is an exaggeration which is favored, both intellectually and morally, by fixation of the early creed.

This fact induces a natural transition from the concept of liberty to that of the individual. The underlying philosophy and psychology of earlier liberalism led to a conception of individuality as something ready-made, already possessed, and needing only the removal of certain legal restrictions to come into full play. It was not conceived as a moving thing, something that is attained only by continuous growth. Because of this failure, the dependence in fact of individuals upon social conditions was made little of. . . .

. . . Individuals, it is implied, have a full-blown psychological and moral nature, having its own set laws, independently of their association with one another. It is the psychological laws of this isolated human nature from which social laws are derived and into which they may be resolved. . . . That the human infant is modified in mind and character by his connection with others in family life and that the modification continues throughout life as his connections with others broaden, is as true as that hydrogen is modified when it combines with oxygen. If we generalize the meaning of this fact, it is evident that while there are native organic or biological structures that remain fairly constant, the actual "laws" of human nature are laws of individuals in association, not of beings in a mythical condition apart from association. In other words, liberalism that takes its profession of the importance of individuality with sincerity must be deeply concerned about the structure of human association. For the latter operates to affect negatively and positively, the development of individuals. Because a wholly unjustified idea of opposition between individuals and society has become current, and because its currency has been furthered by the underlying philosophy of individualistic liberalism, there are many who in fact are working for social changes such that rugged individuals may exist in reality, that have become contemptuous of the very idea of individuality, while others support in the name of individualism institutions that militate powerfully against the emergence and growth of beings possessed of genuine individuality. . . .

The practical consequence was also the logical one. When conditions had changed and the problem was one of constructing social organization from individual units that had been released from old social ties, liberalism fell upon evil times. The conception of intelligence as something that arose from the association of isolated elements, sensations and feelings, left no room for far-reaching experiments in construction of a new social order. It was definitely hostile to everything like collective social planning. The doctrine of *laissez faire* was applied to intelligence as well as to economic action, although the conception of experimental method in science demands a control by comprehensive ideas, projected in possibilities to be realized by action. Scientific method is as much opposed to go-as-you-please in intellectual matters as it is to reliance upon habits of mind whose sanction is that they were formed by "experience" in the past. The theory of mind held by the early liberals advanced beyond dependence upon the past but it did not arrive at the idea of experimental and constructive intelligence.

The dissolving atomistic individualism of the liberal school evoked by way of reaction the theory of organic objective mind. But the effect of the latter theory embodied in idealistic metaphysics was also hostile to intentional social planning. The historical march of mind, embodied in institutions, was believed to account for social changes—all in its own good time. A similar conception was fortified by the interest in history and in evolution so characteristic of the later nineteenth century. The materialistic philosophy of Spencer joined hands with the idealistic doctrine of Hegel in throwing the burden of social direction upon powers that are beyond deliberate social foresight and planning. The economic dialectic of history, substituted by Marx for the Hegelian dialectic of ideas, as interpreted by the social-democratic party in Europe, was taken to signify an equally inevitable movement toward a predestined goal. Moreover, the idealistic theory of objective spirit provided an intellectual justification for the nationalisms that were rising. Concrete manifestation of absolute mind was said to be provided through national states. Today, this philosophy is readily turned to the support of the totalitarian state.

The crisis in liberalism is connected with failure to develop and lay hold of an adequate conception of intelligence integrated with social movements and a factor in giving them direction. We cannot mete out harsh blame to the early liberals for failure to attain such a conception. The first scientific society for the study of anthropology was founded the year in which Darwin's *Origin of Species* saw the light of day. I cite this particular fact to typify the larger fact that the sciences of society, the controlled study of man in his relationships, are the product of the later nineteenth century. Moreover, these disciplines not only came into being too late to influence the formulation of liberal social theory, but they themselves were so much under the influence of the more advanced physical sciences that it was supposed that their findings were of merely theoretic import. By this statement, I mean that although the conclusions of the social disciplines were about man, they were treated as if they were of the same nature as the conclusions of physical science about remote galaxies of stars. Social and historical inquiry is in fact a part of the social process itself, not something outside of it. The consequence of not perceiving this fact was that the conclusions of the social sciences were not made (and still are not made in any large measure) integral members of a program of social action. When the conclusions of inquiries that deal with man are left outside the program of social action, social policies are necessarily left without the guidance that knowledge of man can provide, and that it must provide if social action is not to be directed either by mere precedent and custom or else by the happy intuitions of individual minds. The social conception of the nature and work of intelligence is still immature; in consequence, its use as a director of social action is inchoate and sporadic. It is the tragedy of earlier liberalism that just at the time when the problem of social organization was most urgent, liberals could bring to its solution nothing but the conception that intelligence is an individual possession. . . .

The inchoate state of social knowledge is reflected in the two fields where intelligence might be supposed to be most alert and most continuously active, education and the formation of social policies in legislation. Science is taught in our schools. But very largely it appears in schools simply as another study, to be acquired by much the same methods as are employed in "learning" the older studies that are part of the curriculum. If it were treated as what it is, the method of intelligence itself in action, then the method of science would be incarnate in every branch of study and every detail of learning. Thought would be connected with the possibility of action, and every mode of action would be reviewed to see its bearing upon the habits and ideas from which it sprang. Until science is treated educationally in this way, the introduction of what is called science into the schools signifies one more opportunity for the mechanization of the material and methods of study. When "learning" is treated not as an expansion of the understanding and judgment of meanings but as an acquisition of information, the method of coöperative experimental intelligence finds its way into the working structure of the individual only incidentally and by devious paths.

Of the place and use of socially organized intelligence in the conduct of public affairs, through legislation and administration, I shall have something to say in the next chapter. At this point of the discussion I am content to ask the reader to compare the force it now exerts in politics with that of the interest of individuals and parties in capturing and retaining office and power, with that exercised by the propaganda of publicity agents and that of organized pressure groups.

Humanly speaking, the crisis in liberalism was a product of particular historical events. Soon after liberal tenets were formulated as eternal truths, it became an instrument of vested interests in opposition to further social change, a ritual of lip-service, or else was shattered by new forces that came in. Nevertheless, the ideas of liberty, of individuality and of freed intelligence have an enduring value, a value never more needed than now. It is the business of liberalism to state these values in ways, intellectual and practical, that are relevant to present needs and forces. If we employ the conception of historic relativity, nothing is clearer than that the conception of liberty is always relative to forces that at a given time and place are increasingly felt to be oppressive. Liberty in the concrete signifies release from the impact of *particular* oppressive forces; emancipation from something once taken as a normal part of human life but now experienced as bondage. At one time, liberty signified liberation from chattel slavery; at another time, release of a class from serfdom. During the late seventeenth and early eighteenth centuries it meant liberation from despotic dynastic rule. A century later it meant release of industrialists from inherited legal customs that hampered the rise of new forces of production. Today, it signifies liberation from material insecurity and from the coercions and repressions that prevent multitudes from participation in the vast cultural resources that are at hand. The direct impact of liberty always has to do with some class or group that is suffering in a special way from some form of constraint exercised by the distribution of powers that exists in contemporary society. Should a classless society ever come into being the formal *concept* of liberty would lose its significance, because the *fact* for which it stands would have become an integral part of the established relations of human beings to one another.

Until such a time arrives liberalism will continue to have a necessary social office to perform. Its task is the mediation of social transitions. This phrase may seem to some to be a virtual admission that liberalism is a colorless "middle of the road" doctrine. Not so, even though liberalism has sometimes taken that form in practice. We are always dependent upon the experience that has accumulated in the past and yet there are always new forces coming in, new needs arising, that demand, if the new forces are to operate and the new needs to be satisfied, a reconstruction of the patterns of old experience. The old and the new have forever to be integrated with each other, so that the values of old experience may become the servants and instruments of new desires and aims. We are always possessed by habits and customs, and this fact signifies that we are always influenced by the inertia and the momentum of forces temporally outgrown but nevertheless still present with us as a part of our being. Human life gets set in patterns, institutional and moral. But change is also with us and demands the constant remaking of old habits and old ways of thinking, desiring and acting. The effective ratio between the old and the stabilizing and the new and disturbing is very different at different times. Sometimes whole communities seem to be dominated by custom, and changes are produced only by irruptions and invasions from outside. Sometimes, as at present, change is so varied and accelerated that customs seem to be dissolving before our very eyes. But be the ratio little or great, there is always an adjustment to be made, and as soon as the need for it becomes conscious, liberalism has a function and a meaning. It is not that liberalism creates the need, but that the necessity for adjustment defines the office of liberalism.

For the only adjustment that does not have to be made over again, and perhaps even under more unfavorable circumstances than when it was first attempted, is that effected through intelligence as a method. In its large sense, this remaking of the old through union with the new is precisely what intelligence is. It is conversion of past experience into knowledge and projection of that knowledge in ideas and purposes that anticipate what may come to be in the future and that indicate how to realize what is desired. Every problem that arises, personal or collective, simple or complex, is solved only by selecting material from the store of knowledge amassed in past experience and by bringing into play habits already formed. . . . What I have called the mediating function of liberalism is all one with the work of intelligence. This fact is the root, whether it be consciously realized or not, of the emphasis placed by liberalism upon the rôle of freed intelligence as the method of directing social action.

Objections that are brought against liberalism ignore the fact that the only alternatives to dependence upon intelligence are either drift and casual improvisation, or the use of coercive force stimulated by unintelligent emotion and fanatical dogmatism—the latter being intolerant by its very constitution. . . . Since the ends of liberalism are liberty and the opportunity of individuals to secure full realization of their potentialities, all of the emotional intensity that belongs to these ends gathers about the ideas and acts that are necessary to make them real.

Again, it is said that the average citizen is not endowed with the degree of intelligence that the use of it as a method demands. This objection, supported by alleged scientific findings about heredity and by impressive statistics concerning the intelligence quotients of the average citizen, rests wholly upon the old notion that intelligence is a ready-made possession of individuals. The last stand of oligarchical and anti-social seclusion is perpetuation of this purely individualistic notion of intelligence. The reliance of liberalism is not upon the mere abstraction of a native endowment unaffected by social relationships, but upon the fact that native capacity is sufficient to enable the average individual to respond to and to use the knowledge and the skill that are embodied in the social conditions in which he lives, moves and has his being. There are few individuals who have the native capacity that was required to invent the stationary steam-engine, locomotive, dynamo or telephone. But there are none so mean that they cannot intelligently utilize these embodiments of intelligence once they are a part of the organized means of associated living. . . .

The crisis in liberalism, as I said at the outset, proceeds from the fact that after early liberalism had done its work, society faced a new problem, that of social organization. Its work was to liberate a group of individuals, representing the new science and the new forces of productivity, from customs, ways of thinking, institutions, that were oppressive of the new modes of social action, however useful they may have been in their day. . . .

Liberalism has to gather itself together to formulate the ends to which it is devoted in terms of means that are relevant to the contemporary situation. The only form of endur-

ing social organization that is now possible is one in which the new forces of productivity are coöperatively controlled and used in the interest of the effective liberty and the cultural development of the individuals that constitute society. Such a social order cannot be established by an unplanned and external convergence of the actions of separate individuals, each of whom is bent on personal private advantage. This idea is the Achilles heel of early liberalism. The idea that liberalism cannot maintain its ends and at the same time reverse its conception of the means by which they are to be attained is folly. The ends can now be achieved *only* by reversal of the means to which early liberalism was committed. Organized social planning, put into effect for the creation of an order in which industry and finance are socially directed in behalf of institutions that provide the material basis for the cultural liberation and growth of individuals, is now the sole method of social action by which liberalism can realize its professed aims. Such planning demands in turn a new conception and logic of freed intelligence as a social force.

Franklin Delano Roosevelt, 1882–1945

Franklin Roosevelt is a name synonymous with the positive state, welfare economics, and activist politics. As thirty-second president of the United States and the only U.S. executive to be elected to four terms, Roosevelt presided over the political and social revolution called the New Deal.

Although associated with the causes of labor, minorities, and the underdog, Roosevelt himself came from a patrician background, attended Groton, Harvard, and Columbia Law School, and often argued that he was "saving capitalism from itself."

After a brief, successful stint as a Democratic state legislator from upstate New York, Roosevelt was brought to Washington by Woodrow Wilson to be his secretary of the navy during World War I. In 1920 he ran as the Democratic candidate for vice president with James Cox, but they were soundly thrashed by the Republicans Warren G. Harding and Calvin Coolidge. Roosevelt returned to private business in 1921 but was stricken with polio, which left him crippled for the remainder of his life.

In 1924 and 1928 he nominated Al Smith for the Democratic candidate for president. In 1928 he successfully ran as governor of New York, while Smith lost the presidency to Herbert Hoover. His progressive record as governor made him a prime candidate for the Democratic nomination for president in 1932. With the Depression as the only real issue, Roosevelt convincingly defeated Herbert Hoover and began four terms as president.

Between election and inauguration, Roosevelt assembled a group of advisors called the Brain Trust—including Raymond Moley, Rexford Tugwell, Adolph Berle, and Harry Hopkins—to plan a reform of the economy. In the first one hundred days of his administration Roosevelt submitted to Congress and had passed fourteen major pieces of legislation designed to stabilize markets and keep the economy afloat. Later programs were designed to deal with the needs of labor, the poor, the elderly, and the unemployed. Social security, the National Labor Relations Board, and the Works Progress Administration are just a few examples of Roosevelt's welfare state proposals.

In the process, Roosevelt revamped the American perception of the presidency and indelibly left it as an activist's office at the center of American politics. With the darkening events in Europe and Asia, Roosevelt's activism took on an international dimension. As the United States inevitably became drawn into World War II, Roosevelt came to represent the essence of activist liberalism—intervention in the economy at home and in foreign affairs abroad.

The speech offered below is Roosevelt's famous "Commonwealth Club Address" which he delivered in San Francisco in 1932. It was his first attempt to give intellectual coherence to the collection of programs that he was about to enact. The speech was drafted by Adolph Berle and remains one of the best expressions of the new liberalism that would soon dominate American politics.

Franklin Delano Roosevelt

Commonwealth Club Address (1932)

I want to speak not of politics but of government. I want to speak not of parties but of universal principles. They are not political, except in that large sense in which a great

SOURCE: *New York Times*, September 24, 1932.

American once expressed a definition of politics—that nothing in all of human life is foreign to the science of politics. . . .

The issue of government has always been whether individual men and women will have to serve some system of government or economics, or whether a system of government and economics exists to serve individual men and women. This question has persistently dominated the discussions of government for many generations. On questions relating to these things, men have differed, and for time immemorial it is probable that honest men will continue to differ.

The final word belongs to no man, yet we can still believe in change and in progress. Democracy, as a dear old friend of mine in Indiana, Meredith Nicholson, has called it, is a quest, a never-ending seeking for better things, and in the seeking for these things and the striving for them, there are many roads to follow. But, if we map the course of these roads, we find that there are only two general directions.

When we look about us, we are likely to forget how hard people have worked to win the privilege of government. The growth of the national governments of Europe was a struggle for the development of a centralized force in the nation, strong enough to impose peace upon ruling barons. In many instances the victory of the central government, the creation of a strong central government, was a haven of refuge to the individual. The people preferred the master far away to the exploitation and cruelty of the smaller master near at hand.

But the creators of national government were perforce ruthless men. They were often cruel in their methods, but they did strive steadily toward something that society needed and very much wanted, a strong central state able to keep the peace, to stamp out civil war, to put the unruly nobleman in his place, and to permit the bulk of individuals to live safely. The man of ruthless force had his place in developing a pioneer country, just as he did in fixing the power of the central government in the development of the nations. Society paid him well for his services and its development. When the development among the nations of Europe, however, had been com-

pleted, ambition and ruthlessness, having served their term, tended to overstep their mark.

There came a growing feeling that government was conducted for the benefit of a few who thrived unduly at the expense of all. The people sought a balancing—a limiting force. There came gradually, through town councils, trade guilds, national parliaments, by constitution and by popular participation and control, limitations on arbitrary power. Another factor that tended to limit the power of those who ruled was the rise of the ethical conception that a ruler bore a responsibility for the welfare of his subjects.

The American colonies were born in this struggle. The American Revolution was a turning point in it. After the Revolution the struggle continued and shaped itself in the public life of the country. There were those who, because they had seen the confusion which attended the years of war for American independence, surrendered to the belief that popular government was essentially dangerous and essentially unworkable. They were honest people, my friends, and we cannot deny that their experience had warranted some measure of fear. The most brilliant, honest, and able exponent of this point of view was Hamilton. He was too impatient of slow-moving methods. Fundamentally he believed that the safety of the republic lay in the autocratic strength of its government, that the destiny of individuals was to serve that government, and that fundamentally a great and strong group of central institutions, guided by a small group of able and public spirited citizens, could best direct all government.

But Mr. Jefferson, in the summer of 1776, after drafting the Declaration of Independence, turned his mind to the same problem and took a different view. He did not deceive himself with outward forms. Government to him was a means to an end, not an end in itself; it might be either a refuge and a help or a threat and a danger, depending on the circumstances. We find him carefully analyzing the society for which he was to organize a government.

> We have no paupers. The great mass of our population is of laborers, our rich who cannot live without labor, either manual or professional, being few and of moderate wealth. Most of the laboring class possess property, cultivate their own lands, have families, and from the demand for their labor are enabled to exact from the rich and the competent such prices as enable them to feed abundantly, clothe above mere decency, to labor moderately, and raise their families.

These people, he considered, had two sets of rights, those of "personal competency" and those involved in acquiring and possessing property. By "personal competency" he meant the right of free thinking, freedom of forming and expressing opinions, and freedom of personal living, each man according to his own lights. To insure the first set of rights, a government must so order its functions as not to interfere with the individual. But even Jefferson realized that the exercise of the property rights might so interfere with the rights of the individual that the government, without whose assistance the property rights could not exist, must intervene, not to destroy individualism but to protect it.

You are familiar with the great political duel which followed; and how Hamilton and his friends, building toward a dominant centralized power, were at length defeated in the great election of 1800 by Mr. Jefferson's party. Out of that duel came the two parties, Republican and Democratic, as we know them today.

So began, in American political life, the new day, the day of the individual against the system, the day in which individualism was made the great watchword of American life. The happiest of economic conditions made that day long and splendid. On the Western frontier, land was substantially free. No one, who did not shirk the task of earning a living, was entirely without opportunity to do so. Depres-

sions could, and did, come and go; but they could not alter the fundamental fact that most of the people lived partly by selling their labor and partly by extracting their livelihood from the soil, so that starvation and dislocation were practically impossible. At the very worst there was always the possibility of climbing into a covered wagon and moving West, where the untilled prairies afforded a haven for men to whom the East did not provide a place. So great were our natural resources that we could offer this relief, not only to our own people but to the distressed of all the world; we could invite immigration from Europe and welcome it with open arms. Traditionally, when a depression came, a new section of land was opened in the West; and even our temporary misfortune served our manifest destiny.

It was in the middle of the nineteenth century that a new force was released and a new dream created. The force was what is called the Industrial Revolution, the advance of steam and machinery and the rise of the forerunners of the modern industrial plant. The dream was the dream of an economic machine, able to raise the standard of living for everyone; to bring luxury within the reach of the humblest; to annihilate distance by steam power and later by electricity, and to release everyone from the drudgery of the heaviest manual toil. It was to be expected that this would necessarily affect government. Heretofore, government had merely been called upon to produce conditions within which people could live happily, labor peacefully, and rest secure. Now it was called upon to aid in the consummation of this new dream. There was, however, a shadow over the dream. To be made real, it required use of the talents of men of tremendous will and tremendous ambition, since by no other force could the problems of financing and engineering and new developments be brought to a consummation.

So manifest were the advantages of the machine age, however, that the United States fearlessly, cheerfully, and, I think, rightly, accepted the bitter with the sweet. It was thought that no price was too high to pay for the advantages which we could draw from a finished industrial system. The history of the last half century is accordingly in large measure a history of a group of financial Titans, whose methods were not scrutinized with too much care and who were honored in proportion as they produced the results, irrespective of the means they used.

The financiers who pushed the railroads to the Pacific were always ruthless, often wasteful, and frequently corrupt; but they did build railroads, and we have them today. It has been estimated that the American investor paid for the American railway system more than three times over in the process; but, despite this fact, the net advantage was to the United States. As long as we had free land; as long as population was growing by leaps and bounds; as long as our industrial plants were insufficient to supply our own needs, society chose to give the ambitious man free play and unlimited reward provided only that he produced the economic plant so much desired.

During this period of expansion, there was equal opportunity for all and the business of government was not to interfere but to assist in the development of industry. This was done at the request of businessmen themselves. The tariff was originally imposed for the purpose of "fostering our infant industry," a phrase I think the older among you will remember as a political issue not so long ago. The railroads were subsidized, sometimes by grants of money, oftener by grants of land; some of the most valuable oil lands in the United States were granted to assist the financing of the railroad which pushed through the Southwest. A nascent merchant marine was assisted by grants of money, or by mail subsidies, so that our steamshipping might ply the seven seas.

Some of my friends tell me that they do not want the government in business. With this I agree; but I wonder whether they realize the implications of the past. For while it has been American doctrine that the government must not go into business in competition with private enterprises, still it has been traditional, particularly in Republican administrations, for business urgently to ask the government to put at private disposal all kinds of government assistance. The same man who tells you that he does not want to see the government interfere in business—and he means it, and has plenty of good reasons for saying so—is the first to go to Washington and ask the government for a prohibitory tariff on his product. When things get just bad enough, as they did two years ago, he will go with equal speed to the United States government and ask for a loan; and the Reconstruction Finance Corporation is the outcome of it. Each group has sought protection from the government for its own special interests, without realizing that the function of government must be to favor no small group at the expense of its duty to protect the rights of personal freedom and of private property of all its citizens.

In retrospect we can now see that the turn of the tide came with the turn of the century. We were reaching our last frontier; there was no more free land and our industrial combinations had become great uncontrolled and irresponsible units of power within the state. Clear-sighted men saw with fear the danger that opportunity would no longer be equal; that the growing corporation, like the feudal baron of old, might threaten the economic freedom of individuals to earn a living. In that hour, our antitrust laws were born. The cry was raised against the great corporations.

Theodore Roosevelt, the first great Republican Progressive, fought a presidential campaign on the issue of "trust busting" and talked freely about malefactors of great wealth. If the government had a policy it was rather to turn the clock back, to destroy the large combinations and to return to the time when every man owned his individual small business. This was impossible; Theodore Roosevelt, abandoning the idea of "trust busting," was forced to work out a difference between "good" trusts and "bad" trusts. The Supreme Court set forth the famous "rule of reason" by which it seems to have meant that a concentration of industrial power was permissible if the method by which it got its power, and the use it made of that power, was reasonable.

Woodrow Wilson, elected in 1912, saw the situation more clearly. Where Jefferson had feared the encroachment of political power on the lives of individuals, Wilson knew that the new power was financial. He saw, in the highly centralized economic system, the despot of the twentieth century, on whom great masses of individuals relied for their safety and their livelihood, and whose irresponsibility and greed (if it were not controlled) would reduce them to starvation and penury. The concentration of financial power had not proceeded as far in 1912 as it has today; but it had grown far enough for Mr. Wilson to realize fully its implications.

It is interesting, now, to read his speeches. What is called "radical" today (and I have reason to know whereof I speak) is mild compared to the campaign of Mr. Wilson. "No man can deny," he said,

> that the lines of endeavor have more and more narrowed and stiffened; no man who knows anything about the development of industry in this country can have failed to observe that the larger kinds of credit are more and more difficult to obtain unless you obtain them upon terms of uniting your efforts with those who already control the industry of the country, and nobody can fail to observe that every man who tries to set himself up in competition with any process of manufacture which has taken place under the control of large combinations of capital will presently find himself either squeezed out or obliged to sell and allow himself to be absorbed.

Had there been no World War—had Mr. Wilson been able to devote eight years to domestic instead of to international affairs—we might have had a wholly different situation at the present time. However, the then distant roar of European cannon, growing ever louder, forced him to abandon the study of this issue. The problem he saw so clearly is left with us as a legacy; and no one of us on either side of the political controversy can deny that it is a matter of grave concern to the government.

A glance at the situation today only too clearly indicates that equality of opportunity as we have known it no longer exists. Our industrial plant is built; the problem just now is whether under existing conditions it is not overbuilt. Our last frontier has long since been reached, and there is practically no more free land. More than half of our people do not live on the farms or on lands and cannot derive a living by cultivating their own property. There is no safety valve in the form of a Western prairie to which those thrown out of work by the Eastern economic machines can go for a new start. We are not able to invite the immigration from Europe to share our endless plenty. We are now providing a drab living for our own people.

Our system of constantly rising tariffs has at last reacted against us to the point of closing our Canadian frontier on the North, our European markets on the East, many of our Latin-American markets to the South, and a goodly proportion of our Pacific markets on the West, through the retaliatory tariffs of those countries. It has forced many of our great industrial institutions which exported their surplus production to such countries, to establish plants in such countries, within the tariff walls. This has resulted in the reduction of the operation of their American plants and opportunity for employment.

Just as freedom to farm has ceased, so also the opportunity in business has narrowed. It still is true that men can start small enterprises, trusting to native shrewdness and ability to keep abreast of competitors; but area after area has been preempted altogether by the great corporations, and even in the fields which still have no great concerns, the small man starts under a handicap. The unfeeling statistics of the past three decades show that the independent businessman is running a losing race. Perhaps he is forced to the wall; perhaps he cannot command credit; perhaps he is "squeezed out," in Mr. Wilson's words, by highly organized corporate competitors, as your corner groceryman can tell you.

Recently, a careful study was made of the concentration of business in the United States. It showed that our economic life was dominated by some 600-odd corporations who controlled two-thirds of American industry. Ten million small businessmen divided the other third. More striking still, it appeared that if the process of concentration goes on at the same rate, at the end of another century we shall have all American industry controlled by a dozen corporations, and run by perhaps 100 men. But plainly, we are steering a steady course toward economic oligarchy, if we are not there already.

Clearly, all this calls for a reappraisal of values. A mere builder of more industrial plants, a creator of more railroad systems, an organizer of more corporations is as likely to be a danger as a help. The day of the great promoter or the financial Titan, to whom we granted anything if only he would build or develop, is over. Our task now is not discovery or exploitation of natural resources, or necessarily producing more goods. It is the soberer, less dramatic business of administering resources and plants already in hand, of seeking to reestablish foreign markets for our surplus production, of meeting the problem of under consumption, of adjusting production to consumption, of distributing wealth and products more equitably, of adapting existing economic organizations to the service of the people. The day of enlightened administration has come.

Just as in older times the central government was first a haven of refuge and then a threat, so now, in a closer economic system, the central and ambitious financial unit is no longer a servant of national desire, but a danger. I would draw the parallel one step further. We did not think because national government had become a threat in the eighteenth century that therefore we should abandon the principle of national government. Nor today should we abandon the principle of strong economic units called corporations merely because their power is susceptible of easy abuse. In other times we dealt with the problem of an unduly ambitious central government by modifying it gradually into a constitutional democratic government. So today we are modifying and controlling our economic units.

As I see it, the task of government in its relation to business is to assist the development of an economic declaration of rights, an economic constitutional order. This is the common task of statesman and businessman. It is the minimum requirement of a more permanently safe order of things.

Happily, the times indicate that to create such an order not only is the proper policy of government but it is the only line of safety for our economic structures as well. We know, now, that these economic units cannot exist unless prosperity is uniform, that is, unless purchasing power is well distributed throughout every group in the nation. That is why even the most selfish of corporations for its own interest would be glad to see wages restored and unemployment ended and to bring the Western farmer back to his accustomed level of prosperity and to assure a permanent safety to both groups. That is why some enlightened industries themselves endeavor to limit the freedom of action of each man and business group within the industry in the common interest of all; why businessmen everywhere are asking a form of organization which will bring the scheme of things into balance, even though it may in some measure qualify the freedom of action of individual units within the business. . . .

The Declaration of Independence discusses the problem of government in terms of a contract. Government is a relation of give and take, a contract, perforce, if we would follow the thinking out of which it grew. Under such a contract, rulers were accorded power, and the people consented to that power on consideration that they be accorded certain rights. The task of statesmanship has always been the redefinition of these rights in terms of a changing and growing social order. New conditions impose new requirements upon government and those who conduct government. . . .

Every man has a right to life; and this means that he has also a right to make a comfortable living. He may by sloth or crime decline to exercise that right; but it may not be denied him. We have no actual famine or dearth; our industrial and agricultural mechanism can produce enough and to spare. Our government, formal and informal, political and economic, owes to everyone an avenue to possess himself of a portion of that plenty sufficient for his needs, through his own work.

Every man has a right to his own property; which means a right to be assured, to the fullest extent attainable, in the safety of his savings. By no other means can men carry the burdens of those parts of life which, in the nature of things, afford no chance of labor: childhood, sickness, old age. In all thought of property, this right is paramount; all other property rights must yield to it. If, in accord with this principle, we must restrict the operations of the speculator, the manipulator, even the financier, I believe we must accept the restriction as needful, not to hamper individualism but to protect it.

These two requirements must be satisfied, in the main, by the individuals who claim and hold control of the great industrial and financial combinations which dominate so large a part of our industrial life. They have under-

taken to be, not businessmen but princes—princes of property. I am not prepared to say that the system which produces them is wrong. I am very clear that they must fearlessly and competently assume the responsibility which goes with the power.

So many enlightened businessmen know this that the statement would be little more than a platitude, were it not for an added implication. This implication is, briefly, that the responsible heads of finance and industry, instead of acting each for himself, must work together to achieve the common end. They must, where necessary, sacrifice this or that private advantage; and in reciprocal self-denial must seek a general advantage. It is here that formal government—political government, if you choose—comes in.

Whenever in the pursuit of this objective the lone wolf, the unethical competitor, the reckless promoter, the Ishmael or Insull whose hand is against every man's, declines to join in achieving an end recognized as being for the public welfare and threatens to drag the industry back to a state of anarchy, the government may properly be asked to apply restraint. Likewise, should the group ever use its collective power contrary to the public welfare, the government must be swift to enter and protect the public interest.

The government should assume the function of economic regulation only as a last resort, to be tried only when private initiative, inspired by high responsibility, with such assistance and balance as government can give, has finally failed. As yet there has been no final failure, because there has been no attempt; and I decline to assume that this nation is unable to meet the situation.

The final term of the high contract was for *common good* liberty and the pursuit of happiness. We have learned a great deal of both in the past century. We know that individual liberty and individual happiness mean nothing unless both are ordered in the sense that one man's meat is not another man's poison. We know that the old "rights of personal competency," the right to read, to think, to speak, to choose, and live a mode of life must be respected at all hazards. We know that liberty to do anything which deprives others of those elemental rights is outside the protection of any compact; and that government in this regard is the maintenance of a balance, within which every individual may find safety if he wishes it; in which every individual may attain such power as his ability permits, consistent with his assuming the accompanying responsibility.

All this is a long, slow task. Nothing is more striking than the simple innocence of the men who insist, whenever an objective is present, on the prompt production of a patent scheme guaranteed to produce a result. Human endeavor is not so simple as that. Government includes the art of formulating a policy and using the political technique to attain so much of that policy as will receive general support; persuading, leading, sacrificing, teaching always, because the greatest duty of a statesman is to educate. But in the matters of which I have spoken, we are learning rapidly, in a severe school. The lessons so learned must not be forgotten, even in the mental lethargy of a speculative upturn. We must build toward the time when a major depression cannot occur again; and if this means sacrificing the easy profits of inflationist booms, then let them go; and good riddance.

Faith in America, faith in our tradition of personal responsibility, faith in our institutions, faith in ourselves demand that we recognize the new terms of the old social contract. We shall fulfill them, as we fulfilled the obligation of the apparent utopia which Jefferson imagined for us in 1776, and which Jefferson, Roosevelt, and Wilson sought to bring to realization. We must do so, lest a rising tide of misery, engendered by our common failure, engulf us all. But failure is not an American habit; and in the strength of great hope we must all shoulder our common load.

Adolph A. Berle, Jr., 1895–1971

Berle was an original Brain Truster who contributed individual programs and coherence to the New Deal, yet he never held an official government position. Berle was a successful New York lawyer and a widely published author. He earned three degrees from Harvard, B.A. (1913), M.A. (1914) and L.L.B. (1916), and at twenty-one became the youngest man ever to have received a Harvard law degree.

Berle specialized in corporate law and Latin American affairs. He lectured at Harvard Business School and was a professor of corporate law at Columbia University from 1927 to 1964.

His most famous book, written with Gardiner Means, is *The Modern Corporation and Private Property* (1932). It was this book which brought him to the attention of Raymond Moley and earned him a spot as a Brain Truster insider. In that work Berle argued that modern corporations were not extensions of their owners, but rather large, complex institutions managed by a neutral set of elite technicians. These technocrats, he believed, could form the basis of a cooperative relationship with government to plan economic activity in the common interest.

Berle was also the author of many other works including *The Twentieth Century Capitalist Revolution* (1954), *Power Without Property* (1959), *Latin America—Diplomacy and Reality* (1962) and *Power* (1963).

The following article was written for the *New York Times Magazine* in 1933 to explain the aims of the New Deal.

Adolph A. Berle, Jr.

The Social Economics of the New Deal (1933)

There is no mystery about the economics of the New Deal. For several generations, governments ran their affairs on the theory that natural economic forces balance themselves out. The law of supply and demand would regulate prices. When there was too little supply, the price would go up, and this would automatically increase the supply. When there was too much, the price would go down, and this would automatically decrease the supply. The efficient producer would succeed, the inefficient would fail, and this would keep the productive capacity of the country about in line with the needs for consumption. When credit was needed, bankers would supply it; when too much credit had been extended, there was a period of general inflation cutting down the debt. All this was comprehended in the governmental theory of the time which was really based on the classical economics of Adam Smith.

A tremendous force came into the world in the middle of the nineteenth century. It is usually tied up with what is called the industrial revolution and the advent of large-scale production. But we know now that the actual

forces released ran further than that. The power and force of organization had come into economics. Originally this collected around great investments of capital in huge plants, such as railroads, steel companies and the like. But as the economic machinery adapted itself to the idea of great organizations to run these plants, it became possible to have great organizations only partly dependent upon such plants.

This has led to a revision in some of our economic thinking. No longer can we rely on the economics of balance to take care of human needs. The effect of organization will distort and delay the forces leading to a balance to a degree as yet unmeasured. A falling price does not mean a falling supply under an agricultural system plus a credit system so organized that when the price went down every one tried to produce more wheat, or more cotton or more sugar in order to get out of debt. A big inefficient plant does not shut down because it cannot make a profit. It reorganizes, cuts its debt to nothing, and goes right on. Then it has no interest charges to pay, and only a small investment. It can accordingly undersell a more efficient producer, and drive him into bankruptcy, too. And this is repeated all through the industry.

Only after the entire industry has been bankrupted, do inefficient plants actually begin to go out of business. This process may take fifteen or twenty years, during which time the capital, the labor, the customers, and the industry generally, suffer from the effects of a disorganized and unsound condition.

The old economic forces still work and they do produce a balance after a while. But they take so long to do it and they crush so many men in the process that the strain on the social system becomes intolerable. Leaving economic forces to work themselves out as they now stand will produce an economic balance, but in the course of it you may have half of the entire country begging in the streets or starving to death.

The New Deal may be said to be merely a recognition of the fact that human beings cannot indefinitely be sacrificed by millions to the operation of economic forces accentuated by this factor of organization. Further, the mere process of organization which could create the economic mechanism can be invoked to prevent the shocking toll on life and health and happiness which readjustment under modern conditions demands.

Whatever the outcome, President Roosevelt will live in history as a great President if only for this one fact. He not only appreciated the situation, but had the courage to grapple with the cardinal economic problem of modern life. And he did so not in the spirit of hatred manifested by the red revolutionary or the black Fascist abroad, but in this typical American spirit of great generosity and great recognition that individual life and individual homes are the precious possessions; all else is merely machinery for the attainment of a full life.

You will find that the forces which the New Deal called into action roughly correspond to the organized forces which economists recognize as the senior controls of our present society. The first and the most important is the control of credit, banking and currency. This, the most important, the most delicate and the most complex, was in obvious collapse on March 4. Wisely, the legislation attending the banking holiday did not commit to any final solution; it is one of the problems with which the administration has yet to deal. The reason is not far to seek.

With five countries around us managing their currency, with the whole problem of the American price level then to be worked out, with the many aspects of that problem in vivid dispute, no one in his senses would have undertaken to lay down a definitive system. What was done was to gather into the hands of the administration many of the tools which could be used on a problem of this sort. It is after all a little naive to assume that there could be any one lever in that vast machinery which would serve as the complete solution.

A second senior control lies in the tremendously concentrated domination of certain groups over industry. Now industry heretofore has been assumed to be an enterprise conducted for private profit, providing goods and services which the country needs. But it is a great deal more than that. It is one of the principal avenues by which the national income is distributed through the form of wages, dividends, bond interest and so forth. In this item wages are distinctly the largest factor.

Now distribution of the national income is something more than a problem in social welfare. America, in a most intense form, is struggling with a problem that is common to all countries which are highly developed industrially. This is the fact that no industrial civilization can function at all unless there is a tremendous body of people able and willing to buy the products of industry.

The very process of building big factories means that there is a great output of goods which were formerly called luxuries, but which become necessities as the standard of living rises. In order to keep these plants going at all there have to be customers. Which means, when you carry it one step further, that there have to be people whose wages are high enough and steady enough to enable them to buy these goods. In the economist's jargon, it means that the national income has to be widely diffused. A national income of, say, 80 millions will not support an industrial civilization if 5 percent of the country has most of it and 95 percent divides the remnant. We got into exactly that position—we are there yet, for that matter—and it is one of the great obstacles to recovery.

This is, in political thinking, a new approach to the problem of wealth. The Communist has talked about having no property at all and distributing goods and services currently, because he thought of it in terms of social justice. Sociologists have talked about an evenly distributed income, on the theory that a large middle class, or rather, a nation of people of moderate means, formed the basis for a healthier national life. It remained for the hard-boiled student to work out the simple equation that unless the national income was pretty widely diffused there were not enough customers to keep the plants going; and as the plants shut down the wages shut down, too, and you became engaged in a vicious spiral in which there was less production, hence less wages, hence less income, hence still fewer customers, still less production, and so on down the scale.

We hit the bottom of that mad spiral some time last February, at which point roughly 40 percent of all wage-earners were out of a job. At that time, as a necessary result, no factories had orders enough to carry on with; only a few railroads had traffic enough to pay their current bills, and the whole machinery threatened to fall into absolute collapse. To this problem the incoming administration addressed itself.

It was conceived that by mobilizing industry through the National Recovery Administration and requiring it to meet the responsibilities of an income distributing group much could be done toward achieving the balance and distribution of income which is required to keep a system like ours afloat. When people talk of "creating purchasing power" what they really mean is that the national income goes not into stagnant pools of unneeded investment but into the hands of people who need goods.

Mobilization of this kind cannot be wholesale in scope; it has to be worked out industry by industry, in an intimateness of detail which can be coped with only by men thoroughly familiar with that industry. This accounts for the machinery of the National Recovery Administration. It involves, incidentally, a problem of education of a large order; for business men are not accustomed to work together, or to realize that if every one pursues his individual interest the result may be bankruptcy for all. I am not quite clear whether the hearings on national codes are not quite as important from the point of view of education as they are from the point of view of industrial organization.

The third and extremely important lever was grasped through the medium of the agricultural legislation—the first time in America that machinery has been devised to control production. We had the paradox that the more successful farming was, the more bankrupt was the farmer. And this in turn meant fewer markets for our industrial goods and ultimately unemployment in the cities. Prosperity to one section while another was in difficulties meant nothing; Mr. Roosevelt's now famous dictum that a country cannot endure "half boom and half broke" was an accurate bit of economic diagnosis as well as a brilliant phrase.

Still another of the senior controls is transportation. Through the various processes of regulation, we have held more control over railroads and transportation than over other parts of the national economy. It is plain, however, that the system was, and for that matter still is, badly askew. After conferences with the railroads themselves, the law creating a railroad coordinator was passed, with the object of setting up a nucleus of organization and at the same time providing sufficient "punch," so that the results of cooperation in railroading could be made available and could be passed on to the public either in the form of wages or in the form of lower rates or in the form of a solvent railroad; and preferably through the medium of all three.

An effective bit of machinery was the Reconstruction Finance Corporation which, properly rejuvenated, became during the early days of the administration the focus of most of the private finance of the country. Jesse Jones, the chairman of that board, took on a job the like of which has not been seen in history; for, from the beginning of the bank holiday until well through into the Summer, the Reconstruction Finance Corporation under his leadership was the principal support of our entire fabric, both of long-term and of short-term finance.

I am aware of the many criticisms leveled at the Reconstruction Finance Corporation largely arising out of its early operations, when it was conceived principally as an aid to certain great railroads and banks. Under the philosophy of a new administration, however, it became an instrument for safeguarding and making available the banking and credit structure which is the life blood of all trade. For a period the Reconstruction Finance Corporation virtually took over the great bulk of the work normally done by Wall Street and by the financial centres throughout the country; and as it has completed job after job it has turned the situation back to the respective communities in far better shape than ever before.

The overpowering burden of debt with which the country was struggling as a result of the prosperous decade threatened, and, for that matter, still threatens to engulf much of the economic activity liberated as these various great mechanisms are brought into play. That problem is by no means solved; but I merely mention the Agricultural Credit Corporation, the Home Owners Loan Corporation and other similar institutions designed to take up part of this burden and to reduce it to manageable form.

As a necessary supplement there is the program of public works designed to inject as and when necessary (and it is necessary now) additional activity into the commercial system.

There are many more similar levers and controls, but space does not permit description of them all. It is enough to say that in the aggregate they aim at introducing a power of organization into the economic system which can be used to counterbalance the effects of organization gone wrong; and to make sure that the burdens of readjustment are equitably distributed, and that no group of individuals will be ground to powder in order to satisfy the needs of an economic balance.

The overwhelming question today is, will this gigantic attempt to mold an individualist, capitalist system into a directed economic effort produce the result?

Before answering that question, it is well to look at the alternative. For myself, this alternative, drastic as it may sound, has far less terror than a general breakdown. Those of us who had the privilege of working on the original plan began with the assumption that what we needed most was a machine that worked. Whether it was rugged individualism, Fascism, Communism, Socialism, or what-not, made not the slightest bit of difference. Actually, the job was to satisfy the perfectly legitimate needs of a huge mass of people, all of whom were entitled to their right to live. If it cannot be done one way, it must be done another; but we may as well face with entire frankness what might have to be done should the present experiment fail.

A question has been asked which has not yet been answered. Every one is familiar with it. Why is it that with more food, more clothing, more housing, more luxuries, than we know what to do with, there are some 25 million people in the United States who are hungry, naked, living most precariously, and with little more than the bare necessities of subsistence? Every civilized human being is asking that question; and the fact that there are millions of people to whom civilization offers nothing just now means that the question will go right on being asked until an answer is found.

Now there is an answer possible. If, let us say, the government of the United States, forgetting all about the Constitution, were to commandeer everything and every one tomorrow afternoon, it could make a program that would look something like this:

It would say to every department store, and small retailer, "You are now a government distributing office." It could say the same to every wholesaler, every jobber, every warehouse. It could say to every manufacturer of finished goods, and every supplier of raw material, "You are now a government production agency." It could say to every railroad, truckman and the like, "You are now a government transportation agency." It could say to every one working in any capacity, as president, as day laborer, or as roustabout, employed or unemployed, "You are now enrolled as a part of the government labor supply."

It could say at the same time, "All of you will now go back to work. You will produce until we tell you to stop. When we have more than enough of what you happen to be producing, we will give you a furlough, until we need some more." It could say to the miner, "You will produce copper, or coal, or iron"; to the manufacturer, "You will produce finished products and we will supply your requisitions for raw materials." It could say to the transportation agencies, "You will requisition what you need to run your railroad with, and you will transport as we direct." So far, this is very much what we do in war time.

But it would have to say something more than that. A government tackling a solution on these lines would have to say: "Nobody will be paid anything. Debts and interest are canceled. Instead of that, we will give to every

one a red card entitling him to go to the nearest government distributing agency (for which you can read the department store, the little shop on the corner of Third Avenue, the drug store in the little town, the grocery shop you habitually deal with), and can get your share of the goods produced. You can use this for a small motor car, or you can use it for a barrel of flour, or for a loaf of bread. We shall have difficulties in distribution, and there may be shortages. We shall have to have regulations—you cannot step up to an automobile store (now a government distributing agency), and ask for 10 big cars. But we can arrange things, as organization proceeds, so that everybody gets his share."

If such a method of distribution were arranged, and it was carefully and thoroughly done, and industry maintained its efficiency, pretty much every one in the United States would have, in terms of goods and of services, an income equivalent to somewhere in the vicinity of $5,000 a year—or rather, equivalent to what $5,000 a year income will buy now.

There are two great difficulties with this kind of solution. One of them is that no one knows whether the industrial efficiency we now have would keep up—that is, whether our productive capacity would be great enough to meet the demand, once the incentive of private profit is taken out. I do not regard this objection as very serious. We know enough about production for private profit today to know that it is as often inefficient as efficient; that while private profit in a small enterprise makes for efficiency, in a large enterprise it is quite as likely to make for wholesale plunder. Also, in time we could expect efficiency at least as great as that which we now get out of the United States Postoffice—and that is, on the whole, in season and out, a pretty dependable institution.

The other objection is, however, infinitely more serious. Supposing some one happened to be living on a scale of life which assumed that he had a cook. There are people who serve civilization best by having cooks. Perhaps they are artists, authors, musicians, college professors even; perhaps they are the kind of men and women who have to manage these various enterprises, and it is sheer waste for them to be sweeping the front entry when we need them to see that the industrial program and the esthetic needs of the country are taken care of.

How is any government to say to me that I have to be a cook, and to you, that you can be manager of a plant or a leader of a symphony orchestra! Will not the cook say, "This is all very well; but I have no particular interest in being a servant in your house, while you have a position of importance. Your red card looks exactly the same as mine; it is good for the same thing at the local department store."

A government could, of course, maintain discipline by saying to me, "Unless you go on cooking, you get no food cards." But that is substantially the same as imposing sentence of death by starvation unless I go on working at a job which perhaps I may not like. Consequently, the government would have to begin working out classifications—giving the manager of a plant a food card which entitled him to have a cook, on the ground that he was more highly trained and more highly valuable, while the day laborer had a food card merely entitling him to a decent house, an adequate supply of food and clothing, a small motor car and a reasonable allowance of moving pictures and beer.

I can imagine an American Government doing this if it had to—but only if it had to. If there is a general break-down, it will have to do temporarily at least, something very like this; but it is the last resort; a counsel of despair; an indication that we cannot run our private lives effectively enough to solve the situation. Moreover, under the stress of that kind of experiment, a great deal of the grace of life and human values, which we all of us

hold dear, might very easily go out. Complicated and difficult as it may seem to manipulate private industry and private economic processes, this is still preferable to attempting a wholesale solution, so long as there is any hope of success.

This is why the experiment of the Roosevelt administration not only is historic, but why it must succeed. This is why the only intelligent attitude to take is one of cooperation. This is why, though all of us will undoubtedly have moments of discouragement at the slowness of it, we build more strongly than we might were we either to attempt a wholesale revolution, or to plunge back into the chaos which was failing dismally only a few months ago.

I have perhaps less fear of the sweeping solution than most people, because I have perhaps more faith than most people in the ability of the United States to take almost any scheme of society and manipulate it into a satisfactory solution. People do not change their habits easily; and the kind of economic system people want is the kind which, in the long run, they are likely to get.

If, for example, we were to adopt the Russian Soviet system entire, it would look a good deal more like the Rotary Club or the four railway brotherhoods than like the Moscow Soviet; the skyline of New York and life in Peoria, Ill., or St. Louis, Mo., would be a good deal more like life as it is now in New York, or Peoria, or St. Louis, than like life in Petrograd, or Kieff, or Odessa.

But it is one thing not to be afraid of a change, and quite another to abandon the civilization which, by and large, has served us well, modifying it only enough to meet changed conditions. In a world in which revolutions just now are coming easily, the New Deal chose the more difficult course of moderation and rebuilding. This, in a word, is the social economics—the political economics, in the old phrase—of the New Deal.

Voices of Dissent

From Left and Right

Herbert Hoover

Campaign Speech, It Is a False Liberalism . . . (1932)

. . . We have heard a great deal in this campaign about reactionaries, conservatives, progressives, liberals, and radicals. I have not yet heard an attempt by any one of the orators who mouth these phrases to define the principles upon which they base these classifications. There is one thing I can say without any question of doubt—that is, that the spirit of liberalism is to create free men; it is not the regimentation of men. It is not the extension of bureaucracy. I have said in this city before now that you can not extend the mastery of government over the daily life of a people without somewhere making it master of people's souls and thoughts. Expansion of government in business means that the Government in order to protect itself from the political consequences of its errors is driven irresistibly without peace to greater and greater control

of the Nation's press and platform. Free speech does not live many hours after free industry and free commerce die. It is a false liberalism that interprets itself into Government operation of business. Every step in that direction poisons the very roots of liberalism. It poisons political equality, free speech, free press, and equality of opportunity. It is the road not to liberty but to less liberty. True liberalism is found not in striving to spread bureaucracy, but in striving to set bounds to it. True liberalism seeks all legitimate freedom first in the confident belief that without such freedom the pursuit of other blessings is in vain. Liberalism is a force truly of the spirit proceeding from the deep realization that economic freedom can not be sacrificed if political freedom is to be preserved.

Even if the Government conduct of business could give us the maximum of efficiency instead of least efficiency, it would be purchased at the cost of freedom. It would increase rather than decrease abuse and corruption, stifle ini-

SOURCE: William Starr Myers, ed., *The State Papers and Other Public Writings of Herbert Hoover* (New York: Doubleday, Doran and Company, 1934).

tiative and invention, undermine development of leadership, cripple mental and spiritual energies of our people, extinguish equality of opportunity, and dry up the spirit of liberty and progress. Men who are going about this country announcing that they are liberals because of their promises to extend the Government in business are not liberals, they are reactionaries of the United States.

And I do not wish to be misquoted or misunderstood. I do not mean that our government is to part with one iota of its national resources without complete protection to the public interest. I have already stated that democracy must remain master in its own house. I have stated that abuse and wrongdoing must be punished and controlled. Nor do I wish to be misinterpreted as stating that the United States is a free-for-all and devil-take-the-hindermost society.

The very essence of equality of opportunity of our American system is that there shall be no monopoly or domination by any group or section in this country, whether it be business, sectional or a group interest. On the contrary, our American system demands economic justice as well as political and social justice; it is not a system of laissez faire.

I am not setting up the contention that our American system is perfect. No human ideal has ever been perfectly attained, since humanity itself is not perfect. But the wisdom of our forefathers and the wisdom of the thirty men who have preceded me in this office hold to the conception that progress can only be attained as the sum of accomplishments of free individuals, and they have held unalterably to these principles.

In the ebb and flow of economic life our people in times of prosperity and ease naturally tend to neglect the vigilance over their rights. Moreover, wrongdoing is obscured by apparent success in enterprise. Then insidious diseases and wrongdoings grow apace. But we have in the past seen in times of distress and difficulty that wrongdoing and weakness come to the surface and our people, in their endeavors to correct these wrongs, are tempted to extremes which may destroy rather than build.

It is men who do wrong, not our institutions. It is men who violate the laws and public rights. It is men, not institutions, which must be punished.

In my acceptance speech four years ago at Palo Alto I stated that—"One of the oldest aspirations of the human race was the abolition of poverty. By poverty I mean the grinding by under-nourishment, cold, ignorance, fear of old age to those who have the will to work." I stated that—"In America today we are nearer a final triumph over poverty than in any land. The poorhouse has vanished from amongst us; we have not reached that goal, but given a chance to go forward, we shall, with the help of God, be in sight of the day when poverty will be banished from this Nation."

Our Democratic friends have quoted this passage many times in this campaign. I do not withdraw a word of it. When I look about the world even in these times of trouble and distress I find it more true in this land than anywhere else under the traveling sun. I am not ashamed of it, because I am not ashamed of holding ideals and purposes for the progress of the American people. Are my Democratic opponents prepared to state that they do not stand for this ideal or this hope? For my part, I propose to continue to strive for it, and I hope to live to see it accomplished.

One of the most encouraging and inspiring phases of this whole campaign has been the unprecedented interest of our younger men and women. It is in this group that we find our new homes being founded, our new families in which the children are being taught those basic principles of love and faith and patriotism. It is in this group that we find the starting of business and professional careers with courageous and hopeful faces turned to the future and its promise. It is this group who must undertake the guardianship of our American system and carry it forward to its greater achievements.

Inevitably in the progress of time, our country and its institutions will be entirely in their hands. The burdens of the depression have fallen on the younger generation with equal and perhaps greater severity than upon the elders. It has affected not only their economic well-being, but has tended also to shatter many illusions. But their faith in our country and its institutions has not been shaken. I am confident that they will resist any destruction to our American system of political, economic and social life.

It is a tribute to America and its past and present leaders and even more a tribute to this younger generation that, contrary to the experience of other countries, we can say tonight that the youth of America is more staunch than many of their elders. I can ask no higher tribute from my party for the maintenance of the American system and the program of my administration than the support being given by the younger men and women of our country. It has just been communicated to me that tonight at this time, in every county and almost every precinct of our country, 3 million members of the Young Republican League are meeting for the support of a Republican victory November 8th—a victory for the American system.

My countrymen, the proposals of our opponents represent a profound change in American life—less in concrete proposal, bad as that may be, than by implication and by evasion. Dominantly in their spirit they represent a radical departure from the foundations of 150 years which have made this the greatest nation in the world. This election is not a mere shift from the ins to the outs. It means deciding the direction our Nation will take over a century to come.

My conception of America is a land where men and women may walk in ordered liberty, where they may enjoy the advantages of wealth not concentrated in the hands of a few but diffused through the lives of all, where they build and safeguard their homes, give to their children full opportunities of American life, where every man shall be respected in the faith that his conscience and his heart direct him to follow, where people secure in their liberty shall have leisure and impulse to seek a fuller life. That leads to the release of the energies of men and women, to the wider vision and higher hope; it leads to opportunity for greater and greater service not alone of man to man in our country but from our country to the world. It leads to health in body and a spirit unfettered, youthful, eager with a vision stretching beyond the farthest horizons with an open mind, sympathetic and generous. But that must be builded upon our experience with the past, upon the foundations which have made our country great. It must be the product of our truly American system.

Milton Friedman, 1912–

Milton Friedman is one of America's leading critics of Keynesian economics and the welfare state. In both scholarly and popular books, articles, and TV series, Friedman has maintained that the key to lessening recession and inflation is to be found in a tighter control of the money supply and a return to free market economics. Fiscal policy that attempts to fine-tune the economy by altering tax rates and levels of public spending will only aggravate economic problems and generally reduces individual discretion over one's own income. The result is an economic loss and a net loss in personal freedom.

Friedman graduated from Rutgers University in 1932, received an M.A. from the University of Chicago in 1933, and after a series of jobs in government research bureaus, received his Ph.D. from Columbia in 1946. By 1948 he was a full professor at the University of Chicago and was a critical member of the conservative "Chicago School."

Through his popular books, written with his wife Rose—*Capitalism and Freedom* (1962) and *Free to Choose* (1979)—and his columns in *Newsweek* magazine, Friedman has become one of the most popular critics of the assumptions of welfare state liberalism. His classic *Monetary History of the United States 1867–1960,* written with Anna J. Schwartz, is one of the most influential works in economics in the past two decades.

The following selection from *Capitalism and Freedom* is a good example of Friedman's attack on welfare state liberalism and his advocacy of classical, individualist liberalism.

Milton Friedman

Capitalism and Freedom (1962)

THE ROLE OF GOVERNMENT IN A FREE SOCIETY

A common objection to totalitarian societies is that they regard the end as justifying the means. Taken literally, this objection is clearly illogical. If the end does not justify the means, what does? But this easy answer does not dispose of the objection; it simply shows that the objection is not well put. To deny that the end justifies the means is indirectly to assert that the end in question is not the ultimate end, that the ultimate end is itself the use of the proper means. Desirable or not, any end

SOURCE: Reprinted from Milton Friedman, "The Role of Government in a Free Society," in *Capitalism and Freedom* (Chicago: University of Chicago Press, 1962), by permission of the University of Chicago Press. Copyright © 1962.

that can be attained only by the use of bad means must give way to the more basic end of the use of acceptable means.

To the liberal, the appropriate means are free discussion and voluntary co-operation, which implies that any form of coercion is inappropriate. The ideal is unanimity among responsible individuals achieved on the basis of free and full discussion. This is another way of expressing the goal of freedom. . . .

From this standpoint, the role of the market . . . is that it permits unanimity without conformity; that it is a system of effectively proportional representation. On the other hand, the characteristic feature of action through explicitly political channels is that it tends to require or to enforce substantial conformity. The typical issue must be decided "yes" or "no"; at most, provision can be made for a fairly limited number of alternatives. Even the use of proportional representation in its explicitly political form does not alter this conclusion. The number of separate groups that can in fact be represented is narrowly limited, enormously so by comparison with the proportional representation of the market. More important, the fact that the final outcome generally must be a law applicable to all groups, rather than separate legislative enactments for each "party" represented, means that proportional representation in its political version, far from permitting unanimity without conformity, tends toward ineffectiveness and fragmentation. It thereby operates to destroy any consensus on which unanimity with conformity can rest.

These are clearly some matters with respect to which effective proportional representation is impossible. I cannot get the amount of national defense I want and you, a different amount. With respect to such indivisible matters we can discuss, and argue, and vote. But having decided, we must conform. It is precisely the existence of such indivisible matters—protection of the individual and the nation from coercion are clearly the most basic—that prevents exclusive reliance on individual action through the market. If we are to use some of our resources for such indivisible items, we must employ political channels to reconcile differences.

The use of political channels, while inevitable, tends to strain the social cohesion essential for a stable society. The strain is least if agreement for joint action need be reached only on a limited range of issues on which people in any event have common views. Every extension of the range of issues for which explicit agreement is sought strains further the delicate threads that hold society together. If it goes so far as to touch an issue on which men feel deeply yet differently, it may well disrupt the society. Fundamental differences in basic values can seldom if ever be resolved at the ballot box; ultimately they can only be decided, though not resolved, by conflict. The

religious and civil wars of history are a bloody testament to this judgment.

The widespread use of the market reduces the strain on the social fabric by rendering conformity unnecessary with respect to any activities it encompasses. The wider the range of activities covered by the market, the fewer are the issues on which explicitly political decisions are required and hence on which it is necessary to achieve agreement. In turn, the fewer the issues on which agreement is necessary, the greater is the likelihood of getting agreement while maintaining a free society.

Unanimity is, of course, an ideal. In practice, we can afford neither the time nor the effort that would be required to achieve complete unanimity on every issue. We must perforce accept something less. We are thus led to accept majority rule in one form or another as an expedient. That majority rule is an expedient rather than itself a basic principle is clearly shown by the fact that our willingness to resort to majority rule, and the size of the majority we require, themselves depend on the seriousness of the issue involved. If the matter is of little moment and the minority has no strong feelings about being overruled, a bare plurality will suffice. On the other hand, if the minority feels strongly about the issue involved, even a bare majority will not do. Few of us would be willing to have issues of free speech, for example, decided by a bare majority. Our legal structure is full of such distinctions among kinds of issues that require different kinds of majorities. At the extreme are those issues embodied in the Constitution. These are the principles that are so important that we are willing to make minimal concessions to expediency. Something like essential consensus was achieved initially in accepting them, and we require something like essential consensus for a change in them.

The self-denying ordinance to refrain from majority rule on certain kinds of issues that is embodied in our Constitution and in similar written or unwritten constitutions elsewhere, and the specific provisions in these constitutions on their equivalents prohibiting coercion of individuals, are themselves to be regarded as reached by free discussion and as reflecting essential unanimity about means.

I turn now to consider more specifically, though still in very broad terms, what the areas are that cannot be handled through the market at all, or can be handled only at so great a cost that the use of political channels may be preferable.

It is important to distinguish the day-to-day activities of people from the general customary and legal framework within which these take place. The day-to-day activities are like the actions of the participants in a game when they are playing it; the framework, like the rules of the game they play. And just as a good game requires acceptance by the players both of the rules and of the umpire to interpret and enforce them, so a good society requires that its members agree on the general conditions that will govern relations among them, on some means of arbitrating different interpretations of these conditions, and on some device for enforcing compliance with the generally accepted rules. As in games, so also in society, most of the general conditions are the unintended outcome of custom, accepted unthinkingly. At most, we consider explicitly only minor modifications in them, though the cumulative effect of a series of minor modifications may be a drastic alteration in the character of the game or of the society. In both games and society also, no set of rules can prevail unless most participants most of the time conform to them without external sanctions; unless that is, there is a broad underlying social consensus. But we cannot rely on custom or on this consensus alone to interpret and to enforce the rules; we need an umpire. These then are the basic roles of government in a free society: to provide a means whereby we can modify the rules, to mediate differences among us on the meaning of the rules, and to enforce compliance with the rules on the part of those few who would otherwise not play the game.

The need for government in these respects arises because absolute freedom is impossible. However attractive anarchy may be as a philosophy, it is not feasible in a world of imperfect men. Men's freedoms can conflict, and when they do, one man's freedom must be limited to preserve another's—as a Supreme Court Justice once put it, "My freedom to move my fist must be limited by the proximity of your chin."

The major problem in deciding the appropriate activities of government is how to resolve such conflicts among the freedoms of different individuals. In some cases, the answer is easy. There is little difficulty in attaining near unanimity to the proposition that one man's freedom to murder his neighbor must be sacrificed to preserve the freedom of the other man to live. In other cases, the answer is difficult. In the economic area, a major problem arises in respect of the conflict between freedom to combine and freedom to compete. What meaning is to be attributed to "free" as modifying "enterprise"? In the United States, "free" has been understood to mean that anyone is free to set up an enterprise, which means that existing enterprises are not free to keep out competitors except by selling a better product at the same price or the same product at a lower price. In the continental tradition, on the other hand, the meaning has generally been that enterprises are free to do what they want, including the fixing of prices, division of markets, and the adoption of other techniques to keep out potential competitors. Perhaps the most difficult specific problem in this area arises with respect to combinations among laborers, where the problem of freedom to combine and freedom to compete is particularly acute.

A still more basic economic area in which the answer is both difficult and important is the definition of property rights. The notion of property, as it has developed over centuries and as it is embodied in our legal codes, has become so much a part of us that we tend to take it for granted, and fail to recognize the extent to which just what constitutes property and what rights the ownership of property confers are complex social creations rather than self-evident propositions. Does my having title to land, for example, and my freedom to use my property as I wish, permit me to deny to someone else the right to fly over my land in his airplane? Or does his right to use his airplane take precedence? Or does this depend on how high he flies? Or how much noise he makes? Does voluntary exchange require that he pay me for the privilege of flying over my land? Or that I must pay him to refrain from flying over it? The mere mention of royalties, copyrights, patents; shares of stock in corporations; riparian rights, and the like, may perhaps emphasize the role of generally accepted social rules in the very definition of property. It may suggest also that, in many cases, the existence of a well specified and generally accepted definition of property is far more important than just what the definition is.

Another economic area that raises particularly difficult problems is the monetary system. Government responsibility for the monetary system has long been recognized. It is explicitly provided for in the constitutional provision which gives Congress the power "to coin money, regulate the value thereof, and of foreign coin." There is probably no other area of economic activity with respect to which government action has been so uniformly accepted. This habitual and by now almost unthinking acceptance of governmental responsibility makes thorough understanding of the grounds for such responsibility all the more necessary, since it enhances the danger that the scope of government will spread from activities that are, to those that are not, appropriate in a free society, from providing a monetary framework to determining the allocation of resources among individuals. . . .

In summary, the organization of economic activity through voluntary exchange presumes that we have provided, through government, for the maintenance of law and order to prevent coercion of one individual by another, the enforcement of contracts voluntarily entered into, the definition of the meaning of property rights, the interpretation and enforcement of such rights, and the provision of a monetary framework.

Action through Government on Grounds of Technical Monopoly and Neighborhood Effects

The role of government just considered is to do something that the market cannot do for itself, namely, to determine, arbitrate, and enforce the rules of the game. We may also want to do through government some things that might conceivably be done through the market but that technical or similar conditions render it difficult to do in that way. These all reduce to cases in which strictly voluntary exchange is either exceedingly costly or practically impossible. There are two general classes of such cases: monopoly and similar market imperfections, and neighborhood effects.

Exchange is truly voluntary only when nearly equivalent alternatives exist. Monopoly implies the absence of alternatives and thereby inhibits effective freedom of exchange. In practice, monopoly frequently, if not generally, arises from government support or from collusive agreements among individuals. With respect to these, the problem is either to avoid governmental fostering of monopoly or to stimulate the effective enforcement of rules such as those embodied in our anti-trust laws. However, monopoly may also arise because it is technically efficient to have a single producer or enterprise. I venture to suggest that such cases are more limited than is supposed but they unquestionably do arise. A simple example is perhaps the provision of telephone services within a community. I shall refer to such cases as "technical" monopoly.

When technical conditions make a monopoly the natural outcome of competitive market forces, there are only three alternatives that seem available: private monopoly, public monopoly, or public regulation. All three are bad so we must choose among evils. Henry Simons, observing public regulation of monopoly in the United States, found the results so distasteful that he concluded public monopoly would be a lesser evil. Walter Eucken, a noted German liberal, observing public monopoly in German railroads, found the results so distasteful that he concluded public regulation would be a lesser evil. Having learned from both, I reluctantly conclude that, if tolerable, private monopoly may be the least of the evils.

If society were static so that the conditions which give rise to a technical monopoly were sure to remain, I would have little confidence in this solution. In a rapidly changing society, however, the conditions making for technical monopoly frequently change and I suspect that both public regulation and public monopoly are likely to be less responsive to such changes in conditions, to be less readily capable of elimination, than private monopoly.

Railroads in the United States are an excellent example. A large degree of monopoly in railroads was perhaps inevitable on technical grounds in the nineteenth century. This was the justification for the Interstate Commerce Commission. But conditions have changed. The emergence of road and air transport has reduced the monopoly element in railroads to negligible proportions. Yet we have not eliminated the ICC. On the contrary, the ICC, which started out as an agency to protect the public from exploitation by the railroads, has become an agency to protect railroads from competition by trucks and other means of transport, and more recently even to protect existing truck companies from competition by new entrants. Similarly, in

England, when the railroads were nationalized, trucking was at first brought into the state monopoly. If railroads had never been subjected to regulation in the United States, it is nearly certain that by now transportation, including railroads, would be a highly competitive industry with little or no remaining monopoly elements.

The choice between the evils of private monopoly, public monopoly, and public regulation cannot, however, be made once and for all, independently of the factual circumstances. If the technical monopoly is of a service or commodity that is regarded as essential and if its monopoly power is sizable, even the shortrun effects of private unregulated monopoly may not be tolerable, and either public regulation or ownership may be a lesser evil.

Technical monopoly may on occasion justify a *de facto* public monopoly. It cannot by itself justify a public monopoly achieved by making it illegal for anyone else to compete. For example, there is no way to justify our present public monopoly of the post office. It may be argued that the carrying of mail is a technical monopoly and that a government monopoly is the least of evils. Along these lines, one could perhaps justify a government post office but not the present law, which makes it illegal for anybody else to carry mail. If the delivery of mail is a technical monopoly, no one will be able to succeed in competition with the government. If it is not, there is no reason why the government should be engaged in it. The only way to find out is to leave other people free to enter.

The historical reason why we have a post office monopoly is because the Pony Express did such a good job of carrying the mail across the continent that, when the government introduced transcontinental service, it couldn't compete effectively and lost money. The result was a law making it illegal for anybody else to carry the mail. That is why the Adams Express Company is an investment trust today instead of an operating company. I conjecture that if entry into the mail-carrying business were open to all, there would be a large number of firms entering it and this archaic industry would become revolutionized in short order.

A second general class of cases in which strictly voluntary exchange is impossible arises when actions of individuals have effects on other individuals for which it is not feasible to charge or recompense them. This is the problem of "neighborhood effects." An obvious example is the pollution of a stream. The man who pollutes a stream is in effect forcing others to exchange good water for bad. These others might be willing to make the exchange at a price. But it is not feasible for them, acting individually, to avoid the exchange or to enforce appropriate compensation.

A less obvious example is the provision of highways. In this case, it is technically possible to identify and hence charge individuals for their use of the roads and so to have private operation. However, for general access roads, involving many points of entry and exit, the costs of collection would be extremely high if a charge were to be made for the specific services received by each individual, because of the necessity of establishing toll booths or the equivalent at all entrances. The gasoline tax is a much cheaper method of charging individuals roughly in proportion to their use of the roads. This method, however, is one in which the particular payment cannot be identified closely with the particular use. Hence, it is hardly feasible to have private enterprise provide the service and collect the charge without establishing extensive private monopoly.

These considerations do not apply to long-distance turnpikes with high density of traffic and limited access. For these, the costs of collection are small and in many cases are now being paid, and there are often numerous alternatives, so that there is no serious monopoly problem. Hence, there is every reason why these should be privately owned and operated.

If so owned and operated, the enterprise running the highway should receive the gasoline taxes paid on account of travel on it.

Parks are an interesting example because they illustrate the difference between cases that can and cases that cannot be justified by neighborhood effects, and because almost everyone at first sight regards the conduct of National Parks as obviously a valid function of government. In fact, however, neighborhood effects may justify a city park; they do not justify a national park, like Yellowstone National Park or the Grand Canyon. What is the fundamental difference between the two? For the city park, it is extremely difficult to identify the people who benefit from it and to charge them for the benefits which they receive. If there is a park in the middle of the city, the houses on all sides get the benefit of the open space, and people who walk through it or by it also benefit. To maintain toll collectors at the gates or to impose annual charges per window overlooking the park would be very expensive and difficult. The entrances to a national park like Yellowstone, on the other hand, are few; most of the people who come stay for a considerable period of time and it is perfectly feasible to set up toll gates and collect admission charges. This is indeed now done, though the charges do not cover the whole costs. If the public wants this kind of an activity enough to pay for it, private enterprises will have every incentive to provide such parks. And, of course, there are many private enterprises of this nature now in existence. I cannot myself conjure up any neighborhood effects or important monopoly effects that would justify governmental activity in this area.

Considerations like those I have treated under the heading of neighborhood effects have been used to rationalize almost every conceivable intervention. In many instances, however, this rationalization is special pleading rather than a legitimate application of the concept of neighborhood effects. Neighborhood effects cut both ways. They can be a reason for limiting the activities of government as well as for expanding them. Neighborhood effects impede voluntary exchange because it is difficult to identify the effects on third parties and to measure their magnitude; but this difficulty is present in governmental activity as well. It is hard to know when neighborhood effects are sufficiently large to justify particular costs in overcoming them and even harder to distribute the costs in an appropriate fashion. Consequently, when government engages in activities to overcome neighborhood effects, it will in part introduce an additional set of neighborhood effects by failing to charge or to compensate individuals properly. Whether the original or the new neighborhood effects are the more serious can only be judged by the facts of the individual case, and even then, only very approximately. Furthermore, the use of government to overcome neighborhood effects itself has an extremely important neighborhood effect which is unrelated to the particular occasion for government action. Every act of government intervention limits the area of individual freedom directly and threatens the preservation of freedom indirectly for reasons elaborated in the first chapter.

Our principles offer no hard and fast line how far it is appropriate to use government to accomplish jointly what it is difficult or impossible for us to accomplish separately through strictly voluntary exchange. In any particular case of proposed intervention, we must make up a balance sheet, listing separately the advantages and disadvantages. Our principles tell us what items to put on the one side and what items on the other and they give us some basis for attaching importance to the different items. In particular, we shall always want to enter on the liability side of any proposed government intervention, its neighborhood effect in threatening freedom, and give this effect considerable weight. Just how much weight to give to it, as to other items, depends upon the circumstances. If,

for example, existing government intervention is minor, we shall attach a smaller weight to the negative effects of additional government intervention. This is an important reason why many earlier liberals, like Henry Simons, writing at a time when government was small by today's standards, were willing to have government undertake activities that today's liberals would not accept now that government has become so overgrown.

Action through Government on Paternalistic Grounds

Freedom is a tenable objective only for responsible individuals. We do not believe in freedom for madmen or children. The necessity of drawing a line between responsible individuals and others is inescapable, yet it means that there is an essential ambiguity in our ultimate objective of freedom. Paternalism is inescapable for those whom we designate as not responsible.

The clearest case, perhaps, is that of madmen. We are willing neither to permit them freedom nor to shoot them. It would be nice if we could rely on voluntary activities of individuals to house and care for the madmen. But I think we cannot rule out the possibility that such charitable activities will be inadequate, if only because of the neighborhood effect involved in the fact that I benefit if another man contributes to the care of the insane. For this reason, we may be willing to arrange for their care through government.

Children offer a more difficult case. The ultimate operative unit in our society is the family, not the individual. Yet the acceptance of the family as the unit rests in considerable part on expediency rather than principle. We believe that parents are generally best able to protect their children and to provide for their development into responsible individuals for whom freedom is appropriate. But we do not believe in the freedom of parents to do what they will with other people. The children are responsible individuals in embryo, and a believer in freedom believes in protecting their ultimate rights.

To put this in a different and what may seem a more callous way, children are at one and the same time consumer goods and potentially responsible members of society. The freedom of individuals to use their economic resources as they want includes the freedom to use them to have children—to buy, as it were, the services of children as a particular form of consumption. But once this choice is exercised, the children have a value in and of themselves and have a freedom of their own that is not simply an extension of the freedom of the parents.

The paternalistic ground for governmental activity is in many ways the most troublesome to a liberal; for it involves the acceptance of a principle—that some shall decide for others—which he finds objectionable in most applications and which he rightly regards as a hallmark of his chief intellectual opponents, the proponents of collectivism in one or another of its guises, whether it be communism, socialism, or a welfare state. Yet there is no use pretending that problems are simpler than in fact they are. There is no avoiding the need for some measure of paternalism. As Dicey wrote in 1914 about an act for the protection of mental defectives, "The Mental Deficiency Act is the first step along a path on which no sane man can decline to enter, but which, if too far pursued, will bring statesmen across difficulties hard to meet without considerable interference with individual liberty."[1] There is no formula that can tell us where to stop. We must rely on our fallible judgment and, having reached a judgment, on our ability to persuade our fellow men that it is a correct judgment, or their ability to persuade us to modify our views. We must put our faith, here as elsewhere, in a consensus reached by imperfect and biased men through free discussion and trial and error.

Conclusion

A government which maintained law and order, defined property rights, served as a means whereby we could modify property rights and other rules of the economic game, adjudicated disputes about the interpretation of the rules, enforced contracts, promoted competition, provided a monetary framework, engaged in activities to counter technical monopolies and to overcome neighborhood effects widely regarded as sufficiently important to justify government intervention, and which supplemented private charity and the private family in protecting the irresponsible, whether madman or child—such a government would clearly have important functions to perform. The consistent liberal is not an anarchist.

Yet it is also true that such a government would have clearly limited functions and would refrain from a host of activities that are now undertaken by federal and state governments in the United States, and their counterparts in other Western countries. Succeeding chapters will deal in some detail with some of these activities, and a few have been discussed above, but it may help to give a sense of proportion about the role that a liberal would assign government simply to list, in closing this chapter, some activities currently undertaken by government in the U.S., that cannot, so far as I can see, validly be justified in terms of the principles outlined above:

1. Parity price support programs for agriculture.

2. Tariffs on imports or restrictions on exports, such as current oil import quotas, sugar quotas, etc.

3. Governmental control of output, such as through the farm program, or through prorationing of oil as is done by the Texas Railroad Commission.

---

[1] A. V. Dicey, *Lectures on the Relation between Law and Public Opinion in England during the Nineteenth Century*, 2d. ed. (London: Macmillan & Co., 1914), p. li.

4. Rent control, such as is still practiced in New York, or more general price and wage controls such as were imposed during and just after World War II.

5. Legal minimum wage rates, or legal maximum prices, such as the legal maximum of zero on the rate of interest that can be paid on demand deposits by commercial banks, or the legally fixed maximum rates that can be paid on savings and time deposits.

6. Detailed regulation of industries, such as the regulation of transportation by the Interstate Commerce Commission. This had some justification on technical monopoly grounds when initially introduced for railroads; it has none now for any means of transport. Another example is detailed regulation of banking.

7. A similar example, but one which deserves special mention because of its implicit censorship and violation of free speech, is the control of radio and television by the Federal Communications Commission.

8. Present social security programs, especially the old-age and retirement programs compelling people in effect (a) to spend a specified fraction of their income on the purchase of retirement annuity, (b) to buy the annuity from a publicly operated enterprise.

9. Licensure provisions in various cities and states which restrict particular enterprises or occupations or professions to people who have a license, where the license is more than a receipt for a tax which anyone who wishes to enter the activity may pay.

10. So-called "public-housing" and the host of other subsidy programs directed at fostering residential construction such as F.H.A. and V.A. guarantee of mortgage, and the like.

11. Conscription to man the military services in peacetime. The appropriate free market arrangement is volunteer military forces; which is to say, hiring men to serve. There is no justification for not paying whatever price is necessary to attract the required number of men. Present arrangements are inequitable and arbitrary, seriously interfere with the freedom of young men to shape their lives, and probably are even more costly than the market alternative. (Universal military training to provide a reserve for war time is a different problem and may be justified on liberal grounds.)

12. National parks, as noted above.

13. The legal prohibition on the carrying of mail for profit.

14. Publicly owned and operated toll roads, as noted above.

This list is far from comprehensive.

Norman M. Thomas, 1884–1968

Upon the death of Eugene V. Debs in 1926, Norman Thomas became the head of the Socialist party. He ran for president six times (1928–1948) as the Socialist candidate, and in 1932 gained almost 900,000 votes.

Thomas' socialism was as much a product of his church background and his devotion to the Social Gospel of Walter Rauschenbusch as it was the consequence of the influence of Karl Marx. Thomas graduated from Princeton in 1905 at the top of his class and after some travel and settlement house work, attended the Union Theological Seminary. He graduated in 1911, was ordained a Presbyterian minister, and became pastor of a church in the East Harlem area of New York City. He was distressed by the poverty that he daily encountered and slowly began to reject the conservatism of his earlier years. During World War I he became a pacifist, and he held to this view through another world war much to his political detriment.

Thomas was an unrelenting, if civil, critic of New Deal Democrats as well as traditionally conservative Republicans. Although many of his proposals were adopted by the Democrats—low-cost public housing, five-day work week, minimum wages, the abolition of child labor, social security—Thomas felt that all reforms would fall short unless coupled with nationalization of major industries and banks and extensive public planning. Production for profit could only continue to maldistribute income and wealth. The New Deal sought to preserve capitalism, he believed, just when it was clear that capitalism was the problem.

Thomas and the Socialist party were doomed by the political success of the New Deal and by Thomas' opposition to U.S. involvement in World War II, although he supported the war effort after Pearl Harbor.

Despite his commitment to collective values, Thomas' brand of socialism was well laced with liberal values. He was a staunch defender of individual rights and a founder of the American Civil Liberties Union. He was a fierce critic of Stalinism yet supported the rights of Communists to speak and organize.

The following selection is an example of Thomas' attack on the limits of the New Deal.

Norman Thomas

Why I Am a Socialist (1936)

This little pamphlet is neither a confession, a true story, nor an autobiography. There is no reason why I am a Socialist which does not apply with equal force to other men and women. I am a Socialist because I believe that in Socialism, in this day and generation lies our best, indeed our only hope of plenty, peace and freedom. Or to put the matter negatively, I am a Socialist because I believe that in Socialism lies our only escape from a long

Source: Norman Thomas, *Why I Am a Socialist* (New York: League for Industrial Democracy, 1936).

cycle of poverty, dictatorship and war. . . .

. . . One of the striking facts about our present improvement in business conditions (this is written early in 1936) is the widespread recognition, even by its beneficiaries, that "recovery" is insecure and impermanent.

Despite the present belief of our Tories that a return to the Coolidge epoch is possible and would be Paradise for them, not only is their hope fantastically impossible, but their Paradise was a sorry place at best. Its frantic gamblers' prosperity carried within it the seeds of the catastrophic depression which ended it, and while it lasted it was not far from hell for millions of exploited workers. At the height of our prosperity in 1929 we did not produce what we should have and we distributed what we produced with a cruel and grotesque lack of fairness or justice. As conservative a study as that of the Brookings Institution in *America's Capacity to Produce* tells us that a reasonable use of our then capacity to produce would have given us enough more to raise the annual income of every family in the United States to the $2,000 level without cutting off any at the top. (That also would have been worth doing.) There were 16.4 million families with incomes below that level. A third of our people then needed to be rehoused. There were then between 2 and 3 million unemployed. And many more million of share croppers and other tenant farmers had an annual income of less than $500 for each family.

But instead of going to work to use our productive capacity more efficiently in order to banish poverty, our system went into a kind of nose-spin. From an annual earned income of about $83 billion we dropped to an earned income of about $38 billion in 1932. Whatever the degree of our recovery since then, because of the New Deal or in spite of the New Deal, we have by no means regained the ground that was lost. The rate of increase of our production does not equal the rate of increase of our debt. Re-employment lags far behind the rate of increase in production since "recovery" began. There is no reason to expect the standing army of the unemployed to fall below 8 million; they must be kept quiet under the most hard-boiled administration by the old prescription of bread and circuses. Nothing else is in sight except a temporary boom of wild inflation with the dreadful aftermath of depression.

Now it is important to observe that the great depression which began in October, 1929, was not caused by any terrible natural disaster or by any new war. It was certainly not caused by any "radical" tinkering with our machinery. God, presumably, was in His Heaven, the Republicans in Washington, and the banker captains of capitalism were in full command. There was not even a New Deal for the conservatives to blame until 1933. For what happened, it is plain enough that the system itself and the captains and kings who ruled under it must bear the responsibility.

To my mind this simple statement of fact more than completes whatever might have been lacking in the proof which the Great War and the faults of the Coolidge prosperity afforded that the capitalist system was disintegrating beyond the possibility of a few simple reforms to set it right. It is easy enough in retrospect to criticize the various efforts of Mr. Roosevelt's New Deal in pursuit of "recovery and reform" from the standpoint of a sound progressivism theoretically possible under capitalism. Practically I do not believe that any reform measures *within the limitations of the American political and economic situation*, would have been feasible or successful to a greater degree than the New Deal has been. And that, even the friendly critic must agree, has brought no sense of permanence or security to masses of Americans who suffer all the pangs of poverty in the midst of potential abundance.

What are we to blame for this failure of men to use the natural resources, the machinery and the power which already are sufficient for modest abundance for all, for security and abundance rather than for insecurity and poverty? What indeed can we blame but the system itself, whether under the forms of the old deal or of the new? What is the nature of that system? For Mr. Hoover it was, curiously enough, a system of "rugged individualism." In order to justify capitalism he talked as if we lived in the age of the pioneers although, at the very time he spoke, that age had gone forever. The characteristic mark of the ownership of the means of production under Hoover, as under Roosevelt, is irresponsibility. Multitudes of absentee owners give no thought, no effort, no direction whatsoever, to the industries from whence they derive their incomes. A lucky guess with the investment of a comparatively small sum of money may make a man a millionaire. When the guess is on the Irish sweepstakes and the reward is not in the millions Mr. Hoover and the conservative economists call it gambling; when it is on stocks, oil wells, or corner lots, they call it investment and its rewards the profits of rugged individualism. Moreover, this system before the depression was no longer regulated by competition. It was largely subject to private monopoly. The hundred largest corporations controlled 50 percent of the business wealth of America and were, in turn, controlled by less than 2,000 directors, most of whom, our various investigations have discovered, did not direct.

The characteristic mark of our system is that it leaves in the hands of private owners the land, the natural resources, the great machinery, the power, necessary for our common life. And these private owners or the managers who act for them, use or fail to use what they own, solely in accordance with what they think will make for their own profit. Their profit depends upon relative scarcity. There would be no rent on land if there was not a limitation on convenient lots in the cities and a great difference in fertility and accessibility in the country. To keep up the price of bananas many a cargo boat has been partially lightened of its load in New York or New Orleans harbor. To put up the price of cotton under the New Deal we were taxed to pay great landowners not to plant cotton even though the children of the workers had no cotton for underclothes. This dependence of profit upon relative scarcity was somewhat obscured during the nineteenth and early twentieth century by the extraordinary increase in productive capacity and by the utilization of new lands in America by a rapidly increasing population. Today's technological improvement only

makes more glaring our incapacity to use it for abundance under the profit system.

The New Deal did, indeed, impose various regulations and some reforms on private capitalism. It even increased the amount of government ownership. But it still clung to the principle of production for profit. To a certain extent it replaced private capitalism by state capitalism. The distinction between state capitalism and Socialism must be kept in mind. Government ownership under Socialism is for the purpose of rewarding workers for their toil and for providing abundance. Government ownership and government regulation under capitalism, in the last analysis, are for the purpose of stabilizing and perpetuating the profit system and the division of the national income under which an owning class gets the cream and the workers get the skimmed milk.

I am a Socialist because reflection on these facts makes it so plain to me that it is idle to talk about using our machinery for abundance or of planning for abundance under the profit system. The whole theory of the profit system was that it worked automatically; it made planning unnecessary. True enough, it is an impossible task to plan successfully for the social use of what individuals own. It is plain nonsense to say that we don't have to plan for abundance. How can we expect to have anything but scarcity and insecurity if, in this age of specialization and great machinery, there is no plan *by cooperative effort* to see that we get what we need, and what can be produced?

The case for Socialism arises logically and reasonably out of our examination of the development of capitalism and its present failure to use the machinery of abundance for the conquest of poverty. Socialism says: "Let us go about the business of making machinery provide abundance directly. Let us begin by asking, not what price will bring profit to private owners, but how much food, clothing and shelter do we need for the good life for men. Then let us produce for the use of men, women, and children, in order to supply them with abundance."

Clearly this requires social ownership of the principal means of production and distribution. This not in order to abolish all private property but to give to the exploited workers, for the first time in the long history of mankind, the good things of life which labor of hand and brain, applied to the power-driven machine, can produce. We may make mistakes in social planning, but we can learn by our experience—without planning our whole economic system becomes one tragic mistake. Abundance is possible when we can set our engineers and technicians to planning for society, instead of planning, in so far as they can plan at all, for the profits of an owning class. . . .

But this is only part of the reason why I am a Socialist. It is not merely plenty that we want, but peace. Everybody knows that machinery which can conquer poverty also makes war incredibly disastrous. Yet war is more appropriate to the strife and hate and exploitation of our capitalist-nationalist system than is peace. You will observe that I have added to *capitalist* the word *nationalist* as a more comprehensive description of our disintegrating system. Men are divided not only into economic classes but into nations. And nations as well as men are divided into the Houses of Have and Have-not. We live in an interdependent world where not even the capitalist nations with the most resources, the United States, the British and French empires, are fully self-sufficient. Yet each nation claims absolute sovereignty, absolute sway over its citizens, and blindly sees its economic prosperity, not in cooperation, but in shutting out its neighbors from its own markets. Meanwhile it seeks aggressively to capture the markets of the world, to obtain sources of raw materials outside its borders, and a place for its capitalists to invest more profitably than at home the surplus wealth they have acquired by the successful exploitation of the workers who are their own fellow countrymen.

Modern wars arise out of the clash of nations for power and profit. The heady wine of an emotional patriotism makes men blind and drunk so that they cannot see that out of this struggle for power and profit there can be neither true prosperity nor true peace. Some things indeed we may do now to make our participation in war less likely. We cannot make peace secure or glorious under the loyalties of the institutions of capitalist-nationalism. It was my conviction of this truth which finally made me a Socialist during the Great War of 1914–1918. It is a conviction which has ever deepened. The hardest task for Socialism, as recent history shows, is to bring about a real unity of workers with hand and brain across the lines of nation, race and creed. Yet it is only in the federation of cooperative commonwealths, to which, alas, even Socialists have been more loyal in word than in deed, that there is hope of lasting peace.

The third reason that I have already suggested for my faith in Socialism is that I want a world of freedom. This we do not have and cannot have under the shadow of war and the bondage of capitalist exploitation. Diogenes, with his lantern, might find an honest man in our present society, but it would take a strong searchlight to find a free man. Of course in all generations there is a sense in which freedom is something which must be won. It is also, if it is to be real, something which must be shared. None of us is free in a country where Tom Mooney and Warren K. Billings are still in jail; where a Governor like McNutt of Indiana can arbitrarily proclaim military law superseding the ordinary civil law for purposes of keeping labor in order; where the hideous floggings of Florida and the terror of night riding in Arkansas and Alabama are used to keep workers in subjection. All workers live more or less in fear of those who control their jobs or the tools without which they have no jobs. There is, for a great many of us, a kind of haunting fear of a jobless tomorrow or an unwanted and unrecompensed old age. These things can be ended. They can be ended with the end of exploitation which a proper control of a machine age makes possible. They can be ended by a society of comrades. The Tree of Freedom today has feeble roots for itself except as it may grow in the soil of shared abundance.

But it is just at this point that Socialism is most often challenged. It is asserted that Socialism is an end to freedom, not the beginning of a larger liberty. Those who make that assertion very often are people like the members of the present Liberty League in America to whom freedom means only the right to grab all you can and keep all you have grabbed. This is not true freedom at all. The freedom we seek is the freedom which guarantees to the individual, justice even from those who do not wish to be just to him; which assures to him to the right "to know, to utter, and to argue freely according to conscience"—in short that noble company of rights: free speech, free press, free assemblage, free association, for which man has so long struggled. It is true enough that under the circumstances of a machine age which make some collectivism imperative we cannot have the freedom of Daniel Boone or one of the pioneers whose ideal was to live so far from his neighbors that he could not hear his neighbor's hound dog bark. The price of our freedom is freedom in fellowship or in cooperation. Moreover it is true that there is a discipline which the struggle against tyranny requires which may sometimes compel a subordination of individual "rights" in the essential struggle to change the system.

Nevertheless I am a Socialist and not a Communist largely because I believe that even in a transition period we must maintain civil and religious liberty for the individual. Very great things have been accomplished in Russia. The most disquieting fact about Russia is that there is so little sign that the dictatorship is withering away. That dictatorship still imposes a rigid regimentation and at times prostitutes justice to terrorism. When Kirov was assassinated by

a former Communist it was a terrible crime. But when the Russian government thereupon put to death more than a hundred persons on its blacklist and increased the bitterness of imprisonment or surveillance for unknown hundreds it was a greater crime. It was a crime not excused by the exigencies of a revolutionary crisis. It was a crime directly derived from the Communist theory that justice is to be understood *only* in terms of the safety of that abstraction, the "working masses" which safety is infallibly interpreted by the dictatorship of the one party in power. In this sort of justice lies neither security nor liberty for the new society. They are to be found only in realizing true democracy. This must be more than nose counting if it is to have power or value. Those who really desire to maintain democracy will prove it by their understanding of civil liberty. This fact organized Socialism has accepted to a degree that Communism has not. Loyalty to the idea of justice and civil liberty for the individual may sometimes prove difficult in the hour of struggle. It is the only loyalty which can prevent the gradual degeneration of men under the new society to the level of a community of more or less well fed and well tended cows.

I am a Socialist, then, because I believe in freedom, peace, and plenty and know that they cannot be realized in my generation, or my children's or for many which may follow hereafter, unless they are realized promptly in a cooperative commonwealth or rather in a Federation of Cooperative Commonwealths which will embrace the world. . . .

* * * * *

. . . There has been encouraging progress made in the cooperation of men in the management of their own affairs. I ask you to consider with me the history of labor unionism. It is a magnificent record of the onward march of exploited workers. I ask you to consider what consumers' cooperatives have accomplished. They have shown the capacity of plain men and women to manage in voluntary association the distribution of goods on another principle than the principle of private profit. I ask you to examine the success of a great deal of public ownership—roads, schools, waterworks, etc.—even under the handicap of capitalist institutions and the profit system. The record is far better than a press belonging to big business would lead you to believe. Finally, I ask you to ponder with me the record that Socialists have made. It is not a perfect record. They have made mistakes. They have met defeat. But even in our own country the best governed city over the longest period of time is Milwaukee, Wisconsin, and the leader in that good government is the Socialist Party which has kept Mayor Hoan continuously in office for almost 20 years. Then look at the enormous progress already made toward socialism under the Communist Party in Russia. That progress has been made out of the pit of Czarist tyranny, war, revolution and attempted counter-revolution. Consider also the substantial progress, without domestic or foreign war, in the Scandinavian countries toward a new society under the political initiative of Socialist parties. I am a Socialist because examination of these achievements convinces me that Socialism is practicable.

Furthermore, reflection on all these things and upon the logic of the system persuades me that we need not look forward in America to a Socialism frustrated and corrupted by the lordship of an almighty political state. We can have industrial democracy. Socialized railroads and coal mines can be administered under directorates representing consumers and producers. Our general strategy in the holy war against poverty can be laid down by a council of war, an economic planning council, representative of agriculture as well as industry.

While we work out this change we can take better, not worse care of the unemployed, the old and the children. The change to the new order can take account of immediate demands of workers. They need not be fed only with the bread of hope in a better tomorrow. In proportion to the number of workers who awake and organize for themselves and their children the struggle can be carried on in orderly and peaceful fashion. Separate an owning class from its dupes and its resistance will be weak. The more peaceful the revolution the more priceless its boon. This does not imply passivism or faith in romantic parliamentarianism. The Socialism in which I believe must have the courage to stand out against tyrants and their dupes in face of war and fascism. We dare not stop with merely asking vested privilege and an owning class to grant us as a concession what is ours by right.

In this struggle the appeal is big enough for mankind. There is no man in the world who would not be better off with the menace of war and poverty and insecurity banished. There are few men in the world who would not, as individuals, be better off economically under the abundance of planned production for use. The appeal which moves me is an appeal to men and women of goodwill to bring in this Socialist society. But the very nature of our predatory society makes the appeal of Socialism strongest to workers. The term includes all who do the necessary, honorable and useful tasks of the world, who create its material or cultural wealth. We shall never have a true cooperative commonwealth until men think of their reward as workers who create all wealth and not any longer of their reward as owners of property which enables them to exploit other men's labor. That is one of the reasons why our great Socialist appeal must be always to the workers with hand and brain, in city and country. It is they who have so long been exploited. It is they who can and must be free.

Martin Luther King, Jr., 1929–1968

Martin Luther King, Jr., was both the active leader and symbol of the civil rights movement that altered American society in the 1960s. He was a passionate orator and writer. His words and deeds reaffirmed the underlying principles and rights of American democracy while he struggled to extend their protection to black Americans. Moreover, he espoused a philosophy of nonviolence, and his writings on nonviolent civil disobedience stand as classics within that tradition.

King came from a family of Baptist ministers. In 1947, he was ordained at Atlanta's Ebenezer Baptist Church where his father was pastor and which his grandfather had helped found. King received a divinity degree from Crozer Theological Seminary in Chester, Pennsylvania, in 1948, and then a Ph.D. in Systematic Theology in 1955 from Boston University. In 1954, he became minister of the Dexter Avenue Baptist Church in Montgomery, Alabama.

King's arrival in Montgomery was fortuitous. In 1955, he led the city's black community in its boycott of segregated municipal buses, which, unexpectedly, soon became an event of national importance. After the success of that year-long struggle, King helped establish the Southern Christian Leadership Conference (SCLC) in 1957 in order to help direct protests across the entire South.

King soon rose to national prominence helping to organize nonviolent protests for the cause of civil rights. In the late 1950s and early 1960s, King led a series of protests that captured the attention of the nation, and also its new president, John F. Kennedy. In August 1963, he helped lead a massive civil rights march on Washington, D.C. The crowning event of the march was Dr. King's "I Have A Dream" speech, which electrified the nation and laid the groundwork for a series of major civil rights acts which, ultimately, dismantled the institutions of legal segregation.

In 1964, Dr. King won the Nobel Peace Prize for his work on civil rights and his commitment to nonviolence. Yet King was not willing to rest on his laurels. Now that blacks had gained many formal legal rights, King sought to lead the struggle for fuller equality of participation in American life. He also began to speak out against the war in Vietnam, which, he believed, violated our tradition of respect for the sovereignty of other peoples and also threatened progress at home.

In 1965, King helped lead a massive voter registration drive in Selma, Alabama, a black-belt city where only 1 percent of blacks were able to vote. King and other marchers encountered massive opposition. They were beaten by counterdemonstrators and attacked with clubs, cattle prods, and dogs by local law enforcement officials and state troopers. Selma became an important national symbol, helping give President Lyndon Johnson the political support necessary to pass the Voting Rights Act of 1965. Declaring that "We Shall

Overcome," Johnson passed legislation banning a variety of devices and tactics that had prevented most southern blacks from voting.

After Selma, King turned his attention to the problems of urban and northern blacks. His nonviolent tactics and concern for rights were being challenged by younger, militant black leaders. Many argued that violent revolutionary tactics were needed to gain real freedom for blacks; "Black Power," not mere rights, was the only road for real emancipation. King held true to nonviolence, but he struggled mightily to build a domestic agenda that could address the economic needs of black and poor Americans, along with their legal rights to equal treatment.

In 1967, King joined with others to plan a "Poor Peoples Campaign," a nonviolent mass movement aimed at a major federal commitment to ending poverty. By this time, King's relationship with President Johnson was greatly strained, especially in the wake of King's antiwar stance and Johnson's further anger over a series of black riots in major American cities.

In March 1968, in the midst of planning for the Poor Peoples Campaign, King left for Memphis, Tennessee, to help lend support to striking sanitation workers in that city. Standing on the balcony of his motel room in Memphis, King was assassinated by a white sniper, James Earl Ray. His attempt to shape the next stage of the civil rights movement died with him.

Martin Luther King, Jr.

Letter from Birmingham Jail (1963)

My Dear Fellow Clergymen:

While confined here in the Birmingham city jail, I came across your recent statement calling my present activities "unwise and untimely." Seldom do I pause to answer criticism of my work and ideas. . . . But since I feel that you are men of genuine good will and that your criticisms are sincerely set forth, I want to try to answer your statement in what I hope will be patient and reasonable terms. . . .

I am here because I have organizational

SOURCE: Martin Luther King, Jr., *Why We Can't Wait* (New York: Harper & Row, 1963).

ties here. . . . But more basically, I am in Birmingham because injustice is here. . . .

I am cognizant of the interrelatedness of all communities and states. I cannot sit idly by in Atlanta and not be concerned about what happens in Birmingham. Injustice anywhere is a threat to justice everywhere. We are caught in an inescapable network of mutuality, tied in a single garment of destiny.

Whatever affects one directly, affects all indirectly. Never again can we afford to live with the narrow, provincial "outside agitator" idea. Anyone who lives inside the United States can never be considered an outsider anywhere within its bounds. It is unfortunate that demonstrations are taking place in Birmingham, but it is even more unfortunate that the city's white power structure left the Negro community with no alternative.

In any nonviolent campaign there are four basic steps: collection of the facts to determine whether injustices exist; negotiation; self-purification; and direct action. We have gone through all these steps in Birmingham.

There can be no gainsaying the fact that racial injustice engulfs this community. Birmingham is probably the most thoroughly segregated city in the United States. Its ugly record of brutality is widely known. Negroes have experienced grossly unjust treatment in the courts. There have been more unsolved bombings of Negro homes and churches in Birmingham than in any other city in the nation. These are the hard, brutal facts of the case. . . .

On the basis of these conditions, Negro leaders sought to negotiate with the city fathers. But the latter consistently refused to engage in good-faith negotiation. Then, last September, came the opportunity to talk with leaders of Birmingham's economic community. In the course of the negotiations, certain promises were made by the merchants—for example, to remove the stores' humiliating racial signs.

On the basis of these promises, the Reverend Fred Shuttlesworth and the leaders of the Alabama Christian Movement for Human Rights agreed to a moratorium on all demonstrations. As the weeks and months went by, we realized that we were the victims of a broken promise. A few signs, briefly removed, returned; the others remained.

As in so many past experiences, our hopes had been blasted, and the shadow of deep disappointment settled upon us. We had no alternative except to prepare for direct action, whereby we would present our very bodies as a means of laying our case before the conscience of the local and the national community.

Mindful of the difficulties involved, we decided to undertake the process of self-purification. We began a series of workshops on nonviolence, and we repeatedly asked ourselves: "Are you able to accept blows without retaliation?" "Are you able to endure the ordeal of jail?" . . .

You may well ask, "Why direct action? Why sit-ins, marches, and so forth? Isn't negotiation a better path?" You are quite right in calling for negotiation. Indeed, this is the very purpose of direct action. Nonviolent direct action seeks to create such a crisis and foster such a tension that a community which has constantly refused to negotiate is forced to confront the issue. It seeks so to dramatize the issue that it can no longer be ignored.

My citing the creation of tension as part of the work of the nonviolent resister may sound rather shocking. But I must confess that I am not afraid of the word "tension." I have earnestly opposed violent tension, but there is a type of constructive, nonviolent tension which is necessary for growth.

Just as Socrates felt that it was necessary to create a tension in the mind so that individuals could rise from the bondage of myths and half-truths to the unfettered realm of creative analysis and objective appraisal, so must we see the need for nonviolent gadflies to create the kind of tension in society that will help men rise from the dark depths of prejudice and racism to the majestic heights of understanding and brotherhood.

The purpose of our direct-action program is to create a situation so crisis-packed that it will inevitably open the door to negotiation. I therefore concur with you in your call for negotiation. Too long has our beloved Southland been bogged down in a tragic effort to live in monologue rather than dialogue.

One of the basic points in your statement is that the action that I and my associates have taken in Birmingham is untimely. Some have asked: "Why didn't you give the new city administration time to act?" The only answer that I can give to this query is that the new

Birmingham administration must be prodded about as much as the outgoing one, before it will act. . . .

Lamentably, it is an historical fact that privileged groups seldom give up their privileges voluntarily. Individuals may see the moral light and voluntarily give up their unjust posture; but, as Reinhold Niebuhr has reminded us, groups tend to be more immoral than individuals.

We know through painful experience that freedom is never voluntarily given by the oppressor. It must be demanded by the oppressed. Frankly, I have yet to engage in a direct-action campaign that was "well timed" in view of those who have not suffered unduly from the disease of segregation.

For years now I have heard the word "Wait!" It rings in the ear of every Negro with piercing familiarity. This "Wait!" has almost always meant "Never." We must come to see, with one of our distinguished jurists, that "justice too long delayed is justice denied."

We have waited for more than 340 years for our constitutional and God-given rights. The nations of Asia and Africa are moving with jetlike speed toward gaining political independence, but we still creep at horse-and-buggy pace toward gaining a cup of coffee at a lunch counter. Perhaps it is easy for those who have never felt the stinging darts of segregation to say, "Wait."

But when you have seen vicious mobs lynch your mothers and fathers at will and drown your sisters and brothers at whim;

when you have seen hate-filled policemen curse, kick and even kill your black brothers and sisters;

when you see the vast majority of your twenty million Negro brothers smothering in an airtight cage of poverty in the midst of an affluent society;

when you suddenly find your tongue twisted and your speech stammering as you seek to explain to your six-year-old daughter why she can't go to the public amusement park that has just been advertised on televi-sion, and see tears welling up in her eyes when she is told that Funtown is closed to colored children, and see ominous clouds of inferiority beginning to form in her little mental sky, and see her beginning to distort her personality by developing an unconscious bitterness toward white people;

when you have to concoct an answer for a five-year-old son who is asking, "Daddy, why do white people treat colored people so mean?";

when you take a cross-country drive and find it necessary to sleep night after night in the uncomfortable corners of your automobile because no motel will accept you;

when you are humiliated day in and day out by nagging signs reading "white" and "colored";

when your first name becomes "nigger," your middle name becomes "boy" (however old you are) and your last name becomes "John," and your wife and mother are never given the respected title "Mrs.";

when you are harried by day and haunted by night by the fact that you are a Negro, living constantly at tiptoe stance, never quite knowing what to expect next, and are plagued with inner fears and outer resentments;

when you are forever fighting a degenerating sense of "nobodiness"—then you will understand why we find it difficult to wait.

There comes a time when the cup of endurance runs over, and men are no longer willing to be plunged into the abyss of despair. I hope, sirs, you can understand our legitimate and unavoidable impatience. . . .

One may well ask: "How can you advocate breaking some laws and obeying others?" The answer lies in the fact that there are two types of laws: just and unjust. I would be the first to advocate obeying just laws. One has not only a legal but a moral responsibility to obey just laws. Conversely, one has a moral responsibility to disobey unjust laws. I would agree with St. Augustine that "an unjust law is no law at all."

Now, what is the difference between the

two? How does one determine whether a law is just or unjust? A just law is a man-made code that squares with the moral law or the law of God. An unjust law is a code that is out of harmony with the moral law.

To put it in the terms of St. Thomas Aquinas: An unjust law is a human law that is not rooted in eternal law and natural law. Any law that uplifts human personality is just. Any law that degrades human personality is unjust.

All segregation statutes are unjust because segregation distorts the soul and damages the personality. It gives the segregator a false sense of superiority and the segregated a false sense of inferiority. . . .

Let us consider a more concrete example of just and unjust laws. An unjust law is a code that a numerical or power majority group compels a minority group to obey but does not make binding on itself. This is *difference* made legal. By the same token, a just law is a code that a majority compels a minority to follow and that it is willing to follow itself. This is *sameness* made legal.

Let me give another explanation. A law is unjust if it is inflicted on a minority that, as a result of being denied the right to vote, had no part in enacting or devising the law. Who can say that the legislature of Alabama which set up that state's segregation laws was democratically elected?

Throughout Alabama all sorts of devious methods are used to prevent Negroes from becoming registered voters, and there are some counties in which, even though Negroes constitute a majority of the population, not a single Negro is registered. Can any law enacted under such circumstances be considered democratically structured?

Sometimes a law is just on its face and unjust in its application. For instance, I have been arrested on a charge of parading without a permit. Now, there is nothing wrong in having an ordinance which requires a permit for a parade. But such an ordinance becomes unjust when it is used to maintain segregation and to deny citizens the First-Amendment privilege of peaceful assembly and protest.

I hope you are able to see the distinction I am trying to point out. In no sense do I advocate evading or defying the law, as would the rabid segregationist. That would lead to anarchy.

One who breaks an unjust law must do so openly, lovingly and with a willingness to accept the penalty. I submit that an individual who breaks a law that conscience tells him is unjust, and who willingly accepts the penalty of imprisonment in order to arouse the conscience of the community over its injustice, is in reality expressing the highest respect for law.

Of course, there is nothing new about this kind of civil disobedience. It was evidenced sublimely in the refusal of Shadrach, Meshach, and Abednego to obey the laws of Nebuchadnezzar, on the ground that a higher moral law was at stake. It was practiced superbly by the early Christians, who were willing to face hungry lions and the excruciating pain of chopping blocks rather than submit to certain unjust laws of the Roman Empire.

To a degree, academic freedom is a reality today because Socrates practiced civil disobedience. In our own nation, the Boston Tea Party represented a massive act of civil disobedience.

We should never forget that everything Adolf Hitler did in Germany was "legal" and everything the Hungarian freedom fighters did in Hungary was "illegal." It was "illegal" to aid and comfort a Jew in Hitler's Germany. Even so, I am sure that, had I lived in Germany at the time, I would have aided and comforted my Jewish brothers. If today I lived in a Communist country where certain principles dear to the Christian faith are suppressed, I would openly advocate disobeying that country's anti-religious laws.

I must make two honest confessions to you, my Christian and Jewish brothers. First, I must confess that over the past few years I have been gravely disappointed with the white moderate. I have almost reached the regrettable conclusion that the Negro's great stumbling block in his stride toward freedom is not the White Citizen's Counciler or the Ku Klux Klanner, but the white moderate, who is more devoted to "order" than to justice; who prefers a negative peace which is the absence of tension to a positive peace which is the presence of justice; who constantly says, "I agree with you in the goal you seek, but I cannot agree with your methods of direct action"; who paternalistically believes he can set the timetable for another man's freedom; who lives by a mythical concept of time and who constantly advises the Negro to wait for a "more convenient season."

Shallow understanding from people of good will is more frustrating than absolute misunderstanding from people of ill will. Lukewarm acceptance is much more bewildering than outright rejection.

I had hoped that the white moderate would understand that law and order exist for the purpose of establishing justice and that when they fail in this purpose they become the dangerously structured dams that block the flow of social progress.

I had hoped that the white moderate would understand that the present tension in the South is a necessary phase of the transition from an obnoxious negative peace, in which the Negro passively accepted his unjust plight, to a substantive and positive peace, in which all men will respect the dignity and worth of human personality.

Actually, we who engage in nonviolent direct action are not the creators of tension. We merely bring to the surface the hidden tension that is already alive. We bring it out in the open, where it can be seen and dealt with. Like a boil that can never be cured so long as it is covered up but must be opened with all its ugliness to the natural medicines of air and light, injustice must be exposed, with all the tension its exposure creates, to the light of human conscience and the air of national opinion, before it can be cured. . . .

Human progress never rolls in on wheels of inevitability; it comes through the tireless efforts of men willing to be co-workers with God, and without this hard work, time itself becomes an ally of the forces of stagnation. We must use time creatively, in the knowledge that the time is always ripe to do right.

Now is the time to make real the promise of democracy and transform our pending national elegy into a creative psalm of brotherhood. Now is the time to lift our national policy from the quicksand of racial injustice to the solid rock of human dignity.

You speak of our activity in Birmingham as extreme. At first I was rather disappointed that fellow clergymen would see my nonviolent efforts as those of an extremist. I began thinking about the fact that I stand in the middle of two opposing forces in the Negro community.

One is a force of complacency, made up in part of Negroes who, as a result of long years of oppression, are so drained of self-respect and a sense of "somebodiness" that they have adjusted to segregation; and in part of a few middle-class Negroes who, because of a degree of academic and economic security and because in some ways they profit by segregation, have become insensitive to the problems of the masses.

The other force is one of bitterness and hatred, and it comes perilously close to advocating violence. It is expressed in the various black nationalist groups that are springing up across the nation, the largest and best-known being Elijah Muhammad's Muslim movement. Nourished by the Negro's frustration over the continued existence of racial discrimination, this movement is made up of people who have lost faith in America, who have absolutely repudiated Christianity, and who have concluded that the white man is an incorrigible "devil."

I have tried to stand between these two

forces, saying that we need emulate neither the "do-nothingism" of the complacent nor the hatred and despair of the black nationalist. For there is the more excellent way of love and nonviolent protest. I am grateful to God that, through the influence of the Negro church, the way of nonviolence became an integral part of our struggle. . . .

Oppressed people cannot remain oppressed forever. The yearning for freedom eventually manifests itself, and that is what has happened to the American Negro. Something within has reminded him of his birthright of freedom, and something without has reminded him that it can be gained. Consciously or unconsciously, he has been caught up by the Zeitgeist, and with his black brothers of Africa and his brown and yellow brothers of Asia, South America and the Caribbean, the United States Negro is moving with a sense of great urgency toward the promised land of racial justice.

If one recognizes this vital urge that has engulfed the Negro community, one should readily understand why public demonstrations are taking place. The Negro has many pent-up resentments and latent frustrations, and he must release them. So let him march; let him make prayer pilgrimages to the city hall; let him go on freedom rides— and try to understand why he must do so.

If his repressed emotions are not released in nonviolent ways, they will seek expression through violence; this is not a threat but a fact of history. So I have not said to my people, "Get rid of your discontent." Rather, I have tried to say that this normal and healthy discontent can be channeled into the creative outlet of nonviolent direct action. And now this approach is being termed extremist. . . .

Was not Jesus an extremist for love: "Love your enemies, bless them that curse you, do good to them that hate you, and pray for them which despitefully use you, and persecute you."

Was not Amos an extremist for justice: "Let justice roll down like waters and righteousness like an ever-flowing stream.". . .

And John Bunyan: "I will stay in jail to the end of my days before I make a butchery of my conscience."

And Abraham Lincoln: "This nation cannot survive half slave and half free." And Thomas Jefferson: "We hold these truths to be self-evident, that all men are created equal. . . ."

So the question is not whether we will be extremists, but what kind of extremists we will be. Will we be extremists for hate or for love? Will we be extremists for the preservation of injustice or for the extension of justice? . . . Perhaps the South, the nation, and the world are in dire need of creative extremists.

I had hoped that the white moderate would see this need. Perhaps I was too optimistic; perhaps I expected too much. I suppose I should have realized that few members of the oppressor race can understand the deep groans and passionate yearnings of the oppressed race, and still fewer have the vision to see that injustice must be rooted out by strong, persistent, and determined action.

I am thankful, however, that some of our white brothers in the South have grasped the meaning of this social revolution and committed themselves to it. They are still all too few in quantity, but they are big in quality. Some— such as Ralph McGill, Lillian Smith, Harry Golden, James McBride Dabbs, Ann Braden, and Sarah Patton Boyle—have written about our struggle in eloquent and prophetic terms.

Others have marched with us down nameless streets of the South. They have languished in filthy, roach-infested jails, suffering the abuse and brutality of policemen who view them as "dirty nigger-lovers." Unlike so many of their moderate brothers and sisters, they have recognized the urgency of the moment and sensed the need for powerful "action" antidotes to combat the disease of segregation.

Let me take note of my other major disappointment. I have been so greatly disappointed with the white church and its leadership.

Of course, there are some notable exceptions. I am not unmindful of the fact that each of you has taken some significant stands on this issue. I commend you, Reverend Stallings, for your Christian stand on this past Sunday, in welcoming Negroes to your worship service on a nonsegregated basis. I commend the Catholic leaders of this state for integrating Spring Hill College several years ago. . . .

In spite of my shattered dreams, I came to Birmingham with the hope that the white religious leadership of this community would see the justice of our cause and, with deep moral concern, would serve as the channel through which our just grievances could reach the power structure. I had hoped that each of you would understand. But again I have been disappointed. . . .

I hope the church as a whole will meet the challenge of this decisive hour. But even if the church does not come to the aid of justice, I have no despair about the future. I have no fear about the outcome of our struggle in Birmingham, even if our motives are at present misunderstood. We will reach the goal of freedom in Birmingham and all over the nation, because the goal of America is freedom.

Abused and scorned though we may be, our destiny is tied up with America's destiny. Before the pilgrims landed at Plymouth, we were here. For more than two centuries our forebears labored in this country, without wages; they made cotton king; they built the homes of their masters while suffering gross injustice and shameful humiliation—and yet out of a bottomless vitality they continued to thrive and develop.

If the inexpressible cruelties of slavery could not stop us, the opposition we now face will surely fail. We will win our freedom because the sacred heritage of our nation and the eter-

nal will of God are embodied in our echoing demands.

Before closing I feel impelled to mention one other point in your statement that has troubled me profoundly. You warmly commended the Birmingham police force for keeping "order" and "preventing violence."

I doubt that you would have so warmly commended the police force if you had seen its dogs sinking their teeth into unarmed, nonviolent Negroes. I doubt that you would so quickly commend the policemen if you were to observe their ugly and inhumane treatment of Negroes here in the city jail; if you were to watch them push and curse old Negro women and young Negro girls; if you were to see them slap and kick old Negro men and young boys; if you were to observe them, as they did on two occasions, refuse to give us food because we wanted to sing our grace together. I cannot join you in your praise of the Birmingham police department.

It is true that the police have exercised a degree of discipline in handling the demonstrators. In this sense they have conducted themselves rather "nonviolently" in public. But for what purpose? To preserve the evil system of segregation. . . .

I wish you had commended the Negro sit-inners and demonstrators of Birmingham for their sublime courage, their willingness to suffer, and their amazing discipline in the midst of great provocation. One day the South will recognize its real heroes. They will be the James Merediths, with the noble sense of purpose that enables them to face jeering and hostile mobs, and with the agonizing loneliness that characterizes the life of the pioneer. They will be old, oppressed, battered Negro women, symbolized in a seventy-two-year-old woman in Montgomery, Alabama, who rose up with a sense of dignity and with her people decided not to ride segregated buses, and who responded with ungrammatical profundity to one who inquired about her weariness: "My feets is tired, but my soul is at rest."

They will be the young high school and college students, the young ministers of the gospel and a host of their elders, courageously and nonviolently sitting in at lunch counters and willingly going to jail for conscience' sake. One day the South will know that when these disinherited children of God sat down at lunch counters, they were in reality standing up for what is best in the American dream and for the most sacred values in our Judaeo-Christian heritage, thereby bringing our nation back to those great wells of democracy which were dug deep by the founding fathers in their formulation of the Constitution and the Declaration of Independence.

Never before have I written so long a letter. I'm afraid it is much too long to take your precious time. I can assure you that it would have been much shorter if I had been writing from a comfortable desk, but what else can one do when he is alone in a narrow jail cell, other than write long letters, think long thoughts and pray long prayers? . . .

Yours for the cause of peace and brotherhood,

Martin Luther King, Jr.

Students for a Democratic Society (1962)

Students for a Democratic Society (SDS) was the leading voice of the student movement of the early 1960s. It grew out of the old left Democratic Socialist League for Industrial Democracy, but by the early 1960s, SDS members began to develop a vision and analysis that differed from those of their elders.

New Left students saw themselves first and foremost as critics of liberalism, a system they derisively labeled "corporate liberalism." They assumed that conservative capitalism was irrelevant as a future model of political economy, but they also believed that welfare-state capitalism ultimately served conservative ends. Liberals, they contended, used the Cold War to promote military spending in order to stimulate the economy, and thus avoid unemployment and stagnation. They argued that liberals had joined with anticommunist conservatives in the 1950s to oppose left-leaning governments in Iran and Guatemala in order to provide U.S. firms with new markets for the surplus production of American factories and farms. Moreover, New Left critics maintained that capitalism required high levels of mass consumption and large numbers of docile, trained technicians. Liberals, they charged, provided those needs by promoting programs like social security and unemployment insurance, and building and financing large state universities. In each instance, they contended, corporate liberalism had taken the egalitarian instincts of most Americans and used them to serve the needs of the growing corporate system.

New Left students on campuses across the country began to organize a movement that they believed could move "beyond" liberalism to a true "participatory democracy." They attacked the bureaucracy and repression of communist regimes, and also the inequality of capitalist regimes. Welfare-state bureaucracy came under attack as both remote and demeaning. They spoke in vague terms of "empowering" people so that they could exercise authority over the institutions that affected their lives. They spoke glowingly of decentralized government and economic democracy.

The Port Huron Statement articulated the fundamental values and purposes of the SDS, and was approved by the SDS convention held in Port Huron, Michigan, in 1962. Its primary author was Tom Hayden. Well over 100,000 copies of this document were distributed on college campuses all over the United States.

The Port Huron Statement represents the New Left in its most innocent and, perhaps, appealing moment. Within six years, the New Left was splintered into many competing factions; almost all of which had become far more Leninist (and far less democratic) in their outlook. Nonetheless, their democratic, egalitarian, and antiestablishment views have continued to influence American political thinking in a variety of ways, often unanticipated by New Left members themselves.

Students for a Democratic Society

Port Huron Statement (1962)

INTRODUCTION: AGENDA FOR A GENERATION

We are people of this generation, bred in at least modest comfort, housed now in universities, looking uncomfortably to the world we inherit.

When we were kids the United States was the wealthiest and strongest country in the world; the only one with the atom bomb, the least scarred by modern war, an initiator of the United Nations that we thought would distribute Western influence throughout the world. Freedom and equality for each individual, government of, by, and for the people—these American values we found good, princi-

SOURCE: Massimo Teodori, ed., *The New Left: A Documentary History* (Indianapolis: Bobbs-Merrill, 1969).

ples by which we could live as men. Many of us began maturing in complacency.

As we grew, however, our comfort was penetrated by events too troubling to dismiss. First, the permeating and victimizing fact of human degradation, symbolized by the Southern struggle against racial bigotry, compelled most of us from silence to activism. Second, the enclosing fact of the Cold War, symbolized by the presence of the Bomb, brought awareness that we ourselves, and our friends, and millions of abstract "others" we knew more directly because of our common peril, might die at any time. We might deliberately ignore, or avoid, or fail to feel all other human problems, but not these two, for these were too immediate and crushing in their impact, too challenging in the demand that we as individuals take the responsibility for encounter and resolution.

While these and other problems either directly oppressed us or rankled our consciences and became our own subjective concerns, we began to see complicated and disturbing paradoxes in our surrounding America. The declaration "all men are created equal . . ." rang hollow before the facts of Negro life in the South and the big cities of the North. The proclaimed peaceful intentions of the United States contradicted its economic and military investments in the Cold War status quo.

Not only did tarnish appear on our image of American virtue, not only did disillusion occur when the hypocrisy of American ideals was discovered, but we began to sense that what we had originally seen as the American Golden Age was actually the decline of an era. The worldwide outbreak of revolution against colonialism and imperialism, the entrenchment of totalitarian states, the menace of war, overpopulation, international disorder, supertechnology—these trends were testing the tenacity of our own commitment to democracy and freedom and our abilities to visualize their application to a world in upheaval.

Our work is guided by the sense that we may be the last generation in the experiment with living. But we are a minority—the vast majority of our people regard the temporary equilibriums of our society and world as eternally-functional parts. In this is perhaps the outstanding paradox: we ourselves are imbued with urgency, yet the message of our society is that there is no viable alternative to the present. Beneath the reassuring tones of the politicians, beneath the common opinion that America will "muddle through," beneath the stagnation of those who have closed their minds to the future, is the pervading feeling that there simply are no alternatives, that our times have witnessed the exhaustion not only of Utopias, but of any new departures as well. Feeling the press of complexity upon the emptiness of life, people are fearful of the thought that at any moment things might

be thrust out of control. They fear change itself, since change might smash whatever invisible framework seems to hold back chaos for them now. For most Americans, all crusades are suspect, threatening. The fact that each individual sees apathy in his fellows perpetuates the common reluctance to organize for change. The dominant institutions are complex enough to blunt the minds of their potential critics, and entrenched enough to swiftly dissipate or entirely repel the energies of protest and reform, thus limiting human expectancies. Then, too, we are a materially improved society, and by our own improvements we seem to have weakened the case for further change.

Some would have us believe that Americans feel contentment amidst prosperity—but might it not better be called a glaze above deeply-felt anxieties about their role in the new world? And if these anxieties produce a developed indifference to human affairs, do they not as well produce a yearning to believe there *is* an alternative to the present, that something *can* be done to change circumstances in the school, the workplaces, the bureaucracies, the government? It is to this latter yearning, at once the spark and engine of change, that we direct our present appeal. The search for truly democratic alternatives to the present, and a commitment to social experimentation with them, is a worthy and fulfilling human enterprise, one which moves us and, we hope, others today. On such a basis do we offer this document of our convictions and analysis: as an effort in understanding and changing the conditions of humanity in the late twentieth century, an effort rooted in the ancient, still unfulfilled conception of man attaining determining influence over his circumstances of life.

VALUES

Making values explicit—an initial task in establishing alternatives—is an activity that has been devalued and corrupted. The conventional moral terms of the age, the politician moralities—"free world," "people's democracies"—reflect realities poorly, if at all, and seem to function more as ruling truths than as descriptive principles. But neither has our experience in the universities brought us moral enlightenment. Our professors and administrators sacrifice controversy to public relations; their curriculums change more slowly than the living events of the world; their skills and silence are purchased by investors in the arms race; passion is called unscholastic. The questions we might want raised—what is really important? can we live in a different and better way? if we wanted to change society, how would we do it?—are not thought to be questions of a "fruitful, empirical nature," and thus are brushed aside.

Unlike youth in other countries we are used to moral leadership being exercised and moral dimensions being clarified by our elders. But today, for us, not even the liberal and socialist preachments of the past seem adequate to the forms of the present. Consider the old slogans: Capitalism Cannot Reform Itself, United Front Against Fascism, General Strike, All Out on May Day. Or, more recently, No Cooperation with Commies and Fellow Travellers, Ideologies Are Exhausted, Bipartisanship, No Utopias. These are incomplete, and there are few new prophets. It has been said that our liberal and socialist predecessors were plagued by vision without program, while our own generation is plagued by program without vision. All around us there is astute grasp of method, technique—the committee, the *ad hoc* group, the lobbyist, the hard and soft sell, the make, the projected image—but, if pressed critically, such expertise is incompetent to explain its implicit ideals. It is highly fashionable to identify oneself by old categories, or by naming a respected political figure, or by explaining "how we would vote" on various issues.

Theoretic chaos has replaced the idealistic thinking of old—and, unable to reconstitute theoretic order, men have condemned idealism itself. Doubt has replaced hopefulness—and men act out a defeatism that is labelled realistic. The decline of utopia and hope is in fact one of the defining features of social life today. The reasons are various: the dreams of the older left were perverted by Stalinism and never recreated; the congressional stalemate makes men narrow their view of the possible; the specialization of human activity leaves little room for sweeping thought; the horrors of the twentieth century, symbolized in the gas-ovens and concentration camps and atom bombs, have blasted hopefulness. To be idealistic is to be considered apocalyptic, deluded. To have no serious aspirations, on the contrary, is to be "toughminded."

In suggesting social goals and values, therefore, we are aware of entering a sphere of some disrepute. Perhaps matured by the past, we have no sure formulas, no closed theories—but that does not mean values are beyond discussion and tentative determination. A first task of any social movement is to convince people that the search for orienting theories and the creation of human values is complex but worthwhile. We are aware that to avoid platitudes we must analyze the concrete conditions of social order. But to direct such an analysis we must use the guideposts of basic principles. Our own social values involve conceptions of human beings, human relationships, and social systems.

We regard *men* as infinitely precious and possessed of unfulfilled capacities for reason, freedom, and love. In affirming these principles we are aware of countering perhaps the dominant conceptions of man in the twentieth century: that he is a thing to be manipulated, and that he is inherently incapable of directing his own affairs. We oppose the depersonalization that reduces human beings to the status of things—if anything, the brutalities of the twentieth century teach that means and ends are intimately related, that vague appeals to "posterity" cannot justify the mutilations of the present. . . .

This kind of independence does not mean egotistic individualism—the object is not to have one's way so much as it is to have a way that is one's own. Nor do we deify man— we merely have faith in his potential.

Human relationships should involve fraternity and honesty. Human interdependence is contemporary fact: human brotherhood must be willed, however, as a condition of future survival and as the most appropriate form of social relations. Personal links between man and man are needed, especially to go beyond the partial and fragmentary bonds of function that bind men only as worker to worker, employer to employee, teacher to student, American to Russian.

Loneliness, estrangement, isolation describe the vast distance between man and man today. These dominant tendencies cannot be overcome by better personnel management, nor by improved gadgets, but only when a love of man overcomes the idolotrous worship of things by man. As the individualism we affirm is not egoism, the selflessness we affirm is not self-elimination. On the contrary, we believe in generosity of a kind that imprints one's unique individual qualities in the relation to other men, and to all human activity. Further, to dislike isolation is not to favor the abolition of privacy; the latter differs from isolation in that it occurs or is abolished according to individual will.

We would replace power rooted in possession, privileged, or circumstance by power and uniqueness rooted in love, reflectiveness, reason, and creativity. As a *social system* we seek the establishment of a democracy of individual participation, governed by two central aims: that the individual share in those social decisions determining the quality and direction of his life; that society be organized to encourage independence in men and provide the media for their common participation.

In a participatory democracy, the political life would be based in several root principles:

that decision-making of basic social consequence be carried on by public groupings;

that politics be seen positively, as the art of collectively creating an acceptable pattern of social relations;

that politics has the function of bringing people out of isolation and into community, thus being a necessary, though not sufficient, means of finding meaning in personal life;

that the political order should serve to clarify problems in a way instrumental to their solution; it should provide outlets for the expression of personal grievance and aspiration; opposing views should be organized so as to illuminate choices and facilitate the attainment of goals; channels should be commonly available to relate men to knowledge and to power so that private problems—from bad recreation facilities to personal alienation—are formulated as general issues.

The economic sphere would have as its basis the principles:

that work should involve incentives worthier than money or survival. It should be educative, not stultifying; creative, not mechanical; self-directed, not manipulated, encouraging independence, a respect for others, a sense of dignity and a willingness to accept social responsibility, since it is this experience that has crucial influence on habits, perceptions and individual ethics;

that the economic experience is so personally decisive that the individual must share in its full determination;

that the economy itself is of such social importance that its major resources and means of production should be open to democratic participation and subject to democratic social regulation.

Like the political and economic ones, major social institutions—cultural, educational, rehabilitative, and others—should be generally organized with the well-being and dignity of man as the essential measure of success.

In social change or interchange, we find

violence to be abhorrent because it requires generally the transformation of the target, be it a human being or a community of people, into a depersonalized object of hate. It is imperative that the means of violence be abolished and the institutions—local, national, international—that encourage nonviolence as a condition of conflict be developed.

These are our central values, in skeletal form. It remains vital to understand their denial or attainment in the context of the modern world. . . .

POLITICS WITHOUT PUBLICS

The American political system is not the democratic model of which its glorifiers speak. In actuality it frustrates democracy by confusing the individual citizen, paralyzing policy discussion, and consolidating the irresponsible power of military and business interests.

A crucial feature of the political apparatus in America is that greater differences are harbored within each major party than the differences existing between them. Instead of two parties presenting distinctive and significant differences of approach, what dominates the system is a natural interlocking of Democrats from Southern states with the more conservative elements of the Republican party. This arrangement of forces is blessed by the seniority system of Congress which guarantees congressional committee domination by conservatives—ten of seventeen committees in the Senate and thirteen of twenty-one in the House of Representatives are chaired currently by Dixiecrats.

The party overlap, however, is not the only structural antagonist of democracy in politics. First, the localized nature of the party system does not encourage discussion of national and international issues: thus problems are not raised by and for people, and political representatives usually are unfettered from any responsibilities to the general public except those regarding parochial matters. Second, whole constituencies are divested of the full

political power they might have: many Negroes in the South are prevented from voting, migrant workers are disenfranchised by vari-.ous residence requirements, some urban and suburban dwellers are victimized by gerrymandering, and poor people are too often without the power to obtain political representation. Third, the focus of political attention is significantly distorted by the enormous lobby force, composed predominantly of business interests, spending hundreds of millions each year in an attempt to conform facts about productivity, agriculture, defense, and social services, to the wants of private economic groupings.

What emerges from the party contradiction and insulation of privately held power is the organized political stalemate: calcification dominates flexibility as the principle of parliamentary organization, frustration is the expectancy of legislators intending liberal reform, and Congress becomes less and less central to national decision-making, especially in the area of foreign policy. In this context, confusion and blurring are built into the formulation of issues, long-range priorities are not discussed in the rational manner needed for policy-making, the politics of personality and "image" become a more important mechanism than the construction of issues in a way that affords each voter a challenging and real option. The American voter is buffeted from all directions by pseudo-problems, by the structurally-initiated sense that nothing political is subject to human mastery. Worried by his mundane problems which never get solved, but constrained by the common belief that politics is an agonizingly slow accommodation of views, he quits all pretense of bothering. . . .

THE UNIVERSITY AND SOCIAL CHANGE

There is perhaps little reason to be optimistic about the above analysis. True, the Dixiecrat-GOP coalition is the weakest point in the dominating complex of corporate, military and political power. But the civil rights, peace, and student movements are too poor and socially slighted, and the labor movement too quiescent, to be counted with enthusiasm. From where else can power and vision be summoned? We believe that the universities are an overlooked seat of influence.

First, the university is located in a permanent position of social influence. Its educational function makes it indispensable and automatically makes it a crucial institution in the formation of social attitudes. Second, in an unbelievably complicated world, it is the central institution for organizing, evaluating, and transmitting knowledge. Third, the extent to which academic resources presently are used to buttress immoral social practice is revealed first, by the extent to which defense contracts make the universities engineers of the arms race. Too, the use of modern social science as a manipulative tool reveals itself in the "human relations" consultants to the modern corporations, who introduce trivial sops to give laborers feelings of "participation" or "belonging," while actually deluding them in order to further exploit their labor. And, of course, the use of motivational research is already infamous as a manipulative aspect of American politics. But these social uses of the universities' resources also demonstrate the unchangeable reliance by men of power on the men and storehouses of knowledge: this makes the university functionally tied to society in new ways, revealing new potentialities, new levers for change. Fourth, the university is the only mainstream institution that is open to participation by individuals of nearly any viewpoint.

These, at least, are facts, no matter how dull the teaching, how paternalistic the rules, how irrelevant the research that goes on. Social relevance, the accessibility to knowledge, and internal openness—these together make the university a potential base and agency in a movement of social change.

1. Any new left in America must be, in large measure, a left with real intellectual skills, committed to deliberativeness, honesty, reflection as working tools. The university permits the political life to be an adjunct to the academic one, and action to be informed by reason.

2. A new left must be distributed in significant social roles throughout the country. The universities are distributed in such a manner.

3. A new left must consist of younger people who matured in the post-war world, and partially be directed to the recruitment of younger people. The university is an obvious beginning point.

4. A new left must include liberals and socialists, the former for their relevance, the latter for their sense of thoroughgoing reforms in the system. The university is a more sensible place than a political party for these two traditions to begin to discuss their differences and look for political synthesis.

5. A new left must start controversy across the land, if national policies and national apathy are to be reversed. The ideal university is a community of controversy, within itself and in its effects on communities beyond.

6. A new left must transform modern complexity into issues that can be understood and felt close-up by every human being. It must give form to the feelings of helplessness and indifference, so that people may see the political, social, and economic sources of their private troubles and organize to change society. In a time of supposed prosperity, moral complacency, and political manipulation, a new left cannot rely on only aching stomachs to be the engine force of social reform. The case for change, for alternatives that will involve uncomfortable personal efforts, must be argued as never before. The university is a relevant place for all of these activities.

But we need not indulge in illusions: the university system cannot complete a movement of ordinary people making demands for a better life. From its schools and colleges across the nation, a militant left might awaken its allies, and by beginning the process towards peace, civil rights, and labor struggles, reinsert theory and idealism where too often reign confusion and political barter. The power of students and faculty united is not only potential; it has shown its actuality in the South, and in the reform movements of the North.

The bridge to political power, though, will be built through genuine cooperation, locally, nationally, and internationally, between a new left of young people, and an awakening community of allies. In each community we must look within the university and act with confidence that we can be powerful, but we must look outwards to the less exotic but more lasting struggles for justice.

To turn these possibilities into realities will involve national efforts at university reform by an alliance of students and faculty. They must wrest control of the educational process from the administrative bureaucracy. They must make fraternal and functional contact with allies in labor, civil rights, and other liberal forces outside the campus. They must import major public issues into the curriculum—research and teaching on problems of war and peace is an outstanding example. They must make debate and controversy, not dull pedantic cant, the common style for educational life. They must consciously build a base for their assault upon the loci of power.

As students for a democratic society, we are committed to stimulating this kind of social movement, this kind of vision and program in campus and community across the country. If we appear to seek the unattainable, as it has been said, then let it be known that we do so to avoid the unimaginable.

Betty Friedan, 1921–

Betty Friedan has been a leading feminist thinker and activist for more than two decades. Her most famous book, *The Feminine Mystique* (1963), had a cataclysmic effect on the early women's movement, and Friedan has remained at the center of the movement ever since. She was a founder of the National Organization of Women (NOW) and served as its first president from 1966 to 1970. Friedan took the lead in efforts to reform laws covering abortion, divorce, child support, and eligibility for insurance and credit in ways that she felt would enhance the independence of women. Like Charlotte Perkins Gilman, Friedan pushed beyond the demand for equal political rights to discuss the effects of family, home, church, and workplace on the development of the free female personality.

The following selection is a speech that Friedan delivered to the NOW convention in 1968. It is a good example of mainstream reformist feminism and the tensions that it faces in trying to achieve women's freedom and equality without threatening the institutions of marriage and family or the liberal democratic state.

Betty Friedan

Our Revolution Is Unique (1968)

We new feminists have begun to define ourselves—existentially—through action. We have learned that while we had much to learn from the black civil rights movement and their revolution against economic and racial oppression, our own revolution is unique: it must define its own ideology.

We can cut no corners; we are, in effect, where the black revolution was perhaps fifty years ago; but the speed with which our revolution is moving now is our unearned historical benefit from what has happened in that revolution. Yet there can be no illusion on our part that a separatist ideology copied from black power will work for us. Our tactics and strategy and, above all, our ideology must be firmly based in the historical, biological, economic, and psychological reality of our two-sexed world, which is not the same as the black reality and different also from the reality of the first feminist wave.

Thanks to the early feminists, we who have mounted this second stage of the feminist revolution have grown up with the right to vote, little as we may have used it for our own purposes. We have grown up with the right to higher education and to employment, and with some, not all, of the legal rights of equality. Insofar as we have moved on the periphery of the mainstream of society, with the skills and the knowledge to command its paychecks, even if insufficient; and to make decisions, even if not consulted beyond housework; we begin to have a self-respecting image of our-

selves, as women, not just in sexual relation to men, but as full human beings in society. We are able, at least some of us, to see men, in general or in particular, without blind rancor or hostility, and to face oppression as it reveals itself in our concrete experience with politicians, bosses, priests, or husbands. We do not need to suppress our just grievances. We now have enough courage to express them. And yet we are able to conceive the possibility of full affirmation for man. Man is not the enemy, but the fellow victim of the present half-equality. As we speak, act, demonstrate, testify, and appear on television on matters such as sex discrimination in employment, public accommodations, education, divorce-marriage reform, or abortion repeal, we hear from men who feel they can be freed to greater self-fulfillment to the degree that women are released from the binds that now constrain them.

This sense of freeing men as the other half of freeing women has always been there, even in the early writings of Mary Wollstonecraft, Elizabeth Stanton, and the rest; our action-created new awareness has confirmed this.

Another point we are conscious of in the new feminism is that we are a revolution for all, not for an exceptional few. This, above all, distinguishes us from those token spokeswomen of the period since women won the vote, the Aunt Toms who managed to get a place for themselves in society, and who were, I think, inevitably seduced into an accommodating stance, helping to keep the others quiet.

SOURCE: The President's Report to *NOW*, 1968.

We are beginning to know that no woman can achieve a real breakthrough alone, as long as sex discrimination exists in employment, under the law, in education, in mores, and in denigration of the image of women.

. . . We cannot say that all American women want equality, because we know that women, like all oppressed people, have accepted the traditional denigration by society. Some women have been too much hurt by denigration from others, by self-denigration, by lack of the experiences, education, and training needed to move in society as equal human beings, to have the confidence that they can so move in a competitive society. They say they don't want equality—they have to be happy, adjust to things as they are. Such women find us threatening. They find equality so frightening that they must wish the new feminists did not exist. And yet we see so clearly from younger women and students that to the degree that we push ahead and create opportunities for movement in society, in the process creating the "new women" who are *people first,* to that degree the threat will disappear.

We do not speak for every woman in America, but we speak for the *right* of every woman in America to become all she is capable of becoming—on her own and/or in partnership with a man. And we already know that we speak not for a few, not for hundreds, not for thousands, but for millions—especially for millions in the younger generation who have tasted more equality than their elders. We know this simply from the resonance, if you will, that our actions have aroused in society.

That wave of resonance is world wide. In Canada, they want to have an affiliate of our National Organization for Women, and propose that, ultimately, there will be a World Organization for Women. From Great Britain, France, Italy, the Scandinavian countries, Germany, Japan, New Zealand, women— young, vital new feminists—have asked for guidance.

WOMEN AND SEX

As an example of the new feminism in action, consider the matter of abortion law repeal. NOW was the first organization to speak on the basic rights of women on the question of abortion. We said that it is the inalienable human right of every woman to control her own reproductive process. To establish that right would require that all laws penalizing abortion be repealed, removed from the penal code; the state would not be empowered either to force or prevent a woman from having an abortion. Now many groups are working on abortion law repeal, while at the same time California and Washington, D.C., court decisions have spelled out the right of a woman to control her own reproduction.

What right has any man to say to any woman, "You must bear this child"? What right has any state to say it? The child-bearing decision is a woman's right and not a technical question needing the sanction of the state, nor should the state control access to birth control devices.

This question can only really be confronted in terms of the basic personhood and dignity of woman, which is violated forever if she does not have the right to control her own reproductive process. And the heart of this idea goes far beyond abortion and birth control.

Women, almost too visible as sex objects in this country today, are at the same time invisible people. As the Negro was the invisible man, so women are the invisible people in America today. To be taken seriously as people, women have to share in the decisions of government, of politics, of the church—not just to cook the church supper, but to preach the sermon; not just to look up the zip codes and address the envelopes, but to make the political decisions; not just to do the housework of industry, but to make some of the executive decisions. Women, above all, want to say what their own lives are going to be, what their own personalities are going to be, not permitting male experts to define what is "feminine" or isn't or should be.

The essence of the denigration of women is their definition as sex objects. And to confront our inequality, we must confront our own self-denigration and our denigration by society in these terms.

Am I saying therefore, that women must be liberated from sex? No. I am saying that sex will only be liberated, will only cease to be a sniggering dirty joke and an obsession in this society, when women are liberated, self-determining people, liberated to a creativity beyond motherhood, to a full human creativity.

Nor am I saying that women must be liberated from motherhood. I am saying that motherhood will only be liberated to be a joyous and responsible human act, when women are free to make, with full conscious choice and full human responsibility, the decision to be mothers. Then and only then, will they be able to embrace motherhood without conflict. When they are able to define themselves as people, not just as somebody's mother, not just as servants of children, not just as breeding receptacles, but as people for whom motherhood is a freely chosen part of life, and for whom creativity has many dimensions, as it has for men.

. . . I maintain that motherhood is a bane and a curse, or at least partly that, as long as women are forced to be mothers—and only mothers—against their will. Women today are forced to live too much through their children and husband—too dependent on them, and, therefore, forced to take too much varied resentment, vindictiveness, inexpressible resentment, and rage out on their husbands and their children.

Perhaps the least understood fact of American political life is the enormous buried violence of women in this country today. Like all oppressed people, women have been taking their violence out on their own bodies, in all the maladies with which they plague the doctors' offices and the psychoanalysts. They have been taking out their violence inadvertently and in subtle and in insidious ways on their children and on their husbands. And sometimes, they are not so subtle, for the battered child syndrome that we are hearing more and more about in our hospitals is almost always to be found in the instance of unwanted children, and women are doing the battering, as much or more than men.

Man, we have said, is not the enemy. Men will only be truly liberated, to love women and to be fully themselves, when women are liberated to be full people. Until that happens, men are going to bear the burden and the guilt of the destiny they have forced upon women, the suppressed resentment of that passive stage—the sterility of love, when love is not between two fully active, fully participant, fully joyous people, but has in it the element of exploitation. And men will also not be fully free to be all they can be as long as they must live up to an image of masculinity that denies to a man all the tenderness and sensitivity that might be considered feminine. Men have in them enormous capacities that they have to repress and fear in themselves, in living up to this obsolete and brutal man-eating, lion-killing, Ernest Hemingway image of masculinity—the image of all-powerful masculine superiority. All the burdens and responsibilities that men are supposed to shoulder alone, make them, I think, resent women's pedestal, while the burden to women is enforced passivity.

So the real sexual revolution is not the cheap headlines in the papers—at what age boys and girls go to bed with each other and whether they do it with or without the benefit of marriage. That's the least of it. The real sexual revolution is the emergence of women from passivity, from thingness, to full self-determination, to full dignity. And insofar as they can do this, men are also emerging from the stage of identification with brutality and masters to full and sensitive complete humanity.

A revolutionary theory that's adequate to the current demand of the sexual revolution must also address itself to the concrete realities of our society. We can only transcend the reality of the institutions that oppress us by confronting them in our actions now; confronting reality, we change it; we begin to create alternatives, not in abstract discussion, but here and now.

Some women who call themselves revolutionaries get into abstractions. They say, "What's really wrong is marriage altogether. What's wrong is having babies altogether; let's have them in test tubes. Man is the oppressor, and women are enslaved. We don't want jobs because who wants to be equal to men who aren't free. All jobs today are just a rat race anyway."

Now we are rationalizing in radical terms of the extremists of the women's liberation ideology. This is a rationalization for inaction, because in the end we're going to weep and go home and yell at our husbands and make life miserable for a while, but we'll eventually conclude that it's hopeless, that nothing can be done.

If we are going to address ourselves to the need for changing the social institutions that will permit women to be free and equal individuals, participating actively in their society and changing that society—with men—then we must talk in terms of what is possible, and not accept what is as what must be. In other words, don't talk to me about test tubes because I am interested in leading a revolution for the foreseeable future of my society. And I have a certain sense of optimism that things can be changed.

Twenty-five years from now test-tube babies may be a reality. But it is my educated guess as an observer of the scene—both from what I know of psychology and what I've observed of actual women and men, old and young, conservative and radical, in this country and other countries—that for the foreseeable future people are going to want to enjoy sexual relationships and control the procreative act and make more responsible, human decisions whether and when to have babies.

We need not accept marriage as it's currently structured with the implicit idea of man, the breadwinner, and woman, the housewife. There are many different ways we could posit marriage. But there seems to be a reasonable guess that men and women are going to want relationships of long-term intimacy tied in with sexual relationship, although we can certainly posit a larger variety of sex relationships than now seem conventional. And it's not possible, much less conducive to health, happiness, or self-fulfillment, for women or men to completely suppress their sexual needs.

We can change institutions, but it is a fantasy deviation from a really revolutionary approach to say that we want a world in which there will be no sex, no marriage, that in order for women to be free they must have a manless revolution. We have to deal with the world of reality if we are going to have a real revolution.

I don't happen to think that women and men are so completely different that it is impossible for us to see each other as human beings. I think that it is as possible for men to put themselves finally in woman's place by an act of empathy or by guilt or by awareness of human rights as it has been possible for some whites to do for blacks. But it's perhaps not much more possible than that, though there are more bonds between men and women, and really men's stake in this revolution is greater, because a woman can make a man's life hell if it isn't solved. But I think it would be as much of a mistake to expect men to hand this to women as to consider all men as the enemy, all men as oppressors. This revolution can have the support of men, but women must take the lead in fighting it as any other oppressed group has had to.

I think that it is possible in education to create and disseminate the radical ideology that is needed to influence the great change in expectations and institutions for the revolution of women. In the education of women, I think it is nonsense to keep talking about optional life styles and the freedom of choice that American women have. They do not have them, and we should face this right away. You cannot tell a woman aged eighteen to twenty that she can make a choice to just stay home all her life with her children, her friends, and her husband. This girl is going to live close to a hundred years. There won't be children home to occupy her all her life. If she has intelligence and the opportunity for education it is telling her simply, "Put yourself in a garbage can, except for the years when you have a few little children at home."

. . . Some have the idea that there is another choice—and it is immediately implicit that this is a very freakish and exceptional choice—which is to be single-minded about a career like a man. The idea is, don't marry, don't have children, if you really want a demanding profession. Of course, if you do it this way, forget equality for women. I don't want to forget equality for women. I don't accept for most women the necessity of making a choice that no man has to make. This is not to say that women are not to have a free choice to have children or not to have children, to marry or not to marry; but the idea that this choice has to be influenced by professional or political pursuits, that you are going to be sexually frustrated by choosing to be a scientist, is nonsense.

It is a perversion of the new feminism for some to exhort those who would join this revolution to cleanse themselves of sex and the need for love or to refuse to have children. This not only means a revolution with very few followers—but is a cop-out from the problem of moving in society for the *majority* of women, who do want love and children. To enable *all* women, not just the exceptional few, to participate in society we must confront the fact of life—as a temporary fact of most women's lives today—that women do give birth to children. But we must challenge the idea that a woman is primarily responsible for raising children. Man and society have to be educated to accept their responsibility for that role as well. And this is first of all a challenge to education.

In Sweden I was impressed that these expectations are considered absolutely normal. The need for child-care centers is accepted as so important by all the fathers as well as the mothers of the younger generation that every major young politician has it high on his agenda. The equivalent of the Sunday editor of *The New York Times* in Sweden, or a rising state senator, would each tell me how both he and his wife have part-time schedules so that they can both go on with their professions, and how this is fine but they realize it's only makeshift because what's really needed is more child-care centers. And the editor would pick up the baby and say proudly that she relates to him more than to his wife. And in the Volvo factory, even the public relations man with a crew cut says the same thing.

I couldn't believe it! I asked, "How do you explain this? Why do so many have these attitudes?" And they said, "Education." Eight years ago they decided that they were going to have absolute equality, and the only way to achieve this was to challenge the sex-role idea. The sex-role debate is not considered a woman question, not even an individual woman question or a societal woman question, but a question for men and women alike. In the elementary schools boys and girls take cooking and child care, and boys and girls take shop. Boys and girls take higher mathematics. In the universities the dormitories are sexually integrated. They all have kitchens and boys and girls learn to live together, to cook and study as equals. The kitchens are very important—a boy will boast how good a cook he is, and the idea that this is woman's work is gone. This has been done in the course of one generation, and if Sweden can do it, the United States can do it.

. . . Let's talk about what could be done that isn't just tinkering or tokenism. Every university should have a child-care center. A child development department in any university that doesn't address itself to this need is not confronting its own professional challenge. Another thing we could do, which NOW is trying to do, is to tackle sex discrimination in the universities in the broadest sense. If we get sex into Title VI as well as Title VII of the Civil Rights Act, so that sex discrimination in education is outlawed as well as race discrimination, we could then demand the removal of government contracts from any university that discriminated against women in assigning fellowships. We could then establish, by going to the Supreme Court, that it was discrimination against women not to give them maternity leave rather than requiring them to drop out of medical school. It is as much discrimination against women not to give them a maternity leave as it would be unconscionable to make a boy who has to go into military service lose his chance to get back into graduate school. And it is discrimination against a woman for the graduate school not to have a child-care center, much less not to give her a scholarship or fellowship. If more than a very few women are to enjoy equality, we have an absolute responsibility to get serious political priority for child-care centers, to make it possible for women not to have to bow out of society for ten or fifteen years when they have children. Or else we are only going to be talking of equal opportunities for a few.

Professional schools, and architecture especially, should change their approach. In Sweden, the more sophisticated young architects and planners are professionally confronting the problems of using technology to create new kinds of living places that don't require the slave work on the part of women that makes such a misuse of women's time. These architects do not accept the status quo of "woman as the servant of the house."

WOMEN AS A POLITICAL POWER

On the question of self-determination, we became painfully aware, in our attempts to get a bill of rights for women into the platforms of both political parties at the last presidential election and as a major issue in the election for all candidates for national office, that we need *political power*. Our only success then was getting the word "sex" added to a rather vague antidiscrimination sentence in the Republican platform.

We must overcome our diversity of varied political beliefs. Our common commitment is to equality for women. And we are not single-issue people; we want a voice for all women, to raise our voices in decision making on all matters from war and peace to the kinds of cities we're going to inhabit. Many large issues concern all of us; on these things we may differ. We will surmount this. Political power is necessary to change the situation of the oppressed 51 percent, to realize the power potential in the fact that women *are* 51 percent.

We will do it by getting into city hall ourselves, or by getting into Congress ourselves, regardless of whether our political party is Republican or Democratic or Peace and Freedom. We're only going to do it by getting there ourselves; that's the nitty-gritty of self-determination for us—not to rely on Richard Nixon or a Senate with only one female or a House with only a few women to do it for us.

. . . We must begin to use the power of our actions: to make women finally *visible* as people in America, as conscious political and social power; to change our society *now*, so all women can move freely, as people, in it.

Herbert Marcuse, 1898–1979

Marcuse was a leading exponent in the United States of the Frankfort School of Critical Theory which had flourished in Weimar Germany under the tutelage of Max Horkheimer and Theodor Adorno. This school combined Marx with Freud to offer a startling critique of capitalist industrial life. Marcuse was the Frankfort School member most influenced by Hegel, and his works retained a most Hegelian character.

Marcuse came to this country after he fled Nazi oppression in Europe. Unlike many other Frankfort School members, he remained in the United States after the war and taught at Columbia, Brandeis, and finally the University of California at San Diego. His *Eros and Civilization* (1954) and *Soviet Marxism* (1958) were well-received attacks on both capitalism and bureaucratic communism, but Marcuse was little known outside of the academic community until the publication of *One-Dimensional Man* in 1965. Coming at precisely the time that middle-class college students were beginning to become politically active in support of minority rights and in opposition to the war in Vietnam, Marcuse's work found an adoring audience for its psychological critique of welfare state, consumerist capitalism. Within a few years, *One-Dimensional Man* became requisite reading for a newly politicized generation of college radicals. Essentially Marcuse argued that the modern capitalist system required unnecessary consumption for its survival. Individuals became captives of artificially created needs, which in turn required that they repress their natural instincts if these needs were to be fulfilled even temporarily. Thus amid material plenty, modern men and women were still the objects of extreme repression.

An Essay on Liberation (1969), parts of which are reprinted below, is one of Marcuse's last works. It is the one most clearly written as an appeal to the young radicals of the late 1960s, and he looks to them as the potential bearers of revolutionary change.

Herbert Marcuse

An Essay on Liberation (1969)

INTRODUCTION

Up to now, it has been one of the principal tenets of the critical theory of society (and particularly Marxian theory) to refrain from what might be reasonably called utopian speculation. Social theory is supposed to analyze existing societies in the light of their own functions and capabilities and to identify demonstrable tendencies (if any) which might lead beyond the existing state of affairs. By logical inference from the prevailing conditions and institutions, critical theory may also be able to determine the basic institutional changes which are the prerequisites for the transition to a higher stage of development: "higher" in the sense of a more rational and equitable use of resources, minimization of destructive conflicts, and enlargement of the realm of freedom. But beyond these limits, critical theory did not venture for fear of losing its scientific character.

I believe that this restrictive conception must be revised, and that the revision is suggested, and even necessitated, by the actual evolution of contemporary societies. The dynamic of their productivity deprives "utopia" of its traditional unreal content: what is denounced as "utopian" is no longer that which has "no place" and cannot have any place in the historical universe, but rather that which is blocked from coming about by the power of the established societies.

Utopian possibilities are inherent in the technical and technological forces of advanced capitalism and socialism: the rational utilization of these forces on a global scale would terminate poverty and scarcity within a very foreseeable future. But we know now that neither their rational use nor—and this is decisive—their collective control by the "immediate producers" (the workers) would by itself eliminate domination and exploitation: a bureaucratic welfare state would still be a state of repression which would continue even into the "second phase of socialism," when each is to receive "according to his needs."

What is now at stake are the needs themselves. At this stage, the question is no longer: how can the individual satisfy his own needs without hurting others, but rather: how can he satisfy his needs without hurting himself, without reproducing, through his aspirations and satisfactions, his dependence on an exploitative apparatus which, in satisfying his needs, perpetuates his servitude? The advent of a free society would be characterized by the fact that the growth of well-being turns into an essentially new quality of life. This qualitative change must occur in the needs, in the infrastructure of man (itself a dimension of the infrastructure of society): the new direction, the new institutions and relationships of production, must express the ascent of needs and satisfactions very different from and even antagonistic to those prevalent in the exploitative societies. Such a change would constitute the instinctual basis for freedom which the long history of class society has blocked. Freedom would become the environment of an organism which is no longer capable of adapting to the competitive performances required for well-being under domination, no longer capable of tolerating the aggressiveness, brutality, and ugliness of the established way of life. The rebellion would then have taken root in the very nature, the "biology" of the individual; and on these new grounds, the rebels would redefine the objectives and the strategy of the political struggle, in which alone the concrete goals of liberation can be determined.

Is such a change in the "nature" of man conceivable? I believe so, because technical progress has reached a stage in which reality no longer need be defined by the debilitating competition for social survival and advancement. The more these technical capacities outgrow the framework of exploitation within which they continue to be confined and abused, the more they propel the drives and aspirations of men to a point at which the necessities of life cease to demand the aggressive performances of "earning a living," and the "non-necessary" becomes a vital need. This proposition, which is central in Marxian theory, is familiar enough, and the managers and publicists of corporate capitalism are well aware of its meaning; they are prepared to "contain" its dangerous consequences. The radical opposition also is aware of these prospects, but the critical theory which is to guide political practice still lags behind. Marx and Engels refrained from developing concrete concepts of the possible forms of freedom in a socialist society; today, such restraint no longer seems justified. The growth of the productive forces suggests possibilities of human liberty very different from, and beyond those envisaged at the earlier stage. Moreover, these real possibilities suggest that the gap which separates a free society from the existing societies would be wider and deeper precisely to the degree to which the repressive power and productivity of the latter shape man and his environment in their image and interest.

For the world of human freedom cannot be built by the established societies, no matter how much they may streamline and rationalize their dominion. Their class structure, and the perfected controls required to sustain it, generate needs, satisfactions, and values which reproduce the servitude of the human existence. This "voluntary" servitude (voluntary inasmuch as it is introjected into the individuals), which justifies the benevolent masters, can be broken only through a political practice which reaches the roots of containment and contentment in the infrastructure of man, a political practice of methodical disengagement from and refusal of the Establishment, aiming at a radical transvaluation of values. Such a practice involves a break with the familiar, the routine ways of seeing, hearing, feeling, understanding things so that the organism may become receptive to the potential forms of a nonaggressive, nonexploitative world.

No matter how remote from these notions the rebellion may be, no matter how destructive and self-destructive it may appear, no matter how great the distance between the middle-class revolt in the metropoles and the life-and-death struggle of the wretched of the earth—common to them is the depth of the Refusal. It makes them reject the rules of the game that is rigged against them, the ancient strategy of patience and persuasion, the reliance on the Good Will in the Establishment, its false and immoral comforts, its cruel affluence.

I.

A BIOLOGICAL FOUNDATION FOR SOCIALISM?

In the affluent society, capitalism comes into its own. The two mainsprings of its dynamic—

the escalation of commodity production and productive exploitation—join and permeate all dimensions of private and public existence. The available material and intellectual resources (the potential of liberation) have so much outgrown the established institutions that only the systematic increase in waste, destruction, and management keeps the system going. The opposition which escapes suppression by the police, the courts, the representatives of the people, and the people themselves, finds expression in the diffused rebellion among the youth and the intelligentsia, and in the daily struggle of the persecuted minorities. The armed class struggle is waged outside: by the wretched of the earth who fight the affluent monster.

The critical analysis of this society calls for new categories: moral, political, aesthetic. I shall try to develop them in the course of the discussion. The category of obscenity will serve as an introduction.

This society is obscene in producing and indecently exposing a stifling abundance of wares while depriving its victims abroad of the necessities of life; obscene in stuffing itself and its garbage cans while poisoning and burning the scarce foodstuffs in the fields of its aggression; obscene in the words and smiles of its politicians and entertainers; in its prayers, in its ignorance, and in the wisdom of its kept intellectuals.

Obscenity is a moral concept in the verbal arsenal of the Establishment, which abuses the term by applying it, not to expressions of its own morality but to those of another. Obscene is not the picture of a naked woman who exposes her pubic hair but that of a fully clad general who exposes his medals rewarded in a war of aggression; obscene is not the ritual of the Hippies but the declaration of a high dignitary of the Church that war is necessary for peace. Linguistic therapy—that is, the effort to free words (and thereby concepts) from the all but total distortion of their meanings by the Establishment—demands the transfer of moral standards (and of their validation) from the Establishment to the revolt against it. Similarly, the sociological and political vocabulary must be radically reshaped: it must be stripped of its false neutrality; it must be methodically and provocatively "moralized" in terms of the Refusal. Morality is not necessarily and not primarily ideological. In the face of an amoral society, it becomes a political weapon, an effective force which drives people to burn their draft cards, to ridicule national leaders, to demonstrate in the streets, and to unfold signs saying, "Thou shalt not kill," in the nation's churches.

The reaction to obscenity is shame, usually interpreted as the physiological manifestation of the sense of guilt accompanying the transgression of a taboo. The obscene exposures of the affluent society normally provoke neither shame nor a sense of guilt, although this society violates some of the most fundamental moral taboos of civilization. The term obscenity belongs to the sexual sphere; shame and the sense of guilt arise in the Oedipal situation. If in this respect social morality is rooted in sexual morality, then the shamelessness of the affluent society and its effective repression of the sense of guilt would indicate a decline of shame and guilt feeling in the sexual sphere. And indeed, the exposure of the (for all practical purposes) naked body is permitted and even encouraged, and the taboos on pre- and extramarital intercourse are considerably relaxed. Thus we are faced with the contradiction that the liberalization of sexuality provides an instinctual basis for the repressive and aggressive power of the affluent society.

This contradiction can be resolved if we understand that the liberalization of the Establishment's own morality takes place within the framework of effective controls; kept within this framework, the liberalization strengthens the cohesion of the whole. The relaxation of taboos alleviates the sense of guilt and binds (though with considerable ambivalence) the "free" individuals libidinally to the institutionalized fathers. They are powerful but also tolerant fathers, whose management of the nation and its economy delivers and protects the liberties of the citizens. On the other hand, if the violation of taboos transcends the sexual sphere and leads to refusal and rebellion, the sense of guilt is not alleviated and repressed but rather transferred: not we, but the fathers, are guilty; they are not tolerant but false; they want to redeem their own guilt by making us, the sons, guilty; they have created a world of hypocrisy and violence in which we do not wish to live. Instinctual revolt turns into political rebellion, and against this union, the Establishment mobilizes its full force.

This union provokes such a response because it reveals the prospective scope of social change at this stage of development, the extent to which the radical political practice involves a cultural subversion. The refusal with which the opposition confronts the existing society is affirmative in that it envisages a new culture which fulfills the humanistic promises betrayed by the old culture. Political radicalism thus implies moral radicalism: the emergence of a morality which might precondition man for freedom. This radicalism activates the elementary, organic foundation of morality in the human being. Prior to all ethical behavior in accordance with specific social standards, prior to all ideological expression, morality is a "disposition" of the organism, perhaps rooted in the erotic drive to counter aggressiveness, to create and preserve "ever greater unities" of life. We would then have, this side of all "values," an instinctual foundation for solidarity among human beings—a solidarity which has been effectively repressed in line with the requirements of class society but which now appears as a precondition for liberation.

To the degree to which this foundation is itself historical and the malleability of "human nature" reaches into the depth of man's instinctual structure, changes in morality may "sink down" into the "biological"[1] dimension and modify organic behavior. Once a specific morality is firmly established as a norm of social behavior, it is not only introjected—it also operates as a norm of "organic" behavior: the organism receives and reacts to certain stimuli and "ignores" and repels others in accord with the introjected morality, which is thus promoting or impeding the function of the organism as a living cell in the respective society. In this way, a society constantly recreates, this side of consciousness and ideology, patterns of behavior and aspiration as part of the "nature" of its people, and unless the revolt reaches into this "second" nature, into these ingrown patterns, social change will remain "incomplete," even self-defeating.

The so-called consumer economy and the politics of corporate capitalism have created a second nature of man which ties him libidinally and aggressively to the commodity form. The need for possessing, consuming, handling, and constantly renewing the gadgets, devices, instruments, engines, offered to and imposed upon the people, for using these wares even at the danger of one's own destruction, has become a "biological" need in the

---

[1] I use the terms "biological" and "biology" not in the sense of the scientific discipline, but in order to designate the process and the dimension in which inclinations, behavior patterns, and aspirations become vital needs which, if not satisfied, would cause dysfunction of the organism. Conversely, socially induced needs and aspirations may result in a more pleasurable organic behavior. If biological needs are defined as those which must be satisfied and for which no adequate substitute can be provided, certain cultural needs can "sink down" into the biology of man. We could then speak, for example, of the biological need of freedom, or of some aesthetic needs as having taken root in the organic structure of man, in his "nature," or rather "second nature." This usage of the term "biological" does not imply or assume anything as to the way in which needs are physiologically expressed and transmitted.

sense just defined. The second nature of man thus militates against any change that would disrupt and perhaps even abolish this dependence of man on a market ever more densely filled with merchandise—abolish his existence as a consumer consuming himself in buying and selling. The needs generated by this system are thus eminently stabilizing, conservative needs: the counterrevolution anchored in the instinctual structure.

The market has always been one of exploitation and thereby of domination, insuring the class structure of society. However, the productive process of advanced capitalism has altered the form of domination: the technological veil covers the brute presence and the operation of the class interest in the merchandise. Is it still necessary to state that not technology, not technique, not the machine are the engines of repression, but the presence, in them, of the masters who determine their number, their life span, their power, their place in life, and the need for them? Is it still necessary to repeat that science and technology are the great vehicles of liberation, and that it is only their use and restriction in the repressive society which makes them into vehicles of domination?

Not the automobile is repressive, not the television set is repressive, not the household gadgets are repressive, but the automobile, the television, the gadgets which, produced in accordance with the requirements of profitable exchange, have become part and parcel of the people's own existence, own "actualization." Thus they have to buy part and parcel of their own existence on the market; this existence is the realization of capital. The naked class interest builds the unsafe and obsolescent automobiles, and through them promotes destructive energy; the class interest employs the mass media for the advertising of violence and stupidity, for the creation of captive audiences. In doing so, the masters only obey the demand of the public, of the masses; the famous law of supply and demand establishes the harmony between the rulers and the ruled. This harmony is indeed preestablished to the degree to which the masters have created the public which asks for their wares, and asks for them more insistently if it can release, in and through the wares, its frustration and the aggressiveness resulting from this frustration. Self-determination, the autonomy of the individual, asserts itself in the right to race his automobile, to handle his power tools, to buy a gun, to communicate to mass audiences his opinion, no matter how ignorant, how aggressive, it may be. Organized capitalism has sublimated and turned to socially productive use frustration and primary aggressiveness on an unprecedented scale—unprecedented not in terms of the quantity of violence but rather in terms of its capacity to produce long-range contentment and satisfaction, to reproduce the "voluntary servitude." To be sure, frustration, unhappiness, and sickness remain the basis of this sublimation, but the productivity and the brute power of the system still keep the basis well under control. The achievements justify the system of domination. The established values become the people's own values: adaptation turns into spontaneity, autonomy; and the choice between social necessities appears as freedom. In this sense, the continuing exploitation is not only hidden behind the technological veil, but actually "transfigured." The capitalist production relations are responsible not only for the servitude and toil but also for the greater happiness and fun available to the majority of the population—and they deliver more goods than before.

Neither its vastly increased capacity to produce the commodities of satisfaction nor the peaceful management of class conflicts rendered possible by this capacity cancels the essential features of capitalism, namely, the private appropriation of surplus value (steered but not abolished by government intervention) and its realization in the corporate interest. Capitalism reproduces itself by transforming itself, and this transformation is mainly in the improvement of exploitation. Do exploitation and domination cease to be what they are and what they do to man if they are no longer suffered, if they are "compensated" by previously unknown comforts? Does labor cease to be debilitating if mental energy increasingly replaces physical energy in producing the goods and services which sustain a system that makes hell of large areas of the globe? An affirmative answer would justify any form of oppression which keeps the populace calm and content; while a negative answer would deprive the individual of being the judge of his own happiness.

The notion that happiness is an objective condition which demands more than subjective feelings has been effectively obscured; its validity depends on the real solidarity of the species "man," which a society divided into antagonistic classes and nations cannot achieve. As long as this is the history of mankind, the "state of nature," no matter how refined, prevails: a civilized *bellum omnium contra omnes,* in which the happiness of the ones must coexist with the suffering of the others. The First International was the last attempt to realize the solidarity of the species by grounding it in that social class in which the subjective and objective interest, the particular and the universal, coincided (the International is the late concretization of the abstract philosophical concept of "man as man," human being, *"Gattungswesen,"* which plays such a decisive role in Marx' and Engels' early writings). Then, the Spanish civil war aroused this solidarity, which is the driving power of liberation, in the unforgettable, hopeless fight of a tiny minority against the combined forces of fascist and liberal capitalism. Here, in the international brigades which, with their poor weapons, withstood overwhelming technical superiority, was the union of young intellectuals and workers—the union which has become the desperate goal of today's radical opposition.

Attainment of this goal is thwarted by the integration of the organized (and not only the organized) laboring class into the system of advanced capitalism. Under its impact, the distinction between the real and the immediate interest of the exploited has collapsed. This distinction, far from being an abstract idea, was guiding the strategy of the Marxist movements; it expressed the necessity transcending the economic struggle of the laboring classes, to extend wage demands and demands for the improvement of working conditions to the political arena, to drive the class struggle to the point at which the system itself would be at stake, to make foreign as well as domestic policy, the national as well as the class interest, the target of this struggle. The real interest, the attainment of conditions in which man could shape his own life, was that of no longer subordinating his life to the requirements of profitable production, to an apparatus controlled by forces beyond his control. And the attainment of such conditions meant the abolition of capitalism.

It is not simply the higher standard of living, the illusory bridging of the consumer gap between the rulers and the ruled, which has obscured the distinction between the real and the immediate interest of the ruled. Marxian theory soon recognized that impoverishment does not necessarily provide the soil for revolution, that a highly developed consciousness and imagination may generate a vital need for radical change in advanced material conditions. The power of corporate capitalism has stifled the emergence of such a consciousness and imagination; its mass media have adjusted the rational and emotional faculties to its market and its policies and steered them to defense of its dominion. The narrowing of the consumption gap has rendered possible the mental and instinctual coordination of the laboring classes: the majority of organized labor shares the stabilizing, counterrevolutionary needs of the middle classes, as evidenced by their behavior as consumers of the material and cultural merchandise, by their emotional revulsion against the nonconformist intelligentsia. Conversely, where the consumer gap is still wide, where the capitalist culture has not yet reached into every house or hut, the system of stabilizing needs has its limits; the glaring contrast between the privileged class and the exploited leads to a radicalization of the underprivileged. This is the case of the ghetto population and the unemployed in the United States; this is also the case of the laboring classes in the more backward capitalist countries.

By virtue of its basic position in the production process, by virtue of its numerical weight and the weight of exploitation, the working class is still the historical agent of revolution; by virtue of its sharing the stabilizing needs of the system, it has become a conservative, even counterrevolutionary force. Objectively, "in-itself," labor still is the potentially revolutionary class; subjectively, "for-itself," it is not. This theoretical conception has concrete significance in the prevailing situation, in which the working class may help to circumscribe the scope and the targets of political practice.

In the advanced capitalist countries, the radicalization of the working classes is counteracted by a socially engineered arrest of consciousness, and by the development and satisfaction of needs which perpetuate the servitude of the exploited. A vested interest in the existing system is thus fostered in the instinctual structure of the exploited, and the rupture with the continuum of repression—a necessary precondition of liberation—does not occur. It follows that the radical change which is to transform the existing society into a free society must reach into a dimension of the human existence hardly considered in Marxian theory—the "biological" dimension in which the vital, imperative needs and satisfactions of man assert themselves. Inasmuch as these needs and satisfactions reproduce a life in servitude, liberation presupposes changes in this biological dimension, that is to say, different instinctual needs, different reactions of the body as well as the mind.

The qualitative difference between the existing societies and a free society affects all needs and satisfactions beyond the animal level, that is to say, all those which are essential to the *human* species, man as rational animal. All these needs and satisfactions are permeated with the exigencies of profit and exploitation. The entire realm of competitive performances and standardized fun, all the symbols of status, prestige, power, of advertised virility and charm, of commercialized beauty—this entire realm kills in its citizens the very disposition, the organs, for the alternative: freedom without exploitation.

Triumph and end of introjection: the stage where the people cannot reject the system of domination without rejecting themselves, their own repressive instinctual needs and values. We would have to conclude that liberation would mean subversion against the will and against the prevailing interests of the great majority of the people. In this false identification of social and individual needs, in this deep-rooted, "organic" adaptation of the people to a terrible but profitably functioning society, lie the limits of democratic persuasion and evolution. On the overcoming of these limits depends the establishment of democracy.

It is precisely this excessive adaptability of the human organism which propels the perpetuation and extension of the commodity form and, with it, the perpetuation and extension of the social controls over behavior and satisfaction.

> The ever-increasing complexity of the social structure will make some form of regimentation unavoidable, freedom and privacy may come to constitute antisocial luxuries and their attainment to involve real hardships. In consequence, there may emerge by selection a stock of human beings suited genetically to accept as a matter

of course a regimented and sheltered way of life in a teeming and polluted world, from which all wilderness and fantasy of nature will have disappeared. The domesticated farm animal and the laboratory rodent on a controlled regimen in a controlled environment will then become true models for the study of man.

Thus, it is apparent that food, natural resources, supplies of power, and other elements involved in the operation of the body machine and of the individual establishment are not the only factors to be considered in determining the optimum number of people that can live on earth. Just as important for maintaining the *human qualities* of life is an environment in which it is possible to satisfy the longing for quiet, privacy, independence, initiative, and some open space. . . .[2]

Capitalist progress thus not only reduces the environment of freedom, the "open space" of the human existence, but also the "longing," the need for such an environment. And in doing so, quantitative progress militates against qualitative change even if the institutional barriers against radical education and action are surmounted. This is the vicious circle: the rupture with the self-propelling conservative continuum of needs must *precede* the revolution which is to usher in a free society, but such rupture itself can be envisaged only in a revolution—a revolution which would be driven by the vital need to be freed from the administered comforts and the destructive productivity of the exploitative society, freed from smooth heteronomy, a revolution which, by virtue of this "biological" foundation, would have the chance of turning quantitative technical progress into qualitatively different ways of life—precisely because it would be a revolution occurring at a high level of material and intellectual development, one which would enable man to conquer scarcity and

poverty. If this idea of a radical transformation is to be more than idle speculation, it must have an objective foundation in the production process of advanced industrial society, in its technical capabilities and their use.

For freedom indeed depends largely on technical progress, on the advancement of science. But this fact easily obscures the essential precondition: in order to become vehicles of freedom, science and technology would have to change their present direction and goals; they would have to be reconstructed in accord with a new sensibility—the demands of the life instincts. Then one could speak of a technology of liberation, product of a scientific imagination free to project and design the forms of a human universe without exploitation and toil. But this *gaya scienza* is conceivable only after the historical break in the continuum of domination—as expressive of the needs of a new type of man.[3]

The idea of a new type of man as the member (though not as the builder) of a socialist society appears in Marx and Engels in the concept of the "all-round individual," free to

---

[2] René Dubos, *Man Adapting* (New Haven and London: Yale University Press, 1965), pp. 313–14.

---

[3] The critique of the prevailing scientific establishment as ideological, and the idea of a science which has really come into its own, was expressed in a manifesto issued by the militant students of Paris in May 1968 as follows:

"Refusons aussi la division de la *science* et de *l'idéologie*, la plus pernicieuse de toutes puisqu'elle est *sécrétée* par nous-mêmes. Nous ne voulons pas plus être gouvernés passivement par les lois de la *science* que par celle de l'économie ou les *impératifs* de la technique. La science est un art dont l'originalité est d'avoir des applications possibles hors d'elle-même.

"Elle ne peut cependant être normative que pour elle-même. Refusons son impérialisme mystificant, caution de tous les abus et reculs, y compris en som sein, et remplaçons-le par un choix réel parmi les possibles qu'elle nous offre."

(*Quelle Université? Quelle Société?* Textes réunis par le centre de regroupement des informations universitaires. Paris: Editions de Seuil, 1968, p. 148).

engage in the most varying activities. In the socialist society corresponding to this idea, the free development of individual faculties would replace the subjection of the individual to the division of labor. But no matter what activities the all-round individual would choose, they would be activities which are bound to lose the quality of freedom if exercised "en masse"—and they would be "en masse," for even the most authentic socialist society would inherit the population growth and the mass basis of advanced capitalism. The early Marxian example of the free individuals alternating between hunting, fishing, criticizing, and so on, had a joking-ironical sound from the beginning, indicative of the impossibility anticipating the ways in which liberated human beings would use their freedom. However, the embarrassingly ridiculous sound may also indicate the degree to which this vision has become obsolete and pertains to a stage of the development of the productive forces which has been surpassed. The later Marxian concept implies the continued separation between the realm of necessity and the realm of freedom, between labor and leisure—not only in time, but also in such a manner that the same subject lives a different life in the two realms. According to this Marxian conception, the realm of necessity would continue under socialism to such an extent that real human freedom would prevail only outside the entire sphere of socially necessary labor. Marx rejects the idea that work can ever become play.[4] Alienation would be reduced with the progressive reduction of the working day, but the latter would remain a day of unfreedom, rational but not free. However, the development of the productive forces beyond their capitalist organization

suggests the possibility of freedom *within* the realm of necessity. The quantitative reduction of necessary labor could turn into quality (freedom), not in proportion to the reduction but rather to the transformation of the working day, a transformation in which the stupefying, enervating, pseudo-automatic jobs of capitalist progress would be abolished. But the construction of such a society presupposes a type of man with a different sensitivity as well as consciousness: men who would speak a different language, have different gestures, follow different impulses; men who have developed an instinctual barrier against cruelty, brutality, ugliness. Such an instinctual transformation is conceivable as a factor of social change only if it enters the social division of labor, the production relations themselves. They would be shaped by men and women who have the good conscience of being human, tender, sensuous, who are no longer ashamed of themselves—for "the token of freedom attained, that is, no longer being ashamed of ourselves" (Nietzsche, *Die Fröhliche Wissenschaft,* Book III, 275). The imagination of such men and women would fashion their reason and tend to make the process of production a process of creation. This is the utopian concept of socialism which envisages the ingression of freedom into the realm of necessity, and the union between causality by necessity and causality by freedom. The first would mean passing from Marx to Fourier; the second from realism to surrealism.

A utopian conception? It has been the great, real, transcending force, the *"idée neuve,"* in the first powerful rebellion against the whole of the existing society, the rebellion for the total transvaluation of values, for qualitatively different ways of life: the May rebellion in France. The graffiti of the *"jeunesse en colère"* joined Karl Marx and André Breton; the slogan *"l'imagination au pouvoir"* went well with *"les comités (soviets) partout";* the piano with the jazz player stood well between the barricades;

---

[4] For a far more "utopian" conception see the by now familiar passage in the *Grundrisse der Kritik der Politischen Oekonomie* (Berlin: Dietz, 1953), pp. 596 ff.

the red flag well fitted the statue of the author of *Les Misérables;* and striking students in Toulouse demanded the revival of the language of the Troubadours, the Albigensians. The new sensibility has become a political force.

It crosses the frontier between the capitalist and the communist orbit; it is contagious because the atmosphere, the climate of the established societies, carries the virus.

Irving Kristol, 1920–

An author, influential editor, and professor at New York University, Irving Kristol is a leading member of a contemporary school of thought that has been called neoconservative. Usually former liberals or democratic socialists, neoconservative writers have written extensively in opposition to many of the political events and values of the late 1960s and 1970s. Specifically, various neoconservatives have been worried by the slackening of anticommunism, the decline in traditional values, and the rise in racial and sexual quotas in schools, political parties, and corporations.

Kristol himself was a member of the anti-Stalinist Young People's Socialist League while a student at City College of New York. After serving in the U.S. army in World War II, he began to write for *Commentary* and later helped found and edit *Encounter* with the British poet Stephen Spender. After leaving the *Encounter,* Kristol edited the liberal, anticommunist magazine *The Reporter.* In 1960 he left *The Reporter* to become an editor at Basic Books and to take a position on the faculty at New York University. Since 1965 Kristol has been one of the editors of the *Public Interest,* a leading popular journal with a decidedly conservative orientation. Furthermore, he is a frequent contributor to *The Wall Street Journal* and a member of its editorial board.

In *On the Democratic Idea in America* (1972), Kristol argued that politics needed to be the activity of "moderate men using moderate means." Liberalism, he argued, had become a utopian ideology that was destructive of long-held social values in the name of social justice. His *Two Cheers for Capitalism* (1978), part of which is reprinted below, is a collection of essays exploring the virtues of "democratic capitalism."

Irving Kristol

When Virtue Loses All Her Loveliness, Some Reflections on Capitalism and the Free Society (1978)

When we lack the will to see things as they really are, there is nothing so mystifying as the obvious. This has been the case, I think, with the upsurge of radicalism since the 1960s that has been shaking much of Western society to its foundations. We have constructed the most ingenious sociological and psychological theories—as well as a few disingenuously naive ones—to explain this phenomenon. But there is in truth no mystery here. Our youthful rebels are anything but inarticulate; and though they utter a great deal of nonsense, the import of what they have been saying is clear enough. What they are saying is that they dislike—to put it mildly—the liberal, individualist, capitalist civilization that stands ready to receive them as citizens. They are rejecting this offer of citizenship and are declaring their desire to see some other kind of civilization replace it.

It is consoling to think that the turmoil among them is provoked by the extent to which our society falls short of realizing its ideals. But the plain truth is that it is these ideals themselves that are being rejected. Our young radicals are far less dismayed at America's failure to become what it ought to be

than they are contemptuous of what it thinks it ought to be. For them, as for Oscar Wilde, it is not the average American who is disgusting; it is the ideal American.

This is why one can make so little impression on them with arguments about how much progress has been made in the past decades, or is being made today, toward racial equality, or abolishing poverty, or fighting pollution, or whatever it is that we conventionally take as a sign of "progress." The obstinacy with which they remain deaf to such "liberal" arguments is not all perverse or irrational, as some would like to think. It arises, rather, out of a perfectly sincere, if often inchoate, animus against the American system itself. This animus stands for a commitment—*to* what, remains to be seen, but *against* what is already only too evident.

CAPITALISM'S THREE PROMISES

Dissatisfaction with the liberal-capitalist ideal, as distinct from indignation at failures to realize this ideal, are coterminous with the history of capitalism itself. Indeed, the cultural history of the capitalist epoch is not much more than a record of the varying ways such dissatisfaction could be expressed—in poetry, in the novel, in the drama, in painting, and today even in the movies. Nor, again, is there any great mystery why, from the first stirrings of the romantic movement, poets and philosophers have ever had much regard for the capitalist civilization in which they lived and worked. But to understand this fully, one must be able to step outside the "progressive" ideology which makes us assume that liberal capitalism is the "natural" state of man toward which humanity has always aspired. There is nothing more natural about capitalist civilization than about many others that have had, or will have, their day. Capitalism represents a sum of human choices about the good life and the good society. These choices inevitably have their associated costs, and after 200 years the conviction seems to be spreading that the costs have got out of line.

What did capitalism promise? First of all, it promised continued improvement in the material conditions of all its citizens, a promise without precedent in human history. Second, it promised an equally unprecedented measure of individual freedom for all of these same citizens. And lastly, it held out the promise that, amidst this prosperity and liberty, the individual could satisfy his instinct for self-perfection—for leading a virtuous life that satisfied the demands of his spirit (or, as one used to say, his soul)—and that the free exercise of such individual virtue would aggregate into a just society.

Now, it is important to realize that, though these aims were in one sense more ambitious than any previously set forth by a political ideology, in another sense they were far more modest. Whereas, as Joseph Cropsey has pointed out, Adam Smith defined "prudence" democratically as "the care of the health, of the fortune, of the rank of the individual," Aristotle had defined that term aristocratically, to mean "the quality of mind concerned with things just and noble and good for man." By this standard, all pre-capitalist systems had been, to one degree or another, Aristotelian: they were interested in creating a high and memorable civilization even if this were shared only by a tiny minority. In contrast,

capitalism lowered its sights, but offered its shares in bourgeois civilization to the entire citizenry. Tocqueville, as usual, astutely caught this difference between the aristocratic civilizations of the past and the new liberal capitalism he saw emerging in the United States:

> In aristocratic societies the class that gives the tone to opinion and has the guidance of affairs, being permanently and hereditarily placed above the multitude, naturally conceives a lofty idea of itself and man. It loves to invent for him noble pleasures, to carve out splendid objects for his ambition. Aristocracies often commit very tyrannical and inhuman actions, but they rarely entertain groveling thoughts. . . .
>
> [In democracies, in contrast] there is little energy of character but customs are mild and laws humane. If there are few instances of exalted heroism or of virtues of the highest, brightest, and purest temper, men's habits are regular, violence is rare, and cruelty almost unknown. . . . Genius becomes rare, information more diffused. . . . There is less perfection, but more abundance, in all the productions of the arts.

It is because "high culture" inevitably has an aristocratic bias—it would not be "high" if it did not—that, from the beginnings of the capitalist era, it has always felt contempt for the bourgeois mode of existence. That mode of existence purposively depreciated the very issues that were its *raison d'être*. It did so by making them, as no society had ever dared or desired to do, matters of personal taste, according to the prescription of Adam Smith in his *Theory of Moral Sentiments:*

> Though you despise that picture, or that poem, or even that system of philosophy, which I admire, there is little danger of our quarreling upon that account. Neither of us can reasonably be much interested about them. They ought all of them to be matters of great indifference to us both; so that, though our opinions may be opposite, our affections shall be very nearly the same.

In short, an amiable philistinism was inherent in bourgeois society, and this was bound to place its artists and intellectuals in an antagonistic posture toward it. This antagonism was irrepressible—the bourgeois world could not suppress it without violating its own liberal creed; the artists could not refrain from expressing their hostility without denying their most authentic selves. But the conflict could, and was, contained so long as capitalist civilization delivered on its three basic promises. It was only when the third promise, of a virtuous life and a just society, was subverted by the dynamics of capitalism itself, as it strove to fulfill the other two—affluence and liberty—that the bourgeois order came, in the minds of the young especially, to possess a questionable legitimacy.

FROM BOURGEOIS SOCIETY TO A "FREE SOCIETY"

I can think of no better way of indicating the distance that capitalism has traveled from its original ideological origins than by contrasting the most intelligent defender of capitalism today with his predecessors. I refer to Friedrich von Hayek, who has as fine and a powerful a mind as is to be found anywhere, and whose *Constitution of Liberty* is one of the most thoughtful works of the last decades. In that book, he offers the following argument against viewing capitalism as a system that incarnates any idea of justice:

> Most people will object not to the bare fact of inequality but to the fact that the differences in reward do not correspond to any recognizable differences in the merit of those who receive them. The answer commonly given to this is that a free society on the whole achieves this kind of justice. This, however, is an indefensible contention if by justice is meant proportionality of reward to moral merit. Any attempt to found the case for freedom on this argument is very damaging to it, since it concedes that material rewards ought to be made to correspond to recognizable merit and then opposes the conclusion that most people will draw from this by an assertion which is untrue. The proper answer is that in a free society it is neither desirable nor practicable that material rewards should be made generally to correspond to what men recognize as merit and that it is an essential characteristic of a free society that an individual's position should not necessarily depend on the views that his fellows hold about the merit he has acquired. . . . A society in which the position of the individual was made to correspond to human ideas of moral merit would therefore be the exact opposite of a free society. It would be a society in which people were rewarded for duty performed instead of for success. . . . But if nobody's knowledge is sufficient to guide all human action, there is also no human being who is competent to reward all efforts according to merit.

This argument is admirable both for its utter candor and for its firm opposition to all those modern authoritarian ideologies, whether rationalist or irrationalist, which give a self-selected elite the right to shape men's lives and fix their destinies according to its preconceived notions of good and evil, merit and demerit. But it is interesting to note what Hayek is doing: he is opposing a *free* society to a *just* society—because, he says, while we know what freedom is, we have no generally accepted knowledge of what justice is. Elsewhere he writes:

> Since they [i.e., differentials in wealth and income] are not the effect of anyone's design or intentions, it is meaningless to describe the manner in which the market distributed the good things of this world among particular people as just or unjust. . . . No test or criteria have been found or can be found by which such rules of "social justice" can be assessed. . . . They would have to be determined by the arbitrary will of the holders of power.

Now, it may be that this is the best possible defense that can be made of a free society. But if this is the case, one can fairly say that "capitalism" is (or was) one thing, and a "free society" another. For capitalism, during the first hundred years or so if its existence, did lay claim to being a just social order, in the meaning later given to that concept by Paul Elmer More: ". . . Such a distribution of power and privilege, and of property as the symbol and instrument of these, as at once will satisfy the distinctions of reason among the superior, and will not outrage the feelings of the inferior." As a matter of fact, capitalism at its apogee saw itself as the most just social order the world has ever witnessed, because it replaced all arbitrary (e.g., inherited) distributions of power, privilege, and property with a distribution that was directly and intimately linked to personal merit—this latter term being inclusive of both personal abilities and personal virtues.

Writing shortly before the Civil War, George Fitzhugh, the most gifted of Southern apologists for slavery, attacked the capitalist North in these terms:

> In a free society none but the selfish virtues are in repute, because none other help a man in the race of competition. In such a society virtue loses all her loveliness, because of her selfish aims. Good men and bad men have the same end in view—self-promotion and self-elevation. . . .

> . . . In short, it was a society still permeated by the Puritan ethic, the Protestant ethic, the capitalist ethic—call it what you will. It was a society in which it was agreed that there was a strong correlation between certain personal virtues—frugality, industry, sobriety, reliability, piety—and the way in which power, privilege, and property were distributed. And this correlation was taken to be the sign of a just society, not merely of a free one. Samuel Smiles or Horatio Alger would have regarded Professor Hayek's writings as slanderous of his fellow Christians, blasphemous of God, and ultimately subversive of the social order. I am not sure about the first two of these accusations, but I am fairly certain of the validity of the last.

This is not the place to recount the history and eventual degradation of the capitalist ethic in America.[1] Suffice it to say that, with every passing decade, Fitzhugh's charge, that "virtue loses all her loveliness, because of her selfish aims," became more valid. From having been a *capitalist, republican community*, with shared values and a quite unambiguous claim to the title of a just order, the United States became a free democratic society where the will to success and privilege was severed from its moral moorings.

THREE CURRENT APOLOGIA

But can men live in a free society if they have no reason to believe it is also a just society? I do not think so. My reading of history is that, in the same way as men cannot for long tolerate a sense of spiritual meaninglessness in their individual lives, so they cannot for long accept a society in which power, privilege, and property are not distributed according to some morally meaningful criteria. Nor is equality itself any more acceptable than inequality—neither is more "natural" than the other—if equality is merely a brute fact rather than a consequence of an ideology or social philosophy. This explains what otherwise seems paradoxical: that small inequalities in capitalist countries can become the source of intense controversy while relatively larger inequalities in socialist or communist countries are blandly overlooked. Thus, those same young radicals who are infuriated by trivial inequalities in the American economic system are quite blind to grosser inequalities in the Cuban system. This is usually taken as evidence of hypocrisy or self-deception. I would

---

[1] See Daniel Bell's book, *The Cultural Contradictions of Capitalism,* for a more detailed analysis of what happened and why.

say it shows, rather, that people's notions of equality or inequality have extraordinarily little to do with arithmetic and almost everything to do with political philosophy.

I believe that what holds for equality also holds for liberty. People feel free when they subscribe to a prevailing social philosophy; they feel unfree when the prevailing social philosophy is unpersuasive; and the existence of constitutions or laws or judiciaries have precious little to do with these basic feelings. The average working man in nineteenth-century America had far fewer "rights" than his counterpart today; but he was far more likely to boast about his being a free man.

So I conclude, despite Professor Hayek's ingenious analysis, that men cannot accept the historical accidents of the marketplace—seen merely as accidents—as the basis for an enduring and legitimate entitlement to power, privilege, and property. And, in actual fact, Professor Hayek's rationale for modern capitalism is never used outside a small academic enclave; I even suspect it cannot be believed except by those whose minds have been shaped by overlong exposure to scholasticism. Instead, the arguments offered to justify the social structure of capitalism now fall into three main categories:

(1) The Protestant Ethic. This, however, is now reserved for the lower socioeconomic levels. It is still believed, and it is still reasonable to believe, that worldly success among the working class, lower-middle class, and even middle class has a definite connection with personal virtues such as diligence, rectitude, sobriety, honest ambition, etc., etc. And, so far as I can see, the connection is not only credible but demonstrable. It does seem that the traditional bourgeois virtues are efficacious among these classes; at least, it is rare to find successful men emerging from these classes who do not to a significant degree exemplify them. But no one seriously claims that these traditional virtues will open the cor-ridors of corporate power to anyone, or that those who now occupy the executive suites are—or even aspire to be—models of bourgeois virtue.

(2) The Darwinian Ethic. This is to be found mainly among small businessmen who are fond of thinking that their "making it" is to be explained as "the survival of the fittest." They are frequently quite right, of course, in believing the metaphor appropriate to their condition and to the ways in which they achieved it. But it is preposterous to think that the mass of men will ever accept as legitimate a social order formed in accordance with the laws of the jungle. Men may be animals, but they are political animals and, what comes to not such a different thing, moral animals too. The fact that for several decades after the Civil War, the Darwinian ethic, as popularized by Herbert Spencer, could be taken seriously by so many social theorists represents one of the most bizarre and sordid episodes in American intellectual history. It could not last, and did not.

(3) The Technocratic Ethic. This is the most prevalent justification of corporate capitalism today, and finds expression in an insistence on "performance." Those who occupy the seats of corporate power, and enjoy the prerogatives and privileges thereof, are said to acquire legitimacy by their superior ability to achieve superior "performance"—in economic growth, managerial efficiency, and technological innovation. In a sense, what is claimed is that these men are accomplishing social tasks, and fulfilling social responsibilities, in an especially efficacious way.

There are, however, two fatal flaws in this argument. First, if one defines "performance" in a strictly limited and measurable sense, then one is applying a test that any ruling class is bound, on fairly frequent occasions, to fail. Life has its ups and downs; so do history and economics; and those who can only claim legitimacy *via* performance are going to have to spend an awful lot of time and energy explaining why things are not going as well as they ought to. . . .

Secondly, if one tries to avoid this dilemma by giving the term "performance" a broader and larger meaning, then one inevitably finds oneself passing beyond the boundaries of bourgeois propriety. It is one thing to say with Samuel Johnson that men honestly engaged in business are doing the least mischief that men are capable of; it is quite another thing to assert that they are doing the greatest good: this is only too patently untrue. For the achievement of the greatest good, more than successful performance in business is necessary. Witness how vulnerable our corporate managers are to accusations that they are befouling our environment. What these accusations really add up to is the statement that the business system in the United States does not create a beautiful, refined, gracious, and tranquil civilization. To which our corporate leaders are replying: "Oh, we can perform that mission too—just give us time." But there is no good reason to think they can accomplish this non-capitalist mission; nor is there any reason to believe that they have any proper entitlement even to try.

* * * * *

A CASE OF REGRESSION

For a system of liberal, representative government to work, free elections are not enough. The results of the political process and of the exercise of individual freedom— the distribution of power, privilege, and property—must also be seen as in some profound sense expressive of the values that govern the lives of individuals. An idea of self-government, if it is to be viable, must encompass both the private and the public sectors. If it does not—if the principles that organize public life seem to have little relation to those

that shape private lives—you have "alienation," and anomie, and a melting away of established principles of authority.

Milton Friedman, arguing in favor of Hayek's extreme libertarian position, has written that the free man "recognizes no national purpose except as it is the consensus of the purposes for which the citizens severally strive." If he is using the term "consensus" seriously, then he must be assuming that there is a strong homogeneity of values among the citizenry, and that these values give a certain corresponding shape to the various institutions of society, political and economic. Were that the case, then it is indeed true that a "national purpose" arises automatically and organically out of the social order itself. Something like this did happen when liberal capitalism was in its prime, vigorous and self-confident. But is that our condition today? I think not, just as I think Mr. Friedman doesn't really mean "consensus" but rather the mere aggregation of selfish aims. In such a blind and accidental arithmetic, the sum floats free from the addenda, and its legitimacy is infinitely questionable.

The inner spiritual chaos of the times, so powerfully created by the dynamics of capitalism itself, is such as to make nihilism an easy temptation. A "free society" in Hayek's sense gives birth in massive numbers to "free spirits," emptied of moral substance but still driven by primordial moral aspirations. Such people are capable of the most irrational actions. Indeed, it is my impression that, under the strain of modern life, whole classes of our population—and the educated classes most of all—are entering what can only be called, in the strictly clinical sense, a phase of infantile regression. With every passing year, public discourse becomes sillier and more petulant, while human emotions become, apparently, more ungovernable. Some of our most intelligent university professors are now loudly saying things that, had they been uttered by one of their students twenty years ago, would have called forth gentle and urbane reproof.

THE REFORMING SPIRIT AND THE CONSERVATIVE IDEAL

And yet, if the situation of liberal capitalism today seems so precarious, it is likely nevertheless to survive for a long while, if only because the modern era has failed to come up with any plausible alternatives. Socialism, communism, and fascism have all turned out to be either utopian illusions or sordid frauds. So we shall have time, though not an endless amount of it, for we have already wasted a great deal. We are today in a situation not very different from that described by Herbert Croly in *The Promise of American Life* (1912):

> The substance of our national Promise has consisted of an improving popular economic condition, guaranteed by democratic political institutions, and resulting in moral and social amelioration. These manifold benefits were to be obtained merely by liberating the enlightened self-enterprise of the American people. . . . The fulfillment of the American Promise was considered inevitable because it was based upon a combination of self-interest and the natural goodness of human nature. On the other hand, if the fulfillment of our national Promise can no longer be considered inevitable, if it must be considered as equivalent to a conscious national purpose instead of an inexorable national destiny, the implication necessarily is that the trust reposed in individual self-interest has been in some measure betrayed. No pre-established harmony can then exist between the free and abundant satisfaction of private needs and the accomplishment of a morally and socially desirable result.

Croly is not much read these days. He was a liberal reformer with essentially conservative goals. So was Matthew Arnold, fifty years earlier, and he isn't much read these days, either. Neither of them can pass into the conventional anthologies of liberal or conservative thought. I think this is a sad commentary on the ideological barrenness of the liberal and conservative creeds. I also think it is a great pity. For if our private and public worlds are ever again, in our lifetimes, to have a congenial relationship—if virtue is to regain her lost loveliness—then some such combination of the reforming spirit with the conservative ideal seems to me to be what is most desperately wanted.

I use the word "conservative" advisedly. Though the discontents of our civilization express themselves in the rhetoric of "liberation" and "equality," one can detect beneath the surface an acute yearning for order and stability—but a legitimate order, of course, and a legitimized stability. In this connection, I find the increasing skepticism as to the benefits of economic growth and technological innovation most suggestive. Such skepticism has been characteristic of conservative critics of liberal capitalism since the beginning of the nineteenth century. One finds it in Coleridge, Carlyle, and Newman—in all those who found it impossible to acquiesce in a "progressive" notion of human history or social evolution. Our dissidents today may think they are exceedingly progressive; but no one who puts greater emphasis on "the quality of life" than on "mere" material enrichment can properly be placed in that category. For the idea of progress in the modern era has always signified that the quality of life would inevitably be improved by material enrichment. To doubt this is to doubt the political metaphysics of modernity and to start the long trek back to pre-modern political philosophy—Plato, Aristotle, Thomas Aquinas, Hooker, Calvin, etc. It seems to me that this trip is quite necessary. Perhaps there we shall discover some of those elements that are most desperately needed by the spiritually impoverished civilization that we have constructed on what once seemed to be sturdy bourgeois foundations.

PART VII

The Republic as World Power: Internationalism, Intervention, and a World Safe for Democracy

An America actively involved in the affairs of foreign nations, obligated by alliances, and protected by a peacetime standing army would have been anathema to American republicans of the eighteenth and nineteenth centuries. Alliances with other nations smacked of balance-of-power politics and the moral decay of Europe. The American republic was to have been different.

From John Winthrop's speech to the Pilgrims on the *Arabella* through historian Frederick Jackson Turner's "frontier thesis," Americans spoke of themselves as unique recipients of Providence's gifts. It was America's great fortune to create in the wilderness a new world grounded in sound "first principles" free from the taint of the old world. America was the "new Israel," a model of piety and republican liberty, "a beacon unto the nations." As Thomas Jefferson promised his friend James Madison in 1787, virtue could be reborn in each generation if Americans turned west in search of new land to farm. Turning inward to the great garden of the American frontier instead of outward across the ocean toward the great cities of Europe was America's route to a constant regeneration.

If the United States could remain free of entangling alliances, George Washington warned in his Farewell Address, it could avoid the danger of standing army. This was possible, Alexis de Tocqueville noted, as long as the oceans provided America with the security that other peoples bought with large peacetime armies. American republicans feared that a military establishment would concentrate power in a central government, burden individuals and small businesses with heavy taxes, and transfer resources and population from the countryside to the large urban centers that housed heavy industry. In their view, republics defended themselves with militias and citizen-soldiers; but militias were the luxury only of those nations free from constant threat of attack and the demands of alliances.

To be sure, American practice did not strictly follow isolationist and republican theory. The Monroe Doctrine, the Mexican War, and American aspirations along the Canadian border did not bespeak a purely isolationist, defensive America. However these events were in our own hemisphere—often on our own borders—and were designed in part to keep European powers away from our borders and in part to increase the sphere for our own agrarian republican experiment.

America's isolation ended—although not once and for all—with the Spanish-American War (1898), perhaps not coincidentally just as the census confirmed the end of the frontier. The U.S. decision to place the Philippines under colonial rule after the war ended, advocated by many in the Progressive wing of the Republican party including Albert J. Beveridge, showed a willingness to extend activist government beyond American shores. Advocates of the new imperialism produced a melange of arguments for their position, including racist and religious rationales as well as the more expected appeals to strategic and economic interests. Opponents such as Carl Schurz, Adlai Stevenson, and William Jennings Bryan responded with republican and liberal individualist arguments about limited government, self-determination, and the debilitating economic effects of militarism.

Although the Spanish-American War and its colonial aftermath in the Philippines and Puerto Rico signaled a new U.S. presence in the world, the twin issues of permanent alliances and a military establishment were by no means settled. The United States did not enter World War I until 1917 and then only with assurances to the American people that it was the "war to end all wars." It is interesting to observe how Wilson grappled with the task of justifying a foreign war to the American people. Rather than appealing to balance of power or national self-interest, Wilson argued that the United States must take up arms to make the "world safe for democracy" and to secure the right of all peoples to national self-determination. By justifying American involvement with an appeal to universal and internationalist principles that transcended the particular interest of the United States, Wilson returned to an earlier American self-image as the "new Israel." He articulated a political theory of foreign affairs that simultaneously rejected long-term colonial ambitions at the same time that it committed the United States to active participation in a new world order. Wilson failed in his attempt to build a peaceful world order through the League of Nations. Nonetheless, he succeeded in defining an activist theory of foreign relations that Americans could accept as compatible with the ideals of republican government.

Even as Wilsonian internationalism became the new orthodoxy of American diplomacy, it was subject to attack from a variety of sources. During the war, Randolph Bourne criticized Herbert Croly and other Progressives at

The New Republic magazine and urged them to reconsider their enthusiasm for war. Rather than promote reform and a noble national purpose as Croly had hoped, Bourne suggested that war would simply stifle freedom and diversity. This type of argument was common in the post–World War I era. Prior to U.S. entry in World War II, traditional conservatives, especially from the Midwest, opposed steps to aid the British in their struggle against German expansion. With the exception of a few xenophobic and anti-Semitic fringe groups, these conservatives usually echoed traditional republican concerns about the cost of a military establishment and its consequent destruction of limited government. More to the left, Robert La Follette, Sr. and Jr., associated rearmament with resurgent imperialism and openly worried that munitions manufacturers were corrupting government. Moreover, they felt that military involvement was the greatest threat to domestic social reform.

Once the Japanese attacked Pearl Harbor, this debate ended. President Roosevelt successfully employed Wilsonian language in justifying America's entry into the war in Europe as well as in the Pacific. After the war, President Truman reaffirmed the principle that the United States was the guarantor of a democratic world. Like Wilson and Roosevelt, he reaffirmed the American commitment to new international institutions such as the United Nations, and also pledged to uphold democratic ideals throughout the world. Despite a brief postwar resurgence of isolationism, successive presidents repeated Wilsonian themes as the basis for U.S. opposition to Soviet expansion and communist revolution. Along with internationalist ideals, the American people accepted a large peacetime army, conscription, a series of alliances such as NATO and SEATO, and "limited wars" in Korea and Vietnam.

While a few critics such as George Kennan (whose 1947 "Mr. X" article ironically encouraged U.S. involvement in the Cold War) had questioned the crusading spirit of American internationalism, the first serious challenge to the postwar consensus came during the Vietnam War. Especially to critics on the left, United States involvement in Vietnam was merely another in a series of attempts to shore up authoritarian regimes in order to further our own material ambitions. The desire for trade and investment in third-world countries, many argued, led us to support any regime that painted itself as a foe of communism. In the name of self-determination, these critics argued, the United States had come to police world counterrevolution. Others, such as Senator William Fulbright, appealed to more traditional republican and isolationist themes. American involvement abroad inevitably dissipated our domestic economy and hindered democratic and republican goals at home.

In the wake of opposition to the war and its unsuccessful conclusion, it is safe to say that no clear consensus exists concerning U.S. foreign policy. Daniel Moynihan, among others, has called for a neo-Wilsonian policy of American support for human rights. Moynihan began to put his theory to practice during a short stint as ambassador to the United Nations during the Ford administration. President Carter gave human rights a prominent place in his administration's foreign policy, although the goal was most difficult to implement.

However, many conservatives and Republicans argued that Carter's policy simply undermined "authoritarian" third-world countries that were friendly to American interests, while neglecting the far greater threat of "totalitarian" Marxist revolutions. Jeanne Kirkpatrick, former Ambassador to the United Nations, articulated this theme in an article in *Commentary* magazine titled "Dictatorships and Double Standards" that became an important theoretical document in the Reagan administration.

On the other hand, contemporary liberals have generally countered that American internationalism requires opposition to human rights violations wherever they occur. Economic development and greater equality—not merely protecting the traditional rights of liberal individualism—others have maintained, must be the goals of U.S. foreign policy. Some conservatives have also criticized the resurgent internationalism of the Reagan administration suggesting that it is imprudently expansionist. This view, represented in this text by Christopher Layne, is in the minority among conservative thinkers, but reminds us that conservatives in America come in many varieties.

All of these cases, it should be noted, show a demand that our foreign policy aims be consistent philosophically with our conception of the nature and goals of American democracy. The debate over a foreign policy appropriate to the American republic continues.

The Old Orthodoxy:

The Republic as Isolationist

George Washington, 1732–1799

George Washington's adult life was intertwined with that of the emerging American Republic. From his involvement in the French and Indian War through his leadership of the Continental Army, and later as the new nation's first president, Washington's life was a public one. His "Farewell Address" (1796) was his attempt to leave his nation on a sound footing as he left office.

As president, Washington usually sided with the Federalists and with Alexander Hamilton on most policy questions. Yet in government, as in the army, Washington strove to remain above the conflict and to lead with an almost distant coldness. He had hoped to represent the public good without descending into partisan politics. In a sense, Washington hoped for a similar international role for America—one above the petty intrigue and costly maneuvering of world power politics.

Washington worked hard to keep the United States neutral during the wars following the French Revolution, declaring a Neutrality Proclamation in 1793. He was pressured by many Republicans who favored supporting the French, but Washington held firm, even demanding the recall of the French emissary Citizen Genet' who had sought American volunteers.

Having decided not to run for a third term, Washington delivered his famous "Farewell Address" in which he implored his fellow-countrymen to avoid debilitating regional, partisan, and international involvements. This "isolationist" position on foreign relations was deemed the one appropriate for a republican government for most of the nineteenth century and remains influential in different guises in contemporary political dialogue.

The following two selections are different drafts of the foreign policy sections of the Farewell Address. The first was written in Washington's own hand and is in many respects a clearer but less eloquent document. The second is taken from the actual Farewell Address as rewritten by Alexander Hamilton.

George Washington

Original Draft of Farewell Address (1796)

Had the situation of our public affairs continued to wear the same aspect they assumed at the time the foregoing address was drawn I should not have taken the liberty of troubling you, my fellow citizens, with any new sentiments or with a repetition, more in detail, of those which are therein contained; but considerable changes having taken place both at home and abroad, I shall ask your indulgence while I express with more lively sensibility, the following most ardent wishes of my heart.

That party disputes, among all the friends and lovers of their country may subside, or, as the wisdom of Providence has ordained that men, on the same subjects, shall not always think alike, that charity and benevolence when they happen to differ may so far shed their benign influence as to banish those invectives which proceed from illiberal prejudices and jealousy.

That as the all-wise dispenser of human blessings has favored no nation of the Earth with more abundant, and substantial means of happiness than United America, that we may not be so ungrateful to our Creator; so wanting to ourselves; and so regardless of Posterity, as to dash the cup of beneficence which is thus bountifully offered to our acceptance.

SOURCE: Robert McCalley, ed., *Federalists, Republicans and Foreign Entanglements* (Englewood Cliffs, N.J.: Prentice Hall, 1969).

That we may fulfill with the greatest exactitude *all* our engagements, foreign and domestic, to the *utmost* of our abilities whensoever, and in whatsoever manner they are pledged: for in public, as in private life, I am persuaded that honesty will forever be found to be the best policy.

That we may avoid connecting ourselves with the politics of any nation, farther than shall be found necessary to regulate our own trade; in order that commerce may be placed upon a stable footing; our merchants know their rights; and the government the ground on which those rights are to be supported.

That every citizen would take pride in the name of an American, and act as if he felt the importance of the character by considering that we ourselves are now a distinct nation, the dignity of which will be absorbed, if not annihilated, if we enlist ourselves (further than our obligations may require) under the banners of any other nation whatsoever. And moreover, that we would guard against the intrigues of *any* and *every* foreign nation who shall endeavor to intermingle (however covertly and indirectly) in the internal concerns of our country; or who shall attempt to prescribe rules for our policy with any other power, if there be no infraction of our engagements with themselves, as one of the greatest evils that can befall us as a people; for whatever may be their professions, be assured fellow citizens and the event will (as it always has) invariably prove, that nations as well as individuals, act for their own benefit, and not for the benefit of others, unless both interests happen to be assimilated (and when that is the case there requires no contract to bind them together). That all their interferences are calculated to promote the former; and in proportion as they succeed, will render us less independent. In a word, nothing is more certain than that, if we receive favors, we must grant favors; and it is not easy to decide beforehand under such circumstances as we are, on which side the balance will ultimately terminate; but easy indeed is it to foresee that it may involve us in disputes and finally in war, to fulfill political alliances. Whereas, if there be no engagements on our part, we shall be unembarrassed, and at liberty at all times, to act from circumstances, and the dictates of justice, sound policy, and our essential interests.

That we may be always prepared for war, but never unsheath the sword except in self-defense so long as justice and our essential rights, and national respectability can be preserved without it; for without the gift of prophecy, it may safely be pronounced, that if this country can remain in peace twenty years longer, and I devoutly pray that it may do so to the end of time, such in all probability will be its population, riches, and resources, when combined with its peculiarly happy and remote situation from the other quarters of the globe, as to bid defiance, in a just cause, to any earthly power whatsoever.

That whensoever and so long as we profess to be neutral, let our public conduct whatever our private affections may be, accord therewith; without suffering partialities on one hand, or prejudices on the other to control our actions. A contrary practice is not only incompatible with our declarations, but is pregnant with mischief, embarrassing to the Administration, tending to divide us into parties, and ultimately productive of all those evils and horrors which proceed from faction, and above all, that our Union may be as lasting as time; for while we are encircled in one band, we shall possess the strength of a Giant and there will be none who can make us afraid. Divide, and we shall become weak, a prey to foreign intrigues and internal discord, and shall be as miserable and contemptible as we are now enviable and happy. And lastly:

That the several departments of government may be preserved in their utmost constitutional purity, without any attempt of one to encroach on the rights or privileges of another; that the general and state governments may move in their proper orbits; and that the authorities of our own constituting may be respected by ourselves as the most certain means of having them respected by foreigners. . . .

George Washington

Farewell Address (1797)

. . . Observe good faith and justice toward all nations. Cultivate peace and harmony with all. Religion and morality enjoin this conduct. And can it be that good policy does not equally enjoin it? It will be worthy of a free, enlightened, and at no distant period a great nation to give to mankind the magnanimous and too novel example of a people always guided by an exalted justice and benevolence. Who can doubt that in the course of time and things the fruits of such a plan would richly repay any temporary advantages which might be lost by a steady adherence to it? Can it be that Providence has not connected the permanent felicity of a nation with its virtue? The experiment, at least, is recommended by every sentiment which ennobles human nature. Alas! is it rendered impossible by its vices?

In the execution of such a plan nothing is more essential than that permanent, inveterate antipathies against particular nations and passionate attachments for others should be excluded, and that in place of them just and amicable feelings toward all should be cultivated. The nation which indulges toward another an habitual hatred or an habitual fondness is in some degree a slave. It is a slave to its animosity or to its affection, either of which is sufficient to lead it astray from its duty and its interest. Antipathy in one nation against another disposes each more readily to offer insult and injury, to lay hold of slight causes of umbrage, and to be haughty and intractable when accidental or trifling occasions of dispute occur.

So, likewise, a passionate attachment of one nation for another produces a variety of evils. Sympathy for the favorite nation, facilitating the illusion of an imaginary common interest in cases where no real common interest exists, and infusing into one the enmities of the other, betrays the former into a participation in the quarrels and wars of the latter without adequate inducement or justification. It leads also to concessions to the favorite nation of privileges denied to others, which is apt doubly to injure the nation making the concessions by unnecessarily parting with what ought to have been retained, and by exciting jealousy, ill will, and a disposition to retaliate in the parties from whom equal privileges are withheld; and it gives to ambitious, corrupted, or deluded citizens (who devote themselves to the favorite nation) facility to betray or sacrifice the interests of their own country without odium, sometimes even with popularity, gilding with the appearances of a virtuous sense of obligation, a commendable deference for public opinion, or a laudable zeal for public good the base or foolish compliances of ambition, corruption, or infatuation. . . .

Against the insidious wiles of foreign influence (I conjure you to believe me, fellow citizens) the jealousy of a free people ought to be *constantly* awake, since history and experience prove that foreign influence is one of the most baneful foes of republican government. But that jealousy, to be useful, must

SOURCE: Henry Steele Commager, *Documents of American History*, 7th ed. (New York: Appleton-Century-Crofts, 1963).

be impartial, else it becomes the instrument of the very influence to be avoided, instead of a defense against it. Excessive partiality for one foreign nation and excessive dislike of another cause those whom they actuate to see danger only on one side, and serve to veil and even second the arts of influence on the other. Real patriots who may resist the intrigues of the favorite are liable to become suspected and odious, while its tools and dupes usurp the applause and confidence of the people to surrender their interests.

The great rule of conduct for us in regard to foreign nations is, in extending our commercial relations to have with them as little *political* connection as possible. So far as we have already formed engagements let them be fulfilled with perfect good faith. Here let us stop.

Europe has a set of primary interests which to us have none or a very remote relation. Hence she must be engaged in frequent controversies, the causes of which are essentially foreign to our concerns. Hence, therefore, it must be unwise in us to implicate ourselves by artificial ties in the ordinary vicissitudes of her politics or the ordinary combinations and collisions of her friendships or enmities.

Our detached and distant situation invites and enables us to pursue a different course. If we remain one people, under an efficient government, the period is not far off when we may defy material injury from external annoyance; when we may take such an attitude as will cause the neutrality we may at any time resolve upon to be scrupulously respected; when belligerent nations, under the impossibility of making acquisitions upon us, will not lightly hazard the giving us provocation; when we may choose peace or war, as our interest, guided by justice, shall counsel.

Why forego the advantages of so peculiar a situation? Why quit our own to stand upon foreign ground? Why, by interweaving our destiny with that of any part of Europe, entangle our peace and prosperity in the toils of European ambition, rivalship, interest, humor, or caprice?

It is our true policy to steer clear of permanent alliances with any portion of the foreign world, so far, I mean, as we are now at liberty to do it; for let me not be understood as capable of patronizing infidelity to existing engagements. I hold the maxim no less applicable to public than to private affairs that honesty is always the best policy. I repeat, therefore, let those engagements be observed in their genuine sense. But in my opinion it is unnecessary and would be unwise to extend them.

Taking care always to keep ourselves by suitable establishments on a respectable defensive posture, we may safely trust to temporary alliances for extraordinary emergencies.

Harmony, liberal intercourse with all nations are recommended by policy, humanity, and interest. But even our commercial policy should hold an equal and impartial hand, neither seeking nor granting exclusive favors or preferences; consulting the natural course of things; diffusing and diversifying by gentle means the streams of commerce, but forcing nothing; establishing with powers so disposed, in order to give trade a stable course, to define the rights of our merchants, and to enable the Government to support them, conventional rules of intercourse, the best that present circumstances and mutual opinion will permit, but temporary and liable to be from time to time abandoned or varied as experience and circumstances shall dictate; constantly keeping in view that it is folly in one nation to look for disinterested favors from another; that it must pay with a portion of its independence for whatever it may accept under that character; that by such acceptance it may place itself in the condition of having given equivalents for nominal favors, and yet of being reproached with ingratitude for not giving more. There can be no greater error than to expect or calculate upon real favors from nation to nation. It is an illusion which experience must cure, which a just pride ought to discard. . . .

Though in reviewing the incidents of my Administration I am unconscious of intentional error, I am nevertheless too sensible of my defects not to think it probable that I may have committed many errors. Whatever they may be, I fervently beseech the Almighty to avert or mitigate the evils to which they may tend. I shall also carry with me the hope that my country will never cease to view them with indulgence, and that, after forty-five years of my life dedicated to its service with an upright zeal, the faults of incompetent abilities will be consigned to oblivion, as myself must soon be to the mansions of rest.

Relying on its kindness in this as in other things, and actuated by that fervent love toward it which is so natural to a man who views in it the native soil of himself and his progenitors for several generations, I anticipate with pleasing expectation that retreat in which I promise myself to realize without alloy the sweet enjoyment of partaking in the midst of my fellow-citizens the benign influence of good laws under a free government—the ever-favorite object of my heart, and the happy reward, as I trust, of our mutual cares, labors, and dangers.

Thomas Jefferson's Letter to Elbridge Gerry (1799)

Although far more sympathetic to the French Revolution than Washington, and more concerned that the United States should represent republican principles, Jefferson essentially agreed that the United States ought to avoid involvement with foreign nations. His arguments for a militia and against a standing army were typical of American republican thought.

Thomas Jefferson

Letter to Elbridge Gerry (1799)

. . . I am for a government rigorously frugal and simple, applying all the possible savings of the public revenue to the discharge of the national debt; and not for a multiplication of officers and salaries merely to make partisans, and for increasing, by every device, the public debt, on the principle of its being a public blessing. I am for relying, for internal defence, on our militia solely, till actual invasion, and for such a naval force only as may protect our coasts and harbors from such depredations as we have experienced; and not for a standing army in time of peace, which may overawe the public sentiment; nor for a

SOURCE: Andrew A. Lipscomb, ed., *The Writings of Thomas Jefferson* (Washington, D.C.: Thomas Jefferson Memorial Assoc., 1903).

navy, which, by its own expenses and the eternal wars in which it will implicate us, will grind us with public burthens, and sink us under them. I am for free commerce with all nations; political connection with none; and little or no diplomatic establishment. And I am not for linking ourselves by new treaties with the quarrels of Europe; entering that field of slaughter to preserve their balance, of joining in the confederacy of kings to war against the principles of liberty. I am for freedom of religion, and against all manoeuvres to bring about a legal ascendancy of one sect over another: for freedom of the press, and against all violations of the Constitution to silence by force and not by reason the complaints or criticisms, just or unjust, of our citizens against the conduct of their agents. And I am for encouraging the progress of science in all its branches; and not for raising a hue and cry against the sacred name of philosophy; for awing the human mind by stories of raw-head and bloody bones to a distrust of its own vision, and to repose implicitly on that of others; to go backward instead of forwards to look for improvement; to believe that government, religion, morality, and every other science were in the highest perfection in ages of the darkest ignorance, and that nothing can ever be devised more perfect than what was established by our forefathers. To these I will add, that I was a sincere well-wisher

to the success of the French revolution, and still wish it may end in the establishment of a free and well-ordered republic; but I have not been insensible under the atrocious depredations they have committed on our commerce. The first object of my heart is my own country. In that is embarked my family, my fortune, and my own existence. I have not one farthing of interest, nor one fibre of attachment out of it, nor a single motive of preference of any one nation to another, but in proportion as they are more or less friendly to us. But though deeply feeling the injuries of France, I did not think war the surest means of redressing them. I did believe, that a mission sincerely disposed to preserve peace, would obtain for us a peaceable and honorable settlement and retribution; and I appeal to you to say, whether this might not have been obtained, if either of your colleagues had been of the same sentiment with yourself.

These, my friend, are my principles; they are unquestionably the principles of the great body of our fellow-citizens, and I know there is not one of them which is not yours also. In truth, we never differed but on one ground, the funding system; and as, from the moment of its being adopted by the constituted authorities, I became religiously principled in the sacred discharge of it to the uttermost farthing, we are united now even on that single ground of difference.

A New Orthodoxy:

America's Flirtation with Colonialism

Albert J. Beveridge, 1862–1927

A U.S. senator from Indiana and a dazzling orator, Beveridge was a leading proponent of American imperialism. He was a keen, young supporter of Theodore Roosevelt and later left the Republican party to support Roosevelt's Bull Moose party. Like Roosevelt and many other nationalist Progressives, Beveridge was both a supporter of industrial reform and regulation, and a believer in Anglo-Saxon supremacy. He championed child labor legislation, tariff reform, food and drug inspection, and at the same time an aggressive expansionist foreign policy, especially toward less developed nations. Beveridge was interested in finding new markets for American industry. In a sense his commitment to tariff reform was consistent with his concern for new colonial markets. He was well aware that beyond the Philippines lay "China's illimitable markets," and he felt an American colonial presence in the Pacific would insure our access. Similarly, lower tariffs could reduce trade barriers with the more developed countries and thus increase trade in those areas as well.

Beveridge's political career was cut short, however, when conservative Republicans withdrew their support for his reelection in 1910. Although he ran unsuccessfully in other elections and supported Roosevelt's later campaigns, Beveridge turned to another career—that of historian. He wrote a four-volume work on John Marshall and was in the midst of a work on Lincoln when he died. While a fiery polemicist as a politician, Beveridge wrote history with the sensitive objectivity of the finest scholar.

The following speech is one of Beveridge's most famous, a bellicose imperialist, even racist, advocacy of American rule in the Philippines. This speech became a Republican campaign document in Indiana, Iowa, and other midwestern states.

Albert J. Beveridge

Campaign Speech, The March of the Flag (1898)

It is a noble land that God has given us; a land that can feed and clothe the world; a land whose coastlines would inclose half the countries of Europe; a land set like a sentinel between the two imperial oceans of the globe, a greater England with a nobler destiny.

It is a mighty people that He has planted on this soil; a people sprung from the most masterful blood of history; a people perpetually revitalized by the virile, man-producing working-folk of all the earth; a people imperial by virtue of their power, by right of their institutions, by authority of their Heaven-directed purposes—the propagandists and not the misers of liberty.

It is a glorious history our God has bestowed upon His chosen people; a history heroic with faith in our mission and our future; a history of statesmen who flung the boundaries of the Republic out into unexplored lands and savage wilderness; a history of soldiers who carried the flag across blazing deserts and through the ranks of hostile mountains, even to the gates of sunset; a history of a multiplying people who overran a continent in half a century; a history of prophets who saw the consequences of evils inherited from the past and of martyrs who died to save us from them; a history divinely logical, in the process of whose tremendous reasoning we find ourselves to-day.

Therefore, in this campaign, the question is larger than a party question. It is an Ameri-

SOURCE: Albert J. Beveridge, *The Meaning of the Times* (New York: Bobbs-Merrill, 1908).

can question. It is a world question. Shall the American people continue their march toward the commercial supremacy of the world? Shall free institutions broaden their blessed reign as the children of liberty wax in strength, until the empire of our principles is established over the hearts of all mankind?

Have we no mission to perform, no duty to discharge to our fellow-man? Has God endowed us with gifts beyond our deserts and marked us as the people of His peculiar favor, merely to rot in our own selfishness, as men and nations must, who take cowardice for their companion and self for their deity—as China has, as India has, as Egypt has?

Shall we be as the man who had one talent and hid it, or as he who had ten talents and used them until they grew to riches? And shall we reap the reward that waits on our discharge of our high duty; shall we occupy new markets for what our farmers raise, our factories make, our merchants sell—aye, and, please God, new markets for what our ships shall carry?

Hawaii is ours; Porto Rico is to be ours; at the prayer of her people Cuba finally will be ours; in the islands of the East, even to the gates of Asia, coaling stations are to be ours at the very least; the flag of a liberal government is to float over the Philippines, and may it be the banner that Taylor unfurled in Texas and Fremont carried to the coast.

The Opposition tells us that we ought not to govern a people without their consent. I answer, The rule of liberty that all just government derives its authority from the consent of the governed, applies only to those who are capable of self-government. We govern the Indians without their consent, we govern our territories without their consent, we govern our children without their consent. How do they know that our government would be without their consent? Would not the people of the Philippines prefer the just, humane, civilizing government of this Republic to the savage, bloody rule of pillage and extortion from which we have rescued them?

And, regardless of this formula of words made only for enlightened, self-governing people, do we owe no duty to the world? Shall we turn these peoples back to the reeking hands from which we have taken them? Shall we abandon them, with Germany, England, Japan, hungering for them? Shall we save them from those nations, to give them a self-rule of tragedy?

They ask us how we shall govern these new possessions. I answer: Out of local conditions and the necessities of the case methods of government will grow. If England can govern foreign lands, so can America. If Germany can govern foreign lands, so can America. If they can supervise protectorates, so can America. Why is it more difficult to administer Hawaii than New Mexico or California? Both had a savage and an alien population; both were more remote from the seat of government when they came under our dominion than the Philippines are to-day.

Will you say by your vote that American ability to govern has decayed; that a century's experience in self-rule has failed of a result? Will you affirm by your vote that you are an infidel to American power and practical sense? Or will you say that ours is the blood of government; ours the heart of dominion; ours the brain and genius of administration? Will you remember that we do but what our fathers did—we but pitch the tents of liberty farther westward, farther southward—we only continue the march of the flag?

The march of the flag! In 1789 the flag of the Republic waves over four million souls in thirteen states, and their savage territory which stretched to the Mississippi, to Canada, to the Floridas. The timid minds of that day said that no new territory was needed, and, for the hour, they were right. But Jefferson, through whose intellect the centuries marched; Jefferson, who dreamed of Cuba as an American state; Jefferson, the first Imperialist of the Republic—Jefferson acquired that imperial territory which swept from the Mississippi to the mountains, from Texas to the British possessions, and the march of the flag began!

The infidels to the gospel of liberty raved, but the flag swept on! The title to that noble land out of which Oregon, Washington, Idaho and Montana have been carved was uncertain; Jefferson, strict constructionist of constitutional power though he was, obeyed the Anglo-Saxon impulse within him, whose watchword then and whose watchword throughout the world to-day is, "Forward!": another empire was added to the Republic, and the march of the flag went on!

Those who deny the power of free institutions to expand urged every argument, and more, that we hear, to-day; but the people's judgment approved the command of their blood, and the march of the flag went on!

A screen of land from New Orleans to Florida shut us from the Gulf, and over this and the Everglade Peninsula waved the saffron flag of Spain; Andrew Jackson seized both, the American people stood at his back, and, under Monroe, the Floridas came under the dominion of the Republic, and the march of the flag went on! The Casandras prophesied every prophecy of despair we hear, today, but the march of the flag went on!

Then Texas responded to the bugle calls of liberty, and the march of the flag went on! And, at last, we waged war with Mexico, and the flag swept over the southwest, over peerless California, past the Gate of Gold to Oregon on the north, and from ocean to ocean its folds of glory blazed.

And, now, obeying the same voice that Jefferson heard and obeyed, that Jackson heard and obeyed, that Monroe heard and obeyed, that Seward heard and obeyed, that Grant heard and obeyed, that Harrison heard and obeyed, our President to-day plants the flag over the islands of the seas, outposts of commerce, citadels of national security, and the march of the flag goes on!

Distance and oceans are no arguments. The fact that all the territory our fathers bought and seized is contiguous, is no argument. In 1819 Florida was farther from New York than Porto Rico is from Chicago to-day; Texas, farther from Washington in 1845 than Hawaii is from Boston in 1898; California, more inaccessible in 1847 than the Philippines are now. Gibraltar is farther from London than Havana is from Washington; Melbourne is farther from Liverpool than Manila is from San Francisco.

The ocean does not separate us from lands of our duty and desire—the oceans join us, rivers never to be dredged, canals never to be repaired. Steam joins us; electricity joins us—the very elements are in league with our destiny. Cuba not contiguous! Porto Rico not contiguous! Hawaii and the Philippines not contiguous! The oceans make them contiguous. And our navy will make them contiguous.

But the Opposition is right—there is a difference. We did not need the western Mississippi Valley when we acquired it, nor Florida, nor Texas, nor California, nor the royal provinces of the far northwest. We had no emigrants to people this imperial wilderness, no money to develop it, even no highways to cover it. No trade awaited us in its savage fastnesses. Our productions were not greater than our trade. There was not one reason for the land-lust of our statesmen from Jefferson to Grant, other than the prophet and the Saxon within them. But, to-day, we are raising more than we can consume, making more than we can use. Therefore we must find new markets for our produce.

And so, while we did not need the territory taken during the past century at the time it was acquired, we do need what we have taken in 1898, and we need it now. The resources and the commerce of these immensely rich dominions will be increased as much as American energy is greater than Spanish sloth. In Cuba, alone, there are 15 million acres of forest unacquainted with the ax, exhaustless mines of iron, priceless deposits of manganese, millions of dollars' worth of which we must buy, to-day, from the Black Sea districts. There are millions of acres yet unexplored.

The resources of Porto Rico have only been trifled with. The riches of the Philippines have hardly been touched by the fingertips of modern methods. And they produce what we consume, and consume what we produce—the very predestination of reciprocity—a reciprocity "not made with hands, eternal in the heavens." They sell hemp, sugar, cocoanuts, fruits of the tropics, timber of price like mahogany; they buy flour, clothing, tools, implements, machinery and all that we can raise and make. Their trade will be ours in time. Do you indorse that policy with your vote?

Cuba is as large as Pennsylvania, and is the richest spot on the globe. Hawaii is as large as New Jersey; Porto Rico half as large as Hawaii; the Philippines larger than all New England, New York, New Jersey and Delaware combined. Together they are larger than the British Isles, larger than France, larger than Germany, larger than Japan.

If any man tells you that trade depends on cheapness and not on government influence, ask him why England does not abandon South Africa, Egypt, India. Why does France seize South China, Germany the vast region whose port is Kaouchou?

Our trade with Porto Rico, Hawaii and the Philippines must be as free as between the states of the Union, because they are American territory, while every other nation on earth must pay our tariff before they can compete with us. Until Cuba shall ask for annexation, our trade with her will, at the very least, be like the preferential trade of Canada with England. That, and the excellence of our goods and products; that, and the convenience of traffic; that, and the kinship of interests and destiny, will give the monopoly of these markets to the American people.

The commercial supremacy of the Republic means that this Nation is to be the sovereign factor in the peace of the world. For the conflicts of the future are to be conflicts of trade—struggles for markets—commercial wars for existence. And the golden rule of peace is impregnability of position and invincibility of preparedness. So, we see England, the greatest strategist of history, plant her flag and her cannon on Gibraltar, at Quebec, in the Bermudas, at Vancouver, everywhere.

So Hawaii furnishes us a naval base in the heart of the Pacific; the Ladrones another, a voyage further on; Manila another, at the gates of Asia—Asia, to the trade of whose hundreds of millions American merchants, manufacturers, farmers, have as good right as those of Germany or France or Russia or England; Asia, whose commerce with the United Kingdom alone amounts to hundreds of millions of dollars every year; Asia, to whom Germany looks to take her surplus products; Asia, whose doors must not be shut against American trade. Within five decades the bulk of Oriental commerce will be ours.

No wonder that, in the shadows of coming events so great, free-silver is already a memory. The current of history has swept past that episode. Men understand, to-day, that the greatest commerce of the world must be conducted with the steadiest standard of value and most convenient medium of exchange human ingenuity can devise. Time, that unerring reasoner, has settled the silver question. The American people are tired of talking about money—they want to make it. Why should the farmer get a half-measure dollar of money any more that he should give a half-measure bushel of grain?

Why should not the proposition for the free coinage of silver be as dead as the proposition of irredeemable paper money? It is the same proposition in a different form. If the Government stamp can make a piece of silver, which you can buy for 45 cents, pass for 100 cents, the Government stamp can make a piece of pewter, worth one cent, pass for 100 cents, and a piece of paper, worth a fraction of a cent, pass for 100 cents. Free-silver is the principle of fiat money applied to metal. If you favor fiat silver, you necessarily favor fiat paper.

If the Government can make money with a stamp, why does the Government borrow money? If the Government can create value out of nothing, why not abolish all taxation?

And if it is not the stamp of the Government that raises the value, but the demand which free coinage creates, why has the value of silver gone down at a time when more silver was bought and coined by the Government than ever before? Again, if the people want more silver, why do they refuse what we already have? And if free silver makes money more plentiful, how will *you* get any of it? Will the silver-mine owner give it to you? Will he loan it to you? Will the Government give or loan it to you? Where do you or I come in on this free-silver proposition?

The American people want this money question settled for ever. They want a uniform currency, a convenient currency, a currency that grows as business grows, a currency based on science and not on chance.

And now, on the threshold of our new and great career, is the time permanently to adjust our system of finance. The American people have the mightiest commerce of the world to conduct. They can not halt to unsettle their money system every time some ardent imagination sees a vision and dreams a dream. Think of Great Britain becoming the commercial monarch of the world with her financial system periodically assailed! Think of Holland or Germany or France bearing their burdens, and, yet, sending their flag to every sea, with their money at the mercy of politicians-out-of-an-issue. Let us settle the whole financial system on principles so sound that no agitation can shake it. And then, like men and not like children, let us on to our tasks, our mission and our destiny.

There are so many real things to be done— canals to be dug, railways to be laid, forests to be felled, cities to be builded, fields to be tilled, markets to be won, ships to be launched, peoples to be saved, civilization to be proclaimed and the flag of liberty flung to the eager air of every sea. Is this an hour to waste upon triflers with nature's laws? Is this a season to give our destiny over to word-mongers and prosperity-wreckers? No! It is an hour to remember our duty to our homes. It is a moment to realize the opportunities fate has opened to us. And so it is an hour for us to stand by the Government.

Wonderfully has God guided us. Yonder at Bunker Hill and Yorktown His providence was above us. At New Orleans and on ensanguined seas His hand sustained us. Abraham Lincoln was His minister and His was the altar of freedom the Nation's soldiers set up on a hundred battle-fields. His power directed Dewey in the East and delivered the Spanish fleet into our hands, as He delivered the elder Armada into the hands of our English sires two centuries ago. The American people can not use a dishonest medium of exchange; it is ours to set the world its example of right and honor. We can not fly from our world duties; it is ours to execute the purpose of a fate that has driven us to be greater than our small intentions. We can not retreat from any soil where Providence has unfurled our banner; it is ours to save that soil for liberty and civilization.

The Old Orthodoxy Reaffirmed

Carl Schurz, 1829–1906

Carl Schurz was a nineteenth-century classical liberal reformer who came to the United States as a political refugee from Germany. While a student, Schurz participated in the revolutionary movements of 1848. Forced to flee, he traveled throughout Western Europe and then came to the United States in 1852.

Schurz became active in American politics when he campaigned for Abraham Lincoln in 1858 and again in 1860. He fought bravely for the Union Army and after the war toured the South on behalf of President Johnson. His report, which argued strongly for civil rights and equal suffrage for blacks, was ignored and finally suppressed by the president.

Schurz remained active in politics, serving as U.S. senator from Missouri (1869–1875) and as secretary of interior for Rutherford B. Hayes. He favored aid to the Indians, conservation, and a merit system for hiring and promotion. Civil service reform became one of his chief concerns, and he worked actively to replace the spoils system with more rational, meritocratic practices.

Schurz was repelled by imperialism. In 1870, he strongly denounced President Grant's attempt to annex Santo Domingo; and later, when imperialist sentiment was greatest, he actively opposed the Spanish-American War and the annexation of the Philippines. Despite his love of his adopted country he refused to be a jingoist: "My country right or wrong; if right, to be kept right; and if wrong, to be set right."

Schurz should not be confused with the neoliberals of his day. He was a believer in laissez-faire, equal rights, and self-government. Yet he ignored the plight of the worker and the farmer that was at the heart of much of the reform sentiment of the late nineteenth and early twentieth centuries.

His vision was that of the Jacksonian liberal, and he feared statist intervention whether at home or abroad.

The following speech was an attack on American imperialism which Schurz delivered at the University of Chicago. In many respects it is a call for a return to older republican principles.

Carl Schurz

The Issue of Imperialism (1899)

By inviting me to address its faculty, its students and its friends upon so distinguished an occasion, the University of Chicago has done me an honor for which I am profoundly grateful. I can prove that gratitude in no better way than by uttering with entire frankness my honest convictions on the great subject you have given me to discuss—a subject fraught with more momentous consequence than any ever submitted to the judgment of the American people since the foundation of our Constitutional Government. . . .

If ever, it behooves the American people to think and act with calm deliberation, for the character and future of the Republic and the welfare of its people now living and yet to be born are in unprecedented jeopardy. To form a candid judgment of what this Republic has been, what it may become and what it ought to be, let us first recall to our minds its condition before the recent Spanish war. Our Government was, in the words of Abraham Lincoln, the greatest American of his time and the most genuine type of true Americanism, "the Government of the people, by the people and for the people." It was the

noblest ambition of all true Americans to carry this democratic government to the highest degree of perfection in justice, in probity, in assured peace, in the security of human rights, in progressive civilization; to solve the problem of popular self-government on the grandest scale, and thus to make this Republic the example and guiding-star of mankind.

We had invited the oppressed of all nations to find shelter here, and to enjoy with us the blessings of free institutions. They came by the millions. Some were not as welcome as others, but, under the assimilating force of American life in our temperate climate, which stimulates the working energies, nurses the spirit of orderly freedom and thus favors the growth of democracies, they became good Americans, most in the first generation, all in the following generations. And so with all the blood-crossings caused by the motley immigration, we became a substantially homogeneous people, united by common political beliefs and ideals, by common interests, laws and aspirations—in one word, a nation. Indeed, we were not without our difficulties and embarrassments, but only one of them, the race antagonism between the negroes and the whites, especially where the negroes live in mass, presents a problem which so far has baffled all efforts at practical solution in harmony with the spirit of our free institutions,

SOURCE: Frederic Bancroft, ed., *Speeches, Correspondences and Political Papers of Carl Schurz* (New York: G. P. Putnams' Sons, 1913). Convocation address delivered before the University of Chicago, January 4, 1899.

and thus threatens complications of a grave character.

We gloried in the marvelous growth of our population, wealth, power and civilization, and in the incalculable richness of the resources of our country capable of harboring three times our present population, and of immeasurable further material development. Our commerce with the world abroad, although we had no colonies, and but a small navy, spread with unprecedented rapidity, capturing one foreign market after another, not only for the products of our farms, but also for many of those of our manufacturing industries, with prospects of indefinite extension.

Peace reigned within our borders, and there was not the faintest shadow of a danger of foreign attack. Our voice, whenever we chose to speak in the councils of nations, was listened to with respect, even the mightiest sea Power on occasion yielding to us a deference far beyond its habit in its intercourse with others. We were considered ultimately invincible, if not invulnerable, in our continental stronghold. It was our boast, not that we possessed great and costly armies and navies, but that we did not need any. This exceptional blessing was our pride as it was the envy of the world. We looked down with pitying sympathy on other nations which submissively groaned under the burden of constantly increasing armaments, and we praised our good fortune for having saved us from so wretched a fate. . . .

Then came the Spanish war. A few vigorous blows laid the feeble enemy helpless at our feet. The whole scene seemed to have suddenly changed. According to the solemn proclamation of our Government, the war had been undertaken solely for the liberation of Cuba, as a war of humanity and not of conquest. But our easy victories had put conquest within our reach, and when our arms occupied foreign territory, a loud demand arose, that, pledge or no pledge to the contrary, the conquests should be kept, even the Philippines on the other side of the globe, and that as to Cuba herself, independence would be only a provisional formality. Why not? was the cry. Has not the career of the Republic almost from its very beginning been one of territorial expansion? Has it not acquired Louisiana, Florida, Texas, the vast countries that came to us through the Mexican war and Alaska, and has it not digested them well? Were not those acquisitions much larger than those now in contemplation? If the Republic could digest the old, why not the new? What is the difference?

Only look with an unclouded eye, and you will soon discover differences enough warning you to beware. There are five of decisive importance.

1. All the former acquisitions were on this continent and, excepting Alaska, contiguous to our borders.

2. They were situated, not in the tropical, but in the temperate zone, where democratic institutions thrive, and where our people could migrate in mass.

3. They were but very thinly peopled—in fact, without any population that would have been in the way of new settlements.

4. They could be organized as territories in the usual manner, with the expectation that they would presently come into the Union as self-governing States with populations substantially homogeneous to our own.

5. They did not require a material increase of our Army and Navy, either for their subjection to our rule or for their defense against any probable foreign attack provoked by their being in our possession.

Acquisitions of that nature we might, since the slavery trouble has been allayed, make indefinitely without in any dangerous degree imperiling our great experiment of democratic institutions on the grandest scale; without putting the peace of the Republic in jeopardy, and without depriving us of the inestimable privilege of comparatively unarmed security on a compact continent which may, indeed, by an enterprising enemy, be scratched on its edges, but is, with a people like ours, virtually impregnable. Even of our far-away Alaska it can be said that, although at present a possession of doubtful value, it is at least mainly on this continent, and may at some future time, when the inhabitants of the British possessions happily wish to unite with us, be within our uninterrupted boundaries.

Compare now with our old acquisitions as to all these important points those at present in view.

They are not continental, not contiguous to our present domain, but beyond seas, the Philippines many thousand miles distant from our coast. They are all situated in the tropics, where people of the Northern races, such as Anglo-Saxons, or generally speaking, people of Germanic blood, have never migrated in mass to stay; and they are more or less densely populated, parts of them as densely as Massachusetts—their populations consisting almost exclusively of races to whom the tropical climate is congenial—Spanish creoles mixed with negroes in the West Indies, and Malays, Tagals, Filipinos, Chinese, Japanese, Negritos and various more or less barbarous tribes in the Philippines.

When the question is asked whether we may hope to adapt those countries and populations to our system of government, the advocates of annexation answer cheerily, that when they belong to us, we shall soon "Americanize" them. This may mean that Americans in sufficiently large numbers will migrate there to determine the character of those populations so as to assimilate them to our own.

This is a delusion of the first magnitude. We shall, indeed, be able, if we go honestly about it, to accomplish several salutary things in those countries. But one thing we cannot do. We cannot strip the tropical climate of those qualities which have at all times deterred men of the Northern races, to which we belong, from migrating to those countries in

mass, to make their homes there, as they have migrated and are still migrating to countries in the temperate zone. This is not a mere theory, but a fact of universal experience.

It is true, you will find in the towns of tropical regions a sprinkling of persons of Anglo-Saxon or of other Northern origin—merchants, railroad builders, speculators, professional men and mechanics; also here and there an agriculturist. But their number is small, and most of them expect to go home again as soon as their money-making purpose is more or less accomplished.

Thus we observe now that business men with plenty of means are casting their eyes upon our "new possessions" to establish mercantile-houses there, or manufactories to be worked with native labor, and moneyed syndicates and "improvement companies" to exploit the resources of those countries, and speculators and promoters to take advantage of what may turn up—the franchise grabber, as reported, is already there—many having perfectly legitimate ends in view, others ends not so legitimate and all expecting to be more or less favored by the power of our Government; in short, the capitalist is thinking of going there, or sending his agents, his enterprises in most cases to be directed from these more congenial shores. But you will find that laboring men of the Northern races, as they have never done so before, so they will not now go there in mass to do the work of the country, agricultural or industrial, and to found there permanent homes; and this not merely because the rate of wages in such countries is, owing to native competition, usually low, but because they cannot thrive there under the climatic conditions.

But it is the working-masses, those laboring in agriculture and the industries, that everywhere form the bulk of the population; and these are the true constituency of democratic government. And as the Northern races cannot do the work of the tropical zone, they cannot furnish such a constituency. It is an incontestable and very significant fact that the British, the best colonizers in history, have, indeed, established in tropical regions governments, and rather absolute ones, but they have never succeeded in establishing there democratic commonwealths of the Anglo-Saxon type, like those in America or Australia. . . .

What, then, shall we do with such populations? Shall we, according, not indeed to the letter, but to the evident spirit of our Constitution, organize those countries as territories with a view to their eventual admission as States? If they become States on an equal footing with the other States they will not only be permitted to govern themselves as to their home concerns, but they will take part in governing the whole Republic, in governing us, by sending Senators and Representatives into our Congress to help make our laws, and by voting for President and Vice-President to give our National Government its Executive. The prospect of the consequences which would follow the admission of the Spanish creoles and the negroes of West India islands and of the Malays and Tagals of the Philippines to participation in the conduct of our Government is so alarming that you may well pause before taking the step.

But this may be avoided, it is said, by governing the new possessions as mere dependencies, or subject provinces. I will waive the Constitutional question and merely point out that this would be a most serious departure from the rule that governed our former acquisitions, which are so frequently quoted as precedents. It is useless to speak of the District of Columbia and Alaska as proof that we have done such things before and can do them again. Every candid mind will at once admit the vast difference between those cases and the *permanent* establishment of substantially arbitrary government over large territories with ten millions of inhabitants, and with a prospect of there being many more of the same kind, if we once launch out on a career of conquest. The question is not merely whether we *can*

do such things, but whether, having the public good at heart, we *should* do them.

If we do adopt such a system, then we shall, for the first time since the abolition of slavery, again have two kinds of Americans: Americans of the first class, who enjoy the privilege of taking part in the Government in accordance with our old Constitutional principles, and Americans of the second class, who are to be ruled in a substantially arbitrary fashion by the Americans of the first class, through Congressional legislation and the action of the National Executive—not to speak of individual "masters" arrogating to themselves powers beyond the law.

This will be a difference no better—nay, rather somewhat worse—than that which a century and a quarter ago still existed between Englishmen of the first and Englishmen of the second class, the first represented by King George and the British Parliament, and the second by the American colonists. This difference called forth that great paean of human liberty, the American Declaration of Independence—a document which, I regret to say, seems, owning to the intoxication of conquest, to have lost much of its charm among some of our fellow-citizens. Its fundamental principle was that "governments derive their just powers from the consent of the governed." We are now told that we have never fully lived up to that principle, and that, therefore, in our new policy we may cast it aside altogether. But I say to you that, if we are true believers in democratic government, it is our duty to move in the direction towards the full realization of that principle and not in the direction away from it. . . .

And I warn the American people that a democracy cannot so deny its faith as to the vital conditions of its being—it cannot long play the King over subject populations without creating in itself ways of thinking and habits of action most dangerous to its own vitality—most dangerous especially to those classes of society which are the least powerful in the assertion, and the most helpless in the defense of their rights. Let the poor and the men who earn their bread by the labor of their hands pause and consider well before they give their assent to a policy so deliberately forgetful of the equality of rights. . . .

* * * * *

Our old acquisitions did not require a material increase of our Army and Navy. What of the new? It is generally admitted that we need very considerable additions to our armaments on land and sea to restore and keep order on the islands taken from Spain, and then to establish our sovereignty there. This is a ticklish business. In the first place, Spain has never been in actual control and possession of a good many of the Philippine Islands, while on others the insurgent Filipinos had well-nigh destroyed the Spanish power when the treaty of Paris was made. The people of those islands will either peaceably submit to our rule or they will not. If they do not, and we must conquer them by force of arms, we shall at once have a war on our hands.

What kind of a war will that be? The Filipinos fought against Spain for their freedom and independence, and unless they abandon their recently proclaimed purpose for their freedom and independence, they will fight against us. To be sure, we promise them all sorts of good things if they will consent to become our subjects. But they may, and probably will, prefer independence to foreign rule, no matter what fair promises the foreign invader makes. For to the Filipinos the American is essentially a foreigner, more foreign in some respects than even the Spaniard was. Subjection to foreign rule is not to everybody's taste; and as to the question of their rights under the principles of international law, you need only read the protest against our treaty of Paris by their representative, Agoncillo, to admit that they make out a strong case. Now, if they resist, what shall we do? Kill them?

Let soldiers marching under the Stars and Stripes shoot them down? Shoot them down because they stand up for their independence, just as the Cubans, who are no better than they, fought for their independence, to which we solemnly declared them to be "of right" entitled? Look at this calmly if you can. The American volunteers, who rushed to arms by the hundreds of thousands to fight for Cuban independence, may not stomach this killing of Filipinos fighting for *their* independence. We shall have to rely upon the regulars, the professional soldiers, and we may need a good many of them. . . .

The American people began their career as one of the colonial offshoots of the English stock. They found a great continent to occupy and to fill with democratic commonwealths. Our country is large enough for several times our present population. Our home resources are enormous, in great part not yet touched. We need not fear to be starved by the completest blockade of our coasts, for we have enough of everything and to spare. On the contrary, such a blockade might rather result in starving others that need our products. We are to-day one of the greatest Powers on earth, without having the most powerful fleet, and without stepping beyond our boundaries. We are sure to be by far the greatest Power of all, as our homogeneous, intelligent and patriotic population multiplies, and our resources are developed, without firing a gun or sacrificing a life for the sake of conquest—far more powerful than the British Empire with all its Hindoos, and than the Russian Empire with all its Mongols. We can exercise the most beneficent influences upon mankind, not by forcing our rule or our goods upon others that are weak by the force of bayonets and artillery, but through the moral power of our example, by proving how the greatest as well as the smallest nation can carry on the government of the people by the people and for the people in justice, liberty, order and peace without large armies and navies.

Let this Republic and Great Britain each follow the course which its conditions and its history have assigned to it, and their ambitions will not clash, and their friendship be maintained for the good of all. And if our British cousins should ever get into very serious stress, American friendship may stand behind them; but then Britain would depend upon our friendship, which, as an American, I should prefer, and not America on British friendship, as our British friends, who so impatiently urge us to take the Philippines, would have it. . . .

What can there be to justify a policy fraught with such direful consequences? Let us pass the arguments of the advocates of such imperialism candidly in review.

The cry suddenly raised that this great country has become too small for us is too ridiculous to demand an answer, in view of the fact that our present population may be tripled and still have ample elbow-room, with resources to support many more. But we are told that our industries are gasping for breath; that we are suffering from overproduction; that our products must have new outlets, and that we need colonies and dependencies the world over to give us more markets. More markets? Certainly. But do we, civilized beings, indulge in the absurd and barbarous notion that we must own the countries with which we wish to trade? Here are our official reports before us, telling us that of late years our export trade has grown enormously, not only of farm products, but of the products of our manufacturing industries; in fact, that "our sales of manufactured goods have continued to extend with a facility and promptitude of results which have excited the serious concern of countries that, for generations, had not only controlled their home markets, but had practically monopolized certain lines of trade in other lands."

There is the British Right Hon. Charles T. Ritchie, President of the Board of Trade, telling a British Chamber of Commerce that "we [Great Britain] are being rapidly overhauled in exports by other nations, especially the United States and Germany," their exports fast advancing while British exports are declining. What? Great Britain, the greatest colonial Power in the world, losing in competition with two nations one of which had, so far, no colonies or dependencies at all, and the other none of any commercial importance? It means that, as proved by the United States and Germany, colonies are not necessary for the expansion of trade, and that, as proved by Great Britain, colonies do not protect a nation against a loss of trade. Our trade expands, without colonies or big navies, because we produce certain goods better and in proportion cheaper than other people do. British trade declines, in spite of immense dependencies and the strongest navy, because it does not successfully compete with us, in that respect. Trade follows, not the flag, but the best goods for the price. Expansion of export trade and new markets! We do not need foreign conquests to get them, for we have them, and are getting them more and more in rapidly increasing growth.

"But the Pacific Ocean," we are mysteriously told, "will be the great commercial battlefield of the future, and we must quickly use the present opportunity to secure our position on it. The visible presence of great power is necessary for us to get our share of the trade of China. Therefore we must have the Philippines." Well, the China trade is worth having, although for a time out of sight the Atlantic Ocean will be an infinitely more important battlefield of commerce than the Pacific, and one European customer is worth more than twenty or thirty Asiatics. But does the trade of China really require that we should have the Philippines and a great display of power to get our share? Read the consular reports, and you will find that in many places in China our trade is rapidly gaining, while in some, British trade is declining, and this while Great Britain had on hand the greatest display of power imaginable and we had none. And in order to increase our trade there, our consuls advise us to improve our commercial methods, saying nothing of the necessity of establishing a base of naval operations, and of our appearing there with war-ships and heavy guns. Trade is developed, not by the biggest guns, but by the best merchants. . . .

"But we must have coaling-stations for our Navy!" Well, can we not get as many coaling-stations as we need, without owning populous countries behind them that would entangle us in dangerous political responsibilities and complications?

"But we must civilize those poor people!" Well, are we not ingenious and charitable enough to do much for their civilization without subjugating and ruling them by criminal aggression?

The rest of the pleas for imperialism consist mostly of those high-sounding catchwords of which a free people, when about to decide great questions, should be especially suspicious. We are admonished that it is time for us to become a "world-power." Well, we *are* a world-power now, and have been one for many years. What is a world-power? A power strong enough to make its voice listened to with deference by the world whenever it chooses to speak. It is necessary for a world-power, in order to be such, to have its finger in every pie? Must we have the Philippines in order to become a world-power? To ask the question is to answer it. . . .

We are told that, having grown so great and strong, we must at last cast off our childish reverence for the teachings of Washington's Farewell Address—those "nursery rhymes that were sung around the cradle of the Republic." I apprehend that many of those who now so flippantly scoff at the heritage the Father of his Country left us in his last words of admonition have never read that venerable document. I challenge those who have, to show me a single sentence of general import in it that would not as a wise rule of National conduct apply to the circumstances of to-day!

What is it that has given to Washington's Farewell Address an authority that was revered by all until our recent victories made so many of us drunk with wild ambitions? Not only the prestige of Washington's name, great as that was and should ever remain. No, it was the fact that under a respectful observance of those teachings this Republic has grown from the most modest beginnings into a Union spanning this vast continent; our people have multiplied from a handful to 75 millions; we have risen from poverty to a wealth the sum of which the imagination can hardly grasp; this American Nation has become one of the greatest and most powerful on earth, and continuing in the same course will surely become the greatest and most powerful of all. Not Washington's name alone gave his teachings their dignity and weight. It was the practical results of his policy that secured to it, until now, the intelligent approbation of the American people. And unless we have completely lost our senses, we shall never despise and reject as mere "nursery rhymes" the words of wisdom left us by the greatest of Americans, following which the American people have achieved a splendor of development without parallel in the history of mankind.

You may tell me that this is all very well, but that by the acts of our own Government we are now in this annexation business, and how can we get decently out of it? I answer that the difficulties of getting out of it may be great; but that they are infinitely less great than the difficulties we shall have to contend with if we stay in it.

Looking them in the face, let us first clear our minds of confused notions about our duties and responsibilities in the premises. That our victories have devolved upon us certain duties as to the people of the conquered islands, I readily admit. But are they the only duties we have to perform, or have they suddenly become paramount to all other duties? I deny it. I deny that the duties we owe to the Cubans and the Porto Ricans and the

Filipinos and the Tagals of the Asiatic islands absolve us from our duties to the 75 millions of our own people and to their posterity. . . .

They fought for deliverance from Spanish oppression, and we helped them to obtain that deliverance. That deliverance they understood to mean independence. I repeat the question whether anybody can tell me why the declaration of Congress that the Cubans *of right ought to be* free and independent should not apply to all of them? Their independence, therefore, would be the natural and rightful outcome. This is the solution of the problem first to be taken in view. It is objected that they are not capable of independent government. They may answer that this is their affairs and that they are at least entitled to a trial. I frankly admit that if they are given that trial, their conduct in governing themselves will be far from perfect. Well, the conduct of no people is perfect, not even our own. They may try to revenge themselves upon their tories in their revolutionary war. But we, too, threw our tories into hideous dungeons during our Revolutionary war and persecuted and drove them away after its close. They may have bloody civil broils. But we, too, have had our civil war which cost hundreds of thousands of lives and devastated one-half of our land; and now we have in horrible abundance the killings by lynch law and our battles of Virden. They may have trouble with their wild tribes. So had we, and we treated our wild tribes in a manner not to be proud of. They may have corruption and rapacity in their Government, but Havana and Ponce may get municipal administration almost as good as New York has under Tammany rule; and Manila may have a city council not much less virtuous than that of Chicago. . . .

No, we cannot expect that the Porto Ricans, the Cubans and the Filipinos will maintain orderly governments in Anglo-Saxon fashion. But they may succeed in establishing a tolerable order of things in their fashion, as Mexico, after many decades of turbulent disorder, succeeded at last, under Porfirio Diaz, in having a strong and orderly government of her kind, not, indeed, such a government as we would tolerate in this Union, but a government answering Mexican character and interests, and respectable in its relations with the outside world. . . .

Thus we shall be their best friends without being their foreign rulers. We shall have done our duty to them, to ourselves and to the world. However imperfect their governments may still remain, they will at least be their own, and they will not with their disorders and corruptions contaminate our institutions, the integrity of which is not only to ourselves, but to liberty-loving mankind, the most important concern of all. We may then await the result with generous patience—with the same patience with which for many years we witnessed the revolutionary disorders of Mexico on our very borders, without any thought of taking her government into our own hands. . . .

Let us never cease to invoke the good sense, the honesty and the patriotic pride of the people. Let us raise high the flag of our country— not as an emblem of reckless adventure and greedy conquest, of betrayed professions and broken pledges, of criminal aggression and arbitrary rule over subject populations—but the old, the true flag, the flag of George Washington and Abraham Lincoln; the flag of the government of, for and by the people; the flag of National faith held sacred and of National honor unsullied; the flag of human rights and of good example to all nations; the flag of true civilization, peace and goodwill to all men. Under it let us stand to the last, whatever betide. . . .

The New Orthodoxy Revised

Liberal Internationalism

Woodrow Wilson, "Making the World Safe for Democracy"

Although historians may debate Wilson's motives in bringing the United States into World War I, his public pronouncements clearly attempted to justify our involvement in terms of universal rights and a new internationalist order. Rejecting all imperialist rhetoric, Wilson argued that the United States had to defend itself and at the same time help restructure the world to make it "safe for democracy" and the self-determination of all people. Furthermore, Wilson hoped to replace secret diplomacy and balance of power politics with open treaties and an international peacekeeping organization, the League of Nations.

Wilson's vision was both idealistic and internationalist. He rejected the cynical realism and colonialism of the older powers while at the same time rejecting the isolationist tradition of American republicanism. Although unsuccessful in his attempt to bring the United States into the League of Nations, Wilson's blend of idealism and internationalist activism continues to provide the legitimating language for much of American foreign policy.

The following addresses by Woodrow Wilson are excellent examples of the underlying principles of Wilsonian internationalism.

Woodrow Wilson

Declaration of War (1917)

GENTLEMEN OF THE CONGRESS:

I have called the Congress into extraordinary session because there are serious, very serious, choices of policy to be made, and made immediately, which it was neither right nor constitutionally permissible that I should assume the responsibility of making.

On the third of February last I officially laid before you the extraordinary announcement of the Imperial German Government that on and after the first day of February it was its purpose to put aside all restraints of law or of humanity and use its submarines to sink every vessel that sought to approach either the ports of Great Britain and Ireland or the western coasts of Europe or any of the ports controlled by the enemies of Germany within the Mediterranean. That had seemed to be the object of the German submarine warfare earlier in the war, but since April of last year the Imperial Government had somewhat restrained the commanders of its undersea craft in conformity with its promise then given to us that passenger boats should not be sunk and that due warning would be given to all other vessels which its submarines might seek to destroy, when no resistance was offered or escape attempted, and care taken that their crews were given at least a fair chance to save their lives in their open boats. The precautions taken were meagre and haphazard enough, as was proved in distressing instance after instance in the progress of the

cruel and unmanly business, but a certain degree of restraint was observed. The new policy has swept every restriction aside. Vessels of every kind, whatever their flag, their character, their cargo, their destination, their errand, have been ruthlessly sent to the bottom without warning and without thought of help or mercy for those on board, the vessels of friendly neutrals along with those of belligerents. Even hospital ships and ships carrying relief to the sorely bereaved and stricken people of Belgium, though the latter were provided with safe conduct through the proscribed areas by the German Government itself and were distinguished by unmistakable marks of identity, have been sunk with the same reckless lack of compassion or of principle.

I was for a little while unable to believe that such things would in fact be done by any government that had hitherto subscribed to the humane practices of civilized nations. International law had its origin in the attempt to set up some law which would be respected and observed upon the seas, where no nation had right of dominion and where lay the free highways of the world. By painful stage after stage has that law been built up, with meagre enough results, indeed, after all was accomplished that could be accomplished, but always with a clear view, at least, of what the heart and conscience of mankind demanded. This minimum of right the German Government has swept aside under the plea of retaliation and necessity and because it had no weapons which it could use at sea except these which

SOURCE: Woodrow Wilson, *President Wilson's Great Speeches* (Chicago: Stanton and Von Vliet, 1917).

it is impossible to employ as it is employing them without throwing to the winds all scruples of humanity or of respect for the understandings that were supposed to underlie the intercourse of the world. I am not now thinking of the loss of property involved, immense and serious as that is, but only of the wanton and wholesale destruction of the lives of noncombatants, men, women, and children, engaged in pursuits which have always, even in the darkest periods of modern history, been deemed innocent and legitimate. Property can be paid for; the lives of peaceful and innocent people cannot be. The present German submarine warfare against commerce is a warfare against mankind.

It is a war against all nations. American ships have been sunk, American lives taken, in ways which it has stirred us very deeply to learn of, but the ships and people of other neutral and friendly nations have been sunk and overwhelmed in the waters in the same way. There has been no discrimination. The challenge is to all mankind. Each nation must decide for itself how it will meet it. The choice we make for ourselves must be made with a moderation of counsel and a temperateness of judgment befitting our character and our motives as a nation. We must put excited feeling away. Our motive will not be revenge or the victorious assertion of the physical might of the nation, but only the vindication of right, of human right, of which we are only a single champion. . . .

With a profound sense of the solemn and even tragical character of the step I am taking and of the grave responsibilities which it involves, but in unhesitating obedience to what I deem my constitutional duty, I advise that the Congress declare the recent course of the Imperial German Government to be in fact nothing less than war against the government and people of the United States; that it formally accept the status of belligerent which has thus been thrust upon it; and that it take immediate steps not only to put the country

in a more thorough state of defense but also to exert all its power and employ all its resources to bring the Government of the German Empire to terms and end the war.

What this will involve is clear. It will involve the utmost practicable cooperation in counsel and action with the governments now at war with Germany, and, as incident to that, the extension to those governments of the most liberal financial credits, in order that our resources may so far as possible be added to theirs. It will involve the organization and mobilization of all the material resources of the country to supply the materials of war and serve the incidental needs of the nation in the most abundant and yet the most economical and efficient way possible. It will involve the immediate full equipment of the navy in all respects, but particularly in supplying it with the best means of dealing with the enemy's submarines. It will involve the immediate addition to the armed forces of the United States already provided for by law in case of war of at least 500,000 men, who should, in my opinion, be chosen upon the principle of universal liability to service, and also the authorization of subsequent additional increments of equal force so soon as they may be needed and can be handled in training. It will involve also, of course, the granting of adequate credits to the Government, sustained, I hope, so far as they can equitably be sustained by the present generation, by well conceived taxation.

I say sustained so far as may be equitable by taxation because it seems to me that it would be most unwise to base the credits which will now be necessary entirely on money borrowed. It is our duty, I most respectfully urge, to protect our people so far as we may against the very serious hardships and evils which would be likely to arise out of the inflation which would be produced by vast loans. . . .

While we do these things, these deeply momentous things, let us be very clear, and make very clear to all the world what our motives and our objects are. My own thought has not been driven from its habitual and normal course by the unhappy events of the last two months, and I do not believe that the thought of the nation has been altered or clouded by them. I have exactly the same things in mind now that I had in mind when I addressed the Senate on the 22d of January last; the same that I had in mind when I addressed the Congress on the third of February and on the 26th of February. Our object now, as then, is to vindicate the principles of peace and justice in the life of the world as against selfish and autocratic power and to set up amongst the really free and self-governed peoples of the world such a concert of purpose and of action as will henceforth ensure the observance of those principles. Neutrality is no longer feasible or desirable where the peace of the world is involved and the freedom of its peoples, and the menace to that peace and freedom lies in the existence of autocratic governments backed by organized force which is controlled wholly by their will, not by the will of their people. We have seen the last of neutrality in such circumstances. We are at the beginning of an age in which it will be insisted that the same standards of conduct and of responsibility for wrong done shall be observed among nations and their governments that are observed among the individual citizens of civilized states.

We have no quarrel with the German people. We have no feeling toward them but one of sympathy and friendship. It was not upon their impulse that their Government acted in entering this war. It was not with their previous knowledge or approval. It was a war determined upon as wars used to be determined upon in the old, unhappy days when peoples were nowhere consulted by their rulers and wars were provoked and waged in the interest of dynasties or of little groups of ambitious men who were accustomed to use their fellow men as pawns and tools. Self-governed nations do not fill their neighbor states with spies or set the course of intrigue to bring about some critical posture of affairs which will give them an opportunity to strike and make conquest. Such designs can be successfully worked out only under cover and where no one has the right to ask questions. Cunningly contrived plans of deception or aggression, carried, it may be, from generation to generation, can be worked out and kept from the light only within the privacy of courts or behind the carefully guarded confidences of a narrow and privileged class. They are happily impossible where public opinion commands and insists upon full information concerning all the nation's affairs.

A steadfast concert for peace can never be maintained except by a partnership of democratic nations. No autocratic government could be trusted to keep faith within it or observe its covenants. It must be a league of honor, a partnership of opinion. Intrigue would eat its vitals away; the plottings of inner circles who could plan what they would and render account to no one would be a corruption seated at its very heart. Only free peoples can hold their purpose and their honor steady to a common end and prefer the interests of mankind to any narrow interest of their own. . . .

We are accepting this challenge of hostile purpose because we know that in such a government, following such methods, we can never have a friend; and that in the presence of its organized power, always lying in wait to accomplish we know not what purpose, there can be no assured security for the democratic governments of the world. We are now about to accept gage of battle with this natural foe to liberty and shall, if necessary, spend the whole force of the nation to check and nullify its pretensions and its power. We are glad, now that we see the facts with no veil of false pretense about them, to fight thus for the ultimate peace of the world and for the liberation of its peoples, the German peoples included: for the rights of nations great and small and the privilege of men everywhere to choose their way of life and of obedience. **The world must be made safe for democracy.** Its peace must be planted upon the tested foundations of political liberty. We have no selfish ends to serve. We desire no conquest, no dominion. We seek no indemnities for ourselves, no material compensation for the sacrifices we shall freely make. We are but one of the champions of the rights of mankind. We shall be satisfied when those rights have been made as secure as the faith and the freedom of nations can make them.

Just because we fight without rancour and without selfish object, seeking nothing for ourselves but what we shall wish to share with all free peoples, we shall, I feel confident, conduct our operations as belligerents without passion and ourselves observe with proud punctilio the principles of right and of fair play we profess to be fighting for.

I have said nothing of the governments allied with the Imperial Government of Germany because they have not made war upon us or challenged us to defend our right and our honor. The Austro-Hungarian Government has, indeed, avowed its unqualified endorsement and acceptance of the reckless and lawless submarine warfare adopted now without disguise by the Imperial German Government, and it has therefore not been possible for this Government to receive Count Tarnowski, the Ambassador recently accredited to this Government by the Imperial and Royal Government of Austria-Hungary; but that Government has not actually engaged in warfare against citizens of the United States on the seas, and I take the liberty, for the present at least, of postponing a discussion of our relations with the authorities at Vienna. We enter this war only where we are clearly forced into it because there are no other means of defending our rights.

It will be all the easier for us to conduct ourselves as belligerents in a high spirit of right and fairness because we act without animus, not in enmity towards a people or with the desire to bring any injury or disadvantage upon them, but only in armed opposition to an irresponsible government which has thrown aside all considerations of humanity and of right and is running amuck. We are, let me say again, the sincere friends of the German people, and shall desire nothing so much as the early re-establishment of intimate relations of mutual advantage between us—however hard it be may for them, for the time being, to believe that this is spoken from our hearts. We have borne with their present government through all these bitter months because of that friendship—exercising a patience and forbearance which would otherwise have been impossible. We shall, happily, still have an opportunity to prove that friendship in our daily attitude and actions towards the millions of men and women of German birth and native sympathy who live amongst us and share our life, and we shall be proud to prove it towards all who are in fact loyal to their neighbors and to the Government in the hour of test. They are, most of them, as true and loyal Americans as if they had never known any other fealty or allegiance. They will be prompt to stand with us in rebuking and restraining the few who may be of a different mind and purpose. If there should be disloyalty, it will be dealt with with a firm hand of stern repression; but, if it lifts its head at all, it will lift it only here and there and without countenance except from a lawless and malignant few.

It is a distressing and oppressive duty, Gentlemen of the Congress, which I have performed in thus addressing you. There are, it may be, many months of fiery trial and sacrifice ahead of us. It is a fearful thing to lead this great peaceful people into war, into the most terrible and disastrous of all wars, civilization itself seeming to be in the balance. But the right is more precious than peace, and we shall fight for the things which we have always carried nearest our hearts—for democracy, for the right of those who submit to authority to have a voice in their own governments, for the rights and liberties of small nations, for a universal dominion of right by such a concert of free peoples as shall bring peace and safety to all nations and make the world itself at last free. To such a task we can dedicate our lives and our fortunes, every-thing that we are and everything that we have, with the pride of those who know that the day has come when America is privileged to spend her blood and her might for the principles that gave her birth and happiness and the peace which she has treasured. God helping her, she can do no other.

Woodrow Wilson

The Fourteen Points Address (1918)

GENTLEMEN OF THE CONGRESS:

. . . It will be our wish and purpose that the processes of peace, when they are begun, shall be absolutely open and that they shall involve and permit henceforth no secret understandings of any kind. The day of conquest and aggrandizement is gone by; so is also the day of secret covenants entered into in the interest of particular governments and likely at some unlooked-for moment to upset the peace of the world. It is this happy fact, now clear to the view of every public man whose thoughts do not still linger in an age that is dead and gone, which makes it possible for every nation whose purposes are consistent with justice and the peace of the world to avow now or at any other time the objects it has in view.

We entered this war because violations of right had occurred which touched us to the quick and made the life of our own people impossible unless they were corrected and the world secured once for all against their recur-rence. What we demand in this war, therefore, is nothing peculiar to ourselves. It is that the world be made fit and safe to live in; and particularly that it be made safe for every peace-loving nation which, like our own, wishes to live its own life, determine its own institutions, be assured of justice and fair dealing by the other peoples of the world as against force and selfish aggression. All the peoples of the world are in effect partners in this interest, and for our own part we see very clearly that unless justice be done to others it will not be done to us. The program of the world's peace, therefore, is our program; and that program, the only possible program, as we see it, is this:

1. Open covenants of peace, openly arrived at, after which there shall be no private international understandings of any kind but diplomacy shall proceed always frankly and in the public view.

2. Absolute freedom of navigation upon the seas, outside territorial waters, alike in peace and in war, except as the seas may be closed in whole or in part by international action for the enforcement of international covenants.

SOURCE: Henry Steele Commager, *Documents of American History,* 7th ed. (New York: Appleton-Century-Crofts, 1963).

3. The removal, so far as possible, of all *economic barriers* and the establishment of an equality of trade conditions among all the nations consenting to the peace and associating themselves for its maintenance.

4. Adequate guarantees given and taken that national armaments will be reduced to the lowest point consistent with domestic safety.

5. A free, open-minded, and absolutely impartial adjustment of all colonial claims, based upon a strict observance of the principle that in determining all such questions of sovereignty the interests of the populations concerned must have equal weight with the equitable claims of the government whose title is to be determined.

6. The evacuation of all Russian territory and such a settlement of all questions affecting Russia as will secure the best and freest coöperation of the other nations of the world in obtaining for her an unhampered and unembarrassed opportunity for the independent determination of her own political development and national policy and assure her of a sincere welcome into the society of free nations under institutions of her own choosing; and, more than a welcome, assistance also of every kind that she may need and may herself desire. The treatment accorded Russia by her sister nations in the months to come will be the acid test of their good will, of their comprehension of her needs as distinguished from their own interests, and of their intelligent and unselfish sympathy.

7. Belgium, the whole world will agree, must be evacuated and restored, without any attempt to limit the sovereignty which she enjoys in common with all other free nations. No other single act will serve as this will serve to restore confidence among the nations in the laws which they have themselves set and determined for the government of their relations with one another. Without this healing act the whole structure and validity of international law is forever impaired.

8. All French territory should be freed and the invaded portions restored, and the wrong done to France by Prussia in 1871 in the matter of Alsace-Lorraine, which has unsettled the peace of the world for nearly fifty years, should be righted, in order that peace may once more be made secure in the interest of all.

9. A readjustment of the frontiers of Italy should be affected along clearly recognizable lines of nationality.

10. The peoples of Austria-Hungary, whose place among the nations we wish to see safeguarded and assured, should be accorded the freest opportunity of autonomous development.

11. Rumania, Serbia, and Montenegro should be evacuated; occupied territories restored; Serbia accorded free and secure access to the sea; and the relations of the several Balkan states to one another determined by friendly counsel along historically established lines of allegiance and nationality; and international guarantees of the political and economic independence and territorial integrity of the several Balkan states should be entered into.

12. The Turkish portions of the present Ottoman Empire should be assured a secure sovereignty, but the other nationalities which are now under Turkish rule should be assured an undoubted security of life and an absolutely unmolested opportunity of autonomous development, and the Dardanelles should be permanently opened as a free passage to the ships and commerce of all nations under international guarantees.

13. An independent Polish state should be erected which should include the territories inhabited by indisputably Polish populations, which should be assured a free and secure access to the sea, and whose political and economic independence and territorial integrity should be guaranteed by international covenant.

14. A general association of nations must

be formed under specific covenants for the purpose of affording mutual guarantees of political independence and territorial integrity to great and small states alike.

In regard to these essential rectifications of wrong and assertions of right we feel ourselves to be intimate partners of all the governments and peoples associated together against the Imperialists. We cannot be separated in interest or divided in purpose. We stand together until the end.

For such arrangements and convenants we are willing to fight and to continue to fight until they are achieved; but only because we wish the right to prevail and desire a just and stable peace such as can be secured only by removing the chief provocations to war, which this program does not remove. We have no jealousy of German greatness, and there is nothing in this program that impairs it. We grudge her no achievement or distinction of learning or of pacific enterprise such as have made her record very bright and very enviable. We do not wish to injure her or to block in any way her legitimate influence or power. We do not wish to fight her either with arms or with hostile arrangements of trade if she is willing to associate herself with us and the other peace-loving nations of the world in covenants of justice and law and fair dealing. We wish her only to accept a place of equality

among the peoples of the world,—the new world in which we now live,—instead of a place of mastery.

Neither do we presume to suggest to her any alteration or modification of her institutions. But it is necessary, we must frankly say, and necessary as a preliminary to any intelligent dealings with her on our part, that we should know whom her spokesmen speak for when they speak to us, whether for the Reichstag majority or for the military party and the men whose creed is imperial domination.

We have spoken now, surely, in terms too concrete to admit of any further doubt or question. An evident principle runs through the whole program I have outlined. It is the principle of justice to all peoples and nationalities, and their right to live on equal terms of liberty and safety with one another, whether they be strong or weak. Unless this principle be made its foundation no part of the structure of international justice can stand. The people of the United States could act upon no other principle; and to the vindication of this principle they are ready to devote their lives, their honor, and everything that they possess. The moral climax of this the culminating and final war for human liberty has come, and they are ready to put their own strength, their own highest purpose, their own integrity and devotion to the test.

Franklin Roosevelt, Four Freedoms Speech (1941)

On January 6, 1941, President Roosevelt went before Congress to ask approval for the Lend-Lease Program to aid the British. Although the United States had not yet entered the war, Roosevelt articulated a foreign policy stance reminiscent of Wilson's. He echoed Wilson's commitment to democracy abroad and expressed a set of internationalist principles that tied together the social goals of the New Deal, traditional American democratic values, and U.S. opposition to fascist aggression. Again in the Wilsonian tradition,

Roosevelt attempted to express American foreign policy goals in universalist and idealist terms rather than in the language of narrow national interest.

Franklin D. Roosevelt

Four Freedoms Speech (1941)

TO THE CONGRESS OF THE UNITED STATES:
I address you, the Members of the 77th Congress, at a moment unprecedented in the history of the Union. I use the word "unprecedented," because at no previous time has American security been as seriously threatened from without as it is today. . . .

It is true that prior to 1914 the United States often had been disturbed by events in other Continents. We had even engaged in two wars with European nations and in a number of undeclared wars in the West Indies, in the Mediterranean and in the Pacific for the maintenance of American rights and for the principles of peaceful commerce. In no case, however, had a serious threat been raised against our national safety or our independence.

What I seek to convey is the historic truth that the United States as a nation has at all times maintained opposition to any attempt to lock us in behind an ancient Chinese wall while the procession of civilization went past. Today, thinking of our children and their children, we oppose enforced isolation for ourselves or for any part of the Americas.

Even when the World War broke out in 1914, it seemed to contain only small threat of danger to our own American future. But, as time went on, the American people began

SOURCE: Henry Steele Commager, *Documents of American History*, 7th ed. (New York: Appleton-Century-Crofts, 1963).

to visualize what the downfall of democratic nations might mean to our own democracy.

We need not over-emphasize imperfections in the Peace of Versailles. We need not harp on failure of the democracies to deal with problems of world reconstruction. We should remember that the Peace of 1919 was far less unjust than the kind of "pacification" which began even before Munich, and which is being carried on under the new order of tyranny that seeks to spread over every continent today. The American people have unalterably set their faces against that tyranny.

Every realist knows that the democratic way of life is at this moment being directly assailed in every part of the world—assailed either by arms, or by secret spreading of poisonous propaganda by those who seek to destroy unity and promote discord in nations still at peace. During sixteen months this assault has blotted out the whole pattern of democratic life in an appalling number of independent nations, great and small. The assailants are still on the march, threatening other nations, great and small.

Therefore, as your President, performing my constitutional duty to "give to the Congress information of the state of the Union," I find it necessary to report that the future and the safety of our country and of our democracy are overwhelmingly involved in events far beyond our borders.

Armed defense of democratic existence is

now being gallantly waged in four continents. If that defense fails, all the population and all the resources of Europe, Asia, Africa and Australasia will be dominated by the conquerors. The total of those populations and their resources greatly exceeds the sum total of the population and resources of the whole of the Western Hemisphere—many times over.

In times like these it is immature—and incidentally untrue—for anybody to brag that an unprepared America, single-handed, and with one hand tied behind its back, can hold off the whole world.

No realistic American can expect from a dictator's peace international generosity, or return of true independence, or world disarmament, or freedom of expression, or freedom of religion—or even good business. Such a peace would bring no security for us or for our neighbors. "Those, who would give up essential liberty to purchase a little temporary safety, deserve neither liberty nor safety." As a nation we may take pride in the fact that we are soft-hearted; but we cannot afford to be soft-hearted. We must always be wary of those who with sounding brass and a tinkling cymbal preach the "ism" of appeasement. We must especially beware of that small group of selfish men who would clip the wings of the American eagle in order to feather their own nests.

I have recently pointed out how quickly the tempo of modern warfare could bring into our very midst the physical attack which we must expect if the dictator nations win this war.

There is much loose talk of our immunity from immediate and direct invasion from across the seas. Obviously, as long as the British Navy retains its power, no such danger exists. Even if there were no British Navy, it is not probable that any enemy would be stupid enough to attack us by landing troops in the United States from across thousands of miles of ocean, until it had acquired strategic bases from which to operate. But we learn much from the lessons of the past years in Europe—particularly the lesson of Norway, whose essential seaports were captured by treachery and surprise built up over a series of years. The first phase of the invasion of this Hemisphere would not be the landing of regular troops. The necessary strategic points would be occupied by secret agents and their dupes—and great numbers of them are already here, and in Latin America.

As long as the aggressor nations maintain the offensive, they—not we—will choose the time and the place and the method of their attack. That is why the future of all American Republics is today in serious danger. That is why this Annual Message to the Congress is unique in our history. That is why every member of the Executive branch of the government and every member of the Congress face great responsibility—and great accountability.

The need of the moment is that our actions and our policy should be devoted primarily—almost exclusively—to meeting this foreign peril. For all our domestic problems are now a part of the great emergency. Just as our national policy in internal affairs has been based upon a decent respect for the rights and dignity of all our fellowmen within our gates, so our national policy in foreign affairs has been based on a decent respect for the rights and dignity of all nations, large and small. And the justice of morality must and will win in the end.

Our national policy is this.

First, by an impressive expression of the public will and without regard to partisanship, we are committed to all-inclusive national defense.

Second, by an impressive expression of the public will and without regard to partisanship, we are committed to full support of all those resolute peoples, everywhere, who are resisting aggression and are thereby keeping war away from our Hemisphere. By this support, we express our determination that the democratic cause shall prevail; and we strengthen the defense and security of our own nation.

Third, by an impressive expression of the public will and without regard to partisanship we are committed to the proposition that principles of morality and considerations for our own security will never permit us to acquiesce in a peace dictated by aggressors and sponsored by appeasers. We know that enduring peace cannot be bought at the cost of other people's freedom.

In the recent national election there was no substantial difference between the two great parties in respect to that national policy. No issue was fought out on this line before the American electorate. Today, it is abundantly evident that American citizens everywhere are demanding and supporting speedy and complete action in recognition of obvious danger. Therefore, the immediate need is a swift and driving increase in our armament production. . . .

Our most useful and immediate role is to act as an arsenal for them as well as for ourselves. They do not need man power. They do need billions of dollars worth of the weapons of defense. . . .

Let us say to the democracies: "We Americans are vitally concerned in your defense of freedom. We are putting forth our energies, our resources and our organizing powers to give you the strength to regain and maintain a free world. We shall send you, in ever-increasing numbers, ships, planes, tanks, guns. This is our purpose and our pledge." In fulfillment of this purpose we will not be intimidated by the threats of dictators that they will regard as a breach of international law and as an act of war our aid to the democracies which dare to resist their aggression. Such aid is not an act of war, even if a dictator should unilaterally proclaim it so to be. When the dictators are ready to make war upon us, they will not wait for an act of war on our part. They did not wait for Norway or Belgium or the Netherlands to commit an act of war. Their only interest is in a new one-way inter-national law, which lacks mutuality in its observance, and, therefore, becomes an instrument of oppression.

The happiness of future generations of Americans may well depend upon how effective and how immediate we can make our aid felt. No one can tell the exact character of the emergency situations that we may be called upon to meet. The Nation's hands must not be tied when the Nation's life is in danger. We must all prepare to make the sacrifices that the emergency—as serious as war itself—demands. Whatever stands in the way of speed and efficiency in defense preparations must give way to the national need.

A free nation has the right to expect full cooperation from all groups. A free nation has the right to look to the leaders of business, of labor, and of agriculture to take the lead in stimulating effort, not among other groups but within their own groups. The best way of dealing with the few slackers or trouble makers in our midst is, first, to shame them by patriotic example, and, if that fails, to use the sovereignty of government to save government.

As men do not live by bread alone, they do not fight by armaments alone. Those who man our defenses, and those behind them who build our defenses, must have the stamina and courage which come from an unshakable belief in the manner of life which they are defending. The mighty action which we are calling for cannot be based on a disregard of all things worth fighting for.

The Nation takes great satisfaction and much strength from the things which have been done to make its people conscious of their individual stake in the preservation of democratic life in America. Those things have toughened the fibre of our people, have renewed their faith and strengthened their devotion to the institutions we make ready to protect. Certainly this is no time to stop thinking about the social and economic problems which are the root cause of the social revolution which is today a supreme factor in the world.

There is nothing mysterious about the foundations of a healthy and strong democracy. The basic things expected by our people of their political and economic systems are simple. They are: equality of opportunity for youth and for others; jobs for those who can work; security for those who need it; the ending of special privilege for the few; the preservation of civil liberties for all; the enjoyment of the fruits of scientific progress in a wider and constantly rising standard of living.

These are the simple and basic things that must never be lost sight of in the turmoil and unbelievable complexity of our modern world. The inner and abiding strength of our economic and political systems is dependent upon the degree to which they fulfill these expectations.

Many subjects connected with our social economy call for immediate improvement. As examples: We should bring more citizens under the coverage of old age pensions and unemployment insurance. We should widen the opportunities for adequate medical care. We should plan a better system by which persons deserving or needing gainful employment may obtain it.

I have called for personal sacrifice. I am assured of the willingness of almost all Americans to respond to that call. . . .

In the future days, which we seek to make secure, we look forward to a world founded upon four essential human freedoms.

The first is freedom of speech and expression—everywhere in the world.

The second is freedom of every person to worship God in his own way—everywhere in the world.

The third is freedom from want—which, translated into world terms, means economic understandings which will secure to every nation a healthy peace time life for its inhabitants—everywhere in the world.

The fourth is freedom from fear—which, translated into world terms, means a worldwide reduction of armaments to such a point and in such a thorough fashion that no nation will be in a position to commit an act of physical aggression against any neighbor—anywhere in the world.

That is no vision of a distant millenium. It is a definite basis for a kind of world attainable in our own time and generation. That kind of world is the very antithesis of the so-called new order of tyranny which the dictators seek to create with the crash of a bomb.

To that new order we oppose the greater conception—the moral order. A good society is able to face schemes of world domination and foreign revolutions alike without fear.

Since the beginning of our American history we have been engaged in change—in a perpetual peaceful revolution—a revolution which goes on steadily, quietly adjusting itself to changing conditions—without the concentration camp or the quick-lime in the ditch. The world order which we seek is the cooperation of free countries, working together in a friendly, civilized society.

This nation has placed its destiny in the hands and heads and hearts of its millions of free men and women; and its faith in freedom under the guidance of God. Freedom means the supremacy of human rights everywhere. Our support goes to those who struggle to gain those rights or keep them. Our strength is in our unity of purpose.

To that high concept there can be no end save victory.

Harry S Truman, 1884–1972

The thirty-third president of the United States, Truman came to the office at the death of Franklin Roosevelt with little knowledge of foreign affairs. Yet in his two terms he successfully concluded World War II, decided to drop the atomic bomb on Hiroshima, defined a bipartisan, anticommunist foreign policy, and fought the Korean War.

Truman was a man of little formal education. Yet he was an avid reader of history, a quick learner, and a man capable of reflecting upon his own experiences in order to apply them to unfamiliar questions.

After finishing high school and a few unsuccessful attempts at business, Truman met success as an officer in World War I. He returned to open a small clothing store in Kansas City, but again failed. Desperate for a job, he was introduced to Tom Pendergast, the Democratic boss of Kansas City, and given a job as an overseer of highways. Soon he became involved in electoral politics and in 1934 was Democratic nominee to the Senate. Reelected in 1940, he was appointed chairman of a special committee which investigated waste and corruption in defense industries. Having gained national recognition, Roosevelt asked Truman to be his vice president, to replace Henry Wallace whose liberalism was offensive to southern Democrats.

At the conclusion of the war, Truman tried to extend the New Deal with a series of reforms—including a national health insurance—which he called the Fair Deal. The conservative shift in the country made this impossible, and his proposals were defeated by Congress. Soon, however, foreign policy began to dominate his administration.

With the withdrawal of British support for the defense of Greece and Turkey, both of whom were fighting against communist revolutionaries, Truman announced the Truman Doctrine, which pledged U.S. support to all governments fighting against communist opposition. He began to take a tough stance against the Soviets who had consolidated their positions in eastern Europe and, with Secretary of State George Marshall, forged the European Recovery Plan (Marshall Plan) to help stave off discontent and to finance economic development in Europe.

In 1948 Truman won an upset victory over Thomas Dewey and returned to office to face a recalcitrant Congress. However, again foreign policy began to dominate as the United States intervened in Korea to prevent the North Korean takeover of the South. An indecisive and difficult war, the Korean War demonstrated the extent to which the Truman Doctrine could be applied. He also set a precedent by fighting the war as a police action without a formal declaration of war.

The following selections of Truman's are (a) a statement of fundamental beliefs—clearly in the Wilsonian mold—delivered after his return from the Potsdam Conference, and (b) the Truman Doctrine. In the latter, Truman continues to use internationalist language to explain American opposition to communist movements and to the Soviet Union.

Harry S Truman

Fundamentals of American Foreign Policy (1945)

. . . **1.** We seek no territorial expansion or selfish advantage. We have no plans for aggression against any other state, large or small. We have no objective which need clash with the peaceful aims of any other nation.

2. We believe in the eventual return of sovereign rights and self-government to all peoples who have been deprived of them by force.

3. We shall approve no territorial changes in any friendly part of the world unless they accord with the freely expressed wishes of the people concerned.

4. We believe that all peoples who are prepared for self-government should be permitted to choose their own form of government by their own freely expressed choice, without interference from any foreign source. That is true in Europe, in Asia, in Africa, as well as in the Western Hemisphere.

5. By the combined and cooperative action of our war Allies, we shall help the defeated enemy states establish peaceful, democratic governments of their own free choice. And we shall try to attain a world in which Nazism, Fascism, and military aggression cannot exist.

6. We shall refuse to recognize any government imposed upon any nation by the force of any foreign power. In some cases it may be impossible to prevent forceful imposition of such a government. But the United States will not recognize any such government.

7. We believe that all nations should have the freedom of the seas and equal rights to the navigation of boundary rivers and waterways and of rivers and waterways which pass through more than one country.

8. We believe that all states which are accepted in the society of nations should have access on equal terms to the trade and the raw materials of the world.

9. We believe that the sovereign states of the Western Hemisphere, without interference from outside the Western Hemisphere, must work together as good neighbors in the solution of their common problems.

10. We believe that full economic collaboration between all nations, great and small, is essential to the improvement of living conditions all over the world, and to the establishment of freedom from fear and freedom from want.

11. We shall continue to strive to promote freedom of expression and freedom of religion throughout the peace-loving areas of the world.

12. We are convinced that the preservation of peace between nations requires a United Nations Organization composed of all the peace-loving nations of the world who are willing jointly to use force if necessary to insure peace.

SOURCE: Henry Steele Commager, *Documents of American History,* 7th ed. (New York: Appleton-Century-Crofts, 1963).

That is the foreign policy which guides the United States now. That is the foreign policy with which it confidently faces the future.

It may not be put into effect tomorrow or the next day. But none the less, it is our policy; and we shall seek to achieve it. It may take a long time, but it is worth waiting for, and it is worth striving to attain. . . .

Harry S Truman

The Truman Doctrine—Speech before Congress (1947)

The gravity of the situation which confronts the world today necessitates my appearance before a joint session of the Congress. The foreign policy and the national security of this country are involved.

One aspect of the present situation, which I wish to present to you at this time for your consideration and decision, concerns Greece and Turkey.

The United States has received from the Greek Government an urgent appeal for financial and economic assistance. Preliminary reports from the American Economic Mission now in Greece and reports from the American Ambassador in Greece corroborate the statement of the Greek Government that assistance is imperative if Greece is to survive as a free nation.

I do not believe that the American people and the Congress wish to turn a deaf ear to the appeal of the Greek Government.

The very existence of the Greek state is today threatened by the terrorist activities of several thousand armed men, led by Communists, who defy the Government's authority at a number of points, particularly along the northern boundaries. A commission appointed by the United Nations Security Council is at present investigating disturbed conditions in Northern Greece and alleged border violations along the frontiers between Greece on the one hand and Albania, Bulgaria and Yugoslavia on the other.

Meanwhile, the Greek Government is unable to cope with the situation. The Greek Army is small and poorly equipped. It needs supplies and equipment if it is to restore the authority to the Government throughout Greek territory.

Greece must have assistance if it is to become a self-supporting and self-respecting democracy. The United States must supply this assistance. We have already extended to Greece certain types of relief and economic aid but these are inadequate. There is no other country to which democratic Greece can turn. No other nation is willing and able to provide the necessary support for a democratic Greek Government.

The British Government, which has been helping Greece, can give no further financial or economic aid after March 31. Great Britain finds itself under the necessity of reducing or liquidating its commitments in several parts of the world, including Greece.

We have considered how the United

Source: Henry Steel Commager, *Documents of American History,* 7th ed. (New York: Appleton-Century-Crofts, 1963).

Nations might assist in this crisis. But the situation is an urgent one requiring immediate action, and the United Nations and its related organizations are not in a position to extend help of the kind that is required. . . .

Greece's neighbor, Turkey, also deserves our attention. The future of Turkey as an independent and economically sound state is clearly no less important to the freedom-loving peoples of the world than the future of Greece. The circumstances in which Turkey finds itself today are considerably different from those of Greece. Turkey has been spared the disasters that have beset Greece. And during the war, the United States and Great Britain furnished Turkey with material aid. Nevertheless, Turkey now needs our support.

Since the war Turkey has sought additional financial assistance from Great Britain and the United States for the purpose of effecting the modernization necessary for the maintenance of its national integrity. That integrity is essential to the preservation of order in the Middle East.

The British Government has informed us that, owing to its own difficulties, it can no longer extend financial or economic aid to Turkey. As in the case of Greece, if Turkey is to have the assistance it needs, the United States must supply it. We are the only country able to provide that help.

I am fully aware of the broad implications involved if the United States extends assistance to Greece and Turkey, and I shall discuss these implications with you at this time.

One of the primary objectives of the foreign policy of the United States is the creation of conditions in which we and other nations will be able to work out a way of life free from coercion. This was a fundamental issue in the war with Germany and Japan. Our victory was won over countries which sought to impose their will, and their way of life, upon other nations.

To ensure the peaceful development of nations, free from coercion, the United States has taken a leading part in establishing the United Nations. The United Nations is designed to make possible lasting freedom and independence for all its members. We shall not realize our objectives, however, unless we are willing to help free peoples to maintain their free institutions and their national integrity against aggressive movements that seek to impose on them totalitarian regimes. This is no more than a frank recognition that totalitarian regimes imposed on free peoples, by direct or indirect aggression, undermine the foundations of international peace and hence the security of the United States.

The peoples of a number of countries of the world have recently had totalitarian regimes forced upon them against their will. The Government of the United States has made frequent protests against coercion and intimidation, in violation of the Yalta Agreement, in Poland, Rumania and Bulgaria. I must also state that in a number of other countries there have been similar developments.

At the present moment in world history nearly every nation must choose between alternative ways of life. The choice is too often not a free one.

One way of life is based upon the will of the majority, and is distinguished by free institutions, representative government, free elections, guarantees of individual liberty, freedom of speech and religion, and freedom from political oppression.

The second way of life is based upon the will of the minority forcibly imposed upon the majority. It relies upon terror and oppression, a controlled press and radio, fixed elections, and the suppression of personal freedoms.

I believe that it must be the policy of the United States to support free peoples who are resisting attempted subjugation by armed minorities or by outside pressures.

I believe that we must assist free peoples to work out their own destinies in their own way.

I believe that our help should be primarily through economic and financial aid which is essential to economic stability and orderly political processes.

The world is not static, and the status quo is not sacred. But we cannot allow changes in the status quo in violation of the charter of the United Nations by such methods as coercion, or by such subterfuges as political infiltration. In helping free and independent nations to maintain their freedom, the United States will be giving effect to the principles of the charter of the United Nations.

It is necessary only to glance at a map to realize that the survival and integrity of the Greek nation are of grave importance in a much wider situation. If Greece should fall under the control of an armed minority, the effect upon its neighbor, Turkey, would be immediate and serious. Confusion and disorder might well spread throughout the entire Middle East.

Moreover, the disappearance of Greece as an independent state would have a profound effect upon those countries in Europe whose peoples are struggling against great difficulties to maintain their freedoms and their independence while they repair the damages of war.

It would be an unspeakable tragedy if these countries, which have struggled so long against overwhelming odds, should lose that victory for which they sacrificed so much. Collapse of free institutions and loss of independence would be disastrous not only for them but for the world. Discouragement and possibly failure would quickly be the lot of neighboring peoples striving to maintain their freedom and independence.

Should we fail to aid Greece and Turkey in this fateful hour, the effect will be far reaching to the west as well as to the east. We must take immediate and resolute action.

I therefore ask the Congress to provide authority for assistance to Greece and Turkey in the amount of $44 million for the period ending June 30, 1948.

In addition to funds, I ask the Congress to authorize the detail of American civilian and military personnel to Greece and Turkey, at the request of those countries, to assist in the tasks of reconstruction, and for the purpose of supervising the use of such financial and material assistance as may be furnished. I recommend that authority also be provided for the instruction and training of selected Greek and Turkish personnel.

Finally, I ask that the Congress provide authority which will permit the speediest and most effective use, in terms of needed commodities, supplies, and equipment, of such funds as may be authorized. . . .

The seeds of totalitarian regimes are nurtured by misery and want. They spread and grow in the evil soil of poverty and strife. They reach their full growth when the hope of a people for a better life has died. We must keep that hope alive. The free peoples of the world look to us for support in maintaining their freedoms.

If we falter in our leadership, we may endanger the peace of the world—and we shall surely endanger the welfare of this nation.

Great responsibilities have been placed upon us by the swift movement of events. I am confident that the Congress will face these responsibilities squarely.

George Kennan, 1904–

Diplomat and historian George Kennan's "Mr. X" article was the theoretical statement that best outlined the American policy of "containment" against the Soviet Union.

Kennan was a graduate of Princeton in 1925 and a year later joined the Foreign Service. He served in a variety of "listening posts" surrounding the Soviet Union and joined the U.S. Embassy in 1933 when it opened in Moscow.

In 1947 Secretary of State Marshall made Kennan director of a State Department policy planning staff whose task was to draw up long-range plans for dealing with the Soviet Union. These views were expressed in the "Mr. X" article in *Foreign Affairs* in July 1947.

Kennan became an advisor to Secretary of State Dean Acheson and in 1952 returned to Moscow as ambassador. His stay there was brief, as the Soviet government declared him persona non grata. Except for brief service as ambassador to Yugoslavia from 1961 to 1963, Kennan has spent most of his time as a professor at the Institute for Advanced Study at Princeton.

He is the author of many books including *American Diplomacy 1908–1950* (1951), *Realities of American Foreign Policy* (1954), and two volumes of *Memoirs* (1967 and 1972). Kennan has been a severe critic of the idealist, internationalist strain in American foreign policy and has argued instead for a "realist" foreign policy which pursues limited foreign policy goals in the national interest.

The following selection is excerpted from the "Mr. X" article "The Sources of Soviet Conduct."

Mr. X (George Kennan)

The Sources of Soviet Conduct (1947)

The political personality of Soviet power as we know it today is the product of ideology and circumstances: ideology inherited by the present Soviet leaders from the movement in which they had their political origin, and circumstances of the power which they now have exercised for nearly three decades in Russia. There can be few tasks of psychological analysis more difficult than to try to trace the interaction of these two forces and the relative rôle of each in the determination of

SOURCE: Mr. X, "The Sources of Soviet Conduct," *Foreign Affairs,* 25, no. 4 (July 1947). Reprinted by permission from *Foreign Affairs,* July 1947, Copyright © 1947 by the Council on Foreign Relations, Inc.

official Soviet conduct. Yet the attempt must be made if that conduct is to be understood and effectively countered.

It is difficult to summarize the set of ideological concepts with which the Soviet leaders came into power. Marxian ideology, in its Russian-Communist projection, has always been in process of subtle evolution. The materials on which it bases itself are extensive and complex. But the outstanding features of Communist thought as it existed in 1916 may perhaps be summarized as follows: *(a)* that the central factor in the life of man, the factor which determines the character of public life and the "physiognomy of society," is the system by which material goods are produced and exchanged; *(b)* that the capitalist system of production is a nefarious one which inevitably leads to the exploitation of the working class by the capital-owning class and is incapable of developing adequately the economic resources of society or of distributing fairly the material goods produced by human labor; *(c)* that capitalism contains the seeds of its own destruction and must, in view of the inability of the capital-owning class to adjust itself to economic change, result eventually and inescapably in a revolutionary transfer of power to the working class; and *(d)* that imperialism, the final phase of capitalism, leads directly to war and revolution.

The rest may be outlined in Lenin's own words: "Unevenness of economic and political development is the inflexible law of capitalism. It follows from this that the victory of Socialism may come originally in a few capitalist countries or even in a single capitalist country. The victorious proletariat of that country, having expropriated the capitalists and having organized Socialist production at home, would rise against the remaining capitalist world, drawing to itself in the process the oppressed classes of other countries." It must be noted that there was no assumption that capitalism would perish without proletarian revolution. A final push was needed from a revolutionary proletariat movement in order to tip over the tottering structure. But it was regarded as inevitable that sooner or later that push be given. . . .

The circumstances of the immediate postrevolution period—the existence in Russia of civil war and foreign intervention, together with the obvious fact that the Communists represented only a tiny minority of the Russian people—made the establishment of dictatorial power a necessity. The experiment with "war Communism" and the abrupt attempt to eliminate private production and trade had unfortunate economic consequences and caused further bitterness against the new revolutionary régime. While the temporary relaxation of the effort to communize Russia, represented by the New Economic Policy, alleviated some of this economic distress and thereby served its purpose, it also made it evident that the "capitalistic sector of society" was still prepared to profit at once from any relaxation of governmental pressure, and would, if permitted to continue to exist, always constitute a powerful opposing element to the Soviet régime and a serious rival for influence in the country. Somewhat the same situation prevailed with respect to the individual peasant who, in his own small way, was also a private producer.

Lenin, had he lived, might have proved a great enough man to reconcile these conflicting forces to the ultimate benefit of Russian society, though this is questionable. But be that as it may, Stalin, and those whom he led in the struggle for succession to Lenin's position of leadership, were not the men to tolerate rival political forces in the sphere of power which they coveted. Their sense of insecurity was too great. Their particular brand of fanaticism, unmodified by any of the Anglo-Saxon traditions of compromise, was too fierce and too jealous to envisage any permanent sharing of power. From the Russian-Asiatic world out of which they had emerged they carried with them a skepticism as to the possibilities of permanent and peaceful coexistence of rival forces. Easily persuaded of their own doctrinaire "rightness," they insisted on the submission or destruction of all competing power. Outside of the Communist Party, Russian society was to have no rigidity. There were to be no forms of collective human activity or association which would not be dominated by the Party. No other force in Russian society was to be permitted to achieve vitality or integrity. Only the Party was to have structure. All else was to be an amorphous mass.

And within the Party the same principle was to apply. The mass of Party members might go through the motions of election, deliberation, decision and action; but in these motions they were to be animated not by their own individual wills but by the awesome breath of the Party leadership and the over-brooding presence of "the word."

Let it be stressed again that subjectively these men probably did not seek absolutism for its own sake. They doubtless believed—and found it easy to believe—that they alone knew what was good for society and that they would accomplish that good once their power was secure and unchallengeable. But in seeking that security of their own rule they were prepared to recognize no restrictions, either of God or man, on the character of their methods. And until such time as that security might be achieved, they placed far down on their scale of operational priorities the comforts and happiness of the peoples entrusted to their care.

Now, the outstanding circumstance concerning the Soviet régime is that down to the present day this process of political consolidation has never been completed and the men in the Kremlin have continued to be predominantly absorbed with the struggle to secure and make absolute the power which they seized in November 1917. They have endeavored to secure it primarily against forces at home, within Soviet society itself. But they have also endeavored to secure it against the outside world. For ideology, as we have seen, taught them that the outside world was hostile and that it was their duty eventually to overthrow the political forces beyond their borders. The powerful hands of Russian history and tradition reached up to sustain them in this feeling. Finally, their own aggressive intransigence with respect to the outside world began to find its own reaction; and they were soon forced, to use another Gibbon-esque phrase, "to chastise the contumacy" which they themselves had provoked. It is an undeniable privilege of every man to prove himself right in the thesis that the world is his enemy; for if he reiterates it frequently enough and makes it the background of his conduct he is bound eventually to be right.

Now it lies in the nature of the mental world of the Soviet leaders, as well as in the character of their ideology, that no opposition to them can be officially recognized as having any merit or justification whatsoever. Such opposition can flow, in theory, only from the hostile and incorrigible forces of dying capitalism. As long as remnants of capitalism were officially recognized as existing in Russia, it was possible to place on them, as an internal element, part of the blame for the maintenance of a dictatorial form of society. But as these remnants were liquidated, little by little, this justification fell away; and when it was indicated officially that they had been finally destroyed, it disappeared altogether. And this fact created one of the most basic of the compulsions which came to act upon the Soviet régime: since capitalism no longer existed in Russia and since it could not be admitted that there could be serious or widespread opposition to the Kremlin springing spontaneously from the liberated masses under its authority, it became necessary to justify the retention of the dictatorship by stressing the menace of capitalism abroad.

This began at an early date. In 1924 Stalin specifically defended the retention of the "organs of suppression," meaning, among others, the army and the secret police, on the ground that "as long as there is a capitalist encirclement there will be danger of intervention with all the consequences that flow from that danger." In accordance with that theory, and from that time on, all internal opposition forces in Russia have consistently been portrayed as the agents of foreign forces of reaction antagonistic to Soviet power.

By the same token, tremendous emphasis has been placed on the original Communist thesis of a basic antagonism between the capitalist and Socialist worlds. It is clear, from many indications, that this emphasis is not founded in reality. The real facts concerning it have been confused by the existence abroad of genuine resentment provoked by Soviet philosophy and tactics and occasionally by the existence of great centers of military power, notably the Nazi régime in Germany and the Japanese Government of the late 1930s, which did indeed have aggressive designs against the Soviet Union. But there is ample evidence that the stress laid in Moscow on the menace confronting Soviet society from the world outside its borders is founded not in the realities of foreign antagonism but in the necessity of explaining away the maintenance of dictatorial authority at home. . . .

As things stand today, the rulers can no longer dream of parting with these organs of suppression. The quest for absolute power, pursued now for nearly three decades with a ruthlessness unparalleled (in scope at least) in modern times, has again produced internally, as it did externally, its own reaction. The excesses of the police apparatus have fanned the potential opposition to the régime into something far greater and more dangerous than it could have been before those excesses began.

But least of all can the rulers dispense with the fiction by which the maintenance of dictatorial power has been defended. For this fiction has been canonized in Soviet philosophy by the excesses already committed in its name; and it is now anchored in the Soviet structure of thought by bonds far greater than those of mere ideology.

II

So much for the historical background. What does it spell in terms of the political personality of Soviet power as we know it today?

Of the original ideology, nothing has been officially junked. Belief is maintained in the basic badness of capitalism, in the inevitability of its destruction, in the obligation of the proletariat to assist in that destruction and to take power into its own hands. But stress has come to be laid primarily on those concepts which relate most specifically to the Soviet régime itself: to its position as the sole truly Socialist régime in a dark and misguided world, and to the relationships of power within it.

The first of these concepts is that of the innate antagonism between capitalism and Socialism. We have seen how deeply that concept has become imbedded in foundations of Soviet power. It has profound implications for Russia's conduct as a member of international society. It means that there can never be on Moscow's side any sincere assumption of a community of aims between the Soviet Union and powers which are regarded as capitalist. It must invariably be assumed in Moscow that the aims of the capitalist world are antagonistic to the Soviet régime, and therefore to the interests of the peoples it controls. If the Soviet Government occasionally sets its signature to documents which would indicate the contrary, this is to be regarded as a tactical manoeuvre permissible in dealing with the enemy (who is without honor) and should be taken in the spirit of *caveat emptor*. Basically, the antagonism remains. It is postulated. And from it flow many of the phenomena which we find disturbing in the Kremlin's conduct of foreign policy: the secretiveness, the lack of frankness, the duplicity, the wary suspiciousness, and the basic unfriendliness of purpose. These phenomena are there to stay, for the foreseeable future. There can be variations of degree and of emphasis. When there is something the Russians want from us, one or the other of these features of their policy may be thrust temporarily into the background; and when that happens there will always be Americans who will leap forward with gleeful announcements that "the Russians have changed," and some who will even try to take credit for having brought about such "changes." But we should not be misled by tactical manoeuvres. These characteristics of Soviet policy, like the postulate from which they flow, are basic to the internal nature of Soviet power, and will be with us, whether in the foreground or the background, until the internal nature of Soviet power is changed.

This means that we are going to continue

for a long time to find the Russians difficult to deal with. It does not mean that they should be considered as embarked upon a do-or-die program to overthrow our society by a given date. The theory of the inevitability of the eventual fall of capitalism has the fortunate connotation that there is no hurry about it. The forces of progress can take their time in preparing the final *coup de grâce*. Meanwhile, what is vital is that the "Socialist fatherland"—that oasis of power which has been already won for Socialism in the person of the Soviet Union—should be cherished and defended by all good Communists at home and abroad, its fortunes promoted, its enemies badgered and confounded. The promotion of premature, "adventuristic" revolutionary projects abroad which might embarrass Soviet power in any way would be an inexcusable, even a counter-revolutionary act. The cause of Socialism is the support and promotion of Soviet power, as defined in Moscow.

This brings us to the second of the concepts important to contemporary Soviet outlook. That is the infallibility of the Kremlin. The Soviet concept of power, which permits no focal points of organization outside the Party itself, requires that the Party leadership remain in theory the sole repository of truth. For if truth were to be found elsewhere, there would be justification for its expression in organized activity. But it is precisely that which the Kremlin cannot and will not permit.

The leadership of the Communist Party is therefore always right, and has been always right ever since in 1929 Stalin formalized his personal power by announcing that decisions of the Politburo were being taken unanimously.

On the principle of infallibility there rests the iron discipline of the Communist Party. In fact, the two concepts are mutually self-supporting. Perfect discipline requires recognition of infallibility. Infallibility requires the observance of discipline. And the two together go far to determine the behaviorism of the entire Soviet apparatus of power. But their effect cannot be understood unless a third factor be taken into account: namely, the fact that the leadership is at liberty to put forward for tactical purposes any particular thesis which it finds useful to the cause at any particular moment and to require the faithful and unquestioning acceptance of that thesis by the members of the movement as a whole. This means that truth is not a constant but is actually created, for all intents and purposes, by the Soviet leaders themselves. It may vary from week to week, from month to month. It is nothing absolute and immutable—nothing which flows from objective reality. It is only the most recent manifestation of the wisdom of those in whom the ultimate wisdom is supposed to reside, because they represent the logic of history. The accumulative effect of these factors is to give to the whole subordinate apparatus of Soviet power an unshakeable stubbornness and steadfastness in its orientation. This orientation can be changed at will by the Kremlin but by no other power. Once a given party line has been laid down on a given issue of current policy, the whole Soviet governmental machine, including the mechanism of diplomacy, moves inexorably along the prescribed path, like a persistent toy automobile wound up and headed in a given direction, stopping only when it meets with some unanswerable force. The individuals who are the components of this machine are unamenable to argument or reason which comes to them from outside sources. Their whole training has taught them to mistrust and discount the glib persuasiveness of the outside world. Like the white dog before the phonograph, they hear only the "master's voice." And if they are to be called off from the purposes last dictated to them, it is the master who must call them off. Thus the foreign representative cannot hope that his words will make any impression on them. The most that he can hope is that they will be transmitted to those at the top, who are capable of changing the party line. But even those are not likely to be swayed by any normal logic in the words of the bourgeois representatives. Since there can be no appeal to common purposes, there can be no appeal to common mental approaches. For this reason, facts speak louder than words to the ears of the Kremlin; and words carry the greatest weight when they have the ring of reflecting, or being backed up by, facts of unchallengeable validity.

But we have seen that the Kremlin is under no ideological compulsion to accomplish its purposes in a hurry. Like the Church, it is dealing in ideological concepts which are of long-term validity, and it can afford to be patient. It has no right to risk the existing achievements of the revolution for the sake of vain baubles of the future. The very teachings of Lenin himself require great caution and flexibility in the pursuit of Communist purposes. Again, these precepts are fortified by the lessons of Russian history: of centuries of obscure battles between nomadic forces over the stretches of a vast unfortified plain. Here caution, circumspection, flexibility and deception are the valuable qualities; and their value finds natural appreciation in the Russian or the oriental mind. Thus the Kremlin has no compunction about retreating in the face of superior force. And being under the compulsion of no timetable, it does not get panicky under the necessity for such retreat. Its political action is a fluid stream which moves constantly, wherever it is permitted to move, toward a given goal. Its main concern is to make sure that it has filled every nook and cranny available to it in the basin of world power. But if it finds unassailable barriers in its path, it accepts these philosophically and accommodates itself to them. The main thing is that there should always be pressure, unceasing constant pressure, toward the desired goal. There is no trace of any feeling in Soviet psychology that that goal must be reached at any given time.

These considerations make Soviet diplomacy at once easier and more difficult to deal with than the diplomacy of individual aggressive leaders like Napoleon and Hitler. On the one hand it is more sensitive to contrary force, more ready to yield on individual sectors of the diplomatic front when that force is felt to be too strong, and thus more rational in the logic and rhetoric of power. On the other hand it cannot be easily defeated or discouraged by a single victory on the part of its opponents. And the patient persistence by which it is animated means that it can be effectively countered not by sporadic acts which represent the momentary whims of democratic opinion but only by intelligent long-range policies on the part of Russia's adversaries—policies no less steady in their purpose, and no less variegated and resourceful in their application, than those of the Soviet Union itself.

In these circumstances it is clear that the main element of any United States policy toward the Soviet Union must be that of a long-term, patient but firm and vigilant containment of Russian expansive tendencies. It is important to note, however, that such a policy has nothing to do with outward histrionics: with threats or blustering or superfluous gestures of outward "toughness." While the Kremlin is basically flexible in its reaction to political realities, it is by no means unamenable to considerations of prestige. Like almost any other government, it can be placed by tactless and threatening gestures in a position where it cannot afford to yield even though this might be dictated by its sense of realism. The Russian leaders are keen judges of human psychology, and as such they are highly conscious that loss of temper and of self-control is never a source of strength in political affairs. They are quick to exploit such evidences of weakness. For these reasons, it is a *sine qua non* of successful dealing with Russia that the foreign government in question should remain at all times cool and collected and that its demands on Russian policy should be put forward in such a manner as to leave the way open for a compliance not too detrimental to Russian prestige.

In the light of the above, it will be clearly seen that the Soviet pressure against the free institutions of the western world is something that can be contained by the adroit and vigilant application of counter-force at a series of constantly shifting geographical and political points, corresponding to the shifts and manoeuvres of Soviet policy, but which cannot be charmed or talked out of existence. The Russians look forward to a duel of infinite duration, and they see that already they have scored great successes. It must be borne in mind that there was a time when the Communist Party represented far more of a minority in the sphere of Russian national life than Soviet power today represents in the world community.

But if ideology convinces the rulers of Russia that truth is on their side and that they can therefore afford to wait, those of us on whom that ideology has no claim are free to examine objectively the validity of that premise. The Soviet thesis not only implies complete lack of control by the west over its own economic destiny, it likewise assumes Russian unity, discipline and patience over an infinite period. Let us bring this apocalyptic vision down to earth, and suppose that the western world finds the strength and resourcefulness to contain Soviet power over a period of ten to fifteen years. What does that spell for Russia itself?

The Soviet leaders, taking advantage of the contributions of modern technique to the arts of despotism, have solved the question of obedience within the confines of their power. Few challenge their authority; and even those who do are unable to make that challenge valid as against the organs of suppression of the state.

The Kremlin has also proved able to accomplish its purpose of building up in Russia, regardless of the interests of the inhabitants, an industrial foundation of heavy metallurgy, which is, to be sure, not yet complete but which is nevertheless continuing to grow and is approaching those of the other major industrial countries. All of this, however, both the maintenance of internal political security and the building of heavy industry, has been carried out at a terrible cost in human life and in human hopes and energies. It has necessitated the use of forced labor on a scale unprecedented in modern times under conditions of peace. It has involved the neglect or abuse of other phases of Soviet economic life, particularly agriculture, consumers' goods production, housing and transportation.

To all that, the war has added its tremendous toll of destruction, death and human exhaustion. In consequence of this, we have in Russia today a population which is physically and spiritually tired. The mass of the people are disillusioned, skeptical and no longer as accessible as they once were to the magical attraction which Soviet power still radiates to its followers abroad. The avidity with which people seized upon the slight respite accorded to the Church for tactical reasons during the war was eloquent testimony to the fact that their capacity for faith and devotion found little expression in the purposes of the régime.

In these circumstances, there are limits to the physical and nervous strength of people themselves. These limits are absolute ones, and are binding even for the cruelest dictatorship, because beyond them people cannot be driven. The forced labor camps and the other agencies of constraint provide temporary means of compelling people to work longer hours than their own volition or mere economic pressure would dictate; but if people survive them at all they become old before their time and must be considered as human casualties to the demands of dictatorship. In either case their best powers are no longer available to society and can no longer be enlisted in the service of the state. . . .

In addition to this, we have the fact that

Soviet economic development, while it can list certain formidable achievements, has been precariously spotty and uneven. Russian Communists who speak of the "uneven development of capitalism" should blush at the contemplation of their own national economy. Here certain branches of economic life, such as the metallurgical and machine industries, have been pushed out of all proportion to other sectors of economy. Here is a nation striving to become in a short period one of the great industrial nations of the world while it still has no highway network worthy of the name and only a relatively primitive network of railways. Much has been done to increase efficiency of labor and to teach primitive peasants something about the operation of machines. But maintenance is still a crying deficiency of all Soviet economy. Construction is hasty and poor in quality. Depreciation must be enormous. And in vast sectors of economic life it has not yet been possible to instill into labor anything like that general culture of production and technical self-respect which characterizes the skilled worker of the west.

It is difficult to see how these deficiencies can be corrected at an early date by a tired and dispirited population working largely under the shadow of fear and compulsion. And as long as they are not overcome, Russia will remain economically a vulnerable, and in a certain sense an impotent, nation, capable of exporting its enthusiasms and of radiating the strange charm of its primitive political vitality but unable to back up those articles of export by the real evidences of material power and prosperity.

Meanwhile, a great uncertainty hangs over the political life of the Soviet Union. That is the uncertainty involved in the transfer of power from one individual or group of individuals to others.

This is, of course, outstandingly the problem of the personal position of Stalin. We must remember that his succession to Lenin's pinnacle of preëminence in the Communist movement was the only such transfer of individual authority which the Soviet Union has experienced. That transfer took 12 years to consolidate. It cost the lives of millions of people and shook the state to its foundations. The attendant tremors were felt all through the international revolutionary movement, to the disadvantage of the Kremlin itself.

It is always possible that another transfer of preëminent power may take place quietly and inconspicuously, with no repercussions anywhere. But again, it is possible that the questions involved may unleash, to use some of Lenin's words, one of those "incredibly swift transitions" from "delicate deceit" to "wild violence" which characterize Russian history, and may shake Soviet power to its foundations. . . .

Thus the future of Soviet power may not be by any means as secure as Russian capacity for self-delusion would make it appear to the men in the Kremlin. That they can keep power themselves, they have demonstrated. That they can quietly and easily turn it over to others remains to be proved. Meanwhile, the hardships of their rule and the vicissitudes of international life have taken a heavy toll of the strength and hopes of the great people on whom their power rests. It is curious to note that the ideological power of Soviet authority is strongest today in areas beyond the frontiers of Russia, beyond the reach of its police power. This phenomenon brings to mind a comparison used by Thomas Mann in his great novel "Buddenbrooks." Observing that human institutions often show the greatest outward brilliance at a moment when inner decay is in reality farthest advanced, he compared the Buddenbrook family, in the days of its greatest glamour, to one of those stars whose light shines most brightly on this world when in reality it has long since ceased to exist. And who can say with assurance that the strong light still cast by the Kremlin on the dissatisfied peoples of the western world is not the powerful afterglow of a constellation which is in actuality on the wane? This cannot be proved. And it cannot be disproved. But the possibility remains (and in the opinion of this writer it is a strong one) that Soviet power, like the capitalist world of its conception, bears within it the seeds of its own decay, and that the sprouting of these seeds is well advanced.

IV

It is clear that the United States cannot expect in the foreseeable future to enjoy political intimacy with the Soviet régime. It must continue to regard the Soviet Union as a rival, not a partner, in the political arena. It must continue to expect that Soviet policies will reflect no abstract love of peace and stability, no real faith in the possibility of a permanent happy coexistence of the Socialist and capitalist worlds, but rather a cautious, persistent pressure toward the disruption and weakening of all rival influence and rival power.

Balanced against this are the facts that Russia, as opposed to the western world in general, is still by far the weaker party, that Soviet policy is highly flexible, and that Soviet society may well contain deficiencies which will eventually weaken its own total potential. This would of itself warrant the United States entering with reasonable confidence upon a policy of firm containment, designed to confront the Russians with unalterable counterforce at every point where they show signs of encroaching upon the interests of a peaceful and stable world. . . .

It would be an exaggeration to say that American behavior unassisted and alone could exercise a power of life and death over the Communist movement and bring about the early fall of Soviet power in Russia. But the United States has it in its power to increase enormously the strains under which Soviet policy must operate, to force upon the Kremlin a far greater degree of moderation and circumspection than it has had to observe in recent years, and in this way to promote tendencies which must eventually find their outlet in either the break-up or the gradual mellowing of Soviet power. For no mystical, Messianic movement—and particularly not that of the Kremlin—can face frustration indefinitely without eventually adjusting itself in one way or another to the logic of that state of affairs.

Thus the decision will really fall in large measure in this country itself. The issue of Soviet-American relations is in essence a test of the over-all worth of the United States as a nation among nations. To avoid destruction the United States need only measure up to its own best traditions and prove itself worthy of preservation as a great nation.

Surely, there was never a fairer test of national quality than this. In the light of these circumstances, the thoughtful observer of Russian-American relations will find no cause for complaint in the Kremlin's challenge to American society. He will rather experience a certain gratitude to a Providence which, by providing the American people with this implacable challenge, has made their entire security as a nation dependent on their pulling themselves together and accepting the responsibilities of moral and political leadership that history plainly intended them to bear.

Lyndon Baines Johnson, 1908–1973

Lyndon Johnson, the thirty-sixth president of the United States, is best remembered for his commitment to civil rights, his Great Society legislation, and his unsuccessful effort to resolve the war in Vietnam.

Johnson first came to Washington as a congressional staffer in 1932 and then returned a congressman in 1937. The New Deal Administration of Franklin Roosevelt shaped his political world view, and it was to these early experiences that he often referred.

Johnson was elected to the Senate in 1948 and by 1953 was minority leader. In 1955 he became majority leader and his reputation as a legislator grew. In 1960 he became John Kennedy's vice president and succeeded him as president after the assassination.

Johnson's proudest moments in office were in helping complete the traditional agenda of New Deal liberalism. After his landslide victory over Barry Goldwater in 1964, he succeeded in passing two major pieces of civil rights legislation and a series of job training and educational programs which he labeled the Great Society.

For Johnson, Vietnam also was to be examined in the light of Roosevelt. The United States had to reject appeasement if the communist threat to democracy was to be repelled. Vietnam was his Munich and the aggressor had to be met head-on. To his critics, this was inadequate. For some the war in Vietnam was an example of a third-world revolution unrelated to great power struggles, while for others it was an area of limited importance worthy of only a limited investment in lives and treasure.

The following speech in which Johnson defends his Vietnam policy is a good example of his idealist and internationalist arguments.

Lyndon Baines Johnson

Speech on Vietnam at Johns Hopkins University (1965)

. . . Over this war, and all Asia, is the deepening shadow of Communist China. The rulers in Hanoi are urged on by Peking. This is a regime which has destroyed freedom in Tibet, attacked India, and been condemned by the United Nations for aggression in Korea. It is a nation which is helping the forces of violence in almost every continent. The contest in Vietnam is part of a wider pattern of aggressive purpose.

SOURCE: Henry Steele Commager, ed., *Documents of American History*, 9th ed. (New York: Appleton-Century-Crofts, 1973).

Why are these realities our concern? Why are we in South Vietnam? We are there because we have a promise to keep. Since 1954 every American President has offered support to the people of South Vietnam. We have helped to build, and we have helped to defend. Thus, over many years, we have made a national pledge to help South Vietnam defend its independence. And I intend to keep our promise.

To dishonor that pledge, to abandon this small and brave nation to its enemy, and to the terror that must follow, would be an unforgivable wrong.

We are also there to strengthen world order. Around the globe, from Berlin to Thailand, are people whose well-being rests, in part, on the belief that they can count on us if they are attacked. To leave Vietnam to its fate would shake the confidence of all these people in the value of American commitment, the value of America's word. The result would be increased unrest and instability, and even wider war.

We are also there because there are great stakes in the balance. Let no one think for a moment that retreat from Vietnam would bring an end to conflict. The battle would be renewed in one country and then another. The central lesson of our time is that the appetite of aggression is never satisfied. To withdraw from one battlefield means only to prepare for the next. We must say in Southeast Asia, as we did in Europe, in the words of the Bible: "Hitherto shalt thou come, but no further."

There are those who say that all our effort there will be futile, that China's power is such it is bound to dominate all Southeast Asia. But there is no end to that argument until all the nations of Asia are swallowed up.

There are those who wonder why we have a responsibility there. We have it for the same reason we have a responsibility for the defense of freedom in Europe. World War II was fought in both Europe and Asia, and when it ended we found ourselves with continued responsibility for the defense of freedom.

Our objective is the independence of South Vietnam, and its freedom from attack. We want nothing for ourselves, only that the people of South Vietnam be allowed to guide their own country in their own way.

We will do everything necessary to reach that objective. And we will do only what is absolutely necessary.

In recent months, attacks on South Vietnam were stepped up. Thus it became necessary to increase our response and to make attacks by air. This is not a change of purpose. It is a change in what we believe that purpose requires.

We do this in order to slow down aggression.

We do this to increase the confidence of the brave people of South Vietnam who have bravely borne this brutal battle for so many years and with so many casualties.

And we do this to convince the leaders of North Vietnam, and all who seek to share their conquest, of a very simple fact:

We will not be defeated.

We will not grow tired.

We will not withdraw, either openly or under the cloak of a meaningless agreement. . . .

Once this is clear, then it should also be clear that the only path for reasonable men is the path of peaceful settlement.

Such peace demands an independent South Vietnam securely guaranteed and able to shape its own relationships to all others, free from outside interference, tied to no alliance, a military base for no other country.

These are the essentials of any final settlement.

We will never be second in the search for such a peaceful settlement in Vietnam.

There may be many ways to this kind of peace: in discussion or negotiation with the governments concerned; in large groups or in small ones; in the reaffirmation of old agreements or their strengthening with new ones.

We have stated this position over and over again fifty times and more, to friend and foe alike. And we remain ready, with this purpose, for unconditional discussions.

And until that bright and necessary day of peace we will try to keep conflict from spreading. We have no desire to see thousands die in battle, Asians or Americans. We have no desire to devastate that which the people of North Vietnam have built with toil and sacrifice. We will use our power with restraint and with all the wisdom we can command. But we will use it. . . .

We will always oppose the effort of one nation to conquer another nation.

We will do this because our own security is at stake.

But there is more to it than that. For our generation has a dream. It is a very old dream. But we have the power and now we have the opportunity to make it come true.

For centuries, nations have struggled among each other. But we dream of a world where disputes are settled by law and reason. And we will try to make it so.

For most of history men have hated and killed one another in battle. But we dream of an end to war. And we will try to make it so.

For all existence most men have lived in poverty, threatened by hunger. But we dream of a world where all are fed and charged with hope. And we will help to make it so.

The ordinary men and women of North Vietnam and South Vietnam—of China and India—of Russia and America—are brave people. They are filled with the same proportions of hate and fear, of love and hope. Most of them want the same things for themselves and their families. Most of them do not want their sons ever to die in battle, or see the homes of others destroyed. . . .

Every night before I turn out the lights to sleep, I ask myself this question: Have I done everything that I can do to unite this country? Have I done everything I can to help unite the world, to try to bring peace and hope to all the peoples of the world? Have I done enough?

Ask yourself that question in your homes and in this hall tonight. Have we done all we could? Have we done enough? . . .

Daniel P. Moynihan, 1927–

A former ambassador to India and the United Nations, Moynihan was elected to the Senate as a Democrat from New York in 1976.

Moynihan was well known as a sociologist who wrote on immigrant and ethnic groups in America. In the late 1960s he was at the center of a great deal of controversy over his views on the decay of the black family and became an object of attack for many former liberal allies. A professor at Harvard University, he took a job in the Nixon administration in 1969–1970 as an advisor on welfare policy and social issues. From 1973 to 1975 he served as ambassador to India. In 1975 he was asked by Henry Kissinger to become ambassador to the United Nations, after the secretary of state had read his *Commentary* article "The United States in Opposition," which appears below.

Moynihan is often included among the neoconservatives. Although it is true that he has the conservative's profound appreciation for the importance of tradition and culture, Moynihan is in many respects a New Deal Democrat uncomfortable with the social views and more extreme egalitarianism of contemporary liberals.

"The United States in Opposition" is an answer to those who suggest that the United States should retreat from its role as an active world power, in light of the Vietnam experience. He suggests that the United States stands for human rights and that our foreign policy must aggressively reflect that fact. Moynihan's article marks a return to Wilsonian idealism in the debate over the future of the American role in world affairs.

Daniel P. Moynihan

The United States in Opposition (1975)

. . . Plainly, not all the new nations of the postwar world were formerly British. There were French colonies. Belgian. Dutch. Portuguese. Political traditions in each case were different from the British. But only *slightly* different: viewed from Mars, London, Paris, and The Hague are not widely separated or disparate places. By the time of the granting of independence, all were democratic with a socialist intelligentsia and often as not a socialist government. With the exception of Algeria—which is marked by the exception—the former French and Dutch colonies came into being in very much the manner the British had laid down. For a prolonged initial period the former British possessions had pride of place in the ex-colonial world—they speak English at the UN, not American—and pretty much set the style of politics which has become steadily more conspicuous in international affairs.

Not everyone has noticed this. Indeed, there is scarcely yet a vocabulary in which to describe it. In part, this is because the event is recent; but also because it was incomplete. As with the liberal revolution which came out of America, and the Communist revolution which came out of Russia, this socialist revolution coming mainly out of Britain carried only

so much of the world in its initial period of expansion. The liberal revolution of America was not exactly a spent force by the mid-twentieth century, but (*pace* the Mekong Delta Development Plan) there was never any great prospect of its expanding to new territories. On the other hand, the heirs of the Russian revolution did capture China, the greatest of all the prizes, in 1948, and at least part of Indochina a bit later. But in the main the Communist revolution stopped right there, and the two older revolutions now hold sway within fairly well-defined boundaries. Since 1950 it has been not they but the heirs of the British revolution who have been expanding.

Almost the first international political act of the new states was to form the nonaligned bloc, distinguishing themselves—partially—from the two blocs into which the immediate postwar world had formed. From politics the emphasis shifted to economic affairs. In 1968 these countries, meeting at Algiers, formed the Group of 77 as a formal economic bloc. Their Joint Statement described the group as "comprising the vast majority of the human race"—and indeed it did. The B's in the list of members gave a sense of the range of nations and peoples involved: Bahrain, Barbados, Bhutan, Bolivia, Botswana, Brazil, Burma, Burundi. And yet there was—now somewhat hidden—unity to the list. Of these eight countries, five were formerly British-

SOURCE: Daniel P. Moynihan, "The United States in Opposition," *Commentary* 59, no. 3 (March 1975). Reprinted by permission of the author.

governed or British-directed. At its second Ministerial Meeting in Lima in 1971, the group (now numbering ninety-six) drew up an Action Program which stated, *inter alia,* that developing countries should encourage and promote appropriate commodity action and, particularly, the protection of the interests of primary producers of the region through intensive consultations among producer countries in order to encourage appropriate policies, leading to the establishment of producers' associations and understandings. . . . This was represented in the press as a major gain for the black African states who carried the point over objections from Latin Americans accustomed to working out raw-material and commodity arrangements with the United States. But the idea was fundamentally a heritage of the British revolution, and if the black Africans took the lead in proclaiming it, there is no reason to think it was any less familiar to Arabs. They had all gone to the same schools. Was it not right for those who have only their labor to sell, or only the products of their soil, to organize to confront capital? Had they not been exploited?

II

How has the United States dealt with these new nations and their distinctive ideology? Clearly we have not dealt very successfully. This past year, in the twenty-ninth General Assembly, we were frequently reduced to a voting bloc which, with variations, consisted of ourselves, Chile, and the Dominican Republic. As this "historic session" closed, the Permanent Representative of India to the United Nations declared: "The activities of the Soviet delegation at the session showed once again that the Soviet Union deeply understands and shares the aspirations of the Third World." This was not Krishna Menon, but a balanced and considerate Asian diplomat. If no equivalent pronouncement on China

comes immediately to hand, this may be because the Chinese feel free to identify themselves as members of the Third World. As such, at the end of 1974 they declared that the new majority had written a "brilliant chapter" during the twelve months previous, that it was "sweeping ahead full sail as the boat of imperialism [the United States] and hegemonism [the Soviet Union] founders." "These days," the Chinese statement continued, "the United Nations often takes on the appearance of an international court with the Third World pressing the charges and conducting the trial." A statement to which many could subscribe. But no such statement could come from an American statesman, no such praise would be accorded American policy. Clearly at some level—we all but *started* the United Nations— there has been a massive failure of American diplomacy.

But why? Why has the United States dealt so unsuccessfully with these nations and their distinct ideology? A first thought is that we have not seen the ideology as distinctive. Not recognizing it, we have made no sustained effort to relate ourselves to it. The totalitarian states, from their point of view, did. They recognize ideologies. By 1971 it was clear enough that the Third World—a few exceptions here and there—was not going Communist. But it was nevertheless possible to encourage it in directions that veered very considerably from any tendency the bloc might have to establish fruitful relations with the West; and this was done. It was done, moreover, with the blind acquiescence and even agreement of the United States which kept endorsing principles for whose logical outcome it was wholly unprepared and with which it could never actually go along. . . .

What happened here was that a "Finlandized" Secretariat (the official in charge of preparing the document was indeed a Finn) found that the developing countries and the Communist countries had an easy common interest in portraying their own progress, justifying the effective suppression of dissent, and in the process deprecating and indicting the seeming progress of Western societies. It is easy enough to see that this would be in the interest of the Soviet bloc. (The Chinese did not participate in the debate.) But why the developing world? First, the developing nations could ally with the totalitarians in depicting social reality in this way, in part because so many, having edged toward authoritarian regimes, faced the same problems the Communists would have encountered with a liberal analysis of civil liberties. Secondly, the developing nations had an interest in deprecating the economic achievements of capitalism, since almost none of their own managed economies was doing well. To deplore, to deride, the social effects of affluence in the United States is scarcely a recent invention. For a generation the British Left has held the patent. Further, there is an almost automatic interest on the Left in delegitimating wealth—prior to redistributing it—much as the opposite interest exists on the Right.

Small wonder that officials could describe the Social Report as the most popular document in the UN series, a statement intended as more than faint praise. Yet it has been more representative than otherwise. There are hundreds like it, suffused with a neototalitarian, anti-American bias.

The blindness of American diplomacy to the process persists. Two large events occurred in 1971, and a series of smaller ones were set in motion. China entered the United Nations, an event the Third World representatives saw as a decisive shift of power to their camp. In that same year the Lima conference established the nonaligned as an economic bloc intent on producer cartels. Less noticed, but perhaps no less important in its implications, a distinctive radicalization began in what might as well be termed world social policy.

This radicalization was first clearly evidenced at the United Nations Conference on the Human Environment, held at Stockholm in 1972, or more precisely at the twenty-sixth General Assembly, which was finally to authorize the conference. The conference was in considerable measure an American initiative, and while American negotiators were primarily concerned with ways to get the Russians to join (which in the end they did not), the Brazilians suddenly stormed onto the scene to denounce the whole enterprise as a conspiracy of the haves to keep the have-nots down and out. The argument was that the rich had got rich by polluting their environments and now proposed to stay that way by preventing anyone else from polluting theirs. This, among other things, would insure that the rich would continue their monopoly on the use of the raw materials of the poor. Thus was it asserted that matters originally put forward as soluble in the context of existing economic and political relations were nothing of the sort. To the contrary, they were symptomatic of economic and political exploitation and injustice which could only be resolved by the most profound transformation: to expropriate the expropriators.

At Stockholm itself, this quickly became the dominant theme—espoused by a dominant majority. "Are not poverty and need the greatest pollutors?" Prime Minister Indira Gandhi of India asked. "There are grave misgivings," she continued, "that the discussion of ecology may be designed to distract attention from the problems of war and poverty." She was wrong in this. They were not so designed. But at Stockholm the nations who feared they might be took control of the agenda. The conference declared as its first principle:

> Man has the fundamental right to freedom, equality, and adequate conditions of life, in an environment of a quality which permits a life of dignity and well being, and bears a solemn responsibility to protect and improve the environment for present and future generations. In this respect, policies promoting or perpetuating apartheid, radical segregation, discrimination, colonial and other forms of oppression

and foreign domination stand condemned and must be eliminated.

The American delegates routinely voted for this resolution. It was, after all, language the new countries wanted. What wholly unwelcome meanings might be attached to "other forms of oppression and foreign domination" which stood "condemned" and had to be "eliminated" was a thought scarcely in keeping with the spirit of the occasion.

The Stockholm Conference had been turbulent. The United Nations World Population Conference, held nearly two years later, in August 1974, had an air of insurrection. . . .

. . . few could have anticipated the wild energy of the Chinese assault on the Western position. China has the strictest of all population-control programs. Yet the Chinese arrived in Rumania to assail with unprecedented fury and devastating zeal the very idea of population control as fundamentally subversive of the future of the Third World. The future, the Chinese proclaimed, is infinitely bright. Only the imperialists and the hegemonists could spoil it, and population control was to be their wrecking device. A theory of "consumerism" emerged: it was excessive consumption in the developed economies which was the true source of the problems of the underdeveloped nations and not the size of the latter's population. None dared oppose the thesis. The Indians, who are thought to have a population problem, went to the conference rather disposed to endorse a Plan of Action. But they did nothing of the sort. Instead, the Maharaja of Jammu and Kashmir, who headed the Indian delegation, found himself denouncing "colonial denudation" of the East, and the "vulgar affluence" of the West. The scene grew orgiastic.

In the end, a doctrine emerged which is almost certainly more true than otherwise, namely that social and economic change is the fundamental determinant of fertility change, compared with which family planning

as such has at most a residual role. There need be no difficulty with this assertion. The difficulty comes with the conclusion said to follow: that economic growth in the West should cease and the wealth of the world be redistributed. We are back to Keir Hardie, expropriating the expropriators. Not to produce wealth, but to redistribute it. As with the environment conference, the population conference turned into another occasion for reminding the West of its alleged crimes and unresolved obligations. . . .

IV

What then is to be done? We are witnessing the emergence of a world order dominated arithmetically by the countries of the Third World. This order is already much too developed for the United States or any other nation to think of opting out. It can't be done. One may become a delinquent in this nascent world society. An outcast in it. But one remains "in" it. There is no escape from a definition of nationhood which derives primarily from the new international reality. Nor does this reality respond much to the kind of painfully impotent threats which are sometimes heard of America's "pulling out." Anyone who doubts that Dubai can pay for UNESCO, knows little of UNESCO, less of what the United States pays, and nothing whatever of Dubai.

In any event, matters of this sort aside, world society and world organization have evolved to the point where palpable interests are disposed in international forums to a degree without precedent. Witness, as an instance, the decisions of the World Court allocating the oil fields of the North Sea among the various littoral states in distinctly weighted (but no doubt proper) manner. Witness the current negotiations at the Law of the Sea Conference. Two-thirds of the world is covered by the sea, and the United Nations claims the seabed. That seabed, especially in the region around Hawaii, is rich in so-called "manganese nodules"—concentrations of ore which America technology is now able to exploit, or will be sooner than anyone else. At this moment we have, arguably, complete and perfect freedom to commence industrial use of the high seas. This freedom is being challenged, however, and almost certainly some form of international regime is about to be established. It can be a regime that permits American technology to go forward on some kind of license-and-royalties basis. Or it can assert exclusive "internationalized" rights to exploitation in an international public corporation. The stakes are considerable. They are enormous.

And then, of course, there remains the overriding interest, a true international interest, in arms control, and here true international government has emerged in a most impressive manner. . . .

What then does the United States do?

The United States goes into opposition. This is our circumstance. We are a minority. We are outvoted. This is neither an unprecedented nor an intolerable situation. The question is what do we make of it. So far we have made little—nothing—of what is in fact an opportunity. We go about dazed that the world has changed. We toy with the idea of stopping it and getting off. We rebound with the thought that if only we are more reasonable perhaps "they" will be. (Almost to the end, dominant opinion in the U.S. Mission to the United Nations was that the United States could not vote against the "have-nots" by opposing the Charter on the Rights and Duties of States— all rights for the Group of 77 and no duties.) But "they" do not grow reasonable. Instead, we grow unreasonable. A sterile enterprise which awaits total redefinition.

Going into opposition requires first of all that we recognize that there is a distinctive ideology at work in the Third World, and that it has a distinctive history and logic. To repeat the point once again, we have not done this, tending to see these new political cultures in our own image, or in that of the totalitarians, with a steady shift in the general perception from the former to the latter. But once we perceive the coherence in the majority, we will be in a position to reach for a certain coherence of opposition.

Three central issues commend themselves as points of systematic attack: first, the condition of international liberalism; second, the world economy; third, the state of political and civil liberties and of the general welfare. The rudiments of these arguments need only be sketched.

It is the peculiar function of "radical" political demands, such as those most recently heard in the international forums, that they bring about an exceptional deprecation of the achievements of liberal processes. Even when the radicalism is ultimately rejected, this is rarely from a sense that established processes do better and promise more. American liberalism experienced this deprecation in the 1960s; international liberalism is undergoing it in the 1970s. But the truth is that international liberalism and its processes have enormous recent achievements to their credit. It is time for the United States to start saying so.

One example is the multinational corporation which, combining modern management with liberal trade policies, is arguably the most creative international institution of the twentieth century. A less controversial example is the World Health Organization. In 1966 it set out to abolish smallpox, and by the time this article is read, the job will more than likely have been successfully completed—in very significant measure with the techniques and participation of American epidemiologists. While not many Americans have been getting smallpox of late, the United States has been spending $140 million a year to keep it that way. Savings in that proportion and more will immediately follow. Here, as in a very long list, a liberal world policy has made national sense.

We should resist the temptation to designate agreeable policies as liberal merely on grounds of agreeableness. There are harder criteria.

Liberal policies are limited in their undertakings, concrete in their means, representative in their mode of adoption, and definable in terms of results. These are surely the techniques appropriate to a still tentative, still emergent world society. It is time for the United States, as the new society's loyal opposition, to say this directly, loudly, forcefully.

The economic argument—which will appear inconsistent only to those who have never been much in politics—is that the world economy is not nearly bad enough to justify the measures proposed by the majority, and yet is much worse than it would otherwise be in consequence of measures the majority has already taken. The first half of this formulation will require a considerable shift in the government mind, and possibly even some movement in American elite opinion also, for we have become great producers and distributors of crisis. The world environment crisis, the world population crisis, the world food crisis are in the main American discoveries—or inventions, opinions differ. Yet the simple and direct fact is that any crisis the United States takes to an international forum in the foreseeable future will be decided to the disadvantage of the United States. (Let us hope arms control is an exception.) Ergo: skepticism, challenge.

The world economy is the most inviting case for skepticism, although it will be difficult to persuade many Americans of this during an American recession, and although the rise in oil prices is now creating a crisis in the Third World which is neither of American contrivance nor of American discovery nor of American invention. But until the dislocations caused by OPEC, things were simply not as bad as they were typically portrayed. *Things were better than they had been.* Almost everywhere. In many places things were very good indeed. Sir Arthur Lewis summed up the evidence admirably:

> We have now had nearly three decades of rapid economic growth. . . . Output per head has been growing in the developed world twice as fast as at any time within the preceding century. In the LDC world, output per head is not growing as fast as in the developed world, but is growing faster than the developed world used to grow.

The data can be quite startling. In 1973, as Sir Arthur was speaking, the "Planetary Product," as estimated by the Bureau of Intelligence and Research of the Department of State, grew at a real rate of 6.8 per cent, an astonishing figure. The Third World product expanded by 5.75 per cent, no less astonishing.

Simultaneously it is to be asserted that these economies do less well than they ought: that the difference is of their own making and no one else's, and no claim on anyone else arises in consequence. This will be hard for us to do, but it is time we did it. It is time we commenced citing men such as Jagdish N. Bhagwati, Professor of Economics at MIT, an Indian by birth, who stated in the Lal Bahadur Shastri lectures in India in 1973:

> In the 1950s our economic programs were considered by the progressive and democratic opinion abroad to be a model of what other developing countries might aspire to and emulate. Today, many of us spend our time trying desperately to convince others that *somehow* all the success stories elsewhere are special cases and that our performance is not as unsatisfactory as it appears. And yet, we must confront the fact that, in the ultimate analysis, despite our socialist patter and our planning efforts, we have managed to show neither rapid growth nor significant reduction of income inequality and poverty.

It is time we asserted, with Sir Arthur—a socialist, a man of the Third World—that economic growth is governed not by Western or American conspiracies, but by its own laws and that it "is not an egalitarian process. It is bound to be more vigorous in some professions, or sectors, or geographical regions than in others, and even to cause some impoverishment.". . .

Well, the time may have come when it is necessary for Americans to say, "Yes, it *is* difficult to understand that." Not least because some Third World economies have done so very well. For if Calcutta has the lowest urban standard of living in the world, Singapore has in some ways the highest. It is time we asserted that inequalities in the world may be not so much a matter of condition as of performance. The Brazilians do well. The Israelis. The Nigerians. The Taiwanese. It is a good argument. Far better, surely, than the repeated plea of *nolo contendere* which we have entered, standing accused and abased before the Tribune of the People. . . .

It is time, that is, that the American spokesman came to be feared in international forums for the truths he might tell. Mexico, which has grown increasingly competitive in Third World affairs, which took the lead in the Declaration of the Economic Rights and Duties, preaches international equity. Yet it preaches domestic equity also. It could not without some cost expose itself to a repeated inquiry as to the extent of equity within its own borders. Nor would a good many other Third World countries welcome a sustained comparison between the liberties they provide their own peoples with those which are common and taken for granted in the United States.

For the United States to go into opposition in this manner not only requires a recognition of the ideology of the Third World, but a reversal of roles for American spokesmen as well. As if to compensate for its aggressiveness about what might be termed Security Council affairs, the United States has chosen at the UN to be extraordinarily passive, even compliant, about the endless goings-on in the Commissions and Divisions and Centers and suchlike elusive enterprises associated with the Economic and Social Council. Men and women were assigned to these missions, but have rarely been given much support, or even much scrutiny. Rather, the scrutiny has been of just the wrong kind, ever alert to deviation from the formula platitudes of UN debate, and hopelessly insensitive to the history of

political struggles of the twentieth century.

In Washington, three decades of habit and incentive have created patterns of appeasement so profound as to seem wholly normal. Delegations to international conferences return from devastating defeats proclaiming victory. In truth, these have never been thought especially important. Taking seriously a Third World speech about, say, the right of commodity producers to market their products in concert and to raise their prices in the process, would have been the mark of the quixotic or the failed. To consider the intellectual antecedents of such propositions would not have occurred to anyone, for they were not thought to have any.

And yet how interesting the results might be. The results, say, of observing the occasion of an Algerian's assuming the Presidency of the General Assembly with an informed tribute to the career of the liberator Ben Bella, still presumedly rotting in an Algerian prison cell. The results of a discourse on the disparities between the (1973) per-capita GNP in Abu Dhabi of $43,000 and that of its neighbor, the Democratic People's Republic of Yemen, with one-thousandth that. Again, this need not be a uniformly scornful exercise; anything but. The Third World has more than its share of attractive regimes, and some attractive indeed—Costa Rica, Gambia, Malaysia, to name but three. Half the people in the world who live under a regime of civil liberties live in India. The point is to differentiate, and to turn their own standards against regimes for the moment too much preoccupied with causing difficulties for others, mainly the United States. If this has been in order for some time, the oil price increase—devastating to the development hopes of half-a-hundred Asian and African and Latin American countries— makes it urgent and opportune in a way it has never been. . . .

The Third World must feed itself, for example, and this will not be done by suggesting that Americans eat too much. It is one thing to stress what is consumed in the West, another to note what is produced there. In 1973, 17.8 per cent of the world's population produced 64.3 per cent of its product—and not just from taking advantage of cheap raw materials.

In the same way, the Third World has almost everywhere a constitutional heritage of individual liberty, and it needs to be as jealous of that heritage as of the heritage of national independence. It should be a source of renown that India, for one, has done that, and of infamy that so many others have not.

Not long ago, Alexander Solzhenitsyn, speaking of the case of a Soviet dissident who had been detained in a mental hospital, asked whether world opinion would ever permit South Africa to detain a black African leader in this fashion. Answering his own question, he said, "The storm of worldwide rage would have long ago swept the roof from that prison!" His point is very like the one Stephen Spender came to in the course of the Spanish Civil War. Visiting Spain, he encountered atrocities of the Right, and atrocities of the Left. But only those of the Right were being written about, and it came to him, as he later put it, that if one did not care about every murdered child indiscriminately, one did not really care about children being murdered at all. Very well. But nothing we finally know about the countries of the Third World (only in part the object of the Solzhenitsyn charge) warrants the conclusion that they will be concerned only for wrongdoing that directly affects *them.* Ethnic solidarity is not the automatic enemy of civil liberties. It has been the foundation of many. If there are any who can blow off the roof of any such prison—

then all credit to them. If you can be against the wrongful imprisonment of a person anywhere, then you can be against wrongful imprisonment everywhere. . . .

And equality, what of it? Here an act of historical faith is required: what is the record? The record was stated most succinctly by an Israeli socialist who told William F. Buckley, Jr. that those nations which have put liberty ahead of equality have ended up doing better by equality than those with the reverse priority. This is so, and being so, it is something to be shouted to the heavens in the years now upon us. *This is our case.* We *are* of the liberty party, and it might surprise us what energies might be released were we to unfurl those banners.

In the spring of 1973, in his first address as director-designate of the London School of Economics—where Harold Laski once molded the minds of so many future leaders of the "new majority"—Ralf Dahrendorf sounded this theme. The equality party, he said, has had its day. The liberty party's time has come once more. It is a time to be shared with the new nations, and those not so new, shaped from the old European empires, and especially the British—and is the United States not one such?—whose heritage this is also. To have halted the great totalitarian advance only to be undone by the politics of resentment and the economics of envy would be a poor outcome to the promise of a world society. At the level of world affairs we have learned to deal with Communism. Our task is now to learn to deal with socialism. It will not be less difficult a task. It ought to be a profoundly more pleasant one.

Jeane J. Kirkpatrick, 1926–

Jeane Kirkpatrick is a leading figure among contemporary neoconservative thinkers and former ambassador to the United Nations during the Reagan administration. As an academic political scientist, both before and after her stint at the United Nations, she has written extensively on a variety of issues including party reform and foreign policy.

Kirkpatrick began her political life as a liberal Democrat. In the 1960s, she was a writer and editor for the liberal *New Leader* magazine and was active in the presidential campaigns of John Kennedy and Hubert Humphrey. In the middle 1970s, she served as a member of the Democratic National Convention committee on party structure and presidential nominations. Yet, at the same time, she found herself disenchanted with post-Vietnam liberal approaches to foreign policy. Kirkpatrick helped found and then lead the Coalition for Democratic Majority, a group of Democrats who held strongly to staunch anticommunist and actively interventionist foreign-policy positions despite post-Vietnam reticence and opposition.

An article that Kirkpatrick wrote in the neoconservative *Commentary* magazine titled "Dictatorship and Double Standards" brought her to the attention of Ronald Reagan. In that essay, Kirkpatrick argued that the United States needed to respond differently toward authoritarian (usually of the right) regimes than we did to totalitarian ones (usually of the left). However abusive of personal liberties, authoritarians, Kirkpatrick argued, did not organize and repress every aspect of social life. They allowed realms of freedom and autonomy that later could evolve into the institutions of democratic regimes. Kirkpatrick argued that totalitarian societies, especially those that were Marxist-Leninist, organized and coerced uniform behavior in every aspect of social life. They left no room for autonomous activity and democratic evolution. Given these differences, Kirkpatrick concluded that U.S. policy should show greater tolerance for authoritarian regimes, especially if they were threatened by totalitarian or Marxist revolutionaries within their own countries.

After serving in candidate Reagan's Foreign Policy Advisory Group, Kirkpatrick served as ambassador to the United Nations. Her term was a stormy one as she aggressively pushed U.S. positions and attacked her vociferous critics. In 1985, she resigned her post and returned to Washington to write and teach.

In 1985, Ambassador Kirkpatrick switched her registration to the Republican party, and speculation remains high about her future political ambitions.

The speech reprinted here was also reprinted in the first edition of *The National Interest,* a neoconservative journal focused on foreign affairs. In it, Ambassador Kirkpatrick distinguishes between U.S. involvement in covert wars abroad and similar involvement on the part of Soviets. It is a good

example of a contemporary justification for aggressive American internationalism as the foreign policy stance appropriate to a democratic republic.

Jeane J. Kirkpatrick

Anti-Communist Insurgency and American Policy (1985)

I propose to speak today about the emergence of guerrilla movements against governments that call themselves Marxist/Leninist,
proclaim socialist solidarity, and have been
incorporated into the "Soviet world system."
I propose to discuss U.S. policy toward these
movements, which exist today in Cambodia,
Afghanistan, Mozambique, Angola, Ethiopia
and, of course, Nicaragua. What our attitude
and policy should be toward such movements
is one of the very hottest questions before
the U.S. government today. It has already
proved a fascinating kind of political litmus
test, one that separates Republicans from
Democrats and liberals from conservatives,
and rouses very strong political passions.

In approaching this subject, it is worth not-
ing that the countries in which these insurgencies have arisen were sucked into the Soviet
orbit after January 1975 and the fall of Saigon.
They are *recent* acquisitions. They were rapidly
incorporated during a period in which the
Soviet Union relied heavily on a military bloc
presence to tie new acquisitions into its system.
Each of these countries is a strategically valuable asset, which the Soviets have displayed
determination to preserve. In each country,
political control was secured and is maintained
with direct Soviet or Soviet bloc military inter-

vention. Each offers the Soviets basing rights.
Each government is protected by its own prae-
torian guard from changing its mind or orientation.

Only in Afghanistan have the Soviets relied
on massive direct military intervention. But
Soviet military resources have played a role
everywhere, even though client states provide
most of the manpower. Vietnamese armies
invaded and occupied Cambodia; Cuban
troops are present in large numbers in Angola,
Ethiopia, Mozambique, and Nicaragua. The
role of foreign troops, so-called "internationalists," in sustaining new communist governments in power may be readily observed in
Ethiopia, with its 20,000 or so Cuban troops;
in Angola with its approximately 40,000 Cuban troops; in Mozambique with its 6,000 to
7,000 Cuban troops and advisors, 1,500 East
German, 2,000 Russian, and 8,000 African
from sympathetic African socialist states.

In Mozambique, Cubans and East Germans
comprise the personal body guards of the
ruler, Samora Machel. Libyans pilot his plane,
a North Vietnamese heads the Mozambique
Air Force. North Koreans have occupied key
roles since 1982. Mozambique not only absorbs resources, it provides resources as well.
Over 10,000 young Mozambiquans were sent
as laborers to East Germany. In Angola,
UNITA and the Angolan government put the

SOURCE: *The National Interest* I, 1 Fall 1985.

members of Cuban troops at 45,000. Their upkeep strains an already disorganized economy and absorbs most of its oil reserves. Soviet and Czech pilots fly helicopters. North Korean reinforcements began disembarking last year. In Nicaragua, Cuban military advisors began arriving the same day as the Sandinista takeover, July 19, 1979. Best estimates suggest there have been about 10,000 Cubans present for most of the time for the last five and one-half years. They are supplemented by "internationalists" from all over the Soviet bloc, including the Soviet Union itself.

In each of these countries, military bases are provided and the country's foreign policy is strictly subordinated to Soviet objectives. Mozambique last year signed a joint communique with Mongolia "firmly supporting" the Soviet occupation of Afghanistan. Five members of Nicaragua's junta swore their support of Soviet policy world-wide, including the occupation of Afghanistan in the first year of their tenure. In each of these countries a pattern has developed that includes thousands of Soviet bloc advisers who surround and prop up the government, occupy key roles in its decision structures, and prevent any second thoughts such as those of Sadat or Sekou Toure. These internationalists symbolize the non-nationalist character of the governments they support. Their presence gives an authentic "nationalist" flavor to the insurgents. The extent of the country's integration into the Soviet empire has revived the demand for national independence, comparable to the earlier colonial period.

In each, the revolutionary government has sought to transform traditional ways of life—including land holding, residence, religion, and education—to fit socialist goals and blueprints. This further enhances the sense that aliens' rule is seeking to wipe out indigenous cultures. In each, economic disorganization, stagnation, and scarcity have followed on the heels of installation of a communist government; so has military mobilization of the coun-

try. In each, the population of political prisoners has greatly increased as has the flow of refugees fleeing the new order. In each, the government itself has come to power by force, and maintains itself in power by force. Its only claim to legitimacy is the possession of the instrumentalities of the state. These governments are one party dictatorships even if, as in the case of Nicaragua, some opposition is *permitted* to exist. Each is a closed system that denies its citizens free press, speech, assembly, and free elections. There are no channels through which the policies or composition of the governments change by peaceable means.

It is against these governments that insurgencies have developed. These are repressive dictatorships of recent vintage, propped up by aliens, subordinated to the needs and disciplines of the Soviet bloc, and part of a military machine that is aimed, ultimately, *they* tell us, at us.

Is it morally and legally acceptable for the United States to support armed indigenous movements against these governments? Or, does such support constitute unjustified and illegal interference in the internal affairs of other nations? Is it ever justified to support an armed attack on a sitting government? If so, when? Is it prudent to do so? Do such movements have any chance of success? Does supporting them risk getting *us* into war?

These more general questions lie just beneath the surface as the Congress considers whether to provide assistance—military or humanitarian—to the contras, the Afghan freedom fighters, the Cambodian KPNLF. They were the questions just beneath the surface when, in 1975, the Congress passed the Clark amendment prohibiting the U.S. government from offering assistance to Jonas Savimbi and Angola's resistance movement. The issues involved here touch directly on the most important questions of politics, morals, and the national interest. Many of the values invoked are mutually incompatible in this context.

The post-Vietnam fear of involvement in

any way, in any military conflict of any kind, anywhere, collides with the American commitment to universal values of freedom and self-determination, and these in turn collide with the commitment to the UN Charter's pledge of non-interference in the internal affairs of others. The right to revolution proclaimed in our Declaration of Independence collides with respect for the sovereignty of other governments. Our interest in staving off a serious threat to our national security collides with fear of putting a foot on the slippery slope to war.

The results of these questions and conflicts are becoming ever more curious, the questions ever more pressing. The Congress has before it proposals to aid the contras, and proposals to prohibit aid even by private citizens. Yet certain things seem to be clear. Americans have traditionally affirmed the existence of universal, basic political and civil rights, insisted that the protection of these rights is the very purpose of government, and asserted that people have the *right* to take up arms against their government if it violates their basic rights to life, liberty, and property.

This doctrine is the basic American position on human rights, legitimacy, and armed revolt. It is most clearly stated in our Declaration of Independence. "We hold these truths to be self-evident, that all men are created equal, that they are endowed by their Creator with certain inalienable Rights, that among these are Life, Liberty and the pursuit of Happiness. That to secure these rights, Governments are instituted among Men, deriving their just powers from the consent of the governed." It could not be clearer. Basic American doctrine affirms that *legitimate* government depends on the consent of the governed and respect for basic inalienable rights. This is the claim of legitimacy on which U.S. government rests. A government is not legitimate merely because it exists. Nazi Germany was a *de facto* government headed by Germans; that did not make it legitimate.

But it may be said that this doctrine of legitimacy applies only to rights of citizens to take up arms against their own government, not to the rights of others to supply arms. Others, it is argued, are bound by the prohibitions contained in Article 2.4 of the UN Charter. This article enjoins all member states to "refrain in the international relations from the threat or use of force against the territorial integrity or political independence of any state." But it is clear that this prohibition of force was never intended to stand on its own, but to be seen in the context of the entire Charter, as complementary to Article 51 (which affirms the inherent right to individual or collective self-defense) and to all the provisions of the Charter concerning guarantees of human rights.

Moreover, the Charter of the United Nations clearly states that member states will be democratic, peace-loving, and committed to the maintenance of world peace. Its whole purpose is to promote just such states and behavior. It is not designed to protect repressive expansionist dictatorships or empires. George Kennan once noted that the American interpretation of international law "ignores the devices of the puppet state and the set of techniques by which states can be converted into puppets with no formal violation of, or challenge to, the outward attributes of their sovereignty and their independence." So does the UN Charter. . . .

The notion of a right to violate the sovereignty of existing states was central to the doctrine of limited sovereignty, otherwise known as the Brezhnev Doctrine, which was propounded in 1968 in relation to the Soviet invasion of Czechoslovakia. In the article in *Pravda* on September 26, 1968, where this doctrine was set forth, the Soviet Union claimed not only the right to invade any Soviet bloc country that threatened to deviate from the path of socialistic regularity, but also claimed the right to intervene in the internal affairs of non-Soviet states on behalf of "progressive" forces, that is, forces contributing to the establishment of Marxist regimes. The same article explained how the Soviet Union reconciles the doctrine of limited sovereignty for the rest of the world with the doctrine of absolute sovereignty for itself.

But am I here claiming that violations of international law by the Soviets justify comparable U.S. violations? If we assist an insurgency (thus interfering in the country's internal affairs) are we being "as wrong as" the Soviet bloc? The question recurs in some form in most discussions of these and related questions: Was the U.S., in using military force in liberating Grenada, being "as bad as" Grenada's violent rulers? Were the U.S. and the OECS in liberating Grenada being "as bad as" the Soviets in invading Afghanistan? Is the U.S., in aiding the contras, being "as bad as" the Nicaraguans, or Cubans, or Soviets, in destabilizing El Salvador's government? Lenin said to the Komsomol that "communist morality is based on the struggle for the consolidation and completion of communism." In aiding those who resist communism are we adopting the same concepts of morality in reverse? The answer is, assuredly not. To suggest otherwise is to deny the relevance of context and consequences to moral and legal judgment: it is like asking us to look only at the knife that cuts into an abdomen without taking account of whether the man wielding it is a surgeon or Jack-the-Ripper, or whether the patient is likely to be cured by the knife or destroyed.

The suggestion that force is force is force denies the difference between the force that liberates and that which subjugates. It denies the difference between Soviet force that devastates Afghan towns and countryside and drives its people into exile and OECS/U.S. force that restores democratic freedoms. The suggestion that force is force is force denies that there is an objective difference between liberation and conquest and treats them both as if it were merely a matter of whose ox is being gored.

Again, legitimacy is crucial. The Soviet invasion of Afghanistan is an illegitimate use of force because it aims at the destruction of an independent state, deprives its people of self-determination, denies political and civil rights, wreaks great violence on land and people, and seeks subjugation. The American and OECS landing is, finally, legitimate because it restores just these rights—independence, self-determination, political and civil rights to the people of Grenada. The legal context and political and human consequences of the two are vastly different. . . .

Legitimacy, however, is not the only concern of foreign policy. There is also the matter of prudence and effectiveness. Is it prudent for the U.S. to support insurgencies? Under what circumstances? Can they win? Will it get us into war? I believe it is prudent if the relation to our national interest is clear, if the costs are not too burdensome, if it does not entail too great a risk of embroiling us in a major conflict, and if the long range costs of not doing so are greater than of doing so. In this case, it is clearly prudent to support insurgencies seeking to re-establish the independence of their nation and to detach it from the Soviet empire. The more strategically important the nation, the more important it is to do so.

All the countries in which insurgencies now rage fall in that category, Nicaragua most clearly of all. The U.S. national interest is involved in all, and most directly in Nicaragua. Proximity gives it special importance. Our experiences with Cuba—including the Kennedy/Khrushchev agreement, the Cienfuegos agreement, the combat brigade agreement—make that clear. Moreover, the continuing Cuban military buildup and increased Soviet military presence suggest the costs of not supporting Nicaraguan insurgencies and permitting the consolidation of communist government will be very high—in dollars and in security. The democratic character of the resistance forces makes the moral grounds of assistance particularly clear and compelling.

Is supporting an insurgency tantamount to putting our foot on the slippery slope to another Vietnam? This is the least persuasive argument of all. Going to war requires sending troops into combat—no one proposes doing that. The United States became involved in combat in Vietnam because we sent troops, not because we helped the South Vietnamese help themselves. The Soviet Union promotes insurgencies all over the world, supplies arms, training, and transport and does not get into war. No one even suggests that they are behaving recklessly in destabilizing governments and supporting insurgencies. Neither would we be behaving recklessly in supporting groups who sought to help their countries escape the imperial grip.

Finally, can these nationalist insurgencies win? The answer to that question must be, "maybe, that depends." At least it is not clear they cannot. Every guerrilla war that succeeds against an entrenched government wins against overwhelming odds—by eroding the will of the stronger. Small armies do defeat larger armies. Guerrilla war, at least as much as international war, is a form of politics. "Politics with bloodshed," said Mao, who was this century's greatest master of guerrilla war, "it is a contest of will and wits as much as arms." "It is people not things that are decisive in a war," Mao counseled. Guerrilla wars are long, difficult, and often successful. Their very existence denies a government the pretense that it is acceptable in the eyes of the people over whom it rules. But guerrilla wars require arms. They cannot prevail with only humanitarian assistance.

Can the contras win in Nicaragua? Of course. The Sandinistas have not fully consolidated power. The number of contras is three times the number of FSLN in July, 1979. Both make it likely the contras can end the Marxist-Leninist monopoly of power. The contras are supported by the people of the countryside. They're well trained, but they can't win without arms. People who don't want them to win, and people who don't care, oppose sending arms. Some people really want them to lose. They would like to prohibit even private aid. We should care. The contras are committed to democracy. Their freedom and security are at stake. We should help.

I believe the policy of denying help to insurgencies seeking independence of their country from the Soviet empire is neither necessary nor prudent. To the contrary, morality and national security recommend the opposite course.

Voices of Dissent

Randolph Bourne, 1886–1918

Randolph Bourne was a brilliant radical essayist during the Progressive era and World War I. His early and untimely death in the midst of an influenza epidemic in 1918 robbed America of an original mind, one not easy to pigeonhole in the ideological categories of his time or any other.

Born in Bloomfield, New Jersey, Bourne attended public schools there and later worked for a firm that made automatic piano music. He left this company to attend Columbia University in 1909 and graduated in 1913. He published a collection of essays in that year—*Youth and Life*—celebrating an emerging American youth movement. Bourne won a Gilder Fellowship in 1913 and traveled to Europe. He returned from Europe concerned about the growing likelihood of war there and submitted a series of essays discussing these concerns to Columbia. He then turned his attention to questions of education and became especially attached to the writings of John Dewey.

For a short time, Bourne became a rather well-known Progressive writer, and had close ties to many of the intellectuals clustering around *The New Republic*. Interestingly, however, Bourne found liberal pragmatism wanting, and was especially concerned about the unquestioning devotion to World War I that he found among many Progressives including Herbert Croly, *The New Republic*'s editor. In a powerful essay titled "War and the Intellectuals," Bourne chided Progressives who looked to war as a tool to create a strong national community with a sound sense of purpose and resolve.

Bourne became a vocal pacifist during the war and began to write radical essays in *The Masses* and *The Seven Arts*. At the time of his death he was working on an analysis of "The State," fragments of which remain. Parts of this unpublished work are reprinted below.

Despite his radical views, Bourne showed a distrust for the state and sensitivity to the claims of other nonpoliticized institutions that make him difficult to place in conventional "left-right" categories. In this way, he preshadowed many ideas of the early, but short-lived New Left in the 1960s.

Randolph Bourne

The State (1918)

I

To most of the Americans of the classes which consider themselves significant the war brought a sense of the sanctity of the State, which, if they had had time to think about it, would have seemed a sudden and surprising alteration in their habits of thought. In times of peace, we usually ignore the State in favor of partisan political controversies, or personal struggles for office, or the pursuit of party policies. It is the Government rather than the State with which the politically minded are concerned. The State is reduced to a shadowy emblem which comes to consciousness only on occasions of patriotic holiday.

Government is obviously composed of common and unsanctified men, and is thus a legitimate object of criticism and even contempt. If your own party is in power, things may be assumed to be moving safely enough; but if the opposition is in, then clearly all safety and honor have fled the State. Yet you do not put it to yourself in quite that way. What you think is only that there are rascals to be turned out of a very practical machinery of offices and functions which you take for granted. . . .

The classes which are able to play an active

SOURCE: Randolph Bourne, *War and the Intellectuals*, ed. Carl Resek (New York: Harper & Row, 1964).

and not merely a passive rôle in the organization for war get a tremendous liberation of activity and energy. Individuals are jolted out of their old routine, many of them are given new positions of responsibility, new techniques must be learnt. Wearing home ties are broken and women who would have remained attached with infantile bonds are liberated for service overseas. A vast sense of rejuvenescence pervades the significant classes, a sense of new importance in the world. Old national ideals are taken out, re-adapted to the purpose and used as universal touchstones, or molds into which all thought is poured. Every individual citizen who in peacetimes had no function to perform by which he could imagine himself an expression or living fragment of the State becomes an active amateur agent of the Government in reporting spies and disloyalists, in raising Government funds, or in propagating such measures as are considered necessary by officialdom. Minority opinion, which in times of peace, was only irritating and could not be dealt with by law unless it was conjoined with actual crime, becomes, with the outbreak of war, a case for outlawry. Criticism of the State, objections to war, lukewarm opinions concerning the necessity or the beauty of conscription, are made subject to ferocious penalties, far exceeding in severity those affixed to actual pragmatic crimes. Public opinion, as expressed in the newspapers, and the pulpits and the schools, becomes one solid block. "Loyalty," or rather war orthodoxy, becomes the sole test for all professions, techniques, occupations. Particularly is this true in the sphere of the intellectual life. There the smallest taint is held to spread over the whole soul, so that a professor of physics is *ipso facto* disqualified to teach physics or to hold honorable place in a university —the republic of learning—if he is at all unsound on the war. Even mere association with persons thus tainted is considered to disqualify a teacher. Anything pertaining to the enemy becomes taboo. His books are suppressed wherever possible, his language is forbidden. His artistic products are considered to convey in the subtlest spiritual way taints of vast poison to the soul that permits itself to enjoy them. So enemy music is suppressed, and energetic measures of opprobrium taken against those whose artistic consciences are not ready to perform such an act of self-sacrifice. The rage for loyal conformity works impartially, and often in diametric opposition to other orthodoxies and traditional conformities, or even ideals. The triumphant orthodoxy of the State is shown at its apex perhaps when Christian preachers lose their pulpits for taking more or less in literal terms the Sermon on the Mount, and Christian zealots are sent to prison for twenty years for distributing tracts which argue that war is unscriptural.

War is the health of the State. It automatically sets in motion throughout society those irresistible forces for uniformity, for passionate cooperation with the Government in coercing into obedience the minority groups and individuals which lack the larger herd sense. The machinery of government sets and enforces the drastic penalties, the minorities are either intimidated into silence, or brought slowly around by a subtle process of persuasion which may seem to them really to be converting them. Of course the ideal of perfect loyalty, perfect uniformity is never really attained. The classes upon whom the amateur work of coercion falls are unwearied in their zeal, but often their agitation, instead of converting, merely serves to stiffen their resistance. Minorities are rendered sullen, and some intellectual opinion bitter and satirical. But in general, the nation in war-time attains a uniformity of feeling, a hierarchy of values culminating at the undisputed apex of the State ideal, which could not possibly be produced through any other agency than war. Other values such as artistic creation, knowledge, reason, beauty, the enhancement of life, are instantly and almost unanimously sacrificed, and the significant classes who have constituted themselves the amateur agents of the State are engaged not only in sacrificing these values for themselves but in coercing all other persons into sacrificing them.

War—or at least modern war waged by a democratic republic against a powerful enemy—seems to achieve for a nation almost all that the most inflamed political idealist could desire. Citizens are no longer indifferent to their Government, but each cell of the body politic is brimming with life and activity. We are at last on the way to full realization of that collective community in which each individual somehow contains the virtue of the whole. In a nation at war, every citizen identifies himself with the whole, and feels immensely strengthened in that identification. The purpose and desire of the collective community live in each person who throws himself wholeheartedly into the cause of war. The impeding distinction between society and the individual is almost blotted out. At war, the individual becomes almost identical with his society. He achieves a superb self-assurance, an intuition of the rightness of all his ideas and emotions, so that in the suppression of opponents or heretics he is invincibly strong; he feels behind him all the power of the collective community. The individual as social being in war seems to have achieved almost his apotheosis. Not for any religious impulse could the American nation have been expected to show such devotion *en masse,* such sacrifice and labor. Certainly not for any secular good, such as universal education or the subjugation of nature, would it have poured forth its treasure and its life, or would it have permitted such stern coercive measures to be taken against it, such as conscripting its money and its men. But for the sake of a war of offensive self-defense, undertaken to support a difficult cause to the slogan of "democracy," it would reach the highest level ever known of collective effort.

For these secular goods, connected with the enhancement of life, the education of man and the use of the intelligence to realize reason and beauty in the nation's communal living, are alien to our traditional ideal of the State. The State is intimately connected with war, for it is the organization of the collective community when it acts in a political manner, and to act in a political manner towards a rival group has meant, throughout all history—war.

There is nothing invidious in the use of the term, "herd," in connection with the State. It is merely an attempt to reduce closer to first principles the nature of this institution in the shadow of which we all live, move and have our being. Ethnologists are generally agreed that human society made its first appearance as the human pack and not as a collection of individuals or of couples. The herd is in fact the original unit, and only as it was differentiated did personal individuality develop. All the most primitive surviving tribes of men are shown to live in a very complex but very rigid social organization where opportunity for individuation is scarcely given. These tribes remain strictly organized herds, and the difference between them and the modern State is one of degree of sophistication and variety of organization, and not of kind.

Psychologists recognize the gregarious impulse as one of the strongest primitive pulls which keeps together the herds of the different species of higher animals. Mankind is no exception. Our pugnacious evolutionary history has prevented the impulse from ever dying out. This gregarious impulse is the tendency to imitate, to conform, to coalesce together, and is most powerful when the herd believes itself threatened with attack. Animals crowd together for protection, and men become most conscious of their collectivity at the threat of war. Consciousness of collectivity brings confidence and a feeling of massed strength, which in turn arouses pugnacity and the battle is on. In civilized man, the gregarious impulse acts not only to produce concerted action for defense, but also to produce identity of opinion. Since thought is a form of behavior, the gregarious impulse floods up into its realms and demands that sense of uniform thought which wartime produces so successfully. And it is in this flooding of the conscious life of society that gregariousness works its havoc. . . .

For just as in modern societies the sex-instinct is enormously over-supplied for the requirements of human propagation, so the gregarious impulse is enormously over-supplied for the work of protection which it is called upon to perform. It would be quite enough if we were gregarious enough to enjoy the companionship of others, to be able to coöperate with them, and to feel a slight malaise at solitude. Unfortunately, however, this impulse is not content with these reasonable and healthful demands, but insists that like-mindedness shall prevail everywhere, in all departments of life. So that all human progress, all novelty, and non-conformity, must be carried against the resistance of this tyrannical herd-instinct which drives the individual into obedience and conformity with the majority. Even in the most modern and enlightened societies this impulse shows little sign of abating. As it is driven by inexorable economic demand out of the sphere of utility, it seems to fasten itself ever more fiercely in the realm of feeling and opinion, so that conformity comes to be a thing aggressively desired and demanded.

The gregarious impulse keeps its hold all the more virulently because when the group is in motion or is taking any positive action, this feeling of being with and supported by the collective herd very greatly feeds that will to power, the nourishment of which the individual organism so constantly demands. You feel powerful by conforming, and you feel forlorn and helpless if you are out of the crowd. While even if you do not get any access of power by thinking and feeling just as everybody else in your group does, you get at least the warm feeling of obedience, the soothing irresponsibility of protection.

Joining as it does to these very vigorous tendencies of the individual—the pleasure in power and the pleasure in obedience—this gregarious impulse becomes irresistible in society. War stimulates it to the highest possible degree, sending the influences of its mysterious herd-current with its inflations of power and obedience to the farthest reaches of the society, to every individual and little group that can possibly be affected. And it is these impulses which the State—the organization of the entire herd, the entire collectivity—is founded on and makes use of.

There is, of course, in the feeling towards the State a large element of pure filial mysticism. The sense of insecurity, the desire for protection, sends one's desire back to the father and mother, with whom is associated the earliest feeling of protection. It is not for nothing that one's State is still thought of as Father or Motherland, that one's relation towards it is conceived in terms of family affection. The war has shown that nowhere under the shock of danger have these primitive childlike attitudes failed to assert themselves again, as much in this country as anywhere. If we have not the intense Father-sense of the German who worships his Vaterland, at least in Uncle Sam we have a symbol of protecting, kindly authority, and in the many Mother-posters of the Red Cross, we see how easily in the more tender functions of war service, the ruling organization is conceived in family terms. A people at war have become in the most literal sense obedient, respectful, trustful children again, full of that naive faith in the all-

wisdom and all-power of the adult who takes care of them, imposes his mild but necessary rule upon them and in whom they lose their responsibility and anxieties. In this recrudescence of the child, there is great comfort, and a certain influx of power. On most people the strain of being an independent adult weighs heavily, and upon none more than those members of the significant classes who have had bequeathed to them or have assumed the responsibilities of governing. The State provides the convenientest of symbols under which these classes can retain all the actual pragmatic satisfaction of governing, but can rid themselves of the psychic burden of adulthood. They continue to direct industry and government and all the institutions of society pretty much as before, but in their own conscious eyes and in the eyes of the general public, they are turned from their selfish and predatory ways, and have become loyal servants of society, or something greater than they—the State. The man who moves from the direction of a large business in New York to a post in the war management industrial service in Washington does not apparently alter very much his power or his administrative technique. But psychically, what a transfiguration has occurred! His is now not only the power but the glory! And his sense of satisfaction is directly proportional not to the genuine amount of personal sacrifice that may be involved in the change but to the extent to which he retains his industrial prerogatives and sense of command.

From members of this class a certain insuperable indignation arises if the change from private enterprise to State service involves any real loss of power and personal privilege. If there is to be pragmatic sacrifice, let it be, they feel, on the field of honor, in the traditionally acclaimed deaths by battle, in that detour to suicide, as Nietzsche calls war. The State in wartime supplies satisfaction for this very real craving, but its chief value is the opportunity it gives for this regression to infantile attitudes. In your reaction to an imagined attack on your country or an insult to its government, you draw closer to the herd for protection, you conform in word and deed, and you insist vehemently that everybody else shall think, speak and act together. And you fix your adoring gaze upon the State, with a truly filial look, as upon the Father of the flock, the quasi-personal symbol of the strength of the herd, and the leader and determinant of your definite action and ideas. . . .

J. William Fulbright, 1905–

As chairman of the Senate Foreign Relations Committee during the Johnson and Nixon administrations, J. William Fulbright was an outspoken and articulate critic of the Vietnam War.

Fulbright graduated from the University of Arkansas in 1925 and studied at Oxford on a Rhodes Scholarship. He went to law school at George Washington University, served in the antitrust division of the Justice Department, and took faculty positions at George Washington and then the University of Arkansas. From 1939 to 1941 he was president of the University, but in 1942 he left to serve as a Democrat in the House of Representatives. Two years later he was elected to the Senate. In 1946, he sponsored the Fulbright Act which has financed thousands of scholarships for students and faculty to study in foreign nations.

Fulbright has been a constant critic of an extended U.S. role abroad. By no means an isolationist, he nevertheless favors scaling down America's involvement in the affairs of the other nations and is distrustful of a powerful military. Among his writings are *Prospects for the West* (1963), *Old Myths and New Realities* (1964), and *The Arrogance of Power* (1967).

The following speech is a good example of the ideas of those who have attacked American involvement in Vietnam as "imperial."

J. William Fulbright

The Price of Empire (1967)

Standing in the smoke and rubble of Detroit, a Negro veteran said: "I just got back from Vietnam a few months ago, but you know, I think the war is here."

SOURCE: *Congressional Record—Senate* 113, part 16, August 9, 1967.

There are in fact two wars going on. One is the war of power politics which our soldiers are fighting in the jungles of southeast Asia. The other is a war for America's soul which is being fought in the streets of Newark and Detroit and in the halls of Congress, in churches and protest meetings and on college campuses, and in the hearts and minds of silent Americans from Maine to Hawaii. I believe that the two wars have something to do with each other, not in the direct, tangibly causal way that bureaucrats require as proof of a connection between two things, but in a subtler, moral and qualitative way that is no less real for being intangible. Each of these wars might well be going on in the absence of the other, but neither, I suspect, standing alone, would seem so hopeless and demoralizing.

The connection between Vietnam and Detroit is in their conflicting and incompatible demands upon traditional American values. The one demands that they be set aside, the other that they be fulfilled. The one demands the acceptance by America of an imperial role in the world, or of what our policy makers like to call the "responsibilities of power," or of what I have called the "arrogance of power." The other demands freedom and social justice at home, an end to poverty, the fulfillment of our flawed democracy, and an effort to create a role for ourselves in the world which is compatible with our traditional values. The question, it should be emphasized, is not whether it is *possible* to engage in traditional power politics abroad and at the same time to perfect democracy at home, but whether it is possible for *us Americans,* without particular history and national character, to combine morally incompatible roles.

Administration officials tell us that we can indeed afford both Vietnam and the Great Society, and they produce impressive statistics of the gross national product to prove it. The statistics show financial capacity but they do not show moral and psychological capacity. They do not show how a President preoccupied with bombing missions over North and South Vietnam can provide strong and consistent leadership for the renewal of our cities. They do not show how a Congress burdened with war costs and war measures, with emergency briefings and an endless series of dra-

matic appeals, with anxious constituents and a mounting anxiety of their own, can tend to the workaday business of studying social problems and legislating programs to meet them. Nor do the statistics tell how an anxious and puzzled people, bombarded by press and television with the bad news of American deaths in Vietnam, the "good news" of enemy deaths—and with vividly horrifying pictures to illustrate them—can be expected to support neighborhood antipoverty projects and national programs for urban renewal, employment and education. Anxiety about war does not breed compassion for one's neighbors; nor do constant reminders of the cheapness of life abroad strengthen our faith in its sanctity at home. In these ways the war in Vietnam is poisoning and brutalizing our domestic life. Psychological incompatibility has proven to be more controlling than financial feasibility; and the Great Society has become a sick society.

I. IMPERIAL DESTINY AND THE AMERICAN DREAM

When he visited America a hundred years ago, Thomas Huxley wrote: "I cannot say that I am in the slightest degree impressed by your bigness, or your material resources, as such. Size is not grandeur, and territory does not make a nation. The great issue, about which hangs the terror of overhanging fate, is what are you going to do with all these things?"

The question is still with us and we seem to have come to a time of historical crisis when its answer can no longer be deferred. Before the Second World War our world role was a *potential* role; we were important in the world for what we *could* do with our power, for the leadership we *might* provide, for the example we *might* set. Now the choices are almost gone: we are *almost* the world's self-appointed policeman; we are *almost* the world defender of the *status quo.* We are well on our way to becoming a traditional great power—an imperial nation if you will—engaged in the exercise of power for its own sake, exercising it to the limit of our capacity and beyond, filling every vacuum and extending the American "presence" to the farthest reaches of the earth. And, as with the great empires of the past, as the power grows, it is becoming an end in itself, separated except by ritual incantation from its initial motives, governed, it would seem, by its own mystique, power without philosophy or purpose. . . .

That is something which none of the great empires of the past has ever done—or tried to do—or wanted to do—but we were bold enough—or presumptuous enough—to think that we might be able to do it. And there are a great many Americans who still think we can do it—or at least they want to try.

That, I believe, is what all the hue and cry is about—the dissent in the Senate and the protest marches in the cities, the letters to the President from student leaders and former Peace Corps volunteers, the lonely searching of conscience by a student facing the draft and the letter to a Senator from a soldier in the field who can no longer accept the official explanations of why he has been sent to fight in the jungles of Vietnam. All believe that their country was cut out for something more ennobling than an imperial destiny. Our youth are showing that they still believe in the American dream, and their protests attest to its continuing vitality.

There appeared in a recent issue of the journal *Foreign Affairs* a curious little article complaining about the failure of many American intellectuals to support what the author regards as America's unavoidable "imperial role" in the world. The article took my attention because it seems a faithful statement of the governing philosophy of American foreign policy while also suggesting how little the makers of that policy appreciate the significance of the issue between themselves and their critics. It is taken for granted—not set forth as an hypothesis to be proved—that,

any great power, in the author's words, "is entangled in a web of responsibilities from which there is no hope of escape," and that "there is no way the United States, as the world's mightiest power, can avoid such an imperial role. . . ."[1] The author's displeasure with the "intellectuals"—he uses the word more or less to describe people who disagree with the Administration's policy—is that, in the face of this alleged historical inevitability, they are putting up a disruptive, irritating and futile resistance. They are doing this, he believes, because they are believers in "ideology"—the better word would be "values" or "ideals"—and this causes their thinking to be "irrelevant" to foreign policy.

Here, inadvertently, the writer puts his finger on the nub of the current crisis. The students and churchmen and professors who are protesting the Vietnam war do not accept the notion that foreign policy is a matter of expedients to which values are irrelevant. They reject this notion because they understand, as some of our policy makers do not understand, that it is ultimately self-defeating to "fight fire with fire," that you cannot defend your values in a manner that does violence to those values without destroying the very thing you are trying to defend. They understand, as our policy makers do not, that when American soldiers are sent, in the name of freedom, to sustain corrupt dictators in a civil war, that when the CIA subverts student organizations to engage in propaganda activities abroad, or when the Export-Import Bank is used by the Pentagon to finance secret arms sales abroad, damage—perhaps irreparable damage—is being done to the very values that are meant to be defended. The critics understand, as our policy makers do not, that, through the undemocratic expedients we have adopted for the defense of American democracy, we are weakening it to a degree that is

---

[1] Irving Kristol, "American Intellectuals and Foreign Policy," *Foreign Affairs*, July 1967, pp. 602, 605.

beyond the resources of our bitterest enemies.

Nor do the dissenters accept the romantic view that a nation is powerless to choose the role it will play in the world, that some mystic force of history or destiny requires a powerful nation to be an imperial nation, dedicated to what Paul Goodman calls the "empty system of power,"[2] to the pursuit of power without purpose, philosophy or compassion.". . .

The critics of our current course also challenge the contention that the traditional methods of foreign policy are safe and prudent and realistic. They are understandably skeptical of their wise and experienced elders who, in the name of prudence, caution against any departure from the tried and true methods that have led in this century to Sarejevo, Munich and Dien Bien Phu. They think that the methods of the past have been tried and found wanting, and two world wars attest powerfully to their belief. . . .

At present much of the world is repelled by America and what America seems to stand for in the world. Both in our foreign affairs and in our domestic life we convey an image of violence; I do not care very much about images as distinguished from the things they reflect, but this image is rooted in reality. Abroad, we are engaged in a savage and unsuccessful war against poor people in a small and backward nation. At home—largely because of the neglect resulting from twenty-five years of preoccupation with foreign involvements—our cities are exploding in violent protest against generations of social injustice. America, which only a few years ago seemed to the world to be a model of democracy and social justice, has become a symbol of violence and undisciplined power. . . .

Far from building a safe world environment for American values, our war in Vietnam and the domestic deterioration which it has aggravated are creating a most uncongenial world atmosphere for American ideas and values. The world has no need, in this age of nationalism and nuclear weapons, for a new imperial power, but there is a great need of moral leadership—by which I mean the leadership of decent example. That role could be ours but we have vacated the field, and all that has kept the Russians from filling it is their own lack of imagination.

At the same time, as we have noted, and of even greater fundamental importance, our purposeless and undisciplined use of power is causing a profound controversy in our own society. This in a way is something to be proud of. We have sickened but not succumbed and just as a healthy body fights disease, we are fighting the alien concept which is being thrust upon us, not by history but by our policy makers in the Department of State and the Pentagon. We are proving the strength of the American dream by resisting the dream of an imperial destiny. We are demonstrating the validity of our traditional values by the difficulty we are having in betraying them.

The principal defenders of these values are our remarkable younger generation, something of whose spirit is expressed in a letter which I received from an American soldier in Vietnam. Speaking of the phony propaganda on both sides, and then of the savagery of the war, or the people he describes as the "real casualties"—"the farmers and their families in the Delta mangled by air strikes, and the villagers here killed and burned out by our friendly Korean mercenaries"—this young soldier then asks ". . . whatever has become of our dream? Where is that America that opposed tyrannies at every turn, without inquiring first whether some particular forms of tyranny might be of use to us? Of the three rights which men have, the first, as I recall, was the right to life. How then have we come to be killing so many in such a dubious cause?"

---

[2] *Like a Conquered Province, The Moral Ambiguity of America* (New York: Random House, 1967), p. 73.

II. THE SICK SOCIETY

While the death toll mounts in Vietnam, it is mounting too in the war at home. During a single week of July 1967, 164 Americans were killed and 1,442 wounded in Vietnam, while 65 Americans were killed and 2,100 were wounded in city riots in the United States. We are truly fighting a two-front war and doing badly in both. Each war feeds on the other and, although the President assures us that we have the resources to win both wars, in fact we are not winning either. . . .

. . . Why should not riots and snipers' bullets bring the white man to an awareness of the Negro's plight when peaceful programs for housing and jobs and training have been more rhetoric than reality? Ugly and shocking thoughts are in the American air and they were forged in the Vietnam crucible. Black power extremists talk of "wars of liberation" in the urban ghettoes of America. A cartoon in a London newspaper showed two Negro soldiers in battle in Vietnam with one saying to the other: "This is going to be great training for civilian life.". . .

An unnecessary and immoral war deserves in its own right to be liquidated; when its effect in addition is the aggravation of grave problems and the corrosion of values in our own society, its liquidation under terms of reasonable and honorable compromise is doubly imperative. Our country is being weakened by a grotesque inversion of priorities, the effects of which are becoming clear to more and more Americans—in the Congress, in the press and in the country at large. Even the *Washington Post*, a newspaper which has obsequiously supported the Administration's policy in Vietnam, took note in a recent editorial of the "ugly image of a world policeman incapable of policing itself" as against the "absolute necessity of a sound domestic base for an effective foreign policy," and then commented: "We are confronted simultaneously with an urgent domestic crisis and an urgent foreign crisis and our commitments to both are clear.". . .

Priorities are reflected in the things we spend money on. Far from being a dry accounting of bookkeepers, a nation's budget is full of moral implications; it tells what a society cares about and what it does not care about; it tells what its values are.

Here are a few statistics on America's values: Since 1946 we have spent over $1,578 billion through our regular national budget. Of this amount over $904 billion, or 57.29 percent of the total, have gone for military power. By contrast, less than $96 billion, or 6.08 percent, were spent on "social functions" including education, health, labor and welfare programs, housing and community development. The Administration's budget for fiscal year 1968 calls for almost $76 billion to be spent on the military and only $15 billion for "social functions."

I would not say that we have shown ourselves to value weapons five or ten times as much as we value domestic social needs, as the figures suggest; certainly much of our military spending has been necessitated by genuine requirements of national security. I think, however, that we have embraced the necessity with excessive enthusiasm, that the Congress has been all too willing to provide unlimited sums for the military and not really very reluctant at all to offset these costs to a very small degree by cutting away funds for the poverty program and urban renewal, for rent supplements for the poor and even for a program to help protect slum children from being bitten by rats. Twenty million dollars a year to eliminate rats—about one one-hundredth of the monthly cost of the war in Vietnam— would not eliminate slum riots but, as Tom Wicker has written, "It would only suggest that somebody cared." The discrepancy of attitudes tells at least as much about our national values as the discrepancy of dollars.

III. THE REGENERATIVE POWER OF YOUTH

While the country sickens for lack of moral leadership, a most remarkable younger generation has taken up the standard of American idealism. Unlike so many of their elders, they have perceived the fraud and sham in American life and are unequivocally rejecting it. Some, the hippies, have simply withdrawn, and while we may regret the loss of their energies and their sense of decency, we can hardly gainsay their evaluation of the state of society. Others of our youth are sardonic and skeptical, not, I think, because they do not want ideals but because they want the genuine article and will not tolerate fraud. Others—students who wrestle with their consciences about the draft, soldiers who wrestle with their consciences about the war, Peace Corps volunteers who strive to light the spark of human dignity among the poor of India or Brazil, and VISTA volunteers who try to do the same for our own poor in Harlem or Appalachia—are striving to keep alive the traditional values of American democracy.

They are not really radical, these young idealists, no more radical, that is, than Jefferson's idea of freedom, Lincoln's idea of equality, or Wilson's idea of a peaceful community of nations. Some of them, it is true, are taking what many regard as radical action, but they are doing it in defense of traditional values and in protest against the radical departure from those values embodied in the idea of an imperial destiny for America.

The focus of their protest is the war in Vietnam and the measure of their integrity is the fortitude with which they refused to be deceived about it. By striking contrast with the young Germans who accepted the Nazi evil because the values of their society had disintegrated and they had no normal frame of reference, these young Americans are demonstrating the vitality of American values. They are demonstrating that, while their country is ca-pable of acting falsely to itself, it cannot do so without internal disruption, without calling forth the regenerative counterforce of protest from Americans who are willing to act in defense of the principles they were brought up to believe in.

The spirit of this regenerative generation has been richly demonstrated to me in letters from student leaders, from former Peace Corps volunteers and from soldiers fighting in Vietnam. I quoted from one earlier in my remarks. Another letter that is both striking and representative was written by an officer still in Vietnam. He wrote:

"For eleven years I was, before this war, a Regular commissioned officer—a professional military man in name and spirit; now—in name only. To fight well (as do the VC), a soldier must believe in his leadership. I, and many I have met, have lost faith in ours. Since I hold that duty to conscience is higher than duty to the administration (not 'country' as cry the nationalists). I declined a promotion and have resigned my commission. I am to be discharged on my return, at which time I hope to contribute in some way to the search for peace in Vietnam."

Some years ago Archibald MacLeish characterized the American people as follows:

"Races didn't bother the Americans. They were something a lot better than any race. They were a People. They were the first self-constituted, self-declared, self-created People in the history of the world. And their manners were their own business. And so were their politics. And so, but ten times so, were their souls."

Now the possession of their souls is being challenged by the false and dangerous dream of an imperial destiny. It may be that the challenge will succeed, that America will succumb to becoming a traditional empire and will reign for a time over what must surely be a moral if not a physical wasteland, and then, like the great empires of the past, will decline or fall. Or it may be that the effort to create so grotesque an anachronism will go up in flames of nuclear holocaust. But if I had to bet my money on what is going to happen, I would bet on this younger generation—this generation who reject the inhumanity of war in a poor and distant land, who reject the poverty and sham in their own country, this generation who are telling their elders what their elders ought to have known, that the price of empire is America's soul and that price is too high.

Robert Heilbroner, 1919–

Robert Heilbroner is the Norman Thomas Professor of Economics at the New School for Social Research in New York City. Since his first book *The Worldly Philosophers* (1953), Heilbroner has earned a reputation as an economist who can attract and write for a mass audience. Most of his works approach economic questions from a broad perspective, and are as much political and social theory as pure economics. One of his abiding concerns has been with the phenomenon of economic growth and its relation to social structure and political institutions. He has consistently addressed the problem of how to break the hold of economic backwardness in third-world economies without extensive political repression. Similarly, he has extensively explored the potential conflict between individual freedom and the need for public planning in developed economies where capital is increasingly concentrated and resources potentially scarce.

A few of Professor Heilbroner's works are *The Great Ascent* (1963), *The Limits of Capitalism* (1966), *An Inquiry Into the Human Prospect* (1974), and *Marxism: For and Against* (1980).

In the following 1967 *Commentary* article, written in the midst of the Vietnam War, Heilbroner examines the relationship between modernization and repressive revolutions in third-world countries, and suggests a dilemma for the United States: either to accept leftist revolutionaries—despite a repugnance for their values—for the sake of modernization, or to reject such modernization and in the process accept an active counterrevolutionary world role.

Robert Heilbroner

Counterrevolutionary America (1967)

Is the United States fundamentally opposed to economic development? The question is outrageous. Did we not coin the phrase, "the revolution of rising expectations"? Have we not supported the cause of development more generously than any nation on earth, spent our intellectual energy on the problems of development, offered our expertise freely to the backward nations of the world? How can it possibly be suggested that the United States might be opposed to economic development?

The answer is that we are not at all opposed to what we conceive economic development to be. The process depicted by the "revolution of rising expectations" is a deeply attractive one. It conjures up the image of a peasant in some primitive land, leaning on his crude plow and looking to the horizon, where he sees dimly, but for the *first time* (and that is what is so revolutionary about it), the vision of a better life. From this electrifying vision comes the necessary catalysis to change an old and stagnant way of life. The pace of work quickens. Innovations, formerly feared and resisted, are now eagerly accepted. The obstacles are admittedly very great—whence the need for foreign assistance—but under the impetus of new hopes the economic mechanism begins to turn faster, to gain traction against the environment. Slowly, but surely, the Great Ascent begins.

SOURCE: Robert Heilbroner, "Counter-revolutionary America," *Commentary*, no. 4 (April 1967). Reprinted with permission.

There is much that is admirable about this well-intentioned popular view of "the revolution of rising expectations." Unfortunately, there is more that is delusive about it. For the buoyant appeal of its rhetoric conceals or passes in silence over by far the larger part of the spectrum of realities of the development process. One of these is the certainty that the revolutionary aspect of development will not be limited to the realm of ideas, but will vent its fury on institutions, social classes, and innocent men and women. Another is the great likelihood that the ideas needed to guide the revolution will not only be affirmative and reasonable, but also destructive and fanatic. A third is the realization that revolutionary efforts cannot be made, and certainly cannot be sustained, by voluntary effort alone, but require an iron hand, in the spheres both of economic direction and political control. And the fourth and most difficult of these realities to face is the probability that the political force most likely to succeed in carrying through the gigantic historical transformation of development is some form of extreme national collectivism or Communism.

In a word, what our rhetoric fails to bring to our attention is the likelihood that development will require policies and programs repugnant to our "way of life," that it will bring to the fore governments hostile to our international objectives, and that its regnant ideology will bitterly oppose capitalism as a system of world economic power. If that is the case, we would have to think twice before denying that the United States was fundamentally opposed to economic development. But is it the case? Must development lead in directions that go counter to the present American political philosophy? Let me try to indicate, albeit much too briefly and summarily, the reasons that lead me to answer that question as I do.

I begin with the cardinal point, often noted but still insufficiently appreciated, that the process called "economic development" is not primarily economic at all. We think of development as a campaign of production to be fought with budgets and monetary policies and measured with indices of output and income. But the development process is much wider and deeper than can be indicated by such statistics. To be sure, in the end what is hoped for is a tremendous rise in output. But this will not come to pass until a series of tasks, at once cruder and more delicate, simpler and infinitely more difficult, has been commenced and carried along a certain distance.

In most of the new nations of Africa, these tasks consist in establishing the very underpinnings of nationhood itself—in determining national borders, establishing national languages, arousing a basic national (as distinguished from tribal) self-consciousness. Before these steps have been taken, the African states will remain no more than names insecurely affixed to the map, not social entities capable of undertaking an enormous collective venture in economic change. In Asia, nationhood is generally much further advanced than in Africa, but here the main impediment to development is the miasma of apathy and fatalism, superstition and distrust that vitiates every attempt to improve hopelessly inefficient modes of work and patterns of resource use: while India starves, a quarter of the world's cow population devours Indian crops, exempt either from effective employment or slaughter because of sacred taboos. In still other areas, mainly Latin America, the principal handicap to development is not an absence of national identity or the presence of suffo-

cating cultures (although the latter certainly plays its part), but the cramping and crippling inhibitions of obsolete social institutions and reactionary social classes. Where landholding rather than industrial activity is still the basis for social and economic power, and where land is held essentially in fiefdoms rather than as productive real estate, it is not surprising that so much of society retains a medieval cast.

Thus, development is much more than a matter of encouraging economic growth within a given social structure. It is rather the *modernization* of that structure, a process of ideational, social, economic, and political change that requires the remaking of society in its most intimate as well as its most public attributes.[1] When we speak of the revolutionary nature of economic development, it is this kind of deeply penetrative change that we mean—change that reorganizes "normal" ways of thought, established patterns of family life, and structures of village authority as well as class and caste privilege.

What is so egregiously lacking in the great majority of the societies that are now attempting to make the Great Ascent is precisely this pervasive modernization.

The trouble is that the social physiology of these nations remains so depressingly unchanged despite the flurry of economic planning on top. The all-encompassing ignorance and poverty of the rural regions, the unbridgeable gulf between the peasant and the urban elites, the resistive conservatism of the village elders, the unyielding traditionalism of family life—all these remain obdurately, maddeningly, disastrously unchanged. In the cities, a few modern buildings, sometimes brilliantly executed, give a deceptive patina of modernity, but once one journeys into the immense countryside, the terrible stasis overwhelms all.

---

[1] See C. E. Black, *The Dynamics of Modernization.*

To this vast landscape of apathy and ignorance one must now make an exception of the very greatest importance. It is the fact that a very few nations, all of them Communist, have succeeded in reaching into the lives and stirring the minds of precisely that body of the peasantry which constitutes the insuperable problem elsewhere. In our concentration on the politics, the betrayals, the successes and failures of the Russian, Chinese, and Cuban revolutions, we forget that their central motivation has been just such a war *à l'outrance* against the arch-enemy of backwardness—not alone the backwardness of outmoded social superstructures but even more critically that of private inertia and traditionalism. . . .

It is less certain that the vise of the past has been loosened in China or Cuba. It may well be that Cuba has suffered a considerable economic decline, in part due to absurd planning, in part to our refusal to buy her main crop. The economic record of China is nearly as inscrutable as its political turmoil, and we may not know for many years whether the Chinese peasant is today better or worse off than before the revolution. Yet what strikes me as significant in both countries is something else. In Cuba, it is the educational effort that, according to the New York *Times,* has constituted a major effort of the Castro regime. In China it is the unmistakable evidence—and here I lean not alone on the sympathetic account of Edgar Snow but on the most horrified descriptions of the rampages of the Red Guards—that the younger generation is no longer fettered by the traditional view of things. The very fact that the Red Guards now revile their elders, an unthinkable defiance of age-old Chinese custom, is testimony of how deeply change has penetrated into the texture of Chinese life. . . .

By way of contrast to this all-out effort, however short it may have fallen of its goal, we must place the timidity of the effort to bring modernization to the peoples of the non-Communist world. Here again I do not merely speak of lagging rates of growth. I refer to the fact that illiteracy in the non-Communist countries of Asia and Central America is increasing (by some 200 million in the last decade) because it has been "impossible" to mount an educational effort that will keep pace with population growth. I refer to the absence of substantial land reform in Latin America, despite how many years of promises. I refer to the indifference or incompetence or corruption of governing elites: the incredible sheiks with their oil-doms; the vague, well-meaning leaders of India unable to break the caste system, kill the cows, control the birthrate, reach the villages, house or employ the labor rotting on the streets; the cynical governments of South America, not one of which, according to Lleras Camargo, former president of Colombia, has ever prosecuted a single politician or industrialist for evasion of taxes. And not least, I refer to the fact that every movement that arises to correct these conditions is instantly identified as "Communist" and put down with every means at hand, while the United States clucks or nods approval.

To be sure, even in the most petrified societies, the modernization process is at work. If there were time, the solvent acids of the twentieth century would work their way on the ideas and institutions of the most inert or resistant countries. But what lacks in the twentieth century is time. The multitudes of the underdeveloped world have only in the past two decades been summoned to their reveille. The one thing that is certain about the revolution of rising expectations is that it is only in its inception, and that its pressures for justice and action will steadily mount as the voice of the twentieth century penetrates to villages and slums where it is still almost inaudible. . . .

But how to achieve haste? How to convince the silent and disbelieving men, how to break through the distrustful glances of women in black shawls, how to overcome the overt hostility of landlords, the opposition of the Church, the petty bickerings of military cliques, the black-marketeering of commercial dealers? I suspect there is only one way. The conditions of backwardness must be attacked with the passion, the ruthlessness, and the messianic fury of a jehad, a Holy War. Only a campaign of an intensity and single-mindedness that must approach the ludicrous and the unbearable offers the chance to ride roughshod over the resistance of the rich and the poor alike and to open the way for the forcible implantation of those modern attitudes and techniques without which there will be no escape from the misery of underdevelopment.

I need hardly add that the cost of this modernization process has been and will be horrendous. If Communism is the great modernizer, it is certainly not a benign agent of change. Stalin may well have exceeded Hitler as a mass executioner. Free inquiry in China has been supplanted by dogma and catechism; even in Russia nothing like freedom of criticism or of personal expression is allowed. Furthermore, the economic cost of industrialization in both countries has been at least as severe as that imposed by primitive capitalism.

Yet one must count the gains as well as the losses. Hundreds of millions who would have been confined to the narrow cells of changeless lives have been liberated from prisons they did not even know existed. Class structures that elevated the flighty or irresponsible have been supplanted by others that have promoted the ambitious and the dedicated. Economic systems that gave rise to luxury and poverty have given way to systems that provide a rough distributional justice. Above all, the prospect of a new future has been opened. It is this that lifts the current ordeal in China above the level of pure horror. The number of human beings in that country who have perished over the past centuries from hunger or neglect, is beyond computation. The present revolution may add its dreadful increment to this number. But it also holds out the hope that China may finally have been galvanized

into social, political, and economic attitudes that for the first time make its modernization a possibility.

Two questions must be answered when we dare to risk so favorable a verdict on Communism as a modernizing agency. The first is whether the result is worth the cost, whether the possible—by no means assured—escape from underdevelopment is worth the lives that will be squandered to achieve it.

I do not know how one measures the moral price of historical victories or how one can ever decide that a diffuse gain is worth a sharp and particular loss. I only know that the way in which we ordinarily keep the books of history is wrong. No one is now toting up the balance of the wretches who starve in India, or the peasants of Northeastern Brazil who live in the swamps on crabs, or the undernourished and permanently stunted children of Hong Kong or Honduras. Their sufferings go unrecorded, and are not present to counterbalance the scales when the furies of revolution strike down their victims. Barrington Moore has made a nice calculation that bears on this problem. Taking as the weight in one pan the 35,000 to 40,000 persons who lost their lives—mainly for no fault of theirs—as a result of the Terror during the French Revolution, he asks what would have been the death rate from preventable starvation and injustice under the *ancien regime* to balance the scales. "Offhand," he writes, "it seems unlikely that this would be very much below the proportion of .0010 which [the] figure of 40,000 yields when set against an estimated population of 24 million."[2]

It is unjust to charge the *ancien regime* in Russia with ten million preventable deaths? I think it not unreasonable. To charge the authorities in pre-revolutionary China with equally vast and preventable degradations? Theodore White, writing in 1946, had this

---

[2] *Social Origins of Dictatorship and Democracy*, p. 104.

to say: . . . "some scholars think that China is perhaps the only country in the world where the people eat less, live more bitterly, and are clothed worse than they were 500 years ago."[3]. . .

But there is an even more terrible second question to be asked. It is clear beyond doubt, however awkward it may be for our moralizing propensities, that historians excuse horror that succeeds; and that we write our comfortable books of moral philosophy, seated atop a mound of victims—slaves, serfs, laboring men and women, heretics, dissenters—who were crushed in the course of preparing the way for our triumphal entry into existence. But at least we are here to vindicate the carnage. What if we were not? What if the revolutions grind flesh and blood and produce nothing, if the end of the convulsion is not exhilaration but exhaustion, not triumph but defeat? . . .

As I make this mental calculation I arrive at an answer which is even more painful than that of revolution. I see the alternative as the continuation, without substantial relief—and indeed with a substantial chance of deterioration—of the misery and meanness of life as it is now lived in the sinkhole of the world's backward regions.

I have put the case for the necessity of revolution as strongly as possible, but I must now widen the options beyond the stark alternatives I have posed. To begin with, there are areas of the world where the immediate tasks are so far-reaching that little more can be expected for some decades than the primary missions of national identification and unification. Most of the new African states fall into this category. These states may suffer capitalist, Communist, Fascist, or other kinds of regimes during the remainder of this century, but whatever the nominal ideology in the saddle, the job at hand will be that of military and political nation-making.

There is another group of nations, less easy to identify, but much more important in the scale of events, where my analysis also does not apply. These are countries where the pressures of population growth seem sufficiently mild, or the existing political and social framework sufficiently adaptable, to allow for the hope of considerable progress without resort to violence. Greece, Turkey, Chile, Argentina, Mexico may be representatives of nations in this precarious but enviable situation. Some of them, incidentally, have already had revolutions of modernizing intent—fortunately for them in a day when the United States was not so frightened or so powerful as to be able to repress them.

In other words, the great arena of desperation to which the revolutionizing impetus of Communism seems most applicable is primarily the crowded land masses and archipelagoes of Southeast Asia and the impoverished areas of Central and South America. But even here, there is the possibility that the task of modernization may be undertaken by non-Communist elites. There is always the example of indigenous, independent leaders who rise up out of nowhere to overturn the established framework and to galvanize the masses—a Gandhi, a Marti, a pre-1958 Castro. Or there is that fertile ground for the breeding of national leaders—the army, as witness Ataturk or Nasser, among many.[4]

Thus there is certainly no inherent necessity that the revolutions of modernization be led

---

[3] *Thunder Out of China*, p. 32.

[4] What are the chances for modernizing revolutions of the Right, such as those of the Meiji Restoration or of Germany under Bismarck? I think they are small. The changes to be wrought in the areas of greatest backwardness are much more socially subversive than those of the nineteenth century, and the timespan allotted to the revolutionists is much smaller. Bourgeois revolutions are not apt to go far enough, particularly in changing property ownership. Still, one could imagine such revolutions with armed support and no doubt Fascistic ideologies. I doubt that they would be any less of a threat than revolutions of the Left.

by Communists. But it is well to bear two thoughts in mind when we consider the likely course of non-Communist revolutionary sweeps. The first is the nature of the mobilizing appeal of any successful revolutionary elite. Is it the austere banner of saving and investment that waves over the heads of the shouting marchers in Jakarta and Bombay, Cairo and Havana? It most certainly is not. The banner of economic development is that of nationalism, with its promise of personal immortality and collective majesty. It seems beyond question that a feverish nationalism will charge the atmosphere of any nation, Communist or not, that tries to make the Great Ascent—and as a result we must expect the symptoms of nationalism along with the disease: exaggerated xenophobia, a thin-skinned national sensitivity, a search for enemies as well as a glorification of the state.

These symptoms, which we have already seen in every quarter of the globe, make it impossible to expect easy and amicable relations between the developing states and the colossi of the developed world. No conceivable response on the part of America or Europe or, for that matter, Russia, will be able to play up to the vanities or salve the irritations of the emerging nations, much less satisfy their demands for help. Thus, we must anticipate an anti-American, or anti-Western, possibly even anti-white animus from any nation in the throes of modernization, even if it is not parroting Communist dogma.

Then there is a second caution as to the prospects for non-Communist revolutions. This is the question of what ideas and policies will guide their revolutionary efforts. Revolutions, especially if their whole orientation is to the future, require philosophy equally as much as force. It is here, of course, that Communism finds its special strength. The vocabulary in which it speaks—a vocabulary of class domination, of domestic and international exploitation—is rich in meaning to the backward nations. The view of history it espouses provides the support of historical inevitability to the fallible efforts of struggling leaders. Not least, the very dogmatic certitude and ritualistic repetition that stick in the craw of the Western observer offer the psychological assurances on which an unquestioning faith can be maintained.

If a non-Communist elite is to persevere in tasks that will prove Sisyphean in difficulty, it will also have to offer a philosophical interpretation of its role as convincing and elevating, and a diagnosis of social and economic requirements as sharp and simplistic, as that of Communism. Further, its will to succeed at whatever cost must be as firm as that of the Marxists. It is not impossible that such a philosophy can be developed, more or less independent of formal Marxian conceptions. . . .

Thus, even if for many reasons we should prefer the advent of non-Communist modernizing elites, we must realize that they too will present the United States with programs and policies antipathetic to much that America "believes in" and hostile to America as a world power. The leadership needed to mount a jehad against backwardness—and it is my main premise that only a Holy War will begin modernization in our time—will be forced to expound a philosophy that approves authoritarian and collectivist measures at home and that utilizes as the target for its national resentment abroad the towering villains of the world, of which the United States is now Number One.

All this confronts American policymakers and public opinion with a dilemma of a totally unforeseen kind. On the one hand we are eager to assist in the rescue of the great majority of mankind from conditions that we recognize as dreadful and ultimately dangerous. On the other hand, we seem to be committed, especially in the underdeveloped areas, to a policy of defeating Communism wherever it is within our military capacity to do so, and of repressing movements that might become

Communist if they were allowed to follow their internal dynamics. Thus, we have on the one side the record of Point Four, the Peace Corps, and foreign aid generally; and on the other, Guatemala, Cuba, the Dominican Republic, and now Vietnam.

That these two policies might be in any way mutually incompatible, that economic development might contain revolutionary implications infinitely more far-reaching than those we have so blandly endorsed in the name of rising expectations, that Communism or a radical national collectivism might be the only vehicles for modernization in many key areas of the world—these are dilemmas we have never faced. Now I suggest that we do face them, and that we begin to examine in a serious way ideas that have hitherto been considered blasphemous, if not near-traitorous.

Suppose that most of Southeast Asia and much of Latin America were to go Communist, or to become controlled by revolutionary governments that espoused collectivist ideologies and vented extreme anti-American sentiments. Would this constitute a mortal threat to the United States?

I think it fair to claim that the purely *military* danger posed by such an eventuality would be slight. Given the present and prospective capabilities of the backward world, the addition of hundreds of millions of citizens to the potential armies of Communism would mean nothing when there was no way of deploying them against us. The prospect of an invasion by Communist hordes—the specter that frightened Europe after World War II with some (although retrospectively, not too much) realism—would be no more than a phantasm when applied to Asia or South America or Africa. . . .

However small the military threat, it is undeniably true that a Communist or radical collectivist engulfment of these countries would cost us the loss of billions of dollars of capital invested there. Of our roughly $50 billions in overseas investment, some $10 bil-

lions are in mining, oil, utility, and manufacturing facilities in Latin America, some $4 billions in Asia including the Near East, and about $2 billions in Africa. To lose these assets would deal a heavy blow to a number of large corporations, particularly in oil, and would cost the nation as a whole the loss of some $3 to $4 billions a year in earnings from those areas.

A Marxist might conclude that the economic interests of a capitalist nation would find such a prospective loss insupportable, and that it would be "forced" to go to war. I do not think this is a warranted assumption, although it is undoubtedly a risk. Against a Gross National Product that is approaching ¾ of a trillion dollars and with total corporate assets over $1.3 trillions, the loss of even the whole $16 billions in the vulnerable areas should be manageable economically. Whether such a takeover could be resisted politically—that is, whether the red flag of Communism could be successfully waved by the corporate interests—is another question. I do not myself believe that the corporate elite is particularly war-minded—not nearly so much so as the military or the congressional—or that corporate seizures would be a suitable issue for purposes of drumming up interventionist sentiment. . . .

But is that not the very point?, it will be asked. Would not a Communist success in a few backward nations lead to successes in others, and thus by degrees engulf the entire world, until the United States and perhaps Europe were fortresses besieged on a hostile planet?

I think the answer to this fear is twofold. First, as many beside myself have argued, it is now clear that Communism, far from constituting a single unified movement with a common aim and dovetailing interests, is a movement in which similarities of economic and political structure and ideology are more than outweighed by divergencies of national interest and character. Two bloody wars have demonstrated that in the case of capitalism, structural similarities between nations do not prevent mortal combat. As with capitalism, so with Communism, Russian Communists have already been engaged in skirmishes with Polish and Hungarian Communists, have nearly come to blows with Yugoslavia, and now stand poised at the threshhold of open fighting with China. Only in the mind of the *Daily News* (and perhaps still the State Department) does it seem possible, in the face of this spectacle, to refer to the unified machinations of "international Communism" or the "Sino-Soviet bloc."

The realities, I believe, point in a very different direction. A world in which Communist governments were engaged in the enormous task of trying to modernize the worst areas of Asia, Latin America, and Africa would be a world in which sharp differences of national interest were certain to arise within these continental areas. . . .

Second, it seems essential to distinguish among the causes of dangerous national and international behavior those that can be traced to the tenets of Communism and those that must be located elsewhere. "Do not talk to me about Communism and capitalism," said a Hungarian economist with whom I had lunch this winter. "Talk to me about rich nations and poor ones."

I think it *is* wealth and poverty, and not Communism or capitalism, that establishes much of the tone and tension of international relations. For that reason I would expect Communism in the backward nations (or national collectivism, if that emerges in the place of Communism) to be strident, belligerent, and insecure. If these regimes fail—as they may—their rhetoric may become hysterical and their behavior uncontrolled, although of small consequence. But if they succeed, which I believe they can, many of these traits should recede. Russia, Yugoslavia, or Poland are simply not to be compared, either by way of internal pronouncement or external behavior, with China,

or, on a smaller scale, Cuba. Modernization brings, among other things, a waning of the stereotypes, commandments, and flagellations so characteristic of (and so necessary to) a nation engaged in the effort to alter itself from top to bottom. The idiom of ceaseless revolution becomes less relevant—even faintly embarrassing—to a nation that begins to be pleased with itself. . . .

Nevertheless, there *is* a threat in the specter of a Communist or near-Communist supremacy in the underdeveloped world. It is that the rise of Communism would signal the end of capitalism as the dominant world order, and would force the acknowledgement that America no longer constituted the model on which the future of world civilization would be mainly based. In this way, as I have written before, the existence of Communism frightens American capitalism as the rise of Protestantism frightened the Catholic Church, or the French Revolution the English aristocracy.

It is, I think, the fear of losing our place in the sun, of finding ourselves at bay, that motivates a great deal of the anti-Communism on which so much of American foreign policy seems to be founded. In this regard I note that the nations of Europe, most of them profoundly more conservative than America in their social and economic dispositions, have made their peace with Communism far more intelligently and easily than we, and I conclude that this is in no small part due to their admission that they are no longer the leaders of the world.

The great question in our own nation is whether we can accept a similar scaling-down of our position in history. This would entail many profound changes in outlook and policy. It would mean the recognition that Communism, which may indeed represent a retrogressive movement in the West, where it should continue to be resisted with full energies, may nonetheless represent a progressive movement in the backward areas, where its advent may be the only chance these areas have of escaping misery. Collaterally, it means the recognition that "our side" has neither the political will, nor the ideological wish, nor the stomach for directing those changes that the backward world must make if it is ever to cease being backward. It would undoubtedly entail a more isolationist policy for the United States *vis-à-vis* the developing continents, and a greater willingness to permit revolutions there to work their way without our interference. It would mean in our daily political life the admission that the ideological battle of capitalism and Communism had passed its point of usefulness or relevance, and that religious diatribe must give way to the pragmatic dialogue of the age of science and technology.

Christopher Layne, 1949–

Christopher Layne, a lawyer in Los Angeles, California, writes on foreign policy questions in a variety of magazines and journals. In 1984, Layne served as an analyst studying NATO and western Europe at the U.S. Army's Arroyo Center think tank.

His essay, "The Real Conservative Agenda," aroused a great deal of controversy with its attack on the neoconservative rhetoric and policies of the Reagan administration and advocacy of older, more traditional conservative concerns about the centralizing effects of a highly activist foreign policy on the polity and economy.

Layne continues to criticize both the overarching ambitiousness of many anticommunists and the noninterventionism of those he sees as still mired in a "Vietnam Syndrome." In both camps, Layne sees a naive utopianism that shares more with enlightenment liberalism than with traditional conservatism. While very much a minority view within the conservative movement, Layne's essay taps a real conservative vein that may well find support in the future.

Christopher Layne

The Real Conservative Agenda (1985)

Pushed by a group of neoconservative intellectuals, global containment is making a comeback as the cornerstone of U.S. foreign policy.

SOURCE: *Foreign Policy* 61, Winter 1985–1986.

It could not happen at a worse time. The United States is running enormous budget and trade deficits, economic growth is slowing, and public support for the Reagan military build-up has all but evaporated. Global containment—recast as the Reagan Doctrine—commits the United States to resisting Soviet and Soviet-supported aggression wherever it arises; to building American-style democracies in Third World countries; and to rolling back communism by aiding anticommunist insurgencies. The Reagan Doctrine aims to create an ideologically congenial world, and it assumes that America's security requires nothing less.

It is now clear that no major challenge to this quixotic quest is likely to come from the Democrats in Congress. They are in disarray, split between the "defense Democrats," who offer a "me-too" policy of getting tough with the Soviets, and those whose outlook on national security policy still is shaped by the Vietnam syndrome—reflecting the mistaken belief that the United States can remain a global power while all but ruling out using military force to protect its vital interests abroad.

Therefore, it is up to the Republican party's real conservatives to offer an alternative to the neoconservative Reagan Doctrine. Because they are not liberals, real conservatives will not subordinate American national interests to the requirements of multilateralist internationalism. Real conservatives do not believe that the United States should sacrifice its political and economic interests to appease Western Europe and Japan. And real conservatives reject the idea that providing development aid, promoting human rights, and supporting international organizations should be major elements of U.S. foreign policy. But because they are not neoconservatives, real conservatives also reject the New Right's crusading ideological internationalism.

Real conservatives represent a tradition deeply rooted in America's political culture and history and associated with figures like Ohio Republican Senator Robert Taft, mid-century America's leading conservative voice, President Dwight Eisenhower, and realist scholar-diplomat George Kennan. As early as the late 1940s these men realized that America's strategic and economic circumstances required the United States to define its interests more realistically than the cold warriors of their day were doing and to reduce the scope of the country's overseas commitments. They knew that the United States has few vital interests in the Third World and that it is futile—and counterproductive—to try to mold the world in America's image. Most of all they knew that the pursuit of global containment imperils important political and economic goals at home not only dear to conservatives, but also vital for America's future: noninflationary growth, lower taxes, and fewer government controls over the private and economic lives of Americans.

The real conservatives' critique of global containment was prescient. But it also was premature. Thus when they challenged the emerging cold war orthodoxy, real conservatives lost the great debate of 1950–1951. They underestimated America's overwhelming military, political, and economic strength during that period, and their warnings about the limits of American power rang hollow. Moreover, their strong aversion to a crusading interventionist foreign policy was overcome by the ideological imperatives of the cold war. Because the real conservatives were intellectually discredited by their defeat in the great debate, the Eisenhower administration—though led by a real conservative president, notwithstanding his earlier military career—trimmed its sails to the political wind and embraced and extended the Truman administration's global containment policy.

But the Taft-Kennan critique of American foreign policy is unusually timely and penetrating today. The geopolitical changes of the last thirty-five years have finally validated their analysis. Thus the real conservatives of America's successor generation are charged with the task of rediscovering their intellectual antecedents and of building upon them to frame a new foreign-policy synthesis that reconciles a realistic policy of selective containment abroad with the advancement of conservative values at home.

Debates about foreign policy often boil down to clashes of ideas about the nature of international politics. This is especially true of the clash between real conservatives and neoconservatives, which forces Americans once again to examine the fundamental objectives of their foreign policy.

Should America attempt to contain the spread of communist ideology worldwide and try to impose democracy on repressive regimes? Or should it follow a more traditional balance-of-power policy that aims only at containing the expansion of Soviet political influence and military power in regions truly vital to U.S. national security? When should the United States intervene militarily in overseas conflicts? How much can America afford to do in the world and what is the proper balance between the country's goals overseas and its domestic aspirations?

NEOCONSERVATIVES VERSUS REAL CONSERVATIVES

Real conservatives and neoconservatives are especially divided over the questions of what America should do and what it can afford to do. To the extent it seriously addresses these questions at all, the Reagan Doctrine offers simple answers. Its neoconservative authors depict world politics as a Manichaean struggle between democracy and communism. . . .

According to the Reagan Doctrine, communist ideology per se threatens American security. Neoconservative intellectuals like Norman Podhoretz and Irving Kristol, who have given the Reagan Doctrine its conceptual underpinnings, stress that America is locked in an ideological struggle with communism rather than in a traditional great-power rivalry with the Soviet Union.[1]

Because it equates American security with an ideologically compatible world, the Reagan Doctrine is classically Wilsonian. Thus Secretary of State George Shultz frequently says that America must use its power to preserve an international environment conducive to the survival of its values, and he warns that the defeat of "democracy" by communism anywhere jeopardizes American security everywhere. Like the political scientist Michael Ledeen, writing in the March 1985 issue of Podhoretz's journal, *Commentary,* neoconservatives believe that America's task "is actively to encourage non-democratic governments to democratize and to aid democratic movements that challenge totalitarian and authoritarian regimes." Like all Wilsonians, neoconservatives justify these beliefs by arguing that the world would be peaceful and harmonious if only nondemocratic states (which are inherently bad) became democratic states (which are inherently good). This explains Shultz's insistence, in a February 1985 speech, that there is a worldwide "democratic revolution" that America must support in word and deed by standing for "freedom and democracy not only for ourselves but for others.". . .

The Reagan Doctrine also holds that the Third World is the critical battleground in the war against communism. It is in Angola, Afghanistan, Cambodia, and Nicaragua that Shultz says America must halt the spread of communism. "It is in the Third World rather than in the United States or Europe," Podhoretz wrote in *Commentary* in 1981, "that Communism remains the greatest ideological menace." Consequently, the Third World is where American neoconservatives are pushing the administration, with some success, to organize an international alliance of "democratic freedom fighters." The president himself declared in February 1985: "We must not break faith with those who are risking their lives—on every continent . . . to defy Soviet-supported aggression and secure rights which have been ours since birth. Support for freedom fighters is self-defense.". . .

[1] See Podhoretz, "The Future Danger," *Commentary* (April 1981).

Like the global containment policy of the pre-Vietnam years, the Reagan Doctrine has no obvious limits. Because it does not differentiate between what is vital and what is merely desirable, the doctrine holds that U.S. security is endangered by communism wherever it takes hold. If so, however, the United States must resist communism and defend democracy everywhere. Such a policy will make America ever more dangerously overextended. Although the administration's policies to date have been restrained, words and ideas do have consequences.

The Reagan Doctrine is a throwback to the global containment policy that characterized the cold war liberalism of Presidents Harry Truman, John Kennedy, and Lyndon Johnson. This strategy, and the Manichaean convictions on which it was based, reached its zenith in Kennedy's ringing inaugural vow in 1961 that the United States would "pay any price, bear any burden" to defeat communism around the world, and in then Secretary of State Dean Rusk's assertion that U.S. national security required nothing less than making the total international political environment ideologically safe. But if these goals ever were realistic, they certainly are not today.

Real conservatives should oppose the Reagan Doctrine on three principal grounds: In current and foreseeable circumstances it can bankrupt America; the American people wisely have no stomach for it; and it is based on a fundamental misreading of America's real interests and of the way in which countries behave.

The Reagan Doctrine calls for extending U.S. foreign commitments precisely at a time when circumstances require their reduction. Before Vietnam, U.S. hegemony was based firmly on strategic nuclear superiority and overwhelming economic muscle. Today, the former is gone and the latter is degenerating. To take one indicator, in 1945 the United States accounted for approximately one-half of world manufacturing output, and in 1953 this figure stood at a still formidable 44.7 per

cent.[2] It was during this period of economic and political predominance that America assumed the commitments to defend Western Europe, Japan and Korea, and the Mediterranean and the Middle East that have formed the core of its global strategy for the past thirty-five years.

By 1980, however, the United States accounted for only 31.5 per cent of world manufactures, and this share could fall to 20 per cent by the end of the century. Yet during the last six years U.S. commitments abroad actually have increased as America has assumed responsibilities in the Persian Gulf and Central America. As a March 1985 Congressional Research Service report entitled *U.S.-Soviet Military Balance, 1980–1985* states, "Our military force structure is inadequate to meet our formal and informal worldwide military commitments." The Reagan Doctrine, however, suggests that America will incur further obligations in the Third World.

THE POWER-INTERESTS GAP

America can balance its power and commitments in two ways: It can increase its power or reduce its commitments. The Reagan Doctrine explicitly rejects the notion of curtailing America's obligations. Former Secretary of Defense James Schlesinger told the Senate Foreign Relations Committee in February 1985: "For any great power—and most notably the protecting superpower of the West—to back away from commitments is more easily said than done. In practice, the loss in prestige may actually reduce our power more than the reduced claims on our military resources enhances that power." Therefore, Reagan Doctrine supporters must assume that the power-interests gap can be closed by increasing America's capabilities. This is extremely doubtful. . . .

---

[2] Paul M. Kennedy, "The First World War and the International Power System," *International Security* 9, no. 1 (Summer 1984): 36–39.

Yet current spending fails to meet the country's present strategic commitments. Indeed, during Reagan's presidency, despite the administration's military build-up, the power-interests gap has widened. The country shows no signs of wanting to pay for the Reagan Doctrine.

Not only has America's international economic and political power waned, but also its domestic economy by any measure is much less robust than during the period of American hegemony. The persistent and worsening federal deficits of the past thirty years symbolize both America's decline and its current economic predicament. The deficit attests to the country's inability to set priorities and to live within its means. As the political scientist David Calleo and many others have suggested, deficits and strategic overextension really are two sides of the same coin. Taken together, they indicate that America's aspirations at home and abroad have outstripped its ability—or willingness—to pay for them. . . .

Moreover, America's ability to sustain any level of strategic commitments depends on its economic strength. In a real sense the economy is the fourth branch of the armed forces. Under the Reagan Doctrine, the country would have to come very close to full mobilization to close the gap between its power and its responsibilities. The threat posed by such a policy to America's prosperity and freedoms is incalculable.

Unlike past and present advocates of global containment, real conservatives have always understood this. As Taft once observed, no country "can be constantly prepared to undertake a full-scale war at any moment and still hope to maintain any of the other purposes in which people are interested and for which nations are founded."[3] Few more poignant statements of these concerns can be found than Eisenhower's April 1953 speech to the American Society of Newspaper Editors declaring that "every gun that is made . . . signifies, in the final sense, a theft from those who hunger and are not fed, and those who are cold and are not clothed."

Real conservatives have recognized that a tension always exists between the needs of an interventionist foreign policy and those of a healthy economy. Taft predicted that global containment would impose "tremendous" economic burdens and threaten the country's prosperity. Eisenhower's Secretary of State John Foster Dulles warned that large defense outlays "unbalance our budget and require taxes so heavy, that they discourage incentive. They so cheapen the dollar that savings, pensions, and Social Security reserves already have lost most of their value."[4] . . .

PAYING THE PRICE

If global containment is economically and politically beyond America's reach, how then can the United States accomplish the admittedly vital objective of containing the Soviet Union? First, by taking advantage of the natural dynamics of the international balance of power. Second, by defining its national interests more realistically.

The Reagan Doctrine implicitly assumes that the United States is not doing enough in the world. But the first objective of U.S. policy must be to compel others—namely, Western Europe and Japan—to do much more so that America can do much less.

One leading cause of America's relative decline in power is the increase in West European and Japanese economic power since the end of World War II. Yet the distribution of military responsibilities in Western Europe and Japan still reflects the conditions of forty years ago. Japan, the world's second-ranking economic power, spends a mere 1 per cent of its GNP on defense and depends completely on the United States for its security. Taken as a unit, the economies of NATO's European

---

[3] *A Foreign Policy for Americans* (Garden City, N.Y.: Doubleday and Co., 1951), 68.

[4] "A Foreign Policy of Boldness," *Life*, 19 May 1952, 146.

members compare favorably to America's, but these countries devote considerably less of their individual GNPs to defense. More to the point, a recent Pentagon study indicates that the U.S. commitment to NATO accounts for some 58 per cent of America's own defense budget.

America's early postwar policy aimed to assist Western Europe and Japan in their respective recoveries in the expectation that they could resume some semblance of their traditional international roles and relieve the United States of its global burdens. The U.S. commitment to this reconstruction—and to its corollary, multilateral free trade—made it inevitable that these countries would be strengthened at America's expense. But this was judged an acceptable price to pay because, on balance, the United States would be better off in a world where Western Europe and Japan could protect themselves. Today, America continues to pay the price for its postwar policy but is not reaping any of the benefits.

The United States should complete its historic postwar mission and devolve to Western Europe and Japan full responsibility for their own defense. What Washington needs—and what real conservatives should offer—is a sequel to the Marshall Plan. This far-sighted program helped Europe recover its economic independence. "Marshall Plan II" would build on the economic strength of Western Europe and Japan and allow them to become politically and militarily independent. To avoid leaving these countries out in the cold, the United States should set a firm timetable for a phased, long-term American withdrawal— perhaps over ten years—coupled with an invitation to Western Europe and Japan to formulate their own postalliance defense plans. Washington would give them the assistance they needed to implement these plans. But when the transition period ended, U.S. defense commitments would terminate. . . .

The older generation of American policymakers—accustomed to U.S. hegemony—is temperamentally unable to contemplate the measures required to balance U.S. commitments and resources. However, because it is the first group of Americans in this century to experience something other than American omnipotence in world politics, the successor generation is more prepared to undertake the major strategic reorientation needed to bring about this balance.

Marshall Plan II also would be opposed on the ground that postalliance Europe would fall under the Kremlin's control. But here American and European Atlanticists join with many neoconservatives in fundamentally misperceiving the nature of world politics. States tend to balance—not to jump on bandwagons. As the Princeton University political scientist Stephen M. Walt wrote in the Spring 1985 issue of *International Security:*

> Threatening states will provoke others to align against them. Because those who seek to dominate others will attract widespread opposition, status quo states can take a relatively sanguine view of threats. Credibility is less important in a balancing world because one's allies will resist threatening states out of their own self-interest, not because they expect others to do it for them. Thus the fear that allies will defect declines. Moreover, if balancing is the norm *and* if statesmen understand this tendency, aggression is discouraged because those who contemplate it will anticipate resistance.

Indeed, history provides many examples of balancing behavior. In the nuclear era, China has balanced against the menacing and proximate power of the Soviet Union by entering into an informal strategic entente with the United States. During the era of U.S. hegemony, Charles de Gaulle's France maximized its independence by moving away from the United States and edging slightly toward the Soviet Union. But in the late 1970s and early 1980s, the shift of the strategic nuclear balance toward Moscow caused Paris to tilt back toward Washington. Benito Mussolini's Italy, in fact, is recent history's only major example of "bandwagoning," and all Europeans know the price his country paid.

West Europeans have strong reasons for exploiting U.S. fears that they will jump on Moscow's bandwagon if America withdraws from the Continent. They find the Atlanticist status quo comfortable. But surely Western Europe's leaders are smart enough to realize that weak states that align themselves with strong states are at the mercy of the stronger powers. Moreover, Europe's diplomatic history is the history of the balance of power. . . .

The emergence of a postalliance world can either strengthen or weaken the United States: It all depends on how America gets there. A managed transition like Marshall Plan II will maximize the likelihood of a positive outcome. An ostrich-like policy that lets events run their course on the assumption that NATO will last forever will make the reverse more likely. Wise leadership does not resist the inevitable; it seeks to turn the inevitable to its own advantage.

CRITERIA FOR INTERVENTION

Balancing the ends and means of U.S. policy also requires the United States to define more realistically its goals for the Third World. The United States has few tangible interests in the Third World that compel military or even extensive political involvement. There is no Third World region or country whose loss would decisively tip the superpower balance against America—including the Persian Gulf, whose oil is vital only to Western Europe and Japan, and whose defense would be handled by these countries under Marshall Plan II. The United States is not economically dependent on Third World markets. And its current reliance on Third World raw materials can be minimized by diversifying sources of supply, by stockpiling, by developing synthetic replacements, and by using natural substitutes.

Instead, U.S. involvement in the Third World flows mainly from intangible concerns. Americans often fear that their failure to step into Third World conflicts will lead to Soviet gains. This is the price Americans pay for regarding the world as both politically and ideologically bipolar. This perspective rules out the existence of marginal areas and depicts international politics as a zero-sum game in which a single setback will inevitably have repercussions elsewhere.

The Reagan Doctrine in fact creates a self-fulfilling prophecy by failing to distinguish vital from secondary interests. When Washington says a particular outcome would be a defeat—or that U.S. interests in some part of the world are "vital"—others believe it. Thus the doctrine's rhetoric presents the country with two equally bad alternatives in the Third World: using American power to prevent political changes defined as "unacceptable," or accepting the unacceptable—with consequent damage to U.S. credibility. A wise foreign policy does not paint policymakers into corners like this. . . .

Ironically, despite Third World fears of U.S. domination, America exercises virtually no control over "friendly" developing countries or over anti-Soviet "freedom fighters." They may be allies, but they are peculiar allies, because they are no more committed to liberal democratic values than are their Marxist opponents. It is naive to imagine that American political values could flourish in countries that have no indigenous democratic traditions and that lack the social, cultural, and economic institutions upon which the U.S. democratic structure rests. America's continuing search for a "third force" between the totalitarians and authoritarians of the Left and the Right is unavailing. Political pluralism in the Third World is not promoted by America's choosing among equally unsavory groups whose brutality is distinguishable only by whether it is used to hold power or to seize it.

U.S. interests may be threatened by Third

World conflicts. But the United States is not threatened by the spread of communism per se. As became apparent when Josip Broz Tito's Yugoslavia broke with the Kremlin, and again when China and the USSR split, nationalism can impel even communist governments to follow anti-Soviet policies. It is other countries' foreign policies, not their domestic systems, with which the United States must be concerned.

THE CENTRAL AMERICA DEBATE

The difference between the neoconservative and the real conservative approaches to America's Third World policy is illustrated by the debate over U.S. Central America policy. Central America is no more hospitable a theater for direct U.S. military involvement than is the rest of the Third World. Yet the United States has a strong interest in maintaining a favorable political and strategic environment in neighboring areas. Moreover, a stable superpower relationship requires each superpower to respect the other's critical sphere of influence. The Soviets are not likely to show such respect, however, unless America so compels them by assertively defending U.S. interests.

Although the loss of Central America would not decisively affect America's core security, America does have important strategic interests in the Caribbean Basin, such as Mexican and Venezuelan oil, the Panama Canal, and the Caribbean sea-lanes. Moreover, America's strategic position obviously would be less comfortable if Mexico turned pro-Soviet. Taken individually, none of these interests is vital enough to justify direct U.S. military involvement. But taken collectively, they are.

Still, Americans must be clear on what does and does not justify U.S. military intervention in Central America. Neoconservatives, until recently at least, have not decided whether the Nicaraguan threat is ideological or geopolitical. If the former, the United States can

accept nothing less than the Sandinistas' overthrow, and direct U.S. military intervention is very likely at some point.

Real conservatives see the threat as geopolitical: They insist that the United States cannot allow Nicaragua to become a Soviet satellite or to use force and subversion to export its revolution. But they do not believe that Washington's interests are threatened by the Sandinistas' domestic policies in and of themselves. These policies are odious, but they are the Nicaraguan people's business, not America's. For real conservatives it is not necessarily the case that the United States must overthrow the Sandinistas, because they can envision the possibility of a political accommodation that would exchange an American guarantee of noninterference in Nicaragua's internal affairs for the withdrawal of all Soviet-bloc, Cuban, Libyan, and Palestine Liberation Organization military advisers from Nicaragua; the cessation of Sandinista support for Central American insurgents; and strict quantitative and qualitative limits on Nicaragua's armed forces. These terms will ensure that Nicaragua does not become a Soviet satellite.

Real conservatives recognize that war is a continuation of politics by other means and that U.S. policy must combine force and diplomacy to compel changes in Nicaraguan policies that threaten regional security. Thus the United States must support the anti-Sandinista *contra* forces and exert other forms of military and economic pressure, because, otherwise, the Sandinistas have little incentive to accommodate U.S. wishes.

Central America, however, is a special case for real conservatives. They agree with neoconservatives that Moscow should not have a free ride in the Third World and that, within well-defined limits, the United States should do what it can to make the Soviets pay for their interventions. But real conservatives also know that vital American interests are not engaged in Afghanistan, Angola, Cambodia, and similar Third World hot spots, and they are under no illusions that the anti-Soviet groups in these places are fighting for liberal democracy. Neoconservatives talk as if the contrary is true, and this is one reason that the Reagan Doctrine's implications are so disturbing. By placing so much emphasis on the "worldwide democratic revolution" and on U.S. support for anti-Soviet forces, the Reagan Doctrine may link American prestige and credibility to the outcome of these peripheral conflicts. The Reagan Doctrine forgets that in the real, balancing world there are, in fact, many areas of only marginal importance to America.

But real conservatives are realists. . . . America's experience as a world power has been unique because for much of that time its power was unchallenged. Obviously, this no longer is true. Everywhere are the signs of a more plural international system—a system America helped create. Yet American foreign-policymakers still do not understand that the era of American predominance was an anomaly, not the historical norm. The Reagan Doctrine's neoconservative authors in particular seem to be caught in some Spielbergian time warp that has transported them back to the early 1950s. They talk as if the relative decline of American power, and Vietnam, had never occurred. They do not understand that the end of American hegemony was brought about by complex, objective geopolitical factors; it is not something that can be reversed merely by an assertion of national will. . . .

The most critical functions of political leaders in a democratic society are to define the national agenda and to educate the public.

. . . The essence of a conservative policy is to preserve national strength, husband resources, and expend them wisely. The successor generation's real conservatives must carry the message that American power is finite and that not even a superpower can impose order on a recalcitrant world. The attempt can lead only to exhaustion, to dangerous overextension, and to lasting damage to the fabric of American society.

Additional Readings: Secondary Sources

GENERAL WORKS

Beitzinger, A. J. *A History of American Political Thought.* New York: Harper & Row, 1972.

Boorstin, Daniel. *The Genius of American Politics.* Chicago: University of Chicago Press, 1953.

Commager, Henry Steele. *The American Mind.* New Haven, Conn.: Yale University Press, 1950.

Dorfman, Joseph. *The Economic Mind in American Civilization.* 3 vols. New York: A. M. Kelly, 1945–1959.

Gabriel, Ralph. *The Course of American Democratic Thought.* New York: Ronald Press, 1940.

Grimes, Alan P. *American Political Thought.* New York: Holt, Rinehart & Winston, 1960.

Hartz, Louis. *The Liberal Tradition in America.* New York: Harcourt Brace Jovanovich, 1955.

Hofstadter, Richard. *The American Political Tradition.* New York: Alfred A. Knopf, 1948.

Krinsky, Fred. *The Politics of Religion in America.* Beverly Hills, Calif.: Glencoe Press, 1969.

Lerner, Max. *America as a Civilization.* New York: Simon & Schuster, 1957.

Marty, Martin. *Righteous Empire: The Protestant Experience in America.* New York: Dial, 1970.

McWilliams, Wilson Carey. *The Idea of Fraternity in America.* Berkeley: University of California Press, 1973.

Parrington, Vernon. *Main Currents in American Thought.* 3 vols. New York: Harcourt Brace Jovanovich, 1954.

Potter, David. *People of Plenty: Economic Abundance and the American Character.* Chicago: University of Chicago Press, 1955.

Roche, John P., ed. *American Political Thought: From Jefferson to Progressivism.* New York: Harper & Row, 1967.

Rossiter, Clinton. *Conservatism in America.* New York: Vintage, 1962.

Schlesinger, Arthur, Jr. and Morton White, eds. *Paths of American Thought.* Boston: Houghton Mifflin, 1970.

Skidmore, Max. *American Political Thought.* New York: St. Martin's Press, 1978.

Wilson, Francis G. *The American Political Mind.* New York: McGraw-Hill, 1949.

I. INTRODUCTION: EUROPEANS IN THE WILDERNESS

Baldwin, Alice M. "Sowers of Sedition: The Political Theories of Some of the New Light Presbyterian Clergy of Virginia and North Carolina." *William and Mary Quarterly* 5, 3d series, 1948.

_____. *The New England Clergy and the American Revolution.* Durham, N.C.: Duke University Press, 1928.

Bercovitch, Sacvan. *The Puritan Origins of the American Self.* New Haven, Conn.: Yale University Press, 1975.

Brockunier, Samuel H. *The Irrepressible Democrat: Roger Williams.* New York: Ronald Press, 1940.

Cook, George Allan. *John Wise: Early American Democrat.* New York: King's Crown Press, 1952.

Ernst, James E. *The Political Thought of Roger Williams.* Port Washington, N.Y.: Kennikat Press, 1966.

Gummere, Richard M. "The Classical Ancestry of the United States Constitution." *American Quarterly* 14, 1962.

Lewis, Ewart. "The Contribution of Medieval Thought to the American Political Tradition." *American Political Science Review* 50, 1956.

Leder, Lawerence H. *Liberty and Authority: Early American Political Ideology 1689–1763.* New York: W. W. Norton, 1976.

MacPhail, Sir Andrew. *Essays in Puritanism.* Port Washington, N.Y.: Kennikat Press, 1969.

Miller, Perry. *Orthodoxy in Massachusetts, 1630–1650.* Boston: Beacon Press, 1959.

_____. *Roger Williams.* New York: Atheneum Publishers, 1962.

_____. *The New England Mind: From Colony to Province.* Cambridge, Mass.: Harvard University Press, 1953.

_____. *The New England Mind: The Seventeenth Century.* New York: Macmillan, 1939.

Morgan, Edmund Sears. *The Puritan Dilemma: The Story of John Winthrop.* Boston: Little, Brown, 1958.

_____. *Prologue to Revolution: Sources and Documents on the Stamp Act Crisis.* Chapel Hill: University of North Carolina Press, 1959.

Nash, Gary B. *Quakers and Politics.* Princeton, N.J.: Princeton University Press, 1968.

Osgood, Herbert L. *The American Colonies in the Seventeenth Century.* New York: Macmillan, 1904.

Pearce, Roy Harvey, ed. *Colonial American Writing.* New York: Holt, Rinehart & Winston, 1956.

Perry, Ralph Barton. *Puritanism and Democracy.* New York: Vanguard, 1944.

Pocock, J. G. A. *The Machiavellian Moment: Florentine Political Thought and the Atlantic Republican Tradition.* Princeton, N.J.: Princeton University Press, 1975.

Roche, John R., ed. *Origins of American Political Thought.* New York: Harper & Row, 1967.

Rutman, Darrett Bruce. *John Winthrop's Decision for America: 1629.* Philadelphia: Lippincott, 1975.

Schneider, Herbert W. *The Puritan Mind*. Ann Arbor: University of Michigan Press, 1958.

Wertenbaker, Thomas J. *The Puritan Oligarchy*. New York: Charles Scribner's Sons, 1947.

Wish, Harvey. *Society and Thought in Early America*. New York: Longmans, Green, 1950.

Wright, B. F. *American Interpretations of Natural Law*. Cambridge, Mass.: Harvard University Press, 1931.

Ziff, Larzer. *Puritanism in America*. New York: Viking Press, 1973.

II. ESTABLISHING AN INDEPENDENT REPUBLIC: THE LANGUAGES OF REVOLUTION

Bailyn, Bernard. *Pamphlets of the American Revolution, 1750–1776*. Cambridge, Mass.: Harvard University Press, 1965.

_____. "Political Experience and Enlightenment Ideas in Eighteenth Century America." *American Historical Review* 67, 1962.

_____. *The Ideological Origins of the American Revolution*. Cambridge, Mass.: Belknap Press, 1967.

_____. "1776 a Year of Challenge." *Journal of Law and Economics* 9, 1976.

Baldwin, Alice M. *The New England Clergy and the American Revolution*. Durham, N.C.: Duke University Press, 1928.

Becker, Carl L. *The Declaration of Independence: A Study in the History of Political Ideas*. New York: Vintage, 1958.

Canfield, Cass. *Samuel Adams' Revolution, 1765–1776*. New York: Harper & Row, 1976.

Colbourn, H. Trevor. *The Lamp of Experience: Whig History and the Intellectual Origins of the American Revolution*. New York: W. W. Norton, 1965.

Conway, Moncure Daniel. *The Life of Thomas Paine*. London: Watts, 1909.

Curti, Merle. "The Great Mr. Locke: America's Philosopher, 1783–1861." *The Huntington Library Bulletin*, April 1937.

Greene, Jack P. "Paine, America, and the Modernization of Political Consciousness." *Political Science Quarterly* 93, 1978.

Hartz, Louis. "American Political Thought and the American Revolution." *American Political Science Review* 46, 1952.

Hyneman, Charles and Donald S. Lutz, eds. *American Political Writing During the Founding Era: 1760–1805*. Indianapolis: Liberty Press, 1983.

Kendall, Wilmore. *John Locke and the Doctrine of Majority Rule*. Urbana: University of Illinois Press, 1959.

Kramnick, Isaac. "Republican Revisionism Revisited." *American Historical Review* 87, 1982.

Lynd, Staughton. *The Intellectual Origins of American Radicalism*. New York: Vintage, 1969.

Penniman, Howard. "Thomas Paine—Democrat." *American Political Science Review* 37, 1943.

Roche, John, ed. *Origins of American Political Thought*. New York: Harper & Row, 1967.

Rossiter, Clinton. "The Political Theory of the American Revolution." *Review of Politics* 15, 1953.

_____. *The Political Thought of the American Revolution. Seedtime of the Republic*. Part III. New York: Harcourt Brace Jovanovich, 1963.

White, Morton. *The Philosophy of the American Revolution*. New York: Oxford University Press, 1978.

Wills, Garry. *Inventing America: Jefferson's Declaration of Independence*. Garden City, N.Y.: Doubleday Publishing, 1978.

Wood, Gordon. *The Creation of the American Republic, 1776–1787*. New York: W. W. Norton, 1972.

III. CREATING AN EXTENDED COMMERCIAL REPUBLIC: THE NEW SCIENCE OF POLITICS

Adair, Douglass. *Fame and the Founding Fathers*. New York: W. W. Norton, 1974.

_____. "That Politic's May Be Reduced to a Science: David Hume, James Madison, and the Tenth Federalist." *Huntington Library Quarterly* 20, 1957.

Agresto, John. "Liberty, Virtue, and Republicanism: 1776–1787." *Review of Politics* 39, 1977.

Appleby, Joyce. "The New Republican Synthesis and the Changing Political Ideas of John Adams." *American Quarterly* 25, 1973.

Banning, Lance. "Republican Ideology and the Triumph of the Constitution, 1789 to 1793." *William and Mary Quarterly* 31, 1974.

Beloff, Max. *Thomas Jefferson and American Democracy*. New York: Collier Books, 1962.

Branson, Roy. "James Madison and the Scottish Enlightenment." *Journal of the History of Ideas* 40, 1979.

Brant, Irving. *James Madison*. 6 vols. Indianapolis: Bobbs-Merrill, 1950.

Burns, Edward McNall. *James Madison: Philosopher of the Constitution*. New Brunswick, N.J.: Rutgers University Press, 1938.

Carey, George W. "Separation of Powers and the Madisonian Model." *American Political Science Review* 72, 1978.

_____. "Publius—A Split Personality?" *Review of Politics* 46, 1984.

Corwin, E. S. *The "Higher Law" Background of American Constitutional Law*. Ithaca, N.Y.: Cornell University Press, 1967.

_____. *John Marshall and the Constitution*. New Haven, Conn.: Yale University Press, 1919.

Crosskey, William W. *Politics and the Constitution in the History of the United States*. Chicago: University of Chicago Press, 1953.

Dauer, Manning J. *The Adams Federalists*. Baltimore: Johns Hopkins University Press, 1953.

_____. "The Political Economy of John Adams." *Political Science Quarterly* 56, 1941.

_____ and Hammond Hans. "John Taylor: Democrat or Aristocrat?" *Journal of Politics* 6, 1944.

Diamond, Martin. *The Founding of the Democratic Republic*. Itasca, Ill.: Peacock, 1981.

_____. "Democracy and the Federalist." *American Political Science Review* 53, 1959.

Dorfman, Joseph. "The Economic Philosophy of Thomas Jefferson." *Political Science Quarterly* 40, 1940.

Eidelberg, Paul. *The Philosophy of the American Constitution: A Re-interpretation of the Intentions of the Founding Fathers.* New York: Free Press, 1968.

Elazar, Daniel, ed. "Republicanism, Representation, and Consent: Views on the Founding." *Publius* 9, 1979.

Griswold, A. Whitney. "The Agrarian Democracy of Thomas Jefferson." *American Political Science Review* 40, 1946.

Hacker, Louis M. *Alexander Hamilton in the American Tradition.* New York: McGraw-Hill, 1957.

Haraszti, Zoltan. *John Adams and the Prophets of Progress.* Cambridge, Mass.: Harvard University Press, 1952.

Horne, Thomas. "Bourgeois Virtue, Property, and Moral Philosophy in America." *History of Political Thought* 4, 1983.

Kasson, John. *Civilizing the Machine.* New York: Penguin Books, 1977.

Kenyon, Cecelia. "Men of Little Faith: The Anti-Federalists on the Nature of Representative Government." *William and Mary Quarterly* 12, 1955.

Koch, Adrienne. *The Philosophy of Thomas Jefferson.* New York: Columbia University Press, 1943.

Levy, Leonard. *Jefferson and Civil Liberties: The Darker Side.* Cambridge, Mass.: Belknap Press, 1963.

Lewis, John D., ed. *Anti-Federalists versus Federalists: Selected Documents.* Scranton, Pa.: Chandler, 1967.

Lienesch, Michael. "In Defense of the Anti-Federalists." *History of Political Thought* 4, 1983.

Malone, Dumas. *Jefferson and the Ordeal of Liberty.* Boston: Little, Brown, 1962.

Roche, John P. "The Founding Fathers: A Reform Caucus in Action." *American Political Science Review* 40, 1961.

Sandoz, Ellis. "Classical and Christian Dimensions of American Political Thought." *Modern Age* 25, 1981.

Shalhope, Robert E. "Republicanism and Early American History." *William and Mary Quarterly* 39, 1982.

Storing, Herbert J. *What the Anti-Federalists Were For.* Chicago: University of Chicago Press, 1981.

Stourzh, Gerald. *Alexander Hamilton and the Idea of Republican Government.* Stanford, Calif.: Stanford University Press, 1970.

_____. "A Symposium on Jefferson." *Ethics* 53, 1943.

Wilson, Douglas C. "The American *Agricola:* Jefferson's Agrarianism and the Classical Tradition." *South Atlantic Quarterly* 80, 1981.

Wiltse, Charles M. *The Jefferson Tradition in American Democracy.* Chapel Hill: University of North Carolina, 1935.

Wood, Gordon. *The Creation of the American Republic, 1776–1787.* New York: W. W. Norton, 1972.

Wright, Benjamin F. "The Philosopher of Jeffersonian Democracy." *American Political Science Review* 22, 1928.

Zvesper, John. "The Madisonian Systems." *Western Political Quarterly* 37, 1984.

IV. EXTENDING THE DEMOCRATIC REPUBLIC: LIBERTY, EQUALITY, AND THE OPEN MARKETPLACE

Anthony, Katherine Susan. *Susan B. Anthony: Her Personal History and Her Era.* New York: Russell and Russell, 1975.

Arieli, Yehoshua. *Individualism and Nationalism in American Ideology.* New York: Penguin Books, 1966.

Arvin, Newton. *Whitman.* New York: Macmillan, 1938.

Basler, Roy P. *The Lincoln Legend.* Boston: Houghton Mifflin, 1935.

Beatty, Richmond C. "Whitman's Political Thought." *Southern Atlantic Quarterly* 46, 1947.

Beer, Samuel. "Liberty and Union: Walt Whitman's Idea of the Nation." *Political Theory* 12, 1984.

Beveridge, Albert J. *Abraham Lincoln.* Boston: Houghton Mifflin, 1928.

Bontemps, Arna Wendell. *Free at Last: The Life of Frederick Douglass.* New York: Dodd, Mead, 1971.

Borrit, G. S. *Lincoln and the Economics of the American Dream.* Memphis: University of Tennessee Press, 1978.

Bruce, Dickson D., Jr. *The Rhetoric of Conservatism: The Virginia Convention of 1829–30 and the Conservative Tradition in the South.* San Marino, Calif.: Huntington Library, 1982.

Buhle, MariJo and Paul Bunie, eds. *The Concise History of Women Suffrage: Selections from the Classic Work of Stanton, Anthony, Gage, and Harper.* Urbana: University of Illinois Press, 1978.

Ceaser, James. "Alexis de Tocqueville on Political Science, Political Culture, and the Role of the Intellectual." *American Political Science Review* 79, 1985.

Corlett, William S., Jr. "The Availability of Lincoln's Political Religion." *Political Theory* 10, 1982.

Degler, Carl N. "The Locofocos: Urban 'Agrarians.'" *Journal of Economic History* 16, 1956.

Dubois, Ellen, ed. *Elizabeth Cady Stanton/Susan B. Anthony.* New York: Schocken Books, 1981.

Ekirch, Arthur A. *The Idea of Progress in America, 1815–1860.* New York: Peter Smith, 1951.

Fields, Wayne. "The Reply to Hayne: Daniel Webster and the Rhetoric of Stewardship." *Political Theory* 11, 1983.

Foner, Eric. *Free Soil, Free Labor, Free Men: The Ideology of the Republican Party before the Civil War.* New York: Oxford University Press, 1970.

Foner, Philip. *Frederick Douglass: A Biography.* New York: Citadel Press, 1964.

_____. *Frederick Douglass on Women's Rights.* Westport, Conn.: Greenwood Press, 1976.

Fredrickson, George M. *The Black Image in the White Mind: The Debate on Afro-American Character and Destiny, 1817–1914.* New York: Harper & Row, 1971.

Freehling, William W. *Prelude to Civil War: The Nullification Controversy in South Carolina, 1816–1836.* New York: Harper & Row, 1966.

Goldman, Perry M. "Political Virtue in the Age of Jackson." *Political Science Quarterly* 87, 1972.

Goldstein, Leslie F. "Morality and Prudence in the States-manship of Frederick Douglass." *Polity* 16, 1984.

Grossman, James. "James Fenimore Cooper: An Uneasy American." *Yale Review* 40, 1951.

Hartz, Louis. "The Reactionary Enlightenment: Southern Political Thought Before the Civil War." *Western Political Quarterly* 35, 1952.

Horton, John T. *James Kent: A Study in Conservatism.* New York: Appleton-Century, 1939.

Howe, Daniel Walker, ed. *The American Whigs: An Anthology.* New York: John Wiley & Sons, 1973.

Hofstadter, Richard. "Andrew Jackson and the Rise of Liberal Capitalism." In *The American Political Tradition,* New York: Vintage, 1958.

Hugins, Walter. *Jacksonian Democracy and the Working Class: A Study of the New York Workingman's Movement, 1829–1837.* Stanford, Calif.: Stanford University Press, 1967.

Jaffa, Harry V. *Crisis of the House Divided: An Interpretation of the Issues in the Lincoln-Douglas Debates.* Garden City, N.Y.: Doubleday Publishing, 1959.

Kessler, Sanford. "Tocqueville on Civil Religion and Liberal Democracy." *Journal of Politics* 39, 1977.

Ladu, Arthur I. "Political Ideas of Orestes A. Brownson, Transcendentalist." *Philogical Quarterly* 12, 1933.

Lerner, Gerda. *The Grimke Sisters from South Carolina.* New York: Schocken Books, 1971.

Lerner, Max. *Tocqueville and American Civilization.* New York: Harper & Row, 1969.

Lerner, Ralph. "Calhoun's New Science of Politics," *American Political Science* 57, December 1963.

Lutz, Alma. *Created Equal, A Biography of Elizabeth Cady Stanton.* New York: Octagon, 1974.

———. *Susan B. Anthony.* Boston: Beacon Press, 1959.

Madison, Charles A. "Henry David Thoreau: Transcendental Individualist." *Ethics* 54, 1944.

McKitrick, Eric L., ed. *Slavery Defended: The Views of the Old South.* Englewood Cliffs, N.J.: Prentice-Hall, 1963.

Meyers, Marvin. *The Jacksonian Persuasion.* Stanford, Calif.: Stanford University Press, 1957.

Nathans, Sydney. *Daniel Webster and Jacksonian Democracy.* Baltimore: Johns Hopkins University Press, 1973.

Niebuhr, Reinhold. "The Religion of Abraham Lincoln." *Christian Century* 82, 1965.

Oakley, Mary Ann B. *Elizabeth Cady Stanton.* Old Westbury, N.Y.: Feminist Press, 1972.

Oates, Stephen B. *With Malice toward None.* New York: Harper & Row, 1977.

Pessen, Edward. "Tocqueville's Misreading of America, America's Misreading of Tocqueville." *The Tocqueville Review* 4, 1982.

Peterson, Merrill D., ed. *Democracy, Liberty, and Property: The State Constitutional Conventions of the Early 1820s.* Indianapolis: Bobbs-Merrill, 1965.

Roemer, Lawrence. *Brownson on Democracy and the Trend toward Socialism.* New York: Philosophical Library, 1953.

Rogin, Michael Paul. *Fathers and Children: Andrew Jackson and the Subjugation of the American Indian.* New York: Alfred A. Knopf, 1975.

Schlesinger, Arthur M., Jr. *The Age of Jackson.* Boston: Little, Brown, 1945.

———. *Orestes A. Brownson: A Pilgrim's Progress.* New York: Octagon, 1939.

Stone, John and Stephen Mennel, eds. *Alexis de Tocqueville on Democracy, Revolution, and Society.* Chicago: University of Chicago Press, 1980.

Thomas, John L., ed. *John C. Calhoun: A Profile.* New York: Hill and Wang, 1968.

Thurow, Glen E. *Abraham Lincoln and American Political Religion.* Albany: State University of New York Press, 1976.

Williamson, Chilton. *American Suffrage from Property to Democracy: 1760–1860.* Princeton, N.J.: Princeton University Press, 1961.

Wiltse, Charles M. *John C. Calhoun.* 3 vols. Indianapolis: Bobbs-Merrill, 1944–1951.

———. "From Compact to National State in American Political Thought." In *Essays in Political Theory.* Ed. by Milton R. Konvitz and Arthur E. Murphy. Ithaca, N.Y.: Cornell University Press, 1948.

Zetterbaum, Marvin. *Tocqueville and the Problem of Democracy.* Stanford, Calif.: Stanford University Press, 1967.

Zuckert, Catherine. "Tocqueville on Religion in America." *Review of Politics* 43, 1981.

V. THE REPUBLIC AS INDUSTRIAL CAPITALISM: SOCIAL DARWINISM AND THE NEW INEQUALITY

Braeman, John. *Woodrow Wilson.* Englewood Cliffs, N.J.: Prentice-Hall, 1972.

Bruce, Robert. *1877: Year of Violence.* New York: Franklin Watts, 1959.

Cochran, Thomas C. and William Miller. *The Age of Enterprise.* New York: Macmillan, 1942.

Commager, Henry Steele. *The American Mind: An Interpretation of American Thought and Character Since the 1800s.* New Haven, Conn.: Yale University Press, 1950.

Cravens, Hamilton and John C. Burnham. "Psychology and Evolutionary Naturalism in American Thought, 1890–1940." *American Quarterly* 23, December 1971.

Destler, Chester. *American Radicalism, 1865–1901.* Chicago: Quadrangle, 1966.

Dick, William M. *Labor and Socialism in America: The Gompers Era.* Port Washington, N.Y.: Kennikat Press, 1972.

Egbert, Donald Drew and Persons Stow, eds. *Socialism and American Life,* vol. 1. Princeton, N.J.: Princeton University Press, 1952.

Fine, Sidney. *Laissez-Faire and the General Welfare State.* Ann Arbor: University of Michigan Press, 1967.

———. "Richard T. Ely, Forerunner of Progressivism, 1880–1901." *Mississippi Valley Historical Review* 37, March 1951.

Franklin, John Hope and Isidore Starr, eds. *The Negro in Twentieth Century America: A Reader on the Struggle for Civil Rights.* New York: Vintage, 1967.

Ginger, Ray. *Eugene V. Debs: A Biography.* New York: Macmillan, 1962.

Goldman, Eric. *Rendezvous with Destiny: A History of Modern American Reform.* New York: Alfred A. Knopf, 1952.

Goodwyn, Lawrence. *The Populist Moment.* New York: Oxford University Press, 1979.

Gutman, Herbert. *Work, Culture and Society.* New York: Vintage, 1977.

Hacker, Louis W. *The World of Andrew Carnegie: 1865–1901.* Philadelphia: Lippincott, 1968.

Hays, Samuel P. *The Response to Industrialism: 1885–1914.* Chicago: University of Chicago Press, 1957.

Herreshoff, David. *The Origins of American Marxism.* New York: Pathfinder Press, 1973.

Hicks, John D. *The Populist Revolt: A History of the Farmer's Alliance and the People's Party.* Minneapolis: University of Minnesota Press, 1931.

Hofstadter, Richard. *Social Darwinism in America.* Boston: Beacon Press, 1944.

_____. "The Spoilsmen: An Age of Cynicism." In *American Political Tradition.* New York: Vintage, 1958.

Logan, Rayford W., ed. *W. E. B. Du Bois: A Profile.* New York: Hill and Wang, 1971.

Madison, Charles A. "Eugene Victor Debs: Evangelical Socialist." In *Critics and Crusaders: A Century of American Protest,* 2d ed. New York: Frederick Ungar, 1959.

Mason, Alpheus T. "American Individualism: Fact and Fiction." *American Political Science Review* 46, March 1952.

Meier, August. *Negro Thought in America, 1880–1915: Racial Ideologies in the Age of Booker T. Washington.* Ann Arbor: University of Michigan Press, 1962.

McClosky, Robert G. *American Conservatism in the Age of Enterprise: A Study of William Graham Summer, Stephen J. Field, and Andrew Carnegie.* Cambridge, Mass.: Harvard University Press, 1951.

Petrella, Frank. "Henry George's Theory of the State's Agenda." *American Journal of Economics and Sociology* 43, July 1984.

Pollack, Norman, ed. *The Populist Mind.* Indianapolis: Bobbs-Merrill, 1967.

_____. *The Populist Response to Industrialized America.* New York: Harper & Row, 1962.

Radosh, Ronald, ed. *Debs.* Englewood Cliffs, N.J.: Prentice-Hall, 1971.

Renshaw, Patrick. *The Wobblies.* New York: Doubleday-Anchor, 1967.

Rudwick, E. M. *W. E. B. Du Bois: A Study in Minority Group Leadership.* Philadelphia: University of Pennsylvania Press, 1961.

Salvatore, Nick. *Eugene V. Debs.* Urbana: University of Illinois, 1982.

Storing, Herbert J., ed. *What Country Have I? Political Writings by Black Americans.* New York: St. Martin's Press, 1970.

Thomas, John L. *Alternative America: Henry George, Edward Bellamy, and Henry Demarest Lloyd and the Adversary Tradition.* Cambridge, Mass.: Harvard University Press, 1983.

Twiss, Benjamin R. *Lawyers and the Constitution: How Laissez-Faire Came to the Supreme Court.* Princeton, N.J.: Princeton University Press, 1942.

Wiebe, Robert. *The Search for Order, 1877–1920.* New York: Hill and Wang, 1967.

VI. THE REPUBLIC AS SOCIAL DEMOCRACY: REINING IN THE MARKET

Abbott, Philip. *Furious Fancies: American Political Thought in the Post-Liberal Era.* Westport, Conn.: Greenwood Press, 1980.

Arnold, Thurman. *The Folklore of Capitalism.* New York: Elliott, 1937.

_____. *The Bottlenecks of Business.* New York: Reynal and Hitchcock, 1940.

Baran, Paul and Paul M. Sweezy. *Monopoly Capital.* New York: Monthly Review Press, 1966.

Bell, Daniel. *The Cultural Contradictions of Capitalism.* New York: Basic Books, 1976.

Berle, A. A. and Gardiner C. Means. *The Modern Corporation and Private Property.* New York: Macmillan, 1932.

Brown, Bruce. *Marx, Freud, and the Critique of Everyday Life.* New York: Monthly Review Press, 1973.

Buckley, William F. *Up from Liberalism.* New York: McDowell, Obolensky, 1959.

_____, ed. *American Conservative Thought in the Twentieth Century.* Indianapolis: Bobbs-Merrill, 1970.

Carmichael, Stokeley and Charles V. Hamilton. *Black Power: The Politics of Liberation in America.* New York: Vintage, 1967.

Chamberlain, John. *Farewell to Reform.* Chicago: Quadrangle, 1965.

Clecak, Peter. *Crooked Paths: Reflections on Socialism, Conservatism, and the Welfare State.* New York: Harper & Row, 1978.

Coker, Francis W. "Some Present-Day Critics of Liberalism." *American Political Science Review* 47, March 1953.

Coser, Lewis and Irving Howe. *The New Conservatives: A Critique from the Left.* New York: Quadrangle, 1965.

Crozier, Michel, Samuel P. Huntington, and Joji Wantanuki. *The Crisis of Democracy.* New York: New York University Press, 1975.

Eisenstein, Zillah, ed. *Capitalist Patriarchy and the Case for Socialist Feminism.* New York: Monthly Review Press, 1979.

Forcey, Charles. *The Crossroads of Liberalism.* New York: Oxford University Press, 1961.

Friedman, Milton and Rose Friedman. *Free to Choose.* New York: Harcourt Brace Jovanovich, 1980.

Fusfeld, Daniel Roland. *The Economic Thought of F. D. R. and the Origins of the New Deal.* New York: Columbia University Press, 1956.

Galston, William. "Defending Liberalism." *American Political Science Review* 76, 1982.

Geiger, George R. *John Dewey in Perspective.* New York: Oxford University Press, 1958.

Gerber, Larry. *The Limits of Liberalism.* New York: New York University Press, 1983.

Gilder, George. *Wealth and Poverty*. New York: Bantam, 1981.

Gottfried, Paul. "On Neoconservatism." *Modern Age* 27, 1983.

Greer, Thomas H. *What Roosevelt Thought: The Social and Political Ideas of Franklin Delano Roosevelt*. Ann Arbor: University of Michigan Press, 1958.

Harrington, Michael. *Decade of Decision*. New York: Simon & Schuster, 1980.

Hofstadter, Richard. *The Age of Reform*. New York: Alfred A. Knopf, 1966.

Hook, Sidney. *John Dewey: An Intellectual Portrait*. New York: John Day, 1939.

Hopkins, Charles H. *The Rise of the Social Gospel in American Protestantism, 1865–1915*. New Haven, Conn.: Yale University Press, 1940.

Kirk, Russell. *The Conservative Mind*. Chicago: Regnery, 1953.

Kolko, Gabriel. *The Triumph of Conservatism, 1900–1916*. New York: Free Press, 1963.

Kurtz, Paul. "Libertarianism as the Philosophy of Moral Freedom." *Modern Age* 26, 1982.

Lane, Robert E. "Personal Freedom in a Market Society." *Society* 18, 1981.

Lasch, Christopher. *The Culture of Narcissism*. New York: W. W. Norton, 1978.

Link, Stanley Arthur. *Woodrow Wilson and the Progressive Era, 1910–1917*. New York: Harper & Row, 1954.

Levy, Michael B. "Illiberal Liberalism: The New Property as Strategy." *Review of Politics* 45, 1983.

Lustig, R. Jeffrey. *Corporate Liberalism: The Origins of American Political Theory 1890–1920*. Berkeley: University of California Press, 1982.

Machan, Tibor. "Wronging Rights." *Policy Review* 17, 1982.

McWilliams, Wilson Carey. "The Bible in the American Political Tradition." *Political Anthropology* 3, 1984.

Meier, August and Elliott Rudwick, eds. *Black Protest in the Sixties*. New York: Franklin Watts, 1970.

Meyer, Frank S., ed. *What Is Conservatism?* New York: Holt, Rinehart & Winston, 1965.

Moley, Raymond. *After Seven Years*. New York: Harper & Row, 1939.

Moore, Edward C. *American Pragmatism: Pierce, James and Dewey*. New York: Columbia University Press, 1961.

Moreno, Jonathan and R. Scott Frey. "Dewey's Critique of Marxism." *Sociological Quarterly* 26, 1985.

Mowry, George E. *The Era of Theodore Roosevelt, 1900–1912*. New York: Harper & Row, 1958.

Nash, Gerald D., ed. *Franklin Delano Roosevelt*. Englewood Cliffs, N.J.: Prentice-Hall, 1967.

Nash, George H. *The Conservative Intellectual Movement in America*. New York: Basic Books, 1976.

Novak, Michael. "The Economic System: The Evangelical Basis of a Social Market Economy." *Review of Politics* 43, 1981.

Parekh, B. "Utopianism and Manicheism: A Critique of Marcuse's Theory of Revolution." *Social Research* 39, 1976.

Rand, Ayn. *Capitalism: The Unknown Ideal*. New York: Signet, 1966.

Rauche, G. A. "Marcuse's Concept of Liberation in Light of His Criticism of Western Capitalism and Soviet Marxism." *Politikon* 4, June 1977.

Reich, Charles. "The New Property." *Yale Law Journal* 73, 1964.

_____. *The Greening of America*. New York: Random House, 1970.

Reich, Robert. *The Next American Frontier*. New York: Times Books, 1983.

Rosenberg, Bernard. "The Example of Norman Thomas." *Dissent* 11, Autumn 1964.

Rossiter, Clinton. "The Political Philosophy of Franklin Delano Roosevelt." *Review of Politics* 11, November 1949.

Sabine, George H. "The Pragmatic Approach to Politics." *American Political Science Review* 24, 1930.

Schlesinger, Arthur M., Jr. *The Crisis of the Old Order, 1919–1933*. (*The Age of Roosevelt*, vol. I.) Boston: Houghton Mifflin, 1957.

_____. *The Coming of the New Deal*. (*The Age of Roosevelt*, vol. II.) Boston: Houghton Mifflin, 1959.

_____. *The Politics of Upheavel*. (*The Age of Roosevelt*, vol. III.) Boston: Houghton Mifflin, 1959.

Seidler, Murray. *Norman Thomas: Respectable Rebel*, 2d ed. Syracuse, N.Y.: Syracuse University Press, 1967.

Steinfels, Peter. *The Neo-Conservatives*. New York: Simon & Schuster, 1979.

_____. "What the Neo-Conservatives Believe." *Social Policy* 10, 1979.

Stolz, Matthew F., ed. *Politics of the New Left*. Beverly Hills, Calif.: Glencoe Press, 1968.

Swanberg, W. A. *Norman Thomas: The Last Idealist*. New York: Charles Scribner's Sons, 1976.

Teodori, Massimo, ed. *The New Left: A Documentary History*. Indianapolis: Bobbs-Merrill, 1969.

Weinstein, James. *The Corporate Ideal in the Liberal State, 1900–1918*. Boston: Beacon Press, 1968.

_____ and David W. Eakins, eds. *For a New America: Essays in History and Politics from Studies on the Left, 1959–1967*. New York: Random House, 1970.

White, Howard. "The Political Faith of John Dewey." *Journal of Politics* 20, 1958.

White, Morton G. *Social Thought in America*. New York: Viking Press, 1949.

Wilson, Joan Hoff. *Herbert Hoover: Forgotten Progressive*. Boston: Little, Brown, 1975.

Wolfe, Harold. *Herbert Hoover: Public Servant and Leader of the Loyal Opposition*. New York: Exposition, 1956.

VII. THE REPUBLIC AS WORLD POWER: INTERNATIONALISM, INTERVENTION, AND A WORLD SAFE FOR DEMOCRACY

Acheson, Dean G. *Present at the Creation*. New York: W. W. Norton, 1969.

Adler, Selig. *The Isolationist Impulse: Its Twentieth-Century Reaction*. London and New York: Abelard-Schuman, 1957.

_____. *The Uncertain Giant, 1921–1941: American Foreign Policy between the Wars*. New York: Macmillan, 1965.

Arendt, Hannah. *The Origins of Totalitarianism*. New York: Harcourt Brace Jovanovich, 1951.

Bemis, S. F. *A Diplomatic History of the United States*. New York: Holt, Rinehart & Winston, 1965.

Billington, Ray Allen. "The Origins of Middle Western Isolationism." *Political Science Quarterly* 40, 1945.

Bohlen, Charles. *The Transformation of American Foreign Policy*. New York: W. W. Norton, 1969.

Coffin, Tristam. *The Armed Society: Militarism in Modern America*. New York: Penguin Books, 1968.

Cutler, Lloyd. "The Right to Intervene." *Foreign Affairs* 64, 1985.

Doenecke, Justus D. *Not to the Swift*. Lewisburg, Pa.: Bucknell University Press, 1979.

Douglass, R. Bruce. "International Economic Justice and the Guaranteed Minimum." *Review of Politics* 44, January 1982.

Elliot, William Y. et al. *The Political Economy of American Foreign Policy*. New York: Holt, Rinehart & Winston, 1955.

Feuer, Lewis. "John Dewey and the Back to the People Movement in American Thought." *Journal of the History of Ideas* 20, 1959.

Gardner, Lloyd C. *Economic Aspects of New Deal Diplomacy*. Madison: University of Wisconsin Press, 1964.

_____. "From Liberation to Containment, 1945–1953." In *From Colony to Empire: Essays in the History of American Foreign Relations*. Ed. by William Appleman Williams. New York: John Wiley & Sons, 1972.

Gaddis, John Lewis. "Harry S. Truman and the Origins of Containment." In *Makers of American Diplomacy: From Benjamin Franklin to Henry Kissinger*. Ed. by Frank J. Merli and Theodore A. Wilson. New York: Charles Scribner's Sons, 1971.

Gilbert, Felix. "The English Background of American Isolationism in the Eighteenth Century." *William and Mary Quarterly* 1, 1944.

_____. *To the Farewell Address: Ideas of Early American Foreign Policy*. Princeton, N.J.: Princeton University Press, 1961.

Graebner, N. A., ed. *Ideas and Diplomacy: Readings in the Intellectual Tradition of American Foreign Policy*. New York: Oxford University Press, 1964.

Horowitz, David. *The Free World Colossus*. New York: Hill and Wang, 1965.

Kaplan, Sidney. "Social Engineers as Saviors: Effects of World War I on Some American Liberals." *Journal of the History of Ideas* 17, 1956.

Kennan, George F. *Memoirs*. New York: Bantam, 1969.

Krauthammer, Charles. "The Poverty of Realism: When Should America Intervene?" *The New Republic*, February 17, 1986.

LaFeber, Walter. *America, Russia, and the Cold War*. New York: John Wiley & Sons, 1968.

Link, Arthur S. *Woodrow Wilson in the Progressive Era, 1910–1917*. New York: Harper Torchbooks, 1954.

Lippmann, Walter. *The Cold War*. New York: Harper & Row, 1947.

_____. *U.S. Foreign Policy: Shield of the Republic*. Boston: Little, Brown, 1943.

Rippy, James Fred and Angie Debo. *The Historical Background of the American Policy of Isolation*. Smith College Studies in History, vol. 9. Northampton, Mass.: Smith College Press, 1924.

Robinson, E. E. and V. J. West, eds. *The Foreign Policy of Woodrow Wilson, 1913–1917*. New York: Macmillan, 1918.

Weinberg, Albert K. *Manifest Destiny*. Baltimore: Johns Hopkins University Press, 1935.

_____. "The Historical Meaning of the American Doctrine of Isolation." *American Political Science Review* 34, June 1940.

Weisband, Edward. *The Ideology of American Foreign Policy: A Paradigm of Lockean Liberalism*. Berkeley Hills, Calif.: Sage Professional Paper, International Studies Series 02–016, 1973.

Williams, William Appleman. *The Tragedy of American Diplomacy*. New York: Dell Publishing, 1962.

Woolery, William Kirk. *The Relations of Thomas Jefferson to American Foreign Policy, 1783–93*. Johns Hopkins Studies in History and Political Science, series 45, no. 2. Baltimore: Johns Hopkins University Press, 1927.

Wright, Louis B. "The Founding Fathers and Splendid Isolation." *Huntington Library Quarterly* 6, February 1943.

ABOUT THE AUTHOR

Michael B. Levy earned his doctorate at Rutgers University and taught as Associate Professor of Political Science at Texas A&M University. He moved to Washington, D.C., to serve on the staff of the Joint Economic Committee and in 1986 became Administrative Assistant to Senator Lloyd Bentsen of Texas. He has been an adjunct instructor at Georgetown University since 1986. In addition to his many scholarly articles and *Political Thought in America*, he edited *The Liberal Future in America: Essays in Renewal* with Philip Abbott and *Handbook of Political Theory and Policy Science* with Edward B. Portis.